"The perfect guide for the overachiever. . . . For stud[...]
to improve their scores and the discipline to achieve i[...]

Donald J. Heider
Associate Director of Admissions
Franklin & Marshall College

"This text is an important teaching tool for students and educators. . . .
there is no quick-fix panacea here, just good, old-fashioned studying."

Richard A. Avitabile
Director of Admissions
Fordham University

"I would not hesitate to recommend it to the motivated student wishing to
better prepare himself/herself for the SAT. I strongly believe that this has
been prepared with the students' best interest in mind. . . ."

Patricia Barrett Hitz
Assistant Director of Guidance
The Rye High School, Rye, New York

". . . a 'super' way for students to prepare for the SAT."

John L. Babcock
Associate Academic Dean
The Culver Educational Foundation, Culver, Indiana

". . . Important for students who live in areas where prep courses are not
offered or are beyond their reach because of cost."

Lee Ann Afton
Assistant Director of Admissions
The University of the South

". . . I am generally very impressed with the quality of this publication. . . .
I would rate this book among the best I have seen."

Daniel Boyer
Assistant Head
Miss Porter's School, Farmington, Connecticut

". . . it clearly replaces all of the test preparation courses that I know of."

William W. Chase
Director of College Counseling
The Gunnery, Washington, Connecticut

". . . I was most impressed . . . and would surely use it in my SAT preparation for juniors and seniors."

Christopher G. Boyle
College Counselor and
English Department Chairman
St. Gregory High School, Tucson, Arizona

"... excellent ... a student using the SuperCourse ... would certainly benefit significantly."

Frederick G.H. Fayen II
Director of Guidance
The Pingry School
Martinsville, New Jersey

"... easy to understand and well-written."

Gail Berson Weaver
Executive Director of Admission and Student Aid
Wheaton College

"Highly motivated students will find an excellent resource for review and test preparation in *SuperCourse for the SAT* ... Those students who use it conscientiously should certainly strengthen their ability to read carefully, think logically, and reason intelligently."

Gwen Cleghorn
Associate Principal
The Westminster Schools
Atlanta, Georgia

ARCO

SAT SuperCourse™

Thomas H. Martinson

MACMILLAN • USA

For Elizabeth, who made me take typing in high school

The sample test questions in this book were written by the author and are not actual SAT questions. The directions, format and scoring data were used by permission of Educational Testing Service. This permission does not constitute review or endorsement by Educational Testing Service or the College Board of this publication as whole or of any sample questions or testing information it may contain.

Photo credits
page 1 © Conklin/Monkmeyer Press
page 53 © Rogers/Monkmeyer Press
page 481 © Robert Issacs/Photo Researchers

Third Edition

Previous editions were published under the title *Supercourse for the SAT.*

Macmillan General Reference
A Simon & Schuster Macmillan Company
1633 Broadway
New York, NY 10019-6785

An Arco Book

MACMILLAN is a registered trademark of Macmillan, Inc.
ARCO is a registered trademark of Prentice-Hall, Inc.

Library of Congress Cataloging-in-Publication data

Martinson, Thomas H.
        SAT supercourse / Thomas H. Martinson. --3rd ed.
            p.   cm.
        At head of title: ARCO
        Rev. ed. of Supercourse for the SAT, 1994.
        ISBN 0-02-861185-3
        1. Scholastic assessment test--Study guides.   I. Martinson, Thomas H   Supercourse for
the SAT.   II. Title.   III. SAT supercourse.
        LB2353.57 .M267   1994
        378' .1662--dc20
                                                                93-43346
                                                                CIP

Manufactured in the United States of America

10 9 8 7 6 5 4 3 2

CONTENTS

A Letter to the Reader vii
Preface ix

Part One   The Anatomy of a Test

Lesson 1   Getting Started 3
Lesson 2   Let's Look at the SAT 7
Lesson 3   The Wizard of Odds 19
Lesson 4   Nuts and Bolts 25
Lesson 5   Test Anxiety 37
Lesson 6   Unlocking the Mystery 43

Part Two   The Coaching Program

Lesson 7   Analogies 55
Lesson 8   Sentence Completions 97
Lesson 9   Critical Reading 127
Lesson 10   Verbal Warm-Up Exercises 175
Lesson 11   Diagnostic Math Test 197
Lesson 12   Problem-Solving: Introduction 209
Lesson 13   Problem-Solving: Arithmetic 231
Lesson 14   Problem-Solving: Algebra 271
Lesson 15   Problem-Solving: Geometry 309
Lesson 16   Problem-Solving Drills 357
Lesson 17   Student-Produced Responses 385
Lesson 18   Quantitive Comparisons 403
Lesson 19   Math Warm-Up Exercises 457

Part Three   Practice Tests

Practice Test 1 483
Practice Test 2 531
Practice Test 3 577
Practice Test 4 621
Practice Test 5 665

A Letter to the Reader

Dear Reader,

The book you have just purchased is worth hundreds of dollars. Never before has a total—and academically respected—SAT preparation course been available in book form.

This year thousands of students will spend $300 to $600 (and even more) for expensive test preparation courses. Yet, this book can provide you with the benefits of an expensive course. You get:

- hundreds of proven strategies that take you inside the SAT
- advice that helps you think like the testmakers
- thousands of practice questions with complete explanations—
  the equivalent of ten SATs
- a diagnostic math test
- successful methods to control test anxiety

I know for a fact that this book offers the same kinds of strategies taught in expensive SAT preparation courses because I personally developed not one but *two* such courses for nationally known test preparation schools.

You will learn

- how to answer algebra questions without using algebra
- how to answer geometry questions just by looking at a picture
- how to avoid logical pitfalls that trap unwary test-takers
- how to answer even when you don't know a key vocabulary word
- when and how to guess

and much more.

In other words, this book contains everything you need to make sure you get your top score on the SAT. In my professional opinion, there is little offered by most commercial test preparation courses that you can't get for yourself by conscientious study of this book.

Thomas H. Martinson

Preface

There are three very important reasons for our publishing this book at this time. One, it proves that it is possible to improve your SAT score. Two, it offers a reasonably priced alternative to expensive schools and tutoring services that now compete among themselves for your preparation dollars. Three, it stands as an antidote to the current mania for quick fixes rather than conscientious preparation and study.

First, this book shows that the SAT is not invincible—that it does have patterns or clues that are inherent to the structure of the test. If you understand these patterns or clues, you can pursue them to your advantage. Consider an example.

> At the beginning of a school year, a student receives a university loan of d dollars, which he deposits into a checking account. Each month, he receives p dollars from his parents and spends s dollars. If p is less than s, and the student makes up the difference by withdrawing from d, in how many months will d be exhausted?
>
> (A) $\dfrac{p-s}{d}$ (B) $\dfrac{d}{s-p}$ (C) $\dfrac{s-p}{d}$ (D) $\dfrac{d-p}{s}$ (E) $\dfrac{d}{p+s}$

This is a difficult math question. Perhaps no more than 15 to 20 percent of all test-takers would be able to answer it. But here is a strategy that lets you answer correctly even if you don't understand the algebra needed to set up a formula.

Just make the situation real by choosing some numbers for the letters in the problem. Assume, for example, that the loan was $1,000 ($d = 1,000$), that the student receives $200 per month from his parents ($p = 200$), and that he spends $300 per month ($s = 300$). The student is spending $100 per month more than his parents send him, which he withdraws from the checking account. At the rate of $100 per month, the checking account will be empty in $1,000 \div 100 = 10$ months.

So, on the assumption that $d = 1,000$, $p = 200$, and $s = 300$, the correct formula will yield the number 10. Just substitute the assumed values into the choices until you find the one that works:

(A) $\dfrac{p-s}{d} = \dfrac{200-300}{1,000} = \dfrac{-100}{1,000} = -\dfrac{1}{10}$ (Wrong answer.)

(B) $\dfrac{d}{s-p} = \dfrac{1,000}{300-200} = \dfrac{1,000}{100} = 10$ (Correct!)

(C) $\dfrac{s-p}{d} = \dfrac{300-200}{1,000} = \dfrac{100}{1,000} = \dfrac{1}{10}$ (Wrong answer.)

(D) $\dfrac{d-p}{s} = \dfrac{1,000-200}{300} = \dfrac{800}{300} = \dfrac{8}{3}$ (Wrong answer.)

(E) $\dfrac{d}{p-s} = \dfrac{1,000}{200+300} = \dfrac{1,000}{500} = 2$ (Wrong answer.)

Nor is success here a matter of luck. Since the SAT is primarily a multiple-choice test, most problems like this one (which asks for an algebraic formula) can be attacked in this way. The correct answer is there for the testing.

Given that there are dozens of strategies like this, common sense dictates that test-takers who know the pattern of the SAT enjoy an important competitive edge over those who do not.

Second, this book is a viable alternative to expensive coaching schools. The 400-plus pages of instructional material are the equivalent to the forty or fifty hours of lecture included in those programs.

Third, this book should help debunk a popular myth. There is currently in vogue an attitude that only a *little* preparation is needed. Exponents of this approach tout methods with names such as "cracking the test," "breaking the code," and "beating the system."

There is nothing really new in these approaches. They offer many of the strategies and methods that have been used effectively on multiple-choice tests for years. What *is* new, however, is the "hype" or indoctrination that accompanies the strategies. Students are encouraged to believe that by learning a few easy rules, they can attain a top score without really having to think.

As you can see, preparation is effective, but it requires hard work. In point of fact, the only sure way to conquer the SAT is through conscientious study and hard work. In sum, the approach of this book can perhaps be best expressed by paraphrasing the claim often heard in a widely aired television commercial: "Our students get higher SAT scores the old-fashioned way—they earn them!"

PART ONE

The Anatomy of a Test

Getting Started

✔ **Objective**

To learn the meanings of certain key terms.

1. What Is the SAT?
2. What Is the CEEB?
3. What Is ETS?
4. How to Register

SYMBOLS

strategy

eliminating
suspects

fact

estimating

common
error

inquiry/
guessing

measuring

pattern

calculating

unlocking
the mystery

Dr. Watson

Sherlock
Holmes

smoking
gun

ladder of
difficulty

What Is the SAT?

Let's begin by sorting out a lot of abbreviations such as SAT, CEEB, and ETS.

The letters S-A-T stand for Scholastic Assessment Test. The Scholastic Assessment Test is a standardized exam that is given several times a year at various locations around the world. Many colleges and universities use SAT scores as part of the admission process.

The SAT I includes both verbal and math questions. The SAT II is a series of subject tests in areas such as History and Science. The questions used on the SAT are primarily multiple-choice questions, and your answers are entered on a special answer sheet. Afterward the test, answer sheets, and testing materials are sent to central locations for processing; and a few weeks later, your scores are sent to you and to others whom you have designated to receive copies (such as the schools to which you are applying).

The letters C-E-E-B stand for College Entrance Examination Board, often called the College Board. The College Board is an association of high schools, colleges, and universities that was created to provide special services to the schools that are members. One of the services the College Board provides to its members is the SAT. You will not, however, need to be in contact with the College Board. You will deal directly with colleges and universities to which you are applying and with ETS, the organization that is in charge of giving the SAT.

The letters E-T-S stand for Educational Testing Service. ETS is a private company with headquarters in Princeton, New Jersey, and offices in many other places. Educational Testing Service, as the name suggests, offers testing services. One of its best known tests is the SAT, which it writes and administers on behalf of the College Board. When you are ready to take the SAT, you will register to take the test with ETS. You can obtain registration materials by telephone.

Princeton, New Jersey
(609) 771-7600 (8:30 a.m.–9:30 p.m. Eastern Time, Monday through Friday)
Berkeley, California
(415) 849-0950 (8:15 a.m.–4:30 p.m. Pacific Time, Monday through Friday)

Let's Look at the SAT

✔ Objectives

To learn the names and forms of the different types of questions used on the SAT I.

To learn how the test is scored and the difference between raw scores and scaled scores.

1. Verbal Questions
   - Antonyms
   - Analogies
   - Sentence Completions
   - Critical Reading

2. Math Questions
   - Problem-Solving
   - Quantitative Comparison
   - Student-Produced Responses

The SAT is divided into seven sections, each either 15 or 30 minutes long. Each section is separately timed. You will have three Verbal Reasoning sections, three Mathematical Reasoning sections, plus a "wild card" section. The wild card section may be either Verbal or Math, but it will not count toward your score. The wild card section contains questions being tried out for future SATs. You will not, however, be told which is the wild card section.

Verbal Questions

The SAT uses three different kinds of verbal questions: analogies, sentence completions, and critical reading.

Analogies

Analogies ask you to find pairs of words that express similar relationships. Here is an example:

Directions: Select the lettered pair of words that best expresses a relationship similar to that expressed by the capitalized pair of words.

OAK : TREE ::   **(A)** coat : tie   **(B)** flower : leaf   **(C)** whale : mammal
(D) chimney : smoke   **(E)** ant : hill

The answer is (C). An OAK is a kind of TREE, and a *whale* is a kind of *mammal*.

Sentence Completions

Sentence completions ask that you select a word or a pair of words that will complete the meaning of a sentence. Here is an example of a sentence completion:

Directions: Select the word that best completes the meaning of the following sentence.

Although the two students seem to have been longtime friends, in reality they met only -----.

(A) spontaneously   **(B)** ethically   **(C)** quietly
(D) recently   **(E)** emotionally

The answer is (D). The idea is to find the word that, inserted in the sentence, will make sense. When (D) is inserted in the sentence, it makes it clear that the students have not been friends for a long time since they met only recently.

Critical Reading

Critical reading questions are based upon a reading selection. They ask about the author's main point, the logic of the selection, some detail mentioned in the selection, or the tone of the selection. Here is an example:

Directions: Read the following selection and answer the questions that follow it.

Those who discover the people of Appalachia through quiet patience and open friendliness will rediscover something characteristically American. Part of it is awareness and appreciation of the individual, which have characterized every aspect of Appalachian history and culture. Since the romance of James Fenimore Cooper's *Leatherstocking Tales* on the "glimmerglass" of New York's Otsego Lake, Davy Crockett's tall tales of the Tennessee frontier, and the realistic character portrayals of North Carolina's mountain son Thomas Wolfe, there have been numerous efforts to "interpret" Appalachian life.

Even George Washington didn't fathom the ferocity of the Appalachian's claim to personal liberty—until the Whiskey Rebellion caused backwoodsmen to take up arms and march east in protest against excessive taxes on their mountain brew. Before and during the Civil War, mountain independence asserted itself once more: many of the Appalachian counties in Virginia, Tennessee, and North Carolina either seceded from their states or refused to support the Confederacy.

1. The author's primary concern is to
   (A) condemn the backwoodsmen for the Whiskey Rebellion
   (B) describe the character of the people of Appalachia
   (C) list the main geographical divisions of Appalachia
   (D) praise the people of Appalachia for ignoring the Civil War
   (E) criticize literary attempts to interpret Appalachian life

2. According to the author, which of the following are characteristics of the Appalachian people?
   I. ferocity
   II. independence
   III. dishonesty
   (A) I only   (B) I and II only   (C) I and III only
   (D) II and III only   (E) I, II, and III

The first question asks about the main point of the selection. The best answer is (B). (A), (D), and (E) are incorrect for pretty much the same reason. Though the author does mention those things, no condemnation, praise, or criticism is implied. As for (C), the author never gives such a list. (B) is the best description of the author's main point. The passage describes the important traits of the Appalachian people.

The second question asks about specific points mentioned in the selection. The best answer is (B). The first sentence of the second paragraph mentions ferocity; the last sentence of the passage mentions independence. No mention, however, is made of dishonesty.

Thirty-minute verbal sections will contain either 30 or 35 questions. Fifteen-minute verbal sections will contain from 10 to 13 questions. Although some minor variations in format are always possible, here is a typical arrangement of questions.

Verbal Format A

1–9	Sentence Completions
10–15	Analogies
16–30	Critical Reading

Verbal Format B

1–10	Sentence Completions
11–23	Analogies
24–35	Critical Reading

Verbal Format C

1–13	Critical Reading

Math Questions

SAT math questions test arithmetic, basic algebra, and elementary geometry. The specific topics that you should know are discussed later in the chapters on math. Math questions on the SAT have one of two different formats: problem-solving or quantitative comparison. There are two answer modes: multiple-choice or student-produced response.

Problem Solving

The problem-solving format is the one you already know about. It includes manipulation questions, word problems, and geometry questions.
Here are some examples:

If $x = 2$, then $2x(3x - 2) =$
(A) -6 (B) 0 (C) 8 (D) 12 (E) 16

The answer to this algebraic manipulation is (E). You solve the problem by substituting 2 in place of x in the expression $2x(3x - 2)$:

$$2(2)[3(2) - 2] = 4[6 - 2] = 4(4) = 16$$

Here is a word problem:

> Elizabeth reads at a constant rate of 45 pages per hour. If she reads without being interrupted, how long will it take her, in hours, to read a book 360 pages long?
> **(A)** 4   **(B)** 6   **(C)** 8   **(D)** 9   **(E)** 10

The answer is (C). To find the length of time, you would divide the total number of pages by the rate at which Elizabeth reads:

> 360 pages ÷ 45 pages per hour = 8 hours

Finally, here is an example of a geometry question:

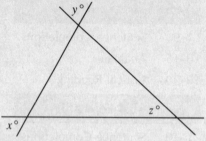

> In the figure above, if $x + y = 100$, then $z =$
> **(A)** 40   **(B)** 50   **(C)** 60   **(D)** 80   **(E)** 90

The answer to this geometry question is (D). Angles x and y, which are outside the triangle, are equal to their opposite angles inside the triangle:

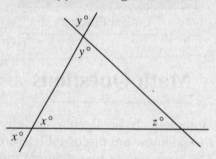

Since the sum of the angles inside a triangle is 180 degrees, we know that $x + y + z = 180$. Then, since $x + y = 100$, we know $100 + z = 180$. So $z = 80$.

Quantitative Comparisons

The other type of math question is called quantitative comparison. Here are the directions for quantitative comparisons plus some examples.

> ***Directions:*** The following questions consist of two quantities, one in Column A and one in Column B.
>
> Answer
> A if the quantity in Column A is greater;
> B is the quantity in Column B is greater;
> C if the two quantities are equal;
> D if the relationship cannot be determined from the information given.

EXAMPLES:

Column A	Column B
0	0 x 5

The answer is (C). Since 0 x 5 = 0, both quantities have the same value.

Column A	Column B
$x - 5$	$x + 5$

The answer is (B). No matter what x is, Column A is 5 less than x while Column B is 5 more than x. Whatever x is, Column B is 10 more than Column A.

Column A	Column B
The cost of a hat that is marked "15% off"	The cost of a hat that is marked "25% off"

The answer is (D). Although you know the percent discount in both cases, you do not know what the original prices were. So it is not possible to determine which cost is greater.

Student-Produced Response

Certain math questions will require you to find the answer without the traditional multiple-choice selections and to record the answer in a grid. The questions will be similar to problem-solving questions. Only your method of responding will differ

EXAMPLE:
What is one possible value of x for which

$$\frac{1}{4} < x < \frac{1}{3}?$$

This question has many possible answers. Staying in fractions, convert both numbers to twenty-fourths: $\frac{6}{24}$ and $\frac{8}{24}$. Thus, one possible answer is $\frac{7}{24}$. You may also convert both numbers to decimals: .250 and .333. In that case, x can have any value between those two decimals. Possible answers include .26, .283, .331, and so on.

The answer grid can be used to show either fractions or decimals. The fraction answer "$\frac{7}{24}$" is gridded like this:

Note: Other possible values of x, such as $\frac{15}{48}$, can also be expressed as fractions. However, such values cannot be used as answers because they will not fit in the space allowed by the grid.

Using decimals, answers would be gridded like this:

Math sections will contain either 10 or 25 questions. Though some minor changes are possible, here is what to expect:

Format A		Format B	
1–25	Problem-Solving	1–15	Quantitative Comparisons
		16–25	Student-Produced Responses

Verbal Format C	
1–10	Problem-Solving

Summary

Here is a summary of what your SAT might look like. Note that the questions on your test could appear in any order, and that the number of questions within individual sections may vary slightly.

SAT

Section 1: Verbal (35 Questions—Time: 30 Minutes)

> Questions   1–5 Sentence Completions
> Questions   6–15 Analogies
> Questions 16–35 Critical Reading

Section 2: Math (25 Questions—Time: 30 Minutes)

> Questions 1–25 Problem-Solving

Section 3: Verbal (10 Questions—Time: 15 Minutes)

> Questions 1–10 Critical Reading

Section 4: Math (10 Questions—Time: 15 Minutes)

> Questions 1–10 Problem-Solving

Section 5: Verbal (35 Questions—Time: 30 Minutes)

> Questions   1–10 Critical Reading
> Questions 11–25 Sentence Completions
> Questions 26–35 Analogies

Section 6: Wild Card (?? Questions—Time: 30 Minutes)

Section 7: Math (25 Questions—Time: 30 Minutes)

> Questions   1–15 Quantitative Comparisons
> Questions 16–25 Student-Produced Responses

Scoring the SAT

SAT results are reported on a scale ranging from 200 (the minimum) to 800 (the maximum). You will receive both a verbal score (200 to 800) and a math score (200 to 800), along with information to help you interpret them.

The first step in scoring is to calculate raw verbal and math scores. Here is how these scores would be calculated for the sample tests in this book.

Calculating Raw Scores

Verbal

Section 1:   _____ − (1/4 × _____) = _____
                   No.   No.
                   Correct   Incorrect

Section 3:   _____ − (1/4 × _____) = _____
                   No.   No.
                   Correct   Incorrect

Section 5:   _____ − (1/4 × _____) = _____
                   No.   No.
                   Correct   Incorrect

Total Verbal raw score   _____

Mathematics

Section 2:   _____ − (1/4 × _____) = _____
                   No.   No.
                   Correct   Incorrect

Section 4:   _____ − (1/4 × _____) = _____
                   No.   No.
                   Correct   Incorrect

Section 6,
Questions
1–15:   _____ − (1/3 × _____) = _____
                   No.   No.
                   Correct   Incorrect

Section 6,
Questions
16–25:   _____ − 0   = _____
                   No.
                   Correct

Total Mathematics raw score   _____

The next step is to round each of the total raw scores. Round all fractions to the nearest whole number. For fractions of one-half or more, round up. For fractions of less than one-half, round down.

The final step is to convert the raw scores to scaled scores using the table on the following page.

SCORE CONVERSION TABLE

	Scaled Scores			Scaled Scores	
Raw Score	SAT-Verbal	SAT-Math	Raw Score	SAT-Verbal	SAT-Math
80	800		40	460	600
79	780		39	450	590
78	760		38	440	580
77	740		37	440	570
76	720		36	430	560
			35	430	550
75	710		34	420	540
74	700		33	410	530
73	690		32	410	530
72	680		31	400	520
71	670		30	390	510
			29	390	500
70	660		28	380	490
69	650		27	370	480
68	640		26	370	470
67	630		25	360	460
66	620		24	350	450
			23	350	440
65	610		22	340	430
64	600		21	330	420
63	600		20	320	420
62	590		19	320	410
61	580		18	310	400
60	580	800	17	300	390
59	570	780	16	300	380
58	570	770	15	290	370
57	560	760	14	280	360
56	550	750	13	270	350
			12	270	350
55	550	740	11	260	340
54	540	730	10	250	330
53	530	720	9	240	320
52	530	710	8	240	310
51	520	700	7	230	300
			6	220	300
50	520	690	5	210	290
49	510	680	4	200	280
48	500	670	3	200	270
47	500	660	2	200	260
46	490	650	1	200	250
45	490	640	0	200	250
44	480	640	−1	200	240
43	470	630	−2	200	230
42	470	620	−3	200	220
41	460	610	−4	200	210
			−5	200	210
			Below	200	200

The Wizard of Odds

✔ **Objective**

To learn the important value of guessing.

1. No Gain, No Pain
2. The Guessing Gold Mine

As you have just learned, part of the scoring of the SAT is an adjustment for wrong answers. This is often called a "guessing penalty," and some test-takers are so afraid of it that they refuse to put down an answer unless they are absolutely certain about it. A serious error!

There is really no "guessing penalty." The adjustment for wrong answers applies to all wrong *answers*, not just to wrong *guesses*. The adjustment is made no matter what reason you have when you give a wrong response. If you are guessing and miss a question, a fraction of a point is subtracted from your total. But the adjustment is also made when you are sincerely trying to answer a question and make an honest mistake. So the wrong answer adjustment is not a punishment. Your problem here is when to guess and when to pass. Let's find out how you can apply common-sense strategies based on some mathematical odds.

No Gain, No Pain

Think about what would happen if you just guessed blindly at every question in a section. Let's take a 35-question verbal section.

Each question has five choices to pick from. So shooting in the dark, on the average, you should get one out of every five, or $\frac{1}{5}$, of the questions right:

$$\frac{1}{5} \text{ of } 35 = 7$$

In other words, random guessing on 35 verbal questions should result in seven correct answers. And that means 28 wrong answers ($35 - 7 = 28$) for a wrong answer adjustment of $28 \times \frac{1}{4} = 7$.

Given seven correct answers and a wrong-answer adjustment of 7, the final result is:

$$7 - 7 = 0$$

In other words, no gain. But then again, no pain.

You should be able to see now that the "guessing penalty" is not really intended as punishment for missing a question. Instead, it is a statistical device that is included in the scoring to neutralize random guessing. On the average, blind guessing neither helps nor hurts.

Of course, on a lucky day, it is theoretically possible that you might be able to guess on every question and get them all right. But the odds of that happening are overwhelmingly against you, and that is certainly not the way you should plan your future.

Does this mean guessing is always a mistake? No! So far, all that has been said is that guessing *randomly* is not a good idea. Sure, you might hit a lucky streak; but you do not really need to rely on luck for a good SAT score.

The Guessing Gold Mine

Many times, mathematical odds make guessing a real gold mine. Remember that "no gain, no pain" results from totally random guessing. The odds change drastically in your favor if you can eliminate one or more of the choices.

Think about what would happen on 35 verbal questions if you were able to eliminate just one choice on each question. You would be in the position of having only four choices per question. What happens if you randomly select from among the four remaining choices?

With only four choices, on the average, you should answer one out of every four questions correctly, for $\frac{1}{4}$ of 35 correct:

$$\frac{1}{4} \text{ of } 35 = 8.75, \text{ or around } 9$$

Answering 9 of 35 correct would mean missing the other 26 questions. So you would incur a wrong-answer adjustment of:

$$\frac{1}{4} \times 26 = 6.5$$

The net result would be:

$$8.75 - 6.5 = 2.25$$

That would be a total gain of a little over 2. Of course, this little "thought experiment" is not totally realistic. It's virtually impossible that you would work a total of 35 problems and be able to eliminate one and only one answer choice on each of them. More realistically, you will be able to answer many of the questions without guessing; but there will be several where you are able to narrow your choice down to two or three possibilities.

Is it still worth guessing on a few questions? Definitely yes! To illustrate, let's assume that there are eight questions in one of the verbal sections that you have a pretty good idea about, but of which you are not certain. You have managed to narrow the possibilities down to two answer choices. Now you have a fifty-fifty chance of guessing correctly. Since you should get one out of two, you should get $\frac{1}{2}$ of the eight correct, for a total of four right. That means four wrong choices, and the adjustment will be $\frac{1}{4}$ of 4, or -1. So the net result of your educated guesses on the eight questions will be $4 - 1 = +3$.

Is +3 worthwhile? Yes; just look back at the conversion tables in the preceding chapter. A gain of just three points on the raw score means a gain of 10 to 20 points on the scaled score. Remember, we are talking just about one section. If you obtained the same results on the other verbal section, that would mean *another* 10 to 20 points, for a total gain on the verbal section of 20 to 40 points on one of the two scores—JUST BY MAKING EDUCATED GUESSES ON A HANDFUL OF QUESTIONS!

3

Summary

To be a Wizard of Odds, remember:

1. For totally random guessing, it's no gain, no pain. Blind guessing is not the way to get your best score.

2. Educated guessing is a gold mine. Anytime you can eliminate one or more answer choices on a question, the odds are definitely in your favor. And even a few more questions can mean an important gain on the scaled score.

Nuts and Bolts

✔ Objectives

To learn how to maximize your performance within the time limit.

To learn how to handle the special time pressure.

To learn how to manage the test booklet and answer sheet so that you get full credit for your performance.

To learn how to respond to the special pressures of the SAT by adjusting your outlook.

1. Maximizing Your Use of Time
   - As Time Goes By...
   - Be in Control
   - Pace Makes the Race
2. The Test Booklet and the Answer Sheet
3. Special Pressures

Lesson 4

Maximizing Your Use of Time

As Time Goes By . . .

Your SAT will consist of seven *separately* timed sections. The proctors will tell you when you can begin working on a section and when your time is up. Once a section is over, you cannot go back to it. So you must answer everything you can in a section during the time given.

In order to do this, you have to keep track of the passing time. Although the proctors do this, there may be problems. First, a proctor may or may not post the time at the exact moment when it changes. For example, a proctor may write on the blackboard "Ten Minutes to Go" when there are really only eight minutes left. Or a proctor may post the time when you're not paying attention. Thus, you might be working away and look up to see "Five Minutes Remaining." But is that a full five minutes, or three minutes, or even 30 seconds?

Be in Control

Bring your own watch to the exam. If you have one with a stop-watch function, use it. A word of warning! Do not use an alarm. The constant "beep-beep" will unfairly distract other test-takers, and the proctors might confiscate your watch for the duration of the exam. Additionally, don't bring a calculator watch. Even if you don't plan to use the calculator function, it might be confiscated until the end of the testing period.

In some ways, a simple watch with a minute hand is the best watch to use. As each period begins, calculate the exact time it will end, either 15 or 30 minutes later. Write that time on your test booklet. That way, you will be able to see at a glance exactly how much time remains.

Pace Makes the Race

Keeping track of time, however, is not your end goal. The real goal is to *use* the time—and to use it effectively. You must pace yourself, working as rapidly as possible without working so quickly that you sacrifice accuracy to speed.

To illustrate the importance of pacing, here are three fictional test-takers: Harriet Hasty, Willie Worrywart, and Teresa Testwise. Their abilities are fairly equal, but they have very different test-taking styles. Let's study their verbal scores. (The point would hold for the math scores as well.)

Harriet Hasty understands the importance of the time limit for each test section, but she believes she has to finish every problem at any cost. Of the 80 verbal questions in the three verbal sections, she makes an attempt at every one and answers 52 of them correctly. That means, however, that she misses 28 questions. Her test report would show:

Correct	minus	$\frac{1}{4}$ (Incorrect)	=	Raw Score	→	Verbal Score
52	−	$\frac{1}{4}$ (28)	=	45	→	490

Willie Worrywort is obsessed with the adjustment for wrong answers. He works very carefully, double- and even triple-checking his work. As a result, he misses very few questions, but there are many questions he does not even have time to look at. He answers correctly on 46 of the 50 questions he attempts, leaving the other 30 questions blank. His test report would show:

Correct	minus	$\frac{1}{4}$ (Incorrect)	=	Raw Score	→	Verbal Score
46	−	$\frac{1}{4}$ (4)	=	45	→	490

Teresa Testwise has a more balanced attitude toward the test. She understands the need to work quickly, but she also knows that needless carelessness is counterproductive. She works quickly enough to answer 74 of the questions in the verbal sections. She leaves the other 6 questions blank since she does not have time even to read them. Of the 74 questions answered, 62 are correct and 12 are incorrect. Her score report would show:

Correct	minus	$\frac{1}{4}$ (Incorrect)	=	Raw Score	→	Verbal Score
62	−	$\frac{1}{4}$ (12)	=	59	→	570

The names I invented for our test-takers tell the whole story. Teresa Testwise's score is the highest. What techniques does a test-wise test-taker use to obtain such results? There are five points you must learn.

1. Don't stop to read directions

No extra time is given for reading the instructions for a section. If you have to read the directions, you are using time that could be better spent answering questions.

There is no reason to read the instructions included in the test booklet. The directions that are used in this book are word for word the same directions that will be in your test booklet. ETS has allowed them to be reprinted here.

2. The tradeoff

The time limit places you in a dilemma. On the one hand, you cannot afford to work so slowly and carefully that you do not try as many questions as you otherwise could. (That is Willie's problem.) On the other hand, you cannot afford to work so quickly that you make foolish errors. (That is Harriet's problem.) Somewhere between the two extremes is the answer.

You will develop your own sense of pacing and find the answer by doing this book's practice exercises. If you find that you are not finishing most of the questions in a practice exercise, then on the next exercise you should speed up. If you find that you are answering most questions but are making a lot of silly mistakes, then slow down.

Finding the best tradeoff is not a science. It is a practical art. Only practice will help you find the answer to the problem.

3. *Climbing the ladder of difficulty*

How much time should you spend on any question? It is, of course, possible to calculate an overall average for a section. Take as an example a verbal section containing 35 questions. To cover all 35 questions in the allotted 30 minutes, on the average, you must dispose of a question every 51 seconds. Unfortunately, this average is really not at all helpful. Things never work out so precisely. Some questions take less time; others take more time.

There is another, more important reason why "average time per question" is not very helpful: the ladder of difficulty. The SAT is designed so that within a section, the questions get progressively more difficult. The following table illustrates this idea for a math section that consists of 25 problem-solving questions.

Question Number	Percent of Students Answering the Question Correctly
1	93%
2	76%
3	82%
4	70%
5	88%
6	81%
7	84%
8	63%
9	65%
10	45%
11	66%
12	61%
13	62%
14	58%
15	48%
16	58%
17	43%
18	41%
19	31%
20	24%
21	29%
22	17%
23	15%
24	19%
25	10%

You can see that questions gradually become more difficult as you work through the section, until they get really tough toward the end. Only 10 percent of test-takers answered the last question correctly.

The increasing difficulty applies only within a particular type of question. In a math section with just one kind of question, the questions go from relatively easy to very hard throughout the section. In other math sections and in the verbal sections, there are groups of different types of questions. Look at what happens in a typical verbal section.

Type of Question	Question Number	Percent of Students Answering the Question Correctly
Sentence Completions	1	93%
	2	88%
	3	82%
	4	82%
	5	77%
	6	61%
	7	67%
	8	55%
	9	36%
	10	47%
	11	26%
	12	29%
	13	28%
	14	31%
	15	26%
Analogies	16	87%
	17	70%
	18	74%
	19	45%
	20	58%
	21	41%
	22	18%
	23	21%
	24	20%
	25	36%

Type of Question	Question Number	Percent of Students Answering the Question Correctly
Critical Reading	26	70%
	27	56%
	28	56%
	29	38%
	30	55%
	31	52%
	32	50%
	33	36%
	34	65%
	35	38%

Questions get progressively more difficult within each group. For example, the first 15 questions are sentence completions. The first sentence completion question (1) is relatively easy, while the last sentence completion question (15) is fairly difficult. The next ten questions (16–25) are analogies. The first analogy (16) is much easier than the last sentence completion (15). (*Note:* When you have several critical reading questions based on the same selection, they are not arranged in strict order. See questions 26 through 35, all ten of which are based on the same selection.)

This "ladder of difficulty" is an important feature of the test design. If you want to attempt all or even most of the questions, you will have to work relatively faster at the beginning of a group, building up a reserve of time to be spent on the more difficult questions in a group.

4. Leapfrogging

A fourth important technique of pacing is leapfrogging, that is, jumping over difficult questions. A question may seem to you to be difficult either because it really is one of the hard ones or because you just happen to have a blind spot for that particular item. Whatever the reason, you cannot afford to spend a lot of time working on a single question.

Remember that each correct answer counts exactly one point toward the raw score—not more, not less. The easiest question on the test adds one point to your raw score; the most difficult question on the test adds one point to your raw score. Why spend five minutes on a difficult analogy when there are easy questions later in the section just waiting to be picked?

Should you automatically skip over groups of questions without making any attempt at all? No. Even when you find that questions are getting more difficult to answer, you should not abandon all hope and move to the next group. This is the time to cut your losses. Quickly look at the questions remaining in that group. Answer the ones you think you can answer without a lot of work; leapfrog over the really difficult ones; and start working on the next group of questions. You can always go back to those you have skipped over if you have time left at the end of the section.

You may find it useful to do some of the questions out of order in a verbal section. Since analogies are shorter than critical reading questions (because of the reading selection), you could do the analogies first. If this works for you, good; if it does not, then do the questions in the order in which they appear.

5. *Throwing in the towel*

The final key to effective pacing is knowing when to give up. You cannot afford to keep working on a question after you have invested a reasonable amount of time with no reward. If you spend three minutes worrying about a question—just waiting for the lightning to strike, so to speak—when you could have used that time to answer four or five other questions, then you are squandering your time.

Once you reach a dead end (you know you do not know what to do or you know it will take too long), throw in the towel. Make your guess and move on to the next question.

The Test Booklet and the Answer Sheet

Your answers to questions must be entered on a separate answer sheet by darkening spaces on a grid. This grid is then read by a machine. The SAT is absolutely unforgiving of mistakes in this respect. If you know the answer to a question but forget to mark your answer sheet, you get no credit. If you mark the wrong space on the answer sheet, you get no credit. If you do not mark your answer sheet clearly, the result is the same: no credit.

It is important to enter your answer choices clearly and correctly. Take a look at a portion of a sample answer sheet:

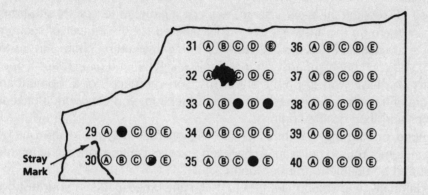

The marks for questions 29 and 35 are made correctly. They are neat and dark, and they completely fill the space. The mark for question 30 does not completely fill the space, so the machine might miss it, giving no credit for the question. The mark for question 31 is not dark enough; and again, the machine might miss it, giving no credit. The mark for question 32 is messy; the machine could read A, B, or C as the intended response.

Question 33 will be graded as an omitted question, since two answers were entered for that question. As with all omitted questions, there is no adjustment for a wrong answer (no "penalty"), but no credit is given either.

Question 34 is blank. It will be treated as an omission. No credit, no wrong-answer adjustment.

Questions 36 through 50 have also been left blank. So assuming there were only 35 questions in the section, this is the correct thing to do with those spaces.

The very worst mistake that you can make with your answer sheet is to enter your responses in the wrong place. You could skip a question in your test booklet and fail to skip the corresponding answer space on your answer sheet. As a result, a whole series of responses is displaced by one question. The correct pattern is there, but it is in the wrong place. The grading machine doesn't grade your intentions, so it reads the marks just as they stand.

You can avoid this error. Aside from taking care in coding answers and checking every now and then to make sure that your problem numbers and answer space numbers match up, there are two further safeguards you should use.

First, keep a separate record of your answer choices in your test booklet. Simply draw a circle around your correct answer choice. If you should make an error in coding responses, this safeguard will allow you to retrieve the information without having to rework every question.

Circle the numbers of any questions that you leapfrog over. This will enable you to locate the questions when you have finished your work and have time to go back and study them. If you do go back and arrive at an answer, blacken in the circle around the number. This lets you know that you have already taken care of the question.

For questions that you answer but are not sure about, place a "?" beside the number. Then, if you have time, you can easily locate the questions and review your solutions. For such questions, if you have definitely eliminated some choices as incorrect, place an "x" over those letters. This will let you concentrate on the remaining choices.

A second method of protecting your answer sheet is entering answers in groups. Why work a problem, shuffle paper, make a mark, work another problem, shuffle paper, make a mark, and so on? This is not only clumsy; it increases the danger of making a silly coding mistake. Instead, work on a group of five or six questions and then mark them on the answer sheet. That will reduce the danger of such errors.

There are natural breaks in a section for doing this coding chore. In the verbal section, you can code your answers when you reach the end of a group. For example, after you have worked on the antonyms, you can pause for a moment and do the chore of transferring answers. In the math section, you can work a page-full of questions and then do the coding.

A word of warning. As time for the section runs out, go to the one-by-one coding system. You do not want to have ten answers waiting for coding in your test booklet and be unable to transfer them.

Additionally, you should feel free to make any other marks in your test booklet that you might find helpful. You can underline phrases, circle words, draw connecting arrows, write notes to yourself, or make any other marks. Do not be afraid to write in the test booklet. You paid for it, and the test booklets are not reused. They are later destroyed.

Go with your choice! Many people do worry about having too many of one letter and not enough of others. When an SAT section is put together, the test-writers make sure that there are approximately equal numbers of each letter. In a section with 40 questions, however, you might have nine (A)s, ten (B)s, eight (C)s, six (D)s, and seven (E)s. The distribution is not perfect.

Also, it is possible to have strings of letters, for example, two or three (D)s in a row. You will not, however, find a string of four or more letters in a row. If you find four (B) answers in a row on your answer sheet, at least one of them is wrong. Unfortunately, you will not know without rechecking each question where the error is.

Special Pressures

The SAT, as you know by now, is different in some very important respects from the teacher-prepared tests you usually get in school. These differences can create special pressures on you.

In the first place, you can expect to experience considerable time pressure. You will probably feel that you are running out of time and that if you only had more time you could definitely answer most if not all of the questions. And this happens not just once, but six times during the test.

Just because you feel time pressure does not mean that you are not doing well. Everyone feels the time pressure. That is part of the design of the test. The objective is to do as many questions as you can within the time limit allowed.

Additionally, you may get the idea that you are not doing very well because you are not answering with confidence. At the back of your mind is the gnawing thought "I like answer (C), but it could be (B), or even (E)." Again, everyone feels this way. Use your best judgment, enter your choice, and do not second-guess yourself.

Finally, you may need to adjust your expectations about performance. What percentage of questions must you answer correctly to get an A or a B on an ordinary exam? You can usually get a B with 80 percent to 90 percent right, and anything above that would be an A. What would 50 percent to 60 percent right be? An F, almost certainly. And no one wants to get an F.

Things are different with the SAT. Getting 50 percent to 60 percent of the questions on the SAT correct does not result in a failing mark. The total number of questions in the verbal sections is 80. Let's assume that your final raw score on the verbal (after the adjustment for wrong answers) is just 50 percent of that, or 40. That would be a raw score of 40 and a scaled score of 460. A verbal score of 460 is 30 to 40 points above the average verbal score nationwide.

A 60 percent is even better. Getting 60 percent of 80 right would give you a raw score of 48 and a scaled score of 500. A score of 500 is nearly 80 points above the national average.

On an ordinary test, 90 percent correct would just barely be a grade of "A." On the SAT, 90 percent of a possible 80 would be a raw score of 72, which would translate into a scaled score of 680!

So you must adjust your expectations slightly. Remember that to get the score you want, you will not need to answer the same number of questions that you would ordinarily have to answer on other tests.

Summary

1. Learn to pace yourself. (1) Don't stop for directions; (2) learn, through practice, the optimal tradeoff for you between speed and accuracy; (3) climb the ladder of difficulty; and (4) know when to leapfrog over a question.

2. Mark your answer sheet carefully, coding in groups. Develop your own record system to keep track of your progress in your test booklet.

3. Understand the special pressures that are created by the SAT and learn to ignore them.

Test Anxiety

✔ Objective

To learn to control the fear of the SAT with knowledge.

1. The SAT and the Fear of Final Judgment
2. Your Contract with ETS
3. Superpeople?
4. They Do Make Mistakes
5. Power to the Test-taker
6. The Score Isn't Everything
7. Exploding the Myth of Final Judgment

The SAT and the Fear of Final Judgment

Many, even most, students experience a sense of dread or foreboding about the SAT. For some, the feeling is no more than an uncomfortable and vague sense of uneasiness. For others, the dread can become unmanageable, leading to what is called test anxiety. In extreme cases, test anxiety can be crippling and can seriously interfere with a person's ability to take a test. This extreme anxiety (the fear of the SAT as a final judgment) is created by a group of mistaken beliefs or impressions that work together to create the greater anxiety. You do not have to experience all of these impressions to feel the strong sense of anxiety. What are these mistaken beliefs and impressions?

Your Contract with ETS

Most people regard the SAT as having a kind of natural authority over them, something like the physical laws that govern the universe. Why is there an SAT? Well, that's like asking why there is gravity. It's just there, a fact of the world. This impression is mistaken.

To see that this impression of natural authority is an error, you need only think about the nature of your relationship to the SAT. When you register to take the SAT, you are entering into a legal contract with ETS (the company that writes and administers the SAT for the College Board). ETS is a company. You are paying that company a fee, and it agrees in turn to provide you with a service. That service is to administer to you a test and to report your scores to the colleges you designate. Because you pay the fee, ETS has a legal obligation to you.

The registration form you sign and the information booklet you receive from ETS set forth in detail the specific provisions of your agreement with the company. Don't worry that all of this is not one single typed document (like a deed); it's still a legal contract. (In fact, most contracts are just verbal agreements, and they are still legally binding.) So you and ETS are parties to a business contract.

Two factors, however, tend to obscure the fact that the relationship between you and ETS is a business contract. First, ETS is a nonprofit corporation. People reason "since ETS is not in business to make a profit, they must administer the SAT for altruistic reasons." This reasoning is mistaken. Though ETS does not show a profit, the people who operate the company are motivated by many of the same concerns that motivate the people who run General Motors or IBM. They are concerned about income, expenses, the quality of their product, their share of the market, customer relations, and so on. In fact, "SAT" is a registered business trademark, like Coca-Cola.

This doesn't mean that the people who work at ETS don't believe in what they do. They believe that they produce a good product and they are proud of it. A nonprofit corporation is not necessarily morally better than any other business.

The second factor that helps to create the impression of natural authority is size. Since ETS is so large, and the SAT is so widespread, it seems almost "natural" to register for the SAT and no other test. But the same can be said of many other large businesses, like power companies. You buy electricity from a particular business because it is the one that services your area. So, too, the SAT "services" a large portion of the country.

Interestingly, ETS does have competitors. Perhaps we will soon see an increase in competition in the area of standardized testing, just as we have seen an increase in competition in telephone communications.

In any event, the SAT really has no natural authority over you. Your relationship is that of a contract—and it takes two parties to make a contract. You are an equal partner to the contract, and you have certain legal rights under it.

Superpeople?

The testing process also creates another impression. You sit down in a classroom at the testing center. You are given the test booklet and told to answer over 200 questions in three hours. You begin to think that the person who wrote these questions must really be superhuman, because you are expected to answer them (and many of them are very difficult) in so short a time. This impression that genius is behind the test is an error.

This test is not written by a single person, nor by two people, nor even three. Rather, the test is the product of a large group of people including teachers, reviewers, and statisticians. Each question is a group effort.

In fact, you will be involved in the process of creating SAT questions. As a final check, questions are included in a non-scoring section of the SAT (the "wild card" section). ETS then uses its computers to check for patterns. Do the questions work in the way they want them to? Student responses on the wild card section of SATs are essential to the development of new versions of the exam.

They Do Make Mistakes

A related impression conveyed by the testing process is that it is free from error. A misconception! In the first place, you are probably aware that every so often ETS slips up. You will find a newspaper report to the effect of "Math Wiz Finds SAT Error." Or on a recent administration, it turned out that many test booklets were defective due to a printing error, and students affected by this ETS error were offered a free make-up. But such errors do not occur very frequently.

The impression of infallibility is a mistake for a more important reason. Built into the scoring of the SAT is a 60-point range of error! The technical term for this is the standard error of measurement. The standard error of measurement for the SAT is 30 points. This means that two-thirds of all scores are within 30 points above or below the "true score." So for most students, an SAT score of 500 represents a true score of anywhere from 470 to 530. And for a full third of the test-takers, the score is even less accurate.

It is an error, therefore, to treat SAT scores as though they are accurate within one or two points. The test is actually a very crude measuring device.

Power to the Test-taker

The testing process can also create a mistaken impression that ETS is all-powerful and that you are powerless. ETS sets the testing dates, the fees, the locations, and the conditions under which you will take the exam. It is true that you have very little say in these matters. Just remember, this is the result of ETS's quasi-monopoly in the area of standardized testing.

ETS controls a large enough share of the market so that you have to do business with it. That is an economic fact of life, like public utilities. But ETS is no more omnipotent than your local electric, gas, or phone company.

This impression of omnipotence can also haunt you as you take the test. You are told where to sit; what you may and may not have with you; when you can use the restroom. And when the proctor reads the rules governing the testing procedure, it may sound as though you are hearing sentence passed. It may be difficult, but try to ignore this feeling. The supervisors and proctors maintain an air of authority to make sure that they can keep control of the situation.

The Score Isn't Everything

One of the most important aspects of the fear of final judgment is the impression of finality created by the testing process. To a certain extent, the result of your test (barring a mistake in scoring) is final. Once graded, that is the score you receive and it doesn't change. But many people have the mistaken impression that bad (or good) things are automatically going to happen as a result of the SAT. In fact, the SAT is a lot less important than you might think.

First, very few colleges (if any) regard SAT scores as either "passing" or "failing." The score is just one more factor used in making a decision, like grades, activities, motivation, and so on. So a "poor" score will not necessarily keep you out of a school, and a "good" score will not guarantee you will get in.

Second, a year after you take the test, no one else will care what your score was. Your college professors will grade you on the basis of your course work. New acquaintances will accept you on the basis of your personality. Student associations will want you as a member for your motivation, energy, and ability.

Exploding the Myth of Final Judgment

I have examined several different impressions about the SAT which I believe are mistaken. No one individual impression would be a very serious cause for concern. But when the individual impressions are taken as a group, they add up to create the fear of final judgment. And it is understandable. You think you are about to be judged by some supreme authority who is both omniscient and omnipotent and that this judgment will be final.

In discussing the "myth" of final judgment, I do not mean to imply that anyone or any group set out to perpetrate a hoax. In particular, I am not suggesting that ETS or the College Board consciously conspired to mislead people. In fact, if you read the information bulletin that comes with the registration materials for the SAT, you will find that ETS and the College Board say many of the same things I have just said.

I suppose that this mistaken impression of final judgment could be just an accident of history, but you do not have to live with it. (After all, at the time of Columbus, almost everyone believed the world was flat.) If you take care to avoid falling under the spell of any one of the individual misconceptions, you should be able to keep any fears you might have about the SAT under control.

Unlocking the Mystery

✔ **Objective**

To learn, through the device of the "Sherlock Holmes SAT Casebook," how to solve the mysteries of the SAT.

1. **Advance Warning**
2. **Multiple-Choice**
3. **Adventures of the SAT**
   - **The Case of the Analogy**
   - **The Case of the Missing Reading Passage**
   - **The Case of the Missing Numbers**
   - **The Case of the Difficult Solution**

Wouldn't it be great to take a test where you had all the questions in advance and the answers right there on the test sheet? Well, the SAT comes close. First, it is almost possible to know in advance what questions will be asked. Second, most answers are actually given to you on the test sheet. These two features of the test form the basis for our system.

Advance Warning

Year after year the SAT is given to millions of students; and, according to ETS, scores are comparable—not just from administration to administration within a given year, but even from year to year. But how is that possible, since different tests are used? The answer is found in the design specifications for the test. Each form of the exam, indeed each question, is written according to special formulas. A question is not acceptable for use on an SAT unless it fits a particular pattern. These patterns are there for you to learn, and that is like having the questions before the test. Of course, you cannot literally have the exact questions that will appear on your particular SAT, but certain patterns are so clearly identifiable that it almost amounts to the same thing.

Multiple-Choice

Additionally, you are actually given the answer to nearly every question on your SAT. Since almost every question on the exam is a multiple-choice question, the right answer is there on the page. Of course, the correct answer is camouflaged in a group of wrong answers; but even though it is partially hidden, it's there for the taking. To demonstrate how important this is, we interrupt this discussion for a:

POP QUIZ

Who was the fourth Chief Justice of the United States Supreme Court?

Time's up! I am not going to give you the correct answer just yet. (If you do know the answer, that's good, and I would want you as my partner in a game of trivia. But for right now, let's assume that you do not know the answer.) It is not the answer to the question that is important to us, but the form of the question.

With a question in this form, you have to come up with an answer from scratch. Either you know the name of the fourth Chief Justice of the Supreme Court or you do not. And if not, you must either leave the question blank or make a wild guess. Either way, your chance of getting credit for the question is very small.

Things change, however, if the question is converted to a multiple-choice format:

POP QUIZ

Who was the fourth Chief Justice of the United States Supreme Court?

(A) xxxxx xxxxxx   **(B)** xxxxx xxxxxx   **(C)** xxxxx xxxxxx
(D) xxxxx xxxxxx   **(E)** xxxxx xxxxxx

Notice that the choices have been covered. Still, even though you cannot read the choices, you are in a much better position than you were before. Given the form of the earlier question, without the knowledge needed to answer the question you had literally no chance of getting credit for it. Now, even though you may not have knowledge that will allow you to answer with confidence, you at least have a fighting chance: pick any letter, and you have a one-out-of-five chance of getting credit for the question.

With real answer choices, you can tip the odds even more in your favor.

POP QUIZ

Who was the fourth Chief Justice of the United States Supreme Court?

(A) Julius Caesar   **(B)** Mickey Mouse   **(C)** Roger Taney
(D) Johnny Carson   **(E)** Madonna

   Enter the letter of your choice here: ____

The answer is (C), and almost everyone can answer correctly even though they have never before seen the name Roger Taney.

How is it possible to answer correctly and even confidently when you don't have the historical fact needed to answer the question? "Easy," you say. "Just eliminate the four choices that could not possibly be correct and select the one that remains."

This method of reasoning is called the Process of Elimination, and it takes advantage of an inherent weakness in the multiple-choice format. One—and only one—of the choices is correct. If you keep eliminating wrong choices, eventually only the correct choice will remain.

Granted, eliminating wrong choices on the SAT will not usually be this easy, but the principle is the same. Even if you cannot eliminate four choices as incorrect, eliminating even one choice tips the odds in your favor and requires a guess. (See Lesson 3, "The Wizard of Odds.")

Patterns and answers are inherent in the SAT. Get rid of either one, and the SAT is no longer the SAT. Therefore, so long as there is an SAT there will be patterns that can be learned and a multiple-choice format that can be taken advantage of.

You are probably familiar with Sherlock Holmes, the fictional detective created by the British writer Sir Arthur Conan Doyle. Using clues and logic, Holmes is able to solve case after case, even though to everyone else the situations seem to present insoluble mysteries. Most people are also familiar with the character of Dr. Watson, Holmes' good-natured friend. Watson, a medical doctor, is clearly a bright person; but his powers of investigation and logical reasoning do not quite equal those of his friend Holmes.

What would happen if these characters took the SAT? I imagine that Watson would do fairly well. He would be able to answer a good many of the questions, but he would likely miss a lot of the more difficult ones. On the other hand, Holmes would surely do very well, getting answers to difficult questions by methods that seem almost magical.

In solving cases, Holmes relies heavily on two techniques: looking for established patterns and the process of elimination. First, in case after case, Holmes refers to his studies of patterns—footprints, cigar ashes, chemicals, and so on. Having foreknowledge of what to look for is often the key to Holmes' solution of a mystery.

Second, Holmes also uses logical reasoning, in particular the process of elimination. In "The Adventure of the Bruce-Partington Plans," Holmes explains to Watson, "When all other contingencies fail, whatever remains, however improbable, must be the truth." That is the process of elimination.

Thus, Holmes succeeded where others failed because he was able to identify patterns and because he reasoned logically. You will notice that these two techniques are the same ones we talked about above.

If Holmes and Watson were to take the SAT, here is what I think would happen.

ADVENTURES OF THE SAT

The Case of the Analogy

One wintery afternoon, Holmes and Watson were riding in the compartment of a train on their way to solve a case. Watson, looking up from a book he was reading, blurted out, "Blast these analogies, Holmes, sometimes they are very tricky. I very nearly missed this one:

> APPLAUSE:APPROVAL::   **(A)** pardon:guilt   **(B)** sound:instrument
> **(C)** laughter:joy   **(D)** vacation:job   **(E)** shout:hearing

I see now that the correct answer must be (C). Applause is a sign of approval, and laughter is a sign of joy. But for a moment I nearly picked (E)."

Sherlock Holmes looked at the question Watson had been studying. "Watson," he said, "you are indeed correct in your analysis of the analogy. Applause is a sign of approval. But you should never even have been tempted to select choice (E). I have made a study of the most common forms of analogies, and this "sign of" analogy is a common one.

"In the past," Holmes continued, "I have seen similar analogies, including: GRIMACE:PAIN, LAUGHTER:JOY, SMILE:HAPPINESS, BLUSH:EMBARRASSMENT, FROWN:DISAPPROVAL, YAWN:BOREDOM, GASP:ASTONISHMENT, NOD: AGREEMENT, GRIN:AMUSEMENT, just to mention a few. In each of these pairs, the first word mentions something that is a sign of what is described by the second word."

Watson immediately objected, "But Holmes, I can't imagine that I would ever find exactly those words on my exam. There are just too many other words that the test-writers could choose."

"Quite right, old friend," responded Holmes. "Those exact words would probably not appear—but the pattern might very well appear. It is the pattern you need to know and look for. Let me write another example for you." Quickly Holmes took a pen and paper and scribbled the following analogy:

> CRINGE:FEAR::   **(A)** flatter:affection   **(B)** announce:usher
> **(C)** eyes:sight   **(D)** shrug:shoulders   **(E)** shudder:disgust

Holmes handed the question to Watson. After a brief glance, Watson nodded, "Of course the answer is (E)!"

"Correct," agreed Holmes. "Once you are familiar with the pattern, the analogy is easy. Of course," he added, "not every question will fall into such a clear pattern. But many do. And, Watson," he continued, "there is always the further technique of logical reasoning, which you have seen me use on so many occasions."

The Case of the Missing Reading Passage

One day Watson came to his friend Holmes with a problem. "Holmes," said Watson, "I have a reading comprehension question that I must answer, but I seem to have lost the reading selection on which the question is based. Now I'll never be able to answer the question."

"Show me the question," insisted Holmes, taking the page offered by Watson. On the page was written:

> The author's attitude toward the new technique of literary criticism about which he is writing is
>
> **(A)** apathetic   **(B)** sentimental   **(C)** scholarly
> **(D)** careless   **(E)** approving

"Why, Watson," exclaimed Holmes, "this is a multiple-choice question! My methods are perfectly suited to it. If we can eliminate four of the five choices by any means whatsoever, then the one choice that remains must be the correct one."

Holmes studied the question for a moment before he spoke further. "We can infer," he began, "from the question itself that in the missing reading selection, the author discussed some new technique of literary criticism. Now let us study the answer choices.

"In the first place, Watson, (A) does not seem to be a possible answer. The question stem informs us that the author has been writing about this new development. But if the author has gone to the trouble of writing an article about something, then it hardly seems likely that the author had no interest in the topic. We conclude, therefore, that the author is not apathetic.

"Now let us examine (B). Could the author's attitude be described as 'sentimental'? Before you answer yes, Watson, let's return to the question. The question asks about the author's attitude toward some *new* development. Is it possible that you would ever describe someone's attitude toward a *new* development as sentimental?"

"No," Watson agreed. "But the author might have regarded the *old* method with affection."

"Perhaps, Watson. But literary criticism does not seem the sort of thing about which one would feel sentimental. And in any case, the question asks for the author's attitude toward the *new* literary criticism—not the old criticism. So you see, (B) cannot be correct."

"So the correct choice must be (C)," offered Watson. "Literary criticism is a scholarly endeavor, so the missing reading passage must have been a scholarly work."

"Not too fast, my dear friend," Holmes interrupted. "Although I readily grant what you say, that does not prove that (C) is the answer we seek. The question does not ask about the author's style but about the author's opinion of the new development. I think you would agree that it makes little sense to say that the author's opinion is scholarly."

"So we must eliminate (C)," said Watson. "Holmes, even if we are not successful in eliminating one of the remaining choices, at least I shall have an even chance of selecting the correct one. It must be either (D) or (E)."

"Well, Watson, it seems to me that we can eliminate (D) on very much the same ground that we eliminated (C). Although 'careless' might describe the author's method in discussing a topic, it would surely not describe the author's attitude toward the new development."

"By Jove, you're right!" Watson exclaimed. "The correct solution is probably (E)."

"Not probably," insisted Holmes. "Certainly! We have eliminated all possibilities but (E) and that *proves* (E) is the correct solution. We now know in fact that the author approves of the new development discussed in the reading selection—even though we do not have a copy of the selection."

The Case of the Missing Numbers

Watson approached Holmes with the following math problem:

> During a sale, the price of a book is reduced by 20 percent. If the price of the book after the reduction is D dollars, what was the original price of the book?
>
> **(A)** $2D$ **(B)** $1.25D$ **(C)** $1.20D$ **(D)** $0.80D$ **(E)** $0.75D$

"I was able to answer this question," announced Watson, "but the algebra took considerable time."

Holmes, smiling, said "Good, Watson! Though I think you might have saved yourself considerable trouble by employing my methods. In the first place, I immediately eliminated choices (D) and (E). They are both *less* than the final reduced price of D dollars, and I know that the original price must be *greater* than D dollars.

"Next I eliminated (A). If a price is reduced from $2D$ dollars to D dollars, it is cut in half. Cutting a price in half reduces it by 50 percent—not 20 percent."

At this point Watson interjected, "But now you are forced to guess. You do have a fifty-fifty chance, but with my approach I can answer with complete certainty."

"Not too quickly," Holmes said. "With one very simple calculation, I can easily arrive at the same position. Since no numbers are provided in the question, I will just supply my own. Let us assume that D, the new price, is $1, a very convenient assumption.

"Now let's test (B). If D, as we assume, is $1, then $1.25D$ is $1.25. Is that consistent with what we are told in the question? Yes. We are told the original price was reduced by 20 percent, or $\frac{1}{5}$. One fifth of $1.25 is $0.25, and if you reduce $1.25 by $0.25, the result is $1. This simple calculation proves that the original price was $1.25D$. (B) is correct."

"But Holmes," objected Watson, "you were merely lucky. Had you selected (C) instead of (B) for your experiment, you would then have had to do two calculations, not just one. And such calculations are time-consuming."

"Not so," countered Holmes. "Even had I selected (C) rather than (B) for my test, I still would have needed only one calculation. When a calculation showed (C) to be incorrect, that, in and of itself, would establish by the process of elimination that the one remaining choice, (B), was correct."

The Case of the Difficult Solution

One afternoon, Watson and Holmes were sitting in the drawing room of their flat. Watson was working through a sample SAT exam, agonizing over a particular question. When he had finally arrived at his solution, he breathed a sigh of relief.

"A knotty problem, Watson?" asked Holmes.

"Yes, the final question in a math section. If you like, I'll share it with you." Watson then read aloud the following:

> Ten players are entered in a chess tournament. If each player is to play every other exactly once, then how many games will be played during the tournament?
>
> **(A)** 100 **(B)** 90 **(C)** 45 **(D)** 10 **(E)** 9

No sooner had Watson finished reading the question than Holmes answered, "An interesting question. The correct choice is (C)."

"You astound me," murmured Watson. "Surely you have seen the question before."

"Not at all," demurred Holmes. "You see, Watson, you told me that this was the last question in the section you had been working on. You know that questions are arranged on a ladder of difficulty. Since this is the last question in the section, it must be very difficult. And difficult questions have difficult solutions.

"Obviously, four of the choices are too easy. If the solution could be obtained just by multiplying 10 by 10, or simply by multiplying 10 by 9, or by the ridiculously easy method of finding the number 10 or the number 9 in the question, the question would not be a difficult one. Since I know by its position in the section that it must be difficult, I eliminated (A), (B), (D), and (E)—leaving only (C) to be correct."

"But Holmes," objected Watson, "there might be some difficult way of arriving at the other choices, making them difficult solutions."

"True. I certainly would not have been this bold were I actually taking an exam. Provided I had the time, I would have worked out an actual solution. But I think my approach is instructive. If you knew that difficult questions have difficult solutions, you would never have been tempted to do something so easy as multiply 9 times 10.

"Having avoided this trap," Holmes went on, "you would be in a position to find the right answer. Each of the ten players does play each of the other nine players, which seems to make for 90 games. But remember, it takes two players to make a game. Although Smith must be matched against Jones and vice versa, this occurs in a single game. Although there are 90 'pairings,' there are only half that number of games."

Most people who take the SAT are in the position of Dr. Watson. They are able to answer most of the easy questions; they answer some of the questions of medium difficulty; but they either leave blank or miss most of the very difficult items. Holmes, on the other hand, with his knowledge of patterns and power of logical thinking, would fare better.

The more you are able to think like Holmes, the better you will do on the SAT. In the chapters that follow, you will read about basic strategies that would be used by Dr. Watson. These strategies are sound, but they are not the final word on attacking the SAT. So you will also learn Holmesian strategies, like those discussed in the stories above, that take advantage of the multiple-choice format of the SAT.

6

PART TWO
The Coaching Program

Lesson 7

Analogies

✔ Objectives

To increase your ability to articulate relationships between verbal concepts.

To recognize answer choices that do not exhibit a necessary relationship.

1. What Is an Analogy?
2. Three Important Facts about SAT Analogies
   - The Ladder of Difficulty
   - Parts of Speech
   - Wrong Answer Choices
3. Watson's Way: The Basic Strategy
4. The Most Common Types of Analogies
5. Tinkering with the Diagnostic Sentence
6. Fine-Tuning the Diagnostic Sentence
7. Tough Calls
8. Shooting in the Dark

55

Your SAT will include 15–20 analogies, one set in each of two verbal sections. In this chapter, you will find many examples of analogies. Some of them may use words with which you are not familiar. If you are not absolutely sure of the meaning of a word, look it up in a dictionary. Then jot a summary of the meaning in the margin of this book by the word. In this way, the meaning will be there for you when you review. Also, you will have added another word to your SAT vocabulary.

7

What Is an Analogy?

In general, an analogy is a parallel that is drawn between two different, but sufficiently similar, events, situations, or circumstances. The SAT uses verbal analogies. A verbal analogy draws a parallel between one pair of words and another pair of words.

Here are the instructions you will find on your SAT for the analogies. Study them now. Don't memorize them; just make sure you understand them. After you are certain you understand the directions, you won't have to look at them ever again. (Remember, when you are taking an SAT, you should not stop to read directions. If you do, you are losing time that could be spent answering questions.)

Each question below consists of a related pair of words or phrases, followed by five lettered pairs of words or phrases. Select the lettered pair that best expresses a relationship similar to that expressed in the original pair.

Example:

YAWN:BOREDOM:: (A) dream:sleep
(B) anger:madness   (C) smile:amusement
(D) face:expression   (E) impatience:rebellion

Ⓐ Ⓑ ● Ⓓ Ⓔ

The single and double colons punctuate the analogy so you know what comparison you are to make. The correct answer is (C): A YAWN is a sign of BOREDOM, and a *smile* is a sign of *amusement*.

YAWN : BOREDOM :: smile : amusement
YAWN *is to* BOREDOM *as* smile *is to* amusement

Verbal analogies are always based on the meanings of words. If you look up *yawn* and *smile* in a dictionary, you will find something like this:

---

yawn   To open the mouth wide, especially involuntarily, and with a deep inhalation, as a
             result of fatigue, drowsiness, or boredom.
smile   To have or take on a facial expression showing pleasure, amusement . . . .

It is part of the meaning of *yawn* that it can be a sign of boredom. And it is a part of the meaning of *smile* that it can be a sign of amusement. All SAT analogies are characterized by this "tight" fit between words.

Another way of describing this "tight" fit is to say that the connection between the pair of words is a *necessary* connection. A *necessary* connection of this sort is based entirely on meaning. You do not need to know anything about the particular facts of the case to understand the connection. All you have to do is think about the meanings of words. To illustrate the point, contrast the following sentences:

This bachelor is not married.
This clerk is not married.

The first sentence is necessarily true because part of the meaning of *bachelor* is "unmarried." The second sentence may or may not be true, depending on the clerk's marital status.

For this reason, you would never find on the SAT a capitalized pair of words such as CLERK:MARRIED. "Clerk:married" could be a *wrong* answer choice; but "clerk:married" could not be a correct answer, nor could it be the capitalized words. BACHELOR:MARRIED, however, could be the basis for an analogy because of the necessary connection between the words.

Knowing that the connections you are looking for must be "tight" can help you to attack verbal analogies.

EXAMPLE:

LOW:CATTLE::   **(A)** run:horses   **(B)** grunt:hogs   **(C)** scratch:chickens
(D) plant:crops   **(E)** store:grain

At first glance, you might think that LOW in this analogy means "not high, close to the ground." Then you are forced to say something like, "Well, some cows might be short." But "short" is not part of the meaning of *cattle,* so that cannot be the meaning intended in the analogy.

LOW also refers to the sound made by cattle, and that is the meaning intended here. Using this meaning, there is a necessary connection between our capitalized words: LOW is the sound made by CATTLE. The correct answer, therefore, is (B): *grunt* is the sound made by *hogs.*

Three Important Facts about SAT Analogies

1. Analogies are presented according to the ladder of difficulty. In a group of ten analogies, the first three are very easy. More than three quarters of all test-takers are able to answer them. The middle three or four analogies are of moderate difficulty. Only about half of the test-takers get them right. The remaining analogies are so difficult that fewer than a third of the test-takers answer them correctly. In fact, the tenth analogy may be so difficult only 10 percent or so of all test-takers are successful in answering it correctly.

What makes one analogy more difficult than another? Two factors: (1) the level of vocabulary used, and (2) the type of relationship tested.

In the first instance, some analogies are difficult because they contain difficult vocabulary words.

EXAMPLES:

BEE:HIVE::   **(A)** horse:carriage   **(B)** rider:bicycle   **(C)** sheep:flock
(D) cow:barn   **(E)** dog:show

BEE:APIARY::   **(A)** horse:carriage   **(B)** rider:bicycle   **(C)** sheep:flock
(D) cow:barn   **(E)** dog:show

The answer to both analogies is (D), and the justification is the same in both cases. A HIVE is a home for BEES, just as a *barn* is a home for *cows*. Similarly, an APIARY is used to house BEES, just as a *barn* is used to house *cows*.

The second analogy, however, is more difficult than the first, because the word APIARY is less well-known than HIVE. In a later section of this lesson ("Shooting in the Dark"), you will be given several Holmesian strategies for dealing with those situations where you encounter one or more words you do not know.

A second reason that some analogies are more difficult is the type of relationship used. Some analogy relationships are concrete. The relationship just discussed ("is a home for") is quite familiar and very concrete. The following analogy is more abstract.

EXAMPLE:

SCRUPULOUS:PRINCIPLES::   **(A)** clever:madness   **(B)** melancholy:joy
(C) ethical:morals   **(D)** altruistic:profits   **(E)** indulgent:denial

The best answer to this more difficult analogy is (C). One who is SCRUPULOUS is by definition someone having PRINCIPLES. Similarly, one who is *ethical* is by definition someone having *morals*.

2. All SAT analogies are constructed using nouns, adjectives, and occasionally verbs. The answer choices will reflect the grammatical structure of the capitalized pair of words. The most common grammatical form is:

NOUN:NOUN::   **(A)** noun:noun   **(B)** noun:noun   **(C)** noun:noun
(D) noun:noun   **(E)** noun:noun

A less common possibility, but one that is used quite a bit, is:

ADJECTIVE:NOUN::   **(A)** adjective:noun   **(B)** adjective:noun
(C) adjective:noun   **(D)** adjective:noun   **(E)** adjective:noun

Since the first capitalized word is an adjective, the first word of each answer choice will also be an adjective. And since the second capitalized word is a noun, the second word of each answer choice will also be a noun.

There are other possibilities, such as VERB:NOUN, and so on, but there is no need to memorize the possibilities. Just remember that the parts of speech of the choices will always reflect those of the capitalized words.

This feature of analogies is important, because some words are ambiguous with respect to part of speech.

EXAMPLE:

PLANT:FERTILIZER::   **(A)** animal:food   **(B)** rose:thorn   **(C)** harvest:plenty   **(D)** season:hunting   **(E)** restaurant:menu

One way of looking at the capitalized pair of words is to say that "you plant something and then you give it fertilizer." But there is no answer choice that corresponds to this relationship. For example, it makes no sense to say "you rose something and then you give it a thorn." What has happened? The word *plant* is ambiguous. It can be either a verb (meaning "to put something in the ground so it will grow") or a noun (referring to a living thing that is not an animal).

In this analogy the word *plant* is meant to be a noun, not a verb. If you treat *plant* as a noun, then you might describe the connection between the two capitalized words in this way: "fertilizer is nourishment for a plant" and "food is nourishment for an animal." But how do you know what part of speech is intended?

You can resolve any ambiguity about part of speech by looking at the answer choices. The parts of speech of the answer choices must be parallel to those of the capitalized words. If you are in doubt as to whether *plant* is intended to be a verb or a noun, look at the first word in some of the answer choices. You will find some words that can be only one part of speech. For example, in choice (A), *animal* can be only a noun. This tells you that *plant* is also intended to be a noun—not a verb.

3. Wrong answer choices are carefully prepared. They must be wrong, but they are not supposed to be so obviously wrong that the analogy is a dead giveaway.

An answer choice will be wrong for one of two reasons. Either (1) it expresses a relationship that is not parallel to the connection between the capitalized words, or (2) it expresses no necessary relationship at all. The next analogy contains both types of wrong answers.

EXAMPLE:

BOAST:VANITY::   **(A)** gloat:satisfaction   **(B)** write:novel   **(C)** primp:humility   **(D)** apologize:profit   **(E)** mail:photograph

The best answer to this analogy is (A). To BOAST is a sign of VANITY, and to *gloat* is a sign of satisfaction. What is wrong with the incorrect choices?

First, a choice may be wrong because it expresses a wrong relationship. This is the case with (B). There is a perfectly good and necessary relation between *write* and *novel*. A novel is a written work, but that is not the connection we found between the capitalized words.

BOAST:VANITY   To BOAST is a sign of VANITY.
(B) write:novel   To *write* is a sign of a *novel*. WRONG!

(C) is wrong for the same reason. Again, there is a necessary relationship between the two words, but that relationship is the opposite of the one connecting the capitalized words.

BOAST:VANITY   To BOAST is a sign of VANITY.
(C) primp:humility   To *primp* is a sign of *humility*. WRONG!

Second, a choice may be wrong because it expresses no relationship at all. Choice (D) is an example of this sort of wrong answer. What relationship could there be between *apologize* and *profit*? You might strain to make a connection, for example, "One might *apologize* for making a *profit*." True, you might; but that is not a necessary connection based on the meanings of the words involved. Remember, a necessary connection based on meanings is the test of an appropriate connection in an SAT verbal analogy.

Choice (E) is wrong for this reason as well. Again, it is possible to say "one could *mail* a *photograph*." That is true, you could. But you could also mail a thousand and one other things. On the other hand, a *photograph* does not, by definition, belong in *mail*.

Eliminating non-answers (pairs that express no necessary relationship) is a powerful attack strategy. The following exercise will help you learn how to identify non-answers.

Identifying Non-Answers (Answers, page 80)

In this exercise, you will find a list of 50 pairs of words. Twenty-five of them are possible analogy items because there is a necessary relationship between the two words. The other 25 pairs are non-answers because there is no necessary relationship between them. Place a check-mark by all of those that are possible analogies and an x by those that are non-answers.

1. OAR:BOAT _____
2. KNIFE:TRUCK _____
3. HORSE:TREE _____
4. CASINO:GAMBLING _____
5. SYRUP:APPLES _____
6. ROOF:CURTAIN _____
7. LISP:SPEECH _____
8. JOG:SPRINT _____
9. PAINT:DRAWER _____
10. ROCK:QUARRY _____
11. SCRIBBLE:WRITE _____
12. BLINK:LISTEN _____
13. UNICORN:CATASTROPHE _____
14. PASTEL:COLOR _____
15. ROGUE:MARKET _____
16. TARGET:WOUND _____
17. KEYSTONE:ARCH _____
18. IMPOSTER:CHEAPSKATE _____
19. BRAZEN:TRUSTWORTHY _____
20. RESTIVE:AGREEMENT _____
21. ARROW:QUIVER _____
22. MELT:LIQUID _____
23. CHAOS:ORDER _____
24. PLATEAU:RIVER _____
25. CREDENTIALS:COMMERCE _____

26. ADMIRATION:COMPETITOR _____
27. PLANT:AMPHIBIAN _____
28. STREAM:RIVER _____
29. MOCKERY:QUALITY _____
30. SYMPHONY:MUSIC _____
31. LINGUISTICS:LANGUAGE _____
32. CONFIDENCE:POSSESSION _____
33. DEBUT:BEGINNING _____
34. IMPULSE:DELIBERATION _____
35. PASSIVE:LONGING _____
36. DISASTER:PREDICTION _____
37. NOMAD:MOUNTAINS _____
38. LANGUISH:PROCUREMENT _____
39. IMITATION:ORIGINALITY _____
40. VOLATILE:VAPORIZATION _____
41. DAIS:SPEAKER _____
42. PHOTOSYNTHESIS:TROPICS _____
43. EPAULET:SHOULDER _____
44. APPROBATION:COMPLIMENT _____
45. INTREPID:FEAR _____
46. OPULENCE:WEALTH _____
47. IMPERATIVE:ILL-FATED _____
48. MALADROIT:SKILL _____
49. LEVITY:CONFUSION _____
50. MOTLEY:VARIETY _____

Watson's Way: The Basic Strategy

Verbal analogies ask that you identify the relationship between two words and find another pair of words that parallel as closely as possible that same relationship.

The first step in analyzing an SAT analogy is to describe the connection between the capitalized words. The best way to do this is to formulate a sentence that expresses the connection between the two words. Since the purpose of this sentence is to analyze or diagnose the nature of the connection between the capitalized words, we will call it the diagnostic sentence, or DXS for short.

After you have formulated a DXS, test each answer choice to find the pair of words that best fits the sentence.

EXAMPLE:

ECSTASY:PLEASURE::   **(A)** hatred:affection   **(B)** condemnation:approval
(C) rage:anger   **(D)** difficulty:understanding   **(E)** privacy:invasion

The first step is to formulate your diagnostic sentence. ECSTASY means "great or overwhelming PLEASURE," so your diagnostic sentence might be "ECSTASY is extreme PLEASURE."

The second step is to test each of the answer choices.

... is extreme ....
(A) *Hatred* is extreme *affection.*
(B) *Condemnation* is extreme *approval.*
(C) *Rage* is extreme *anger.*
(D) *Difficulty* is extreme *understanding.*
(E) *Privacy* is extreme *invasion.*

(C) is the best answer, for (C) has the only pair of words that correctly fit the DXS.

EXAMPLE:

ACCIDENTAL:INTENTION::   **(A)** voluntary:requirement
(B) anticipated:performance   **(C)** interesting:feeling
(D) practical:knowledge   **(E)** insane:correction

A good way of expressing the relation between the capitalized words is "Something that is ACCIDENTAL is done without INTENTION." Now test each of the answer choices in the diagnostic sentence.

Something that is ... is done without ....
(A) Something that is *voluntary* is done without *requirement.*
(B) Something that is *anticipated* is done without *performance.*
(C) Something that is *interesting* is done without *feeling.*
(D) Something that is *practical* is done without *knowledge.*
(E) Something that is *insane* is done without *correction.*

(A) is the best answer, and it is the only substitution that makes sense in the DXS.

This strategy of diagnostic sentences is sound. It would be used by Dr. Watson, and he would be very successful on the first three or four analogies in a group. Then the ladder of difficulty would take over, and Watson would find it more difficult to formulate an effective DXS. To improve his chances, Watson could use some advice from Holmes.

The Most Common Types of Analogies

Holmes was a great student of patterns, and his knowledge of past patterns helped him to understand new situations as he encountered them. Holmes would use common patterns to make it easier to formulate a DXS.

1. ... is a defining characteristic of .... This is by far the most common type of analogy used on the SAT. For example, WISDOM:SAGE. A sage is a person of great wisdom. So a good diagnostic sentence for this pair would be "WISDOM is a defining characteristic of a SAGE."

EXAMPLES:

COURAGE:HERO   COURAGE is a defining characteristic of a HERO.
ELECTION:DEMOCRACY   An ELECTION is a defining characteristic of a DEMOCRACY.
STINGINESS:MISER   STINGINESS is a defining characteristic of a MISER.
DOUBT:SKEPTICISM   DOUBT is a defining characteristic of SKEPTICISM.
SKILL:VIRTUOSO   SKILL is a defining characteristic of a VIRTUOSO.

2. Lack of ... is a defining characteristic of .... This is the mirror image of the connection just discussed, and it too is commonly used on the SAT. For example, RAIN:DROUGHT. Lack of RAIN is a defining characteristic of DROUGHT.

EXAMPLES:

HOPE:PESSIMISM   Lack of HOPE is a defining characteristic of PESSIMISM.
FLAW:PERFECTION   Lack of any FLAW is a defining characteristic of PERFECTION.
COMPANIONSHIP:HERMIT   Lack of COMPANIONSHIP is a defining characteristic of a HERMIT.
IDENTITY:ANONYMITY   Lack of IDENTITY is a defining characteristic of ANONYMITY.
DOMICILE:VAGRANT   Lack of DOMICILE is a defining characteristic of a VAGRANT.

3. ... is a type of .... In this connection, the first word in the pair is a specific type of the second word.

EXAMPLES:

ANGER:EMOTION   ANGER is a type of EMOTION.
ORANGE:FRUIT   An ORANGE is a type of FRUIT.
SONNET:POEM   A SONNET is a type of POEM.
MISDEMEANOR:CRIME   A MISDEMEANOR is a type of CRIME.
MURAL:PAINTING   A MURAL is a type of PAINTING.

4. ... is a part of .... This connection is simply that of part to whole.

EXAMPLES:

LETTER:ALPHABET   A LETTER is a part of an ALPHABET.
CHAPTER:NOVEL   A CHAPTER is a part of a NOVEL.
CREST:WAVE   The CREST is a part of a WAVE.
BRANCH:TREE   A BRANCH is a part of a TREE.
TREAD:TIRE   The TREAD is a part of a TIRE.

5. . . . is the place for . . . . With this sort of analogy, the first word indicates where you would find the person or thing referred to by the second word.

EXAMPLES:

CLINIC:NURSE   A CLINIC is the place for a NURSE.
STAGE:PERFORMER   A STAGE is the place for a PERFORMER.
PULPIT:MINISTER   A PULPIT is the place for a MINISTER.
DICTIONARY:DEFINITION   A DICTIONARY is the place for a DEFINITION.
DRY DOCK:SHIP   A DRY DOCK is the place for a SHIP.

6. Relation of Degree. Some analogy words are connected by a relation of degree.

EXAMPLES:

MOUNTAIN:HILL   A MOUNTAIN is a large HILL.
EPIC:STORY   An EPIC is a long STORY.
HURRICANE:BREEZE   A HURRICANE is more powerful than a BREEZE.
DELUGE:RAIN   A DELUGE is a great RAIN.
EXCLAMATION:STATEMENT   An EXCLAMATION is stronger than a STATEMENT.

7. Tools. Some analogies are based upon the connection between a person and the tool that a person uses or upon a tool and the result that it achieves.

EXAMPLES:

SCALPEL:SURGEON   A SCALPEL is the tool of a SURGEON.
WRENCH:MECHANIC   A WRENCH is the tool of a MECHANIC.
PEN:WRITER   A PEN is the tool of a WRITER.
PAINTING:BRUSH   A PAINTING is the result of a BRUSH.
HOLE:DRILL   A HOLE is the result of a DRILL.

8. . . . is a sign of . . . . In this sort of analogy, one word refers to something that is a sign of something.

EXAMPLES:

TREMBLING:FEAR   TREMBLING is a sign of FEAR.
SIGH:RELIEF   A SIGH is a sign of RELIEF.
MOAN:PAIN   A MOAN is a sign of PAIN.
HISS:DISAPPROVAL   A HISS is a sign of DISAPPROVAL.

9. Order. In this type of connection, one event follows another, either as a matter of logic or sequence, or as an effect follows its cause.

EXAMPLES:

ENGAGEMENT:MARRIAGE   An ENGAGEMENT comes before a MARRIAGE.
CONVICTION:SENTENCE   CONVICTION comes before the SENTENCE.
EXPLOSION:DESTRUCTION   An EXPLOSION causes DESTRUCTION.
VIRUS:ILLNESS   A VIRUS causes ILLNESS.

7

10. Interruption. In this type of connection, one word indicates something that interrupts the events described by the other word.

EXAMPLES:

EXTINGUISHER:FLAME   An EXTINGUISHER stops the FLAME.
LUBRICANT:FRICTION   A LUBRICANT stops the FRICTION.
BREAKDOWN:OPERATION   A BREAKDOWN interrupts OPERATION.
DISMISSAL:EMPLOYMENT   DISMISSAL interrupts EMPLOYMENT.

These are the ten most common connections found in SAT verbal analogies, but you cannot hope to apply them automatically and without thought. The list will help you get organized and be more efficient, but it will not eliminate the need for mental work.

Common Connections (Answers, page 81)

This exercise contains 50 pairs of words that could be used on the SAT. Each pair is an example of one of the ten common analogies. Using the key provided below, write the number of the common analogy each pair of words represents.

Pattern Key	
1. Defining characteristic	**6.** Degree
2. Lack of	**7.** Tool
3. Type of	**8.** Sign of
4. Part of	**9.** Order (Sequence or Cause)
5. Place for	**10.** Interruption

1. JUDGE:COURTROOM ____

2. STAR:GALAXY ____

3. NOTE:SCALE ____

4. SCULPTOR:CHISEL ____

5. SNIFTER:BRANDY ____

6. WHALE:OCEAN ____

7. GRIMACE:PAIN ____

8. VACCINATION:IMMUNITY ____

9. TEA:BEVERAGE ____

10. WORK DAY:LUNCH ____

11. SIP:GUZZLE ____

12. LUMBERJACK:AX ____

13. TIFF:BATTLE ____

14. MAST:SHIP ____

15. CROWN:ROYALTY ____

16. APPETIZER:DESSERT ____

17. JOY:EMOTION ____

18. CELLO:BOW ____

19. SEMINARY:THEOLOGIAN ____

20. SAND:SMOOTHNESS ____

21. CROUCH:SPRING ____

22. EROSION:GULLY ____

23. CRUSADER:CAUSE ____

24. COLANDER:CHEF ____

25. TERMITE:INSECT ____

26. CONDEMNED:EXECUTED ____

27. INVENTION:ORIGINALITY ____

28. ALIEN:CITIZENSHIP ____

29. FALLACIOUS:ERROR ____

30. MORTIFICATION:EMBARRASSMENT ____

31. INEFFABLE:EXPRESS ____

32. EPHEMERAL:PERISH ____

33. ARACHNID:TARANTULA ____

34. PROCRASTINATION:HASTE ____

35. PROSELYTIZE:CONVERSION ____

36. PARIAH:SCORN ____

37. DELIRIUM:SENSE ____

38. PROTAGONIST:CHARACTER ____

39. NEGLIGENCE:CARE ____

40. RECOVERY:RELAPSE ____

41. IDYLL:CARE ____

42. GARRULOUS:TALK ____

43. DEFAULT:FORECLOSURE ____

44. ENTHUSIASM:MANIA ____

45. SOOTHSAYER:PROPHECY ____

46. COMA:CONSCIOUSNESS ____

47. PUNDIT:KNOWLEDGE ____

48. PHILANTHROPIST:BENEVOLENCE ____

49. AUSTERITY:ORNAMENTATION ____

50. EVICTION:RESIDE ____

Tinkering with the DXS

In the examples we have been studying, the capitalized words fit neatly into the suggested DX sentence. Two factors—word order and part of speech—can obscure a relationship, making it slightly more difficult to see.

First, word order can make things a little more difficult because the words do not fit into the format in the right order. What should you do? Just reverse the order of the capitalized words and the words in the choices.

> **EXAMPLE:**
>
> TRAITOR:DISLOYALTY::   **(A)** rebel:defiance   **(B)** general:army
> **(C)** executioner:reliability   **(D)** artist:business   **(E)** banker:marketing

The best answer is (A), and you can easily see this if you reverse the word order:
   DISLOYALTY is a defining characteristic of a TRAITOR.
   (A) *Defiance* is a defining characteristic of a *rebel*.
   (B) *Army* is a defining characteristic of a *general*.
   (C) *Reliability* is a defining characteristic of an *executioner*.
   (D) *Business* is a defining characteristic of an *artist*.
   (E) *Marketing* is a defining characteristic of a *banker*.

A second factor may work to make it difficult to recognize a common relationship: part of speech. The analogies above were all constructed using only nouns. But it is also possible to build analogies using adjectives and verbs. There are two ways of handling this problem. One, change the wording of your DXS; two, change the parts of speech of the analogy words.

First, you can tinker with your DXS by changing its wording. Here's how that works:

> **EXAMPLE:**
>
> BETRAY:TREACHERY::   **(A)** acknowledge:infamy   **(B)** amuse:horror
> **(C)** abandon:desertion   **(D)** inflate:reduction   **(E)** contend:victory

The best answer is (C). The key to this analogy is one of the most common of all relations, the "defining characteristic" connection. But the capitalized words will not fit neatly into the ordinary DXS: BETRAY is a defining characteristic of TREACHERY. This is because BETRAY is a verb, not a noun. You can easily get around the problem by tinkering with your DXS.
   To BETRAY is a defining characteristic of TREACHERY.
   (A) To *acknowledge* is a defining characteristic of *infamy*.
   (B) To *amuse* is a defining characteristic of *horror*.
   (C) To *abandon* is a defining characteristic of *desertion*.
   (D) To *inflate* is a defining characteristic of *reduction*.
   (E) To *contend* is a defining characteristic of *victory*.

An alternative strategy is to change the part of speech of some word in the analogy.

EXAMPLE:

KNOW:IGNORANCE::   **(A)** cure:health   **(B)** construct:school
(C) invite:party   **(D)** educate:graduation   **(E)** breathe:suffocation

The best answer is (E). KNOW and IGNORANCE are joined by a "lack of" connection, but the grammatical form of the analogy (VERB:NOUN) makes this difficult to see. It would be much easier to see the connection if both words were nouns. In your mind, change all the first words to nouns.

Lack of KNOWLEDGE is a defining characteristic of IGNORANCE.

(A) Lack of a *cure* is a defining characteristic of *health*.
(B) Lack of *construction* is a defining characteristic of a *school*.
(C) Lack of *invitation* is a defining characteristic of a *party*.
(D) Lack of *education* is a defining characteristic of *graduation*.
(E) Lack of *breath* is a defining characteristic of *suffocation*.

Now it is easy to see that (E) is the best answer.

7

Formulating DX Sentences (Answers, page 82)

This exercise includes 50 pairs of words. Each pair is joined by a necessary connection. In the blank provided, formulate a diagnostic sentence that describes the connection. **Note:** Not all of the connections fall into one of the categories already discussed. Use your imagination, and feel free to change the part of speech of a word.

1. OAK:TREE _____

2. SOLDIER:WEAPON _____

3. PUN:JOKE _____

4. MAGAZINE:PERIODICAL _____

5. PLANT:HARVEST _____

6. DRIFTING:ANCHOR _____

7. COURAGE:VIRTUE _____

8. STUMBLE:FALL _____

9. TOSS:HURL _____

10. VIOLINIST:ORCHESTRA _____

11. REQUEST:DEMAND _____

12. FROWN:DISAPPROVAL _____

13. PALLOR:COLOR _____

14. CALLIGRAPHY:WRITING _____

15. MYTH:REALITY _____

16. BIRD:NEST _____
_____

17. WIND:KITE _____
_____

18. COW:MEADOW _____
_____

19. LIAR:FALSEHOOD _____
_____

20. PRESERVATIVE:DECAY _____
_____

21. GOOSE:GAGGLE _____
_____

22. DELINQUENT:TIMELINESS _____
_____

23. VEHICLE:CONVOY _____
_____

24. BOOK:LIBRARY _____
_____

25. PIONEER:UNKNOWN _____
_____

26. DIPLOMAT:TACT _____
_____

27. ENDEARMENT:AFFECTION _____
_____

28. TREATMENT:CONVALESCENCE _____
_____

29. RECKLESSNESS:CAUTION _____
_____

30. PERJURER:TRUTH _____
_____

31. DAMPEN:SATURATE _____
_____

32. GROTTO:CAVE _____
_____

33. DITTY:HUMOR _____
_____

34. HUNGRY:RAVENOUS _____
_____

35. DAM:FLOW _____
_____

7

36. SHRIEK : TERROR _____

_____

37. RIPEN : WITHER _____

_____

38. BANALITY : FRESH _____

_____

39. MAGNATE : MERCHANT _____

_____

40. STARVATION : NUTRITION _____

_____

41. PROSE : WRITING _____

_____

42. EXHAUSTION : ENERGY _____

_____

43. GIGGLE : LAUGHTER _____

_____

44. INTERMISSION : PERFORMANCE _____

_____

45. LEAN : EMACIATED _____

_____

46. POEM : ANTHOLOGY _____

_____

47. SHOT : VOLLEY _____

_____

48. STOIC : RESIGNATION _____

_____

49. GOURMAND : SELF-RESTRAINT _____

_____

50. INSOMNIA : SLEEP _____

_____

Fine-Tuning the DXS

You may find that your first formation of a diagnostic sentence is satisfied by more than one answer choice.

> **EXAMPLE:**
>
> VERDICT:TRIAL::   **(A)** audience:play   **(B)** finish:race   **(C)** overture:opera
> **(D)** recovery:operation   **(E)** act:drama

A good first cut at this analogy might be "The VERDICT is a part of the TRIAL." Using this diagnostic sentence, you would have:

  The . . . is a part of the . . . .
  (A) The *audience* is a part of the *play*.
  (B) The *finish* is a part of the *race*.
  (C) The *overture* is a part of the *opera*.
  (D) The *recovery* is a part of the *operation*.
  (E) The *act* is a part of the *drama*.

The diagnostic sentence eliminates both (A) and (D). The *audience* is not a part of the *play*; and the *recovery* is not a part of the *operation*. But we are still left with three possibilities.

  (B) The *finish* is a part of the *race*.
  (C) The *overture* is a part of the *opera*.
  (E) The *act* is a part of the *drama*.

Our original formulation " . . . is a part of . . . " is too crude. It is correct so far as it goes, but we must go further. Try to articulate more precisely the relationship between the capitalized words.

   After studying the capitalized words more carefully, you would probably see that the *verdict* is a particular part of the *trial*: the end. So you would refine your diagnostic sentence:

  The . . . is the final part of the . . . .
  (B) The *finish* is the final part of the *race*.
  (C) The *overture* is the final part of the *opera*.
  (E) The *act* is the final part of the *drama*.

With this refined diagnostic sentence, we can eliminate both (C) and (E). The *overture* is the first, not the last, part of the opera. And an *act* can be any subdivision of a *drama*—the first, second, or last act. Only (B) truly parallels the relationship we are looking for. The *finish* is the final part of the *race*.

Tough Calls

Even after you have fine-tuned your DXS, you still may not be able to settle on a single choice. You may be forced to pick from among two or even three answers. These we term "tough calls." Here are two Holmesian strategies for dealing with "tough calls."

First, even in tough cases, wrong answers are wrong; and they are wrong for specific reasons. Holmes would try to isolate the wrong choices in a tough call by finding weaknesses in those choices. A good technique for finding weaknesses is to try to improve an answer choice. Try changing an answer choice. If you can improve it, it was not correct in its original form.

EXAMPLE:

SUPPORT:PATRON::   **(A)** acceptance:donor   **(B)** loyalty:patriot
(C) apathy:zealot   **(D)** deception:anarchist   **(E)** entertainment:narrator

A good DX sentence for this analogy might use the common linkage of "... is a defining characteristic of ...."
SUPPORT is a defining characteristic of a PATRON.
(A) *Acceptance* is a defining characteristic of a *donor*.
(B) *Loyalty* is a defining characteristic of a *patriot*.
(C) *Apathy* is a defining characteristic of a *zealot*.
(D) *Deception* is a defining characteristic of an *anarchist*.
(E) *Entertainment* is a defining characteristic of a *narrator*.

Our DX sentence allows us easily to eliminate (C) and (D). Let's assume for the purpose of the discussion that you cannot eliminate any other of the remaining choices, because each at least arguably fits into the sentence.

You could say about (A) that unless there is an *acceptance* of something, the *donor* is not really a *donor* at all because nothing has been given. Of (E), you could say that a *narrator* can supply *entertainment*. Ultimately, these choices are wrong, but in what ways are they flawed? Try improving them.

Take (A). What really is the *defining* characteristic of a *donor*? Giving of a gift. So had (A) read *gift:donor*, then it would have fit the sentence: A *gift* is the defining characteristic of a *donor*. So (A), as originally written, really does not fit the sentence, and improving on the original (A) makes us realize that.

Now take (E). What really is the *defining* characteristic of a *narrator*? Telling a story. So had (E) read *story:narrator*, (E) would have fit the sentence: A *story* is the defining characteristic of a *narrator*. So (E), as originally written, does not fit the sentence very precisely. It cannot be the *best* answer.

A second strategy for tough calls is to look for an *indirect* relationship. Thus far we have studied only direct relationships—those that work between the first and second words of a pair. An indirect relationship works between the first word of one pair and the first word of another pair, or between the second word of one pair and the second word of another pair.

The idea of an indirect relationship can be illustrated using a box. Take the analogy TRESPASS:BOUNDARY::exceed:limit:

	direct →
TRESPASS	BOUNDARY
exceed	limit

One way of describing the analogy is to say that "to trespass is to cross a boundary" and that "to exceed is to cross a limit." But there is also a very pronounced indirect relationship between TRESPASS and *exceed* and between BOUNDARY and *limit*.

Indirect relationships are weaker than direct relationships, and not every correct answer choice has a noticeable indirect relationship. But when there is one, this lets you know in a tough case that you have found the correct choice.

EXAMPLE:

SWITCH:TRACK::   **(A)** interchange:freeway   **(B)** elevator:building
(C) lapel:coat   **(D)** investor:account   **(E)** bow:package

The best answer to this analogy is (A), but the connection between SWITCH and TRACK cannot easily be captured by any of our common relationships. A SWITCH is not just a part of the TRACK, it is a kind of TRACK. Still, trying the first idea, we have:

A SWITCH is a part of a TRACK.

(A) An *interchange* is a part of a *freeway*.
(B) An *elevator* is a part of a *building*.
(C) A *lapel* is a part of a *coat*.
(D) An *investor* is a part of an *account*.
(E) A *bow* is a part of a *package*.

This rough DX sentence allows us to eliminate (D), but we are still left with four choices.

At this point, you might look for an indirect relationship. A SWITCH is most like which of the following?

(A) interchange   **(B)** elevator   **(C)** lapel   **(E)** bow

The answer is (A). Both *switches* and *interchanges* have the same function, to re-route traffic. And this is confirmed by a further indirect relationship between TRACK and *freeway*. A TRACK is the route for trains, and a *freeway* is a route for motor vehicles.

In the example above, you can find two fairly clear indirect relationships. Sometimes, however, there will only be one.

EXAMPLE:

BABBLING:SPEECH::   **(A)** climbing:ascent   **(B)** speaker:story
(C) conclusion:beginning   **(D)** grace:acrobat   **(E)** rambling:walking

A good DX sentence for this analogy would use the "... is a type of ..." connection.

BABBLING is a type of SPEECH.

(A) *Climbing* is a type of *ascent*.
(B) A *speaker* is a type of *story*.
(C) A *conclusion* is a type of *beginning*.
(D) *Grace* is a type of *acrobat*.
(E) *Rambling* is a type of *walking*.

Our DX sentence easily eliminates (B), (C), and (D); but we are left with both (A) and (E). BABBLING, however, is characterized by a lack of direction; and *rambling* is characterized by a lack of direction. So there is an indirect relation between BABBLING and *rambling* that confirms (E) is the correct answer.

Caution! The technique of looking for secondary relationships should not be used in place of formulating a DX sentence. If you try to skip the step of the DX sentence, you could be badly misled. In the next analogy, try looking for the secondary relationship without formulating a DX sentence.

EXAMPLE:

PRISON:CELL::   **(A)** dormitory:room   **(B)** criminal:court   **(C)** cage:bird
(D) garage:automobile   **(E)** weather:rain

If you start by looking for secondary relationships, you are likely to be distracted by (B) or (C). After all, there is a connection between PRISON and *criminal*, and a PRISON is like a *cage*. The best answer, however, is (A).

A CELL is a part of a PRISON.

(A) A *room* is a part of a *dormitory*.

In fact, now you should be able to see an indirect relationship between CELL and *room*.

Improving Choices (Answers, page 83)

In this exercise, you will find two pairs of words that almost form an analogy. One word of the second pair is underlined. The analogy fails because of the underlined word. Find a different word which, when substituted for the underlined word, will complete the analogy.

Faulty Analogy	Your Replacement
1. ZOOLOGY:ANIMAL::botany:molecule	*plant*
2. TRIAL:ATTORNEY::surgery:clerk	*doctor*
3. SCROLL:BOOK::parchment:library	
4. GALOSHES:SHOES::laundry:suit	
5. BRANCH:TREE::face:human	
6. ANCIENT:AGE::heavy:skill	
7. INTRODUCTION:CONCLUSION:: salutation:greeting	
8. GUEST:INVITATION::subpoena:jury	
9. TEPID:SCALDING::cool:interested	
10. LUSH:VEGETATION::crowded:traffic	
11. CISTERN:WATER::leaf:tea	
12. LAWN:GRASS::pelt:scalp	
13. TERMITE:WOOD::ant:wool	
14. PAINTING:MUSEUM::hunter:menagerie	
15. SCORE:SYMPHONY::developer:building	
16. SWAGGER:WALK::brag:listen	
17. RULER:CENTIMETER::alarm:minute	
18. LAWYER:CLIENT::doctor:cure	
19. RACQUET:TENNIS::glove:baseball	
20. DRIZZLE:CLOUDBURST::candle:conflagration	
21. SHED:HAIR::molt:bird	
22. CONDOLENCE:LOSS::congratulation:fame	
23. ARID:MOISTURE::bankrupt:plans	
24. BEAR:HIBERNATE::bird:fly	
25. INN:TRAVELER::dormitory:college	

Shooting in the Dark

The analogies section of the SAT is, at least in part, a test of vocabulary, and it is very likely you will see several words that you do not know. In those situations, you must think like Holmes, drawing conclusions from limited information. There is a lot you can do even when you do not know the meaning of one or more words.

Even if you don't know the meaning of both capitalized words, do not give up. Go through the answer choices and eliminate any pairs that do not express a necessary connection.

> **EXAMPLE:**
>
> XXXXXXXXX:XXXX::   **(A)** materialist:horror   **(B)** chauvinist:imagination
> **(C)** parasite:modesty   **(D)** contender:disdain   **(E)** belligerent:war

Here the capitalized words are covered. This is the position you would be in if you did not know either one of the capitalized words. Still, there is a lot you can do.

Begin by eliminating all the non-answers. In this analogy, you can confidently eliminate (A) through (D), because there is no necessary connection between the words of those pairs. There is a necessary connection in (E). A *belligerent* is someone who makes *war*. By process of elimination, (E) must be correct.

Even though the capitalized words are covered, you know that the analogy is based on a " . . . is a defining characteristic of . . . " connection. The entire analogy is:

> MISCREANT:EVIL::   **(A)** materialist:horror   **(B)** chauvinist:imagination
> **(C)** parasite:modesty   **(D)** contender:disdain   **(E)** belligerent:war

EVIL is a defining characteristic of a MISCREANT.

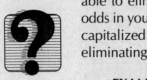

Obviously, you cannot expect to be so lucky all the time. Sometimes you will be able to eliminate only one or two choices as non-answers. Even so, that tips the odds in your favor and you must make a guess. Of course, if you do know one of the capitalized words, then you are in a better position. Again, you should begin by eliminating any non-answers.

> **EXAMPLE:**
>
> XXXXXXXXX:ACTIVITY   **(A)** trivial:significance   **(B)** entertaining:anecdote
> **(C)** logical:persuasion   **(D)** valuable:nature   **(E)** successful:position

This is the situation you would find yourself in if you did not know the meaning of one of the capitalized words.

Begin by eliminating the non-answers—in this analogy, (C), (D), and (E). Either (A) or (B) could be the correct choice:

(A) Lack of *significance* is a defining characteristic of something that is *trivial*.

(B) *Entertainment* is a defining characteristic of an *anecdote*.

Which is the correct answer? There is no sure way to tell when you do not know the meaning of a word, so you would pick either (A) or (B) and move on. In the actual analogy, the missing word was INDOLENT, so the correct answer was (A).

It is also possible that you will find one or more words in the answer choices that you do not know, and you would use the same technique. Eliminate non-answers and guess from among those that remain. Do not, however, automatically eliminate an answer choice just because it contains a word you do not know.

EXAMPLE:

HERMIT:SOLITUDE:: **(A)** warrior:civility **(B)** XXXXXXXX:self-denial **(C)** traitor:loyalty **(D)** researcher:finding **(E)** dreamer:practicality

You can summarize the connection between the capitalized words as "SOLITUDE is a defining characteristic of a HERMIT." You would then eliminate both (A) and (D) as non-answers. Next, you would eliminate both (C) and (E) as having the wrong connection. The result? Choice (B) must be correct, even though you do not know one of the words in (B). In the actual analogy, the missing word is *ascetic*, a difficult vocabulary word meaning "a person who lives a life of self-denial."

Non-answers are so prevalent in analogies that you should make a resolution not to leave any analogy unanswered. At the very worst, you should be able to eliminate at least one non-answer, and that gives you a mathematical edge over the SAT by allowing you to make a calculated guess.

Summary

1. An analogy depends upon a necessary connection between pairs of words based entirely on meaning. Any words that are not joined by a "tight" connection are non-answers.

2. Answer choices always reflect the part of speech of the capitalized words. If you are in doubt about the part of speech of a capitalized word, just look at the corresponding word in one of the choices.

3. Your basic Watsonian attack strategy is to formulate a DXS (diagnostic sentence). This procedure is not automatic. You must be ready to adapt to circumstances, for example, by reversing word order and changing parts of speech.

4. The ten most common analogy connections used on the SAT are:

   1. Defining characteristic
   2. Lack of
   3. Type of
   4. Part of
   5. Place for
   6. Degree
   7. Tool
   8. Sign of
   9. Order (Sequence or Cause)
   10. Interruption

5. On tough calls, use two Holmesian strategies: (a) Try improving an answer choice, and (b) Look for an indirect relationship to confirm the correctness of one choice.

6. Even when you are uncertain about the meaning of a word (or words), you should still be able to make an attempt at an analogy by eliminating all non-answers and guessing. Do not leave blank any analogy that you have had time to read.

7

Explanatory Answers

EXERCISE 1

1. An OAR is the tool used to propel a BOAT.
2. X
3. X
4. A CASINO is a place where GAMBLING occurs.
5. X   Although there is a possible connection here (you might put syrup on apples), there is no "tight" connection.
6. X
7. A LISP is a type of SPEECH.
8. A SPRINT is a faster form of running than a JOG.
9. X   Although DRAWER may mean either "a storage bin" or "a person who sketches," neither meaning has a necessary connection with PAINT.
10. A QUARRY is the place where ROCK is mined.
11. SCRIBBLING is a type of WRITING.
12. X
13. X
14. A PASTEL is a type of COLOR.
15. X
16. X   Although TARGET and WOUND might seem to have something to do with weapons, there is no necessary connection between the words themselves.
17. The KEYSTONE is a part of an ARCH.
18. X
19. X   Although both of these are character traits, there is no necessary connection between BRAZEN and TRUSTWORTHY themselves.
20. X
21. A QUIVER is the place where ARROWS are stored.
22. The process of MELTING forms a LIQUID.
23. CHAOS is the total absence of ORDER.
24. X   Although both are geographical features, there is no necessary connection between a PLATEAU and a RIVER.
25. X
26. X
27. X
28. A STREAM is a small RIVER.
29. X
30. A SYMPHONY is a type of MUSIC.

31. LINGUISTICS is the study of LANGUAGE.

32. X

33. A DEBUT is the BEGINNING of something.

34. To act out of IMPULSE is to act without DELIBERATION.

35. X

36. X Although someone might PREDICT a DISASTER, it is not part of the meaning of DISASTER that it must be PREDICTED. Nor is it a part of the meaning of PREDICT that it must be a prediction of a DISASTER.

37. X Although a NOMAD might live in the MOUNTAINS, it is not necessary to live in the MOUNTAINS to be a NOMAD. Conversely, a MOUNTAIN is still a MOUNTAIN without NOMADS living on it.

38. X

39. IMITATION is the lack of ORIGINALITY.

40. VAPORIZATION is the process that characterizes something that is VOLATILE.

41. A SPEAKER'S place is on the DAIS.

42. X PHOTOSYNTHESIS is characteristic of plants; and though there may be many plants in the TROPICS, PHOTOSYNTHESIS is not confined to the TROPICS.

43. The SHOULDER is the place for an EPAULET.

44. A COMPLIMENT shows APPROBATION.

45. Someone who is INTREPID is without FEAR.

46. OPULENCE is great WEALTH.

47. X

48. Someone who is MALADROIT is totally lacking in SKILL.

49. X Although CONFUSION might sometimes be funny (as in a play or a movie), there is no necessary connection between CONFUSION and LEVITY.

50. Something that is MOTLEY is characterized by VARIETY.

EXERCISE 2

1. 5	**11.** 6	**21.** 9	**31.** 2	**41.** 2
2. 4	**12.** 7	**22.** 9	**32.** 1	**42.** 1
3. 4	**13.** 6	**23.** 1	**33.** 3	**43.** 9
4. 7	**14.** 4	**24.** 7	**34.** 2	**44.** 6
5. 5	**15.** 8	**25.** 3	**35.** 9	**45.** 1
6. 5	**16.** 9	**26.** 9	**36.** 1	**46.** 2
7. 8	**17.** 3	**27.** 1	**37.** 2	**47.** 1
8. 9	**18.** 7	**28.** 2 or 9	**38.** 3	**48.** 1
9. 3	**19.** 5	**29.** 1	**39.** 2	**49.** 2
10. 10	**20.** 9	**30.** 6	**40.** 10 or 2	**50.** 10

EXERCISE 3

1. An OAK is a type of TREE.
2. A WEAPON is the tool of a SOLDIER.
3. A PUN is a type of JOKE.
4. A MAGAZINE is a type of PERIODICAL.
5. (sequence) PLANTING is followed by the HARVEST.
6. DRIFTING is characterized by lack of an ANCHOR. (Or) An ANCHOR can interrupt the process of DRIFTING.
7. COURAGE is a type of VIRTUE.
8. (sequence) A STUMBLE comes before a FALL.
9. HURLING is a more energetic form of TOSSING.
10. A VIOLINIST is a part of an ORCHESTRA. (Or) An ORCHESTRA is a place for a VIOLINIST.
11. A DEMAND is a stronger form of a REQUEST.
12. A FROWN is a sign of DISAPPROVAL.
13. PALLOR is characterized by a lack of COLOR.
14. CALLIGRAPHY is a type of WRITING.
15. MYTH is characterized by a lack of REALITY.
16. A NEST is the place for a BIRD.
17. (tool) WIND is needed to fly a KITE.
18. The MEADOW is a place for a COW.
19. FALSEHOOD is the defining characteristic of a LIAR.
20. A PRESERVATIVE stops the process of DECAY.
21. A GOOSE is a part of a GAGGLE.
22. DELINQUENCY is characterized by a lack of TIMELINESS.
23. A VEHICLE is a part of a CONVOY.
24. A LIBRARY is a place for BOOKS. (Or) One BOOK is part of an entire LIBRARY.
25. The UNKNOWN is a defining characteristic of a PIONEER.
26. TACT is a defining characteristic of a DIPLOMAT.
27. AFFECTION is a defining characteristic of ENDEARMENT.
28. CONVALESCENCE follows TREATMENT.
29. RECKLESSNESS is characterized by a lack of CAUTION.
30. PERJURY is characterized by a lack of TRUTH.
31. SATURATION is more extreme than DAMPENING.
32. A GROTTO is a type of CAVE.
33. HUMOR is a defining characteristic of a DITTY.
34. To be RAVENOUS is more extreme than being HUNGRY.
35. A DAM interrupts the FLOW of something.
36. A SHRIEK is a sign of TERROR.
37. WITHERING follows RIPENING.

38. BANALITY is characterized by a lack of FRESHNESS.
39. A MAGNATE is a type of MERCHANT. (Or) A MAGNATE is much more successful than a simple MERCHANT.
40. STARVATION is characterized by a lack of NUTRITION.
41. PROSE is a type of WRITING.
42. EXHAUSTION is characterized by a lack of ENERGY.
43. GIGGLING is a less extreme form of LAUGHTER.
44. An INTERMISSION interrupts a PERFORMANCE.
45. EMACIATED is a more extreme form of LEAN.
46. A POEM is a part of an ANTHOLOGY.
47. A SHOT is a part of a VOLLEY.
48. RESIGNATION is a defining characteristic of someone who is STOIC.
49. A GOURMAND is characterized by a lack of SELF-RESTRAINT.
50. INSOMNIA is characterized by a lack of SLEEP.

EXERCISE 4

1. plant
2. doctor
3. paper
4. raincoat
5. arm
6. weight
7. closing, farewell
8. witness
9. frigid, frozen
10. people
11. cup, pot
12. fur
13. moth
14. animal
15. blueprint
16. speak, talk
17. clock, watch
18. patient
19. bat
20. fire, flame
21. feather
22. success, achievement
23. funds, money
24. migrate
25. student

Analogies Drills

The following part includes five drills. Each drill consists of ten problems, arranged (but not numbered) just as you might find them on an actual exam.

The first drill is a "walk-through." In the column opposite the questions you will find answers and discussion, so that you can walk through the exercise as you read the explanations.

The other four drills are for practice. There is no time limit. You will find answers and explanations on pages 91–95.

Walk-Through

Directions: Each question below consists of a related pair of words or phrases, followed by five lettered pairs of words or phrases. Select the lettered pair that best expresses a relationship similar to that expressed in the original pair.

1. BICYCLIST:PEDAL::

   (A) referee:contest
   (B) singer:piano
   (C) rower:oar
   (D) runner:marathon
   (E) jockey:horse

1. (C) This analogy is fairly easy, for it is the first in the series. The connection is one of the common types: tool. You might use as a DX sentence "A PEDAL is the tool that is used by a BICYCLIST." Similarly, "An *oar* is the tool that is used by a *rower*."

   Watch out for (E)! It does not fit the DXS (a *horse* is not a tool used by a *jockey*), but some test-takers might be misled by an indirect relationship between BICYCLIST and *jockey*. They ride in similar fashion. Remember, you never use an indirect relationship except in a tough call, and then only *after* you have screened choices with a DXS.

2. SCRIPT:DRAMA::

   (A) writing:page
   (B) photograph:magazine
   (C) lyrics:note
   (D) chapter:book
   (E) score:symphony

2. (E) Again, we have a relatively easy analogy, but this time it does not fit one of the ten most common categories. So you would have to create an original DXS. One way of describing the connection between the capitalized words is "The SCRIPT is the written instructions for the DRAMA." Similarly, "The *score* is the written instructions for the *symphony*."

3. KANGAROO:MAMMAL::

   (A) frog:amphibian
   (B) bear:fur
   (C) giraffe:neck
   (D) bird:pet
   (E) fish:aquarium

3. (A) This analogy fits one of the common categories: type of. A KANGAROO is a type of MAMMAL, and a *frog* is a type of *amphibian*.

   Watch out for (D)! Although a *bird* can be a *pet*, a *bird* is not a type of *pet* in the same way that a KANGAROO is a type of MAMMAL. *Pet* is not a scientific classification like MAMMAL and *amphibian*.

4. TANGLED:KNOT::

   (A) snarled:rope
   (B) crumpled:wrinkle
   (C) mussed:hair
   (D) empty:hole
   (E) canned:preserves

4. (B) Now things begin to get slightly more difficult. This is a "defining characteristic" analogy. You would use this connection to create your DX sentence: A KNOT is a defining characteristic of things that are TANGLED, and a *wrinkle* is a defining characteristic of things that are *crumpled*.

Do not be tricked by (A)! It is true that there is an indirect relation between TANGLED and *snarled*, but (A) is eliminated by the DXS: A *rope* is a defining characteristic of things that are *snarled*. (Wrong!) Many other things can be snarled, such as hair.

5. ROUSTABOUT:CIRCUS::

    (A) electrician:kitchen
    (B) dean:classroom
    (C) stevedore:dock
    (D) engineer:library
    (E) ruffian:factory

5. (C) This analogy reaches a higher level of difficulty because of the word ROUSTABOUT. It's not a word that everyone knows. And to make things more difficult, *stevedore* is not an easy word. The analogy is one of the common types: place for. A ROUSTABOUT is a CIRCUS worker, and a *stevedore* is a *dock* worker.

Even if you did not know these words, you still could have answered correctly by using the Holmesian strategy of elimination. (C) is the only possible choice. (A), (D), and (E) are non-answers. (B) is a little trickier. A *dean* does have something to do with a *classroom*. But try improving (B). For (B) to be a possible choice, it would have to be *dean:college*, or *professor:classroom*.

6. CONCILIATORY:FRIENDLINESS::

    (A) peaceful:litigation
    (B) oblivious:awareness
    (C) inventive:practicality
    (D) toxic:antidote
    (E) rueful:sorrow

6. (E) Again, we have an analogy of medium difficulty. If you know the meanings of CONCILIATORY and *rueful*, you are home free. The analogy is the most common of all. FRIENDLINESS is a defining characteristic of someone who is CONCILIATORY, and *sorrow* is a defining characteristic of someone who is *rueful*. What if you do not know the words? At least you can eliminate both (A) and (C) as incorrect, which gives you a one-out-of-three chance of picking the right choice. And that is pretty good odds if you do not know the meaning of CONCILIATORY or *rueful*.

7. PIT:ABYSS::

    (A) defeat:rout
    (B) impasse:detour
    (C) hurdle:clearance
    (D) improvement:practice
    (E) ambition:success

7. (A) This analogy is based on the common type: degree. An ABYSS is a bottomless PIT, so you might say an ABYSS is more extreme than a PIT. So too, a *rout* is more extreme (serious) than a *defeat*. (C) is obviously wrong. And (D) and (E) are examples of process analogies: *practice* results in *improvement*, and *ambition* results in *success*. Finally, (B) would have been attractive only if you saw the indirect relationship between PIT and *impasse*. But your DXS should have eliminated (B).

8. CACHE:HIDE::

   (A) forgiveness:punish
   (B) stockpile:accumulate
   (C) testimony:falsify
   (D) ignition:extinguish
   (E) intimidation:fear

9. LOQUACITY:TALK::

   (A) garrulity:listen
   (B) piety:disregard
   (C) gluttony:eat
   (D) tenacity:resign
   (E) simplicity:understand

10. NOISE:DIN::

   (A) utterance:voice
   (B) celebration:revelry
   (C) motion:traction
   (D) sanity:treatment
   (E) remonstrance:sin

8. (B) Now things begin to get even more difficult. CACHE is a difficult word. Additionally, CACHE can be either a verb or a noun. In this case, the first word of (A) lets us know CACHE is used here as a noun. As a noun, CACHE refers to a hidden place that is used to store something. So the analogy is the common one of defining characteristic. To HIDE is a defining characteristic of CACHE. (B) fits this DXS: To *accumulate* is a defining characteristic of a *stockpile*.

9. (C) Here is another analogy made harder by a difficult vocabulary word: LOQUACITY. This means "a tendency to be very talkative." So a good DXS might be "TALKING is a defining characteristic of LOQUACITY." (C) neatly fits the DXS: "*Eating* is a defining characteristic of *gluttony*." Do not be tricked by (A). *Garrulity* is a synonym for LOQUACITY, but (A) would definitely be eliminated by the DXS: "*Listening* is a defining characteristic of *garrulity*." (Wrong!) Even without knowing the definitions of the key words, you can eliminate both (B) and (E) as non-answers, giving yourself a decent chance of getting the right answer.

10. (B) This analogy is based on degree. Using a DXS based on degree, you might reason that a DIN is a a very great NOISE, and *revelry* is very great *celebration*. Do not be distracted by (A). Although an *utterance* is a kind of NOISE, you should eliminate (A) with your DXS. Additionally, you can eliminate (C), (D), and (E) as non-answers.

Drill 1 (Answers, page 91)

Each question below consists of a related pair of words or phrases, followed by five lettered pairs of words or phrases. Select the lettered pair that best expresses the relationship similar to that expressed in the original pair.

Example:

YAWN:BOREDOM:: (A) dream:sleep
(B) anger:madness   (C) smile:amusement
(D) face:expression   (E) impatience:rebellion

Ⓐ Ⓑ ● Ⓓ Ⓔ

1. SINGER:CHORUS::
   (A) architect:blueprint
   (B) teacher:student
   (C) author:publisher
   (D) driver:highway
   (E) actor:cast

2. READ:LEGIBLE::
   (A) require:admissible
   (B) purchase:expensive
   (C) hear:audible
   (D) enter:enjoyable
   (E) cater:important

3. BALLAD:SONG::
   (A) spire:church
   (B) ode:poem
   (C) novel:chapter
   (D) envelope:letter
   (E) leopard:jaguar

4. INCISION:SCALPEL::
   (A) hospital:patient
   (B) playground:swing
   (C) kitchen:knife
   (D) electricity:wire
   (E) hole:drill

5. TRANQUILITY:PEACE::
   (A) chaos:disorder
   (B) retraction:indictment
   (C) combustion:waste
   (D) miracle:belief
   (E) tension:relaxation

6. GROTESQUE:DISTORTED::
   (A) fabricated:efficient
   (B) monotonous:constant
   (C) trustworthy:optimistic
   (D) imagined:permanent
   (E) mature:young

7. OBSCURITY:INTELLIGIBILITY::
   (A) ambiguity:clarity
   (B) redundancy:repetition
   (C) novelty:experimentation
   (D) cynicism:philosophy
   (E) insight:communication

8. SVELTE:EMACIATED::
   (A) enriched:impoverished
   (B) large:gargantuan
   (C) still:profound
   (D) routine:inspiring
   (E) permanent:transitory

9. CORNUCOPIA:ABUNDANCE::
   (A) chameleon:lizard
   (B) insignia:banner
   (C) gargoyle:edifice
   (D) phoenix:rebirth
   (E) idolatry:religion

10. REMISSION:DISEASE::
    (A) reduction:procedure
    (B) transportation:goods
    (C) assignment:position
    (D) stay:execution
    (E) impression:security

Drill 2 (Answers, page 92)

1. DRUGGIST:PHARMACY::
   (A) librarian:catalogue
   (B) physician:patient
   (C) chef:restaurant
   (D) carpenter:wood
   (E) musician:night club

2. WEED:GARDEN::
   (A) vegetable:market
   (B) termite:house
   (C) hair:barber
   (D) heretic:asylum
   (E) horse:team

3. HAND:WRIST::
   (A) muscle:bone
   (B) tendon:finger
   (C) foot:ankle
   (D) skull:brain
   (E) ear:hair

4. SUNDIAL:TIME::
   (A) balance:weight
   (B) pyramid:worship
   (C) umpire:score
   (D) thermometer:illness
   (E) metronome:music

5. CHECKPOINT:HIGHWAY::
   (A) postponement:delay
   (B) map:route
   (C) detour:destination
   (D) advertisement:product
   (E) valve:pipe

6. PICKPOCKET:WALLET::
   (A) burglar:night
   (B) embezzler:funds
   (C) detective:fugitive
   (D) merchant:expenses
   (E) innkeeper:guest

7. ANONYMOUS:IDENTITY::
   (A) amorphous:form
   (B) masked:party
   (C) wealthy:income
   (D) motivated:goal
   (E) infamous:report

8. REDUNDANT:REPETITIOUS::
   (A) written:oral
   (B) incomplete:developed
   (C) censured:obscene
   (D) wise:understandable
   (E) verbose:wordy

9. LAPIDARY:GEMS::
   (A) carpenter:stones
   (B) biologist:laboratories
   (C) numismatist:coins
   (D) aviator:students
   (E) cardiologist:hearts

10. INTERLOPER:CONSENT::
    (A) investor:return
    (B) referee:game
    (C) translator:language
    (D) missionary:commitment
    (E) intruder:invitation

Drill 3 (Answers, page 93)

1. GLACIER:ICE::
   - (A) trestle:train
   - (B) dune:sand
   - (C) forest:path
   - (D) bird:feather
   - (E) ship:ocean

2. HEAR:INAUDIBLE::
   - (A) touch:intangible
   - (B) mumble:praiseworthy
   - (C) spend:wealthy
   - (D) prepare:ready
   - (E) enjoy:illegal

3. GARGOYLE:GROTESQUE::
   - (A) magician:elegant
   - (B) elf:serene
   - (C) dragon:friendly
   - (D) troll:beautiful
   - (E) witch:wicked

4. EXTINGUISHED:RELIT::
   - (A) completed:discouraged
   - (B) announced:publicized
   - (C) collapsed:rebuilt
   - (D) evicted:purchased
   - (E) imagined:denied

5. VACUUM:AIR::
   - (A) invitation:host
   - (B) vacancy:occupant
   - (C) love:passion
   - (D) literacy:writing
   - (E) bait:trap

6. BLAME:SCAPEGOAT::
   - (A) explain:answer
   - (B) convict:punishment
   - (C) lionize:hero
   - (D) appreciate:art
   - (E) relate:secret

7. LIBEL:DEFAMATORY::
   - (A) praise:laudatory
   - (B) option:selective
   - (C) value:sparse
   - (D) insult:apologetic
   - (E) struggle:victorious

8. ANNEX:BUILDING::
   - (A) bedroom:apartment
   - (B) fountain:park
   - (C) epilogue:novel
   - (D) dining car:train
   - (E) memory:computer

9. BOOK:TOME::
   - (A) page:binding
   - (B) plot:character
   - (C) omission:diligence
   - (D) library:borrower
   - (E) story:saga

10. GREGARIOUSNESS:SOCIABILITY::
    - (A) courage:fearfulness
    - (B) reliability:esteem
    - (C) forgetfulness:memorability
    - (D) affability:friendliness
    - (E) gullibility:believability

Drill 4 (Answers, page 94)

1. ATTORNEY:CLIENT::
   (A) accountant:taxes
   (B) physician:patient
   (C) conductor:passenger
   (D) detective:case
   (E) trainer:animal

2. FOREST:TREES::
   (A) fleet:ships
   (B) lumber:wood
   (C) rose:thorns
   (D) shelf:books
   (E) camera:film

3. RAMPART:FORTRESS::
   (A) bicycle:wheel
   (B) river:lake
   (C) cage:animal
   (D) ladder:roof
   (E) fence:house

4. SCYTHE:REAPING::
   (A) screws:turning
   (B) crops:planting
   (C) lights:reading
   (D) shears:cutting
   (E) saws:gluing

5. MOISTEN:DRENCH::
   (A) pump:replenish
   (B) chill:freeze
   (C) deny:pretend
   (D) dance:rejoice
   (E) announce:suppress

6. MAVERICK:STRAY::
   (A) hermit:recluse
   (B) expert:ignorance
   (C) trickster:payment
   (D) miser:money
   (E) rumor:truth

7. PLATITUDE:TRITE::
   (A) axiom:geometrical
   (B) prescription:medical
   (C) cuisine:international
   (D) boredom:friendly
   (E) innovation:novel

8. MOTLEY:COLOR::
   (A) bovine:herd
   (B) cacophonous:sound
   (C) legal:codification
   (D) miraculous:apathy
   (E) remedial:expertise

9. BELIE:TRUTH::
   (A) convey:idea
   (B) mask:face
   (C) invite:attention
   (D) succumb:illness
   (E) dawdle:tardiness

10. HARBINGER:BEGINNING::
    (A) ordain:decree
    (B) herald:advent
    (C) amend:correction
    (D) emancipate:freedom
    (E) commiserate:news

Explanatory Answers

DRILL 1

1. (E) A SINGER is a part of a CHORUS, and an *actor* is a part of a *cast*. Although the other choices may show a necessary connection, those connections do not fit the pattern "is a part of."

2. (C) This analogy is based on the "defining characteristic" connection, but you have to play around with the wording to get a workable DX sentence. One possibility is: A defining characteristic of something that is LEGIBLE is that it can be READ, and a defining characteristic of something that is *audible* is that it can be *heard*. Because (A), (D), and (E) do not exhibit a necessary connection, they can be eliminated. (B) is also incorrect.

3. (B) A BALLAD is a type of SONG, and an *ode* is a type of *poem*. The other choices are possible analogies, but they do not fall into the category "is a type of."

4. (E) A SCALPEL is a tool that makes an INCISION, and a *drill* is a tool that makes a *hole*. The other choices, except for (C), do show necessary connections, but none of them fits the "is a tool" pattern.

5. (A) PEACE is a defining characteristic of TRANQUILITY, and *disorder* is a defining characteristic of *chaos*. (B) and (C) are clearly wrong. (E) must be wrong because it fits the pattern "lack of." (D) may seem to show a necessary connection, but it really doesn't. What really is the defining characteristic of a *miracle*? It is a supernatural event, especially a supernatural event caused by a divine agency. So (D) would be better had it read *divinity:miracle*.

6. (B) DISTORTION is a defining characteristic of GROTESQUENESS, and *constancy* is a defining characteristic of *monotony*. (Notice the parts of speech of the words have been changed in order to make the DXS read more smoothly. Your DXS doesn't have to read exactly like this.) (A), (C), and (D) are non-answers. (E) shows a necessary connection (*youth* is characterized by a lack of *maturity*), but it is not the connection we are looking for.

7. (A) Lack of INTELLIGIBILITY is a defining characteristic of something that is OBSCURE, and lack of *clarity* is a defining characteristic of something that is *ambiguous*. (B) and (C) show a necessary connection, but not the one we are looking for. (D) and (E) are non-answers. Finally, you may notice an indirect relationship between OBSCURITY and *ambiguity* and between INTELLIGIBILITY and *clarity*. Although indirect relationships should never be your first line of attack, the indirect relationships here confirm the correctness of (A).

8. (B) EMACIATED is a more intense degree of SVELTE, and *gargantuan* is a more intense degree of *large*. (A), (D), and (E) show analogy-type connections, but not the same one as the capitalized words. (C) is a non-answer.

9. (D) As you might expect with a ninth question, this one includes some difficult vocabulary words. The CORNUCOPIA is a sign of ABUNDANCE, and the *phoenix* is a sign of *rebirth*. Even if you don't know the meaning of CORNUCOPIA, you can eliminate (B). An *insignia* is a badge or an emblem, and that does not seem to have any necessary connection to a *banner*. The other choices,

however, do show necessary connections: (A) a *chameleon* is a type of *lizard*; (C) an *edifice* is the place for a *gargoyle*; and (E) *idolatry* is the lack of *religion*. So you would have to make your guess from among the four remaining choices.

10. (D) REMISSION interrupts the progress of a DISEASE, and a *stay* interrupts an *execution*. Although this analogy may be a little difficult to see, you can definitely find the correct answer by the Holmesian process of elimination.

DRILL 2

1. (C) A PHARMACY is the place for a DRUGGIST, and a *restaurant* is the place for a *chef*.

2. (B) A GARDEN is the place for a WEED, and a *house* is the place for a *termite*. (C) and (E) fairly clearly do not fit this relationship. A *barber* works with *hair*; a *horse* is a part of a *team*. Additionally, you can eliminate (D) as a non-answer. But you might have a little trouble with (A) if you are distracted by the indirect relationship. If you carefully refine your DX sentence, however, you can eliminate (A). A WEED lives in the GARDEN; a *vegetable* does not live in the *market*. Once (A) is eliminated, you can look for a confirming indirect relationship between WEED and *termite*—both are pests, one found in the GARDEN, the other in the *house*.

3. (C) This analogy does not easily fit one of our standardized types, so you will have to work a little to form a DX sentence. You might use: the HAND is at the end of the arm next to the WRIST. So, too, the *foot* is at the end of the leg next to the *ankle*. Using this, you can eliminate the other choices. Now you are permitted to see that there is a confirming indirect relationship. A HAND functions somewhat like a *foot*, and a WRIST like an *ankle*.

4. (A) A SUNDIAL is a tool for measuring TIME, and a *balance* is a tool for measuring *weight*. Here, *balance* must be a noun, and one meaning might be "equilibrium" ("I lost my balance"). But another meaning is "scale." In any case, you should have eliminated the other choices. (B) is incorrect because a *pyramid* is not an object of *worship*. (C) makes no sense because *umpire* and *score* are not related by meaning. An *umpire* might or might not keep the *score*. (D) can also be eliminated by improving it. Had (D) read *thermometer:temperature*, it would have been closer. This shows that it is not correct in its original form. Also, (E) fails for a similar reason. Had (E) read *metronome:tempo*, it would be a candidate for the correct choice. Finally, having eliminated the others, we can see a very pronounced indirect relationship between SUNDIAL and *balance*—both are ancient measuring devices.

5. (E) A CHECKPOINT interrupts the flow of traffic on a HIGHWAY, and a *valve* interrupts the flow of liquid in a *pipe*. This a good analogy to show the importance of ignoring indirect relationships until after screening choices with a DX sentence. Otherwise, you might be misled by (B) or (C).

6. (B) A defining characteristic of a PICKPOCKET is that he steals WALLETS, and a defining characteristic of an *embezzler* is that he steals *funds*. (A) is close and shows the importance of refining your DXS if necessary. It is true that *night* is a defining characteristic of a *burglar* (in the strict sense of the term, a burglar works only at night). But a *burglar* does not steal the *night*.

7. (A) Lack of IDENTITY is the defining characteristic of something that is ANON-YMOUS, and lack of *form* is the defining characteristic of something that is *amorphous*. You can eliminate both (B) and (E) as non-answers. Then, you can eliminate (C) and (D) because they fit the pattern "defining characteristic," not the pattern "lack of."

8. (E) That which is REDUNDANT is by definition REPETITIOUS, and that which is *verbose* is by definition *wordy*. You can eliminate (A) and (B) because those seem to be opposites. You can eliminate (C) and (D) as non-answers.

9. (C) A LAPIDARY is a person who collects GEMS, and a *numismatist* is a person who collects *coins*. This is a difficult analogy, made so by the difficult vocabulary. Even if you do not know the meaning of LAPIDARY, you should be able to eliminate both (A) and (D) as non-answers. But you are still left with (B), (C), and (E). You must, of course, make a guess, but which one? Since this is a difficult analogy, and since difficult items have difficult answers, why not pick the answer choice with the most unusual vocabulary word? That would be (C).

10. (E) An INTERLOPER is someone who meddles in someone else's business with-out his or her CONSENT; and an *intruder* is someone who interferes in someone else's privacy without an *invitation*. This is a very difficult item because of the word INTERLOPER. But even if you do not know its meaning, you are not without your strategies. You can at least eliminate (D) as a non-answer. Admit-tedly, this is not much, but it does tip the guessing odds in your favor, and you should pick one of the other choices.

DRILL 3

1. (B) A GLACIER is made of ICE, and a *dune* is made of *sand*.

2. (A) The defining characteristic of something that is INAUDIBLE is that it cannot be HEARD, and the defining characteristic of something that is *intangible* is that it cannot be *touched*. Additionally, you can eliminate (B), (C), and (E) as non-answers.

3. (E) GROTESQUENESS is a defining characteristic of a GARGOYLE, and *wickedness* is a defining characteristic of a *witch*. (B) and (D) are incorrect because *dragons* and *trolls* are not *friendly* or *beautiful*. And you can eliminate (A) and (B) as non-answers.

4. (C) RELIGHTING follows EXTINGUISHING, and *rebuilding* follows *collapse*. This is an analogy based on sequence. You can eliminate (A), (D), and (E) as non-answers. (B) is a possible analogy, but it does not fit the "sequence" connection.

5. (B) Lack of AIR is a defining characteristic of a VACUUM, and lack of an *occupant* is a defining characteristic of a *vacancy*. The other choices are possible analo-gies, but they do not fit the "lack of" pattern.

6. (C) BLAME is a defining characteristic of a SCAPEGOAT, and *lionize* is a defin-ing characteristic of a *hero*. You can eliminate (A), (D), and (E) as non-answers. Further, (B) does not fit the "defining characteristic" pattern. Interestingly, there is a very pronounced indirect relationship between BLAME and *lionize* and between SCAPEGOAT and *hero*. A SCAPEGOAT is the opposite of a *hero*, and to BLAME is the opposite of to *lionize*.

7. (A) DEFAMATORY is a defining characteristic of what it is to LIBEL, and *laudatory* is a defining characteristic of what it is to *praise*. In any case, the remaining choices are so weak as to be non-answers. Additionally, there is an indirect relationship here similar to that we observed in question 6, above. DEFAMA-TORY is the opposite of *laudatory*, and LIBEL is the opposite of *praise*.

8. (C) This analogy does not fit any of our standard patterns. An ANNEX is not really a part of a BUILDING, but something added to an already existing build-ing. Similarly, an *epilogue* is a section or comment added to a play or a *novel*. Perhaps it best fits into the category of sequence. An ANNEX comes after the original BUILDING, and an *epilogue* comes after the original *novel*. We can eliminate (A), for a *bedroom* is part of, not an addition to, an *apartment*. And for the same reason you can eliminate (D) and (E). Finally, (B) qualifies as a non-answer. A *fountain* is not necessarily found in a *park*, and a *park* does not necessarily contain a *fountain*.

9. (E) A TOME is a large BOOK, and a *saga* is a lengthy *story*. The analogy is one of degree, but to see this you have to be attentive to the precise meaning of TOME. This is what makes the analogy difficult. A TOME is not merely a BOOK; it is a large BOOK. (C) can be eliminated as a non-answer, and the others must be incorrect since they do not fit the pattern "degree."

10. (D) SOCIABILITY is a defining characteristic of GREGARIOUSNESS, and *friendliness* is a defining characteristic of *affability*. The analogy relationship here is the most common one of "defining characteristic," but the analogy uses difficult vocabulary. It is, however, possible to eliminate (B) as a non-answer.

DRILL 4

1. (B) The CLIENT is the customer of the ATTORNEY, and the *patient* is the cus-tomer of the *physician*. This relationship is not one of the common ones you have studied, but this first analogy is fairly easy.

2. (A) A TREE is part of the FOREST, and a *ship* is part of the *fleet*. Once we change the word order, the fairly common "part of" pattern becomes evident. You might, however, need to refine your DXS to eliminate some of the other choices. You might try: a FOREST is a group of TREES, and a *fleet* is a group of *ships*.

3. (E) This is a fairly odd analogy. It doesn't fit any of the patterns. It is based on a physical similarity. A RAMPART is an embankment encircling a FORTRESS, and a *fence* encircles a *house*. Occasionally, the SAT will have analogies based on physical similarities, e.g., FRAME:PICTURE::envelope:letter. (The FRAME surrounds the PICTURE, and the *envelope* surrounds the *letter*.) You could have eliminated both (B) and (D) as non-answers. Then, if you had to make a guess, you could look for an indirect relationship. There is a weak but noticeable indirect relationship between FORTRESS and *house* (places to live).

4. (D) A SCYTHE is a tool for REAPING, and *shears* are a tool for *cutting*. (A), (C), and (E) are non-answers, and (B) does not fit the "tool" pattern.

5. (B) To DRENCH is to do more than just MOISTEN, and to *freeze* is to do more than just *chill*. This analogy is based upon a relationship of degree. You can eliminate (A), (C), and (D) as non-answers; and (E), though a possible analogy, does not fit the pattern we are looking for.

6. (A) A defining characteristic of a MAVERICK is that it is a STRAY, and a defining characteristic of a *hermit* is that he is a *recluse*. You can easily eliminate (C) as a non-answer. And (B) and (E) fail because they are based upon the "lack of" connection. What about (D)? You should eliminate (D) for two reasons. First, it is the love of *money*, or greed, that is the defining characteristic of a *miser*. Had (D) read *miser:greed*, it would have been better. Since we can improve (D), we know it is not the best choice as it originally stands. Two, there is a very strong indirect relationship between MAVERICK and *hermit*. Both are alone. The MAVERICK is an animal outside the herd, and the *hermit* is a person outside society. Remember in close calls (after you have used your DXS), it is permissible to use an indirect relationship to make your final choice.

7. (E) A defining characteristic of a PLATITUDE is that it is TRITE, and a defining characteristic of an *innovation* is that it is *novel*. You can eliminate (C) and (D) as non-answers; and the words in (A) and (B), though arguably related, do not express a connection fitting the "defining characteristic" mold. You may notice also a fairly strong indirect relationship—the opposition between both first words and between both second words of old and new.

8. (B) The defining characteristic of something that is MOTLEY is a variety of COLOR, and the defining characteristic of something that is *cacophonous* is a variety of *sound*. You can eliminate (D) and (E) as non-answers. As for (A) and (C), though there may arguably be a connection there, it does not parallel that which joins the capitalized words.

9. (B) The defining characteristic of BELIE is to hide the TRUTH, and the defining characteristic of *mask* is to hide the *face*. You can eliminate (A) and (C) as non-answers. (D) and (E) do show necessary connections, but not the one we are looking for.

10. (B) To HARBINGER is to announce the BEGINNING of something, and to *herald* is to announce the *advent* of something. This is a difficult analogy because of the word HARBINGER, and it is made more difficult because HARBINGER is used as a verb. (It is usually used as a noun: "The robin is a harbinger of spring.") But even if you do not know the meaning of the key word in this analogy, you should be able to eliminate (E) as a non-answer. And since you would be making a guess anyway, you would be permitted to look for an indirect relationship. There is an indirect relationship between BEGINNING and *advent*—both words mean the same thing.

Sentence Completions

✔ **Objectives**

To learn what is tested by a sentence completion item.

To learn about the important aspects of a sentence completion item.

To learn the basic strategy of anticipating choices.

To learn about the logical patterns of sentence completion items.

To learn test-wise strategies for eliminating wrong answers.

1. **How Do Sentence Completions Work?**
2. **Three Important Facts about Sentence Completions**
   - **The Variety of Topics**
   - **The Ladder of Difficulty**
   - **Why Wrong Choices Are Wrong**
3. **Watson's Way: The Basic Strategy**
4. **Improving A&T: Some Common Patterns**
5. **Holmes' Strategies**
   - **Go to Pieces**
   - **Difficult Questions Have Difficult Answers**

Your SAT will include 15–20 sentence completions divided between two verbal sections. A sentence completion item consists of a sentence, a part or parts of which have been left out, plus answer choices. You must choose an answer that will complete the sentence by correctly filling in the blank or blanks.

Sentence completions are in part a test of reading comprehension, but they are also a test of vocabulary. The examples in this chapter may contain vocabulary words with which you are not familiar. Again, you are encouraged to look up unfamiliar words and jot down their meanings in the margin of this book.

How Do Sentence Completions Work?

The basic idea of a sentence completion is "fill in the blank." Here are the instructions you will find on your SAT. Don't try to memorize them; just make sure you understand them.

Each sentence below has one or two blanks, each blank indicating that something has been omitted. Beneath the sentence are five lettered words or sets of words. Choose the word or set of words that best fits the meaning of the sentence as a whole.

Example:

Although its publicity has been ----, the film itself is intelligent, well-acted, handsomely produced, and altogether ----.

(A) tasteless..respectable
(B) extensive..moderate
(C) sophisticated..amateur
(D) risqué..crude
(E) perfect..spectacular

● Ⓑ Ⓒ Ⓓ Ⓔ

The answer to the example is (A). The overall logical structure of the sentence is determined by the introductory *although*, which signals a contrast of ideas. The film's publicity creates one impression, *but* the film itself is different. The words needed to fill in the blanks must create the appropriate contrast. Additionally, the second word has to make sense in the series "intelligent, well-acted, handsomely produced . . . ."

Choices (D) and (E) can be eliminated because the words in those choices do not supply the needed contrast. *Risqué* and *crude* are not opposites; *perfect* and *spectacular* are not opposites.

Although the words in (B) and (C) would supply the appropriate contrast, the second words are not appropriate. Neither *moderate* nor *amateur* makes any sense in the series of words used to describe the film itself: "intelligent, well-acted, handsomely produced . . . ."

(A) meets both tests. The pair *tasteless. .respectable* provides the needed contrast set up by the *although*, and *respectable* fits well enough into the series of words used to describe the film.

Sentence completions are in part a test of reading comprehension, because they test your ability to understand the overall meaning of a sentence. When you read, you usually don't see each and every word on the page. Some words you pass over and take in "automatically" without actually reading them.

To convince yourself that you do not need to have all the words to make sense of something, imagine that you are listening to a radio broadcast that is occasionally disrupted by static:

Today, the Surgeon General announced the findings of a new ⁓ that concludes that smoking represents a serious ⁓ to nonsmokers as well as to ⁓ . According to the Surgeon General, disease risk due to ⁓ of tobacco smoke is not limited to the ⁓ who is smoking, but can also extend to those who ⁓ tobacco smoke in the same room. Simple ⁓ of smokers and nonsmokers within the same airspace may reduce, but does not ⁓ , exposure of nonsmokers to environmental smoke. A spokesperson for the tobacco industry ⁓ the report, saying the available ⁓ does not support the conclusion that environmental tobacco smoke is a hazard to nonsmokers. On the other hand, the Coalition on Smoking or Health, an antismoking organization, ⁓ the report and called for ⁓ government action to ensure a smoke-free environment for all nonsmokers.

Although several key words are missing from the "broadcast," you still should be able to understand what has been said by supplying the missing pieces yourself. This is the principle of sentence completions.

Of course, for each gap there are several different words that could be substituted, but you should be able to get the gist of the news report.

The Newscast (Answers, page 116)

A sentence completion always includes answer choices. For fun, for each of the numbered gaps in the radio broadcast select an appropriate completion from the list provided below.

Today, the Surgeon General announced the findings of a new ___(1)___ that concludes that smoking represents a serious ___(2)___ to nonsmokers as well as to ___(3)___. According to the Surgeon General, disease risk due to ___(4)___ of tobacco smoke is not limited to the ___(5)___ who is smoking, but can also extend to those who ___(6)___ tobacco smoke in the same room. Simple ___(7)___ of smokers and nonsmokers within the same airspace may reduce, but does not ___(8)___, exposure of nonsmokers to environmental smoke. A spokesperson for the tobacco industry ___(9)___ the report, saying the available ___(10)___ does not support the conclusion that environmental tobacco smoke is a hazard to nonsmokers. On the other hand, the Coalition on Smoking or Health, an antismoking organization, ___(11)___ the report and called for ___(12)___ government action to ensure a smoke-free environment for all nonsmokers.

8

1. **(A)** movie **(B)** election **(C)** report
   (D) advertisement **(E)** plan

2. **(A)** consciousness **(B)** hazard **(C)** remedy
   (D) possibility **(E)** treatment

3. **(A)** cigarettes **(B)** fumes **(C)** alcoholics
   (D) pipes **(E)** smokers

4. **(A)** observation **(B)** criticism **(C)** improvement
   (D) inhalation **(E)** cessation

5. **(A)** individual **(B)** doctor **(C)** campaign
   (D) reporter **(E)** objector

6. **(A)** create **(B)** breathe **(C)** enjoy
   (D) ban **(E)** control

7. **(A)** encouragement **(B)** prohibition **(C)** separation
   (D) intermingling **(E)** prosecution

8. **(A)** imagine **(B)** increase **(C)** prepare
   (D) eliminate **(E)** satisfy

9. **(A)** purchased **(B)** prepared **(C)** understood
   (D) criticized **(E)** worshipped

10. **(A)** alibi **(B)** publicity **(C)** evidence
    (D) reaction **(E)** resources

11. **(A)** praised **(B)** rejected **(C)** prolonged
    (D) denied **(E)** proclaimed

12. **(A)** minimal **(B)** immediate **(C)** reactionary
    (D) uncontrolled **(E)** theoretical

Three Important Facts about

Sentence Completions

1. Sentence completions can be about almost any subject in the world—sports, history, opera, medicine, politics, and so on. But you do not need any special knowledge. The sentence itself will give you all the information you need to complete it. Don't give up on a sentence just because it starts with something strange, such as "The bel canto period of opera was ... " or "The thermonuclear reactions that fuel most mainline stars ...."

Further, don't be intimidated by the sentence by falling into the trap of thinking "Boy, the people who wrote this test must be a lot smarter than I am, so I'll never be able to get this right." Remember that SAT questions are not written by a single person; and no one person is expected to be familiar with all the various topics. Just answer the question based on the information that is given to you in the sentence.

2. Sentence completions are arranged according to the so-called "ladder of difficulty." That is, within each group of sentence completion questions, each succeeding question is generally more difficult than the one before.

What makes one sentence completion more difficult than another? Two factors: (1) vocabulary, and (2) sentence structure. Compare the following two sentence completions.

EXAMPLES:

Although critics denounced the film as silly and inane, people flocked to the theater to see it, guaranteeing its ---- success.

(A) scholarly   (B) hypothetical   (C) secret
(D) financial   (E) occasional

Even the most arbitrary and ---- corporation today must be aware of the attitudes of its employees; management may at times be more or less ----, but all must respect the power of an organized work force.

(A) influential..outraged
(B) prosperous..precipitous
(C) flexible..patronizing
(D) authoritarian..responsive
(E) susceptible..permanent

The first sentence completion is fairly easy; it might appear as the first item in a group. The answer is (D). The film was not a critical success, but it was a success in some way. The film succeeded in attracting customers to the theater, so it must have been a *financial* success.

The second example is more difficult. It might appear as the last item in a group. In the first place, the vocabulary used in the sentence and in the choices is more difficult. Additionally, the logical structure of the sentence is more involved.

The answer to the second sentence completion is (D). We can eliminate both (C) and (E) on the ground of the first word. The structure "arbitrary and ---- corporation" requires an adjective that is somewhat like *arbitrary*. *Flexible* is definitely out. Also, *susceptible*, which means "easily affected," does not fit with *arbitrary*.

(A) and (B) cannot be eliminated on the ground of the first word. A corporation might be *influential* or *prosperous*. But (A) and (B) fail on the second word. The logic of the second clause of the sentence (everything following the semicolon) requires a word like *respect*: management may be more or less "respectful," but they must respect. Neither *outraged* nor *precipitous* (which means "acting hastily") does the trick.

(D) works nicely. With the substitutions, the sentence states that a powerful corporation may be more or less sensitive to its employees, but it must respect their power.

3. Wrong choices are wrong for one of two reasons: one, when inserted in the sentence, the phrase they create is not idiomatic; or two, they fail to support the overall logic of the sentence.

First, many answer choices are wrong because the phrasing they would create is not idiomatic; that is, the words just never go together.

EXAMPLE:

The ease with which the candidate answers difficult questions creates the impression that she has been a public servant for years, but in reality she entered politics only ----.
(A) securely   **(B)** enthusiastically   **(C)** frequently
(D) needfully   **(E)** recently

(E) is the best answer. Every other choice can be eliminated because its substitution would create a phrase that is not idiomatic English:

(A) ... only *securely*.

(B) ... only *enthusiastically*.

(C) ... only *frequently*.

(D) ... only *needfully*.

Try to think up a sentence using one of these words in the phrase: "did something only . . . ." You might find one, but I doubt it. And if you do, it will be so bizarre that it would never show up on the SAT.

Second, although an answer choice may create a meaningful phrase, it may be wrong because it is not consistent with the overall logic of the sentence.

EXAMPLE:

Though afflicted by headaches, nausea, and respiratory difficulties, Nietzsche refused to let his ---- problems prevent him from writing.
(A) imaginary   **(B)** financial   **(C)** emotional
(D) theoretical   **(E)** physical

Here we cannot eliminate any choice on the ground of idiomatic usage:

(A) ... his *imaginary* problems ....

(B) ... his *financial* problems ....

(C) ... his *emotional* problems ....

(D) ... his *theoretical* problems ....

(E) ... his *physical* problems ....

All of these are possible as isolated phrases. With a little thought, you could create sentences in which they could be used. But only (E) sustains the overall logic of the sentence. "...his ---- problems" must refer to the list at the beginning of the sentence, and those are *physical* problems. So (E) is the best choice.

Some sentence completions have two blanks, and the answer choices include two substitutions. For a choice to be correct, both substitutions must work. You may find that one half of the choice seems to work, but the other half fails. In that case, the choice is completely wrong and must be eliminated.

Finally, don't worry about grammar. An answer choice might be wrong because it makes no sense when inserted in the appropriate blank, but answer choices will always be grammatically correct.

Watson's Way: The Basic Strategy

The "radio broadcast" exercise above should have convinced you that it is possible to anticipate appropriate substitutions for missing parts. This is the basis of Watson's method for attacking sentence completions. You should read the sentence through for understanding, trying to imagine what word or words would effectively complete the sentence. Then look at the answer choices to find the one that comes closest to your reading of the sentence. Occasionally, you may find the very words you anticipated, but most of the time you will find words that are similar to those that came to mind as you read the sentence.

A&T (Anticipate and Test) is the basic strategy, and here is how it works. First, take a sentence without the choices.

> **EXAMPLE:**
>
> The university should ---- the function of the alumni fund so that its importance will be better appreciated by the school's graduates who are asked to contribute to it.

What word might complete the sentence? The sentence asserts that something should be done to improve understanding. Thus, you should anticipate that that something is probably explanation. So you turn to the choices, looking for a word like *explain*:

(A) revoke   **(B)** elucidate   **(C)** ascertain
(D) prescribe   **(E)** entice

(B) is the only choice that has a meaning like "explain."

At this point, you should insert your selection into the sentence to test it. Read the sentence through to make sure that your answer choice reads smoothly and correctly:

> The university should *elucidate* the function of the alumni fund so that its importance will be better appreciated by the school's graduates who are asked to contribute to it.

This reading should convince you that you have found the correct choice.

What if a first reading of the sentence does not suggest any possibilities? In that event, the Anticipate step doesn't help, so go on to the Test step. Test each of the answers until you find one that works.

This situation arises fairly often, and not just because you might be having trouble understanding the sentence. There are some sentences that are open-ended; that is, they don't make sense without some sample substitutions.

EXAMPLE:

In spite of the ---- of the minister's sermon, when it was finished, most of the congregation was ---- .

The general structure of the sentence is not difficult to understand, but it's hard to imagine what words should be substituted. Was the effect of the sermon good or bad? If good, then we might look for pairs such as "brevity..moved" or "length..smiling" or "harshness..understanding." On the other hand, if the effect was bad, we might expect pairs such as "beauty..asleep" or "importance..impatient" or "vehemence..unmoved." These are all logical possibilities.

In such cases, you have no alternative but to go to the Test stage of A&T. Here are the choices:

   (A) passion..fidgety
   (B) confidence..fearful
   (C) understanding..merciful
   (D) obtrusiveness..hurt
   (E) veracity..cold

Substituting the pairs one by one, you should find that only (A) is a real possibility:

In spite of the *passion* of the minister's sermon, when it was finished, most of the congregation was *fidgety*.

Anticipating Completions (Answers, page 116)

Below you will find ten sentences, each containing one blank. Using the technique of Anticipation, try to imagine one or more words that might be used to complete the sentence. Write your answers in the space provided.

EXAMPLE:

Although government agencies insist that so-called UFO phenomena can be accounted for by one natural cause or another, for most people these incidents remain -----.
Anticipated words: *unexplainable, mysterious*

1. Good teachers know that study habits learned as a youngster stay with a student for life, so they try to find ways to ---- enthusiasm for studies.
Anticipated words: _____

2. Although he had not been physically injured by the explosion, the violence of the shock left him temporarily ----.
Anticipated words: _____

3. She was one of the most ---- criminals of the 1930s, her name a household word and her face in every post office.
Anticipated words: _____

4. The females of many common species of birds have dull coloring that ---- them when they are sitting on a nest in a tree or other foliage.
Anticipated words: _____

5. The Constitution sets up a system of checks and balances among the executive, the legislative, and the judiciary branches to ensure that no one branch can establish ---- control over the government.
Anticipated words: _____

6. The report is so ---- that it covers all of the main points in detail and at least touches on everything that is even remotely connected with its topic.
Anticipated words: _____

7. The cold weather caused ---- damage to the Florida citrus crop, prompting growers to warn that the reduced yield is likely to result in much higher prices.
Anticipated words: _____

8. Martin's opponent is a ---- speaker who is unable to elicit a reaction from a crowd on even the most emotional of issues.
Anticipated words: _____

9. The ---- of his career, capturing the coveted "Most Valuable Player" award, came at a time of deep personal sadness.
Anticipated words: _____

10. Stress is the reaction an individual feels when he believes the demands of a situation ---- his ability to meet them.
Anticipated words: _____

Improving A&T: Some Common Patterns

This basic strategy of A&T is sound. You should be able to employ it without strain on the first two out of five sentence completions. Then the going gets tougher. But you can improve your chances by learning the common logical patterns that are used in sentence completions.

Although an infinite number of sentences are possible, it is useful to group the possibilities into two general categories. In one category, the substitutions extend (continue) another thought in the sentence. In the other category, the substitutions reverse another thought in the sentence. So our two categories are called *thought-extenders* and *thought-reversers*.

Our first category is *thought-extenders*. In such sentences, the word or words in the correct choice must carry forward some thought in the sentence.

> **EXAMPLE:**
>
> The terms *toad* and *frog* refer to two different animals belonging to different genuses, and careful students ---- the two.
>
> **(A)** intermingle **(B)** ignore **(C)** distinguish **(D)** confuse **(E)** dispute

The key to this question is the logical structure of the sentence. What follows the *and* is supposed to continue or extend the thought that comes before the comma. So we are looking for a thought-extender. Only (C) does this.

The other category is thought-reversers. In this structure, the substitution must convey the reverse of some other thought in the sentence. The example we just studied could easily be changed into a case of a thought-reverser:

> Although the terms *toad* and *frog* refer to two different animals belonging to different genuses, some students ---- the two.
>
> **(A)** distinguish **(B)** confuse **(C)** respect **(D)** observe **(E)** mention

In this variation, the *although* introduces a contrast. What comes after the comma is the reverse of what comes before. Here we need a word to indicate that the distinction between toads and frogs is ignored, and that is choice (B).

Many words in the English language can signal an extension of a thought: *and, so, therefore, since, because, as a result*, and others. Similarly, many words can signal a reversal of a thought: *although, though, but, else, in spite of, despite, however*, and others. Moreover, a sentence may contain both thought-extenders and thought-reversers. For this reason, you cannot just memorize a long list of words. Instead, you must learn to recognize the logical structure of a sentence and pay attention to what that structure requires.

> **EXAMPLES:**
>
> If we continue to consume our fossil fuel supply without restraint, then someday it will be ---- .
>
> **(A)** replenished **(B)** limited **(C)** useless **(D)** available **(E)** exhausted

The best answer is (E). "If—then" signals an extension. The second clause must extend the thought expressed in the first.

The public debates were often ----, finally deteriorating into mudslinging contests.

(A) informative **(B)** bitter **(C)** theoretical **(D)** inspiring **(E)** insightful

The best answer is (B). Here, the punctuation signals that a thought-extender is required. The main clause must suggest that the debates were like mudslinging contests.

Elementary school children, who have not yet been repeatedly disappointed by other people, are much more ---- than older and more cynical high school students.

(A) inquisitive **(B)** relaxed **(C)** enjoyable **(D)** trusting **(E)** enlightened

The best answer is (D). The blank must extend the description of elementary school children. These children have not been disappointed, so they should be more trusting than older children. Or, you might interpret this as needing a thought-reverser to create a contrast between younger children (who are trusting) and older children (who are not). Both elements are present in the sentence.

There is no necessary connection between a dollar and what can be purchased for a dollar; the value of money is ---- and can be ---- by supply and demand.

(A) arbitrary..altered
(B) predetermined..overruled
(C) conventional..inspired
(D) lackluster..improved
(E) optional..prevented

The best answer is (A). What follows the semicolon must be an extension of the thought in the first clause that a dollar has no fixed or necessary value. (A) nicely develops this idea. The value of a dollar is arbitrary and can be changed. Also, the second blank can be seen as extending and explaining the idea expressed in the first blank: what is arbitrary is subject to change.

The critic must have detested the play, for the review was not merely ---- , it was ---- .

(A) unhappy..miserable
(B) laudatory..enthusiastic
(C) sincere..long
(D) appreciative..stinging
(E) critical..scathing

The best answer is (E). The blanks must carry forward the thought that the critic detested the play. Additionally, the second blank must carry forward and strengthen the thought of the first blank. *Scathing* is stronger than just *critical*.

The ascent of the mountain is ----, but anyone who makes it to the top is rewarded by a spectacular view.

(A) helpful **(B)** easy **(C)** unique **(D)** unpleasant **(E)** automatic

The best answer is (D). The *but* signals a reversal of thought. The second clause describes the view in positive terms, but getting there must be described in negative terms. So the ascent is unpleasant, but the view is spectacular.

> Although Barbara argues strongly that current policies are unjust, she does not ----
> any particular changes.
>
> **(A)** reject   **(B)** presume   **(C)** advocate   **(D)** remember   **(E)** oppose

The best answer is (C). The *although* sets up a contrast between the first idea ("current policies are unjust") and the second idea ("she does not ---- change"). (C) completes the reversal. Barbara does not like the present situation, but she has no plans for change.

> Despite the fact that they had clinched the divisional title long before the end of
> regular season play, the team continued to play every game as though it were ---- .
>
> **(A)** superfluous   **(B)** irrational   **(C)** lengthy   **(D)** hopeless   **(E)** vital

The best answer is (E). *Despite the fact* sets up a thought-reversal. One thing would be expected after a team had clinched a title, but another thing actually happened. What would be expected? That the remaining games would be regarded as a boring exercise. But what actually happened? The team played as though the games were really very important, or *vital*.

> Unless we ---- our water resources, there may come a time when our supplies of
> clean water are completely exhausted.
>
> **(A)** predict   **(B)** use   **(C)** conserve   **(D)** replace   **(E)** tap

The best answer is (C). *Unless* sets up a contrast, "either this or that": either conserve or run out.

> Nutritionists have found that certain elements long known to be ---- in large quantities are ---- to life in small amounts.
>
> **(A)** lethal..essential
> **(B)** deadly..painful
> **(C)** healthful..pleasurable
> **(D)** fatal..unbearable
> **(E)** unfashionable..important

The best answer is (A). The "large—small" distinction sets up a thought reversal, so we need a pair of words that are opposites. (A) supplies the needed contrast.

Thought-extenders versus Thought-reversers

(Answers, page 116)

In this exercise, you will find ten sentences with one or two blanks. For each sentence, draw arrows connecting the key elements and indicate whether the elements are similar (thought-extenders[+]) or contrasting (thought-reversers[✔]). Then try to anticipate one or more words that might complete the sentence.

EXAMPLE:

Even though the audience gave the star singer a twenty-minute standing ovation, newspaper reviews of the performance were filled with ---- comments.
Anticipated words: *critical, negative, disapproving*

1. Our modern industrialized societies have been responsible for the greatest destruction of nature and life; indeed, it seems that more civilization results in greater ---- .
Anticipated words: _____

2. The current spirit of ---- among different religions has lead to a number of meetings that their leaders hope will lead to better understanding.
Anticipated words: _____

3. For a child to be happy, his day must be very structured; when his routine is ----, he becomes nervous and irritable.
Anticipated words: _____

4. Because there is always the danger of a power failure and disruption of elevator service, high-rise buildings, while suitable for younger persons, are not recommended for ---- .
Anticipated words: _____

5. The committee report vigorously expounded the bill's strengths but also acknowledged its ---- .
Anticipated words: _____

6. In a pluralistic society, policies are the result of compromise, so political leaders must be ---- and accommodating of the views of others.
Anticipated words: _____

7. The Mayor's proposal for a new subway line, although ---- , is not a final solution to the city's transportation needs.
Anticipated words: _____

8. Due to the ---- nature of the chemical, it can't be used near an open flame.
Anticipated words: _____

9. The guillotine was introduced during the French Revolution as a(n) ---- , an alternative to other less humane means of execution.
Anticipated words: _____

10. The survivors had been drifting for days in the lifeboat, and in their weakness, they appeared to be ---- rather than living beings.
Anticipated words: _____

Holmes' Strategies

By using A&T and by paying attention to the logical structure of a sentence, you should have some idea of how to attack the first three or even four sentence completions. But at some point, you are likely to run up against sentences that are very difficult—both because the logical structure is complicated and because the vocabulary is difficult. Here are two Holmesian strategies. The first is for handling sentences with complex logical structures; the second is for those cases made difficult by vocabulary.

1. Go to pieces. No, not you—the sentence! Take the sentence to pieces. As we have seen, an answer may be incorrect because the phrase it would create would not be idiomatic. So isolate a small part of the sentence, a phrase you do understand. Then test choices, eliminating as many as possible.

EXAMPLES:

The passage of the mass transit bill over the Governor's veto and despite opposition by key leaders in the legislature was a devastating ---- for the party machinery and suggests that other, much-needed legislation may receive similar treatment in the future.

(A) victory   (B) optimism   (C) compromise   (D) slap   (E) setback

The best answer is (E). You may be able to get the answer by the basic process of A&T. You can also arrive at (E) by analyzing the logical structure of the sentence. The blank must continue the thought that the legislation passed despite opposition by some powerful people. How would that affect those powerful people? It would be a defeat or a setback.

You could also use the technique of "going to pieces." Take just the phrase "a devastating ----." Which of the answers, when filled in the blank, creates a meaningful phrase?

(A) a devastating victory?   (NO!)

(B) a devastating optimism?   (NO!)

(C) a devastating compromise?   (NO!)

(D) a devastating slap?   (NO!)

(E) a devastating setback?   (YES!)

By isolating a manageable phrase, you can eliminate every choice but (E).

People who use their desk-top computers for writing can become almost hypnotized by the unbroken succession of letters and text; in such cases, a computer video game can supply a welcome ----.

(A) burden   (B) diversion   (C) handicap   (D) predicament   (E) insight

Take the sentence to pieces:

    (A) a welcome burden   (NO!)

    (B) a welcome diversion   (YES!)

    (C) a welcome handicap   (NO!)

    (D) a welcome predicament   (NO!)

    (E) a welcome insight   (Perhaps.)

You can confidently eliminate (A), (C), and (D), because they do not create a meaningful phrase.

At first, you might think a sentence with two blanks is more difficult than a sentence with just one blank. But when your back is to the wall, two blanks are better than one. Why? Your chances of eliminating an answer are doubled. If an answer choice fails on either substitution, you eliminate the entire answer choice.

> It is highly characteristic of business's ---- attitude that little or no interest was evinced in urban renewal until similar undertakings elsewhere proved that such projects could be ----.
> **(A)** prestigious..feasible
> **(B)** capitalistic..rigid
> **(C)** degrading..completed
> **(D)** mercantile..insensitive
> **(E)** pragmatic..profitable

The best answer is (E), and you can reach this conclusion by "going to pieces":

    (A) business's prestigious attitude . . . projects could be feasible

    (B) business's capitalistic attitude . . . projects could be rigid

    (C) business's degrading attitude . . . projects could be completed

    (D) business's mercantile attitude . . . projects could be insensitive

    (E) business's pragmatic attitude . . . projects could be profitable

You can eliminate (A) and (C) on the ground that their first words do not make a meaningful phrase; and you can eliminate (B) and (D) on the ground that their second words do not make a meaningful phrase. By the process of elimination, (E) must be the correct answer.

    2. Remember that difficult questions have difficult answers. If a sentence is the first in a group, it is highly unlikely that the correct answer is a difficult word. On the other hand, the fifth question in the group may very well have as its correct answer a difficult vocabulary word. Compare the following two sentences. The first represents an item that might be the first one in a group, while the second is an item that might be the last one in a group.

> **EXAMPLES:**
>
> The committee's report is not as valuable as it might have been because it addresses only the symptoms and not the ---- causes of the problem.
> **(A)** unimpeachable **(B)** ephemeral **(C)** underlying
> **(D)** incipient **(E)** superficial
>
> Calvin had long been known for his mendacity, but even those who knew him well were surprised at the ---- explanation he gave for the shortage of funds.
> **(A)** elegant **(B)** disingenuous **(C)** sincere **(D)** dogmatic **(E)** bitter

The first question in a group should not have a difficult solution. So it is not likely that the correct answer to our first example, above, would be (A), (B), or (D). In fact, (C) is the best choice. The sentence requires a contrast between symptoms and underlying causes.

The second example, however, represents a difficult problem. And difficult problems have difficult solutions. If you can eliminate (A), (C), (D), and (E), then do not be afraid to pick a word like "disingenuous"—even if you do not know its meaning. And if you are forced to guess, go ahead and guess the most difficult word of the five. It's more likely to be correct than the easiest word in the group.

8

Going to Pieces (Answers, page 117)

 In this exercise, you will find isolated phrases containing blanks with possible completions. For each item, place an *X* by those words that can be eliminated because they do not create a meaningful phrase.

1. . . . he is capable of _____.
   (A) genius **(B)** error **(C)** knowledge **(D)** trivia **(E)** compromise

2. . . . modern technology is _____.
   (A) generalized **(B)** cynical **(C)** widespread
   (D) backwards **(E)** dangerous

3. . . . this much-needed reform has been _____.
   (A) denied **(B)** thwarted **(C)** ensured **(D)** completed **(E)** avoided

4. . . . conditions are _____.
   (A) improving **(B)** complimentary **(C)** sympathetic
   (D) threatening **(E)** dispassionate

5. . . . _____ to learn more about . . . .
   (A) eager **(B)** seeking **(C)** ignoring **(D)** reluctant **(E)** progressing

6. . . . the story is not _____.
   (A) interesting **(B)** petty **(C)** believable **(D)** wishful **(E)** rumored

7. . . . discussions are often _____.
   (A) apathetic **(B)** lethargic **(C)** exciting **(D)** nascent **(E)** charismatic

8. . . . her capacity for thought has _____.
   (A) atrophied **(B)** diversified **(C)** concerned
   (D) detained **(E)** premeditated

9. . . . the _____ ending of the play.
   (A) dramatic **(B)** exciting **(C)** abstract **(D)** climactic **(E)** fulfilled

10. . . . _____ device.
    (A) disparaging **(B)** versatile **(C)** useful **(D)** vague **(E)** inauspicious

Summary

1. Sentence completions are partly a test of reading comprehension. They test whether or not you understand the logical structure of the sentence by asking you to fill in missing pieces, just as you might have to fill in missing pieces if a communication such as a radio broadcast were intermittently interrupted.

2. Sentence completions can be about virtually any topic, but you don't need any special knowledge to answer them. Also, they are arranged according to the ladder of difficulty. Finally, wrong choices are wrong for one of two reasons. Either they do not create idiomatic phrases, or they fail to support the overall logic of the sentence.

3. The basic attack strategy is called "Watson's Way." Read through the sentence completion item, trying to anticipate what words might be used to complete it. Then try to match your anticipated completions to an answer choice. Alternatively, you can try testing each answer in the sentence until you find a completion that works.

4. Pay careful attention to the logical structure of the sentence. Be particularly alert for thought-extenders (structures that require a later thought to explain or develop an earlier one) and thought-reversers (structures that require a later thought to contrast with an earlier one).

5. When you encounter a sentence with a difficult logical structure, concentrate on the phrases that would be created by the various choices. Eliminate choices that do not form meaningful phrases. Remember, too, that difficult questions have difficult answers. Don't be afraid to select a difficult vocabulary word as the answer to a difficult question. And if all else fails, use a difficult vocabulary word as your guess to a difficult question.

8

Answers

EXERCISE 1

1. C	**7.** C
2. B	**8.** D
3. E	**9.** D
4. D	**10.** C
5. A	**11.** A
6. B	**12.** B

EXERCISE 2

Don't worry if you did not anticipate the exact words that appear below, so long as your words express the same general ideas.

1. generate, spark, increase
2. dazed, confused, disoriented
3. wanted, infamous, notorious
4. hides, camouflages, conceals
5. complete, total, authoritarian
6. complete, comprehensive
7. serious, severe, large-scale
8. boring, dull, uninspiring
9. climax, high point, zenith
10. exceed, surpass

EXERCISE 3

Don't worry if your completions are not exactly those you find below, so long as you have the right idea.

1. Our modern industrialized societies have been responsible for the greatest destruction of nature and life; indeed, it seems that more civilization results in greater ----.

   Anticipated words: destruction, death

2. The current spirit of ---- among different religions has lead to a number of meetings which their leaders hope will lead to better understanding.

   Anticipated word: cooperation

3. For a child to be happy, his day must be very structured when his routine is ---- he becomes nervous and irritable.

   Anticipated words: disrupted, interrupted

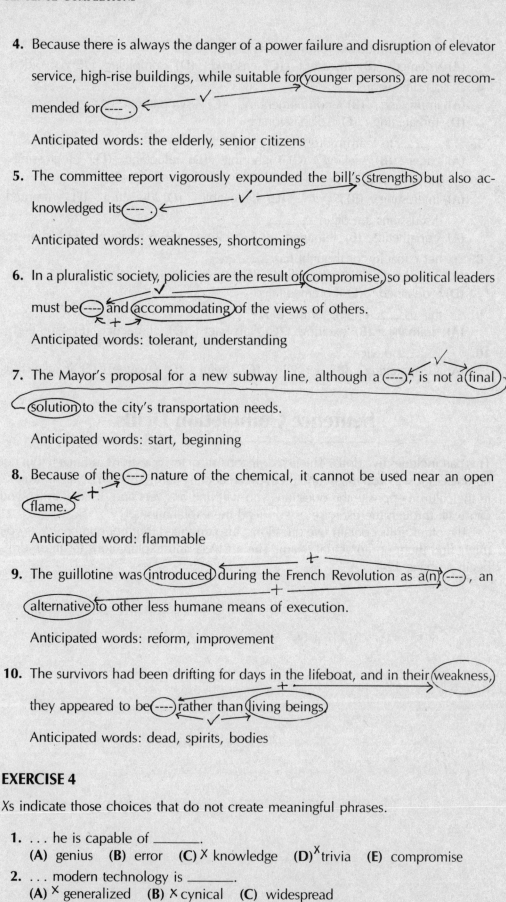

4. Because there is always the danger of a power failure and disruption of elevator service, high-rise buildings, while suitable for younger persons are not recommended for ---- .

Anticipated words: the elderly, senior citizens

5. The committee report vigorously expounded the bill's strengths but also acknowledged its ---- .

Anticipated words: weaknesses, shortcomings

6. In a pluralistic society, policies are the result of compromise so political leaders must be ---- and accommodating of the views of others.

Anticipated words: tolerant, understanding

7. The Mayor's proposal for a new subway line, although a ----, is not a final solution to the city's transportation needs.

Anticipated words: start, beginning

8. Because of the ---- nature of the chemical, it cannot be used near an open flame.

Anticipated word: flammable

9. The guillotine was introduced during the French Revolution as a(n) ----, an alternative to other less humane means of execution.

Anticipated words: reform, improvement

10. The survivors had been drifting for days in the lifeboat, and in their weakness, they appeared to be ---- rather than living beings.

Anticipated words: dead, spirits, bodies

EXERCISE 4

Xs indicate those choices that do not create meaningful phrases.

1. . . . he is capable of _____.
(A) genius **(B)** error **(C)** ˣ knowledge **(D)** ˣ trivia **(E)** compromise

2. . . . modern technology is _____.
(A) ˣ generalized **(B)** ˣ cynical **(C)** widespread
(D) ˣ backwards **(E)** dangerous

3. . . . this much-needed reform has been _____.
   (A) ✗ denied   (B) thwarted   (C) ensured   (D) completed   (E) ✗ avoided

4. . . . conditions are _____.
   (A) improving   (B) ✗ complimentary   (C) ✗ sympathetic
   (D) threatening   (E) ✗ dispassionate

5. . . . _____ to learn more about. . . .
   (A) eager   (B) seeking   (C) ✗ ignoring   (D) reluctant   (E) ✗ progressing

6. . . . the story is not _____.
   (A) interesting   (B) ✗ petty   (C) believable   (D) ✗ wishful   (E) ✗ rumored

7. . . . discussions are often _____.
   (A) ✗ apathetic   (B) lethargic   (C) exciting   (D) ✗ nascent   (E) ✗ charismatic

8. . . . her capacity for thought has _____.
   (A) atrophied   (B) ✗ diversified   (C) ✗ concerned
   (D) ✗ detained   (E) ✗ premeditated

9. . . . the _____ ending of the play.
   (A) dramatic   (B) exciting   (C) ✗ abstract   (D) climactic   (E) ✗ fulfilled

10. . . . _____ device.
    (A) ✗ disparaging   (B) versatile   (C) useful   (D) ✗ vague   (E) ✗ inauspicious

Sentence Completion Drills

This part includes five drills. The first drill consists of ten questions, arranged (but not numbered) just as you might find them on an actual exam. This is a "walk-through." In the column opposite the questions you will find answers and discussion, so you can walk through the exercise as you read the explanations.

The other drills contain five questions, also arranged (but not numbered) as you might find them on an actual exam. The answers and explanations for these drills begin on page 124.

Walk-Through

Directions: Each question below has one or two blanks, each blank indicating that something has been omitted. Beneath the sentence are five lettered words or sets of words. Choose the word or set of words that, when inserted in the sentence, <u>best</u> fits the meaning of the sentence as a whole.

1. Although there are more female students at the college than male students, the women seem to have a(n) ---- influence on the student government.

    (A) enormous   (B) negligible
    (C) provocative   (D) venerable   (E) active

2. Her acceptance speech was ---- , eliciting thunderous applause at several points.

    (A) tedious   (B) well-received   (C) cowardly
    (D) uninteresting   (E) poorly written

3. George Bernard Shaw expressed his ---- for technological progress when he said that the human race is just interested in finding more ---- ways of exterminating itself.

    (A) hope..impartial
    (B) regard..remote
    (C) preference..violent
    (D) support..effective
    (E) contempt..efficient

1. (B) This question is fairly easy. Notice that the choices do not contain difficult vocabulary. The *although* sets up a thought-reverser. Therefore, as you read, you should anticipate that what comes after the comma will contrast with what comes before. So your thinking should be "women are a majority, but something." In this way, you can anticipate that the blank ought to be filled by something like *unimportant* or *insignificant*. Choice (B), *negligible*, neatly does the trick.

2. (B) This question, too, is not very difficult. Again, the choices are all ordinary words. The key to this sentence completion is a thought-extender; what follows the comma must extend or amplify what comes before the comma. So your thinking should be "the speech was something, and that got applause." You might anticipate several completions with positive overtones such as *brilliant, magnificent*, or *persuasive*. None of these appears as an answer choice, so you should match your anticipated response to the best actual choice available. Only choice (B) has the positive overtones you need to complete the parallel between the quality of the speech and the applause.

3. (E) This sentence completion is a bit more difficult than the first two. It is one of those examples for which it may be very difficult to anticipate completions. *Exterminate* is a key word, but you might not immediately see its significance. In such cases, you may need to skip the "anticipate" stage and rely on other techniques. First, you should be able to eliminate both (A) and (B) by "going to pieces." The phrases *impartial ways* and *remote ways* really

are not possibilities. Then you would test the other three choices:

   (C) his preference for . . . finding more
        violent ways . . . .
   (D) his support for . . . finding more
        effective ways . . . .
   (E) his contempt for . . . finding more
        efficient ways . . . .

Given the logical structure of the sentence, (E) is the best choice. For in neither (C) nor (D) does the second element explain the nature of Shaw's judgment described in the first element.

4. Although this disease threatens the lives of several thousand persons every year, the ---- of supplies and equipment has ---- the progress of medical research for a cure.

   (A) discontinuance..ensured
   (B) scarcity..hampered
   (C) rationing..enhanced
   (D) squandering..facilitated
   (E) financing..neglected

4. (B) Again, the technique of anticipation is not by itself the entire solution. The overall structure of the sentence is a thought-reverser introduced by *although*. The blanks themselves, however, are parallel. The second must extend the thought of the first. But the parallel could express either a happy thought or a sad thought, for example "the *availability* of supplies has *ensured* . . . ," or "the *lack* of supplies has *thwarted* . . . ." So you should fall back on the technique of testing. (A), (C), (D), and (E) are all wrong because they do not provide the right connection between the two blanks. (B), however, does. *Scarcity hampers* progress.

5. Despite some bad reviews, Horowitz's stature was not ---- and his fans and critics in Tokyo were unanimous in expressing their ---- of his unique talent.

   (A) distilled..kinship with
   (B) embellished..ignorance of
   (C) criticized..disdain for
   (D) diminished.. appreciation of
   (E) convincing..concern for

5. (D) In this sentence, *despite* introduces a contrast, but notice there is a *not* in the sentence. The blank will actually complete a parallel to bad reviews: Bad reviews but *not* something negative. On this basis, you can eliminate (A), (B), and (E). Then, you should see that the second blank must continue the idea expressed in the first. Only (D) accomplishes this.

6. The Commissioner of Agriculture was so influenced by dairy industry lobbyists that he became a(n) ---- industry goals rather than a ---- of the milk-consuming public.

   (A) apologist for..believer
   (B) spokesperson for ..practitioner
   (C) opponent of..defender
   (D) promoter of..critic
   (E) advocate of..protector

6. (E) This item would be the first sentence completion in the second group (in a verbal section having two groups). Remember that the first sentence completion in the second group is likely to be of above-average difficulty— and then things get even more difficult. This sentence contains a thought-reverser: *rather than.* So the two substitutions must provide a contrast: a something of the industry and not a something of the public. (E) provides this contrast: An *advocate of* industry goals and not a *protector of* the public.

7. The star of the show is a ---- performer, who acts, sings, and dances with equal facility.

    (A) capricious   (B) pretentious   (C) versatile
    (D) myopic   (E) quixotic

7. (C) This sentence requires a thought-extender. What comes after the comma is supposed to amplify or clarify what goes in the blank. What would you call someone who acts, sings, and dances? You might say "talented," or something like that, and a good match would be (C), *versatile*. Notice that this item is made difficult by the vocabulary used in the choices.

8. A skillful ---- , the Dean adopted a posture of patience and ---- toward the protestors, rather than rejecting their demands outright.

    (A) administrator..arrogance
    (B) academician..understanding
    (C) negotiator..compromise
    (D) pundit..tolerance
    (E) pedagogue..obstinacy

8. (C) The logical structure of this sentence completion is not that difficult, but some of the choices contain difficult vocabulary. The first blank sets up a continuation. Whatever follows the comma is supposed to amplify the first completion. Then you can see the second blank as either an extender or a reverser. It must parallel the idea of patience, and it must contrast with the idea of outright rejection. *Compromise* does both jobs. You can eliminate (A) and (E) on the basis of the second elements and (B) and (D) on the basis of their first substitutions.

9. It has been ---- that environment is the ---- factor in the incidence of drug addiction, but recent studies with twins separated at birth indicate that a predisposition to addiction can be inherited.

    (A) proved..crucial
    (B) demonstrated..conclusive
    (C) suggested..predominant
    (D) argued..logical
    (E) urged..unimportant

9. (C) This question is fairly difficult, particularly since (A) and (B) might at first seem like right answers. First, however, let's notice that the *but* introduces a thought-reverser, so we are looking for a contrast between the theory that says environment is responsible and the theory that says heredity is responsible: environment is important, but heredity is important. Thus, you can eliminate (D) and (E) because they do not provide the needed contrast. (A) and (B), however, are more difficult. Ultimately, they are wrong because of their first elements. How could something be *proved* or *demonstrated* and yet be incorrect? The initial evidence really did not prove or demonstrate anything, since it was wrong. Rather, it merely *suggested* an explanation that finally was proved wrong.

10. The delicate aroma and ---- flavor of this fine wine need a sensitive nose and ---- palate to be appreciated.

    (A) insipid..educated
    (B) subtle..discriminating
    (C) pungent..educated
    (D) adulterated..cautious
    (E) savory..untutored

10. (B) The logical structure here is pure thought-extender. The first blank must parallel *delicate*, the second blank must parallel *sensitive*, and both blanks must parallel each other. The item, however, is not easy, because of the vocabulary. Unless you know the meanings of *insipid*, *pungent*, and *savory*, you might have difficulty eliminating (A), (D), and (E). In any event, *subtle* very nicely parallels *delicate*, *discriminating* nicely parallels *sensitive*, and *subtle* and *discriminating* neatly parallel one another.

Drill 1 (Answers, page 124)

> Each sentence below has one or two blanks, each blank indicating that something has been omitted. Beneath the sentence are five lettered words or sets of words. Choose the word or set of words that, when inserted in the sentence, best fits the meaning of the sentence as a whole.
>
> Example:
>
> Although its publicity has been ----, the film itself is intelligent, well-acted, handsomely produced, and altogether ----.
>
> (A) tasteless..respectable
> (B) extensive..moderate
> (C) sophisticated..amateur
> (D) risqué..crude
> (E) perfect..spectacular
>
> ● Ⓑ Ⓒ Ⓓ Ⓔ

1. Although his work was often ---- and ----, he was promoted anyway, simply because he had been with the company longer than anyone else.

    (A) forceful..extraneous
    (B) negligent..creative
    (C) incomplete..imprecise
    (D) predictable..careful
    (E) expeditious..concise

2. Shopping malls account for 60 percent of the retail business done in the United States because they are controlled environments which ---- concerns about the weather.

    (A) eliminate   (B) necessitate   (C) foster
    (D) justify   (E) maintain

3. An oppressive ----, and not the festive mood one might have expected, characterized the gathering.

    (A) senility   (B) capriciousness   (C) inanity
    (D) solemnity   (E) hysteria

4. In order to ---- museums and legitimate investors and to facilitate the ---- of pilfered artifacts, art magazines often publish photographs of stolen archaeological treasures.

    (A) perpetuate..return
    (B) protect..recovery
    (C) encourage..excavation
    (D) undermine..discovery
    (E) confuse..repossession

5. Though the concert had been enjoyable, it was overly ---- and the three encores seemed ---- .
    (A) extensive..curtailed
    (B) protracted..gratuitous
    (C) inaudible..superfluous
    (D) sublime..fortuitous
    (E) contracted..lengthy

Drill 2 (Answers, page 124)

1. Peter, ---- by the repeated rejections of his novel, ---- to submit his manuscript to other publishers.

    (A) encouraged..declined
    (B) elated..planned
    (C) undaunted..continued
    (D) inspired..complied
    (E) undeterred..refused

2. All ---- artists must struggle with the conflict between ---- their own talent and knowledge that very few are great enough to succeed.

    (A) great..neglect of
    (B) aspiring..faith in
    (C) ambitious..indifference to
    (D) prophetic..dissolution of
    (E) serious..disregard of

3. The judge, after ruling that the article had unjustly ---- the reputation of the architect, ordered the magazine to ---- its libelous statements in print.

    (A) praised..communicate
    (B) injured..retract
    (C) sullied..publicize
    (D) damaged..disseminate
    (E) extolled..produce

4. The fact that the office was totally disorganized was one more indication of the ---- of the new manager and of the ---- of the person who had hired him.

    (A) indifference..conscientiousness
    (B) ignorance..diligence
    (C) incompetence..negligence
    (D) tolerance..viciousness
    (E) propriety..confidence

5. Since the evidence of the manuscript's ---- is ---- , its publication will be postponed until a team of scholars has examined it and declared it to be genuine.

    (A) authenticity..inconclusive
    (B) truthfulness..tarnished
    (C) veracity..indubitable
    (D) legitimacy..infallible
    (E) profundity..forthcoming

Drill 3 (Answers, page 125)

1. Although the language was ---- and considered to be inferior to standard English, Robert Burns wrote his love poetry in the language of the Scots.

   (A) interpreted
   (B) belittled
   (C) distinguished
   (D) appreciated
   (E) elevated

2. Given the Secretary of State's ---- the President's foreign policies, he has no choice but to resign.

   (A) reliance upon
   (B) antipathy toward
   (C) pretense of
   (D) support for
   (E) concurrence with

3. In order to ---- the deadline for submitting the research paper, the student tried to ----additional time from the professor.

   (A) extend..wheedle
   (B) accelerate..obtain
   (C) postpone..forego
   (D) sustain..imagine
   (E) conceal..procure

4. Joyce's novel *Finnegan's Wake* continues to ---- critics, including those who find it incomprehensible and call it ---- .

   (A) appall..genial
   (B) enthrall..nonsensical
   (C) baffle..transparent
   (D) bore..compelling
   (E) entertain..monotonous

5. Jazz is an American art form which is now ---- in Europe through the determined efforts of ---- in France, Scandinavia, and Germany.

   (A) foundering..governments
   (B) diminishing..musicians
   (C) appreciated..opponents
   (D) waning..novices
   (E) flourishing..expatriates

Drill 4 (Answers, page 126)

1. The poetry of Mallarmé, like the poetry of most of the symbolists, is not clear and easily accessible but rather vague and ----.

   (A) opaque   (B) redundant   (C) lucid
   (D) straightforward   (E) concrete

2. Mary was very annoyed that her secretary did not meet her deadlines, and she warned her that her laziness and ---- could result in her dismissal.

   (A) procrastination   (B) ambition   (C) zeal
   (D) veracity   (E) fortitude

3. Although a solemn tone was appropriate to the seriousness of the occasion, the speaker lapsed into ----, which was depressing rather than moving.

   (A) reverence   (B) frankness
   (C) loquaciousness   (D) levity   (E) morbidity

4. Due to the ---- of the materials needed to manufacture the product and the ever-increasing demand for it, it is highly probable that the final cost to the consumer will ----.

   (A) immensity..evolve
   (B) paucity..escalate
   (C) scarcity..relax
   (D) acuity..stabilize
   (E) certainty..fluctuate

5. Although the comedian was very clever, many of his remarks were ---- and ---- lawsuits against him for slander.

   (A) derogatory..resulted in
   (B) pithy..came upon
   (C) protracted..forestalled
   (D) depraved..assuaged
   (E) recanted..sparked

Explanatory Answers

DRILL 1

1. (C) The *although* sets up a contrast between the idea of a promotion and the quality of the person's work. So the work must be bad, even though the person was promoted. Additionally, the two blanks must themselves be parallel, since both describe the poor quality of the work.

2. (A) The blank is a thought-extender that explains the result of a controlled environment. What would be the result of a controlled environment? You would not need to worry about the weather.

3. (D) The *not*, a thought-reverser, introduces a contrast. The blank requires a word that means the opposite of a festive mood.

4. (B) The logical structure here requires a thought-extender. The information that comes before the comma must explain why art magazines publish photos of stolen property. Additionally, the two blanks must create a parallel. Publishing the photos must do roughly the same thing for museums and legitimate investors that is done for stolen property. In this case, the result must be good. The museums and investors are protected and the stolen property is recovered.

5. (B) The *though* sets up a contrast. The concert was enjoyable, *but* it suffers from some defect. You can eliminate (D), since to be *sublime* is not to have a defect. Additionally, the two blanks themselves are parallel, for they complete similar thoughts. (A) and (E) contain words opposite in meaning, so they must be wrong. And the words in (C) are unrelated, so they cannot provide the needed contrast.

DRILL 2

1. (C) There are several ways to analyze this item. First, you might see that the overall structure is that of thought-extender. The first blank must complete a phrase set off by commas that explains why Peter does what he does. Also, the word in the first blank must describe an emotional reaction that is an appropriate response to rejection. On this ground you can surely eliminate (A), (B), and (D), since it is not logical for anyone to be *encouraged, elated,* or *inspired* by rejection. (C) and (E) are both possible reactions to rejection, but (E) does not provide the overall logical continuity we need.

2. (B) The sentence sets up a contrast between the artists' view of their own talent and the knowledge that few will succeed. You can eliminate (A), (C), and (E) because they fail to provide a contrast. It would not be surprising that an artist who neglected, or was indifferent to, or disregarded his talent would not succeed. And you can eliminate (D) on the ground that the phrase "*dissolution* of talent" is not meaningful.

3. (B) There are several ways of analyzing this item. First, the overall structure is that of a thought-extender. The second blank must explain the results or consequence of the first blank. Additionally, you can rely on key words such as *unjustly* and *libelous* to learn that the action of the magazine was wrong.

On this basis you can eliminate (A) and (E), since there is nothing wrong with praising or extolling. Then you should eliminate (C) and (D), because they do not explain the natural consequences of the judge's ruling. (C), however, does the job. The judge ruled that the article had wrongly *damaged* the architect's reputation, so he ordered the magazine to make amends by *retracting* what it had printed.

4. (C) The overall structure is that of extender. The blanks must explain why the operation was so disorganized. Additionally, the two blanks describe the same kind of behavior and must be a parallel. You can eliminate (A) and (B) because those word pairs are opposites, not parallels. Then you can eliminate (D) and (E), since they do not supply the needed parallel; they are not related at all. (C) is the choice that supports the overall logical structure of the sentence while providing the parallel between the blanks.

5. (A) The overall structure of the sentence is an extension of a thought signalled by *since*. The blanks must set up the explanation given in the part of the sentence following the comma. Why would the publication need to be postponed until further study? Something is missing. What is it? The two blanks together must provide the answer, and perhaps the most efficient way to arrive at (A) is to test each choice.

DRILL 3

1. (B) The most obvious logical clue to be found here is the parallel between the blank and *inferior*. You must find something that has similar negative overtones; and, of the five choices, only (B) will provide the parallel.

2. (B) Again, we need a parallel. What is the cause of the Secretary's resignation? It cannot be the fact that the Secretary is in favor of the President's policies, so you can eliminate (D) and (E). Then, you can eliminate (A) and (C), because they do not make meaningful statements. (B), however, does provide the reason you are looking for. Since the Secretary is in disagreement with the President, he will resign.

3. (A) We need a thought-extender. The second blank must give the student's reason for doing what is mentioned in the first part of the sentence. Test each choice to see if it does just that. (A) is the only choice that works. The student needs to extend the deadline, so he wheedles some extra time. (B) and (C) make the opposite statement. (D) and (E) create phrases that are not idiomatic English.

4. (B) The key to this item is the parallel set up between *incomprehensible* and the second blank. The second element of the correct choice must be a word like *incomprehensible*.

5. (E) This is the last question in the group, and it is likely to be the most difficult. Even if you had difficulty with the item, you can at least eliminate (A) by "going to pieces." Although a musical style might be famous, or unknown, or fading out of memory, you would not be likely to say that it is *foundering*. Remember that even eliminating one choice allows you to make an educated guess! Beyond that, the second substitution must extend the idea of the first: The music is doing something thanks to the determined efforts of someone. Given the phrase *determined efforts*, you can eliminate (B) and (D), since *diminishing* and *waning* are not things accomplished by determined efforts. And you can eliminate (C),

since opponents do not create an appreciation for the things they oppose. Finally, notice how well (E) works. The sentence states that jazz is an American art form flourishing in Europe. How is that possible? Because of the efforts of American expatriates.

DRILL 4

1. (A) The key here is a thought-extender. The second blank must be filled in by a word that means the same thing as "not clear." This immediately eliminates every choice but (A).

2. (A) There are two logical clues in this item. First, the second blank must extend the idea of *laziness*. Second, the second clause (everything after the comma) must amplify the idea of not meeting deadlines. (A) does both jobs. *Laziness* and *procrastination* are parallel, and the idea of *procrastination* explains why the secretary did not meet her deadlines.

3. (E) The most important logical feature of this sentence is the reverser set up by the *although*. Additionally, there is the parallel between *depressing* and the second substitution. So we are looking for a contrast between *seriousness* and something and a parallel between *depressing* and something. The idea of *morbidity* fits the bill. The morbid tone contrasts with simple solemnity (it goes overboard), and it completes the parallel with *depressing*.

4. (B) This sentence is made difficult by the overall logical structure, so you may want to use the technique of "going to pieces." You can eliminate both (A) and (C) on the basis of their second elements. Cost is not the sort of thing that evolves or relaxes. Then, (D) can be eliminated on the basis of the first element. The phrase *acuity of materials* is meaningless. At this point you would need to analyze the overall logical structure of the sentence. The *due to* signals a thought-extender. What comes before the comma explains the "why" of what comes after the comma. In other words, the something of the raw materials must explain what happens to the cost. You can eliminate (E) because certainty does not explain a fluctuation. And you can eliminate (D) because its first element would not create a meaningful, idiomatic English phrase.

5. (A) This may be a case to go directly to the stage of testing. The logical structure requires that the first blank explain the reasons for what happened in the second blank. Only (A) accomplishes this. Since the remarks were *derogatory*, they *resulted in* lawsuits against the comedian.

Critical Reading

✔ Objectives

To learn what makes Critical Reading difficult and how to avoid being intimidated by a selection.

To learn about the four basic types of Critical Reading questions.

To learn about reading techniques especially suited to the SAT.

To learn the patterns of wrong answers in the Critical Reading section.

1. **Why Critical Reading Is Difficult**
   - **The Choice of Topics**
   - **The Way the Selections Are Edited**
   - **The Double-Passage Format**

2. **The Four Types of Critical Reading Questions**
   - **Vocabulary-in-Context Questions**
   - **Interpretation Questions**
   - **Evaluation Questions**
   - **Synthesis/Analysis Questions**

3. **Reading Techniques**

4. **Question Patterns That Clue You In**

5. **Some Final Words of Advice from Holmes**

6. **A Perfect Format for Holmes's Strategies**

The typical SAT contains up to 40 critical reading questions. These may be divided among four passages of varying length, including one double passage of 700–850 words.

Here are the instructions for critical reading:

> Each passage below is followed by questions based on its content. Answer the questions following each passage on the basis of what is <u>stated</u> or <u>implied</u> in that passage.

This seems easy enough, but the impression of simplicity is misleading.

Why Critical Reading Is Difficult

Answering critical reading questions on the SAT is not nearly as easy as the directions make it sound. Some students attribute the difficulty of reading comprehension to their inability to read quickly enough. They imagine they would do better if they were able to do "speed reading."

This conclusion is completely incorrect! The SAT is not a test of "speed reading." First, the reading selections are rarely long enough to need "speed reading" techniques. Second, the questions test depth of understanding, while in general, "speed reading" emphasizes coverage at the expense of understanding.

Three other factors make SAT critical reading difficult.

1. SAT reading selections can treat virtually any subject. The categories include:

Social Sciences, e.g., history, sociology, archaeology, government, economics

Natural Sciences, e.g., physics, chemistry, astronomy, geology, medicine, botany, zoology

Humanities, e.g., art, literary criticism, philosophy, music, folklore

Narrative, e.g., fiction, biography, true adventure, etc.

And this list does not exhaust the possibilities. Since authors can write about any topic whatsoever, a critical reading selection can be about anything.

Obviously, a reading selection about some unfamiliar topic is more difficult to read than one about material you know something about, and the test-writers go out of their way to find material you've probably not read.

Let's put this into perspective. The test-writers don't select unfamiliar reading selections simply to make the reading more difficult. Rather, they select unfamiliar passages to make sure the questions test *comprehension* rather than knowledge of a subject. The theory is that if a reading selection is about, say, the little-known medieval composer Josquin des Pres, no one will be able to answer questions based on memory.

Additionally, since this is not a test of knowledge, the reading selection will contain everything needed to answer the question. For example, if a critical reading question asks "Why is Josquin des Pres so little known?", the basis for the correct answer will be provided in the reading selection itself.

Finally, don't let the reading selections intimidate you! Imagine the following as the opening of a reading passage:

I say that every Prince should desire to be accounted merciful and not cruel. Nevertheless, he should be on his guard against the abuse of this quality of mercy. Cesare Borgia was reputed cruel, yet his cruelty restored Romagna, united it, and brought it to order and obedience; so that if we look at things in their true light, it will be seen that he was in reality far more merciful than the people of Florence, who, to avoid the imputation of cruelty, suffered Pistoja to be torn to pieces by factions.

Your first reaction to this could be "What on earth is this about? Who is this guy Borgia and where are these places? I'll never be able to answer any questions!" This reaction, though understandable, is the wrong one to have. Instead, you should be thinking, "I've never heard of Cesare Borgia or Pistoja, but neither have most other people who are taking this test. And anyway, everything I need to know will be included in this selection."

Furthermore, each reading passage on the SAT now has a short introduction that will help you place the passage in context. For example, this introduction may tell you who wrote the passage, when it was written, or the author's purpose in writing it. For the reading passage referred to above, the introduction might read as follows:

One of the most frequently read political treatises of all time is The Prince, *by the Italian author Niccolò Machiavelli (1469–1527). In this work, Machiavelli uses examples from his own time and place to explain how a ruler may govern most effectively. Because the policies Machiavelli recommends are sometimes ruthless, the word* Machiavellian *has in our time come to mean "diabolical."*

This introduction gives you a point of reference from which to begin your reading. You will be able to dive into the passage with a clear expectation of what you'll find there. The introduction helps you place the passage in context and can greatly improve your understanding. For this reason, the time you spend reading introductions to SAT reading passages will be time well spent.

2. Many passages are difficult to read because of their old-fashioned grammar, spelling, and even punctuation. The SAT often includes passages from works that were written long ago, and these passages retain their original sentence structure, spelling, and punctuation. As a result, you may have difficulty following the ideas that are expressed in the passage, and words may be used in ways that are not familiar to you. Here is an example:

This passage comes from the diary of Mrs. Sarah Kemble Knight, an eighteenth-century teacher and writer. Her journal tells of a trip she took on horseback from her home in Boston to New York City in the year 1704. Here she describes life in colonial New York, comparing and contrasting it to life in her hometown.

The City of New York is a pleasant, well compacted place, situated on a Commodious River which is a fine harbor for shipping. The Buildings Brick Generally, very stately and high, although not altogether like ours in Boston. The Bricks in some of the Houses are of divers Colors and Laid in Checkers, being glazed look very agreeable. The inside of them are neat to admiration, the wooden work, for only the walls are plastered, and the Summers and Joists are planed and kept very white scour'd as so is all the partitions if made of Boards. The fireplaces have no Jambs (as ours have) But the Backs run flush with the walls, and the Hearth is of Tiles, and is as far out into the Room at the Ends as before the fire, which is Generally Five foot in the Lower rooms, and the piece over where the mantle tree should be is made as ours with Joiners' work, and as I suppose is fasten'd to iron rods inside.

This passage is entirely in old-fashioned style, with grammar, capitalization, and punctuation unlike what we use today. You probably found some parts of it difficult to read, and some words were surely unfamiliar to you. However, the introduction let you know what to expect, and by careful reading you should have been able to understand nearly everything in the passage.

The questions based on a passage like this one shouldn't pose any extra problem for you. They will not ask you anything that you cannot deduce by careful reading, and if they ask you the meaning of an unfamiliar word, there will likely be clues in the passage that will give you the help you need. For example, a question based on the passage above might read as follows:

The *Summers and Joists* referred to in the passage are probably part of which portion of a New York house?

(A) the fireplace
(B) the brickwork
(C) the woodwork
(D) the windows
(E) the tiles

In the passage, you read, "The inside of them are neat to admiration, the wooden work, for only the walls are plastered, and the Summers and Joists are planed and kept very white scour'd as so is all the partitions if made of Boards."

Even if you did not know exactly what "Summers and Joists" are, you are told that they are "planed" (like the "wooden work") and "kept very white" like the partitions made of boards. You should therefore be able to deduce that they are probably another kind of woodwork. In any case, they are clearly not related to any of the other answer choices, so by process of elimination, (C) must be the correct answer choice.

3. The double-passage format increases the difficulty level of critical reading questions. Once on each SAT, you will encounter critical reading questions based not on a single passage but on a pair of passages. One of the passages will support or oppose the viewpoint expressed in the other. You will have to answer questions about each individual passage, and you will also be asked to compare the viewpoints of the two passages. Questions of this type require critical reading skills on an even higher level than those required for questions about single passages.

The Four Types of Critical Reading Questions

Every SAT critical reading question is an "open-book" test; the questions ask about a selection you can look at. And every SAT critical reading question falls into one of four categories.

1. Vocabulary-in-Context Questions. These questions test your understanding of a word or phrase in context. Such questions are usually worded as follows:

> The word *x* in line 23 means . . .
>
> In line 14, what is the best definition of *x*?

2. Interpretation Questions. Interpretation questions require you to understand an author's intent and to interpret words or phrases based on that purpose. Interpretation questions are usually worded in these ways:

> In line 12, why does the author say . . . ?
>
> What does the author mean by . . . ?

3. Evaluation Questions. These questions require you to be a bit more analytical and to discern the author's key assumptions, point of view, or main idea. An evaluation question might be worded in one of these ways:

> How does the author feel about . . . ?
>
> Which of the following would be a good title for . . . ?
>
> Which of these phrases best summarizes the author's intent?

4. Synthesis/Analysis Questions. As their name implies, these questions involve using the whole selection to analyze the author's structural choices and the composition of the passage. Some examples of synthesis/analysis questions are:

Why does the author mention *x*?

How does part 1 of the passage differ from/support part 2?

There are many different ways of wording these four types of questions, but every critical reading question falls into one of the four categories.

9

The Four Types of Questions (Answers, page 153)

The passage below is followed by questions that illustrate the four different types of critical reading questions. Answer the questions on the basis of what is <u>stated</u> or <u>implied</u> in the passage.

On July 19, 1848, Elizabeth Cady Stanton delivered the keynote address at the first women's rights convention in the United States. The Seneca Falls Convention saw a coming together of a variety of women, many of them already involved in the abolition-ist movement. While working for the emancipation of slaves, these women were forced to note similarities between their own disenfranchisement and that of the people they sought to free. Here is the beginning of Stanton's address.

We have met here today to discuss our rights and wrongs, civil and political, and not, as some have supposed, to go into the detail of social life alone. We do not propose to petition the legislature to make our husbands just, generous, and courteous, to seat every man at the head of a cradle, and to clothe every woman in male attire. None of
(5) these points, however important they may be considered by leading men, will be touched in this convention. As to their costume, the gentlemen need feel no fear of our imitating that, for we think it in violation of every principle of taste, beauty, and dignity; notwithstanding all the contempt cast upon our loose, flowing garments, we still admire the graceful folds and consider our costume far more artistic than theirs. Many of the
(10) nobler sex seem to agree with us in this opinion, for the bishops, priests, judges, barristers, and lord mayors of the first nation on the globe, and the Pope of Rome, with his cardinals, too, all wear the loose flowing robes, thus tacitly acknowledging that the male attire is neither dignified nor imposing. No, we shall not molest you in your philo-sophical experiments with stocks, pants, high-heeled boots, and Russian belts. Yours be
(15) the glory to discover, by personal experience, how long the kneepan can resist the terri-ble strapping down which you impose, in how short time the well-developed muscles of the throat can be reduced to mere threads by the constant pressure of the stock, how high the heel of a boot must be to make a short man tall, and how tight the Russian belt may be drawn and yet have wind enough to sustain life.
(20)   But we are assembled to protest against a form of government existing without the consent of the governed—to declare our right to be as free as man is free, to be repre-sented in the government which we are taxed to support, to have such disgraceful laws as give man the power to chastise and imprison his wife, to take the wages which she

(25) earns, the property which she inherits, and, in case of separation, the children of her
love; laws which make her the mere dependent on his bounty. It is to protest against
such unjust laws as these that we are assembled today, and to have them, if possible,
forever erased from our statute books, deeming them a shame and a disgrace to a
Christian republic in the nineteenth century. We have met
      To uplift woman's fallen divinity
(30)   *Upon an even pedestal with man's.*

Vocabulary-in-Context Questions

1. The word *tacitly* in line 12 means
   (A) explicitly
   (B) implicitly
   (C) diplomatically
   (D) gaudily
   (E) violently

2. In line 17, what is the best definition of *stock?*
   (A) equipment
   (B) inventory
   (C) breed
   (D) necktie
   (E) dungeon

Interpretation Questions

3. In line 10, why does Stanton refer to the *nobler sex?*
   (A) She believes that men are worthier than women.
   (B) She is speaking about the upper classes.
   (C) Her audience is made up entirely of women.
   (D) She is using a cliché in a jesting tone.
   (E) She wants to anger her audience.

4. What does Stanton mean by a government "existing without the consent of
   the governed" (lines 20–21)?
   (A) No one has agreed on this form of representation.
   (B) The government has run amok.
   (C) The government does not represent everyone.
   (D) The monarchy subjugates the people.
   (E) There is no such thing as a true democracy.

9

5. When Stanton cites the phrase "fallen divinity," she is referring to
   (A) the abasement of women
   (B) a nation's turning its back on God
   (C) the overthrow of the monarchy
   (D) women's loss of their inherent goodness
   (E) domestic violence

Evaluation Questions

6. How does Stanton feel about men's clothing?
   (A) She prefers it to women's bustles and corsets.
   (B) She thinks women should be able to wear male attire.
   (C) She prefers the comfort of women's flowing garments.
   (D) Clothes do not interest her one way or the other.
   (E) She does not care to waste time discussing fashion.

7. Which of the following would be a good title for paragraph 1 of this selection?
   (A) A Violation of Taste
   (B) Our Serious Mission
   (C) The Unjustness of Fashion
   (D) Clothes Make the Man
   (E) Keep Your Styles; Give Us Our Rights

8. Which of these phrases best summarizes Stanton's intent in paragraph 2?
   (A) "look before you leap"
   (B) "toward justice and parity"
   (C) "with malice toward none"
   (D) "down with men"
   (E) "save us from ourselves"

Synthesis/Analysis Questions

9. Between paragraphs 1 and 2, Stanton changes her tone from
   (A) polite to strained
   (B) humorous to ardent
   (C) glib to maudlin
   (D) puzzled to amused
   (E) serious to frivolous

10. Why does Stanton include the quotation (lines 29–30)?

    (A) to contrast with her flippant tone

    (B) to demonstrate women's artistic abilities

    (C) to support her introduction of the convention's purpose

    (D) to refute her detractor's arguments

    (E) to amuse her audience with a well-known reference

9

Reading Techniques

"You see, Watson," said Holmes, "The tail wags the dog!"

Since Watson, like most people, believes that SAT critical reading is just "reading," he would read the selections just as he might a chapter from a textbook or an article in a magazine. That is an error.

You have just learned that each reading selection is an "excuse" to ask one of the six questions. The test writers don't just find an interesting article and ask questions about it. Instead, they write a passage (by adapting and editing published material) just so they can ask several of the six questions. In other words, the tail is wagging the dog.

Knowing this, the Holmesian strategy for reading the selections is to "read for the four types of questions." Now, this does not mean that you try to anticipate the exact wording of every question that might be asked. (There are many possibilities.) Rather, this means that you adapt your reading techniques to fit the exercise.

SAT critical reading questions are set up to test three levels of reading: understanding of specific points, evaluation of the text, and synthesis. The first level is the most basic. Specific detail questions and questions about the meaning of vocabulary test whether you read carefully.

The second level of reading, evaluation of the text, takes you deeper. These questions ask not just for understanding—they ask for a judgment or an evaluation of what you have read.

The third level requires a total understanding of the selection. You apply your general comprehension of the author's structure of the text.

This does not mean, however, that the three different levels are reached at completely different times. A good reader will be constantly moving back and forth, but there is a logical priority to the levels. That is, without the first level of general understanding, you can't hope to have the precise understanding of the second level. And without the precise understanding of the second level, you can't hope to evaluate or criticize the selection.

The proper method for reading an SAT selection could be represented as a pyramid.

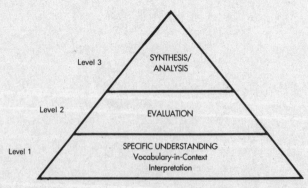

The base of the pyramid represents the basic level of reading on which the other two levels rest, and the second level is needed to support the third level. The easiest questions are usually those on the bottom level, and the most difficult questions are usually found at the top.

Although critical reading questions vary in difficulty, they are usually not arranged in order of difficulty. *This is an exception to the general rule of ladder of difficulty.*

Your first task when you begin reading is to answer the question "What is the topic of the selection?" If the selection consists of more than one paragraph, you may find it useful to preview the first sentence of each paragraph.

The first sentence of a paragraph is often the topic sentence, and it may give you a summary of the content of the paragraph. Here is a sample passage. Everything has been blocked out except the first sentences.

> In the art of the Middles Ages, the personality of the artist as an individual is never present; rather, it is diffused through the artistic genius of centuries embodied in the rules of religious art. Xxx xxx xx xxx xxxxxx xxxx xx xxxxx xxx xxxxxxxx x xxxxxx xxxxx, xxx xxxxxxx xxx xxxxxxxx xx xxxxx xxxx xxxx xxxxxxx. Xxx xxxxxxxx xxxx xxxxxx xxxxxxxxxx xxxxxx xxx xxxx xxxxxxxxx xxxxxxxxx, xxxxx xxx xxxx xxxxxxxxx xxxx x xxxxx xxxxxxxx xxxxxxxx. X xxxxx xxxx x xxxxxx xxxxxxxxx x xxxxxxx; xxx xxxxxx xx xxxxx xx xxxxxxx xxxx xxx xxxxxxxxxx, xxxx xxxx xx xxxxxxx xxxxxxxxx xx Xxxxxxxxx.
>
> Mathematics, too, was an important element of this iconography. "Xxx Xxxxxx Xxxxxx," xxxxx Xxxxx Xxxxxxxxx, "xxxxxxx xxxxxx xxxxxxxxxx xx xxxxxxx," x xxxxxxxx xxxxxxx xxxx xxx xxx-Xxxxxxxxx xxx xxxxxxx xxx xxxxxxxxx xx Xxxxxxxxxx. Xxx xxxxxxx xxxxxxx xxxxxxxx. Xx Xxxxxxxx, x xxxxxxx xxxxx xxxxxx xxxxx xxx xxxx xxxxxxxx Xxxxx, Xxxxxxx, Xxxxxx. xxx Xxxxxxxx xxxxxxxx xx xxxxx xxxxxxxxx xxx xxxx xxxxxxxxxxx Xxxxxxx, Xxxx, Xxxx, xxx Xxxx.
>
> Every painting is also an allegory, showing us one thing and inviting us to see another. Xxxxxxx xxxxxxx, xxx xxxxxx xxx xxxxx xx xxxxxxx Xxx, xxx xxx xxxxxx x xxxxxxxx xxxxxxx xxxxxx xxx xxxxxxx xxx xxx xxxxx xxxxxx xx xx x xxxxx xxxxxx xx xxx. Xx x xxxxxxxx xx xxx xxxxx xxxxxxxx, xx xxx xxx xxxxxxx xxxxxxx xx xxx xxxx xxxx xx Xxxx xxx xxx xxxx xx xxx xxxxx, xxx xx xxxxxxxxxx xxxx xxxx xxxxxxxxx xxxxx xxx xxx xxxx xxx xxxxx xxx xxx xxxxx.
>
> Within such a system even the most mediocre talent was elevated by the genius of the centuries, and the first artists of the Renaissance broke with tradition at great risk. Xxxx xxxx xxxx xxx xxxxx, xxxx xxx xx xxxx xxxx xxx xxxxxx xx xxx xxx xxxxxxx xxx xxxxxxxxx xxxxxxxx xxx xxxxx xxxxx; xxx xxxx xxxx xxx xxx xxxxxxxxxxx, xxxx xxxxxxxx xxxxx xxxxxxxx xxx xxxxxxxxxxxxx xx xxxxx xxxxxxxxx xxxxx.

9

A preview of the first sentences should give you a pretty good idea of the subject discussed in the selection. The passage treats art in the Middle Ages. Additionally, it states that art in the Middle Ages was governed by rules and had numerical and allegorical features. Renaissance painting, however, broke with this tradition.

Given this framework, here is the selection broken down by paragraphs. As you read, consciously ask yourself what point the author is trying to make. And as you come across each new particular point, ask yourself why the author has introduced the point:

> In the art of the Middles Ages, the personality of the artist as an individual is never present; rather, it is diffused through the artistic genius of centuries embodied in the rules of religious art. For art of the Middle Ages is first and foremost a sacred script, the symbols and meanings of which were well settled. The circular halo placed vertically behind the head signifies sainthood, while the halo impressed with a cross signifies divinity. A tower with a window indicates a village; and should an angel be watching from the battlements, that city is thereby identified as Jerusalem.

In the first sentence the author introduces the topic of art in the Middle Ages. In the second sentence, we learn that this art is like a script or writing governed by rules. What function does the rest of the paragraph serve in the overall development? The author provides some illustrations of the assertion about art.

The second paragraph continues the discussion.

> Mathematics, too, was an important element of this iconography. "The Divine Wisdom," wrote Saint Augustine, "reveals itself everywhere in numbers," a doctrine derived from the neo-Platonists who revived the teachings of Pythagoras. And numbers require symmetry. At Chartres, a stained-glass window shows the four prophets Isaac, Ezekiel, Daniel, and Jeremiah carrying on their shoulders the four evangelists Matthew, Mark, Luke, and John.

Why does the author mention mathematics? Because it, too, was part of the rules for painting. And why does the author quote Saint Augustine? To show the importance of numbers in the Middles Ages.

Now, let us introduce another reading technique. This is an "open-book" test, and you can always go back to the selection. Therefore, if something is highly technical or difficult to understand, don't dwell on it. Bracket the information mentally or in writing. You can always come back to it. You should probably do this with the reference to the neo-Platonists. Who were they? It really doesn't matter. Just recognize that they had something to do with numbers, and if you need to learn more about them to answer a question, you can return to the paragraph.

What is the purpose of referring to the stained-glass window in Chartres? It illustrates the way in which numbers might influence art in the Middle Ages.

Now we move to the third paragraph.

> Every painting is also an allegory, showing us one thing and inviting us to see another. In this respect, the artist was asked to imitate God, who had hidden a profound meaning behind the literal and who wished nature to be a moral lesson to man. In a painting of the final judgment, we see the foolish virgins at the left hand of Jesus and the wise at his right, and we understand that this symbolizes those who are lost and those who are saved.

In this paragraph, the author describes another characteristic of painting in the Middle Ages: it contains an allegory. What does the next sentence mean when it compares the artist to God? That's hard to say, and again, this may be a part you should bracket. If a question asks about the analogy between art and Creation, you can always return to the selection to study. And why is the painting of the final judgment mentioned at this point? As an example of an allegorical painting.

Finally, we read the fourth paragraph.

> Within such a system even the most mediocre talent was elevated by the genius of the centuries, and the first artists of the Renaissance broke with tradition at great risk. Even when they are great, they are no more than the equals of the old masters who passively followed the sacred rules; and when they are not outstanding, they scarcely avoid banality and insignificance in their religious works.

What is the meaning of the first sentence of the final paragraph? Roughly, that even mediocre artists could produce good work as long as the rules were followed. Then the selection mentions the first artists of the Renaissance. Why? Because that was the next historical period, and also because it demonstrates how important the rules were to art in the Middle Ages.

Let's summarize the procedure for reading an SAT reading comprehension selection.

Step 1: If the selection is more than one paragraph long, begin with a preview of the first sentence of each paragraph.

Step 2: Read the selection, consciously asking what the author is trying to do.

Step 3: When you encounter material in the selection that seems difficult to understand, bracket it. Try to understand *why* the author introduced it even if you don't understand exactly *what* it means.

A Holmesian strategy—before you begin to read the passage, preview the question stem. The question stem is everything but the answer choices. Take a question stem totally unrelated to anything we have been reading.

> Which of the following comparisons most closely parallels the relationship between specific acts and personality as described in the passage?

This stem tells you something about the passage to which it would be attached. The selection discusses some topic of psychology, specifically the relationship between personality and behavior.

Previewing the question stems may help you find your point of reference. Additionally, a stem can alert you to look for certain things as you do your reading. For example:

> The author's attitude toward corporate contributions to the arts can best be described as

You are alerted to look for the author's judgment about such contributions as you read.

This suggestion must be qualified, however, in three ways. First, some students don't find it useful. The best thing to do, therefore, is to give it a practice shot. Use it only if it helps. Second, don't try to preview the answer choices; they are too long. Additionally, four out of five choices are wrong, so they can't help you at all. In fact, they might actually lead you astray. Third, some stems are not going to be helpful, for they have no content. For example:

> Which of the following is the main point of the passage?

This question stem could go with any selection. Previewing it tells you nothing about what's to come when you read the passage. So just skip over such stems quickly. Preview only the ones that seem likely to provide some substantial information.

Previewing and Reading (Answers, page 154)

The passage below is followed by questions based on its content. Follow the suggestions indicated for previewing and reading. Then answer the questions on the basis of what is <u>stated</u> or <u>implied</u> in the passage.

Dr. Sun Yat-sen (1866–1925) worked for 16 years in exile to promote the overthrow of the Manchu dynasty in China and the elimination of foreign influences there. During the revolution of 1911 he returned to China, where he served briefly as head of the provisional government before being forced into exile again by the new dictator. When he gave his series of lectures on "The Three Principles of the People" in 1924, he was a dying man but was busily planning what would become Chiang Kai-shek's Northern Expedition to liberate and unify all of China. This excerpt is from one of those lectures.

How shall we distinguish clearly between [race and the state]? The most suitable method is by a study of the forces which molded each. In simple terms, the race or nationality has developed through natural forces, while the state has developed through force of arms. To use an illustration from China's political history: Chinese say that
(5) *wang-tao*, royal way or way of right, followed nature; in other words, natural force was the royal way. The group molded by the royal way is the race, the nationality. Armed force is the *pa-tao*, or the way of might; the group formed by the way of might is the state. For example, Hong Kong was not built up because thousands of Hong Kongese wished the British to do it; Hong Kong was taken by the British by armed force.
(10) Because China had been defeated in a war with England, the Hong Kong territory and its people were ceded to England and, in time, the modern Hong Kong was built up. England's development of India is a similar story. The territory of Great Britain now spreads over the whole earth; the English have a saying: "The sun never sets upon the British Empire." In other words, wherever the sun shines in a revolution of the Earth,
(15) there lies some British territory. If we of the Eastern Hemisphere should start with the sun, we would see it shining first upon New Zealand, Australia, Hong Kong, and Singapore; as it turned westward it would shine on Ceylon and India; farther west, upon Aden and Malta; and yet farther, upon England itself; moving into the Western Hemisphere the sun would reach Canada and then complete its revolution at Hong
(20) Kong and Singapore. So, wherever the sun shines in twenty-four hours, there is sure to be British territory. A great territory like Great Britain's has been developed entirely by means of force; since of old, no state has been built up without force. But the development of a race or nationality is quite different: it grows entirely by nature, in no way subject to force. The thousands of Chinese at Hong Kong, for instance, are united in
(25) one race—by nature; whatever force England may employ cannot change the fact. Therefore, we say that a group united and developed by the way of might, by human forces, is a state. This, then, is the difference between a race or nationality and a state.

1. A reasonable definition of *pa-tao* (line 7) might be
   (A) the way of right
   (B) nationality
   (C) the practice of force
   (D) army
   (E) revolution

2. Sun Yat-sen uses the example of Hong Kong to show
   (A) that a state can be created unnaturally
   (B) that nations arise when the people require them to
   (C) how force can destroy a people and their land
   (D) how many people live under British rule
   (E) that nationalism is important in Asia

3. Why does Sun Yat-sen include a listing of nations (lines 16–20)?
   (A) to demonstrate the power of the people
   (B) to show that a state can include many nationalities
   (C) to indicate China's place in the world
   (D) to alarm his audience with Great Britain's domination
   (E) to foment discussion of the use of force

4. Would Sun Yat-sen consider the people of India to be of the British race?
   (A) Yes, because Great Britain rules them by force.
   (B) No, because India is half a world away from England.
   (C) Yes, because the sun shines equally on the two nations.
   (D) No, because only the Chinese are united in that way.
   (E) No, because a race can only be formed naturally.

Step 1: Preview the introductory material.

This paragraph identifies the author and gives you some clues to his point of view.

Step 2: Preview the first and last sentence of the selection or the first sentence of each paragraph.

> How shall we distinguish clearly between [race and the state]?
>
> This, then, is the difference between a race or nationality and a state.

These sentences, taken together, tell you that the topic of the passage is a definition of the difference between a race or nationality and a state.

Step 3: Preview the question stems.

Question 1 tells you to watch for the word *pa-tao*.

Question 2 alerts you to watch for a reference to Hong Kong and to keep in mind the reason for the reference.

Question 3 suggests that a list of nations is included for a particular reason and reminds you to read with that reason in mind.

Question 4 is a synthesis question that requires you to take all you have learned and apply it to a predictive situation. The wording of the question alerts you particularly to look for references to India and to keep in mind the author's purpose as you read those lines.

Step 4: Read the passage.

Lines 5–8 demonstrate the difference between the way of right and the way of might.

Lines 8–22 provide examples of the way of might in action.

Lines 22–25 provide examples of the way of right.

Now you are in a position to answer questions.

Question Patterns That Clue You In

Like most test-takers, Watson is completely preoccupied with finding correct answers to particular questions; but Holmes is keenly aware that answers fall into patterns. Once you know what makes right answers right and wrong answers wrong, you will be able to eliminate incorrect choices and spot the correct answer more easily. Right now, just read through the following double passage selection and familiarize yourself with it. There are no question stems yet to be previewed.

For political reasons, the poet Dante Alighieri was banished from his native city of Florence in 1302. For years he tried to end his exile, but not until 1316 was there a possibility of return. Dante was pardoned, but he was told that in order to return, he must pay a fine and walk in a penitential parade. Centuries later, the writer Madame de Staël was thrown out of Paris by Napoleon after she published an "immoral" work. In the letters below, the exiles express their feelings about their banishments.

Passage 1—Dante Alighieri to a Friend (1316)

From your letter, which I received with due respect and affection, and have diligently studied, I learn with gratitude how my recall to Florence has been the object of your care and concern; and I am the more beholden to you therefor, inasmuch as it rarely happens that an exile finds friends. My reply to what you have written, although per-
(5) chance it be not of such tenor as certain faint hearts would desire, I earnestly beg may be carefully examined and considered by you before judgment be passed upon it.

I gather then, from the letter of your nephew and mine, as well as from those of sundry other friends, that, by the terms of the decree lately promulgated in Florence touching the pardon of exiles, I may receive pardon, and be permitted to return forth-
(10) with, on condition that I pay a certain amount of money, and submit to the stigma of the oblation—two propositions, my father, which in sooth are as ridiculous as they are

ill advised—ill advised, that is to say, on the part of those who have communicated them, for in your letter, which was more discreetly and cautiously formulated, no hint of such conditions was conveyed.

(15)   This, then, is the gracious recall of Dante Alighieri to his native city, after the miseries of well-nigh fifteen years of exile! This is the reward of innocence manifest to all the world, and of the sweat and toil of unremitting study! Far be from a familiar of philosophy such a senseless act of abasement as to submit himself to be presented at the oblation, like a felon in bonds, as one Ciolo and other infamous wretches have done!

(20) Far be it from the preacher of justice, after suffering wrong, to pay of his money to those that wronged him, as though they had deserved well of him!

No! my father, not by this path will I return to my native city. If some other can be found, in the first place by yourself and thereafter by others, which does not derogate from the fame and honor of Dante, that will I tread with no lagging steps. But if by no

(25) such path Florence may be entered, then will I enter Florence never. What! Can I not anywhere gaze upon the face of the sun and the stars? Can I not under any sky contemplate the most precious truths, without first returning to Florence, disgraced, nay dishonored, in the eyes of my fellow citizens? Assuredly bread will not fail me!

Passage 2—Madame de Staël to Napoleon (1810)

Sire, ten years have passed since I saw Your Majesty and eight since I have been exiled.

(30) Eight years of misery modify all characters and destiny teaches resignation to those who suffer.

Ready to embark, I supplicate Your Majesty to grant me the favor of an interview before my departure. I shall permit myself one thing only in this letter, namely, to explain the motives which induce me to leave Europe, if I cannot obtain from Your

(35) Majesty permission to remain in the neighborhood of Paris, in order that my children may live there.

To be in disgrace with Your Majesty casts upon those who suffer it such disfavor in Europe that I cannot make a step without feeling its effects; for while some fear to compromise themselves by holding intercourse with me, and others think themselves

(40) Roman in triumphing over this fear, the simplest courtesies of society become insupportable by a proud spirit. There are some among my friends who have associated their fate with mine with admirable generosity; but I have seen the most friendly sentiments destroyed by the necessity of living with me in solitude, and I have passed eight years of my life between the fear of not obtaining sacrifices and the misery of being their

(45) object. . . .

Your Majesty has been told that I regret Paris because of the Musée and of Talma. This is an agreeable pleasantry upon exile—that is upon the misfortune which Cicero and Bolingbroke have declared the most insupportable of all.

But while I delight in the masterworks of the arts which France owes to Your

(50) Majesty's conquests—while I delight in beautiful tragedies, the representations of heroism—is it for you, Sire, to blame me? The happiness of each individual results from the nature of his faculties; and if heaven has given me talents, are not the enjoyments of the arts and of intellect necessary to my imagination?

Vocabulary-in-Context Questions

EXAMPLES:

By *tenor* (line 5), Dante means
(A) expression
(B) tone
(C) meanness
(D) music
(E) belief

The best answer is (B). To answer a vocabulary-in-context question, first read the choices. Return to the line indicated (here, line 5) and plug the choices into the sentence to see which makes sense. The choices will all be the correct part of speech—in this case, nouns—but only one will fit the context of the sentence or paragraph into which it is being inserted.

Occasionally, the choices you are given will in fact be synonyms for the word in question, but synonyms that have other meanings or shades of meaning than the one required. Here is an example:

In line 46 of Madame de Staël's letter, what does *regret* mean?
(A) mourn
(B) grieve
(C) curse
(D) repent
(E) miss

The correct choice is (E). Nonetheless, all five choices are possible synonyms. However, in the context given, it is clear that Madame de Staël is not *mourning* or *grieving* over Paris, nor is she *cursing* or *repenting*. After rereading the entire paragraph in which the line is located, an alert reader will realize that only (E) is a sensible replacement for *regret*.

> The correct answer for a vocabulary-in-context question will be a synonym that exactly fits the context of the sentence.

Interpretation Questions

EXAMPLE:

What does Dante mean by "Can I not anywhere gaze upon the face of the sun and the stars?"

(A) There is no place like home.

(B) Anywhere is better than Florence.

(C) It would be better to be in jail.

(D) Florence is not the only place in the world.

(E) He misses his hometown.

The answer is (D). Just as you would for a vocabulary-in-context question, you must look closely at the context in which the phrase or sentence occurs in the passage. Dante is waxing indignant over his treatment, and he says that, if this is the way it is going to be, he will never go back to Florence. After all, he can do his work "under any sky"; Florence is not the only place where he can "gaze upon the face of the sun and the stars."

The answer for an interpretation question will be found by looking closely at the context in which the excerpt occurs.

Evaluation Questions

EXAMPLES:

Based on the sentiments expressed in the letter, how does Dante feel toward those who have exiled him?

(A) He forgives them.

(B) He feels sorry for them.

(C) He is contemptuous of them.

(D) He is ashamed of them.

(E) He regrets having offended them.

The best choice is (C). This question requires you to look at the overall tone of the letter. Dante never shows remorse for his actions (E); nor does he show any feelings of pity or forgiveness (A and B). (D) is a possibility, but given Dante's tone of indignation and dislike, (C) is the better answer.

All evaluation questions ask you to summarize in some way; many are phrased like this:

> Which of the following phrases best summarizes Madame de Staël's intent in writing to Napoleon?
> **(A)** I beg your pardon.
> **(B)** I am your servant.
> **(C)** Let my people go.
> **(D)** How dare you?
> **(E)** Your word is your bond.

Here, the correct answer is (A). A thorough reading of the letter shows that Madame de Staël is asking Napoleon to end her exile. She is literally begging his pardon.

Evaluation questions for a double passage such as the one here may require you to evaluate and compare or contrast the two excerpts. Here is an example of that kind of question:

> Unlike Dante, Madame de Staël is
> **(A)** exiled
> **(B)** brave
> **(C)** free
> **(D)** insolent
> **(E)** submissive

The answer is (E). Both writers are exiled (A); neither is free (C). Dante might be considered insolent (D), but Madame de Staël is totally acquiescent in her desire to return to Paris. The submissive posture she assumes throughout her letter cannot be seen as particularly brave (B).

> To answer an evaluation question, read the entire passage and look at it as a whole. Your answer will rely on the tone of the passage as well as its main idea.

Synthesis/Analysis Questions

EXAMPLES:

> Madame de Staël's letter moves from
> **(A)** supplication to explanation to defense
> **(B)** argument to apology
> **(C)** apology to narrative to interpretation
> **(D)** fact to detail
> **(E)** request to prayer to condemnation

The correct response is (A). Synthesis/analysis questions ask you to look at the structure and form of a passage. In Madame de Staël's letter, she begins with a request or supplication, continues with an explanation of why she finds it necessary to make this request, and ends with a defense of her reasons for wanting to return to Paris.

Some synthesis/analysis questions call for a prediction—based on what has occurred so far, what might happen next? Here is an example:

If Dante's letter continued, you might expect him to
(A) beg his friend to intercede on his behalf
(B) promise to return to Florence by springtime
(C) apologize to his friend for wasting his time
(D) agree to pay the fine and walk in the procession
(E) suggest some other means of returning to Florence

The best answer is (E). This is a tricky type of question; it seems subjective, but it is based on what exists in the passage. In Dante's final paragraph, he states that he will not return "by this path," but that "if some other can be found," he might consider returning. He is certainly not about to beg or apologize (A or C); that is not his tone. He will never agree to pay the fine (D), and he cannot return (B) until he does. He might, however, have some suggestions of other ways that he could return without losing face.

> A synthesis/analysis question requires an understanding of the structure and logic of a passage.

Some Final Words of Wisdom from Holmes

Earlier, critical reading was likened to a pyramid, with easier questions as the base and more difficult questions at the top. Remember, however, that critical reading questions are *not* necessarily arranged according to a ladder of difficulty. The first question on a selection might be the most difficult one and the last, the easiest. So don't get bogged down by the first or second question if you happen to find it very difficult.

Additionally, certain questions (usually evaluation or synthesis/analysis questions) can be extremely difficult. But on balance, there are enough of the easier kinds for you to do well on critical reading even if you can't answer one or two of the most difficult questions. Again, don't spend too much time trying to crack a difficult nut.

Remember, also, that you have your own particular strengths, and you will react differently to different topics. For example, if you are very interested in music but relatively less knowledgeable about chemistry, you will find a passage about music easier than one about chemistry. You don't have to do the passages in the order in which they are presented. If you start on one that seems so difficult that you're going nowhere, abandon it and try another.

A Perfect Format for Holmes's Strategies

Some critical reading questions follow a slightly more complicated format. The question stem itself will offer you three alternatives, numbered with Roman numerals. You must decide which of the various alternatives is true. Sometimes just one will be true; other times, two or even all three of the alternatives may be true. You may find this extra level of complication extremely daunting. However, this question format lends itself perfectly to one of Holmes's favorite strategies: the process of elimination. Here is an example:

EXAMPLE:

According to Dante, he cannot abase himself because he is

I. a philosopher
II. an innocent man
III. infamous

(A) I only
(B) II only
(C) III only
(D) I and II only
(E) I and III only

The answer is (D). With a format such as this, the process of elimination becomes a very powerful tool. Start with I. If you look at line 17 in Dante's letter, you see that he refuses, as a "familiar of philosophy," to be abased. Once you know this, you can eliminate any choice that does not include I. So you eliminate (B) and (C). Next you try II. Skim the passage to find the word *innocence* (line 16), and you will see that Dante does consider himself innocent, and that is why he refuses to submit. You can now answer the question, but just to be sure, try III. Nowhere does Dante call himself infamous; he speaks of "infamous wretches" who have submitted. Both I and II work, so the answer must be (D).

> With the Roman numeral format, if you have to guess, first use the process of elimination to narrow down your choices.

Now that you are familiar with the four types of critical reading questions that you're likely to encounter on the SAT, try working your way through the Critical Reading Drills that start on page 155. The first one is a "walk-through" drill with the answers printed alongside the questions; the rest simulate what you'll find on the actual SAT. As you tackle each question, try to determine which type it is, and practice using the strategies described in this section. The more practice you have with critical reading questions, the more confident you'll be when faced with this difficult SAT question type.

9

Summary

1. Critical reading is made difficult by the variety of topics and compact-
    ness of the selections. Don't let the passages intimidate you.
2. Critical reading questions fall into one of four categories: vocabulary-
    in-context, interpretation, evaluation, and synthesis/analysis.
3. Your reading proceeds on three levels (shown on the pyramid). Begin
    by previewing the introduction, first and last sentences, and question
    stems. As you read, try to identify as quickly as possible the main theme
    of the selection. Then, as each new point is introduced, try to fit it into
    the overall development. If material is too difficult, bracket it. Make
    sure you understand why it is in the passage (even if you don't under-
    stand what it says) and continue your reading.
4. Hints for answering questions.

    For a vocabulary-in-context question, find a synonym that precisely fits
the context of the sentence or paragraph.

    For an interpretation question, look closely at the context in which the
excerpt appears. Choose the answer that best fits the author's meaning and
purpose.

    For an evaluation question, think of the passage as a whole. Consider
its tone and purpose as well as its main idea. In a double passage, you may
be asked to compare and contrast main points.

    For a synthesis/analysis question, look at the structure of the passage
and think about why the author arranged it the way he or she did.

Explanatory Answers

EXERCISE 1
Vocabulary-in-Context Questions

1. (B) Stanton says that bishops and judges wear clothing that resembles women's, thus appearing to uphold her opinion that such clothing is better than men's. They do not come right out and say so, however; their support is *tacit*, or *implicit*.

2. (D) The context refers to the tightness of the stock upon the neck. Only *necktie* fits this context.

Interpretation Questions

3. (D) The tone of paragraph 1 is humorous, but the speech's content makes clear that Stanton does not consider men particularly noble.

4. (C) The remaining part of the sentence supports this interpretation of the phrase. Nowhere does she speak of monarchy (D) or democracy (E).

5. (A) Stanton wants to uplift woman to the position of man; over time, woman has fallen, or been abased.

Evaluation Questions

6. (C) The point of paragraph 1 is to allay men's fears that liberated women will start dressing like men; Stanton does this by explaining how much better women's clothing is than men's.

7. (E) Stanton is rejecting male arguments that say that women want to be just like men. In a humorous way, she urges her audience to forego issues of style for issues of substance.

8. (B) Paragraph 2 lists the offenses men have perpetrated against women and ends with a ringing call for equality.

Synthesis/Analysis Questions

9. (B) After drawing listeners in with a humorous beginning, Stanton turns serious and impassioned in paragraph 2.

10. (C) Paragraph 2 tells why the Seneca Falls meeting has been convened; the quotation nicely summarizes the intent of the convention.

9

EXERCISE 2

1. (C) The answer to this vocabulary-in-context question is a simple restating of Sun Yat-sen's own definition, "the way of might."

2. (A) To evaluate Sun Yat-sen's inclusion of this example, you must read carefully. "Hong Kong was not built up because thousands of Hong Kongese wished . . . it . . ."; it was created unnaturally, by force.

3. (B) Great Britain is the state that rules all of these nationalities, but just because the territory belongs to Great Britain does not mean that the people are British.

4. (E) If you understand the answer to Question 3, you will probably answer this question correctly. It requires your application of Sun Yat-sen's definitions of state and nationality to his example of India, which, although controlled by Great Britain, is not naturally British.

Critical Reading Drills

Here are five drills. The first one, a "walk-through," has answers and discussion facing the questions so that you can walk through the exercise as you read the explanations.

The remaining drills contain ten questions each, arranged just as you might find them on an actual SAT. Drill 4 features a double reading passage. The answers and explanations for these drills begin on page 168.

9

Walk-Through

In 1922, after years of activity in the Indian nationalist movement, Mohandas Gandhi was arrested and charged with treason based on his writings in the journal Young India. *By this time, Gandhi's principles of nonviolence and self-denial were the foundation of the movement. His trial was followed closely and attended by hundreds. This is his statement to the court before he was sentenced to six years in prison.*

I am satisfied that many Englishmen and Indian officials honestly believe that they are administering one of the best systems devised in the world and that India is making steady though slow progress. They do not know
(5) that a subtle but effective system of terrorism and an organized display of force on the one hand, and the deprivation of all powers of retaliation or self-defense on the other, have emasculated the people and induced in them the habit of simulation. This awful habit has
(10) added to the ignorance and self-deception of the administrators. Section 124-A, under which I am happily charged, is perhaps the prince among the political sections of the Indian Penal Code designed to suppress the liberty of the citizen. Affection cannot be manufactured
(15) or regulated by law. If one has an affection for a person or system, one should be free to give the fullest expression to his disaffection, so long as he does not contemplate, promote, or incite to violence. But the section under which Mr. Banker and I are charged is one under
(20) which mere promotion of disaffection is a crime. I have studied some of the cases tried under it, and I know that some of the most loved of India's patriots have been convicted under it. I consider it a privilege, therefore, to be charged under that section. I have endeavored to
(25) give in their briefest outline the reasons for my disaffection. I have no personal ill will against any single administrator, much less can I have any disaffection toward the King's person. But I hold it to be a virtue to be disaffected toward a government which in its totality
(30) has done more harm to India than any previous system. India is less manly under the British rule than she ever was before. Holding such a belief, I consider it to be a sin to have affection for the system. And it has been a precious privilege for me to be able to write what I
(35) have in the various articles, tendered in evidence against me.

In fact, I believe that I have rendered a service to India and England by showing in non-co-operation the

This selection is two paragraphs long. You can preview the selection by reading the introduction, which tells you who wrote the passage and sets the stage for the words that follow. Then read the first and last sentences of each of the two paragraphs. In these sentences Gandhi discusses the system in England and India, the evidence brought against him in his trial, his belief in the power of non-co-operation, and his recommendations for his own sentencing. You now know quite a bit about Gandhi's subject matter.

Preview the question stems, looking especially for those that feature words or phrases you may need to look for as you read. Now read the selection.

way out of the unnatural state in which both are living.
(40) In my humble opinion, non-co-operation with evil is as
much a duty as is co-operation with good. But in the
past, non-co-operation has been deliberately expressed
in violence to the evildoer. I am endeavoring to show to
my countrymen that violent non-co-operation only mul-
(45) tiplies evil and that as evil can only be sustained by
violence, withdrawal of support of evil requires complete abstention from violence. Nonviolence implies
voluntary submission to the penalty for non-co-operation with evil. I am here, therefore, to invite and submit
(50) cheerfully to the highest penalty that can be inflicted
upon me for what in law is a deliberate crime and what
appears to me to be the highest duty of a citizen. The
only course open to you, the judge, is either to resign
your post, and thus dissociate yourself from evil if you
(55) feel that the law you are called upon to administer is an
evil and that in reality I am innocent, or to inflict upon
me the severest penalty if you believe that the system
and the law you are assisting to administer are good for
the people of this country and that my activity is there-
(60) fore injurious to the public weal.

1. When Gandhi calls Section 124-A "the prince"
   among laws designed to suppress liberty (line 12),
   he means the law is
   (A) fair
   (B) regal
   (C) chief among such laws
   (D) majestic in its language
   (E) outmoded

2. How does Gandhi feel about the charge leveled
   against him?
   (A) It is absurd to try to legalize affection.
   (B) He is pleased to be in such good criminal
       company.
   (C) He is furious that such a spurious charge has
       been made.
   (D) both A and B
   (E) both B and C

9

1. (C) This interpretation question asks you to look at an unfamiliar use of words and place it in the context of the passage, paying particular attention to Gandhi's purpose and meaning. If you try plugging in the choices one by one, you will see that (A) is exactly opposite to his meaning. (B) and (D) are not supported by the text, and (E), although it may be an opinion held by the author, is not as accurate a choice as (C).

2. (D) To answer an evaluation question in this form, you must take the time to look at all the choices and eliminate all those that do not fit. Gandhi says that "affection cannot be manufactured or regulated by law" (lines 14–15); therefore (A) is correct. However, if you give up at this point and write (A) as your answer, you will receive no points for this question. Check (B). Gandhi points out that "some of the most loved of India's patriots" have been charged with the same crime (line 22); he feels privileged to be in their company. Now you know that (B) is correct as well, so (D) must be your choice. Just to be safe, since you are not being timed here, check (C). Nowhere does Gandhi express anger, nor does he say that the charge is false (spurious).

3. What does Gandhi mean by his statement that he
    has given his reasons for disaffection "in their
    briefest outline" (line 25)?

    (A) He has shared his reasons with a panel of
        lawyers.
    (B) He has explained the basic rationale for his
        feelings.
    (C) He has written down the reasons for his disaf-
        fection.
    (D) both A and B
    (E) both B and C

4. The word *tendered* (line 35) most closely means

    (A) sympathized
    (B) augmented
    (C) projected
    (D) submitted
    (E) ached

5. How does Gandhi feel about non-cooperation?

    (A) It is always the right path.
    (B) It always supports evil.
    (C) It must be expressed nonviolently.
    (D) It cannot win against violence.
    (E) It multiplies and eradicates evil.

6. Why will Gandhi "submit cheerfully to the highest
    penalty"?

    (A) It will offer him a chance at martyrdom.
    (B) He knows his supporters will free him.
    (C) He does not accept the government's right to
        try him.
    (D) His policy of nonviolence requires submission.
    (E) The only penalty he fears is death.

3. (B) This is an interpretation question with a
    process-of-elimination format. Look at the
    choices one by one and plug each into the
    context of the sentence. (A) is unsupported.
    The word *brief* may confuse you and make
    you think of lawyers, but no mention is
    made of any panel of lawyers. (B) is a clear
    restatement of Gandhi's sentence, but just to
    be sure, you must look at (C), because if (C)
    is also correct, then your answer must be (E).
    However, nowhere in the speech does
    Gandhi say that he has written his reasons
    down; he is more likely to have stated them
    aloud in the process of giving testimony.

4. (D) Vocabulary-in-context questions require
    you to try out the various choices in place of
    the word in question. If you have previewed
    the question stems, you are alert in your
    reading to the fact that certain words will be
    tested. The choices here contain some plays
    on *tender* meaning "gentle" (A) and *tender*
    meaning "sore" (E). There are also some syn-
    onyms for the related word *extended* (B and
    C). Only (D) works in context, however.

5. (C) This is an evaluation question. If you
    need to, skim the passage until you find a
    reference to non-co-operation (line 38). Then
    skim to determine which of the choices is
    the best paraphrase of Gandhi's beliefs. In
    this case, (A) is not right; Gandhi says that
    co-operation with good is also correct (line
    41). (B) is not right; violent non-co-operation
    may support evil (line 42), but not all non-
    co-operation does so. (D) and (E) are not
    supported by the text. Only (C) is a good
    restatement of what Gandhi says in para-
    graph 2.

6. (D) Understanding Gandhi's intent will help
    you choose the only answer of the five choices
    that is directly supported by the text. Lines
    47–48 states that "nonviolence implies volun-
    tary submission to the penalty for non-co-oper-
    ation." In order to live by his own creed,
    Gandhi must submit rather than defy the system.

7. Why does Gandhi speak directly to the judge?
   (A) He want's the judge's sympathy for his plight.
   (B) He is tired of addressing an uncaring jury.
   (C) He thinks the judge, being Indian, will understand him.
   (D) He seeks the most severe sentence possible.
   (E) He wants to appeal to the judge's own convictions.

8. What is "the public weal" (line 60)?
   (A) the people's welfare
   (B) the country's difficulties
   (C) civic responsibility
   (D) popular opinion
   (E) the nation's prosperity

9. How does paragraph 1 of the passage strengthen Gandhi's recommendation to the judge?
   (A) It defines evil and lists appropriate penalties for sedition.
   (B) It offers reasons for Gandhi's behavior and suggests that the law under which he is charged is oppressive.
   (C) It accuses the English and Indian systems of terrorist acts.
   (D) It explains Gandhi's service to the people of India and England.
   (E) It states that Gandhi does not personally dislike the King or his administrators.

10. Which of the following sentences might Gandhi use to sum up his argument to the judge?
    (A) Have the courage of your convictions.
    (B) India—love it or leave it!
    (C) Your power has no significance.
    (D) Only the strong survive.
    (E) My country, right or wrong.

7. (E) Gandhi puts his life directly in the hands of the sentencing judge, not allowing the judge blindly to follow the law, but rather encouraging him to decide how he feels about that law. (A), (B), and (C) are unsupported by the text; (D) is true, but it is only part of the story. This kind of question requires you to understand the author's intent.

8. (A) Again, this kind of interpretation question asks you to match a phrase against the author's purpose. The context of the phrase says that Gandhi's "activity is therefore injurious to the public weal." (B), (C), and (D) could hardly be harmed by such activity. (E) suggests that *weal* is related to *wealth*, but it is really closer to *welfare*, as in (A).

9. (B) This synthesis/analysis question involves the structure of the passage and Gandhi's compositional choices. (A) is unsupported by the text. (C) and (E) appear in paragraph 1 (lines 5–6 and 26), but they do not particularly strengthen Gandhi's recommendation to the judge. The reference in (D) appears in paragraph 2, not in paragraph 1.

10. (A) This kind of evaluation asks for a summary of what has gone before. If you have clearly understood Gandhi's words to the judge, there can be no question—(A) is the only possible answer. (B) and (E) are a kind of patriotic prattle in which Gandhi would hardly indulge. (C) is certainly not what Gandhi believes—the judge's power *is* significant, or Gandhi would not be speaking to him. As for (D), Gandhi does not consider himself strong, but he has no doubts about his survival. He is encouraging the judge to vote his conscience (A).

Drill 1 (Answers, page 168)

In June of 1881, the brilliant bacteriologist Louis Pasteur overcame the odds and achieved the results he craved in his experiments on a cure for anthrax, a disease of sheep and cattle. He wrote this letter to his family to announce his success and to describe the reactions of his colleagues.

It is only Thursday, and I am already writing to you; it is because a great result is now acquired. A wire from Melun has just announced it. On Tuesday last, May 31, we inocu-lated all the sheep, vaccinated and non-vaccinated, with
(5) very virulent splenic fever. It is not forty-eight hours ago. Well, the telegram tells me that, when we arrive at two o'clock this afternoon, all the non-vaccinated subjects will be dead; eighteen were already dead this morning, and the others dying. As to the vaccinated ones, they are all well;
(10) the telegram ends by the words "stunning success"; it is from the veterinary surgeon, M. Rossignol.

It is too early yet for a final judgment; the vaccinated sheep might yet fall ill. But when I write to you on Sunday, if all goes well, it may be taken for granted that
(15) they will henceforth preserve their good health, and that the success will indeed have been startling. On Tuesday, we had a foretaste of the final results. On Saturday and Sunday, two sheep had been abstracted from the lot of twenty-five vaccinated sheep, and two from the lot of
(20) twenty-five non-vaccinated ones, and inoculated with a very virulent virus. Now, when on Tuesday all the visitors arrived, amongst whom were M. Tisserand, M. Patinot, the Préfect of Seine et Marne, M. Foucher de Careil, Senator, etc., we found the two unvaccinated sheep dead, and the
(25) others in good health.

I then said to one of the veterinary surgeons who were present, "Did I not read in a newspaper, signed by you, apropos of the virulent little organism of saliva, 'There! one more microbe; when there are 100 we shall make a
(30) cross'?" "It is true," he immediately answered, honestly. "But I am a converted and repentant sinner." "Well," I answered, "allow me to remind you of the words of the Gospel: joy shall be in heaven over one sinner that repen-teth, more than over ninety and nine just persons which
(35) need no repentance." Another veterinary surgeon who was present said, "I will bring you another, M. Colin." "You are mistaken," I replied. "M. Colin contradicts for the sake of contradicting, and does not believe because he will not believe. You would have to cure a case of neurosis, and
(40) you cannot do that!" Joy reigns in the laboratory and in the house. Rejoice, my dear children.

1. The best definition of *virulent* (line 5) might be
   (A) benign
   (B) bitter
   (C) deadly
   (D) violent
   (E) sarcastic

2. When Pasteur refers to "a final judgment" (line 12), he means
   (A) the measure of his worth by God
   (B) payment for services rendered
   (C) a life-or-death decision
   (D) other scientists' belief in his methods
   (E) a ruling of success or failure

3. The word *abstracted* (line 18) means
   (A) abridged
   (B) removed
   (C) occupied
   (D) agitated
   (E) pledged

4. How does Pasteur feel about the results of his experi-ment?
   (A) impassive
   (B) unsure
   (C) bewildered
   (D) astounded
   (E) apprehensive

5. Why does Pasteur include his conversation with the veterinary surgeon?
   (A) as a measure of his concern for others
   (B) to discredit the scientific community
   (C) to demonstrate the need for accurate surgery
   (D) as a way of poking fun at medical scholarship
   (E) to show that his detractors have been won over

6. Why does Pasteur quote the Gospel?

   (A) He believes that his work is approved by God.
   (B) He exults in the change of heart of his adversary.
   (C) He wants to express his humility.
   (D) His experiments have vanquished the ways of God.
   (E) He thinks that everyone should have agreed with him.

7. How does Pasteur feel about M. Colin?

   (A) The man cannot be cured of his cynicism.
   (B) He is too much of a "yes-man" for Pasteur's taste.
   (C) M. Colin does not understand scientific inquiry.
   (D) both A and B
   (E) both B and C

8. Pasteur's letter moves from

   (A) report of results to description of reactions
   (B) conclusions to hypotheses
   (C) hypotheses to experiments to results
   (D) reports of failure to reports of success
   (E) discussion of his feelings to interpretation of results

9. A good title for the final paragraph of the letter might be

   (A) "Experimental Setback"
   (B) "From the Sublime to the Ridiculous"
   (C) "Abandon Hope!"
   (D) "So There, Doubters!"
   (E) "God Is Great"

10. The tone of the letter as a whole is

    (A) upbeat
    (B) indifferent
    (C) tactful
    (D) solemn
    (E) naive

9

Drill 2 (Answers, page 169)

Gertrude Simmons Bonnin (1876–1938) was born and raised on a Sioux reservation in South Dakota. She began to write in 1900, and took the pen name Zitkala-Sa, *meaning "red bird." After marrying Raymond Bonnin, she moved to the Uintah Reservation in Utah. She became increasingly involved in Native American politics, and her literary output declined. The passage below is from one of her early short stories, "The Soft-Hearted Sioux," published first in* Harper's Monthly *in 1901.*

Beside the open fire I sat within our teepee. With my red blanket wrapped tightly about my crossed legs, I was thinking of the coming season, my sixteenth winter. On either side of the wigwam were my parents. My father was
(5) whistling a tune between his teeth while polishing with his bare hand a red stone pipe he had recently carved. Almost in front of me, beyond the centre fire, my old grandmother sat near the entranceway.

She turned her face toward her right and addressed
(10) most of her words to my mother. Now and then she spoke to me, but never did she allow her eyes to rest upon her daughter's husband, my father. It was only upon rare occasions that my grandmother said anything to him. Thus his ears were open and ready to catch the smallest wish she
(15) might express. Sometimes when my grandmother had been saying things which pleased him, my father used to comment upon them. At other times, when he could not approve of what was spoken, he used to work or smoke silently.

(20) On this night my old grandmother began her talk about me. Filling the bowl of her red stone pipe with dry willow bark, she looked across at me.

"My grandchild, you are tall and are no longer a little boy." Narrowing her old eyes, she asked, "My grandchild,
(25) when are you going to bring here a handsome young woman?" I stared into the fire rather than meet her gaze. Waiting for my answer, she stooped forward and through the long stem drew a flame into the red stone pipe.

I smiled while my eyes were still fixed upon the
(30) bright fire, but I said nothing in reply. Turning to my mother, she offered her the pipe. I glanced at my grandmother. The loose buckskin sleeve fell off at her elbow and showed a wrist covered with silver bracelets. Holding up the fingers of her left hand, she named off the desirable
(35) young women of our village.

"Which one, my grandchild, which one?" she questioned.

"Hoh!" I said, pulling at my blanket in confusion. "Not yet!" Here my mother passed the pipe over the fire to my
(40) father. Then she too began speaking of what I should do.

"My son, always be active. Do not dislike a long hunt. Learn to provide much buffalo meat and many buckskins before you bring home a wife." Presently my father gave

the pipe to my grandmother, and he took his turn in the
(45) exhortations.

"Ho, my son, I have been counting in my heart the bravest warriors of our people. There is not one of them who won his title in his sixteenth winter. My son, it is a great thing for some brave of sixteen winters to do."
(50) Not a word had I to give in answer. I knew well the fame of my warrior father. He had earned the right of speaking such words, though he himself was a brave only at my age. Refusing to smoke my grandmother's pipe because my heart was too much stirred by their words, and
(55) sorely troubled with a fear lest I should disappoint them, I arose to go. Drawing my blanket over my shoulder, I said, as I stepped toward the entranceway: "I go to hobble my pony. It is now late in the night."

1. The purpose of paragraph 1 seems to be to
   (A) set the scene
   (B) introduce the characters
   (C) reveal the theme
   (D) both A and B
   (E) both B and C

2. When the narrator refers to "her daughter's husband" (lines 11–12), he implies
   (A) a close relationship between husband and wife
   (B) a formal relationship between mother-in-law and son-in-law
   (C) a strained relationship between father and son
   (D) a loving relationship between mother and daughter
   (E) a distant relationship between daughter-in-law and mother-in-law

3. How does the narrator feel toward his grandmother?
   (A) doting and indulgent
   (B) repulsed but polite
   (C) nervous but respectful
   (D) hostile but afraid
   (E) annoyed and angry

4. The word *stem* in line 28 is used to mean
   - (A) shaft
   - (B) rein
   - (C) leash
   - (D) yoke
   - (E) stalk

5. When the narrator says "Not yet!" (line 38–39), he means
   - (A) he will resume this discussion after his parents leave
   - (B) he will make a decision after the buffalo hunt
   - (C) he is not ready to choose a bride
   - (D) the girls of the village are not ready to marry
   - (E) he cannot choose until he has become a warrior

6. The word *exhortations* (line 45) means
   - (A) warnings
   - (B) instructions
   - (C) rejoicings
   - (D) inspirations
   - (E) lamentations

7. When the narrator says that his father "was a brave only at my age," he means that his father
   - (A) won his own title and fame at a later age
   - (B) became a brave at age 16
   - (C) was a brave for only one year before becoming a warrior
   - (D) was exceptionally courageous at an early age
   - (E) became a warrior at age 16

8. The best summation of the narrator's feelings as he leaves the teepee at the end of the passage might be
   - (A) elated and excited
   - (B) weary and depressed
   - (C) optimistic and expectant
   - (D) frightened and insulted
   - (E) flustered and worried

9. In line 57, what does *hobble* mean?
   - (A) tether
   - (B) falter
   - (C) stagger
   - (D) stumble
   - (E) ride

10. A good title for this selection might be
   - (A) "My Sixteenth Winter"
   - (B) "Father Teaches Me a Lesson"
   - (C) "Grandmother's Opinion"
   - (D) "Advice from My Family"
   - (E) "Life in the Wigwam"

9

Drill 3 (Answers, page 170)

The Italian physicist Galileo Galilei (1564–1642), among hundreds of scientific innovations, was responsible for overturning Aristotle's theories of motion and proving that bodies in freefall do not fall at a speed proportional to their weight. His discoveries anticipated Newtonian physics; Isaac Newton was born the year Galileo died. This passage is from Chapter 1 of Galileo's treatise On Motion.

We are going to explain later on that all natural motion, whether upward or downward, is the result of the essential heaviness or lightness of the moving body. We have there-fore thought it logical first to discuss on what basis we are
(5) to say that one thing is lighter or heavier than another thing, or is equally heavy. And it is necessary to settle this, for it often happens that what is lighter is called heavier, and conversely. Thus, we sometimes say that a large piece of wood is heavier than a small piece of lead, though lead,
(10) as such, is heavier than wood. And we say that a large piece of lead is heavier than a small piece of lead, though lead is not heavier than lead.

Therefore, to avoid pitfalls of this kind, we define as equally heavy two substances which, when they are equal
(15) in size [i.e., in volume], are also equal in weight. Thus, if we take two pieces of lead which are equal in volume and equal also in weight, we shall have to say that they are equally heavy. And clearly, therefore, we must not say that wood and lead are equally heavy. For a piece of wood
(20) which weighs the same as a piece of lead will far exceed the piece of lead in volume.

Again, one substance should be called heavier than a second substance, if a piece of the first, equal in volume to a piece of the second, is found to weigh more than the sec-
(25) ond. For example, if we take a piece of lead and a piece of wood equal in volume to each other, and the piece of lead is heavier than the piece of wood, then we shall certainly be right in asserting that lead is heavier than wood. There-fore, if we find a piece of wood equal in weight to a piece
(30) of lead, surely we must not conclude that wood and lead are equally heavy. For we shall find that in such a case a volume of the lead is far exceeded by the volume of the wood.

And, finally, we must define, in converse fashion, that
(35) which is lighter. That is, one substance is to be considered lighter than a second substance, if a portion of the first, equal in volume to a portion of the second, is found to weigh less than the second. Thus, if we take two pieces, one of wood and one of lead, equal to each other in vol-
(40) ume, and the piece of wood weighs less than the piece of lead, then we shall properly conclude that wood is lighter than lead.

1. When Galileo states that "it is necessary to settle this" (line 6) he means that
   (A) experiments will prove what he is alleging
   (B) people do not believe what he has been saying
   (C) he can proceed no further without consensus
   (D) without an accepted definition, we cannot make comparisons
   (E) the arguments of earlier scientists are absurd

2. In line 8, what is the best definition of *conversely*?
   (A) as shall be proven
   (B) *vice versa*
   (C) *vis-à-vis*
   (D) as we discussed
   (E) in the scheme of things

3. Why does Galileo point out that "lead is not heavier than lead" (line 12)?
   (A) He wants to confuse his readers.
   (B) He is making a play on words.
   (C) He is showing that a substance is as heavy as itself, albeit a small piece weighs less than a large piece.
   (D) He wants to prove the absurdity of comparing one unrelated substance to another in terms of weight.
   (E) He is demonstrating that comparing wood to lead is just as useless as comparing lead to lead.

4. Galileo includes paragraph 2 in order to
   (A) disprove an earlier theory
   (B) provide a counterpoint to paragraph 1
   (C) remind his readers of his topic
   (D) explain his experimental theory
   (E) define some of his terms

5. Which sentence best summarizes Galileo's point in paragraph 3?

   (A) *X* is heavier than *Y* if a piece of *X* is heavier than an equal-sized piece of *Y*.
   (B) *X* is heavier than *Y* if a piece of *X* is always heavier than a piece of *Y*.
   (C) *X* is heavier than *Y* if a piece of *Y* is heavier than a smaller piece of *X*.
   (D) *X* is heavier than *Y* if a piece of *X* can be considered heavier than *Y*.
   (E) *X* is heavier than *Y* if *X* is lead-based and *Y* is not.

6. The word *asserting* in line 28 means

   (A) validating
   (B) claiming
   (C) witnessing
   (D) denying
   (E) accusing

7. The purpose of paragraph 3 seems to be to

   (A) nullify paragraph 2
   (B) introduce the concept of "equal weight"
   (C) introduce the concept of "heavier"
   (D) both A and B
   (E) both B and C

8. The structure of paragraph 4 could be charted as

   (A) introduction, cause, effect
   (B) introduction, definition, illustration
   (C) hypothesis, proof, resolution
   (D) definition, explication, refutation
   (E) theory, experiment, analysis

9. The word *properly* in line 41 is used to mean

   (A) agreeably
   (B) erroneously
   (C) prudishly
   (D) decorously
   (E) correctly

10. A good title for this selection might be

   (A) "Heat and Motion"
   (B) "A Falling Body"
   (C) "Wood and Lead: Which Weighs More?"
   (D) "Heavier, Lighter, and Equal in Weight"
   (E) "A Definition of *Heavy*"

9

Drill 4 (Answers, page 171)

The philosopher/writer Jean Jacques Rousseau lived for a time in the 1750s at a cottage built for him by his friend and patron, Madame d'Épinay. He was not an easy man to befriend; hotheaded and temperamental, he tended to alienate people and make enemies. Not long after this exchange of letters on the subject of friendship, Rousseau and d'Épinay had a falling-out, and they never again reconciled.

Passage 1—Jean Jacques Rousseau to Madame d'Épinay (1756)

. . . Since we are on this topic, I should like to tell you what I demand of friendship and what I, on my side, am willing to give. Don't be afraid to find fault with my rule for friendship, but don't expect me to be easily turned
(5) from it, for it is the result of my temperament which I cannot alter.

Firstly, I want my friends to be my friends and not my masters: to advise me but not try to rule me: to have every claim upon my heart but none upon my liberty. I consider
(10) it extraordinary—the way people interfere, in friendship's name, in my affairs, without telling me of theirs.

. . . Their great eagerness to do me a thousand services wearies me: there is a touch of patronage about it that annoys me: besides, anyone else could do as much. I
(15) would rather that they should just love me and let me love them: that's the one thing a friend is for. Especially does it make me indignant when any newcomer can take my place with them, whilst, in all the world, they are the only ones whose society I can stand. It is only their affection that
(20) makes me endure their kindnesses: but when I bring myself to accept their kindness I do wish that they would consult my tastes and not their own, for we think so differently on so many points that often what they consider good I consider bad.
(25) If there should happen to be a falling out, I say distinctly that it is for him who is in fault to offer the olive branch first, but that means nothing, for we all think we are in the right: right or wrong, he who began the quarrel should end it. If I take his censure ill, if I get vexed unrea-
(30) sonably, if I get angry without good cause, it is not for him to follow my example: he does not love me, if he does. On the contrary, I would have him be very loving with me and embrace me tenderly, do you see, Madame? In a word, let him commence by appeasing me, and that assuredly will
(35) not take long, for never was there a conflagration in my heart that a tear could not quench. Then, when I am melted, calmed, ashamed, covered with confusion, let him rate me well, and tell me straight where I'm wrong, and assuredly he will be satisfied with me. . . .

Passage 2—Madame d'Épinay to Jean Jacques Rousseau (1756)

(40) . . .There are two general rules—essential and indispensable in friendship, to which everyone must subscribe—tolerance and liberty. There's no tie that will not snap without these two things, and that—or practically that— is my code, in a nutshell. I should not demand from a friend
(45) a love that is hot, tender, well-pondered, or effusive, but I simply ask him to love me as best he can, according to his temperament, for all my wishing will not alter him, be he reserved, fickle, grave, or gay, and to be forever dwelling on some quality that he lacks, and which I am set on his
(50) possessing, would result in my not being able to stand him. See—we should love our friends as true lovers of art love pictures: they keep their eyes fixed on the good points and do not notice the others.

If a quarrel should arise, you say, if my friend treats
(55) me badly, etc., etc. Oh! I don't understand this talk of "my friend has treated me badly." In friendship I know but one bad treatment—mistrust. But when you say—one day he keeps things from me—another day he prefers this or that to the pleasure of my society or to paying me proper atten-
(60) tion—or he should have given up that for me. And then there are black looks! Oh, leave these petty complaints to the empty-hearted and empty-headed! . . . Believe me, he who really understands human nature will not find it hard to pardon his fellow creatures' weaknesses, and will love
(65) them for their good deeds, knowing how hard it is to be good. . . .

1. How does Rousseau feel about advice from friends?

    (A) It must be kept to a minimum.
    (B) It is always kindly meant.
    (C) It is fine as long as it is not tyrannical.
    (D) It is often given and rarely taken.
    (E) It is oppressive.

2. The word *censure* in line 29 of Rousseau's letter means

    (A) criticism
    (B) inspection
    (C) praise
    (D) restriction
    (E) sanction

3. How should a friend behave if Rousseau has treated him badly?

   (A) He should react with anger.
   (B) He should follow Rousseau's example.
   (C) He should criticize Rousseau's actions.
   (D) He should calm Rousseau with kindness.
   (E) He should accept the blame for the fight.

4. In line 36, what does Rousseau mean by "when I am melted"?

   (A) when we are united
   (B) when I feel more warmhearted
   (C) after I cry
   (D) when I've been fed
   (E) as soon as spring arrives

5. In line 38 of Rousseau's letter, what does *rate* mean?

   (A) grade
   (B) merit
   (C) evaluate
   (D) scold
   (E) measure

6. Madame d'Épinay compares friendship to love of art in terms of

   (A) respect for the worthy goods humankind can produce
   (B) our tendency to place people and artworks "on a pedestal"
   (C) our delight in possessing beautiful things
   (D) the need to overlook flaws in order to appreciate the whole
   (E) art's ability to soothe and divert

7. In paragraph 2 of her letter, Madame d'Épinay deals with

   (A) remarks Rousseau has made
   (B) her rules for friendship
   (C) her quarrel with Rousseau
   (D) Rousseau's quarrel with Diderot
   (E) her desire to be friends

8. Madame d'Épinay feels that Rousseau's complaints are

   (A) valid
   (B) intolerant
   (C) well-pondered
   (D) philosophic
   (E) the result of mistrust

9. Which attribute of friendship do Rousseau and d'Épinay agree is essential?

   (A) tenderness
   (B) similar tastes
   (C) admonition
   (D) tolerance
   (E) liberty

10. Which of these best summarizes the difference between Rousseau's and Madame d'Épinay's philosophy of friendship?

   (A) Madame d'Épinay is less tolerant of the foibles of others.
   (B) Rousseau believes that love should be blind.
   (C) Madame d'Épinay never quarrels with her true friends.
   (D) Rousseau is far less trusting.
   (E) Madame d'Épinay realizes that she cannot mold people to fit her requirements.

9

Explanatory Answers

DRILL 1

1. (C) Remember, with a vocabulary-in-context question, you must plug the possible choices into the context of the sentence. The animals are injected with splenic fever; shortly thereafter, many are dead. Certainly, the fever is not *benign* (A). *Sarcastic* (E) makes no sense. The fever may be *bitter* or *violent* (B and D) but it is certainly *deadly*; (C) is the best answer.

2. (E) For any interpretation question, read the context in which the phrase is found. Pasteur says that it is too early for a final judgment because "the vaccinated sheep might yet fall ill." His experiment cannot yet be deemed a success.

3. (B) Both (D) and (C) are synonyms for *abstracted*, but only (B) makes sense in context. Two sheep have been *abstracted* from the group and inoculated; they have been taken away, or *removed*.

4. (D) To answer this evaluation question, look for clues to Pasteur's frame of mind. M. Rossignol has written that the experiment is a "stunning success"; Pasteur seems to agree when he says that "the success will indeed have been startling" (line 16). He is not *impassive* (A), *unsure* (B), or *apprehensive* (E); all of these imply a negative reaction. He seems too joyous to be *bewildered* (C). He is stunned, startled, *astounded* (D).

5. (E) Responses (B), (D), and (E) are possible, but Pasteur is not angry with his detractors, so (B) is not accurate. He is poking fun at the surgeon, but not at medical scholarship *per se*, so (D) is not accurate. Only (E) is exactly right; Pasteur is happy to show his family that his opponents have had a change of heart.

6. (B) A careful reading of the context in which he quotes the Gospel proves that Pasteur is simply goading his colleague in good humor. He rejoices that he has won over this particular "sinner" to his own point of view.

7. (A) Evaluation questions in this form require you to use a process of elimination. Determining that (A) is true is not enough, because (A) is included in answer (D) as well. You must eliminate (B) to prove that (D) is not the correct response. M. Colin is certainly not a "yes-man"; on the contrary, he disagrees with everything.

8. (A) This synthesis/analysis question asks you to look at the form of the letter as a whole and to summarize its parts. Pasteur begins by talking about his experiment's results; he continues in paragraph 2. In paragraph 3, he talks about the reactions of his colleagues.

9. (D) This is the kind of evaluation question that asks you to summarize and title all or part of the selection. Skim the final paragraph and compare it to the choices. (A) is wrong; there has been no setback. (B) makes no sense. (C) is exactly opposite to Pasteur's mood and tone, and (E) is for those readers

who get stuck on the word *Gospel* and ignore the sense of the paragraph. Only (D) reflects Pasteur's gentle chiding of those who did not believe his experiment would work.

10. (A) This is a question that is easily answered by using the first sentence/last sentence previewing technique. Pasteur's happy mood is revealed by his words: "great result" and "rejoice" are clearly upbeat expressions.

DRILL 2

1. (D) This analysis question forces you to look at the beginning of the story as it relates to the whole. The form of the question requires you to look at all the answers before choosing one. Answer (A) is true; the paragraph introduces the setting. Answer (B) is true; the paragraph introduces the characters. It is not possible to guess the theme from paragraph 1, however; therefore, the correct answer incorporates (A) and (B): answer (D).

2. (B) As with all interpretation questions, this one calls upon you to interpret a phrase based on the author's intent. The narrator refers to his father in relation to his grandmother only in terms of his father's relationship to his grandmother's daughter, the narrator's mother. This intimation of distance or formality is upheld by the rest of paragraph 2.

3. (C) This is an evaluation question. You need to analyze the narrator's feelings based on evidence in the text. Because each choice contains two words, you must read carefully to choose the response in which both words are accurate. You might call the narrator *indulgent* (A), but he is not *doting*. He is *polite* (B) but not *repulsed*. He may be somewhat *afraid* (D), but he is never *hostile*. And although he may be a little *annoyed* at his grandmother's interference (E), he is not really *angry*. The only response in which both words fit is (C).

4. (A) In this vocabulary-in-context question, each response relates to a meaning of the word in question. Only (A) and (E) are close to the appropriate meaning of *stem*, however; and *shaft* is a better description of the stem of a pipe than *stalk* is. This example shows why it is vital to reread the context in which the word is found before you select a response.

5. (C) This is another interpretation question. Since you are given a line number, it is a good idea to return to that line and reread the context: The narrator's grandmother is asking which of the village women the narrator wants. None of the answers besides (C) is supported by the text.

6. (B) *Exhortations* can have several meanings. You must return to the text to find the context in which the word is used. Choices (C) and (E) relate to a similar but unrelated word: *exultations*. The family's advice cannot be considered *warnings* (A) or *inspirations* (D); only (B) works in context.

7. (A) This is a tricky interpretation question. The unusual wording of the sentence can make it difficult to interpret unless you consider the text that surrounds it. The narrator says that his father has "earned the right" to speak of winning a title in one's sixteenth winter "though he himself was a brave only" at that age. In other words, the father, a great warrior, wants his son to do something that even he had not done at such an early age.

9

8. (E) This evaluation question is similar to question 3. You must check each word's validity before choosing a response. In this case, you have an excellent clue in lines 54–55 in the final paragraph. The narrator's heart is stirred, but he is troubled. (E) is the only analogous choice.

9. (A) This vocabulary question presents you with four synonyms for the word in question and one logical replacement (E) in terms of the context of the sentence. Neither (B), (C), nor (D) makes sense in context, and the fact that "It is now late in the night" (line 58) makes it unlikely that the narrator would be going for a ride. This leaves you with (A), the only reasonable choice.

10. (D) This kind of evaluation question asks you to summarize a selection and give it an appropriate title. Often, as here, more than one title will be possible, but only one will be the best. Titles (A) and (E) are too general, whereas (B) and (C) are too specific. Choice (D) neatly summarizes the action of the whole selection, in which the narrator hears advice from three members of his family.

DRILL 3

1. (D) An interpretation question requires a look back at the passage in order to place the phrase in context. First, you need to find an antecedent for this: to what is Galileo referring when he says that *this* must be settled? Rereading the sentences before and after the excerpted phrase tells you that Galileo wants to "discuss on what basis we are to say that one thing is lighter or heavier than another thing" (line 4). The problem is that sometimes "what is lighter is called heavier" (line 7). Thus, we need to agree on a definition of light and heavy in order to compare objects (D). None of the other choices is substantiated by the text.

2. (B) You must plug each vocabulary-in-context choice into the sentence in question and eliminate those that do not work. Try (A). "It often happens that what is lighter is called heavier, and *as shall be proven.*" Try (B). ". . . what is lighter is called heavier, and *vice versa.*" Even if you do not know the meaning of that Latin phrase, trying out the other choices in this way will lead you to (B) by process of elimination.

3. (C) This interpretation question requires a bit of analysis as well. You must recognize Galileo's purpose, review the context in which the phrase is found, and compare both of these things to the choices you are given. Galileo's purpose is not to entertain, so (A) and (B) are unlikely choices. In context, he is not comparing wood to lead (E); in fact he is comparing two like substances, not two unrelated substances, as (D) would indicate. Only (C) is possible.

4. (E) This synthesis/analysis question should only be approached once you have read the entire selection. You need to look at the selection as a whole in order to determine what role each part plays. Then reread paragraph 2, having first previewed the choices. (A) and (D) are clearly not true. (B) might be, and so might (C), but of all the choices, (E) is most precise. Paragraph 2 defines the concept of "equally heavy."

5. (A) To answer this evaluation question, you must summarize the information in paragraph 3. It is a good idea to reread the paragraph and distill the information in your own mind into a single sentence. Then compare your summary to the choices you are given. Only (A) is a faithful summary of Galileo's postulate.

6. (B) Four of the choices for this vocabulary-in-context question are possible synonyms for *asserting*. You must refer to the context of the sentence before choosing one word that works best: ". . . we shall certainly be right in (___) that lead is heavier than wood." (A) is possible, but (B) is better. None of the other choices makes sense.

7. (C) You have already summarized paragraph 3 for question 5; this should help you answer this related question. Since the format includes choices that combine other choices, you *must* look at all of the possible answers before choosing one. (A) is not true; paragraph 3 does not negate or nullify information in paragraph 2. (B) is not true; equal weight is a concept that is discussed in paragraph 2. The answer must be (C). Just to be sure, look at (D) and (E); since both contain one or more wrong answers, neither can be correct.

8. (B) Synthesis/analysis questions oblige you to understand the structure of a selection or one of its parts. In this case, you are asked to look closely at the final paragraph. Taking that paragraph apart, you can see that sentence 1 introduces the concept of "lighter." Sentence 2 defines "lighter" in terms of two substances. Sentence 3 gives an example or illustration to support this definition. Now select the one choice that fits your analysis: introduction, definition, illustration—choice (B).

9. (E) This is one type of vocabulary question—one that uses a very familiar word and asks you to choose one of its possible multiple meanings by looking at the word in context. Once again, take the line in question and plug the choices into it in place of the word *properly*. (A) is possible, but an odd choice. (B) would make sense if Galileo were showing how to disprove something. (C) and (D) are connotations of *properly* that make no sense in this particular context. (E) is the best choice. Do not be misled because it is such a simple word—often the most obvious choices are the best.

10. (D) This kind of evaluation question asks you to choose a title that fits the selection. You must summarize the selection in your head and compare your analysis to the choices you are given. Here, (A) and (B) have nothing to do with the passage. (E) is too limited in scope—it would be a good title for paragraph 3 but not for the whole selection. (C) is possible, but Galileo is really only using wood and lead as examples; he is not particularly interested in determining which weighs more. That leaves you with (D), which summarizes the discussion in paragraphs 1–4.

DRILL 4

1. (C) This evaluation question asks you to get inside the author's head. Reference to advice appears in line 8; Rousseau says that he wants his friends "to advise me but not try to rule me." (C) is a fairly accurate paraphrase of this thought. He may think (A) or (D), but there is no direct evidence of this. He certainly does not think all advice is kindly meant (B), or he would not go on to talk about interference; nor does he think that all advice is oppressive (E), or he would not want friends to advise him.

2. (A) As with all vocabulary-in-context questions, this one asks you to find a word in the passage and check five possible replacements against the context in which that word is found. Rousseau is discussing his possible unreasonable reactions to the action of a friend. Only (A) and (C) refer to likely actions of a friend; of these, (C) is unlikely to produce a negative response. Only (A) makes sense in context.

3. (D) To answer this evaluation question, you must summarize Rousseau's last paragraph. He says clearly that in such a case, it is *not* "for him to follow my example" (B); he wants his friend to begin by acting loving and tender until Rousseau relents, and, contrary to (E), himself accepts the blame.

4. (B) To answer this interpretation question, go back to the line in question and read what precedes it. Rousseau wants his friend to appease him, which should not be hard, because no matter how angry he is, a few tears will do the trick. In other words, the friend is to cry, not Rousseau himself (C). Then the ice will melt, and Rousseau will feel warmer toward his friend.

5. (D) This is a tricky vocabulary question, in that it involves an archaic meaning for a familiar word. By returning to the line in question, you can see that "rate me well" is parallel to "tell me straight where I'm wrong." *Rate* is, in fact, a form of *berate*, or *scold*.

6. (D) Here you are asked to evaluate d'Épinay's use of a particular simile. First find the reference (line 51); then read what comes before and after. The author says that true lovers of art "keep their eyes fixed on the good points and do not notice the others." This fits well with her prior call for tolerance; she urges Rousseau to appreciate the good and ignore the bad.

7. (A) Here you must analyze paragraph 2 and determine its purpose. The author begins by referring to Rousseau's remarks—"you say" is a good clue. She may be hinting at a particular quarrel, as in (C) or (D), but there is no direct evidence of this. Her rules for friendship (B) were covered in paragraph 1. Nowhere does she discuss her desire to be friends (E).

8. (B) This evaluation question asks you again to look at d'Épinay's second paragraph, this time to summarize it. In fact, she calls Rousseau's complaints "petty" in line 61; put into the context of her discussion of intolerance, you can see that only one answer is possible.

9. (E) This is a difficult evaluation question, because it requires you to summarize and compare both passages. Testing each response and eliminating those that do not work will prove the most useful method for answering questions of this kind. First try (A). Rousseau wants tenderness (line 33); d'Épinay remarks that she cannot demand it (line 44). Try (B). Rousseau says that his friends think differently from him (line 23); d'Épinay says that she cannot dwell on some quality her friend lacks (line 48). (C) does not make sense in context. (D) is something cherished by d'Épinay, who counts it among her essential rules of friendship (line 41). However, as d'Épinay makes clear throughout, Rousseau is intolerant when it comes to friends. The

only answer they have in common is (E)—again, liberty is one of d'Épinay's rules of friendship, and Rousseau wants friends to have no claim upon his liberty (line 9).

10. (E) Just as question 9 asked you to compare the passages, this question asks you to summarize and *contrast* the passages. Again, you can use the process of elimination. (A) is certainly not true, and there is no support for (B), (C), or (D). Madame d'Épinay certainly believes (E), and a close reading of Rousseau's letter proves that he does not—he wants friends to bend to his will.

9

Verbal Warm-Up Exercises

✔ Objectives

To practice under timed conditions the techniques and strategies learned in lessons 7 through 9.

To reinforce the material learned in lessons 7 through 9 by study of practice items.

To learn to answer questions within the time limits of the actual test.

1. Section 1, 35 Questions, Time—30 minutes
2. Section 2, 35 Questions, Time—30 minutes
3. Answers and Review Explanations

Use a No. 2 pencil only. Be sure each mark is dark and completely fills the intended oval. Completely erase any errors or stray marks.

☐ A R C O ☐

Start with number 1 for each new section. If a section has fewer than 40 questions, leave the extra answer spaces blank.

SECTION 1

1 Ⓐ Ⓑ Ⓒ Ⓓ Ⓔ	11 Ⓐ Ⓑ Ⓒ Ⓓ Ⓔ	21 Ⓐ Ⓑ Ⓒ Ⓓ Ⓔ	31 Ⓐ Ⓑ Ⓒ Ⓓ Ⓔ
2 Ⓐ Ⓑ Ⓒ Ⓓ Ⓔ	12 Ⓐ Ⓑ Ⓒ Ⓓ Ⓔ	22 Ⓐ Ⓑ Ⓒ Ⓓ Ⓔ	32 Ⓐ Ⓑ Ⓒ Ⓓ Ⓔ
3 Ⓐ Ⓑ Ⓒ Ⓓ Ⓔ	13 Ⓐ Ⓑ Ⓒ Ⓓ Ⓔ	23 Ⓐ Ⓑ Ⓒ Ⓓ Ⓔ	33 Ⓐ Ⓑ Ⓒ Ⓓ Ⓔ
4 Ⓐ Ⓑ Ⓒ Ⓓ Ⓔ	14 Ⓐ Ⓑ Ⓒ Ⓓ Ⓔ	24 Ⓐ Ⓑ Ⓒ Ⓓ Ⓔ	34 Ⓐ Ⓑ Ⓒ Ⓓ Ⓔ
5 Ⓐ Ⓑ Ⓒ Ⓓ Ⓔ	15 Ⓐ Ⓑ Ⓒ Ⓓ Ⓔ	25 Ⓐ Ⓑ Ⓒ Ⓓ Ⓔ	35 Ⓐ Ⓑ Ⓒ Ⓓ Ⓔ
6 Ⓐ Ⓑ Ⓒ Ⓓ Ⓔ	16 Ⓐ Ⓑ Ⓒ Ⓓ Ⓔ	26 Ⓐ Ⓑ Ⓒ Ⓓ Ⓔ	36 Ⓐ Ⓑ Ⓒ Ⓓ Ⓔ
7 Ⓐ Ⓑ Ⓒ Ⓓ Ⓔ	17 Ⓐ Ⓑ Ⓒ Ⓓ Ⓔ	27 Ⓐ Ⓑ Ⓒ Ⓓ Ⓔ	37 Ⓐ Ⓑ Ⓒ Ⓓ Ⓔ
8 Ⓐ Ⓑ Ⓒ Ⓓ Ⓔ	18 Ⓐ Ⓑ Ⓒ Ⓓ Ⓔ	28 Ⓐ Ⓑ Ⓒ Ⓓ Ⓔ	38 Ⓐ Ⓑ Ⓒ Ⓓ Ⓔ
9 Ⓐ Ⓑ Ⓒ Ⓓ Ⓔ	19 Ⓐ Ⓑ Ⓒ Ⓓ Ⓔ	29 Ⓐ Ⓑ Ⓒ Ⓓ Ⓔ	39 Ⓐ Ⓑ Ⓒ Ⓓ Ⓔ
10 Ⓐ Ⓑ Ⓒ Ⓓ Ⓔ	20 Ⓐ Ⓑ Ⓒ Ⓓ Ⓔ	30 Ⓐ Ⓑ Ⓒ Ⓓ Ⓔ	40 Ⓐ Ⓑ Ⓒ Ⓓ Ⓔ

SECTION 2

1 Ⓐ Ⓑ Ⓒ Ⓓ Ⓔ	11 Ⓐ Ⓑ Ⓒ Ⓓ Ⓔ	21 Ⓐ Ⓑ Ⓒ Ⓓ Ⓔ	31 Ⓐ Ⓑ Ⓒ Ⓓ Ⓔ
2 Ⓐ Ⓑ Ⓒ Ⓓ Ⓔ	12 Ⓐ Ⓑ Ⓒ Ⓓ Ⓔ	22 Ⓐ Ⓑ Ⓒ Ⓓ Ⓔ	32 Ⓐ Ⓑ Ⓒ Ⓓ Ⓔ
3 Ⓐ Ⓑ Ⓒ Ⓓ Ⓔ	13 Ⓐ Ⓑ Ⓒ Ⓓ Ⓔ	23 Ⓐ Ⓑ Ⓒ Ⓓ Ⓔ	33 Ⓐ Ⓑ Ⓒ Ⓓ Ⓔ
4 Ⓐ Ⓑ Ⓒ Ⓓ Ⓔ	14 Ⓐ Ⓑ Ⓒ Ⓓ Ⓔ	24 Ⓐ Ⓑ Ⓒ Ⓓ Ⓔ	34 Ⓐ Ⓑ Ⓒ Ⓓ Ⓔ
5 Ⓐ Ⓑ Ⓒ Ⓓ Ⓔ	15 Ⓐ Ⓑ Ⓒ Ⓓ Ⓔ	25 Ⓐ Ⓑ Ⓒ Ⓓ Ⓔ	35 Ⓐ Ⓑ Ⓒ Ⓓ Ⓔ
6 Ⓐ Ⓑ Ⓒ Ⓓ Ⓔ	16 Ⓐ Ⓑ Ⓒ Ⓓ Ⓔ	26 Ⓐ Ⓑ Ⓒ Ⓓ Ⓔ	36 Ⓐ Ⓑ Ⓒ Ⓓ Ⓔ
7 Ⓐ Ⓑ Ⓒ Ⓓ Ⓔ	17 Ⓐ Ⓑ Ⓒ Ⓓ Ⓔ	27 Ⓐ Ⓑ Ⓒ Ⓓ Ⓔ	37 Ⓐ Ⓑ Ⓒ Ⓓ Ⓔ
8 Ⓐ Ⓑ Ⓒ Ⓓ Ⓔ	18 Ⓐ Ⓑ Ⓒ Ⓓ Ⓔ	28 Ⓐ Ⓑ Ⓒ Ⓓ Ⓔ	38 Ⓐ Ⓑ Ⓒ Ⓓ Ⓔ
9 Ⓐ Ⓑ Ⓒ Ⓓ Ⓔ	19 Ⓐ Ⓑ Ⓒ Ⓓ Ⓔ	29 Ⓐ Ⓑ Ⓒ Ⓓ Ⓔ	39 Ⓐ Ⓑ Ⓒ Ⓓ Ⓔ
10 Ⓐ Ⓑ Ⓒ Ⓓ Ⓔ	20 Ⓐ Ⓑ Ⓒ Ⓓ Ⓔ	30 Ⓐ Ⓑ Ⓒ Ⓓ Ⓔ	40 Ⓐ Ⓑ Ⓒ Ⓓ Ⓔ

Now that you have studied each of the three types of verbal questions and drilled on each, it is time to do some practice under the same time constraints you will have to work within on the test.

   In this chapter, you will find two verbal sections, each with a 30-minute time limit. It is recommended that you work one of them, review it, and do the other at a later time.

   Set aside a half hour during which you won't be interrupted. Use a watch or a clock to time yourself. Stop working when time is up.

   After you have done as much as you can in 30 minutes, go back and review your work. Finish any questions you did not have time to finish. Then study the explanations that begin on page 188. If anything is not clear to you, return to the appropriate chapter and review the material.

SECTION 1   Time—30 Minutes
                35 Questions   For each question in this section, choose the best answer.

The passage below is followed by questions based on its content. Answer all questions following the passage on the basis of what is <u>stated</u> or <u>implied</u> in the passage.

Henry Highland Garnet (1815–1882) was born a slave but escaped with his parents to New York. He became a missionary and a famous abolitionist, and later served as ambassador to Liberia. This excerpt is from Garnet's "Address to the Slaves of the United States of America," delivered at an 1843 abolitionists' convention in Buffalo, New York.

Brethren and Fellow Citizens:

Your brethren of the north, east, and west have been accustomed to meet together in National Conventions, to sympathize with each other, and to weep over your unhappy
(5) condition. In these meetings we have addressed all classes of the free, but we have never until this time, sent a word of consolation and advice to you. We have been contented in sitting still and mourning over your sorrows, earnestly hoping that before this day, your sacred liberties would have
(10) been restored. But, we have hoped in vain. Years have rolled on, and tens of thousands have been borne on streams of blood, and tears, to the shores of eternity. While you have been oppressed, we have also been partakers with you; nor can we be free while you are enslaved. We therefore
(15) write to you as being bound with you.

Many of you are bound to us, not only by the ties of a common humanity, but we are connected by the more tender relations of parents, wives, husbands, children, brothers, and sisters, and friends. As such we most affectionately
(20) address you.

Slavery has fixed a deep gulf between you and us, and while it shuts out from you the relief and consolation which your friends would willingly render, it afflicts and persecutes you with a fierceness which we might not expect to
(25) see in the fiends of hell. But still the Almighty Father of Mercies has left to us a glimmering ray of hope, which shines out like a lone star in a cloudy sky. Mankind are becoming wiser, and better—the oppressor's power is fading, and you, every day, are becoming better informed, and
(30) more numerous. Your grievances, brethren, are many. We shall not attempt, in this short address, to present to the world, all the dark catalogue of this nation's sins, which have been committed upon an innocent people. Nor is it indeed, necessary, for you feel them from day to day, and
(35) all the civilized world look upon them with amazement.

Two hundred and twenty-seven years ago, the first of our injured race were brought to the shores of America. They came not with glad spirits to select their homes, in the New World. They came not with their own consent, to
(40) find an unmolested enjoyment of the blessings of this fruitful soil. The first dealings which they had with men calling themselves Christians, exhibited to them the worst features of corrupt and sordid hearts; and convinced them that no cruelty is too great, no villainy, and no robbery too
(45) abhorrent for even enlightened men to perform, when influenced by avarice, and lust. Neither did they come flying upon the wings of Liberty, to a land of freedom. But,

they came with broken hearts, from their beloved native land, and were doomed to unrequited toil, and deep degradation. Nor did the evil of their bondage end at their emancipation by death. Succeeding generations inherited their chains, and millions have come from eternity into time, and have returned again to the world of spirits, cursed, and ruined by American Slavery.

1. The speech refers to brethren of the north, east, and west because

   (A) that is where slaves have met in the past
   (B) those people have been free to convene
   (C) it is addressed to slaves in the south
   (D) both A and B
   (E) both B and C

2. What does Garnet mean by "We therefore write to you as being bound with you"?

   (A) we were slaves, and you are still in chains
   (B) this speech is being dispatched to you
   (C) we address you out of a shared connection
   (D) our hearts leap up to join you
   (E) we are constrained from seeing you in person

3. Why does Garnet include paragraph 2?

   (A) to announce his intentions
   (B) to reveal his opinions
   (C) to express his feelings
   (D) both A and B
   (E) both B and C

4. The word *fixed* (line 21) most closely means

   (A) repaired
   (B) determined
   (C) created
   (D) mended
   (E) corrected

5. How does Garnet feel about the future?

   (A) despondent
   (B) grateful
   (C) fearful
   (D) hopeful
   (E) angry

6. The word *grievances* (line 30) most closely means

   (A) sorrows
   (B) complaints
   (C) opposition
   (D) illnesses
   (E) exceptions

7. What does Garnet mean by "dark catalogue" (line 32)?

   (A) roll call of Africans
   (B) the Book of Revelations
   (C) classification of slaves
   (D) list of names
   (E) grim inventory

8. Why does Garnet include paragraph 4?

   (A) to give a brief history of slavery
   (B) to remind his audience of their past
   (C) to express his alliance with all slaves
   (D) both A and B
   (E) both B and C

9. How does Garnet feel toward the Christians he refers to in paragraph 4?

   (A) He disapproves of their religion.
   (B) He thinks they have broken their vows.
   (C) They did not consent to become Christians.
   (D) They do not behave as Christians should.
   (E) He is bound to them by a common religion.

10. What does the word *unrequited* (line 49) mean?

    (A) unnecessary
    (B) unrewarded
    (C) unending
    (D) unreserved
    (E) optional

11. When Garnet says that "millions have come from eternity into time," he means that millions

    (A) have been born
    (B) have toiled
    (C) have come from Africa
    (D) have died
    (E) have returned to their homes

12. Garnet's intent in this opening to his speech is to

    (A) address a new and important audience
    (B) express an affiliation with slaves
    (C) censure white slaveholders
    (D) both A and B
    (E) both B and C

Each sentence below has one or two blanks, each blank indicating that something has been omitted. Beneath the sentence are five lettered words or sets of words. Choose the word or set of words that <u>best</u> fits the meaning of the sentence as a whole.

Example:

Although its publicity has been ----, the film itself is intelligent, well-acted, handsomely produced, and altogether ----.

(A) tasteless..respectable
(B) extensive..moderate
(C) sophisticated..amateur
(D) risqué..crude
(E) perfect..spectacular

13. John's parents could not ---- why he was doing so poorly in school, since his diagnostic test scores indicated a high degree of ---- which his grades did not reflect.

    (A) resolve..laziness
    (B) comprehend..aptitude
    (C) refute..agility
    (D) conclude..experience
    (E) understand..volition

14. The film was ----, completely lacking in plot, just a series of beautiful images with no particular connection.

    (A) incoherent
    (B) morbid
    (C) moral
    (D) romantic
    (E) fictitious

15. The diva's autobiography was largely ----; when she wasn't saying wonderful things about herself, she ---- her mother, who said them for her.

    (A) confidential..repudiated
    (B) anecdotal..angered
    (C) self-congratulatory..quoted
    (D) critical..rebuked
    (E) misunderstood..flouted

16. The image of the Native American brave on his pinto pony is so common that most people don't realize that horses are not ---- North America but were ---- by the Europeans.

    (A) raised in..purchased
    (B) indigenous to..introduced
    (C) native to..trained
    (D) worshipped in..bred
    (E) unknown in..imported

10

17. Sally had ---- taste in clothing and always dressed
     very fashionably; but she was totally ---- her sur-
     roundings, and her apartment and office were drab
     and disorganized.

     (A) impeccable..indifferent to
     (B) dreadful..dependent on
     (C) pedestrian..fascinated by
     (D) bizarre..suspicious of
     (E) unimaginative..enamored of

Each question below consists of a related pair of
words or phrases, followed by five lettered pairs of
words or phrases. Select the lettered pair that <u>best</u>
expresses a relationship similar to that expressed in
the original pair.

Example:

YAWN : BOREDOM::

(A) dream : sleep
(B) anger : madness
(C) smile : amusement
(D) face : expression
(E) impatience : rebellion

---

18. CONDUCTOR : BATON::

     (A) blacksmith : hammer
     (B) professor : university
     (C) page : book
     (D) strings : guitar
     (E) handle : door

19. THEME : SYMPHONY::

     (A) plot : novel
     (B) ranch : horse
     (C) sky : cloud
     (D) petal : flower
     (E) lake : stream

20. LID : EYE::

     (A) spectacles : sight
     (B) window : wall
     (C) shutter : camera
     (D) glove : hand
     (E) highway : tunnel

21. ACQUAINTANCE : CONFIDANT::

     (A) president : meeting
     (B) novice : master
     (C) teacher : class
     (D) minister : pulpit
     (E) actor : role

22. PALLID : COLOR::

     (A) arid : moisture
     (B) rugged : terrain
     (C) libelous : suit
     (D) drenched : water
     (E) hearty : meal

23. IMMORAL : ETHICS::

     (A) monotonous : boredom
     (B) factual : history
     (C) chaotic : order
     (D) disturbing : memory
     (E) infamous : reputation

24. FLOW CHART : PROCESS::

     (A) plan : architect
     (B) menu : check
     (C) graph : globe
     (D) painting : investor
     (E) blueprint : construction

25. FACETIOUS : SINCERITY::

     (A) hasty : insanity
     (B) farcical : gravity
     (C) ponderous : reticence
     (D) precise : amiability
     (E) anxious : intensity

The passage below is followed by questions based on its content. Answer the questions following the passage on the basis of what is <u>stated</u> or <u>implied</u> in the passage.

Best known for her serialized works such as Little Women *and* Jo's Boys, *Louisa May Alcott began writing as a way of supporting her family. Despite a modest success, she remained relatively penniless. In this letter to her older sister, Anna, written in the 1860s, Alcott comments wryly on the frugal inventiveness that led to her new hat.*

My Lass:

This must be a frivolous and dressy letter, because you always want to know about our clothes, and we have been at it lately. May's bonnet is a sight for gods and men. Black and white outside, with a great cockade boiling over the front to meet a red ditto surging from the interior, where a red rainbow darts across the brow, and a surf of white lace foams up at either side. I expect to hear that you and John fell flat in the dust with horror on beholding it.

My bonnet has nearly been the death of me; for, thinking some angel might make it possible for me to go to the mountains, I felt a wish for a tidy hat, after wearing an old one till it fell in tatters from my brow. Mrs. P. promised a bit of gray silk, and I built on that; but when I went for it I found my hat was founded on sand; for she let me down with a crash, saying she wanted the silk herself, and kindly offering me a flannel petticoat instead. I was in woe for a spell, having one dollar in the world, and scorning debt even for that prop of life, a "bonnet." Then I roused myself, flew to Dodge, demanded her cheapest bonnet, found one for a dollar, took it, and went home wondering if the sky would open and drop me a trimming. I am simple in my tastes, but a naked straw bonnet is a little too severely chaste even for me. Sky did not open; so I went to the "Widow Cruise's oil bottle"—my ribbon box—which, by the way, is the eighth wonder of the world, for nothing is ever put in, yet I always find some old dud when all other hopes fail. From this salvation bin I extracted the remains of an old white ribbon (used up, as I thought, two years ago), and the bits of black lace that have adorned a long line of departed hats. Of the lace I made a dish, on which I thriftily served up bows of ribbon, like meat on toast. Inside put the lace bow, which adorns my form anywhere when needed. A white flower A.H. gave me sat airily on the brim—fearfully unbecoming, but pretty in itself, and in keeping. Strings are yet to be evolved from chaos. I feel that they await me somewhere in the dim future. Green ones *pro tem.* hold this wonder of the age upon my gifted brow, and I survey my hat with respectful awe. I trust you will also, and see in it another great example of the power of mind over matter, and the convenience of a colossal brain in the primeval wrestle with the unruly atoms which have harassed the feminine soul ever since Eve clapped on a modest fig-leaf and did up her hair with a thorn for a hairpin. . . .

26. The word *frivolous* (line 2) is used to mean

(A) petty
(B) flippant
(C) serious
(D) ardent
(E) negligent

27. Why does Alcott include the paragraph about May's hat?

(A) to impress her reader with May's excellent taste
(B) to provide a contrast to her description of her own hat
(C) for humorous effect
(D) both A and B
(E) both B and C

28. How does Alcott feel about May's hat?

(A) It is ungodly.
(B) It is absurd.
(C) It is sensible.
(D) It is beautiful.
(E) It is substandard.

29. "Widow Cruise's oil" (line 25) is probably a reference to

(A) Alcott's marital status
(B) striking it rich
(C) voyages through history
(D) the lost and found
(E) a cure-all elixir

30. When Alcott refers in line 31 to "departed hats," she means that the hats

(A) are worn to funerals
(B) have been lost
(C) have been sold
(D) were long ago worn out
(E) are made of pieces of scrap

31. When Alcott says that "strings are yet to be evolved from chaos," she is referring to

(A) various theories of the birth of the universe
(B) her inability to knit
(C) her present lack of hat fasteners
(D) her desire to be serenaded
(E) a Biblical story

10

32. In line 38, what is the best definition of *pro tem.*?

    (A) professional temporary
    (B) each day
    (C) as I have said
    (D) haphazardly
    (E) for the time being

33. Alcott mentions Eve in order to compare their respective

    (A) ingenuity
    (B) shortage of materials
    (C) modesty
    (D) both A and B
    (E) both B and C

34. How does Alcott feel about her own hat?

    (A) It is unbecoming, but it is stylish.
    (B) She is proud of her ability to make do with little.
    (C) She wishes she could have a hat like May's.
    (D) It is a mockery of hats everywhere.
    (E) It is quite sophisticated but rather awful.

35. Alcott's intent in this letter seems to be to

    (A) brag about her abilities
    (B) convince Anna to visit
    (C) poke fun at May
    (D) entertain Anna
    (E) make Anna feel sorry for her

IF YOU FINISH BEFORE TIME IS CALLED, YOU MAY CHECK YOUR WORK ON **S T O P**
THIS SECTION ONLY. DO NOT WORK ON ANY OTHER SECTION IN THE TEST.

SECTION **2** Time—30 Minutes
35 Questions   For each question in this section, choose the best answer.

Each sentence below has one or two blanks, each blank indicating that something has been omitted. Beneath the sentence are five lettered words or sets of words. Choose the word or set of words that best fits the meaning of the sentence as a whole.

Example:

Although its publicity has been ----, the film itself is intelligent, well-acted, handsomely produced, and altogether ----.

(A) tasteless..respectable
(B) extensive..moderate
(C) sophisticated..amateur
(D) risqué..crude
(E) perfect..spectacular

1. Although all of the guests at the dinner party were ----, the food was so poorly prepared no one ate more than a small portion.

(A) elegant
(B) ravenous
(C) invited
(D) forewarned
(E) surly

2. Galileo finally ---- his theories, for it was heresy to ---- the teachings of the Church.

(A) composed..assuage
(B) recanted..contradict
(C) invoked..deploy
(D) demonstrate..delude
(E) protracted..ameliorate

3. As a ---- he was a disaster, for his students rarely understood his lectures; yet he was a ---- scholar.

(A) dean..banal
(B) philosopher..failed
(C) teacher..formidable
(D) professor..second-rate
(E) speaker..contemptuous

4. Judging by the ---- of new talent on Broadway and the large number of revivals, we may assume that the era of the American musical is over.

(A) temerity
(B) versatility
(C) laxity
(D) verbosity
(E) paucity

5. Although he wanted to write a lengthy novel of grand proportions, he found himself writing ---- about his carefree childhood in rural America.

(A) vignettes
(B) tragedies
(C) editorials
(D) epic poetry
(E) elegies

6. Amidst the din at the day-care center, she alone remained ----; it seemed nothing could agitate her.

(A) imperturbable
(B) impermeable
(C) implausible
(D) impassioned
(E) immoderate

7. Far from the ---- crowds of the city, I find refuge at my ---- cabin on Big Lake.

(A) pervasive..dominant
(B) aggressive..listless
(C) petrified..motivating
(D) overwhelming..secluded
(E) extensive..scanty

8. With little ---- we went about our business, asking only that the ---- leave us alone to work in peace.

(A) ado..management
(B) fanfare..regulations
(C) alarm..community
(D) strain..effluvium
(E) truth..overseer

9. This pamphlet is about ----, the art of ---- spirits.

(A) brewing..founding
(B) bartending..manufacturing
(C) sorcery..imparting
(D) necromancy..conjuring
(E) juicing..eliminating

10. Please do not ---- at the man on the corner; he will see you.

(A) trill
(B) gawk
(C) chortle
(D) behold
(E) saunter

10

11. His suggestion to amend the club charter was met with ----, if not outright hostility, by the other members who ---- disagreed with him.

   (A) gratitude..allegedly
   (B) elation..tacitly
   (C) disapprobation..vehemently
   (D) profusion..summarily
   (E) disdain..reluctantly

12. Although it may seem a contradiction, psychologists agree that a good marriage is based on the ---- of the partners as well as on their ---- one another.

   (A) financial security..animosity toward
   (B) infallibility..manipulation of
   (C) conformity..denial of
   (D) compatibility..independence from
   (E) eccentricity..perusal of

13. The exhibit was a complete ----, thereby confirming the rumors from Paris of the artist's ----.

   (A) victory..malfeasance
   (B) triumph..apathy
   (C) disaster..virtuosity
   (D) failure..geniality
   (E) success..brilliance

14. The press was shocked when they interviewed the famous author, for despite the ---- of his writing, he revealed himself to be a ----.

   (A) incomprehensibility..philanthropist
   (B) simplicity..dolt
   (C) power..scholar
   (D) erudition..philistine
   (E) humor..miser

15. In contrast with the early architecture of the Northeast, which was basically utilitarian, the Georgian homes of the early South were far more ----.

   (A) supine
   (B) inconsequential
   (C) grandiose
   (D) acrimonious
   (E) crude

Each question below consists of a related pair of words or phrases, followed by five lettered pairs of words or phrases. Select the lettered pair that best expresses a relationship similar to that expressed in the original pair.

Example:

YAWN:BOREDOM::

   (A) dream : sleep
   (B) anger : madness
   (C) smile : amusement
   (D) face : expression
   (E) impatience : rebellion   Ⓐ Ⓑ ● Ⓓ Ⓔ

16. COMMAND : REQUEST::

   (A) discover : announce
   (B) malign : criticize
   (C) decline : remember
   (D) admire : fulfill
   (E) revere : envision

17. SOB : GRIEF::

   (A) laugh : smile
   (B) scream : whisper
   (C) expression : reaction
   (D) applause : hand
   (E) groan : pain

18. ELEVATION : MOUNTAIN::

   (A) level : plateau
   (B) boundary : geographic
   (C) altitude : population
   (D) area : climate
   (E) depth : ocean

19. WAR : CEASEFIRE::

   (A) trial : recess
   (B) legend : hero
   (C) government : constitution
   (D) painting : frame
   (E) dust : moisture

20. ENERVATE : EXHAUSTED::

   (A) digress : attentive
   (B) decelerate : motionless
   (C) invoke : bewitched
   (D) alter : manufactured
   (E) imitate : original

21. FRUGAL : MISERLY::

   (A) unhappy : morose
   (B) tentative : welcome
   (C) gracious : talkative
   (D) forthcoming : undecided
   (E) capricious : stable

22. CORRUPT : INTEGRITY::
    (A) talented : ability
    (B) available : argument
    (C) restrained : argument
    (D) irresolute : commitment
    (E) scarce : desire

23. EPISTLE : POSTSCRIPT::
    (A) missive : envelope
    (B) novel : epilogue
    (C) drama : screenplay
    (D) catalogue : brochure
    (E) opera : aria

24. HEDONIST : PLEASURE::
    (A) perpetrator : gain
    (B) introvert : library
    (C) epicure : food
    (D) athlete : victory
    (E) model : applause

25. PESTILENCE : DISEASE::
    (A) desert : oasis
    (B) lightning : storm
    (C) holocaust : fire
    (D) celebration : marriage
    (E) vessel : inundation

10

The passage below is followed by questions based on its content. Answer the questions following the passage on the basis of what is <u>stated</u> or <u>implied</u> in the passage.

John James Audubon (1785–1851) was an ornithologist and naturalist whose descriptions and paintings of wild birds remain among the best ever made. In this essay on the wild turkey, his superb powers of observation are evident.

The great size and beauty of the Wild Turkey, its value as a delicate and highly prized article of food, and the circumstance of its being the origin of the domestic race now generally dispersed over both continents, render it one of
(5) the most interesting of the birds indigenous to the United States of America.

The unsettled parts of the States of Ohio, Kentucky, Illinois, and Indiana, an immense extent of country to the northwest of these districts, upon the Mississippi and
(10) Missouri, and the vast regions drained by these rivers from their confluence to Louisiana, including the wooded parts of Arkansas, Tennessee, and Alabama, are the most abundantly supplied with this magnificent bird. It is less plentiful in Georgia and the Carolinas, becomes still scarcer in
(15) Virginia and Pennsylvania, and is now very rarely seen to the eastward of the last mentioned States. In the course of my rambles through Long Island, the State of New York, and the country around the Lakes, I did not meet with a single individual, although I was informed that some exist
(20) in those parts. Turkeys are still to be found along the whole line of the Allegheny Mountains, where they have become so wary as to be approached only with extreme difficulty. While, in the Great Pine Forest, in 1829, I found a single feather that had been dropped from the tail of a
(25) female, but saw no bird of the kind. Farther eastward, I do not think they are now to be found. I shall describe the manners of this bird as observed in the countries where it is most abundant, and having resided for many years in Kentucky and Louisiana, may be understood as referring
(30) chiefly to them.

The Turkey is irregularly migratory, as well as irregularly gregarious. With reference to the first of these circumstances, I have to state, that whenever the *mast* of one portion happens greatly to exceed that of another, the
(35) Turkeys are insensibly led toward that spot, by gradually meeting in their haunts with more fruit the nearer they advance towards the place where it is most plentiful. In this manner flock follows after flock, until one district is entirely deserted, while another, as it were, overflowed
(40) with them. But as these migrations are irregular, and extend over a vast expanse of country, it is necessary that I should describe the manner in which they take place.

About the beginning of October, when scarcely any of the seeds and fruits have yet fallen from the trees, these
(45) birds assemble in flocks, and gradually move towards the rich bottom lands of the Ohio and Mississippi. The males, or, as they are more commonly called, the *gobblers*, associate in parties of from ten to a hundred, and search for food apart from the females; while the latter are seen
(50) either advancing singly, each with its brood of young, then about two-thirds grown, or in connexion with other families, forming parties often amounting to seventy or eighty individuals, all intent on shunning the old cocks, which,

even when the young birds have attained this size, will
(55) fight with, and often destroy them by repeated blows on the head. Old and young, however, all move in the same course, and on foot, unless their progress be interrupted by a river, or the hunter's dog force them to take wing. When they come upon a river, they betake themselves to the
(60) highest eminences, and there often remain a whole day, or sometimes two, as if for the purpose of consultation. During this time, the males are heard *gobbling*, calling, and making much ado, and are seen strutting about, as if to raise their courage to a pitch befitting the emergency. Even
(65) the females and young assume something of the same pompous demeanor, spread out their tails, and run round each other, *purring* loudly, and performing extravagant leaps. At length, when the weather appears settled, and all around is quiet, the whole party mounts to the tops of the
(70) highest trees, whence, at a signal, consisting of a single *cluck*, given by a leader, the flock takes flight for the opposite shore.

26. The word *indigenous* (line 5) most closely means

(A) piqued
(B) genuine
(C) inborn
(D) confined
(E) native

27. What does the word *unsettled* mean in line 7?

(A) troubled
(B) uninhabited
(C) upset
(D) disorganized
(E) disturbed

28. The sentence that begins "I shall describe . . ." and ends "referring chiefly to them" (lines 26–30) could be paraphrased

(A) I will talk about the turkey's behavior in the states where it is most prevalent, those being Kentucky and Louisiana.
(B) I will talk about the bird as it behaves in the places it is most common, and since I'm a longtime resident of Kentucky and Louisiana, I'll focus on those states.
(C) I will discuss turkeys since they are most commonly found in Kentucky and Louisiana.
(D) I will describe the birds of Kentucky and Louisiana, focusing particularly on that longtime resident, the turkey.
(E) none of the above

29. The reason for including paragraph 2 is to

(A) describe the range of the turkey
(B) compare the turkey to other birds
(C) describe turkey coloration
(D) explain one kind of turkey behavior
(E) review what is known about the turkey

30. The word *mast* (line 33) apparently refers to

(A) part of a ship
(B) any vertical pole or tree
(C) a disciplinary action
(D) a large cell
(E) nuts and berries

31. Paragraph 3 introduces the concept of

(A) turkey behavior
(B) turkey mating patterns
(C) turkey hibernation
(D) turkey migration
(E) turkey eating habits

32. The word *eminences* (line 60) means

(A) excellences
(B) nobilities
(C) prominences
(D) heights
(E) reputations

33. The "emergency" referred to in line 64 is

(A) rising flood waters
(B) lack of food
(C) an obstacle in the path of migration
(D) inability to fly
(E) a sudden flight of turkeys

34. How does Audubon feel about turkeys?

(A) mystified
(B) nettled
(C) repelled
(D) amused
(E) fascinated

35. Audubon is apparently writing based on

(A) his memoirs
(B) scientific experiments
(C) diaries of early explorers
(D) his own observations
(E) laboratory studies

10

IF YOU FINISH BEFORE TIME IS CALLED, YOU MAY CHECK YOUR WORK ON **S T O P**
THIS SECTION ONLY. DO NOT WORK ON ANY OTHER SECTION IN THE TEST.

Explanatory Answers

Were you able to pace yourself so that you covered all or most of the questions? Did you remember the ladder of difficulty? Did you remember to "leapfrog" over difficult questions?

Did you try to eliminate answers and make educated guesses?

SECTION 1

1. E	**11.** A	**21.** B	**31.** C
2. C	**12.** D	**22.** A	**32.** E
3. C	**13.** B	**23.** C	**33.** D
4. C	**14.** A	**24.** E	**34.** B
5. D	**15.** C	**25.** B	**35.** D
6. B	**16.** B	**26.** B	
7. E	**17.** A	**27.** E	
8. D	**18.** A	**28.** B	
9. D	**19.** A	**29.** E	
10. B	**20.** C	**30.** D	

1. (E) This is an interpretation question whose format requires you to look at all five choices. You must understand that by omitting "south" in his list, Garnet implies that he is addressing people in the south (C); but by including the list at all, he is listing those places from which free people have come to meet (B). The best choice is a combination of (B) and (C)—(E).

2. (C) This interpretation is confirmed by a close reading of the sentences before and after the line in question. Garnet discusses the ways in which the conventioneers and their fellow slaves are bound, or connected.

3. (C) Again, look at all the choices to answer this synthesis question. Reread paragraph 2 to determine its focus, and you will see that Garnet defines a connection he feels to his audience and expresses his affection.

4. (C) For any vocabulary-in-context question you must return to the line in question to try out the choices in place of the word being tested. Here, all of the choices are synonyms for *fixed*, but only one makes sense.

5. (D) This evaluation question requires you to skim the passage for reference to the future, which you will find in lines 27–28. He speaks of mankind becoming wiser and better, and expresses some hope.

6. (B) Plug in the choices for this vocabulary question, and you will see that (A), (B), and (D) make sense in context, but (B) is definitely the best and most meaningful choice.

7. (E) This interpretation asks you to decipher a metaphor used by Garnet. Return to the line cited, and try out the choices in context. Only (E) fits; (B) is never mentioned, and the other choices do not make sense.

8. (D) This synthesis question asks you to look at the selection as a whole and paragraph 4 in particular. By summarizing the paragraph mentally, you can determine its substance and purpose. It does give a history (A), and it does talk about the audience's past (B). It does *not* express an alliance with slaves (C); that was expressed earlier.

9. (D) The words "calling themselves Christians" (line 42) alert you to Garnet's feelings in this evaluation question. (A), (B), and (E) are unsupported by the text; (C) is a misreading of the paragraph.

10. (B) Plugging in the choices reveals that (B) and (C) are possible, but only (B) is a synonym for *unrequited*.

11. (A) Continue with the sentence (lines 53–54) and you will see that Garnet is talking about a lifetime in slavery, from birth to death.

12. (D) Look at all of the choices to answer this evaluation question. (A) is true; (B) is true; (C) is never stated. Since (A) and (B) both work, the answer must be (D).

13. (B) There are several ways of attacking this item. You can use A & T (Anticipate and Test) while taking advantage of the verbal clues included in the sentence. You might anticipate, therefore, that the second substitution would be *ability* or *talent*. Those words don't appear themselves, but a good match would be *aptitude*. Then you would substitute both words of (B) back into the sentence and read it through in its entirety.

    You could also "go to pieces" and use the process of elimination. Eliminate (A) and (C) on the basis of the first words. "Resolve why" and "refute why" just aren't meaningful English phrases. You can do the same thing with the second words of (D) and (E). Neither "a high degree of experience" nor "a high degree of volition" are likely to create meaningful English phrases.

14. (A) This sentence is governed by a thought-extender. Everything that follows the blank is intended to explain what goes in the blank. You might anticipate words such as *disconnected* or *disjointed*, and (A), *incoherent*, provides a pretty good match. None of the other choices is equivalent to the idea of an absence of plot and a montage of images.

15. (C) This sentence is also governed by a thought-extender. The material following the semicolon explains what comes before. So the first substitution must be equivalent to "saying wonderful things about herself." You might anticipate such substitutions as *self-serving* or *self-congratulatory*. Additionally, the second clause (everything following the semicolon) is also governed by a thought-extender: "when she wasn't saying . . . , she . . ." So the second substitution must be parallel to *saying*, and *quoted* works nicely.

    None of the other choices gives you the overall parallelism of the sentence, along with the parallelism of the second clause.

16. (B) This sentence is characterized by a thought-reverser. The structure "not . . . but" sets up a contrast between the two blanks. Only (B) provides that contrast. *The horses were not indigenous to North America but were introduced later.* Although the other choices create meaningful phrases when taken in isolation, they fail to provide this needed contrast.

17. (A) This sentence contains both a thought-reverser and an extender. The *but* sets up a contrast between the first blank and the second. Additionally, the comma in the second clause sets up a parallel. Taking the second idea first,

10

the second blank must be filled in by a word that explains why someone's apartment and office are drab and disorganized. Only *indifferent to* will do the trick. None of the other possibilities explains the state of her surroundings. Additionally, (A) gives the needed contrast: *her taste in clothes was impeccable, but she was totally indifferent to her surroundings.*

18. (A) This analogy is based on the relationship of tool. So your diagnostic sentence (DXS) might take the form "A BATON is the tool of a CONDUCTOR, and a *hammer* is the tool of a *blacksmith*. Every other choice is eliminated by this DXS. (B) is a "place of" connection; and (C), (D), and (E) all express "part of" connections.

    You may also notice a secondary connection. Both a baton and a hammer are things held by the hand, and there is the additional suggestion of similarity of movement. Remember, however, a secondary relation can be used only for confirmation—not as your first line of attack.

19. (A) This analogy is based upon the "part of" connection, so your DXS might say "The THEME is part of the SYMPHONY." This eliminates (B), (C), and (E), but it seems to accept both (A) and (D). The next step would be to refine the DXS. Exactly how is the theme a part of a symphony? It's the melody that holds together the various parts; it connects things.

    This refinement allows you to eliminate (D), for the *petal* does not hold the *flower* together. Additionally, there are confirming secondary relations operating here. A THEME is like a *plot.*

20. (C) This analogy is based on the "part of" connection. Your first formulation of a DXS might be "a LID is a part of the EYE." Unfortunately, this can accept both (B) and (C), so you need to refine the sentence. State more precisely the function of the lid. It is the part of the eye that regulates light. This may or may not lead you to eliminate (B), since the window lets in light. So at this point, you could look for a secondary relationship, and you find a very nice one. The *camera* is like an EYE, and the *shutter* and the LID have similar functions. This secondary relationship would confirm (C).

21. (B) This item is based on the "sequence" connection. You might express the connection as "In friendship, one might progress from ACQUAINTANCE to CONFIDANT." This eliminates (A), (C), (D), and (E), since those choices do not express a relationship of sequence. The DXS accepts only (B): In work, one might progress from *novice* to *master.*

22. (A) This item is based on the "lack of" connection. You could say: "PALLID is characterized by a total lack of COLOR." Again, this eliminates every choice but the correct one: *arid* is characterized by a total lack of *moisture.*

23. (C) This analogy is also based on the "lack of" connection. You may feel more comfortable with your DXS if you change the parts of speech: IMMORALITY is characterized by a lack of ETHICS, and *chaos* is characterized by a lack of *order.* No other choice is accepted by the testing sentence.

24. (E) This item cannot be fit into any of the ten standard analogy forms. Your DXS might read: "A FLOW CHART is the tangible outline for a PROCESS, and a *blueprint* is the tangible outline for *construction.* And there is a very nice, confirming secondary relationship. Both FLOW CHART and *blueprint* are directions for doing something.

    Even if you did not see the analogy connection, you should have been able to eliminate some of the wrong choices as non-answers. You could have eliminated (B), (C), and (D). There is no necessary connection between those pairs of terms. Then, you would have had to guess between (A) and (E)—but that's a fifty-fifty proposition, and well worth the guess.

25. (B) This item is based on the "lack of" connection. Your DXS could be "lack of SINCERITY is the defining characteristic of FACETIOUSNESS." This DXS accepts only choice (B): lack of *gravity* is the defining characteristic of the *farcical*. Additionally, three of the wrong choices can be eliminated as non-answers: (A), (C), and (E).

26. (B) This vocabulary-in-context question asks you to find the best replacement for the word being tested. Return to the cited line and plug in the choices. (A) and (B) are possible synonyms, but (B) is a better choice in context.

27. (E) This synthesis question asks you to analyze Alcott's inclusion of a particular part of her letter. Look at all the choices and compare them with paragraph 1. (A) is certainly not true; Alcott's tone is amused but not impressed. (B) is true; May's hat is stylish and fine, whereas Alcott's is plain and unbecoming. (C) is also true; the description of May's hat is hilarious. If (B) and (C) are true, the answer must be (E).

28. (B) A quick skim of paragraph 1 reveals Alcott's feelings; she is describing a force of nature, not a hat. Despite a certain wistfulness, she is laughing at May's bonnet.

29. (E) Read the context surrounding this citation. Alcott's ribbon box is proven to cure her plain-hat troubles, just as an elixir might cure her ills.

30. (D) Again, this is an interpretation question that asks you to look at an unusual use of words. Rereading the cited phrase in context will help you here. Alcott must be speaking of hats no longer in use, but she never says that they were either lost (B) or sold (C).

31. (C) Alcott's amusingly flowery language makes her a good source of interpretation questions. Again, look back at the context in which the phrase is found. Lines before and after refer to the decoration of the bonnet and the fact that it is being held on her "gifted brow" by "green ones." *Ones* must refer back to *strings*, which evidently are hat ties.

32. (E) Only one choice here makes sense in context. If you do not take the time to plug the choices into the phrase, you might miss this one.

33. (D) This synthesis question asks you to explain Alcott's intent in citing a particular figure. The reference to Eve is quite short and centers around Eve's use of found materials (B) to manufacture creative clothing (A). Since (A) and (B) both work, (D) is correct.

34. (B) This is an evaluation question. Alcott never comes right out and says how she feels, but you can infer that she feels somewhat proud of her accomplishment. Her hat is neither stylish (A) nor sophisticated (E). She does not seem to want May's hat (C); she makes fun of it. Nor does she criticize her own hat (D). Only (B) works here.

35. (D) This evaluation question asks you to look both at purpose and at tone. The letter is neither boastful (A) nor pitiful (B). It pokes some fun at May's hat, but that is not its primary focus (C). Nowhere does Alcott ask Anna to visit (B). The only appropriate answer is (D).

10

SECTION 2

1. B	**11.** C	**21.** A	**31.** D
2. B	**12.** D	**22.** D	**32.** D
3. C	**13.** E	**23.** B	**33.** C
4. E	**14.** D	**24.** C	**34.** E
5. A	**15.** C	**25.** C	**35.** D
6. A	**16.** B	**26.** E	
7. D	**17.** E	**27.** B	
8. A	**18.** E	**28.** B	
9. D	**19.** A	**29.** A	
10. B	**20.** B	**30.** E	

1. (B) This sentence is governed by the thought-reverser *although*. The blank must describe the guests in terms that will contrast with the fact that they ate very little. You would anticipate possible substitutions such as *hungry, voracious,* or *ravenous.* And *ravenous* is the correct choice.

2. (B) This sentence is governed by two thought-extenders. The first blank must establish an action that can be explained by the fact that something was heresy. Additionally, the second blank must explain what *heresy* means. As for the second relationship, *heresy* is a word meaning "an idea or doctrine that is contrary to accepted religious teachings." The second element of (B) correctly defines *heretic.* Additionally, *recanted* provides the overall parallel needed. The idea of *heresy* explains why Galileo recanted his theories.

3. (C) This sentence has both thought-extender and thought-reverser. The first clause (everything up to the semicolon) requires a continuer; the blank sets up what is to be explained by the phrase "students rarely understood." Additionally, the entire second clause, with an appropriate completion, must contrast with the idea of the first clause.

   We start with the first blank. What kind of a person would be giving lectures? A *teacher*, a *professor*, or even a *speaker*, but we eliminate (A) and (B). Next, what kind of scholar could be contrasted with a teacher who is a failure? A good scholar, or a respected scholar, or a conscientious scholar. The closest match available to us is *formidable*. So (C) must be the best choice.

4. (E) This sentence is governed by a thought-extender, but its logic is so simple that the item is ultimately a vocabulary question. The blank must explain why the era of the musical is concluded. The logical explanation is that there is a lack of new talent.

   The word *lack* does not itself appear as a choice, so you must try to match it to the best available choice. The answer is *paucity*, a word that means "lack of" or "scarcity." There are two other difficult vocabulary words in the choices, both of which were also included in the list. *Temerity* means "audacity" or "boldness," and *laxity* means "looseness."

5. (A) Again we have a question that is primarily a vocabulary item. The logic of the sentence is fairly simple. The correct substitution must contrast with the idea of a lengthy and grand work yet be consistent with a carefree childhood as a topic. You can eliminate (B) because it fails to complete the

parallel with carefree childhood. And you can eliminate (D) because it fails to make a contrast with the idea of a lengthy and grand work. (An epic is lengthy and grand.) And (C), too, fails to supply the needed contrast.

At this point, the choice between (A) and (E) depends on your familiarity with the words *vignette* and *elegy.* The correct answer is *vignette*, which means "a short story or sketch." *Vignette* nicely provides the overall contrast with *grand* and *lengthy* and is consistent with the idea of a happy childhood. *Elegies* is inconsistent with writing about a happy childhood, because an elegy is a poem about death and is therefore sad or mournful.

6. (A) This is primarily a vocabulary question. *Din* and "nothing could agitate her" are your clues; you must look for the word that means "undisturbed by noise." Only (A), meaning "even-tempered," fits.

7. (D) The logic of this sentence is based on contrast; the clues are *crowds, refuge,* and *cabin.* In choices (A) and (B), the first substitution works, but the second is meaningless. In choices (C) and (E), neither word makes sense in context.

8. (A) The first substitution in choices (A), (B), and (D) makes sense in context, but *regulations* (B) cannot leave someone in peace, and *effluvium*, or outflowing, makes no sense. Your choice must be (A).

9. (D) This sentence has a thought-extender logic; the phrase that follows the comma defines the first word in question. *Spirits* is the clue, and, of course, it is a word with more than one meaning. If you take it to mean *alcohol*, you might look at (A), (B), or (E). In (A), *brewing* is not the art of *founding* spirits, but rather the art of distilling them. In (B), *bartending* is not the art of *manufacturing* spirits, but rather the art of mixing and serving them. (E) makes little sense. Turn to the other meaning of *spirits: apparitions. Sorcery* (C) is not the art of imparting spirits, but may be the art of invoking them. Only (D) works—*necromancy* (a form of sorcery) is the art of *conjuring* or calling forth spirits.

10. (B) This is a vocabulary question. The clues are *do not* and *see.* If you were to *trill* (A) or *chortle* (C) at the man on the corner, the danger would not be his seeing you but rather his hearing you. You can *behold* (D) someone without being rude or risking danger. It would be odd to *saunter* (E) or amble at someone. *Gawk*, meaning "stare rudely," is the best choice.

11. (C) The overall structure of the sentence is that of thought-extender. The second substitution must echo the first. Additionally, the first substitution must introduce an idea that is somewhat less intense than hostility but still expresses that general idea. (C) does the job. *Disapprobation* suggests *hostility*, and *hostility* is in turn paralleled by *vehement disagreement.*

(A), (B), and (D) can be eliminated on the ground that they do not set up the continuation of *hostility. Gratitude, elation,* and *profusion* are not forms of *hostility.*

(E) at least has the merit of using disdain, a word that works well in the first blank. But (E) fails to carry forward the parallel between the first and second blanks. *Reluctantly disagree* is not the result of disdain and hostility.

12. (D) In this sentence, the language of the introductory clause sets up a contrast between the blanks; it may seem a contradiction, this as well as that. But it is difficult to anticipate what words should be used, since many different pairs would be acceptable so long as they expressed a contrast; for

10

example, *love* and *hatred for*, *respect* and *disdain for*, and so on. So the best thing to do is skip the Anticipate stage and go straight to the choices.

Only (D) provides the needed contrast: the partners are *compatible* (they go well together), but still they are *independent* of one another.

13. (E) The logical key to this sentence is the parallel set up by *confirming*. The second substitution must echo the first one. But it's impossible to tell from other verbal clues whether we should anticipate substitutions with positive or negative overtones. (E) provides the needed continuation. The exhibit was a *success* because the artist is *brilliant*.

The other choices fail to create a parallel between the two blanks. A *victory* is not the result of *malfeasance*; a *triumph* is not the result of *apathy*; a *disaster* is not the result of *virtuosity*; nor is a *failure* the result of *geniality*.

14. (D) This sentence is governed by a thought-reverser, *despite*. The two substitutions must be opposite of each other. *Incomprehensibility* is not the opposite of *philanthropist*; *simplicity* is certainly not the opposite of *dolt*; *power* is not the opposite of *scholar*; and *humor* is not the opposite of *miser*. But *erudition* is not something one expects of a *philistine*.

To a certain extent, this question is made difficult by the level of vocabulary. *Erudition* means "deep, scholarly learning"; *philistine* (a word based on a reference in the Bible) means "narrowly conventional in views and tastes."

15. (C) This sentence is characterized by a thought-reverser, *in contrast to*. So the blank must be something that contrasts with *utilitarian*. The only possibility is *grandiose*. Both *inconsequential* and *crude* seem too much like *utilitarian* ("stark, not adorned").

Again, this item is to a certain extent a matter of vocabulary. If you know the meanings of *supine* and *acrimonious*, you can eliminate (A) and (D), since a house could not be described in those terms.

16. (B) This analogy is based upon a connection of degree. First, make sure you know what parts of speech you are dealing with. After all, both COMMAND and REQUEST can be either noun or verb. A quick look at the choices lets you know that the capitalized words are both verbs, since all of the answer choices are verbs.

The relationship is one of degree since a command is stronger than a request. Your diagnostic sentence might have the form: COMMANDING is stronger than REQUESTING. Only (B) fits this DXS: *Maligning* is stronger than *criticizing*.

17. (E) This analogy is based on the "is a sign of" connection. A SOB is a sign of GRIEF. The only choice that also fits this sentence is (E): A *groan* is a sign of *pain*. Incidentally, you may also notice a pronounced secondary relationship here. SOB and *groan* are both audible indications of emotions; and GRIEF and *pain* are both emotions that people would prefer to avoid. Remember, however, that such relationships are to be used only after constructing and refining a DXS, and then only to increase confidence about the correct choice.

18. (E) This analogy is based on the connection "is a defining characteristic of." ELEVATION is a defining characteristic of a MOUNTAIN, and *depth* is a defining characteristic of an *ocean*.

19. (A) This analogy is based on the connection "interruption." A CEASEFIRE is a temporary interruption of a WAR, and a *recess* is a temporary interruption of

a *trial*. Additionally, there is a very prominent secondary relationship operating here. A war and a trial are both interactions between two hostile sides.

20. (B) It's difficult to classify the connection on which this analogy is based, and this reminds us that not every analogy can be easily fitted into one of the ten categories. On the one hand, it might be considered a matter of degree (EXHAUSTED is more severe than ENERVATED); but on the other hand, it could be described as a matter of sequence (first you are ENERVATED, then you are EXHAUSTED).

   For purposes of discussion, we will take the second view. Using a DXS of "EXHAUSTION follows ENERVATION," we select (B) as the best choice: *motionless* follows *deceleration*. Importantly, even though it is difficult to articulate precisely the connection here, there is a very pronounced pair of secondary relationships that confirm (B) to be correct. ENERVATION (a weakening) is similar to a *deceleration* (running down), and EXHAUSTION, like *motionless*, is a complete lack of energy.

21. (A) This analogy is clearly based on degree. MISERLINESS is an extreme form of FRUGALITY, and *moroseness* is an extreme form of *unhappiness*.

22. (D) This analogy is based on the connection "lack of." Lack of INTEGRITY is a defining characteristic of someone who is CORRUPT, and lack of *commitment* is a defining characteristic of someone who is *irresolute*.

23. (B) This analogy is based on the "part of" connection. So your diagnostic sentence might be "A POSTSCRIPT is a part of an EPISTLE." But this accepts both (B) and (E). An *epilogue* is a part of a *novel*, and an *aria* is a part of an *opera*. So you need to refine the DXS. Precisely what part of an epistle is a postscript? It is the very last part. This eliminates (E), since an *aria* can come anywhere in an opera. But an *epilogue* can come only at the end of a *novel*.

24. (C) This analogy is based on the connection "defining characteristic." But you need to know that HEDONIST means "a seeker of PLEASURE." Thus PLEASURE is a defining characteristic of what it is to be a HEDONIST. And *food* is a defining characteristic of what it is to be an *epicure*. (An *epicure* is a person who loves *food*.)

   But even if you don't know the meanings of HEDONIST and EPICURE, you can still get the right answer by the process of elimination. Every answer but (C) can be eliminated as a non-answer. There is no necessary connection between *perpetrator* and *gain*, *introvert* and *library*, *athlete* and *victory*, or *model* and *applause*.

25. (C) This analogy is based upon degree. A PESTILENCE is a particularly widespread and destructive DISEASE, and a *holocaust* is a very large and destructive *fire*.

26. (E) Choices (B) through (E) are potential synonyms for *indigenous* [(A) is a play on a sound-alike word: *indignant*]; however, only (E) truly works in the context of the sentence.

27. (B) This is another vocabulary-in-context question, this time featuring choices all of which are synonyms for *unsettled*. Only (B) is the meaning required by the context, however; the other choices refer to an unrelated connotation for *unsettled*.

28. (B) This interpretation question asks you to select the best restatement of a difficult sentence. Reread the sentence in question, paying attention to the

10

sentence that precedes it as well. If you were to parse the sentence, you would find that "having resided" refers back to the subject of the sentence, "I." It is "I" who "may be understood," and it is "I" who has resided for many years in Kentucky and Louisiana. Only (B) matches this meaning.

29. (A) Review paragraph 2 before making a choice, and you will see that the entire paragraph is dedicated to listing the places in which the bird is found—its range. Even if you did not know this meaning of the word *range,* you could select this choice by a process of elimination, since none of the other choices for this synthesis question is true.

30. (E) The meaning of this unfamiliar vocabulary word can only be drawn from context. In this case, you must read more than the sentence in which the word is found. All of the choices are related to the various meanings of *mast;* only (E) relates to turkeys hunting for "more fruit."

31. (D) This evaluation question requires you to summarize paragraph 3 in order to locate its main idea. (E) is discussed briefly, but is too specific. (A) is true, but is too general. (B) and (C) are not mentioned at all.

32. (D) All of these choices are synonyms for *eminences,* but the eminences here refer to someplace to which turkeys might "betake themselves." The answer must be (D).

33. (C) This interpretation question calls on your ability to decipher an expression in terms of its referent. The turkeys have flocked to trees or high ground, and they are spending time strutting and calling. Why? Skimming the paragraph reminds you that their progress has been "interrupted by a river, or the hunter's dog. . . ." An obstacle (C) has led them to behave this way.

34. (E) This is an evaluation question. It can be answered after reading the entire selection, but it is supported by the first paragraph, in which Audubon refers to turkeys as "one of the most interesting . . . birds. . . ."

35. (D) Previewing the selection by reading the introduction will help you here, but so will clues in paragraph 2, especially the last sentence. Audubon is speaking of things he himself has seen in the wild. There is no evidence that he is writing from anything other than his own notes and memory.

Diagnostic Math Test

✔ Objectives

To diagnose and pinpoint any weaknesses in arithmetic, algebra, and geometry.

To determine whether a general review of math is required.

To explain key concepts.

To refer you to areas needing review.

1. Diagnostic Test, 40 Questions
   - Arithmetic
   - Algebra
   - Geometry
2. Explanatory Answers with References to Math Review

11

The SAT tests arithmetic, basic algebra, and elementary geometry. To help you decide what you must study, here is a diagnostic test.

MATH DIAGNOSTIC TEST
40 Questions
No Time Limit

Directions: Enter your answers to the following questions in the blanks provided. Use the available space for scratch work. Although there is no time limit for the exercise, you should work as quickly as possible. After you have finished, review your work using the explanations that follow.

1. To increase the number 12,345,678 by exactly 10,000, it is necessary to increase which digit by one? _____

2. $\dfrac{(7 + 2)(16 \div 4)}{(2 \times 3)(6 \div 2)} =$ _____

3. List all of the factors of 36: _____

4. List all of the prime numbers greater than 10 but less than 30: _____
_____

Questions 5–7

Indicate whether or not the following *must always* be an even number. Enter *yes* or *no*.

5. Even Number × Odd Number _____

6. Odd Number + Odd Number _____

7. Even Number ÷ Even Number _____

8. In a string of consecutive odd numbers, what is the fifth number following the number 13? _____

9. $\dfrac{\left(\dfrac{5}{6}+\dfrac{1}{2}\right) \times \left(\dfrac{4}{3} \times \dfrac{1}{4}\right)}{\left(\dfrac{3}{2}-\dfrac{1}{3}\right)-\left(\dfrac{2}{3} \div \dfrac{8}{2}\right)} = \underline{\hspace{2cm}}$

10. Convert $2\dfrac{2}{5}$ to a decimal: _____

11. Convert 1.125 to a fraction: _____

12. $0.001 + 0.01 + 0.227 - 0.027 =$ _____

13. $0.1 \times 0.01 =$ _____

14. $1.5 \div 0.75 =$ _____

15. Convert $2\dfrac{3}{4}$ to a percent: _____

16. 2 is what percent of 10? _____

17. The price of a certain item increased from $2.00 to $2.50. What was the percent increase in the price? _____

18. $\dfrac{(3-6) \times (12 \div -2)}{(6-8)} =$ _____

19. Bob's average score on five tests was 85. If he received scores of 90, 80, 78, and 82 on four of the five tests, what was his score on the remaining test? _____

20. In a certain class, a student's final grade is a function of the grades she receives on a midterm exam, a final exam, and a term paper. The term paper counts twice as much as the final exam, and the final exam counts twice as much as the midterm exam. If a student receives a midterm score of 75, a final exam score of 80, and a grade of 90 on the term paper, what is the student's final grade for the course? _____

21. A jar contains black and white marbles in the ratio 2:3. If the jar contains a total of 30 marbles, how many of the marbles are black? _____

22. In a certain game, if 2 wixsomes are worth 3 chags, and 4 chags are worth 1 plut, then 6 pluts are worth how many wixsomes? _____

23. In the proportion $\dfrac{x}{6} = \dfrac{12}{24}$, $x =$ _____

24. What is the value of 3 raised to the third power? _____

25. $\sqrt{4} + \sqrt{9} =$ _____

26. $y - x + 3x - 4y + 3y =$ _____

27. $\dfrac{(x^3 y^4)^2}{(x^2 y^2)(x^4 y^6)} =$ _____

28. $(a+b)(a+b) =$ _____

29. Factor the expression $12x^3 + 3x^2 + 18x$: _____

30. Factor the expression $x^2 + 2xy + y^2$: _____

31. If $2x + y = 12$ and $y - x = 3$, then $x =$ _____

32. If $x^2 + x = 2$, and $x > 0$, then $x =$ _____

33. If $x + y \leqq 5$ and $y \geqq 2$, then what is the maximum possible value of x? _____

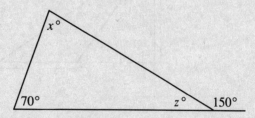

34. In the figure above, what is the value of x? _____

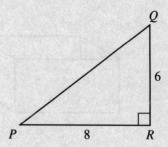

35. In the figure above, what is the length of side PQ? _____

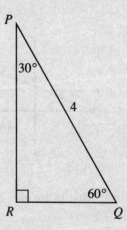

36. In the figure above, what is the length of sides PR and RQ?

PR: _____ RQ: _____

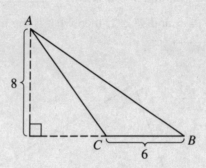

37. In the figure above, what is the area of triangle *ABC*? _____

38. A circle has a diameter of 4. What is the area of the circle? _____

What is the circumference of the circle? _____

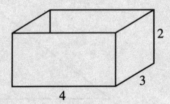

39. What is the volume of the rectangular box shown above? _____

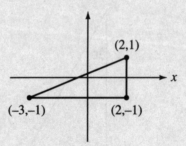

40. In the figure above, what is the area of the triangle? _____

Explanatory Answers

1. Changing the digit 4 to 5 will increase the number by 10,000 to 12,355,678.

2. 2
$$\frac{(7 + 2)(16 \div 4)}{(2 \times 3)(6 \div 2)} = \frac{(9)(4)}{(6)(3)} = \frac{36}{18} = 2$$

3. 1 and 36; 2 and 18; 3 and 12; 4 and 9; and 6 and 6

4. 11, 13, 17, 19, 23, and 29

5. Yes. For example, 2×3 is 6, which is even.
6. Yes. For example, $3 + 5$ is 8, which is even.
7. No. For example, $2 \div 4$ is a fraction and therefore not an even number.

11

8. 23

	First	Second	Third	Fourth	Fifth
13	15	17	19	21	23

9. $\dfrac{4}{9}$

$$\frac{\left(\dfrac{5}{6}+\dfrac{1}{2}\right)\times\left(\dfrac{4}{3}\times\dfrac{1}{4}\right)}{\left(\dfrac{3}{2}-\dfrac{1}{3}\right)-\left(\dfrac{2}{3}\div\dfrac{8}{2}\right)}=\frac{\left(\dfrac{8}{6}\right)\left(\dfrac{4}{12}\right)}{\left(\dfrac{7}{6}\right)-\left(\dfrac{1}{6}\right)}=\frac{\dfrac{4}{9}}{1}=\frac{4}{9}$$

10. 2.4

$$2\frac{2}{5}=\frac{12}{5}=2.4$$

11. $1\dfrac{1}{8}$

$$1.125=1+0.125=1+\frac{125}{1,000}=1+\frac{1}{8}=1\frac{1}{8}$$

12.

$$
\begin{array}{r}
0.001 \\
0.010 \\
+\ 0.227 \\
\hline
0.238 \\
-\ 0.027 \\
\hline
0.211
\end{array}
$$

13. 0.001

$$
\begin{array}{r}
0.01 \\
\times\quad .1 \\
\hline
0.001
\end{array}
$$

14. 2

$$0.75\overline{)1.50}\ \ \overset{2}{}$$

15. 275%

$$2\frac{3}{4} = \frac{11}{4} = 2.75 = 275\%$$

16. 20%

$$\frac{2}{10} = 0.20 = 20\%$$

17. 25%

$$\frac{\text{Increase}}{\text{Original Price}} = \frac{\$0.50}{\$2.00} = \frac{1}{4} = 25\%$$

18. −9

$$\frac{(3-6) \times (12 \div -2)}{(6-8)} = \frac{-3 \times -6}{-2} = \frac{18}{-2} = -9$$

19. 95

$$\frac{90 + 80 + 78 + 82 + x}{5} = 85$$

$$\frac{330 + x}{5} = 85$$

$$330 + x = 85(5)$$

$$x = 425 - 330$$

$$x = 95$$

20. 85

$$\frac{75 + 2(80) + 4(90)}{7} = \frac{595}{7} = 85$$

21. 12

There are $2 + 3 = 5$ ratio parts. So each part has the value $30 \div 5 = 6$. Two of the parts are black marbles, and $2 \times 6 = 12$.

22. 16

Since 2 wixsomes equal 3 chags, 8 wixsomes equal 12 chags. Since 4 chags equal 1 plut, 12 chags equal 3 pluts. Therefore, 8 wixsomes equal 3 pluts, and 16 wixsomes equal 6 pluts.

23. $x = 3$

Cross-multiply: $24x = 72$

Divide by 24: $x = 3$

11

24. 27

$3 \times 3 \times 3 = 27$

25. 5

$\sqrt{4} = 2$ and $\sqrt{9} = 3$, and $2 + 3 = 5$

26. $2x$

$y - x + 3x - 4y + 3y = 3x - x + y - 4y + 3y = 2x$

27. 1

$$\frac{(x^3 \, y^4)^2}{(x^2 \, y^2)(x^4 \, y^6)} = \frac{x^6 \, y^8}{x^6 \, y^8} = 1$$

28. $a^2 + 2ab + b^2$

29. $3x(4x^2 + x + 6)$

30. $(x + y)(x + y)$

31. $x = 3$

Since $y - x = 3$, $y = 3 + x$. Therefore,

$2x + (3 + x) = 12$

$3x + 3 = 12$

$3x = 9$

$x = 3$

32. $x = 1$

Rewrite the original equation: $x^2 + x - 2 = 0$.

Factor: $(x + 2)(x - 1) = 0$.

So the two solutions are $x = -2$ or $x = +1$.

33. 3

x will be the greatest when y is the least. So let's use the minimum possible value for y: $x + 2 \leqq 5$, so $x \leqq 3$. The maximum value for x is 3.

34. 80°
The unlabeled angle with the 150° angle form a straight line, for a total of 180°. Therefore the unlabeled angle is 180° less 150°, or 30°. Then, the interior angles of the triangle total 180°. So:
$70° + 30° + x° = 180°$
$x + 100 = 180$
$x = 80$

35. 10
This is a right triangle, so you can use the Pythagorean Theorem to find the length of the hypotenuse:
$PR^2 + QR^2 = PQ^2$
$(8)^2 + (6)^2 = PQ^2$
$64 + 36 = PQ^2$
$PQ^2 = 100$
$PQ = 10$

36. $PR = 2\sqrt{3}$ and $RQ = 2$
In a triangle with angles of 30°, 60°, and 90°, the side opposite the 30° angle is one-half the length of the hypotenuse, while the side opposite the 60° angle is one-half the length of the hypotenuse times the square root of 3.

37. 24
The area of a triangle is equal to $\frac{1}{2}$ × altitude × base. So $\frac{1}{2} \times 8 \times 6 = 24$.

38. The radius of a circle is one-half the diameter, so the radius of this circle is 2.
Area $= \pi r^2 = \pi(2)^2 = 4\pi$
Circumference $= 2\pi r = 2\pi(2) = 4\pi$

39. 24
To find the volume of a rectangular solid, multiply the length by the width by the depth: $2 \times 3 \times 4 = 24$.

40. 5
The length of the altitude is 2; the length of the base is 5; so the area is $\frac{1}{2}(2)(5) = 5$.

11

Problem-Solving: Introduction

✔ Objectives

To learn the general rules that govern problem-solving items.

To learn about figures that may not be drawn to scale.

To learn what is tested in the problem-solving sections.

To learn to avoid attractive but wrong choices.

To learn to use the ladder of difficulty to eliminate wrong choices.

To learn when to use a calculator.

1. The Directions for Problem-Solving
2. What Is Tested in Problem-Solving?
   - Arithmetic Manipulation
   - Arithmetic Application
   - Algebra Manipulation
   - Algebra Application
   - Geometry Manipulation
   - Geometry Application
3. Important Facts about Problem-Solving Items
   - The Ladder of Difficulty
   - The Selection of Wrong Answer Choices
   - Calculator Use

12

The SAT uses two different kinds of math questions: problem-solving and quantitative comparisons. Problem-solving items are mostly standard multiple-choice questions (a few call for student-produced responses), but quantitative comparisons involve a special set of instructions. In this and the next five lessons we will study the problem-solving type, saving quantitative comparisons for Lesson 18.

The Directions for Problem-Solving

Here are the instructions for multiple-choice problem-solving items just as they will appear on the exam. You don't need to memorize this material. Just familiarize yourself with it, then you won't need to read it ever again.

> In this section solve each problem, using any available space on the page for scratchwork. Then decide which is the best of the choices given and fill in the corresponding oval on the answer sheet.

Reference:

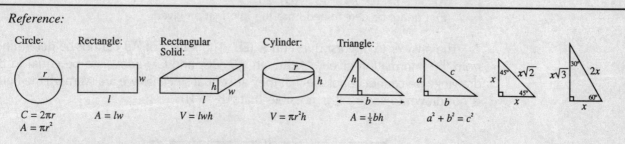

- The measure in degrees of a straight angle is 180.
- The number of degrees of arc in a circle is 360.
- The sum of the measures of the angles of a triangle is 180.

Notes: The figures accompanying the problems are drawn as accurately as possible unless otherwise stated in specific problems. Again, unless otherwise stated, all figures lie in the same plane. All numbers used in these problems are real numbers. Calculators are permitted for this test.

There is nothing very unusual in these directions. As in other sections, you solve a problem and indicate your response on your answer sheet. You can and should do scratchwork in the available space. No one expects you to do all of your thinking and figuring in your head. As for the formulas and symbols, these should already be familiar to you. If they are not, you should consult a mathematics textbook.

One point, however, does need clarification. Unless otherwise specifically noted, the figures included as illustrations are drawn to scale.

EXAMPLE:

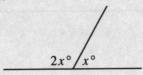

In the figure above, $x =$
(A) 15   (B) 30   (C) 45   (D) 60   (E) 120

Since the sum of the measures in degrees of the angles of a straight line is 180, $2x + x = 180°$. So $3x = 180°$, and $x = 60°$. If you measure angle x with a protractor, you will find it is indeed 60°.

Sometimes, however, a figure will include a warning note.

EXAMPLE:

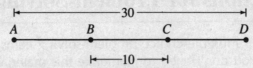

Note: Figure not drawn to scale.

In the figure above, $AB =$
(A) 5   (B) 10   (C) 15   (D) 20
(E) Cannot be determined from the information given.

In the figure above, $AB + CD =$
(A) 5   (B) 10   (C) 15   (D) 20
(E) Cannot be determined from the information given.

The answer to the first question is (E). The length of AB cannot be determined from the information given. Although AB, BC, and CD *appear* to be equal in the drawing, we cannot conclude that they are equal since (as we are warned) the figure is not drawn to scale. It is possible that $AB > 10$:

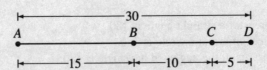

And it is also possible that $AB < 10$:

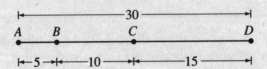

The answer to the second question, however, is (D)—not (E). Although the note indicates that the figure is not drawn to scale, you may assume that points $ABCD$ are on line AD in the order shown. Therefore, regardless of the accuracy of the drawing, you can deduce mathematically that $AB + CD$ must be 20. The entire line segment

AD is 30 units long. *BC* is 10 units long, so the other two segments together, *AB plus CD*, must be 30 − 10 = 20.

Here are other examples to illustrate the difference between valid and invalid conclusions based on figures that are not drawn to scale:

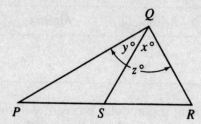

Which of the following must be true?
I. $PS < SR$
II. $z = 90$
III. $x > y$
(A) I only   (B) I and II only   (C) I and III only
(D) I, II, and III   (E) Neither I, II, nor III

Which of the following must be true?
I. $PR > PS$
II. $z > x$
III. $x + y = z$
(A) I only   (B) I and II only   (C) II and III only
(D) I, II, and III   (E) Neither I, II, nor III

The answer to the first question is (E). Although all three statements look like they are true the way the figure is drawn, the figure might also be drawn as follows:

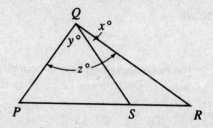

Notice that the lines and points in this redrawn figure are in the same position relative to each other as they are above. But in this figure, it appears that all three statements are false. Therefore, none of the three statements is necessarily true.

The answer to the second question, however, is (D). No matter how the figure is drawn, all three of these statements must be true. Statement I must be true, since *PS* is only a part of *PR*. For the same reason, II must be true; angle *x* is only a part of angle *z*. And III must be true since *x* and *y* are the only two parts of *z*.

What Is Tested in Problem-Solving?

Problem-solving items test arithmetic, basic algebra, and elementary geometry. Some of the questions will look as though they might have been taken from one of your math textbooks; others will require you to apply your knowledge of math to new situations.

Therefore, we can classify problem-solving questions according to whether they just test your ability to do mathematical manipulations or require you to do some original thinking:

	Arithmetic	Algebra	Geometry
Manipulation	1	3	5
Application	2	4	6

Your methods for attacking a particular problem will depend on what type of problem you have. The following problems illustrate the six categories.

1. Arithmetic Manipulation

EXAMPLE:

What is the average of 8.5, 7.8, and 7.7?

(A) 8.3   (B) 8.2   (C) 8.1   (D) 8.0   (E) 7.9

No original thinking is needed to solve this question. To find the average of the three numbers, you simply total them and divide the sum by 3:

$$\frac{8.5 + 7.8 + 7.7}{3} = \frac{24.0}{3} = 8.0$$

So the answer is (D).

2. Arithmetic Application

EXAMPLE:

If the price of fertilizer has been decreased from 3 pounds for $2 to 5 pounds for $2, how many more pounds of fertilizer can be purchased for $10 than could have been purchased before?

(A) 2   (B) 8   (C) 10   (D) 12   (E) 15

The operations required here are the basic ones of arithmetic, but applying them to this new situation requires some original thinking.

To solve the question, you have to determine how many pounds of fertilizer could have been purchased at the old price and how many can be purchased at the new price. With $10, it's possible to buy five $2 measures of fertilizer (10 ÷ 2 = 5). At the old price, this would mean 5 × 3 = 15 pounds. At the new price, this would be 5 × 5 = 25 pounds. Therefore, it's possible to buy 25 − 15 = 10 more pounds at the new price than at the old price. So the correct choice is (C).

3. Algebra Manipulation

EXAMPLE:

If $x - 5 = 3 - x$, then $x =$

(A) −8   (B) −2   (C) 2   (D) 4   (E) 8

To answer this question, you need only to solve for *x*—one of the basic manipulations of algebra:

$x - 5 = 3 - x$

Add *x* to both sides: $x - 5 + x = 3 - x + x$

$2x - 5 = 3$

Add 5 to both sides: $2x - 5 + 5 = 3 + 5$

$2x = 3 + 5$

$2x = 8$

Divide both sides by 2: $2x \div 2 = 8 \div 2$

$x = 4$

So the correct choice is (D).

4. Algebra Application

EXAMPLE:

A vending machine dispenses *k* cups of coffee, each at a cost of *c* cents, every day. During a period *d* days long, what is the amount of money in *dollars* taken in by the vending machine from the sale of coffee?

(A) $\dfrac{100kc}{d}$ (B) kcd (C) $\dfrac{dk}{c}$ (D) $\dfrac{kcd}{100}$ (E) $\dfrac{kc}{100d}$

This question requires more than just basic manipulation. You must apply your knowledge of algebra to a new situation. Let's first find the total amount of money received by the vending machine in cents. It sells *k* cups each day at *c* cents per cup, so it takes in *k* times *c* or *kc* cents every day. And it does this for *d* days, so the total taken in (in cents) is *kc* times *d*, or *kcd*. But the question asks for the amount expressed in dollars. Since there are 100 cents in every dollar, we need to divide *kcd* by 100. So the final answer is $\frac{kcd}{100}$, or (D).

5. Geometry Manipulation

EXAMPLE:

If a circle has a radius of 1, what is its area?

(A) $\dfrac{\pi}{2}$ (B) π (C) 2π (D) 4π (E) π^2

This very easy question just requires that you substitute 1 into the formula πr^2: $\pi(1)^2 = \pi(1 \times 1) = \pi(1) = \pi$

Very few SAT geometry questions are as easy as this. Virtually all require that you apply your knowledge of formulas to a new situation.

6. Geometry Application

EXAMPLE:

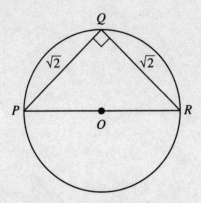

In the figure above, a triangle is inscribed in a circle with center O. What is the area of the circle?

(A) $\dfrac{\pi}{2}$ (B) $\dfrac{\pi}{\sqrt{2}}$ (C) π (D) $\pi\sqrt{2}$ (E) 2π

To answer this question, we will have to find the radius of the circle. Since the hypotenuse of the triangle is also the diameter of the circle, we can find the radius of the circle by calculating the length of the hypotenuse of the triangle. First we use the Pythagorean Theorem:

$$PR^2 = PQ^2 + QR^2$$
$$PR^2 = (\sqrt{2})^2 + (\sqrt{2})^2$$
$$PR^2 = 2 + 2 = 4$$
$$PR = \sqrt{4} = 2$$

So the diameter of the circle is 2, which means the radius of the circle = 1. Now we use the formula for calculating the area of a circle, just as we did above: $\pi r^2 = \pi(1)^2 = \pi$. So the correct choice is (C).

Important Facts about

Problem-Solving Items

1. Problem-solving questions are arranged according to the ladder of difficulty. In the two sections that consist solely of problem-solving items, the first few are likely to be relatively easy; three-quarters or more of all test-takers answer them correctly. The middle items are of moderate difficulty, and about half of the test-takers will answer them correctly. The final questions are very difficult, and fewer than one-third of all test-takers are likely to answer them correctly.

In the third math section, the problem-solving items, numbered 16 through 25, are all of the student-produced response type. Like other problem-solving questions, they too are arranged according to the ladder of difficulty.

2. The wrong answer choices for multiple-choice problem-solving items are very carefully selected. In fact, from a question writer's perspective, each wrong choice is as important as the correct answer. Why? Since the correct answer is one of the five, it has to be carefully camouflaged by the wrong choices. To accomplish this, a question writer keeps in mind three points.

First, the correct choice must blend into the background of the wrong answers. Study the following "dummy" question.

> Xx x xxxxxxx xxxx, xxx xxxxxx xx xxxxx xxx xxxxxxxxx xxxx Xxxx Xxxx Xxxxxx xxx xxxxx xxx xxxxxx xx xxxx. Xx xxx xx xxx xxxxx xxx xxx xx xxx xxxx xxxx xx xxxxxxx xxxxxxxxxxx xxxxx xxxxxxxxxx, xxxx xxxxxxxx xx xxx xxxxxxxxx xxxx xxxx xxxx xx xxxxxxx xxxxxxxxxxx xxxxx xxxxxxxxxx?
>
> (A) $\frac{5}{36}$ (B) $\frac{16}{27}$ (C) $\frac{7}{9}$ (D) $\frac{29}{36}$ (E) $\frac{31}{36}$

Even without a real question stem, you can see that each choice seems at least a plausible answer. The answer is hidden by the camouflage of wrong responses.

You would never have an array of choices like this:

> (A) π^3 (B) $\sqrt{143.111}$ (C) $\frac{7}{9}$ (D) k^{33} (E) 120°

In this array, the wrong choices could not conceal the right one. Given an actual question stem, one of these choices would stick out as obviously correct:

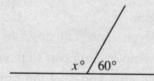

> In the figure above, $x =$
>
> (A) π^3 (B) $\sqrt{143.111}$ (C) $\frac{7}{9}$ (D) k^{33} (E) 120°

The answer is obviously (E)—the only choice that makes any sense. So the choices will be similar enough to one another that you can't spot the correct one at a glance.

Second, you can see that the answer choices are arranged in an order. Sometimes they are arranged from smallest to largest, sometimes from largest to smallest; but they are always in some order. Even algebraic expressions are arranged in some order:

> (A) x (B) x^2 (C) x^3 (D) x^4 (E) x^5

Or:

> (A) x (B) $x + y$ (C) $x^2 + y$ (D) $x^2 + y^2$ (E) $(x + y)^2$

The only exception to this rule would be a question like the following.

> Which of the following fractions is the largest?
>
> (A) $\frac{12}{29}$ (B) $\frac{108}{129}$ (C) $\frac{76}{130}$ (D) $\frac{11}{12}$ (E) $\frac{101}{200}$

12

In a question like this, choices will not be arranged in order for the obvious reason that the order would give away the solution. Here, the largest answer (and correct choice) is (D).

Third, many answer choices correspond to possible mistakes (incorrect reading or some other misunderstanding). The following example illustrates this point:

> In a certain year, the number of girls who graduated from City High School was twice the number of boys. If $\frac{3}{4}$ of the girls and $\frac{5}{6}$ of the boys went to college immediately after graduation, what fraction of the graduates that year went to college immediately after graduation?
>
> **(A)** $\frac{5}{36}$ **(B)** $\frac{16}{27}$ **(C)** $\frac{7}{9}$ **(D)** $\frac{29}{36}$ **(E)** $\frac{31}{36}$

The correct choice is (C), and the problem requires that you apply your knowledge of fractions. Since the ratio of girls to boys was 2:1, girls were $\frac{2}{3}$ of the graduating class and boys $\frac{1}{3}$. Let us write this as $\frac{2}{3}T$ and $\frac{1}{3}T$, where T stands for Total (all graduates). Of the $\frac{2}{3}T$, $\frac{3}{4}$ went directly to college: $\frac{3}{4}$ of $\frac{2}{3}T = \frac{3}{4} \times \frac{2}{3}T = \frac{6}{12}T = \frac{1}{2}T$. Of the $\frac{1}{3}T$, $\frac{5}{6}$ went directly to college: $\frac{5}{6}$ of $\frac{1}{3}T = \frac{5}{6} \times \frac{1}{3}T = \frac{5}{18}T$. The fraction of boys and girls combined was $\frac{1}{2}T + \frac{5}{18}T = \frac{14}{18}T = \frac{7}{9}T$, so $\frac{7}{9}$ of all the graduating students went directly to college.

The wrong choices, however, represent possible misreadings or misunderstandings. Take (D) as an example. Suppose that you carelessly misread the question thinking that $\frac{5}{6}$ of the girls and $\frac{3}{4}$ of the boys went directly to college (rather than vice versa). Given that misreading, you would multiply: $\frac{5}{6}$ of $\frac{2}{3}T = \frac{5}{9}T$ and $\frac{3}{4}$ of $\frac{1}{3}T = \frac{1}{4}$; and adding $\frac{5}{9}T + \frac{1}{4}T = \frac{29}{36}T$, which is choice (D).

Or imagine that you read the problem correctly and got as far as $\frac{1}{2}$ and $\frac{5}{18}$, but then multiplied instead of adding: $\frac{1}{2} \times \frac{5}{18} = \frac{5}{36}$, which is choice (A).

Such wrong answers are "distractors" (they distract attention from the correct choice). Distractors are an important part of the design of a question. After all, imagine what would happen if you made one of the mistakes described above but couldn't find a choice to fit your solution. Obviously, you would try another tack. So distractors are like misleading clues that lead you to a wrong conclusion.

3. The use of calculators *is* permitted on the SAT. You may bring to your exam any of the following types of calculators:

- four-function
- scientific
- graphing

You may *not* bring calculators of the following types:

- calculators with paper tape or printers
- laptop computers
- pocket organizers
- "hand-held" microcomputers

Make sure that the calculator you bring is one you are familiar with.

No question requires the use of a calculator. For some questions a calculator may be helpful; for others it may be inappropriate. In general, the calculator may be useful for any question which involves arithmetic computations. Remember, though, that the calculator is only a tool. It can help you avoid inaccuracies in computation, but it cannot take the place of understanding how to set up and solve a mathematical problem.

Here is a sample problem for which a calculator would be useful:

> The cost of two dozen apples is $3.60. At this rate, what is the cost of 10 apples?
>
> **(A)** $1.75   **(B)** $1.60   **(C)** $1.55   **(D)** $1.50   **(E)** $1.25

The correct answer is (D).
Make a ratio of apples to dollars:

$$\frac{apples}{dollars} : \frac{24}{3.60} = \frac{10}{x}$$

$$24x = 36$$

$$x = \frac{36}{24} = \$1.50$$

A calculator would be useful in solving this problem. Although the calculations are fairly simple, the calculator can improve your speed and accuracy.

Here is a problem for which a calculator would *not* be useful.

> Joshua travels a distance of d miles in $t - 6$ hours. At this rate, how many miles will he travel in $t^2 - 36$ hours?
>
> **(A)** $d(t + 6)$ **(B)** $d(t - 6)$ **(C)** $\dfrac{d}{t + 6}$ **(D)** $\dfrac{d}{t - 6}$ **(E)** $\dfrac{t + 6}{d}$

The correct answer is (A).

$$rate = \frac{distance}{time}$$

$$Joshua's\ rate = \frac{d}{t - 6}$$

To calculate his new distance, use $d = rt$:

$$Distance = \left(\frac{d}{t + 6}\right)(t^2 - 36)$$

$$= \left(\frac{d}{t - 6}\right)(t + 6)(t - 6)$$

$$= d(t + 6)$$

This is an algebra question. Using a calculator would not be helpful.

Here is a problem for which a calculator would be of minimal help. Its use might mask the more appropriate method of solution.

> If $x = \left(\dfrac{1}{2}\right)\left(\dfrac{1}{3}\right)\left(\dfrac{3}{2}\right)\left(\dfrac{4}{81}\right)$, then $\sqrt{x} =$
>
> **(A)** $\dfrac{1}{5}$ **(B)** $\dfrac{1}{9}$ **(C)** $\dfrac{1}{11}$ **(D)** $\dfrac{1}{13}$ **(E)** $\dfrac{1}{17}$

12

The correct answer is (B).

Without a calculator:

Reduce the fraction by canceling.

$$x = \frac{\cancel{(3)}\cancel{(4)}}{\cancel{(2)}\cancel{(3)}\cancel{(2)}(81)} = \frac{1}{81}$$

$$\sqrt{x} = \frac{1}{9}$$

With a calculator :

$$x = \frac{(3)(4)}{(2)(3)(2)(81)} = \frac{12}{972} = \frac{1}{81}$$

$$\sqrt{x} = \frac{1}{9}$$

Fractions can be reduced. Fractions can be multiplied rapidly after cancel-ing. Using a calculator for this problem does not simplify the arithmetic.

Some Words to the Wise

1. Don't be misled by sloppy detective work! Although this part of the SAT is a "math" test, you must also read carefully. While this is always important, there are two special cases where it becomes even more important: capitalized and underlined words.

First, pay very careful attention to any words in the question stem that are capitalized. When a question stem contains a thought-reverser, it is usually cap-italized. Why? To catch your attention. A thought-reverser is a negative word that turns a question around.

EXAMPLE:

A jar contains black and white marbles. If there are ten marbles in the jar, which of the following could NOT be the ratio of black to white marbles?

(A) 9:1   **(B)** 7:3   **(C)** 1:1   **(D)** 1:4   **(E)** 1:10

Ordinarily, questions are phrased in the affirmative, such as "Which of the following is . . . ?" or "Which of the following could be . . . ?" This question, however, contains the thought-reverser NOT. So a wrong answer here would ordinarily be a right answer, and vice versa.

The answer is (E). Since there are ten marbles, the number of ratio parts in the ratio must be a factor of 10. (E) is not possible since 1 + 10 = 11, and 10 is not evenly divisible by 11.

The question above might also have been phrased as:

A jar contains black and white marbles. If there are ten marbles in the jar, all of the following could be the ratio of black to white marbles EXCEPT

(A) 9:1   **(B)** 7:3   **(C)** 1:1   **(D)** 1:4   **(E)** 1:10

Or as:

A jar contains black and white marbles. If there are ten marbles in the jar, which of the following CANNOT be the ratio of black to white marbles?

(A) 9:1   **(B)** 7:3   **(C)** 1:1   **(D)** 1:4   **(E)** 1:10

Another word that functions like a thought-reverser is "LEAST."

EXAMPLE:

If *n* is a negative number, which of the following is the LEAST?

(A) $-n$ (B) $n - n$ (C) $n + n$ (D) n^2 (E) n^4

The word *least* is capitalized here to make sure that you don't do what most of us would ordinarily do, which is to look for the largest value. The correct choice is (C). Since *n* is a negative number, (A), (D), and (E) are all positive. Then (B) is just zero, since it is one number subtracted from itself. (C) is the smallest since a negative added to a negative yields a negative number.

The second group of words requiring special attention contains those that are underlined. If the question is one that requires an answer choice in special units, the test-writer may underline the special units to avoid a possible misunderstanding.

EXAMPLE:

If a machine produces 240 thingamabobs per hour, how many <u>minutes</u> are needed for the machine to produce 30 thingamabobs?

(A) 6   (B) 7.5   (C) 8   (D) 12   (E) 12.5

The answer is (B). A machine that produces 240 units per hour produces 240 units/60 minutes = 4 units/minute. To produce 30 units will take $30 \div 4 = 7.5$ *minutes.*

2. Don't fall off the ladder of difficulty! The last few problem-solving items are very difficult, and difficult items require difficult solutions. So an answer choice that can be obtained by a simple calculation must be a distractor.

EXAMPLES:

25. Three friends are playing a game in which each person simultaneously displays one of three hand signs, a clenched fist, an open palm, or two extended fingers. How many different combinations of the signs are possible?

(A) 3   (B) 9   (C) 10   (D) 12   (E) 27

Watson is most likely to pick (B) or (E), reasoning that $3 \times 3 = 9$ or that $3 \times 3 \times 3 = 27$. But (B) and (E) are both incorrect. Since this is question number 25, a difficult item, it could not possibly be handled so easily as simply multiplying 3×3 or $3 \times 3 \times 3$.

The answer is (C). One way of approaching the problem is simply to count on your fingers the different possibilities (using *F* to mean "fist," *P* to mean "palm," and *T* to mean "two fingers extended"): (1) *FFF,* (2) *PPP,* (3) *TTT,* (4) *FPP,* (5) *FTT,* (6) *PFF,* (7) *PTT,* (8) *TFF,* (9) *TPP,* and (10) *FPT.*

Here is another difficult problem for which Watson is likely to pick an obvious but wrong answer.

23. If $\frac{1}{3}$ of the girls at a school equals $\frac{1}{5}$ of the total number of students, then what is the ratio of girls to boys at the school?

(A) 5:3   (B) 3:2   (C) 2:5   (D) 1:3   (E) 1:5

With a question such as this, Watson is likely to create a ratio using $\frac{1}{3}$ and $\frac{1}{5}$: $\frac{1}{5}/\frac{1}{3}/\frac{1}{5} = 5:3$, and then breathe a sigh of relief: "That was easy." But it should not have been easy, and the fact that Watson thinks it is an easy question should prompt him to think "Uh-oh, I have fallen off the ladder of difficulty."

The answer is (B). Since $\frac{1}{3}$ of girls $= \frac{1}{5}$ of total: $\frac{1}{3}G = \frac{1}{5}T$ and $G = \frac{3}{5}T$, which means girls account for $\frac{3}{5}$ of total students. That means boys $= \frac{2}{5}$ of total, so the ratio of girls to boys is $\frac{3}{5}/\frac{2}{5} = 3:2$.

The main point of this Holmesian strategy is that you should avoid trying to find easy answers for difficult questions. Such choices are almost certain to be wrong. But you can actually use the strategy even more aggresively. If you come to a difficult question and you are not sure of your solution, eliminate any choice that can be gotten either by a single step or by just copying a number from the problem.

There is a special case when this strategy is useful. Some questions include as a possible choice "(E) Cannot be determined from the information given." What is Watson's likely reaction when he sees such a choice on a difficult problem? "This is so hard it seems impossible," he reasons, "so the correct choice must be (E)."

This line of reasoning is incorrect. If simple frustration were enough to guarantee a right answer to the question, then the problem would not be a difficult one at all. Rather, it would be very easy. Everyone able to do the math would answer correctly *plus* everyone unable to do the math would also answer correctly.

In fact, if the problem is a difficult one and seems difficult to you, the correct solution is unlikely to be (E) Cannot be deteremined from the information given." As a general rule, don't guess. "Cannot be determined" on difficult questions.

Summary

1. Unless otherwise indicated, a figure is drawn to scale. If a figure is not accompanied by any disclaimer then you can rely upon the apparent magnitudes (angles, lines, etc.). If the figure is accompanied by the disclaimer: "*Note:* Figure not drawn to scale," then you *cannot* rely on the apparent magnitudes, but you can trust that lines drawn as straight are straight and that points are in the order shown.
2. Problem-solving tests both basic manipulations and further applications of arithmetic algebra and geometry.
3. The distractors are carefully selected and represent possible misreadings or misunderstandings.
4. Circle any word in the question stem that is emphasized (capitalized or underlined). Once you've finished the problem, consciously ask yourself whether you have answered what the question asked.
5. Difficult questions require difficult solutions.
   A. If you find an easy answer to a difficult question, throw it out.
   B. Additionally, as a guessing strategy you can eliminate as incorrect any choice that is one of the numbers in the question stem or that can be obtained by some simple operation.
   C. Finally, with difficult questions, avoid a "cannot be determined" answer.

Problem-Solving (Answers, page 226)

Directions: The following questions are representative of the more difficult problem-solving items. As you work them, be alert for possible Watson-type errors. Eliminate any choice that is a number found in the problem itself. If you try an approach that generates an easy answer, eliminate that answer and try again.

1. Peter walked from point P to point Q and back again, a total distance of 2 miles. If he averaged 4 miles per hour on the trip from P to Q and 5 miles per hour on the return trip, what was his average walking speed for the entire trip?

   (A) $2\frac{2}{9}$ **(B)** 4 **(C)** $4\frac{4}{9}$ **(D)** $4\frac{1}{2}$ **(E)** 5

2. A square floor with sides of 8 feet is to be completely covered with non-overlapping square tiles, each with sides of 1 foot. If every tile along the outer edge of the floor is black and all other tiles are white, how many black tiles are needed?

   (A) 28 **(B)** 29 **(C)** 30 **(D)** 32 **(E)** 64

3. After a 20-percent decrease in price, the cost of an item is D dollars. What was the price of the item before the decrease?

   (A) $0.75D$ **(B)** $0.80D$ **(C)** $1.20D$ **(D)** $1.25D$ **(E)** $1.5D$

4. On a certain trip, a motorist drove 10 miles at 30 miles per hour, 10 miles at 40 miles per hour, and 10 miles at 50 miles per hour. What portion of her total driving time was spent driving 50 miles per hour?

   (A) $\frac{5}{7}$ **(B)** $\frac{5}{12}$ **(C)** $\frac{1}{3}$ **(D)** $1\frac{13}{51}$ **(E)** $\frac{12}{47}$

Pile A   Pile B

| 1 | 2 | 3 | | 4 | 5 | 6 |

5. In a certain game, to determine how many spaces to move, a player selects a card from pile A and another card from pile B. If the player then moves a number of spaces equal to the sum of the two cards selected, how many different possible moves are there?

   (A) 5 **(B)** 6 **(C)** 7 **(D)** 8 **(E)** 9

6. What is the largest number of non-overlapping sectors that can be created when a circle is crossed by three straight lines?

   (A) 3 **(B)** 4 **(C)** 5 **(D)** 6 **(E)** 7

12

7. At Glenridge High School, 20 percent of the students are seniors. If all of the seniors attended the school play, and 60 percent of all the students attended the play, what percent of the *non-seniors* attended the play?

   (A) 20%   (B) 40%   (C) 50%   (D) 60%   (E) 100%

8. Sally has an amount of money equal to the amount Charles has plus $6. If the amount Charles has is equal to 0.6 the amount that Sally has, then how much money does Charles have?

   (A) $9   (B) $12   (C) $36   (D) $100   (E) $120

9. On a certain street, the houses on the west side have consecutive odd numbers and those on the east side have consecutive even numbers. If only the houses on the east side with numbers 122 through 182 are painted blue, how many houses on the street are painted blue?

   (A) 120   (B) 60   (C) 59   (D) 31   (E) 30

10. The ratio of Victor's weight to Mike's weight is 2:7, and the ratio of Victor's weight to Hank's weight is 3:5. What is the ratio of Hank's weight to Mike's weight?

    (A) 6:35   (B) 5:12   (C) 10:21   (D) 12:5   (E) 35:6

Water Usage in Cubic Feet

11. The water meter at a factory displays the reading above. What is the MINIMUM number of cubic feet of water the factory must use before four of the five digits on the meter are the same?

    (A) 10,000   (B) 1,000   (C) 999   (D) 666   (E) 9

12. During a certain chess tournament, each of six players will play every other player exactly once. How many matches will be played during the tournament?

    (A) 12   (B) 15   (C) 18   (D) 30   (E) 36

13. A telephone call from City *X* to City *Y* costs $1.00 for the first three minutes and $0.25 for every minute thereafter. What is the maximum length of time (in minutes) that a caller could talk for $3.00?

    (A) 8   (B) 10   (C) 11   (D) 12   (E) 13

14. For a certain student, the average of ten test scores is 80. If the highest and the lowest scores are dropped, the average of the remaining scores is 82. What is the average of the highest and lowest scores?

    (A) 68   (B) 72   (C) 78   (D) 81
    (E) Cannot be determined from the information given.

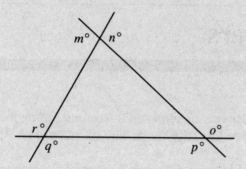

15. In the figure above, $m + n + o + p + q + r =$

(A) 360   (B) 540   (C) 720   (D) 900

(E) Cannot be determined from the information given.

12

Explanatory Answers

1. (C) Watson would almost surely pick (D) here, reasoning that $4\frac{1}{2}$ is the average of 4 and 5, but that's too easy for a difficult question. And, in fact, (D) is incorrect.

   The average speed for the entire trip is the total distance travelled divided by the total time of the trip. Since the entire trip was 2 miles, each leg was 1 mile. Therefore, the time it took Peter to walk from P to Q was $\frac{1}{4}$ hour, and the time it took to walk back from Q to P was $\frac{1}{5}$ hour. So the total walking time was $\frac{1}{4} + \frac{1}{5}$ $= \frac{9}{20}$ hours. The total distance walked was 2 miles, so the average rate of travel was $2 \div \frac{9}{20} = 2 \times \frac{20}{9} = 4\frac{4}{9}$.

2. (A) Most likely, Watson will pick (D), reasoning that there are four sides to a square and that $4 \times 8 = 32$. But this is much too easy. This reasoning overlooks the fact that a corner tile belongs to both of its sides:

8	9	10	11	12	13	14	15
7							16
6							17
5							18
4							19
3							20
2							21
1	28	27	26	25	24	23	22

3. (D) Here Watson is likely to pick (C) (or perhaps [B]), reasoning that $1.2D - .2D = 1D = D$. But the fact that this is so easy should make him suspicious. The correct answer is $1.25D$: 20% of $1.25D = .25D$ and $1.25D - .25D = D$.

4. (E) In this item, there are several misleading clues for Watson to use. He could add 30, 40, and 50 to get 120, and put 50 over that: $\frac{50}{120} = \frac{5}{12}$. Too easy, and wrong. Or he might place 50 over 30 plus 40: $\frac{50}{70} = \frac{5}{7}$. Again, easy but wrong. He might even be so foolish as to think "the leg driven at 50 miles per hour was one of three legs of the journey and 1 out of 3 is $\frac{1}{3}$ and pick (C)." (Ouch! That's really falling off the ladder of difficulty.)

   The correct solution is similar to that for question 1, above. We must find the time spent driving for each of the legs. Again, time is found by the formula: Time = Distance ÷ Rate. So the times for the three legs are:

   $10 \div 30 = \dfrac{1}{3}$

   $10 \div 40 = \dfrac{1}{4}$

   $10 \div 50 = \dfrac{1}{5}$

   Total: $\dfrac{47}{60}$

So the fraction of the time spent driving at 50 miles per hour was $\frac{1}{5} \div \frac{47}{60} = \frac{12}{47}$.

5. (A) Again, there are two easy mistakes for Watson to make. Since there are three cards in each pile, he can reason either that $3 + 3 = 6$ or $3 \times 3 = 9$. Both are too easy, and both are wrong!

    The easiest way to get the correct answer is just to test all of the possibilities. The addition is easy and there aren't that many:

$A + B =$	$A + B =$	$A + B =$
$1 + 4 = 5$	$2 + 4 = 6$	$3 + 4 = 7$
$1 + 5 = 6$	$2 + 5 = 7$	$3 + 5 = 8$
$1 + 6 = 7$	$2 + 6 = 8$	$3 + 6 = 9$

How many *different* moves are possible? Only five: five, six, seven, eight, and nine spaces.

6. (E) Here we have a difficult geometry question with several appealing distractors. First, on a bad day, Watson might think "Three lines, three sectors." But that's clearly wrong. On second reading, he might draw a figure:

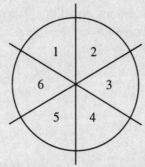

But that's too obvious, so it must be wrong. Trying again:

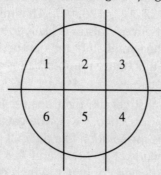

No improvement. At this point, a Holmesian test-taker would reason, "It's got to be more than 6, so the correct choice must be (E)." And (E) it is:

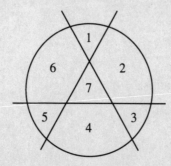

7. (C) Now we're learning how to avoid the typical errors. In this problem, it is very unlikely that (A) or (D) will be correct. And it's a foregone conclusion that (B) is wrong. Since $60 - 20 = 40$, (B) is too easy and must be wrong.

   The solution requires more thought. From the number of those who attended the play, take away the number of seniors:

60% of student body minus 20% of student body = 40% of student body

This 40 percent of the student body comes from the 80 percent who are not seniors. So half, or 50 percent, of the non-seniors must have attended.

8. (A) Here, Watson would be very content to select either (B) ($6 + 6 = 12$) or, more likely, (C) ($6 \times 6 = 36$). The answer, however, is (A).

   Using S to stand for the amount Sally has and C for the amount Charles has, we can express the information as follows:

$S = C + 6$

$C = 0.6S$

Treating these as simultaneous equations, we can substitute $C + 6$ for S in the second equation and solve for C:

$C = 0.6(C + 6)$

$C = 0.6C + 0.36$

$0.4C = 0.36$

$C = 9$

9. (D) Here, the misleading clues point in two different directions. One, a careless reader might overlook the fact that the east side of the street uses consecutive *even* numbers, e.g., 122, 124, 126, etc. That mistake leads to (B) or (C). Two, even disregarding that error, Watson is likely to reason: $182 - 122 = 60$, and (since we have only the even half of the numbers, not the odds) $60 \div 2 = 30$. Too easy! The trick is that house number 122 is also painted blue, so there are $30 + 1 = 31$ blue houses.

10. (C) Here you can almost get the right answer just by eliminating misleading clues. If you multiply 2×3 and 7×5, you get the numbers 6 and 35. Such a simple process can't be the solution to a difficult problem, so you can eliminate both (A) and (E). Similarly, $2 + 3 = 5$ and $7 + 5 = 12$; also too easy, so you eliminate (B) and (D), leaving only (C), which is correct.

   The solution requires that you find a common multiple for 2 and 3 and change the ratios so that the Victor term is the same in both:

$\frac{2}{7} = \frac{2 \times 3}{7 \times 3} = \frac{6}{21}$

$\frac{3}{5} = \frac{3 \times 2}{5 \times 2} = \frac{6}{10}$

Now you have the ratios:

Victor:Mike::6:21

Victor:Hank::6:10

So Hank:Mike::10:21.

11. (D) The most common error here would be (A). Watson recognizes that 71,111 plus 10,000 is equal to 81,111—a number in which four of the digits are the same. The difficulty with this reasoning is that 10,000 is not the smallest number that will do the trick. 71,111 plus 666 is equal to 71,777—a number in which four of the digits are the same!

12. (B) Here, Watson is likely to be tempted to do something as easy as multiplying 6×6 to get 36. But it's too easy. So in an attempt to think like Holmes, Watson reasons, "That's too easy. I bet I need to divide or multiply by 2. So it's either (C) or (E)." Good try, Watson, but that's still too easy.

  The solution is to see that each player plays the other five players: $6 \times 5 = 30$. But each match involves two players: $30 \div 2 = 15$.

13. (C) By this point we may assume that Watson has learned not to take the bait, so there is no chance that he will think $3.00 \div 0.25 = 12$. So the correct choice cannot be (D). Once over this hurdle, if he reasons carefully, he can answer correctly. Out of the $3.00, the first dollar is for the first three minutes. This leaves $2.00 for the additional minutes: $\$2.00 \div \$0.25 = 8$. So the total time is the original three minutes plus the additional eight, or 11 minutes.

14. (B) The one thing Watson should not guess here is (E). Remember, it is unlikely that the answer to a difficult question will be "cannot be determined." The correct choice is (B). Since the average of the ten scores is 80, the total of the ten scores is $80 \times 10 = 800$. The total of the eight scores remaining after the high and low scores are dropped is $8 \times 82 = 656$. This means that the two dropped scores totalled $800 - 656 = 144$, so their average is $144 \div 2 = 72$.

15. (C) Here we have a similar situation. Watson will be tempted to pick (E), since the drawing doesn't provide much information. But the solution is supposed to be difficult, since this is a difficult question.

  One way of understanding the problem is to see that each of the lettered angles, when combined with an angle of the triangle, forms a straight line:

$m + x = 180$

$n + x = 180$

$o + y = 180$

$p + y = 180$

$q + z = 180$

$r + z = 180$

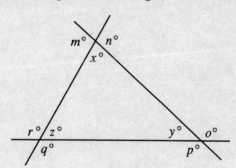

This means that:

$m + x + n + x + o + y + p + y + q + z + r + z = 6(180)$

$m + n + o + p + q + r + x + y + z + x + y + z = 6(180)$

And since $x + y + z = 180$:

$m + n + o + p + q + r + 180 + 180 = 6(180)$

$m + n + o + p + q + r = 4(180) = 720$

Problem-Solving: Arithmetic

✔ **Objectives**

To learn basic attack strategies for arithmetic items.

To learn advanced Holmesian strategies to simplify or avoid arithmetic manipulations.

To learn to handle complicated application problems.

To learn specific strategies for the five most important areas of arithmetic.

To learn to use the answer choices themselves to generate solutions.

1. **Arithmetic Manipulations**
   - **Simplifying**
   - **Factoring**
   - **Calculation Shortcuts**

2. **Arithmetic Applications**

3. **Common Types of Problem-Solving**
   - **Properties of Numbers**
   - **Percents**
   - **Ratios**
   - **Averages**
   - **Proportions**

4. **Testing the Test**

13

In this chapter, we discuss three topics: techniques for handling pure arithmetic manipulations, strategies for dealing with problems that require some original thinking, and hints for dealing with some often-used question types.

Arithmetic Manipulations

Watson's Favorites

Some easy problem-solving questions ask for nothing more than simple addition, subtraction, multiplication, or division. These are Watson's favorites, since the obvious and correct strategy is to perform the indicated operation.

FOR SIMPLE ARITHMETIC MANIPULATIONS, JUST DO THE OPERATIONS.

EXAMPLES:

$\frac{8}{9} - \frac{7}{8} =$

(A) $\frac{1}{72}$ (B) $\frac{15}{72}$ (C) $\frac{1}{7}$ (D) $\frac{1}{8}$ (E) $\frac{15}{7}$

The answer is (A), and the arithmetic is so simple that you should not hesitate to perform the subtraction indicated:

$$\frac{8}{9} - \frac{7}{8} = \frac{64 - 63}{72} = \frac{1}{72}$$

$\sqrt{1 - \left(\frac{2}{9} + \frac{1}{36} + \frac{1}{18}\right)} =$

(A) $\frac{1}{5}$ (B) $\sqrt{\frac{2}{3}}$ (C) $\frac{5}{6}$ (D) 1 (E) $\sqrt{3}$

Again, the arithmetic is not that complicated, so you should perform the indicated operations:

$$\sqrt{1 - \left(\frac{2}{9} + \frac{1}{36} + \frac{1}{18}\right)} =$$

$$\sqrt{1 - \left(\frac{8}{36} + \frac{1}{36} + \frac{2}{36}\right)} =$$

$$\sqrt{1 - \frac{11}{36}} = \sqrt{\frac{36}{36} - \frac{11}{36}} = \sqrt{\frac{25}{36}} = \frac{5}{6}$$

Holmes Helps

Other manipulation questions are so complicated that it would take too long to perform them as written. In such cases, the questions were not written to test whether you know the basic manipulation but whether you can find an alternative solution. The test-writer has provided you with an escape route from the maze—if you can find it.

IF THE ARITHMETIC IS TOO COMPLICATED, LOOK FOR ONE OF THE FOLLOWING ESCAPE ROUTES: SIMPLIFYING, FACTORING, OR APPROXIMATING.

1. Simplifying

EXAMPLE:

$$\frac{1}{2} \times \frac{2}{3} \times \frac{3}{4} \times \frac{4}{5} \times \frac{5}{6} \times \frac{6}{7} \times \frac{7}{8} =$$

(A) $\frac{1}{56}$ **(B)** $\frac{1}{8}$ **(C)** $\frac{28}{37}$ **(D)** $\frac{41}{43}$ **(E)** $\frac{55}{56}$

The fact that performing this operation as it is written would be tedious is a clue that an alternate route has been provided. The alternative is to simplify by cancelling:

$$\frac{1}{2} \times \frac{2}{3} \times \frac{3}{4} \times \frac{4}{5} \times \frac{5}{6} \times \frac{6}{7} \times \frac{7}{8} = \frac{1}{8}$$

2. Factoring

EXAMPLES:

$$48(1) + 48(2) + 48(3) + 48(4) =$$

(A) 48   **(B)** 96   **(C)** 480   **(D)** 960   **(E)** 7,200

You could do the operations as indicated, but the fact that the process would be very time-consuming indicates that there is an alternate solution. You can factor:

$$48(1) + 48(2) + 48(3) + 48(4) =$$
$$48(1 + 2 + 3 + 4) = 48 \times 10 = 480$$

So the correct choice is (C).

$$86(37) - 37(85) =$$

(A) 0   **(B)** 1   **(C)** 37   **(D)** 85   **(E)** 86

Again, factoring is the shorter route:

$$86(37) - 37(85) = 37(86 - 85) = 37(1) = 37$$

So the correct choice is (C).

There are three factoring patterns you should memorize and always be alert for.

LEARN THE FOLLOWING PATTERNS AND BE ON THE LOOKOUT FOR OPPORTUNITIES TO USE THEM.

$$m^2 - n^2 = (m + n)(m - n)$$

$$m^2 + 2mn + n^2 = (m + n)(m + n)$$

$$m^2 - 2mn + n^2 = (m - n)(m - n)$$

The first is the most important. The second is less important, but it is still used occasionally. The third is the least important, but it is something you should know; and it is a pattern that is easily spotted.

The first pattern is called the "difference of two squares." (It is the square of one number minus the square of another.)

EXAMPLES:

$74^2 - 26^2 =$
(A) 26   **(B)** 48   **(C)** 74   **(D)** 4,800   **(E)** 5,678

The answer is (D):

$$74^2 - 26^2 = (74 + 26)(74 - 26) = 100 \times 48 = 4,800$$

$125^2 - 25^2 =$
(A) 25   **(B)** 100   **(C)** 125   **(D)** 175   **(E)** 15,000

The answer is (E):

$$125^2 - 25^2 = (125 + 25)(125 - 25) = 150 \times 100 = 15,000$$

Here are some questions in the second pattern.

EXAMPLES:

$36^2 + 2(36)(64) + 64^2 =$
(A) 3,600   **(B)** 6,400   **(C)** 10,000   **(D)** 10,300   **(E)** 14,400

The answer is (C):

$$36^2 + 2(36)(64) + 64^2 = (36 + 64)(36 + 64) = 100 \times 100 = 10,000$$

$14^2 + 2(14)(16) + 16^2 =$
(A) 28   **(B)** 48   **(C)** 360   **(D)** 900   **(E)** 2,700

The answer is (D):

$$14^2 + 2(14)(16) + 16^2 = (14 + 16)(14 + 16) = 30 \times 30 = 900$$

Finally, here is a question using the last pattern.

EXAMPLE:

$25^2 - 2(25)(15) + 15^2 =$
(A) 100   **(B)** 400   **(C)** 900   **(D)** 1,600   **(E)** 2,500

The answer is (A):

$$25^2 - 2(25)(15) + 15^2 = (25 - 15)(25 - 15) = 10 \times 10 = 100$$

13

3. Approximation

EXAMPLES:

$\dfrac{0.2521 \times 8.012}{1.014}$ is approximately equal to

(A) 0.25   **(B)** 0.5   **(C)** 1.0   **(D)** 1.5   **(E)** 2.0

The operations indicated here are very tedious, so you are not expected to do all the arithmetic. Instead, you are specifically invited to approximate. Round 0.2521 to 0.25, 8.012 to 8, and 1.014 to 1:

$\dfrac{0.25 \times 8}{1} = 2$

And (E) must be the correct answer.

Which of the following fractions is the largest?

(A) $\dfrac{111}{221}$ **(B)** $\dfrac{75}{151}$ **(C)** $\dfrac{333}{998}$ **(D)** $\dfrac{113}{225}$ **(E)** $\dfrac{101}{301}$

One way of comparing fractions is to convert them to decimals by dividing the numerator by the denominator. That process, however, would obviously be time-consuming, so there must be an alternative.

The alternative is to approximate. A quick glance reveals that (A), (B), and (D) are all very close to $\frac{1}{2}$. (Their denominators are just about twice their numerators.) (C) and (E) are closer to $\frac{1}{3}$. Since $\frac{1}{3} < \frac{1}{2}$, you can eliminate (C) and (E).

Now take a closer look at the remaining three choices. (A) and (D) are both slightly more than $\frac{1}{2}$ (the numerator is a little more than double the denominator), but (B) is slightly less than $\frac{1}{2}$ (the numerator is slightly less than double the denominator). So we eliminate (B).

Now the choice is between (A) $\frac{111}{221}$ and (D) $\frac{113}{225}$. Since $\frac{1}{221}$ is larger than $\frac{1}{225}$, (A) is slightly larger than (D). And that's all that's needed to prove that (A) is the answer.

Calculation Shortcuts

Here are some hints to help you do calculations more quickly.

1. Divisibility

If a number is even, then it is divisible by 2; for example, 9,999,992 is divisible by 2.

If a number ends in 0 or 5, it is divisible by 5; for example, 1,005 and 1,230 are divisible by 5.

If the sum of the digits of a number is divisible by 3, then the number is divisible by 3; for example, 12,327. Since $1 + 2 + 3 + 2 + 7 = 15$ and 15 is divisible by 3, 12,327 is divisible by 3.

2. The Flying-X

Ordinarily when we add or subtract fractions, we look for a lowest common denominator. But that's only because we want the result in lowest terms for reasons of convenience. As long as you are prepared to reduce your final result, you don't really need to use a lowest common denominator. Instead, you can add or subtract any two fractions in the following way:

THE FLYING-X METHOD OF ADDING AND SUBTRACTING FRACTIONS

$$\frac{a}{b} + \frac{c}{d} = \frac{a}{b} + \frac{c}{d} = \frac{ad + bc}{bd}$$

$$\frac{a}{b} - \frac{c}{d} = \frac{a}{b} - \frac{c}{d} = \frac{ad - bc}{bd}$$

The method is called the "flying-x" because of the picture it creates—an x flying above the ground. (Also, it helps you fly through the calculation.) The steps are:

1. Find the new denominator by multiplying the old denominators.
2. Multiply the numerator of the first fraction by the denominator of the second fraction.
3. Multiply the denominator of the first fraction by the numerator of the second fraction.
4. Add (or subtract) the results of steps (2) and (3).

EXAMPLES:

$$\frac{4}{5} + \frac{3}{4} = \frac{4}{5} + \frac{3}{4} = \frac{16 + 15}{20} = \frac{31}{20}$$

$$\frac{4}{5} - \frac{3}{4} = \frac{4}{5} - \frac{3}{4} = \frac{16 - 15}{20} = \frac{1}{20}$$

Of course, this method does not guarantee your results will be in lowest terms, but you can correct that by reducing.

3. Decimal/Fraction Equivalents

You should memorize the following decimal/fraction equivalents:

$\frac{1}{2} = 0.50$

$\frac{1}{3} = 0.33\frac{1}{3} = 0.333 \ldots$

$\frac{1}{4} = 0.25$

$\frac{1}{5} = 0.20$

$\frac{1}{6} = 0.16\frac{2}{3} = 0.1666 \ldots$

$\frac{1}{7} = 0.14\frac{2}{7} = 0.1428 \ldots$

$\frac{1}{8} = 0.125$

$\frac{1}{9} = 0.11\frac{1}{9} = 0.1111 \ldots$

13

What about fractions like $\frac{4}{9}$ or $\frac{5}{8}$? There is no need to memorize more equivalents; just multiply. Since $\frac{1}{9}$ is approximately 0.111, $\frac{4}{9}$ is approximately 4×0.111, or 0.444; and since $\frac{1}{8}$ is 0.125, $\frac{5}{8}$ is 5×0.125, or 0.625.

Sometimes it is easier to use fractions than decimals in a calculation.

EXAMPLES:

$0.125 \times 0.125 \times 64 =$
(A) 0.625   **(B)** 0.125   **(C)** 0.5   **(D)** 1   **(E)** 8

The answer is (D). The problem can be solved quickly if you convert 0.125 to its fraction equivalent $\frac{1}{8}$:

$$\frac{1}{8} \times \frac{1}{8} \times 64 = \frac{1}{64} \times 64 = 1$$

$\dfrac{0.111 \times 0.666}{0.166 \times 0.125}$ is approximately

(A) 6.8   **(B)** 4.3   **(C)** 3.6   **(D)** 1.6   **(E)** 0.9

Convert the decimals to their fractional approximations.

$$\frac{\dfrac{1}{9} \times \dfrac{2}{3}}{\dfrac{1}{6} \times \dfrac{1}{8}} = \frac{2}{27} \div \frac{1}{48} = \frac{2}{27} \times 48 =$$

$$\frac{96}{27} = 3\frac{5}{9} \cong 3.555$$

The final conversion can even be done in your head. Since $\frac{1}{9} \cong .111$, $\frac{5}{9} \cong 5 \times .111 = .555$.

Arithmetic Manipulations (Answers, page 263)

1. $\frac{1}{9} + \frac{1}{10} =$

   (A) $\frac{1}{90}$ (B) $\frac{1}{45}$ (C) $\frac{2}{19}$ (D) $\frac{19}{90}$ (E) $\frac{1}{3}$

2. $\frac{1}{3} + \frac{1}{4} + \frac{1}{5} =$

   (A) $\frac{1}{60}$ (B) $\frac{1}{20}$ (C) $\frac{1}{10}$ (D) $\frac{47}{60}$ (E) $\frac{65}{64}$

3. $\frac{12}{11} - \frac{11}{12} =$

   (A) $\frac{1}{121}$ (B) $\frac{1}{12}$ (C) $\frac{1}{11}$ (D) $\frac{23}{132}$ (E) $\frac{1}{2}$

4. $\frac{8}{7} - \frac{8}{9} =$

   (A) $-\frac{16}{63}$ (B) 0 (C) $\frac{16}{63}$ (D) $\frac{1}{4}$ (E) 4

5. $\dfrac{\frac{3}{5} \times \frac{5}{9} \times \frac{9}{13}}{\frac{13}{12} \times \frac{12}{11} \times \frac{11}{3}} =$

   (A) $\frac{9}{169}$ (B) $\frac{12}{123}$ (C) $\frac{7}{47}$ (D) $\frac{3}{5}$ (E) 1

6. $\frac{3}{11} \times \frac{11}{13} \times \frac{13}{15} \times \frac{15}{17} =$

   (A) $\frac{1}{17}$ (B) $\frac{1}{11}$ (C) $\frac{3}{17}$ (D) $\frac{1}{5}$ (E) $\frac{1}{3}$

7. Which of the following numbers is divisible by both 3 and 88?
   (A) 88,888,888 (B) 8,888,888 (C) 888,888 (D) 88,888 (E) 8,888

8. Which of the following numbers is divisible by both 11 and 3?
   (A) 111,111,111 (B) 11,111,111 (C) 1,111,111 (D) 111,111 (E) 11,111

9. $(0.506 \times 4.072) \div 4.08$ is approximately

   (A) $\frac{1}{4}$ (B) $\frac{1}{2}$ (C) 1 (D) 2 (E) 4

10. $\left(\frac{0.889}{0.666}\right) \div \left(\frac{0.333}{0.625}\right)$ is approximately

    (A) $\frac{1}{27}$ (B) $\frac{1}{16}$ (C) $\frac{1}{2}$ (D) $\frac{5}{7}$ (E) $\frac{5}{2}$

11. Which of the following fractions is the LEAST?

    (A) $\frac{12}{119}$ (B) $\frac{1}{10}$ (C) $\frac{2}{21}$ (D) $\frac{4}{39}$ (E) $\frac{7}{69}$

13

12. $12,345(1) + 12,345(2) + 12,345(3) + 12,345(4) =$

(A) 66,667   (B) 81,818   (C) 99,999   (D) 123,450   (E) 127,978

13. $510^2 - 490^2 =$

(A) 16,000   (B) 18,917   (C) 19,470   (D) 20,000   (E) 24,000

14. $(16)^2 + 2(9)(16) + 81 =$

(A) 444   (B) 500   (C) 625   (D) 875   (E) 900

15. $\dfrac{1}{10^{22}} - \dfrac{1}{10^{23}} =$

(A) $\dfrac{1}{10}$ (B) $\dfrac{9}{10^{23}}$ (C) $\dfrac{1}{10^{23}}$ (D) $\dfrac{-1}{10}$ (E) $\dfrac{-1}{10^{22}}$

Arithmetic Applications

On each SAT, there are a few arithmetic questions that require some original thinking, and Watson often has difficulty with these items. Why should Watson have trouble with arithmetic questions? Because he fails to attack them in a systematic fashion. When Watson can't envision the needed sequence of operations all at once, he goes off in just any direction, adding and subtracting, multiplying and dividing, until he finally gets a wrong answer or gets so discouraged he abandons the problem as too difficult.

Holmes, on the other hand, thrives on such items because he analyzes them step by step. He knows that the question stem gives him all the clues needed to solve the mystery, if he can only put them together in the right order. Even when the correct answer to the question is "Cannot be determined," Holmes can *prove* that is the correct answer. (He doesn't pick "Cannot be determined" just because he finds the question difficult.)

Holmes' Method for Solving Complicated Problems

1. What is the question to be answered?
2. What information have I been given?
3. How can I bridge the gap between (1) and (2)?
4. Execute the needed operations.

Notice that Holmes doesn't start doing arithmetic (4) until he has formulated his solution to the problem.

Here is how the method works:

EXAMPLE:

If the senior class has 360 students, of whom $\frac{5}{12}$ are women, and the junior class has 350 students, of whom $\frac{4}{7}$ are women, how many more women are there in the junior class than in the senior class?

(A) $(350-360)(\frac{4}{7}-\frac{5}{12})$

(B) $\dfrac{(350-360)(\frac{4}{7}-\frac{5}{12})}{2}$

(C) $(\frac{4}{7} \times \frac{5}{12})(360-350)$

(D) $(\frac{4}{7} \times 350) - (\frac{5}{12} \times 360)$

(E) $(\frac{5}{12} \times 350) - (\frac{4}{7} \times 350)$

This is a good question to illustrate logical thinking, because you don't even have to do the arithmetic. All you need to do is set up the problem.

Step 1: **What is the question to be answered?** If the senior class has 360 students, of whom $\frac{5}{12}$ are women, and the junior class has 350 students, of whom $\frac{4}{7}$ are women, how many more women are there in the junior class than in the senior class?

13

Depending on how complex the problem is, Holmes might make a note of what is required:

Women Juniors – Women Seniors

Step 2: **What information am I given?** The question states the total number of students in each class and the fraction who are women.

Step 3: **How can I bridge the gap?** Multiplying the total number by the fraction who are women will fill in the blanks in the statement in Step 1.

Step 4: **Execute.** The solution is ($\frac{4}{7} \times 350$) minus ($\frac{5}{12} \times 360$), which is choice (D).

Here is another question to illustrate how Holmes breaks a solution down into several steps:

> **EXAMPLE:**
>
> If the price of candy increases from 5 pounds for $7 to 3 pounds for $7, how much less candy (in pounds) can be purchased for $3.50 at the new price than at the old price?
>
> (A) $\frac{2}{7}$ (B) $1\frac{17}{35}$ (C) $3\frac{34}{35}$ (D) 1   (E) 2

Step 1: **What is the question to be answered?** If the price of candy increases from 5 pounds for $7 to 3 pounds for $7, how much less candy (in pounds) can be purchased for $3.50 at the new price than at the old price? In other words, you are looking for the amount $3.50 used to buy minus the amount $3.50 now buys. And because the question is fairly complex, Holmes might write this down:

---

amt. $3.50 old – amt. $3.50 new

Step 2: **What information am I given?** The question gives pounds and dollars for two different prices.

Step 3: **How can I bridge the gap?** Find the cost per pound and divide the amount you have to spend by the cost per pound. The result is the quantity you can buy.

Step 4: **Execute.** If $7 buys 5 pounds, the cost is $7 \div 5 = \frac{7}{5}$ dollars per pound. $3.50 = \frac{7}{2}$ dollars, and $\frac{7}{2} \div \frac{7}{5} = \frac{7}{2} \times \frac{5}{7} = \frac{5}{2}$. If $7 buys 3 pounds, the cost is $7 \div 3 = \frac{7}{3}$ dollars per pound, and $\frac{7}{2} \div \frac{7}{3} = \frac{7}{2} \times \frac{3}{7} = \frac{3}{2}$. Finally, $\frac{5}{2} - \frac{3}{2} = 1$. So the correct answer is (D). (As was suggested above, we used fractions rather than decimals. This made the arithmetic in Step 4 easier.)

Learning to think in a systematic way is not easy, nor is it a skill that can be acquired just by reading about it. In this respect, systematic thinking is like playing a sport or a musical instrument. You can't just read a book about basketball or the violin and expect to become a star player or virtuoso overnight. Still, the more you practice logical thinking, the better you'll become at it. So as you do practice problems later in this book, try to break down your solutions to difficult questions into steps.

Some Common Types of Problem-Solving

There are some common types of math problems that appear so frequently that you must be familiar with them and know how to solve them almost automatically.

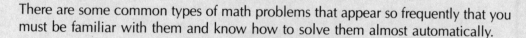

Properties of Numbers

You should be familiar with the following principles of odd and even numbers:

EVEN + EVEN = EVEN (and EVEN − EVEN = EVEN)
EVEN + ODD = ODD (and EVEN − ODD = ODD)
ODD + EVEN = ODD (and ODD − EVEN = ODD)
ODD + ODD = EVEN (and ODD − ODD = EVEN)
EVEN × EVEN = EVEN
EVEN × ODD = EVEN
ODD × EVEN = EVEN
ODD × ODD = ODD

Note: The multiplication properties do *not* hold for division. This is because division may not result in a whole number; for example, $2 \div 4 = \frac{1}{2}$, a fraction. Odd and even are properties of integers, not fractions.

Questions based on these principles usually ask that you make a judgment about the "structure" of a number.

> **EXAMPLE:**
>
> If n is an odd integer, which of the following must also be odd?
> I. $n + n$
> II. $n + n + n$
> III. $n \times n \times n$
> (A) I only   (B) II only   (C) III only   (D) II and III only   (E) I, II, and III

The answer is (D). As for I, since n is odd, $n + n$ must be even. As for II, since $n + n$ is even, $n + (n + n)$ must be odd. And as for III, since n is odd, $n \times n$ is odd, and so $n \times (n \times n)$ also is odd.

In the example just studied, the question specifies that n is an odd number. You get a different answer if the question is changed to specify that n is an even number.

> **EXAMPLE:**
>
> If n is an even integer, which of the following must also be even?
> I. $n + n$
> II. $n + n + n$
> III. $n \times n \times n$
> (A) I only   (B) II only   (C) III only   (D) II and III only   (E) I, II, and III

Now the answer is (E).

Some structures are odd or even no matter what the value of n.

13

> **EXAMPLE:**
>
> If n is an integer, which of the following must be even?
>   I. $2n$
>   II. $2n + n$
>   III. $2n \times n$
>   (A) I only   (B) II only   (C) III only   (D) I and II only   (E) I and III only

The answer is (E). As for item I, $2n$ has the structure $2 \times n$, so no matter what the value of n, $2n$ must be even. As for III, since $2n$ is even, $2n \times n$ must be even (an even number times any other number always yields an even number). II, however, may or may not be even. Although we know that $2n$ is even, $2n + n$ will be even only if n is even (even plus even); if n is odd, $2n + n$ will be odd (even plus odd).

A variation on this type of question uses the phrase *consecutive integers*.

CONSECUTIVE INTEGERS ARE INTEGERS IN A ROW: 3, 4, 5, AND 6 ARE CONSECUTIVE INTEGERS, AS ARE -2, -1, 0, 1, AND 2.

Since a number in a series of consecutive integers is just one more than its predecessor and one less than its successor, consecutive integers can be represented as: n, $n + 1$, $n + 2$, $n + 3$, and so on.

> **EXAMPLE:**
>
> Which of the following represents the product of two consecutive integers?
>   (A) $2n + 1$ (B) $2n + n$ (C) $2n^2$ (D) $n^2 + 1$ (E) $n^2 + n$

The answer is (E). If n is an integer, the next larger consecutive integer is just one more: $n + 1$. And the product of n and $n + 1$ is $n(n + 1) = n^2 + n$.

Sometimes a question will ask about consecutive even numbers or consecutive odd numbers.

> **EXAMPLES:**
>
> If n is an odd number, which of the following represents the third odd number following n?
>   (A) $n + 3$ (B) $n + 4$ (C) $n + 6$ (D) $3n + 3$ (E) $4n + 4$

The answer is (C). If n is an odd number, the next odd number is $n + 2$, then $n + 4$, then $n + 6$.

> If n is the first number in a series of three consecutive even numbers, which of the following represents the sum of the three numbers?
>   (A) $n + 2$ (B) $n + 4$ (C) $n + 6$ (D) $3n + 6$ (E) $6(3n)$

The answer is (D). Since n is even, the next even number is $n + 2$ and the one following that is $n + 4$. The sum of n, $n + 2$, and $n + 4$ is $n + n + 2 + n + 4 = 3n + 6$.

Notice that in the two previous examples, it was stipulated that n was either odd or even. This is important, because $n + 2$ can be either odd or even, depending on whether n is odd or even.

EXAMPLES:

If n is any integer, which of the following is always an odd integer?
(A) $n - 1$ **(B)** $n + 1$ **(C)** $n + 2$ **(D)** $2n + 1$ **(E)** $2n + 2$

The answer is (D). Since n can be either even or odd, $n - 1$, $n + 1$, and $n + 2$ can be either even or odd. $2n + 1$, however, must always be odd. No matter what n is, $2n$ is even, and $2n + 1$ must be odd. By the same reasoning, (E) must always be even.

The behavior of positive and negative numbers is also a basis for questions. You should know the following principles:

POSITIVE × POSITIVE = POSITIVE (and POSITIVE ÷ POSITIVE = POSITIVE)
POSITIVE × NEGATIVE = NEGATIVE (and POSITIVE ÷ NEGATIVE = NEGATIVE)
NEGATIVE × POSITIVE = NEGATIVE (and NEGATIVE ÷ POSITIVE = NEGATIVE)
NEGATIVE × NEGATIVE = POSITIVE (and NEGATIVE ÷ NEGATIVE = POSITIVE)

If n is a negative number, which of the following must be positive?
  I. $2n$
  II. n^2
  III. n^5
(A) I only   **(B)** II only   **(C)** III only   **(D)** I and II only   **(E)** II and III only

The answer is (B). Since n is negative, $2n$ must also be negative. As for III, since n is negative, $(n \times n) \times (n \times n) \times n$ is a positive times a positive, which is a positive, multiplied by a negative. So the final result is negative. II, however, must be positive, since n^2 is just $n \times n$, and a negative times a negative yields a positive.

Finally, fractions have a peculiar characteristic that might be the basis for a question.

THE RESULT OBTAINED FROM MULTIPLYING A FRACTION BY ITSELF IS SMALLER THAN THE ORIGINAL FRACTION; FOR EXAMPLE, $\frac{1}{2} \times \frac{1}{2} \times \frac{1}{2} = \frac{1}{8}$ AND $\frac{1}{8} < \frac{1}{2}$.

EXAMPLE:

If $0 < x < 1$, which of the following is the largest?
(A) x **(B)** $2x$ **(C)** x^2 **(D)** x^3 **(E)** $x + 1$

The answer is (E). When a fraction is raised to a power, the result is smaller than the original fraction, so (C) and (D) are smaller than (A). (B), however, is double (A), so (B) is larger. But finally, (E) is larger than (B). $2x$ is equal to $x + x$, and since $1 > x$, (E) must be larger than (B).

If you know the general principles just discussed and apply them correctly, you should be able to handle any question about properties of numbers. If, however, you find that you are having trouble, fall back on the simplistic yet very effective technique of substitution.

AS A LAST RESORT, TRY SUBSTITUTING NUMBERS.

Just pick some values and test them in the choices.

EXAMPLE:

If $-1 < x < 0$, which of the following is the largest?

(A) -1 (B) x (C) $2x$ (D) x^3 (E) $x - 1$

The correct choice is (D), but the problem is a little tricky. You might want to test a value, for example, $-\frac{1}{2}$. On the assumption that $x = -\frac{1}{2}$, the choices have these values:

(A) -1 (B) $-\frac{1}{2}$ (C) -1 (D) $-\frac{1}{8}$ (E) $-1\frac{1}{2}$

The largest of these is $-\frac{1}{8}$.

Properties of Numbers (Answers, page 264)

1. If n is an even number, all of the following must also be even EXCEPT
   (A) n^3 **(B)** n^2 **(C)** $2n$ **(D)** $2n + n$ **(E)** $2n + 5$

2. If $3n$ is an even number, which of the following must be an odd number?
   (A) n **(B)** $2n$ **(C)** $n + 1$ **(D)** $n + 2$ **(E)** n^2

3. If n is an integer, which of the following must be an odd number?
   (A) $n + 1$ **(B)** $2n$ **(C)** $2n + 1$ **(D)** $2(n + 1)$ **(E)** $3(n + 1)$

4. If $m, n, o, p,$ and q are integers, then $m(n + o)(p - q)$ must be even when which of the following is even?
   (A) $m + n$ **(B)** $n + p$ **(C)** m **(D)** o **(E)** p

5. If n is an integer, which of the following *must* be even?
   (A) $n - 1$ **(B)** $n + 1$ **(C)** $3n + 1$ **(D)** $2n + 2$ **(E)** $2n + n$

6. If p is the smallest of three consecutive integers, $p, q,$ and r, what is the sum of q and r expressed in terms of p?
   (A) $3p + 3$ **(B)** $3p + 1$ **(C)** $2p + 3$ **(D)** $2p + 1$ **(E)** $2p$

7. If the fifth number in a series of five consecutive integers has the value $n + 3$, what is the first number in the series expressed in terms of n?
   (A) 0 **(B)** 1 **(C)** $n - 1$ **(D)** $n - 3$ **(E)** $-4n$

8. If n is negative, all BUT which of the following must also be negative?
   (A) n^5 **(B)** n^3 **(C)** $\frac{1}{n}$ **(D)** $\frac{1}{n^2}$ **(E)** $\frac{1}{n^3}$

9. If $x = -1$, which of the following is the largest?
   (A) $2x$ **(B)** x **(C)** $\frac{x}{2}$ **(D)** x^2 **(E)** x^3

10. If x is greater than zero but less than 1, which of the following is the largest?
    (A) $\frac{1}{x^2}$ **(B)** $\frac{1}{x}$ **(C)** x **(D)** x^2 **(E)** x^3

Percents

Aside from the very basic operation of taking a percent of some number (for example, 25 percent of 60 = 15), there are really only two different kinds of percent questions. One question asks for the ratio of two numbers expressed as a percent (for example, 4 is what percent of 20?); the other asks about percent change in a quantity.

All percent questions in the first category can be solved by a simple Holmesian device called the "this-of-that" strategy. Compare the following questions:

What percent is 4 of 20?

4 is what percent of 20?

Of 20, what percent is 4?

The questions are equivalent, for they all ask for the same thing: express $\frac{4}{20}$ as a percent. Notice also that in each there is the phrase "of 20" and the other number, 4.

Generally, then, these questions all have the form:

What percent is this of that?

This is what percent of that?

Of that, what percent is this?

You can solve any question of this type using the "this-of-that" strategy.

THIS-OF-THAT: CREATE A FRACTION IN WHICH THE NUMBER IN THE PHRASE "OF THAT" IS THE DENOMINATOR AND THE OTHER NUMBER IN THE QUESTION (THE "THIS") IS THE NUMERATOR. CONVERT THE FRACTION TO A PERCENT.

EXAMPLES:

If a jar contains 24 white marbles and 48 black marbles, then what percent of all the marbles in the jar are black?

(A) 20%   (B) 25%   (C) $33\frac{1}{3}$%   (D) 60%   (E) $66\frac{2}{3}$%

Using the "this-of-that" strategy, we create a fraction:

$$\frac{\text{black marbles}}{\text{of all marbles}} = \frac{48}{24 + 48} = \frac{48}{72} = \frac{2}{3} = 66\frac{2}{3}\%$$

Three friends shared the cost of a tape recorder. If Andy, Barbara, and Donna each paid $12, $30, and $18, respectively, then Donna paid what percent of the cost of the tape recorder?

(A) 10%   (B) 20%   (C) $33\frac{1}{3}$%   (D) 50%   (E) $66\frac{2}{3}$%

In this question, the phrase "of the cost" establishes the denominator. The cost is 12 + 30 + 18 = 60. The numerator is the other item in the question, Donna's contribution:

$$\frac{\text{Donna's}}{\text{Total}} = \frac{18}{60} = \frac{3}{10} = 30\%$$

The other type of percent question asks about the percent change in a quantity. The Holmesian strategy for such questions is the "change-over" formula.

EXAMPLE:

If the price of an item increased from $5.00 to $5.25, what was the percent increase in the price?

(A) 50%　**(B)** 25%　**(C)** 20%　**(D)** 5%　**(E)** 4%

The answer is (D).

CHANGE-OVER STRATEGY: TO FIND PERCENT CHANGE, CREATE A FRACTION. PUT THE CHANGE IN THE QUANTITY OVER THE ORIGINAL AMOUNT. CONVERT THE FRACTION TO A PERCENT.

$$\frac{\text{Change}}{\text{Original Amount}} = \frac{5.25 - 5.00}{5.00} = \frac{0.25}{5.00} = 0.05 = 5\%$$

The "change-over strategy" works for decreases as well.

EXAMPLE:

If the population of a town was 20,000 in 1970 and 16,000 in 1980, what was the percent decline in the town's population?

(A) 50%　**(B)** 25%　**(C)** 20%　**(D)** 10%　**(E)** 5%

$$\frac{\text{Change}}{\text{Original Amount}} = \frac{20,000 - 16,000}{20,000} = \frac{4,000}{20,000} = \frac{1}{4} = 20\%$$

So there was a 20-percent decline in the town's population.

Be careful that you don't confuse the two strategies. Compare the following three questions.

EXAMPLES:

If 20 people attended Professor Rodriguez's class on Monday and 25 attended on Tuesday, the number of people who attended on Monday was what percent of the number who attended on Tuesday?

(A) 5%　**(B)** 20%　**(C)** 25%　**(D)** 80%　**(E)** 125%

If 20 people attended Professor Rodriguez's class on Monday and 25 attended on Tuesday, the number of people who attended on Tuesday was what percent of the number who attended on Monday?

(A) 5%　**(B)** 20%　**(C)** 25%　**(D)** 80%　**(E)** 125%

If 20 people attended Professor Rodriguez's class on Monday and 25 attended on Tuesday, what was the percent increase in attendance from Monday to Tuesday?

(A) 5%　**(B)** 20%　**(C)** 25%　**(D)** 80%　**(E)** 125%

Only the third question asks about percent *change*; the first two questions are of the form "this-of-that." So the answer to the first question is $\frac{20}{25} = \frac{4}{5} = 80\%$, or (D). The answer to the second question is $\frac{25}{20} = \frac{5}{4} = 125\%$, or (E). And the answer to the third question, using the "change-over" strategy, is $\frac{25-20}{20} = \frac{5}{20} = \frac{1}{4} = 25\%$, or (C).

13

Percents (Answers, page 265)

1. A certain company has 120 employees. If 24 of the employees are in the union, what percent of the employees are *not* in the union?

    (A) 12%   (B) 24%   (C) 48%   (D) 80%   (E) 96%

2. In 1960, a certain tree was 12 meters tall. If the tree measured 15 meters in 1985, by what percent did its height increase?

    (A) 3%   (B) 25%   (C) 40%   (D) 80%   (E) 125%

3. At 9:00 a.m. on Monday the price of gold was $450 per ounce. If the price of gold at 3:00 that same day was $441 per ounce, what was the percent decrease in the price of gold during the day?

    (A) 98%   (B) 9.8%   (C) 9%   (D) 2%   (E) 0.2%

4. In 1940, the price of a certain item was $0.20. If the same item cost $1.00 in 1987, what was the percent increase in the price of the item?

    (A) 20%   (B) 80%   (C) 120%   (D) 400%   (E) 500%

5. In a certain school, 40 percent of the students are boys. If there are 80 boys in the school, what is the total number of students in the school?

    (A) 32   (B) 50   (C) 120   (D) 200   (E) 320

6. The price of an item increased by 25 percent. If the price of the item after the increase is $2.00, what was the *original* price?

    (A) $1.50   (B) $1.60   (C) $1.75   (D) $2.50   (E) $3.20

Average Price of Metal X (per ounce)	
1981	$10
1982	$11
1983	$12
1984	$15
1985	$18
1986	$21

7. The greatest percent increase in the average price per ounce of metal X occurred during which period?

   (A) 1981–1982   **(B)** 1982–1983   **(C)** 1983–1984
   (D) 1984–1985   **(E)** 1985–1986

   Use the following table for questions 8–10.

Number of Fires in City Y	
1982	100
1983	125
1984	140
1985	150
1986	135

8. The number of fires in 1982 was what percent of the number of fires in 1983?
   (A) 25%   **(B)** $66\frac{2}{3}$%   **(C)** 80%   **(D)** 100%   **(E)** 125%

9. The number of fires in 1986 was what percent of the number of fires in 1985?
   (A) 90%   **(B)** 82%   **(C)** 50%   **(D)** 25%   **(E)** 10%

10. What was the percent decrease in the number of fires from 1985 to 1986?
    (A) 10%   **(B)** 25%   **(C)** 50%   **(D)** 82%   **(E)** 90%

13

Ratios

In addition to understanding the basic idea of a ratio, you may be asked to divide a quantity according to ratio parts or to work with a three-part ratio.

First, you may be asked to divide a quantity according to a ratio.

TO DISTRIBUTE A QUANTITY ACCORDING TO A RATIO, DIVIDE THE QUANTITY BY THE TOTAL NUMBER OF RATIO PARTS. THEN MULTIPLY THAT RESULT BY THE NUMBER OF PARTS TO BE DISTRIBUTED.

EXAMPLE:

A groom must divide 12 quarts of oats between two horses. If Dobbin is to receive twice as much as Pegasus, how many quarts of oats should the groom give to Dobbin?

(A) 4   (B) 6   (C) 8   (D) 9   (E) 10

The answer is (C). The oats must be divided according to the ratio 2:1. There are 2 + 1 = 3 ratio parts, so each part is 12 ÷ 3 = 4 quarts. Dobbin gets two parts, or 2 x 4 = 8 quarts.

The other type of ratio question involves three parts.

EXAMPLE:

If the ratio of John's allowance to Lucy's allowance is 3:2, and the ratio of Lucy's allowance to Bob's allowance is 3:4, what is the ratio of John's allowance to Bob's allowance?

(A) 1:6   (B) 2:5   (C) 1:2   (D) 3:4   (E) 9:8

The answer is (E). In a problem like this, the middle term (the one that appears in both ratios) joins the other two terms like a common denominator. Here, the common term is Lucy's allowance. Adjust the ratios so that the "Lucy" term has the same value in both ratios. The ratio of John's allowance to Lucy's is 3:2, and that is equivalent to 9:6. The ratio of Lucy's allowance to Bob's is 3:4, and that is equivalent to 6:8. So the ratio John:Lucy:Bob is 9:6:8, and the ratio John:Bob is 9:8.

Ratios (Answers, page 266)

1. In a certain box of candy, the ratio of light chocolates to dark chocolates is 4:5. If the box contains 36 candies, how many of the candies are dark chocolates?
   (A) 9   (B) 18   (C) 20   (D) 24   (E) 27

2. In a certain school, the ratio of Seniors to Juniors is 5:4, and the ratio of Seniors to Sophomores is 6:5. What is the ratio of Sophomores to Juniors?
   (A) 2:3   (B) 25:24   (C) 1   (D) 24:25   (E) 3:2

3. In a certain library, the ratio of fiction to nonfiction books is 3:5. If the library contains a total of 8,000 books, how many of the books are nonfiction?
   (A) 2,400   (B) 3,000   (C) 3,600   (D) 4,800   (E) 5,000

4. In a certain game, 3 nurbs are equal to 2 zimps, and 6 clabs are equal to 1 zimp. 4 clabs are equal to how many nurbs?
   (A) 1   (B) 2   (C) 3   (D) 4   (E) 5

5. A $1,000 bonus is to be divided among three people so that Jane receives twice as much as Robert, who receives $\frac{1}{5}$ as much as Wendy. How much money should Wendy receive?
   (A) $100   (B) $125   (C) $250   (D) $375   (E) $625

13

Averages

Aside from the very simple questions that ask you to calculate the average of several numbers, there are two questions about averages that you should know about.

The first kind asks about a missing element.

EXAMPLE:

If the average of 35, 38, 41, 43, and x is 37, what is x?

(A) 28   **(B)** 30   **(C)** 31   **(D)** 34   **(E)** 36

The answer is (A). Using the general idea of average:

$$\frac{35 + 38 + 41 + 43 + x}{5} = 37$$

So: $35 + 38 + 41 + 43 + x = 5(37)$

$157 + x = 185$

$x = 28$

THE DIFFERENCE OF THE SUMS METHOD FOR FINDING THE MISSING QUANTITY (OR QUANTITIES) OF AN AVERAGE:

(1) FIND THE SUM OF ALL THE QUANTITIES BY MULTIPLYING THE AVERAGE BY THE TOTAL NUMBER OF QUANTITIES.
(2) ADD UP THE KNOWN QUANTITIES.
(3) SUBTRACT THE RESULT OF (2) FROM THE RESULT OF (1).
     THE DIFFERENCE IS THE MISSING QUANTITY (OR THE SUM OF THE MISSING QUANTITIES).

In the question above, the total of all five elements in the average had to be 185. But the total of the four we were given was only 157. So the missing element had to be 185 − 157 = 28.

There is a Holmesian shortcut you can use with this type of problem.

THE AVERAGE IS THE "MIDPOINT" OF THE NUMBERS AVERAGED.

So if the average of 35, 38, 41, 43, and x is 37, the values in excess of 37 must equal the values below 37. Instead of doing an "official" calculation, you can reason that 35 is 2 below the average, or −2; 38 is one over, or +1; 41 is 4 over, or +4; and 43 is 6 over, or +6. Now you add up those numbers: −2 + 1 + 4 + 6 = +9. To offset this overage and bring the average down to 37, the missing number must be 9 less than 37, or 28. You can check this result by calculating the average using 28.

As you might have already guessed, there are some variations on this theme, but all can be solved in essentially the same way.

EXAMPLES:

For a certain student, the average of ten test scores is 80. If the high and low scores are dropped, the average is 81. What is the average of the high and low scores?

(A) 76   **(B)** 78   **(C)** 80   **(D)** 81   **(E)** 82

The answer is (A). The sum of the ten test scores is 80 x 10 = 800. The sum of the eight scores after the two scores have been dropped is 8 x 81 = 648. So the two scores that were dropped total 800 − 648 = 152. And since there are two of them, their average is 152 ÷ 2 = 76.

> In a certain shipment, the average weight of six packages is 50 pounds. If another package is added to the shipment, the average weight of the seven packages is 52 pounds. What is the weight (in pounds) of the additional package?
> **(A)** 2   **(B)** 7   **(C)** 52   **(D)** 62   **(E)** 64

The answer is (E). The total weight of the original six packages is $6 \times 50 = 300$ pounds. The total weight of the seven packages is $7 \times 52 = 364$ pounds. So the weight of the final package is $364 - 300 = 64$ pounds.

The other unusual average question that you might encounter is a weighted average.

> **EXAMPLES:**
>
> In a certain course, a student's final exam grade is weighted twice as heavily as his midterm grade. If a student receives a score of 84 on his final exam and 90 on his midterm, what is his average for the course?
> **(A)** 88   **(B)** 87.5   **(C)** 86   **(D)** 86.5   **(E)** 85

The answer is (C). You have to be sure you weight the final exam grade twice as much as the midterm grade:

$$\frac{90 + 2(84)}{3} = \frac{258}{3} = 86$$

In calculating a weighted average, there are two things to watch out for. One, make sure you have the average weighted properly. Two, make sure you divide by the correct number of quantities.

> In a certain group of children, three of the children are ten years old and two of the children are five years old. What is the average age in years of the children in the group?
> **(A)** 6   **(B)** 6.5   **(C)** 7   **(D)** 7.5   **(E)** 8

The answer is (E).

$$\frac{3(10) + 2(5)}{5} = \frac{40}{5} = 8$$

Notice that we weight the ages according to the number of children in the group, and then we divide by 5 (the number of children in the group).

13

Averages (Answers, page 267)

1. If the average of six numbers—12, 15, 18, 14, 13, and x—is 14, what is x?
   (A) 10 **(B)** 11 **(C)** 12 **(D)** 13 **(E)** 14

2. The average weight of four packages on a scale is 16 pounds. When one of those packages is removed, the average of the remaining three packages is 14 pounds. What is the weight in pounds of the package that was removed?
   (A) 16 **(B)** 18 **(C)** 21 **(D)** 22 **(E)** 24

3. Herman purchased three books that cost $2, five books that cost $3, and one book that cost $6. What was the average cost of the books?
   (A) $3 **(B)** $4 **(C)** $5 **(D)** $6 **(E)** $7

4. On a certain toll road, the toll charge is 10 cents per mile for the first 50 miles, 20 cents per mile for the next 20 miles, and 30 cents per mile for the last 10 miles. What is the average cost per mile (in cents) for the entire trip?
   (A) 10.5 **(B)** 12 **(C)** 12.5 **(D)** 15 **(E)** 18

5. The average weight of ten people sitting in a boat is 145 pounds. If one person gets out of the boat, the average weight of the remaining people is 150 pounds. What is the weight in pounds of the person who got out of the boat?
   (A) 90 **(B)** 100 **(C)** 120 **(D)** 150 **(E)** 175

Proportions

The simplest of all problems with a proportion asks that you solve for an unknown quantity.

EXAMPLE:

If $\frac{2}{3} = \frac{x}{12}$, $x =$

(A) 3   (B) 4   (C) 6   (D) 8   (E) 9

To solve, you cross-multiply:

$$\frac{2}{3} = \frac{x}{12}$$

$$2(12) = 3x$$

$$3x = 24$$

Then you divide both sides by 3:

$$3x \div 3 = 24 \div 3$$

$$x = 8$$

Proportions also provide you with a powerful Holmesian strategy for solving word problems that ask about things like cost, output, distance, and so on.

IF A QUESTION INVOLVES QUANTITIES THAT CHANGE IN THE SAME DIRECTION WITH ONE ANOTHER, USE A PROPORTION TO SOLVE FOR UNKNOWN QUANTITIES.

EXAMPLES:

If 4.5 pounds of chocolate cost $10, how many pounds of chocolate can be purchased for $12?

(A) $4\frac{3}{4}$ (B) $5\frac{2}{5}$ (C) $5\frac{1}{2}$ (D) $5\frac{3}{4}$ (E) 6

13

This is not a difficult question, and Watson will probably get it right. He reasons that $10 buys $4\frac{1}{2}$ pounds of chocolate, so the cost per pound is $10 \div 4\frac{1}{2} = \$2\frac{2}{9}$. (We use a fraction to avoid the repeating decimal 2.222 . . . .) Next, Watson divides: $12 \div 2\frac{2}{9} = 5\frac{2}{5}$. So (B) is the answer.

There is nothing conceptually wrong with what Watson has done, but the same result can be achieved more easily by using a proportion:

$$\frac{\text{Amount } x}{\text{Amount } y} = \frac{\text{Cost } x}{\text{Cost } y}$$

Cross-multiply: $\frac{4.5}{x} = \frac{10}{12}$

$$54 = 10x$$

Solve for x: $x = 5\frac{2}{5}$

At a certain school, 45 percent of the students purchased a yearbook. If 540 students purchased yearbooks, how many students did *not* buy a yearbook?

(A) 243 **(B)** 540 **(C)** 575 **(D)** 660 **(E)** 957

Set up a proportion. Since 45 percent bought a yearbook, 55 percent did not:

$$\frac{45\%}{55\%} = \frac{540}{x}$$

First, you can cancel the percent signs:

$$\frac{45\%}{55\%} = \frac{540}{x}$$

Cross-multiply: $45x = 55(540)$

Solve for x: $x = \frac{55(540)}{45} = \frac{11(540)}{9} = 660$

This method will work in all of the following situations and more:

The greater (or less) the quantity, the greater (or less) the cost (and vice versa).

The greater (or less) the quantity, the greater (or less) the weight (and vice versa).

The greater (or less) the number, the greater (or less) the percent of the whole (and vice versa).

The longer (or shorter) the working time, the greater (or less) the output, assuming constant rate of operation (and vice versa).

The longer (or shorter) the travel time, the greater (or less) the distance traveled, assuming constant speed (and vice versa).

The only things to watch for are those situations in which the quantities vary indirectly.

EXAMPLE:

Walking at a constant rate of 4 miles per hour, it takes Jill exactly one hour to walk home from school. If she walks at a constant rate of 5 miles per hour, how many *minutes* will the trip take?

(A) 48 **(B)** 54 **(C)** 56 **(D)** 72 **(E)** 112

In this case, the faster the speed, the shorter the time. So we use an indirect proportion. Set up the proportion as usual (being sure to group like terms):

$$\frac{60}{x} = \frac{4}{5}$$

Then invert the right side of the proportion:

$$\frac{60}{x} = \frac{5}{4}$$

And solve for x:

$$5x = 4(60)$$

$$x = \frac{4(60)}{5} = 48 \text{ minutes}$$

Proportions (Answers, page 267)

1. A roll of metal ribbon that weighs 12 pounds is cut into two pieces. One piece is 75 feet long and weighs 9 pounds. What was the length, in feet, of the original roll?
   (A) 60 **(B)** 90 **(C)** 100 **(D)** 120 **(E)** 150

2. A car traveling at a constant 50 miles per hour covers the same distance in one hour as a car traveling at a constant 25 miles per hour for how many hours?
   (A) $\frac{1}{3}$ **(B)** $\frac{1}{2}$ **(C)** 1 **(D)** 2 **(E)** 3

3. A recipe calls for three eggs and two cups of milk. If a quantity of the recipe is prepared using eight eggs, how many cups of milk should be used?
   (A) 4 **(B)** $4\frac{2}{3}$ **(C)** $5\frac{1}{3}$ **(D)** $5\frac{1}{2}$ **(E)** $5\frac{2}{3}$

4. If 8 pounds of coffee cost $50, how much do 12 pounds of coffee cost?
   (A) $25.00 **(B)** $62.50 **(C)** $75.00 **(D)** $80.00 **(E)** $84.00

5. Three printing presses can finish a certain job in 60 minutes. How many minutes will it take five such printing presses to do the same job?
   (A) 15 **(B)** 20 **(C)** 30 **(D)** 36 **(E)** 100

6. If 4 gallons of water occupy 30 cubic feet of space, how many gallons are needed to fill a tank with a capacity of 360 cubic feet?
   (A) 12 **(B)** 24 **(C)** 30 **(D)** 36 **(E)** 48

7. A repair shop can paint three cars every four hours. At that rate, how many hours will it take the shop to paint five cars?
   (A) $6\frac{1}{3}$ **(B)** $6\frac{2}{3}$ **(C)** $7\frac{1}{3}$ **(D)** $7\frac{1}{2}$ **(E)** $7\frac{3}{4}$

8. If a machine seals cans at the rate of $4\frac{1}{2}$ cans every three seconds, how many *minutes* will it take the machine to seal 720 cans?
   (A) 6 **(B)** 8 **(C)** 18 **(D)** 36 **(E)** 48

9. At a certain factory, it takes five metal fasteners to attach a muffler to a car. If a box containing 500 fasteners costs $42, how much will it cost to buy the exact number of fasteners needed to attach 300 mufflers?
   (A) $14 **(B)** $36 **(C)** $56 **(D)** $126 **(E)** $4,200

10. In a certain population, only 0.03 percent of the people have physical trait X. On the average, it will be necessary to screen how many people to find six with trait X?
    (A) 180 **(B)** 200 **(C)** 1,800 **(D)** 2,000 **(E)** 20,000

13

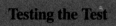

It cannot be said often enough that for every math problem except the small number that require student-produced responses, the correct answer is right there on the page. This sets up a Holmesian strategy that can be applied to many different kinds of problems:

TEST THE TEST.

Instead of trying to devise a mathematical solution to a problem, just test the available choices until you find one that works.

> **EXAMPLE:**
>
> Which of the following is the larger of two numbers the product of which is 600 and the sum of which is five times the difference between the two?
> **(A)** 10   **(B)** 15   **(C)** 20   **(D)** 30   **(E)** 50

It would be foolish to try to devise some mathematical approach to this question. All you need to do is test answers until you find one that works. First, we can eliminate (A), (B), and (C). Though those are factors of 600, they are not the *larger* of their respective pairs, as required by the question.

Next we test (D). $30 \times 20 = 600$, and $30 + 20 = 50$, which is $5 \times 30 - 20 = 10$. Since 30 meets the requirements, it must be the correct choice.

Testing the Test (Answers, page 270)

Directions: Solve each of the following questions by testing answer choices.

1. If $\frac{1}{3}$ of a number is 3 more than $\frac{1}{4}$ of the number, then what is the number?

   (A) 18 **(B)** 24 **(C)** 30 **(D)** 36 **(E)** 48

2. If $\frac{3}{5}$ of a number is 4 more than $\frac{1}{2}$ of the number, then what is the number?

   (A) 20 **(B)** 28 **(C)** 35 **(D)** 40 **(E)** 56

3. When both 16 and 9 are divided by n, the remainder is 2. What is n?

   (A) 3 **(B)** 4 **(C)** 5 **(D)** 6 **(E)** 7

4. The sum of the digits of a three-digit number is 16. If the tens digit of the number is 3 times the units digit, and the units digit is $\frac{1}{4}$ of the hundreds digit, then what is the number?

   (A) 446 **(B)** 561 **(C)** 682 **(D)** 862 **(E)** 914

5. If the sum of five consecutive integers is 40, what is the smallest of the five integers?

   (A) 4 **(B)** 5 **(C)** 6 **(D)** 7 **(E)** 8

13

Summary

1. If a problem presents an easy arithmetic manipulation, just do the indicated operations. If the indicated operations are too complex, look for an alternative approach such as simplifying, factoring, or approximating.

2. If a problem is very complicated, break your solution of the problem down into steps:
   (1) What is the question to be answered?
   (2) What information have I been given?
   (3) How can I bridge the gap between (1) and (2)?
   (4) Execute the needed operations.

3. The following principles are often tested:
   (a) properties of numbers (odd and even, positive and negative, and fractions)
   (b) percents (the "this of that" and the "change over" strategies)
   (c) ratios (basic ratios and ratio parts)
   (d) averages (simple averages and weighted averages)
   (e) proportions (direct and indirect)

4. Sometimes the best attack strategy is just to test answer choices until you find the correct one.

Explanatory Answers

EXERCISE 1

1. (D) This is a case for the "flying x":

$$\frac{1}{9} + \frac{1}{10} = \frac{9+10}{90} = \frac{19}{90}$$

2. (D) Don't worry about common denominators. Just perform the "flying x" twice:

$$\frac{1}{3} + \frac{1}{4} = \frac{4+3}{12} = \frac{7}{12}$$

$$\frac{7}{12} + \frac{1}{5} = \frac{35+12}{60} = \frac{47}{60}$$

3. (D) Again, the "flying x."

$$\frac{12}{11} - \frac{11}{12} = \frac{144-121}{132} = \frac{23}{132}$$

4. (C) The mighty "flying x."

$$\frac{8}{7} - \frac{8}{9} = 72 - \frac{56}{63} = \frac{16}{63}$$

5. (A) The escape route out of this maze of calculations is cancelling to simplify:

$$\frac{\frac{3}{5} \times \frac{5}{9} \times \frac{9}{13}}{\frac{13}{12} \times \frac{12}{11} \times \frac{11}{3}} = \frac{3}{13} \div \frac{13}{3} = \frac{3}{13} \times \frac{3}{13} = \frac{9}{169}$$

6. (C) Again, you can cancel:

$$\frac{3}{11} \times \frac{11}{13} \times \frac{13}{15} \times \frac{15}{17} = \frac{3}{17}$$

7. (C) A quick check shows that (B) and (D) are not divisible by 88. After that, if a number is divisible by 3, then the sum of its digits, divisible by 3. As for (A), the sum of the digits, $8 \times 8 = 64$, is not divisible by 3. As for (E), the sum of the digits is $4 \times 8 = 32$, not divisible by 3. But the sum of the digits of (C) is $6 \times 8 = 48$, which is divisible by 3.

8. (D) Only (B) and (D) are divisible by 11. (B) is not divisible by 3 since the sum of the digits is 8. But the sum of the digits of (D) is divisible by 3.

9. (B) The question specifically invites approximation:
$(0.5 \times 4.0) \div 4 = 0.5$, which is $\frac{1}{2}$.

13

10. (E) You are specifically invited to approximate, and approximation makes the operations manageable. 0.889 is approximately $\frac{8}{9}$; 0.666 is approximately $\frac{2}{3}$; 0.333 is approximately $\frac{1}{3}$; and 0.625 is $\frac{5}{8}$.

$$\frac{8}{9} \div \frac{2}{3} = \frac{8}{9} \times \frac{3}{2} = \frac{4}{3}$$

$$\frac{1}{3} \div \frac{5}{8} = \frac{1}{3} \times \frac{8}{5} = \frac{8}{15}$$

$$\frac{4}{3} \div \frac{8}{15} = \frac{4}{3} \times \frac{15}{8} = \frac{5}{2}$$

11. (C) Look for a benchmark. In this case, $\frac{1}{10}$ will do very well. Since $\frac{12}{120} = \frac{1}{10}$, $\frac{12}{119}$ is larger than $\frac{1}{10}$, (A) can be eliminated. Similarly, $\frac{4}{39}$ and $\frac{7}{69}$ are larger than $\frac{1}{10}$ and can be eliminated. Finally, since $\frac{2}{20}$ would be exactly $\frac{1}{10}$, (C) is slightly smaller than $\frac{1}{10}$. So (C) is the smallest fraction.

12. (D) Look for an escape. In this case, you can factor:

$$12{,}345(1) + 12{,}345(2) + 12{,}345(3) + 12{,}345(4) =$$

$$12{,}345(1 + 2 + 3 + 4) = 12{,}345 \times 10 = 123{,}450$$

13. (D) Notice that this expression is the difference of two squares. Factor:

$$510^2 - 490^2 = (510 + 490)(510 - 490) = 1{,}000 \times 20 = 20{,}000$$

14. (C) Finding the escape route here is a little more difficult. $81 = 9^2$, and $16^2 + 2(9)(16) + 9^2$ is the second pattern you were asked to learn:

$$16^2 + 2(9)(16) + 9^2 = (16 + 9)(16 + 9) = (25)(25) = 625$$

15. (B) Here, your escape is accomplished by factoring.

$$\frac{1}{10^{22}} - \frac{1}{10^{23}} = \frac{1}{10^{22}}\left(1 - \frac{1}{10}\right) = \frac{1}{10^{22}}\left(\frac{9}{10}\right) = \frac{9}{10^{23}}$$

EXERCISE 2

1. (E) $2n$ must be even, so $2n + 5$, which is an even number plus an odd number, must be odd. Or, you could substitute a number such as 2 into each choice. (E) turns out to be $2(2) + 5 = 9$, an odd number.

2. (C) The only way 3 times n can be even is if n is even. Since n is even, $n + 1$ is odd.

3. (C) Since $2n$ will be even no matter what the value of n, $2n + 1$ must be odd. Again, you can substitute numbers to prove to yourself that the other choices do not guarantee an odd number.

4. (C) Regardless of whether $n + o$ or $p - q$ is even, as long as m is even the entire number is even.

5. (D) Regardless of whether n is itself odd or even, $2n$ must be even, and $2n + 2$ must be even as well.

6. (C) Since p is the smallest of the three, the next number is $p + 1$ and the one after that is $p + 2$. So the sum of the next two consecutive integers is $p + 1 + p + 2 = 2p + 3$.

7. (C) Since these are consecutive integers, each number in the series is one less than the number that follows it. So the number before $n + 3$ is $n + 2$; the number before that is $n + 1$; the one before that is just n; and the one before that is $n - 1$. So the first of the five numbers is $n - 1$.

8. (D) A negative times a negative is a positive, so n^2 must be positive. So $\frac{1}{n^2}$ is positive.

9. (D) Just substitute -1 for x in each choice:

   (A) $2x = 2(-1) = -2$

   (B) $x = -1$

   (C) $\frac{x}{2} = -\frac{1}{2} = -\frac{1}{2}$

   (D) $x^2 = (-1)(-1) = 1$

   (E) $x^3 = (-1)(-1)(-1) = -1$

10. (A) When a fraction is raised to a power, the result is smaller than the original fraction. Therefore, (D) and (E) are both smaller than (C). On the other hand, when you divide by a fraction, the result is larger than the number divided, so both (A) and (B) are larger than 1 and so larger than (C). Between (A) and (B), since x^2 is smaller than x, $\frac{1}{x^2}$ will be larger than $\frac{1}{x}$. You can arrive at the same conclusion by testing a number such as $\frac{1}{2}$.

EXERCISE 3

1. (D) $120 - 24 = 96$ are not in the union. Next, use the "this-of-that" strategy.

   $\frac{\text{Nonmembers}}{\text{Of Employees}} = \frac{96}{120} = 0.8 = 80\%$.

2. (B) This is a percent increase question. Use the "change-over" strategy. Change $= 15 - 12 = 3$. Original amount $= 12$. $\frac{3}{12} = \frac{1}{4} = 25\%$.

3. (D) Though this question involves a percent decrease, you still use the "change-over" strategy. Change $= 450 - 441 = 9$. Original amount $= 450$. $\frac{9}{450} = 0.02 = 2\%$.

4. (D) This question asks about percent change, so you use the "change-over" strategy. Change $= 1.00 - 0.20 = 0.80$. Original amount $= 0.20$. $\frac{0.80}{0.20} = 4 = 400\%$.

5. (D) This question can be answered using the "this-of-that" strategy. $\frac{80}{\text{Of Total}} = 40\%$. $80 = 40\%$ of Total, so Total $= \frac{80}{0.4} = 200$.

13

6. (B) This question can be answered with the "change-over" strategy even though you don't know the change or the original price. The key is to see that the original price is equal to $2.00 minus the change.

$$\frac{\text{Change}}{\$2.00 - \text{Change}} = 25\%$$

Let C stand for Change:

$$\frac{C}{2 - C} = 0.25$$

$$C = 0.25\,(2 - C)$$

$$C = 0.5 - 0.25C$$

$$C + 0.25C = 0.5 - 0.25C + 0.25C$$

$$1.25C = 0.5$$

$$C = 0.5 \div 1.25$$

$$C = 0.4$$

So the change was $0.40, which means the original price was $2.00 − $0.40 = $1.60. You can check this result by using the "change-over" formula to calculate the percent increase from 1.60 to 2.00.

7. (C) This question calls for the "change-over" strategy. Since you are only interested in finding the largest percent growth, you can compare your fractions and skip the step of converting them to percents:

(A) $\frac{1}{10}$　**(B)** $\frac{1}{11}$　**(C)** $\frac{3}{12}$ or $\frac{1}{4}$　**(D)** $\frac{3}{15}$ or $\frac{1}{5}$　**(E)** $\frac{3}{18}$ or $\frac{1}{6}$

8. (C) Use the "this-of-that" strategy. $\frac{100}{125} = \frac{4}{5} = 80\%$.

9. (A) Use the "this-of-that" strategy. $\frac{135}{150} = \frac{9}{10} = 90\%$.

10. (A) Use the "change-over" strategy. Change = 150 − 135 = 15.
$\frac{15}{150} = \frac{1}{10} = 10\%$.

EXERCISE 4

1. (C) Add the ratio parts: 4 + 5 = 9. Divide the total quantity by that result: 36 ÷ 9 = 4. So each ratio part is worth 4. Since five of the ratio parts are dark chocolates, the number of dark chocolates is 5 × 4 = 20.

2. (B) "Seniors" must function as a common term. Change 5:4 to 30:24, and 6:5 to 30:25. The ratio of Seniors to Juniors is 30:24, and the ratio of Seniors to Sophomores is 30:25. So the ratio of Sophomores to Juniors is 25:24.

3. (E) Find the total number of ratio parts: 3 + 5 = 8. Divide: 8,000 ÷ 8 = 1,000. Then multiply by the number of parts that are nonfiction: 5 × 1,000 = 5,000.

4. (A) Since 6 clabs = 1 zimp, 12 clabs = 2 zimps. Therefore, 3 nurbs = 12 clabs, and 4 clabs = 1 nurb.

5. (E) The tricky thing here is setting up the ratio. The ratio of Robert's share to Wendy's share is 1:5, and the ratio of Robert's share to Jane's share is 1:2. So the ratio of the shares of Wendy:Jane:Robert is 5:2:1. Now you add ratio parts: $5 + 2 + 1 = 8$. Divide: $\$1,000 \div 8 = \$125$. And finally, multiply by the number of parts Wendy is to receive: $5 \times \$125 = \$625$.

EXERCISE 5

1. (C) The total of all the numbers must be $14 \times 6 = 84$. The total of the known quantities is only 72. So the missing number is $84 - 72 = 12$.

Or, you might have used the "midpoint" method. 12 is 2 below 14, for -2. 15 is 1 above 14, and (keeping a running total) $-2 + 1 = -1$. Then, 18 is 4 above 14, and $4 - 1 = +3$. 14 is equal to 14, so our running total is still $+3$. Finally, 13 is 1 less than 14, which brings our running total to $+3 - 1 = +2$. This means that the missing number must offset this $+2$ by being 2 less than 14, or 12.

2. (D) The total weight of the four packages is $16 \times 4 = 64$. The weight of the remaining three is $3 \times 14 = 42$. The difference is $64 - 42 = 22$. So the package that was removed weighed 22 pounds.

3. (A) Here you must use a weighted average:

$$\frac{3(\$2) + 5(\$3) + 1(\$6)}{9} = \frac{6 + 15 + 6}{9} = \frac{27}{9} = 3$$

4. (D) Again, you can use a weighted average:

$$\frac{50(10) + 20(20) + 10(30)}{80} = \frac{50 + 40 + 30}{80} = \frac{120}{80} = 015$$
$0.15 = 15$ cents

5. (B) The weight of the ten people is $145 \times 10 = 1,450$. The weight of the remaining nine is $9 \times 150 = 1,350$. So the person who got out of the boat weighed $1,450 - 1,350 = 100$ pounds.

EXERCISE 6

1. (C) The longer the piece, the greater the weight. So you can use a direct proportion:

$$\frac{\text{Length } x}{\text{Length } y} = \frac{\text{Weight } x}{\text{Weight } y}$$

$$\frac{75}{x} = \frac{9}{12}$$

Simplify: $\dfrac{75}{x} = \dfrac{3}{4}$

Cross-multiply: $4(75) = 3x$

Solve for x: $x = \dfrac{4(75)}{3} = 100$

2. (D) The faster the speed, the shorter the time (and vice versa). So here you must use an indirect proportion. Set up a normal proportion, being sure to group like terms:

$$\frac{\text{Speed } x}{\text{Speed } y} = \frac{\text{Time } x}{\text{Time } y}$$

$$\frac{50}{25} = \frac{1}{x}$$

Invert the right side: $= \frac{50}{25} = \frac{x}{1}$

Cross-multiply: $50(1) = 25x$

Solve for x: $x = \frac{50}{25} = 2$

3. (C) The more eggs, the more milk, so you should use a direct proportion:

$$\frac{\text{Eggs } x}{\text{Eggs } y} = \frac{\text{Milk } x}{\text{Milk } y}$$

$$\frac{3}{8} = \frac{2}{x}$$

Cross-multiply: $3x = 16$

Solve for x: $x = \frac{16}{3} = 5\frac{1}{3}$

4. (C) The more of a thing purchased, the greater the cost. Use a direct proportion:

$$\frac{\text{Quantity } x}{\text{Quantity } y} = \frac{\text{Cost } x}{\text{Cost } y}$$

$$\frac{8}{12} = \frac{50}{x}$$

Cross-multiply: $8x = 50(12)$

Solve for x: $x = \frac{50(12)}{8} = 75$

5. (D) The more machines working, the shorter the time needed to do a job. Here you need an indirect proportion. Set up a proportion, being sure to group like terms:

$$\frac{\text{Number of Machines } x}{\text{Number of Machines } y} = \frac{\text{Time } x}{\text{Time } y}$$

$$\frac{3}{5} = \frac{60}{x}$$

Invert the right side: $\frac{3}{5} = \frac{x}{60}$

Cross-multiply: $5x = 3(60)$

Solve for x: $x = \frac{3(60)}{5} = 36$

6. (E) The more water, the greater the space occupied. So you can use a direct proportion:

$$\frac{\text{Water } x}{\text{Water } y} = \frac{\text{Space } x}{\text{Space } y}$$

$$\frac{4}{x} = \frac{30}{360}$$

Cross-multiply: $30x = 4(360)$

Solve for x: $x = \frac{4(360)}{30} = 48$

7. (B) The greater the number of cars, the longer the time needed for the job. So use a direct proportion:

$$\frac{\text{Cars } x}{\text{Cars } y} = \frac{\text{Time } x}{\text{Time } y}$$

$$\frac{3}{5} = \frac{4}{x}$$

Cross-multiply: $3x = 4(5)$

Solve for x: $x = \frac{4(5)}{3} = 6\frac{2}{3}$

8. (B) The more cans, the longer the time. So you can use a direct proportion, but you must take care that the final result is expressed in minutes and not seconds. First, set up a proportion to find how many seconds will be needed:

$$\frac{\text{Cans } x}{\text{Cans } y} = \frac{\text{Time in Seconds } x}{\text{Time in Seconds } y}$$

$$\frac{4\frac{1}{2}}{720} = \frac{3}{x}$$

Cross-multiply: $\frac{4\frac{1}{2}}{720} = \frac{3}{x}$

Solve for x: $x = 3(720) \div 4\frac{1}{2} = 480$ seconds

To convert that number of seconds to minutes, divide by 60:
$$480 \div 60 = 8 \text{ minutes.}$$

9. (D) This problem is a bit complex, but we will take it step by step. To find the total cost of the fasteners, we must first find how many we need. Since more mufflers means more fasteners, use a direct proportion:

$$\frac{\text{Mufflers } x}{\text{Mufflers } y} = \frac{\text{Fasteners } x}{\text{Fasteners } y}$$

$$\frac{1}{300} = \frac{5}{x}$$

Cross-multiply: $x = 1,500$

13

Now, to figure cost, you set up another direct proportion:

$$\frac{\text{Cost } x}{\text{Cost } y} = \frac{\text{Number } x}{\text{Number } y}$$

$$\frac{500}{1,500} = \frac{42}{x}$$

Cross-multiply: $500x = 42(1,500)$

Solve for x: $x = \dfrac{42(1,500)}{500} = 126$

10. (E) Here, too, you can use a direct proportion:

$$\frac{\text{Percent } x}{\text{Percent } y} = \frac{\text{Number } x}{\text{Number } y}$$

$$\frac{0.03\%}{100\%} = \frac{6}{x}$$

Clear the percents: $\dfrac{0.03}{100} = \dfrac{6}{x}$

Cross-multiply: $0.03x = 6(100)$

Solve for x: $x = \dfrac{600}{0.03} = 20,000$

EXERCISE 7

1. (D) 36
$\frac{1}{3}$ of 36 = 12. $\frac{1}{4}$ of 36 = 9. And 12 is 3 more than 9. So (D) fits the requirements.

2. (D) 40
$\frac{3}{5}$ of 40 = 24. $\frac{1}{2}$ of 40 = 20. And 24 is 4 more than 20. So (C) fits the requirements.

3. (E) 7
$16 \div 7 = 2$ plus remainder 2. $9 \div 7 = 1$ plus remainder 2. So (E) fits the requirements.

4. (D) 862
The sum of the three digits of 862 is $8 + 6 + 2 = 16$. The tens digit is 6, which is three times the units digit, which is 2. Finally, 2, the units digit, is $\frac{1}{4}$ of 8, the hundreds digit.

5. (C) 6
If the smallest integer is 6, then the sum is $6 + 7 + 8 + 9 + 10 = 40$.

Problem-Solving: Algebra

✔ Objectives

To learn to use the answer choices to generate solutions to algebra problems.

To review key concepts needed to solve the most common types of algebra problems.

1. Testing the Test
2. Algebra Manipulations
   - Evaluating Expressions
   - Exponents
   - Factoring
   - Defined Functions
   - Equations with One Variable
   - One Equation with Two Variables
   - Two Equations with Two Variables
   - Quadratic Equations
3. Algebra Applications

14

We now move to algebra, and you might think that the problems are suddenly going to get very difficult. Fortunately, this is not the case. SAT algebra questions cover the range of difficulty, from very easy to very difficult. Very often the first question in a math section is an algebra question; but since it is the first question, it will be an easy one.

EXAMPLE:

1. If $a^3 + b = 3 + a^3$, then $b =$
   (A) 3^3 (B) $3\sqrt{3}$ (C) 3 (D) $\sqrt[3]{3}$ (D) $-\sqrt{3}$

The problem is solved by a simple manipulation. Subtract a^3 from both sides of the equation:

$$a^3 + b - (a^3) = 3 + a^3 - (a^3)$$
$$a^3 - a^3 + b = 3 + a^3 - a^3$$
$$b = 3$$

So the answer is (C). And you can almost pick (C) without even doing the manipulation, because the other choices (like $\sqrt[3]{3}$) are answers for difficult questions, not easy ones.

Of course, not all algebra problems are so simple. Here is one of moderate difficulty.

EXAMPLE:

Diana spent $\frac{1}{2}$ of her allowance on a book and another \$3 on lunch. If she still had $\frac{1}{6}$ of her original allowance, how much is Diana's allowance?

(A) \$24 (B) \$18 (C) \$15 (D) \$12 (E) \$9

You can solve the problem by setting up an equation. In words, the problem states:

Diana's allowance minus $\frac{1}{2}$ her allowance minus another \$3 is equal to $\frac{1}{6}$ of Diana's allowance.

If you use x for Diana's allowance, your equation is:

$$x - \frac{1}{2}x - 3 = \frac{1}{6}x$$

And now you solve for x. First, combine like terms:

$$\left(x - \frac{1}{2}x\right) - 3 = \frac{1}{6}x$$

$$\frac{1}{2}x - 3 = \frac{1}{6}x$$

Next, get all of the x terms on one side (by subtracting $\frac{1}{6}x$ from both sides of the equation):

$$\left(\frac{1}{2}x - \frac{1}{6}x\right) - 3 = \frac{1}{6}x - \frac{1}{6}x$$

$$\left(\frac{3}{6}x - \frac{1}{6}x\right) - 3 = 0$$

$$\frac{2}{6}x - 3 = 0$$

$$\frac{1}{3}x - 3 = 0$$

Then, isolate the x term by adding 3 to both sides of the equation:

$$\frac{1}{3}x - 3 + 3 = 0 + 3$$

$$\frac{1}{3}x = 3$$

Finally, solve for x by multiplying both sides by 3:

$$(3)\frac{1}{3}x = 3(3)$$

$$x = 9$$

   The solution was described in excruciating detail. The problem can actually be solved in fewer steps. Even so, wouldn't it be nice if there were a way to avoid the algebra altogether? Well, there is an alternative.
   If Holmes were studying the above problem, he would begin by thinking, "The guilty party is one of the five suspects. I only need to prove which one." This sets up two Holmesian strategies which we will discuss before we talk any further about algebra.

One of the Five Suspects:

Testing the Test

We concluded our discussion of arithmetic problems with the topic "Testing the Test." You learned that it is sometimes possible to get a right answer just by testing choices. That principle can be extended to cover algebra questions.

Let's apply the principle to the problem of Diana's allowance. Start by testing (A). If Diana's allowance is $24, then after she spends $\frac{1}{2}$ on a book, she has $12. Subtract the $3 for lunch, and she has $9. But $\frac{9}{24}$ is not equal to $\frac{1}{6}$—so (A) cannot be correct.

Next, try (B). If her allowance is $18, then she has $9 after she buys the book and $6 after she pays for lunch. But $\frac{6}{18}$ is not $\frac{1}{6}$,—so (B), too, is incorrect.

Next, try (C), $15. Half of that is $7.50, which, less the $3 for lunch, leaves Diana with $4.50. But $\frac{4.5}{15}$, which is $\frac{9}{2} \div 15 = \frac{9}{30}$, is not $\frac{1}{6}$. So you would try (D), $12. Half of $12 is $6, which less $3 more for lunch is $3; but $\frac{3}{12}$ is not $\frac{1}{6}$.

By this point you *know* that the correct answer must be (E). But we will check it anyway. Half of $9 is $4.50, which less $3 is $1.50. And $\frac{1.5}{9} = \frac{3/2}{9} = \frac{3}{18} = \frac{1}{6}$.

But, you object, that is too many calculations! Yes and no. Yes, but the algebra itself required several steps. And with the "five suspects" strategy, at least you may be able to do something if the algebra proves impossible. And no, because the process really doesn't require all of those calculations.

Answer choices to questions like this one are arranged in order, from largest to smallest or vice versa. This cuts the calculations to a maximum of two. Start by testing choice (C). Your result is $\frac{3}{12}$, which is $\frac{1}{4}$ (which proves [C] is wrong). So ask yourself, is (C) incorrect because $15 is too much money or too little? Since $\frac{1}{4}$ is more than $\frac{1}{6}$, $15 must be too much money. So you should test the next smaller number.

You test (D). It doesn't work. By the process of elimination, (E) must be correct —and you don't need to do that calculation (unless you are ahead of schedule and can afford the time for a failsafe check).

We will apply this "five suspects" strategy to some other problems.

14

EXAMPLES:

In a certain game, a player had five successful turns in a row, and after each one the number of points added to his total score was double what was added the preceding turn. If the player scored a total of 465 points, how many points did he score on the first play?

(A) 15   **(B)** 31   **(C)** 93   **(D)** 155   **(E)** 270

Start with (C). If the player scored 93 points on the first turn, he scored $2 \times 93 = 186$ on the second, for a total of $93 + 186 = 279$. Then, on the third turn, he scored $2 \times 279 = 558$. But wait! This cannot possibly be the correct answer. We have already exceeded the total number of points scored.

Which suspect should we grill next? If 93 generated a result that was too large, logically, we should try the next smaller number. Assuming the player won 31 points on the first turn, he won $2 \times 31 = 62$ on the second, for a total of $31 + 62 = 93$. On the third, he won $2 \times 62 = 124$, for a total of $93 + 124 = 217$. On the fourth, he won $2 \times 124 = 248$, for a total of $217 + 248 = 465$, with still another round to go. (B) must be wrong.

By the process of elimination, therefore, (A) is correct. And if you care, you can prove it by doing the calculation.

Notice that in both of our examples, the answer was located at the extreme —either (E) or (A). This was to demonstrate that even with the worst luck, only two calculations are required. Sometimes you will be lucky and hit upon the correct choice on the first try.

The principle of the five suspects gives rise to another strategy called "If you don't see what you want, ask for it." This "ask for it" strategy is useful when the problem asks you to invent a formula.

> At a certain firm, d gallons of fuel are needed per day for each truck. At this rate, g gallons of fuel will supply t trucks for how many days?
>
> (A) $\dfrac{dt}{g}$ (B) $\dfrac{gt}{d}$ (C) dgt (D) $\dfrac{t}{dg}$ (E) $\dfrac{g}{dt}$

This is a fairly difficult question. And what makes it difficult is the use of unknowns. The question wouldn't be difficult if it read:

> At a certain firm, 20 gallons of fuel are needed per day for each truck. At this rate, 1,000 gallons of fuel will supply five trucks for how many days?

You would reason that five trucks using 20 gallons of fuel per day would consume $5 \times 20 = 100$ gallons per day. So 1,000 gallons would be used up in $1,000 \div 100 = 10$ days.

Numbers are what you want. You don't see them, so ask for them. Or rather, make them up as we just did. On the assumption that there are five trucks ($t = 5$), and that each truck consumes 20 gallons per day ($d = 20$), and that we have 1,000 gallons of fuel ($g = 1,000$), the correct formula should generate the number 10.

(A) $\dfrac{dt}{g} = \dfrac{20(5)}{1,000} = \dfrac{100}{1,000} = \dfrac{1}{10}$ (Wrong answer.)

(B) $\dfrac{gt}{d} = \dfrac{1,000(5)}{20} = \dfrac{5,000}{20} = 250$ (Wrong answer.)

(C) $dgt = (20)(1,000)(5) = 100(1,000)$ (Wrong answer.)

(D) $\dfrac{t}{dg} = \dfrac{5}{(20)(1,000)} = \dfrac{5}{20,000}$ (Wrong answer.)

(E) $\dfrac{g}{dt} = \dfrac{1,000}{20(5)} = \dfrac{1,000}{100} = 10$ (BINGO!)

> Y years ago Paul was twice as old as Bob. If Bob is now 18 years old, how old is Paul in terms of Y?
>
> (A) $36 + Y$ (B) $18 + Y$ (C) $18 - Y$ (D) $36 - Y$ (E) $36 - 2Y$

In our first example, we used realistic numbers. A truck might use 20 gallons of fuel per day, and a firm might have five trucks and a 1,000-gallon tank. But an unknown can stand for any number at all (as long as you don't divide by zero). So pick numbers that are easy to work with.

For starters, why not assume that $Y = $ zero, which is to say that right now Paul is twice as old as Bob. Since Bob is now 18, Paul is 36. So with $Y = $ zero, the correct formula should generate the value 36.

(A) $36 + Y = 36 + 0 = 36$

(B) $18 + Y = 18 + 0 = 18$

(C) $18 - Y = 18 - 0 = 18$

(D) $36 - Y = 36 - 0 = 36$

(E) $36 - 2Y = 36 - 0 = 36$

What happened? Our strategy yielded three choices, not one. There's nothing wrong with the strategy. The problem is with the value we used. (A), (D), and (E) all yielded 36 because -0, $+0$, and $-2(0)$ are all zero. To eliminate the two incorrect choices, just pick another easy number.

Assume that $Y = 1$. On that assumption, a year ago Bob was 17 years old and Paul was 34 years old. And today, one year later, he is $34 + 1 = 35$. So if $Y = 1$, the correct choice should yield 35:

(A) $36 + Y = 36 + 1 = 37$ (Definitely incorrect.)

(D) $36 - Y = 36 - 1 = 35$ (Bingo!)

(E) $36 - 2Y = 36 - 2 = 34$ (Wrong.)

You may also encounter a problem if you use the value 1, because $1 \times 1 = 1 \div 1$. For example, if you assume that $X = 1$, the formula XY will give you the same result as the formula $\frac{Y}{X}$. This doesn't mean you should never use 1. You can and should use 1 as an assumption; but if you get more than one seemingly correct formula, try another set of numbers.

14

It Must Be One of the Five. (Answers, page 297)

Directions: Solve the following problems using one of the two strategies just discussed. Don't even be tempted to use algebra.

1. On a shopping trip, Peter spent $\frac{1}{3}$ of his money for a jacket and another $5 for a hat. If Peter still had $\frac{1}{2}$ of his money left, how much money did he have originally?

   (A) $18   **(B)** $24   **(C)** $30   **(D)** $48   **(E)** $60

2. After filling the car's fuel tank, a driver drove from P to Q and then to R. She used $\frac{2}{5}$ of the fuel driving from P to Q. If she used another 7 gallons to drive from Q to R and still had $\frac{1}{4}$ of a tank left, how many gallons does the tank hold?

   (A) 12   **(B)** 18   **(C)** 20   **(D)** 21   **(E)** 35

3. A school meeting was attended only by sophomores, juniors, and seniors. $\frac{5}{12}$ of those who attended were juniors, and $\frac{1}{3}$ were seniors. If 36 sophomores attended, what was the total number of students who attended the meeting?

   (A) 108   **(B)** 144   **(C)** 252   **(D)** 288   **(E)** 300

4. If p pounds of coffee costs d dollars, how many pounds of coffee can be purchased for x dollars?

   (A) $\frac{pd}{x}$ **(B)** $\frac{x}{pd}$ **(C)** $\frac{xp}{d}$ **(D)** $\frac{d}{xp}$ **(E)** xpd

5. If p pounds of coffee costs d dollars, how many pounds of coffee can be purchased for $x + 10$ dollars?

   (A) $\frac{pd}{x + 10}$ **(B)** $\frac{x + 10}{pd}$ **(C)** $\frac{10px}{d}$ **(D)** $\frac{p(x + 10)}{d}$ **(E)** $pd(x + 10)$

6. If pencils costs x cents each, how many pencils can be purchased for y dollars?

   (A) $\frac{100}{xy}$ **(B)** $\frac{xy}{100}$ **(C)** $\frac{100y}{x}$ **(D)** $\frac{y}{100x}$ **(E)** $100xy$

7. If the profit on an item is $2 and the sum of the cost and the profit is $10, what is the cost of the item?

   (A) $6   **(B)** $8   **(C)** $10   **(D)** $12   **(E)** $14

8. A candy bar weighing 4 ounces costs c cents. If the size of the candy bar is reduced to 3.6 ounces while the price remains the same, then the old price per ounce is what fraction of the new price per ounce?

   (A) $\frac{10c}{9}$ **(B)** $\frac{9c}{10}$ **(C)** $\frac{10}{9c}$ **(D)** $\frac{9}{10c}$ **(E)** $\frac{9}{10}$

9. A merchant increased the original price of an item by 10 percent. If she then reduces the new price by 10 percent, the final result in terms of the original price is
   (A) a decrease of 11 percent
   (B) a decrease of 1 percent
   (C) no net change
   (D) an increase of 1 percent
   (E) an increase of 11 percent

10. Harold is twice as old as Jack, who is three years older than Dan. If Harold's age is five times Dan's age, how old in years is Jack?

(A) 2   (B) 4   (C) 5   (D) 8   (E) 10

11. A tank with capacity T gallons is empty. If water flows into the tank from Pipe X at the rate of X gallons per minute, and water is pumped out by Pipe Y at the rate of Y gallons per minute, and X is greater than Y, in how many minutes will the tank be filled?

(A) $\dfrac{T}{Y-X}$ (B) $\dfrac{T}{X-Y}$ (C) $\dfrac{T-X}{Y}$ (D) $\dfrac{X-Y}{60T}$ (E) $\dfrac{60T}{XY}$

12. If 144 pencils cost d dollars, how many pencils can be purchased for $0.50?

(A) $72d$ (B) $288d$ (C) $\dfrac{72}{d}$ (D) $\dfrac{d}{72}$ (E) $\dfrac{720}{d}$

13. Machine X produces w widgets in five minutes. Machine X and Machine Y, working at the same time, produce w widgets in two minutes. How long will it take Machine Y working alone to produce w widgets?

(A) 2 min. 30 sec.
(B) 2 min. 40 sec.
(C) 3 min. 20 sec.
(D) 3 min. 30 sec.
(E) 3 min. 40 sec.

14. If a train travels m miles in h hours and 45 minutes, what is its average speed in miles per hour?

(A) $\dfrac{m}{h+\frac{3}{4}}$ (B) $\dfrac{m}{1\frac{3}{4}h}$ (C) $m\left(h+\dfrac{3}{4}\right)$ (D) $\dfrac{m+45}{h}$ (E) $\dfrac{h}{m+45}$

15. In a playground, there are x seesaws. If 50 children are all riding on seesaws, two to a seesaw, and five seesaws are not in use, what is x?

(A) 15   (B) 20   (C) 25   (D) 30   (E) 35

16. Of a group of 27 students, 18 belong to the French Club and 15 belong to the Spanish Club. If each student belongs to at least one club, how many students belong to both clubs?

(A) 3   (B) 6   (C) 8   (D) 10   (E) 24

17. In a certain population group, 57 percent of the people have characteristic X and 63 percent have characteristic Y. If every person in the group has at least one of the two characteristics, what percent of the people have both X and Y?

(A) 6%   (B) 12%   (C) 18%   (D) 20%   (E) 23%

18. Mike is older than Ned but younger than Oscar. If m, n, and o are the ages of Mike, Ned, and Oscar, respectively, then which of the following is true?
(A) $m < n < o$
(B) $n < m < o$
(C) $o < n < m$
(D) $o < m < n$
(E) $n < o < m$

19. If $2 < x < 5$ and $3 < y < 6$, which of the following describes all of the possible values of $x + y$?
(A) $1 < x + y < 6$
(B) $1 < x + y < 11$
(C) $2 < x + y < 6$
(D) $3 < x + y < 5$
(E) $5 < x + y < 11$

14

20. If $2 < x < 5$ and $3 < y < 6$, which of the following describes all of the possible values of $x - y$?

(A) $-4 < x - y < 1$

(B) $-4 < x - y < 2$

(C) $-1 < x - y < 1$

(D) $-1 < x - y < 11$

(E) $5 < x - y < 11$

Algebraic Manipulations

On each exam, a few of the math problems require algebraic manipulation. And sometimes there is no better way to attack the problem than to do the operations indicated. We will divide our discussion of algebraic manipulations into two parts: rewriting expressions and solving equations.

Rewriting Expressions

1. Evaluating Expressions

The easiest rewriting problems ask you to change an algebraic expression into a number by having you substitute values. This is called "evaluating an expression."

EXAMPLE:

If $x = 2$, what is the value of $x^2 + 2x - 2$?
(A) -2 **(B)** 0 **(C)** 2 **(D)** 4 **(E)** 6

We use the same strategy here that we would employ for an analogous arithmetic problem: if the operations are manageable, just do them. Here, you substitute 2 for x and do the easy arithmetic:

$$x^2 + 2x - 2 = 2^2 + 2(2) - 2 = 4 + 4 - 2 = 8 - 2 = 6$$

A test-writer might try to make a problem like this more difficult by using fractions.

EXAMPLE:

If $x = 2$, then $\frac{1}{x^2} + \frac{1}{x} - \frac{x}{2} =$
(A) $\frac{-3}{4}$ **(B)** $\frac{-1}{4}$ **(C)** 0 **(D)** $\frac{1}{4}$ **(E)** $\frac{1}{2}$

The answer is (B). Just substitute 2 for each occurrence of x:

$$\frac{1}{x^2} + \frac{1}{x} - \frac{x}{2} = \frac{1}{2^2} + \frac{1}{2} - \frac{2}{2} =$$

$$\frac{1}{4} + \frac{1}{2} - 1 = \frac{3}{4} - 1 = -\frac{1}{4}$$

And just as was the case with arithmetic manipulations, there is a limit to the complexity of manipulations. You might find something like this.

EXAMPLE:

If $p = 1$, $q = 2$, and $r = 3$, then $\frac{(q \times r)(r - q)}{(q - p)(p \times q)} =$
(A) -3 **(B)** -1 **(C)** 0 **(D)** 3 **(E)** 6

14

You just substitute for the different letters and execute:

$$\frac{(q \times r)(r - q)}{(q - p)(p \times q)} = \frac{(2 \times 3)(3 - 2)}{(2 - 1)(1 \times 2)} = \frac{(6)(1)}{(1)(2)} = \frac{6}{2} = 3$$

Such manipulations shouldn't get any more complicated than this; but if they do, you know to look for an escape route.

2. *Exponents*

A knowledge of the rules for manipulating exponents is essential for many algebraic manipulations:

1. $(x^m)(x^n) = x^{m + n}$

2. $\left(\dfrac{x^m}{x^n}\right) = x^{m - n}$

3. $(x^m)^n = x^{m \cdot n}$

4. $(x^m \cdot y^m)^n = x^{mn} \cdot y^{mn}$

5. $\left(\dfrac{x^m}{y^m}\right)^n = \dfrac{x^{mn}}{y^{mn}}$

Occasionally, you may be asked to demonstrate your knowledge of these rules.

EXAMPLE:

$\dfrac{9(x^2y^3)^6}{(3x^6y^9)^2} =$

(A) 1   **(B)** 3   **(C)** x^2y^3 **(D)** $3x^2y^3$ **(E)** $x^{12}y^{12}$

The answer is (A).

$$\frac{9(x^2y^3)^6}{(3x^6y^9)^2} = \frac{9(x^{2 \cdot 6}y^{3 \cdot 6})}{3^2x^{6 \cdot 2}y^{9 \cdot 2}} = \frac{9x^{12}y^{18}}{9x^{12}y^{18}} = 1$$

3. *Factoring*

Although factoring of algebraic expressions is an important part of most high school algebra classes, it's really not that important for the SAT. Of course, you might be asked to do simple factoring.

EXAMPLE:

$2x^3 + 4x^2 + 6x =$
(A) $2x(2x^2 + 2x + 6)$
(B) $2x(x^2 + 2x + 3)$
(C) $2x(x + 5)$
(D) $3x(x + 2x + 2)$
(E) $6x(x + 2x + 1)$

The answer is (B), as you can prove to yourself by multiplying:

$2x(x^2 + 2x + 3) = 2x^3 + 4x^2 + 6x$

Generally, the factoring procedures you learned in the chapter on arithmetic are all you need to know. If you need to factor a quadratic expression, you follow the formats you learned in the preceding chapter:

$$x^2 - y^2 = (x + y)(x - y) \quad \text{(Called the difference of two squares)}$$
$$x^2 + 2xy + y^2 = (x + y)(x + y) \quad \text{(Also written } [x + y]^2)$$
$$x^2 - 2xy + y^2 = (x - y)(x - y) \quad \text{(Not used that often, but easy to recognize)}$$

Whenever you see one of these three expressions, you should have an irresistible urge to factor.

EXAMPLE:

$$\frac{x^2 - y^2}{x + y} =$$

(A) $x^2 - y^2$ **(B)** $x^2 + y^2$ **(C)** $x^2 + y$ **(D)** $x + y^2$ **(E)** $x - y$

The answer is (E). Just factor the numerator, using the method for the difference of two squares:

$$\frac{x^2 - y^2}{(x + y)} = \frac{(x + y)(x - y)}{x + y} = x - y$$

It is theoretically possible, though unlikely, that you could be asked to factor a quadratic expression that is not one of the three shown above. But then you would look for an escape route:

EXAMPLE:

$$\frac{x^2 - x - 6}{x + 2} =$$

(A) $x^2 - \frac{1}{2}x - 3$ **(B)** $x^2 - 2$ **(C)** $x - 2$ **(D)** $x - 3$ **(E)** x

The answer is (D). And the trick is to see that $x + 2$ must be a factor of $x^2 - x - 6$. (Otherwise, what is the question doing on the SAT?) Now you can figure out what the other factor is:

$$(x + 2)(? \quad ?) = x^2 - x - 6$$

The first question mark must be filled in by an x. That's the only way to get x^2 in the final result:

$$(x + 2)(x \quad ?) = x^2 - x - 6$$

The second question mark must be 3:

$$(x + 2)(x \quad 3) = x^2 - x - 6$$

Finally, to get -6 in the final result, the sign must be $-$:

$$(x + 2)(x - 3) = x^2 - 3x + 2x - 6 = x^2 - x - 6$$

14

Once you know this, you rewrite the original expression:

$$\frac{x^2 - x - 6}{x + 2} = \frac{(x + 2)(x - 3)}{x + 2} = x - 3$$

And what happens if you fail to see the trick? You can use one of the other techniques we have already used to good advantage. Try numbers. Assume that $x = 1$:

$$\frac{x^2 - x - 6}{x + 2} = \frac{1^2 - 1 - 6}{1 + 2} = \frac{1 - 1 - 6}{3} = -\frac{6}{3} = -2$$

So substituting 1 for x into the correct choice will yield -2:

(A) $x^2 - \frac{1}{2}x - 3 = 1^2 - \frac{1}{2}(1) - 3 = -3\frac{1}{2}$ (Wrong.)

(B) $x^2 - 2 = 1^2 - 2 = 1 - 2 = -1$ (Wrong.)

(C) $x - 2 = 1 - 2 = -1$ (Wrong.)

(D) $x - 3 = 1 - 3 = -2$ (Correct.)

(E) $x = 1$ (Wrong.)

4. Defined Functions

In algebra, you learned about the expression $f(\ )$, which signals a function. $f(x)$ tells you to do something to the term inside the parentheses. Algebraic functions are tested by the SAT using strange drawings.

EXAMPLE:

If $\underline{\bigtriangledown x}= x^2 - x$ for all whole numbers, then $\underline{\bigtriangledown -2}=$
(A) -6 **(B)** -2 **(C)** 0 **(D)** 4 **(E)** 6

The answer is (E). The weird drawing does the job of $f(\ )$. $\bigtriangledown$ tells you to take whatever is inside the $\bigtriangledown$ and do "$x^2 - x$" to it. If $x = -2$, then $\underline{\bigtriangledown x} = (-2^2) - (-2) = 4 + 2 = 6$.

Some function questions are easy (the one above), while others are fairly difficult. But even the easy ones can seem difficult because of the unusual format. To make them seem more familiar, you might want to give them a name, say, your own name. If your name is Ted, you could analyze a function in the following way.

EXAMPLE:

If $\underline{\bigtriangledown x}= x^2 - x$ for all whole numbers, then $\underline{\bigtriangledown 3}=$
(A) 27 **(B)** 30 **(C)** 58 **(D)** 72 **(E)** 121

The answer is (B). You must ted the result of tedding 3. To ted 3, you square 3 and subtract 3 from that result: $3^2 - 3 = 9 - 3 = 6$. Now you do ted to that. To ted 6, you square 6 and subtract 6 from that result: $6^2 - 6 = 36 - 6 = 30$. The main thing is to take the problem one step at a time.

Sometimes functions come in pairs. Then, the first question will just ask that you perform the defined operation on a number. The second will ask for something more complicated.

EXAMPLES:

For all numbers, $x * y = xy + y$.
What is $4 * 5$?
(A) 12   **(B)** 18   **(C)** 24   **(D)** 25   **(E)** 30

If $3 * 2 = 7 * k$, then $k =$
(A) 1   **(B)** 2   **(C)** 3   **(D)** 4   **(E)** 5

The first question just asks you to apply the definition of "*." Using Ted's name (or your own), 4 ted 5 means 4 times 5 plus 5: $(4 \times 5) + 5 = 20 + 5 = 25$. So the correct choice is (D).

The second question is more difficult. First, let's find the value of 3 ted 2. 3 ted 2 means 3 times 2 plus 2: $(3 \times 2) + 2 = 6 + 2 = 8$. So $7 * k = 8$, but what is k? Fall back on one of our strategies. Test the choices starting with (C).

$7 * 3$ means 7 times 3 plus 3: $(7 \times 3) + 3 = 21 + 3 = 24$. But that's not equal to 8, so (C) is wrong. Since (C) is too large, try (B).

$7 * 2$ means 7 times 2 plus 2: $(7 \times 2) + 2 = 14 + 2 = 16$. Again too large, so the correct choice must be (A): $7 * 1$ means 7 times 1 plus 1: $(7 \times 1) + 1 = 7 + 1 = 8$.

So (A) is correct.

Solving Equations

1. One Equation with One Simple Variable

These questions are generally in the easiest third of a section and require nothing more than that you solve for x.

EXAMPLE:

If $(2 + 3)(1 + x) = 25$, then $x =$

(A) $\frac{1}{5}$ **(B)** $\frac{1}{4}$ **(C)** 1   **(D)** 4   **(E)** 5

The answer is (D).
Solve for x:

$$(2 + 3)(1 + x) = 25$$

$$5(1 + x) = 25$$

Divide both sides by 5:

$$\frac{5(1 + x)}{5} = \frac{25}{5}$$

$$1 + x = 5$$

Subtract 1:

$$1 + x (-1) = 5 - 1$$

$$x = 4$$

14

It is possible to employ our "test the test" technique by substituting the choices back into the equation. But given that the equation is so simple, it's probably easier to solve for *x* directly. You may, however, use the testing technique to check your solution. Substitute 4 back into the original equation: $(2 + 3)(1 + 4) = (5)(5) = 25$. This proves our solution is correct.

Sometimes the test-writers will attempt to jazz up their simple equations a bit by using decimals or fractions, but this really doesn't change things much.

EXAMPLE:

If $T \times \frac{3}{7} = \frac{3}{7} \times 9$, then T =

(A) $\frac{1}{9}$ **(B)** $\frac{1}{7}$ **(C)** 1 **(D)** 7 **(E)** 9

Once you divide both sides by $\frac{3}{7}$ to eliminate the fractions, the equation becomes $T = 9$. So there's no need for a strategy other than just doing the simple algebra.

There is one variation on this theme for which you might look for something different.

EXAMPLE:

If $2x + 3 = 7$, then $2x =$
(A) 4   **(B)** 6   **(C)** 8   **(D)** 14   **(E)** 21

The correct choice is (A), and it would not be wrong to solve for *x*. $2x = 4$, so $x = 2$. Therefore, $2x = 2(2) = 4$. You don't really need to do the last two steps. Once you have $2x = 4$, you have your solution.

EXAMPLE:

If $\frac{1}{3}x = 10$, then $\frac{1}{6}x =$

(A) $\frac{1}{15}$ **(B)** $\frac{2}{3}$ **(C)** 2   **(D)** 5   **(E)** 30

The answer is (D). And again it would not be wrong to solve for *x* and then substitute your solution for *x* in $\frac{1}{6}x$. But you can save a few seconds if you can see that $\frac{1}{6}$ is one-half of $\frac{1}{3}$, so $\frac{1}{6}x$ is half of $\frac{1}{3}x$. Therefore, half of 10 is 5.

In general, then, if the problem is an equation with one simple variable, you are safe solving for the variable. But if the question asks for a multiple or a fraction of the variable, you can save a little time if you can compare things directly without solving for the variable itself.

2. One Equation with Two Variables

With one equation and one variable, you can solve for the variable. But with two variables and only one equation, you won't be able to get a solution for either variable alone.

EXAMPLE:

If $x + y = 3$, then $2x + 2y =$

(A) $\frac{2}{3}$ (B) $\frac{1}{2}$ (C) $\frac{2}{3}$ (D) 6

(E) Cannot be determined from the information given.

The answer is (D). Although it is not possible to find values for x and y individually, $2x + 2y = 2(x + y)$, so $2x + 2y$ is double 3, which is 6.

For questions with two variables and only one equation, look for a way of transforming the first expression into the second. The transformation will give you a solution.

3. Two Equations with Two Variables

With two equations and two variables, you solve using the technique of simultaneous equations:

Given two equations with two variables, x and y, to solve for x:

Step 1:   **In one of the equations, define y in terms of x (y = some form of x).**

Step 2:   **Substitute the value of y (from step 1) for every occurrence of y in the other equation.**   (This will eliminate the ys leaving only xs.)

Step 3:   **Solve for x.**   (And, if necessary, substitute the value of x for x into either equation to get the value of y.)

In simplest form, such problems look like this:

EXAMPLE:

If $2x + y = 8$ and $x - y = 1$, then $x =$
(A) -2 (B) -1 (C) 0   (D) 1   (E) 3

The answer is (E).

First, use one of the equations to define y in terms of x. Since the second is simpler, use it:

$x - y = 1$

$x = 1 + y$

$x - 1 = y$, so $y = x - 1$.

Second, substitute $x - 1$ into the other equation for every occurrence of y. (There is only one occurrence of y in the other equation.)

$2x + y = 8$

$2x + (x - 1) = 8$

Third, solve for x:

$$2x + (x - 1) = 8$$
$$3x - 1 = 8$$
$$3x = 9$$
$$x = 3$$

Sometimes it may be necessary to continue the process to solve for the second variable.

EXAMPLE:

If $2x + y = 8$ and $x - y = 1$, then $x + y =$
(A) -1 (B) 1 (C) 2 (D) 3 (E) 5

The answer is (E), and this is the question we just answered, except that we are looking for $x + y$, not just x. You follow the same procedure, and once you know $x = 3$, substitute 3 for x into either equation. Since the second is simpler, we will use it:

$$x - y = 1$$
$$3 - y = 1$$
$$y = 2$$
So $x + y = 5$.

If you keep your eyes open, you might find a chance to make a direct substitution, thereby avoiding some algebra.

EXAMPLE:

If $7x = 2$ and $3y - 7x = 10$, then $y =$
(A) 2 (B) 3 (C) 4 (D) 5 (E) 6

The answer is (C). The problem can be solved using the procedure outlined above; but in solving for x, you get a fraction. And fractions are a pain in the neck. You can avoid the problem, however, if you see not only that $7x = 2$ but that $7x$ is one of the terms of the second equation. Just substitute 2 for $7x$ in the second equation:

$$3y - 2 = 10$$
$$3y = 12$$
$$y = 4$$

And such shortcuts become absolutely necessary with more difficult problems.

EXAMPLE:

If $4x + 5y = 12$ and $3x + 4y = 5$, then $7(x + y) =$
(A) 7 (B) 14 (C) 49 (D) 77 (E) 91

The answer is (C). You could, if you had to, solve for both x and y, but it would be a tedious process. The best attack on this question is to see that the final answer requires the *sum* of x and y ($x + y$), not the individual values of x and y.

We can simply rewrite our equations so that we get a value for $x + y$:

$$4x + 5y = 12$$
$$- [3x + 4y = 5]$$
$$\overline{x + y = 7}$$

Since $x + y = 7$, $7(x + y) = 7(7) = 49$.

In general, then, "two equation/two variable" questions should be attacked as simultaneous equations, unless that process would be too complicated. Then look for an alternative.

4. Quadratic Equations (Equations with a Squared Variable)

Perhaps one of the most important topics in high school algebra is solving quadratic equations. These are equations with squared variables.

> **EXAMPLE:**
>
> If $x^2 - 3x = 4$, then which of the following shows all possible values of x?
> **(A)** 4, 1   **(B)** 4, −1   **(C)** −4, 1   **(D)** −4, −1   **(E)** −4, 1, 4

To *solve* a quadratic equation:

Step 1:   **Set all the terms equal to zero.**

Step 2:   **Factor.**

Step 3:   **Set each of the factors equal to zero.**

Step 4:   **Solve each equation.**

First, set all the terms equal to zero:

$$x^2 - 3x = 4$$
$$x^2 - 3x - 4 = 0$$

Next, factor:

$$(x - 4)(x + 1) = 0$$

Now, create equations with each of the factors equal to zero:

$$x - 4 = 0 \quad \text{or} \quad x + 1 = 0$$

Finally, solve each equation:

$$x - 4 = 0 \quad \text{or} \quad x + 1 = 0$$
$$x = 4 \qquad x = -1$$

And if you need to, you can check these solutions by reinserting 4 and −1 in the original equation.

Although this procedure is a big deal in math class, you probably *will not* need to do it on the SAT. And in the extremely unlikely event that you do need to do it, the factoring will probably fit one of three patterns:

$$x^2 - y^2 = (x - y)(x + y)$$

$$x^2 + 2xy + y^2 = (x + y)(x + y)$$

$$x^2 - 2xy + y^2 = (x - y)(x + y)$$

You should recognize these three patterns. They are the same three you were asked to memorize in Lesson 13 as a way of avoiding lengthy calculations. Once again, the first and second are more important than the third. In the context of algebra, it is possible you could get a problem like the following.

EXAMPLE:

If $x^2 - y^2 = 0$ and $x + y = 1$, then $x - y =$
(A) -1 **(B)** 0 **(C)** 1 **(D)** 2
(E) Cannot be determined from the information given.

The answer is (B). Factor:

$$x^2 - y^2 = 0$$

$$(x + y)(x - y) = 0$$

Either $x + y = 0$ or $x - y = 0$.

The question stipulates that $x + y = 1$ and not zero, so $x - y$ must be zero.

In general, then, you probably will not need to solve a quadratic equation. If you should, it will probably fit one of the two patterns: $x^2 - y^2$ or $x^2 + 2xy + y^2$. And remember, most quadratic equations have two solutions. (Some, like $x^2 - 2x + 1 = 0$, have only one solution.)

Algebraic Manipulations (Answers, page 301)

1. Which of the following is equal to $3x^3 + 3x^2 + 3x$?
    (A) $9x^6$ **(B)** $3x^6$ **(C)** $3x(x^3 + x^2 + x)$ **(D)** $3x(3x^2 + 3x + 3)$ **(E)** $3x(x^2 + x + 1)$

2. $\dfrac{x^2 + 2xy + y^2}{x + y} =$
    (A) $x + y$ **(B)** $x - y$ **(C)** $x^2 + y$ **(D)** $x + y^2$ **(E)** $x^2 + y^2$

3. If $x - y = 3$, then $\dfrac{x^2 - y^2}{x + y} =$
    (A) 0 **(B)** 1 **(C)** 3 **(D)** 9
    (E) Cannot be determined from the information given.

4. $(x + y)^2 - (x - y)^2 =$
    (A) $4xy$ **(B)** x^2 **(C)** $x + y$ **(D)** $x - y$ **(E)** $x^2 + y^2$

5. $\dfrac{x^2 + 2x + 1}{x + 1} =$
    (A) x **(B)** $x + 1$ **(C)** $x - 1$ **(D)** x^2 **(E)** x^3

6. If ⟨x⟩ denotes the greatest integer that is less than or equal to x, then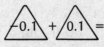
    (A) -2 **(B)** -1 **(C)** 0 **(D)** 1 **(E)** 2

Questions 7 and 8
For all numbers x and y, $x \diamondsuit y = xy + x$

7. $4 \diamondsuit 5 =$
    (A) 9 **(B)** 24 **(C)** 25 **(D)** 36 **(E)** 41

8. If $2 \diamondsuit 3 = x \diamondsuit 7$, then $x =$
    (A) 0 **(B)** 1 **(C)** 4 **(D)** 5 **(E)** 7

Questions 9 and 10
For all real numbers except 0, $x \diamondsuit y \diamondsuit z = \dfrac{(x \diamondsuit y)}{z}$

9. $9 \diamondsuit 3 \diamondsuit 1 =$
    (A) 1 **(B)** 3 **(C)** 9 **(D)** 10 **(E)** 12

10. $x \diamondsuit y \diamondsuit (x \diamondsuit y \diamondsuit z) =$
    (A) $\dfrac{z}{x + y}$ **(B)** $\dfrac{x + y}{z}$ **(C)** x **(D)** y **(E)** z

11. If $n + n + 1 + n + 2 = 12$, then $n =$
    (A) 0 **(B)** 1 **(C)** 2 **(D)** 3 **(E)** 4

12. $\dfrac{1}{x} + \dfrac{1}{x} = 4$, then $x =$
    (A) $\dfrac{1}{4}$ **(B)** $\dfrac{1}{2}$ **(C)** 1 **(D)** 2 **(E)** 4

14

13. If $x + y = 9$, then $\frac{1}{3}x + \frac{1}{3}y =$

    (A) 1 **(B)** 3 **(C)** 18 **(D)** 27 **(E)** 54

14. If $2x + y = 5$ and $x + y = 3$, then $x =$

    (A) 0 **(B)** 1 **(C)** 2 **(D)** 4 **(E)** 5

15. If $3m = 5$ and $4n - 3m = 3$, then $n =$

    (A) 0 **(B)** 1 **(C)** 2 **(D)** 4 **(E)** 8

16. If $7m - 2 = 3k$, then $\frac{7m - 2}{3} =$

    (A) $\frac{k}{3}$ **(B)** k **(C)** $3k$ **(D)** $9k$ **(E)** $27k$

17. If $x = 4y$, then $12y - 3x =$

    (A) 0 **(B)** 1 **(C)** 7 **(D)** 15

    (E) Cannot be determined from the information given.

18. If $x + \frac{1}{3} = \frac{x + 2}{3}$, then $x =$

    (A) $\frac{1}{2}$ **(B)** 1 **(C)** $\frac{3}{2}$ **(D)** 2 **(E)** 3

19. If $(x + y)^2 = x^2 + y^2$, then $xy =$

    (A) 0 **(B)** 1 **(C)** 2 **(D)** 5

    (E) Cannot be determined from the information given.

20. If $(x + y)^2 - (x - y)^2 = 20$, then $xy =$

    (A) 0 **(B)** 1 **(C)** 2 **(D)** 5

    (E) Cannot be determined from the information given.

Algebraic Applications

Some questions ask for you to apply your algebra skills to practical situations. The problems in Exercise 1 are examples. And this raises an interesting question. If it is possible to solve algebra questions by testing choices or by assuming numbers, why bother with algebra at all?

There are two answers to this question. One, sometimes you may not be able to find an alternative solution, in which case, you can use the "official" algebra approach. Two, a direct solution using algebra may be faster than working backwards or assuming numbers.

You can brush up on your algebra by doing the following problems.

14

Algebraic Applications (Answers, page 304)

Directions: These problems appeared in Exercise 1. Solve them using algebra. To make sure you don't try to use your Holmesian strategies, there are no answer choices. You will have to arrive at your own solutions.

1. On a shopping trip, Peter spent $\frac{1}{3}$ of his money for a jacket and another $5 for a hat. If Peter still had $\frac{1}{2}$ of his money left, how much money did he have originally? _____

2. After filling the car's fuel tank, a driver drove from P to Q and then to R. She used $\frac{2}{5}$ of the fuel driving from P to Q. If she used another 7 gallons to drive from Q to R and still had $\frac{1}{4}$ of a tank left, how many gallons does the tank hold? _____

3. A school meeting was attended only by sophomores, juniors, and seniors. $\frac{5}{12}$ of those who attended were juniors, and $\frac{1}{3}$ were seniors. If 36 sophomores attended, what was the total number of students who attended the meeting? _____

4. If p pounds of coffee costs d dollars, how many pounds of coffee can be purchased for x dollars? _____

5. If p pounds of coffee costs d dollars, how many pounds of coffee can be purchased for x + 10 dollars? _____

6. If pencils costs x cents each, how many pencils can be purchased for y dollars? _____

7. If the profit on an item is $2 and the sum of the cost and the profit is $10, what is the cost of the item? _____

8. A candy bar weighing 4 ounces costs c cents. If the size of the candy bar is reduced to 3.6 ounces while the price remains the same, then the old price per ounce is what fraction of the new price per ounce? _____

9. A merchant increased the original price of an item by 10 percent. If she then reduces the new price by 10 percent, what is the final result in terms of the original price? _____

10. Harold is twice as old as Jack, who is three years older than Dan. If Harold's age is five times Dan's age, how old in years is Jack? _____

11. A tank with capacity T gallons is empty. If water flows into the tank from Pipe X at the rate of X gallons per minute, and water is pumped out by Pipe Y at the rate of Y gallons per minute, and X is greater than Y, in how many minutes will the tank be filled? _____

12. If 144 pencils cost d dollars, how many pencils can be purchased for $0.50? _____

13. Machine X produces w widgets in five minutes. Machine X and Machine Y, working at the same time, produce w widgets in two minutes. How long will it take Machine Y working alone to produce w widgets? _____

14. If a train travels m miles in h hours and 45 minutes, expressed in terms of m and h, what is its average speed in miles per hour? _____

15. In a playground, there are x seesaws. If 50 children are all riding on seesaws, two to a seesaw, and five seesaws are not in use, what is x? _____

16. Of a group of 27 students, 18 belong to the French Club and 15 belong to the Spanish Club. If each student belongs to at least one club, how many students belong to both clubs? _____

17. In a certain population group, 57 percent of the people have characteristic X and 63 percent have characteristic Y. If every person in the group has at least one of the two characteristics, what percent of the people have both X and Y? _____

14

Summary

1. Some problems require simple algebraic manipulations such as evaluating an expression, working with exponents, or factoring. Do the operations.

2. Defined functions use a nonstandardized symbol to define a short series of algebraic operations. Do the indicated operations step by step. For a difficult function problem, try working backwards from the answer choices.

3. If the question stem is an equation (or equations), solve for an unknown or find a way of directly transforming one expression into another.

4. The Holmesian principle "one of the five suspects" is the basis for two powerful strategies: (a) test answer choices, and (b) assume actual numbers for unknowns.

Explanatory Answers

EXERCISE 1

1. (C) Test choices starting with (C). If Peter spent $\frac{1}{3}$ of his money for a jacket, he spent $\frac{1}{3}$ of $30 = $10. This would leave him with $30 − $10 = $20. Take away another $5 for the hat, and he is left with $20 − $5 = $15. And $\frac{$15}{$30}$ is equal to $\frac{1}{2}$, so (C) is correct.

2. (C) Test choices starting with (C). On the assumption that the tank originally contained 20 gallons, the driver used $\frac{2}{5}$ of 20, or 8, gallons going from P to Q, which left her with $20 − 8 = 12$ gallons. Take away another 7 gallons, and she is left with $12 − 7 = 5$. $\frac{5}{20}$ is $\frac{1}{4}$, so (C) is correct.

3. (B) We will test choices, but first we must determine what fraction of the students are *not* sophomores. $\frac{5}{12} + \frac{1}{3} = \frac{5}{12} + \frac{4}{12} = \frac{9}{12} = \frac{3}{4}$. If $\frac{3}{4}$ are not sophomores, $\frac{1}{4}$ are sophomores. So 36 over the total number must be $\frac{1}{4}$. Start with (C). $\frac{36}{252}$ is not $\frac{1}{4}$, so (C) is wrong. And since $\frac{36}{252}$ is less than $\frac{1}{4}$, the number of students is less than 252, so we should try a smaller number. (The smaller the denominator, the larger the fraction.) So we try (B). $\frac{36}{144} = \frac{1}{4}$. So (B) is correct.

4. (C) Assume some numbers. Suppose coffee costs $5 for 2 pounds and that you have $10. You could buy 4 pounds. So if $p = 2$, $d = 5$, and $x = 10$, the correct formula generates the value 4:

(A) $\frac{pd}{x} = \frac{2(5)}{10} = \frac{10}{10} = 1$ (Wrong.)

(B) $\frac{x}{pd} = \frac{10}{2(5)} = \frac{10}{10} = 1$ (Wrong.)

(C) $\frac{xp}{d} = \frac{10(2)}{5} = \frac{20}{5} = 4$ (Correct.)

(D) $\frac{d}{xp} = \frac{5}{10(2)} = \frac{5}{20} = \frac{1}{4}$ (Wrong.)

(E) $xpd = (10)(2)(5) = 100$ (Wrong.)

5. (D) Again, assume that $p = 2$ and $d = 5$. And let's assume that $x = 0$. If $x = 0$, then $x + 10 = 10$, and so again the correct answer should be 4.

(A) $\frac{pd}{x + 10} = \frac{(2)(5)}{0 + 10} = \frac{10}{10} = 1$ (Wrong.)

(B) $\frac{x + 10}{pd} = \frac{0 + 10}{(2)(5)} = \frac{10}{10} = 1$ (Wrong.)

(C) $\frac{10px}{d} = \frac{10(2)(0)}{5} = \frac{0}{5} = 0$ (Wrong.)

(D) $\frac{p(x + 10)}{d} = \frac{2(0 + 10)}{5} = \frac{20}{5} = 4$ (Correct.)

(E) $pd(x + 10) = 2(5)(0 + 10) = 100$ (Wrong.)

14

6. (C) Assume some numbers. Assume pencils cost 2 cents apiece and that you
have $2 to spend. You can buy 100 pencils. So if $x = 2$ and $y = 2$, the correct
formula generates 100.

  (A) $\dfrac{100}{xy} = \dfrac{100}{(2)(2)} = \dfrac{100}{4} = 25$ (Wrong.)

  (B) $\dfrac{xy}{100} = \dfrac{(2)(2)}{100} = \dfrac{4}{100} = \dfrac{1}{25}$ (Wrong.)

  (C) $\dfrac{100y}{x} = \dfrac{100(2)}{2} = \dfrac{200}{2} = 100$ (Correct.)

  (D) $\dfrac{y}{100x} = \dfrac{2}{100(2)} = \dfrac{2}{200}$ (Wrong.)

  (E) $100xy = 100(2)(1) = 200$ (Wrong.)

7. (B) Test numbers, starting with (C). If the cost of the item is $10, then the sum
of the cost and profit is $10 + $2 = $12, which is more than $10. So try a
smaller number, (B). If the cost of the item is $8, then the sum of the cost and
profit is $8 + $2 = $10. So (B) is correct.

8. (E) Assume some numbers. Since the numbers you assume will have to be
divided by both 4 and 3.6, choose 36. So the cost per ounce at the old price
was 36 cents per 4 ounces = 9 cents per ounce. At the new price, it is 36 cents
per 3.6 ounces = 10 cents per ounce. So if $c = 36$, the correct choice will
yield the value $\frac{9}{10}$.

   You don't even need to calculate for (A) through (D). You can see immedi-
ately that once you put in 36 for c, they will not equal $\frac{9}{10}$. Only (E) is $\frac{9}{10}$—but
(E) doesn't have c as part of it. That's true. And the correct formula should not
have c as part of it.

9. (B) Assume some numbers. Assume the original price of the item is $100.
Increase that by 10 percent: 10% of $100 = $10, and $100 + $10 = $110.
Now decrease $110 by 10 percent: 10% of $110 = $11, and $110 − $11 =
$99. The original price was $100 and the new price is $99, so there is a net
decrease of 1 percent. (Change/Original Total $= \frac{\$1}{\$100} = 1\%$.)

10. (C) Test choices starting with (C). If Jack is five, then Harold (who is twice as
old) is ten. And Dan must be two (Jack is three years older than Dan). If Harold
is ten and Dan is two, then Harold is five times older than Dan. So (C) is
correct.

11. (B) Assume some numbers. Assume the tank has a capacity of 10 gallons, and
that water is flowing in at the rate of 2 gallons per minute and being pumped out
at the rate of 1 gallon per minute. That's a net gain of 1 gallon per minute, and
at that rate it will take 10 ÷ 1 = 10 minutes to fill the tank. So on the assumption that $T = 10$, $X = 2$, and $Y = 1$, the correct formula generates 10.

(A) $\dfrac{10}{1-2} = \dfrac{10}{-1} = -10$ (Wrong.)

(B) $\dfrac{10}{2-1} = \dfrac{10}{1} = 10$ (Correct.)

(C) $\dfrac{10-2}{1} = \dfrac{8}{1} = 8$ (Wrong.)

(D) $\dfrac{2-1}{60(10)} = \dfrac{1}{600}$ (Wrong.)

(E) $\dfrac{60(10)}{(2)(1)} = 5$ (Wrong.)

12. (C) Assume numbers. Assume that 144 pencils cost \$1, so for 50 cents you can get $\frac{1}{2}$ of 144, or 72. So assuming $d = 1$, the correct choice will generate 72.

(A) $72d = 72(1) = 72$

(B) $288d = 288(1) = 288$ (Wrong.)

(C) $\dfrac{72}{d} = \dfrac{72}{1} = 72$

(D) $\dfrac{d}{72} = \dfrac{1}{72}$ (Wrong.)

(E) $\dfrac{720}{d} = 720$ (Wrong.)

And we seem to have two right answers. But that sometimes happens when you use 1. So let's try again with $d = 2$. If 144 pencils cost \$2, for 50 cents you can buy $\frac{1}{4}$ of 144 = 36.

(A) $72(2) = 144$ (Wrong.)

(C) $\dfrac{72}{2} = 36$ (Correct.)

13. (C) Assume some numbers. Assume that n is 100 widgets—a nice round number that is easily divided by a lot of other numbers. On that assumption, Machine X operates at $100 \div 5 = 20$ widgets per minute. At that rate, when the two machines are working together, Machine X contributes at the rate of 20 widgets per minute, which means Machine X produces only 40 of the 100 widgets. So Machine Y produces the other 60 in two minutes, which is 30 widgets per minute. To produce 100 widgets would take Machine Y $100 \div 30$ $= 3\frac{1}{3}$ minutes, which is three minutes and 20 seconds.

14. (A) Assume some numbers, and let's make them easy. Say that the train traveled for $2\frac{3}{4}$ hours and covered 275 miles. That would be 100 miles per hour. So assuming that $m = 275$ and $h = 2$, the correct formula generates 100.

14

(A) $\dfrac{275}{2\frac{3}{4}} = \dfrac{275}{2.75} = 100$ (Correct.)

(B) $\dfrac{275}{1\frac{3}{4}(2)} = \dfrac{275}{1.75(2)} = \dfrac{275}{3} = 91\frac{2}{3}$ (Wrong.)

(C) $275\left(2 + \dfrac{3}{4}\right) = 275 \times 2.75$ (Wrong.)

(D) $\dfrac{275 + 45}{2} = \dfrac{310}{2} = 155$ (Wrong.)

(E) $\dfrac{2}{275 + 45} = \dfrac{2}{310} = \dfrac{1}{155}$ (Wrong.)

15. (D) Test numbers, starting with (C). Since 50 children need 25 seesaws, if x (the total number of seesaws in the park) is 25, all the seesaws are in use. So 25 is too small; try (D). If there are 30 seesaws in the park and five are not in use, that makes 25 seesaws in use. So (D) is correct.

16. (B) Test numbers. Start with (C). If eight students belong to both clubs, that means that there are $(18 + 15) - 8 = 25$ total students. But that is incorrect. Since 25 is less than 27, fewer than eight must belong to both clubs. So try (B). $(18 + 15) - 6 = 27$. So (B) is correct.

   Incidentally, this sets up a very easy method for solving problems like this. The total membership of the two clubs is $18 + 15 = 33$, but there are only 27 different students. So $33 - 27 = 6$ must belong to both clubs.

17. (D) Test choices, starting with (C). If 18 percent have both characteristics, then $(57 + 63) - 18 = 102$ percent. But the total population cannot exceed 100 percent. So try the next larger number: $(57 + 63) - 20 = 100$ percent.

   And now you can use the method devised in our explanation to the previous question. $(57 + 63) - 100 = 20$.

18. (B) You can make up numbers for the ages. Assume that Mike is two, and Ned (who is younger) is one, and Oscar (who is older) is three. So $m = 2$, $n = 1$, and $o = 3$. The proper order is n, m, o.

19. (E) You don't need any fancy algebraic technique to answer this question. Just try to figure out under what circumstance $x + y$ will be the largest, and under what conditions it will be the smallest. Since x must be larger than 2 and y larger than 3, $x + y$ must be larger than 5. And since x is smaller than 5 and y smaller than 6, $x + y$ must be smaller than 11, which is choice (E).

20. (B) Though this item is a little trickier than the last, you can use the same technique of picking numbers. The least value for $x - y$ will come with the smallest possible value for x and the largest possible value for y: $2 - 6 = -4$. So the smallest possible value for $x - y$ is greater than -4. And the largest value will come with the largest possible value for x and the smallest possible value for y: $5 - 3 = 2$. So $x - y$ must be less than 2.

EXERCISE 2

1. (E) Factor by removing the common factor of $3x$ from each of the terms: $3x^3 + 3x^2 + 3x = 3x(x^2 + x + 1)$.

2. (A) The numerator fits the second of the three factoring patterns you learned: $(x + y)(x + y)$. Simplify by cancelling the $(x + y)$. The final result is $x + y$.

3. (C) Again, you should have an irresistible urge to factor. The numerator of the expression is the difference of two squares, the first of the three factoring patterns you learned. So the numerator is equal to $(x + y)(x - y)$. Next, cancel the $(x + y)$ terms. The result is $x - y$, which is said to be equal to 3.

4. (A) Do the indicated operations, and subtract.

$$(x + y)^2 = (x + y)(x + y) = x^2 + 2xy + y^2$$

$$(x - y)^2 = (x - y)(x - y) = \frac{x^2 - 2xy + y^2}{0 + 4xy + 0}$$

5. (B) $x^2 + 2x + 1$ fits the pattern $x^2 + 2xy + y^2$, where $y = 1$. But even if you didn't recognize that, you should think that $(x + 1)$ is one of the factors of the numerator and work backwards to find the other factor, which is also $(x + 1)$. Then cancel, and the final result is $x + 1$.

6. (B) This is a function problem. To "ted" a number (perform the defined operation on it), you do one of two things. If the number is already an integer, the number stays the same. If the number is not an integer, it is rounded down to the next lowest integer. So tedding -0.1 yields -1. (-1 is the next integer smaller than -0.1.) And tedding 0.1 yields 0. And $-1 + 0 = -1$.

7. (B) Here is the first of a pair of function questions. Use the name *Ted* (or your own name, if you prefer). To *ted* means to multiply the first number by the second and add to that product the first number. So 4 ted 5 is (4 times 5) plus 4 $= 20 + 4 = 24$.

8. (B) This question is more difficult than the previous one. But you can solve it by working backwards. 2 ted 3 is equal to $(2 \times 3) + 2 = 8$. Which of the answer choices, when substituted for x, will yield 8? Try (C). 4 ted 7 is equal to $(4 \times 7) + 4 = 32$. (C) is too large, so try the next smaller choice. 1 ted 7 is equal to $(1 \times 7) + 7 = 8$. Which proves that (B) is correct.

9. (E) The first question of this pair just requires that you plug in numbers. 9 ted 3 ted 1 means 9 plus 3 divided by 1, which is equal to 12.

10. (E) This second question is more difficult, because you must work with unknowns. First, x ted y ted z means $\frac{x+y}{z}$. Now we use that result as the third element of another ted. x ted y ted $\frac{x+y}{z}$ is equal to $x + y$ divided by $\frac{x+y}{z}$. $x + y \div \frac{x+y}{z} = (x + y)(\frac{z}{x+y}) = z$.

11. (D) Solve for n:

$$n + n + 1 + n + 2 = 12$$

$$3n + 3 = 12$$

$$3n = 9$$

$$n = 3$$

14

12. (B) Solve for x:

$$\frac{1}{x} + \frac{1}{x} = 4$$

$$\frac{2}{x} = 4$$

$$2 = 4x$$

$$x = \frac{2}{4} = \frac{1}{2}$$

13. (B) Before you start solving for x, look for a way of converting $x + y$ to $\frac{1}{3}x + \frac{1}{3}y$. You can do that by multiplying $x + y$ by $\frac{1}{3}$: $\frac{1}{3}(x + y) = \frac{1}{3} + \frac{1}{3}y$. So $\frac{1}{3}x + \frac{1}{3}y$ must be equal to $\frac{1}{3}(9)$, or 3.

14. (C) Two variables and two equations calls for the simultaneous equations technique. To solve for x, first isolate y in one of the equations. We will use the second, since it is simpler:

$$x + y = 3$$

$$y = 3 - x$$

Now substitute $3 - x$ for y in the first equation:

$$2x + (3 - x) = 5$$

And solve for x:

$$2x + 3 - x = 5$$

$$2x - x + 3 = 5$$

$$x + 3 = 5$$

$$x = 2$$

15. (C) Simultaneous equations again, so to solve for n, you isolate m: $3m = 5$, so $m = \frac{5}{3}$. Now substitute $\frac{5}{3}$ for m in the second equation:

$$4n - 3\left(\frac{5}{3}\right) = 3$$

$$4n - 5 = 3$$

$$4n = 8$$

$$n = 2$$

Or you might have recognized that since $3m = 5$, you can substitute 5 for $3m$ in the second equation without solving for m.

16. (B) You could solve for m in the first equation, getting m in terms of k:

$$7m = 3k + 2$$

$$m = \frac{3k + 2}{7}$$

Then substitute this into $\frac{7m - 2}{3}$:

$$\frac{7\left(\dfrac{3k + 2}{7}\right) - 2}{3} = \frac{3k + 2 - 2}{3} = \frac{3k}{3} = k$$

That's conceptually correct, but it's too much work. Instead, you should see that you can turn $7m - 2$ into $\frac{7m - 2}{3}$ by dividing by 3. So $\frac{7m - 2}{3} = \frac{3k}{3} = k$.

17. (A) Notice that $12y$ is 3 times $4y$ and that $3x$ is 3 times x. Start by multiplying $x = 4y$ by 3:

$$3(x) = 4y(3)$$

$$3x = 12y$$

Now, to turn $3x = 12y$ into $12y - 3x$, subtract $3x$ from both sides of the equation:

$$3x = 12y$$

$$3x - 3x = 12y - 3x$$

$$0 = 12y - 3x$$

So $12y - 3x$ is equal to 0.

18. (A) You can solve for x:
First, multiply both sides of the equation by 3:

$$3\left(x + \frac{1}{3}\right) = x + 2$$

$$3x + 1 = x + 2$$

$$2x = 1$$

$$x = \frac{1}{2}$$

Or, if you need to, you can use the technique of substituting numbers.

14

19. (A) The natural starting point is to do the indicated multiplication. (It's one of the patterns you memorized.)

$(x + y)^2 = (x + y)(x + y) = x^2 + 2xy + y^2$

So, $x^2 + 2xy + y^2 = x^2 + y^2$.

Subtract x^2 and y^2 from both sides. The result is:

$2xy = 0$

So $xy = 0$.

20. (D) First do the multiplication. You should be able to do this by memory.

$(x + y)^2 = x^2 + 2xy + y^2$
$(x - y)^2 = x^2 - 2xy + y^2$

So:

$x^2 + 2xy + y^2 - (x^2 - 2xy + y^2) = 20$
$x^2 + 2xy + y^2 - x^2 + 2xy - y^2 = 20$
$x^2 - x^2 + 2xy + 2xy + y^2 - y^2 = 20$
$4xy = 20$
$xy = 5$

EXERCISE 3

1. 30

The original amount minus $\frac{1}{3}$ of the original amount minus another \$5 is equal to $\frac{1}{4}$ of the original amount. With x designating the original amount, in algebra:

$x - \frac{1}{3}x - 5 = \frac{1}{2}x$

$\frac{2}{3}x - 5 = \frac{1}{2}x$

$\frac{2}{3}x - \frac{1}{2}x = 5$

$\frac{1}{6}x = 5$

$x = 30$

2. 20

A tank full minus $\frac{2}{5}$ of a tank minus another 7 gallons is equal to $\frac{1}{4}$ of a tank. Let x be the number of gallons the tank holds:

$$x - \frac{2}{5}x - 7 = \frac{1}{4}x$$

$$\frac{3}{5}x - 7 = \frac{1}{4}x$$

$$\frac{3}{5}x - \frac{1}{4}x = 7$$

$$\frac{7}{20}x = 7$$

$$x = 7\left(\frac{20}{7}\right) = 20$$

3. 144

$\frac{5}{12}$ of the total number who attended plus $\frac{1}{3}$ of the total number who attended plus 36 students is equal to the total number who attended. Let T represent the total number who attended:

$$\frac{5}{12}T + \frac{1}{3}T + 36 = T$$

$$\frac{9}{12}T + 36 = T$$

$$36 = T - \frac{3}{4}T$$

$$36 = \frac{1}{4}T$$

$$T = 36 \times 4 = 144$$

4. $\frac{xp}{d}$

To find how much of something can be purchased for a certain amount, you divide the amount of money by the cost. The cost of coffee is d dollars per p pounds, or $\frac{d}{p}$. Then divide x dollars by $\frac{d}{p}$: $x \div \frac{d}{p} = x\left(\frac{p}{d}\right) = \frac{xp}{d}$.

5. $\frac{p(x + 10)}{2}$

Follow the same procedure. The cost of coffee is $\frac{d}{p}$. Next, divide $x + 10$ by $\frac{d}{p}$: $(x + 10) \div \frac{d}{p} = (x + 10)\left(\frac{p}{d}\right) = \frac{p(x + 10)}{2}$.

6. $\frac{100y}{x}$

Again, divide the amount available by the cost. The cost of a pencil is $\frac{x}{1}$. The available amount is y dollars, which is $100y$ cents. $100y \div x = \frac{100y}{x}$.

7. 8

Cost plus $2 = $10. Let C be cost:

$$C + 2 = 10$$

$$C = 8$$

14

8. $\frac{9}{10}$

The old price was $\frac{c}{4}$ ounces, and the new price is $\frac{c}{3.6}$ ounce. Using the "this-of-that" strategy:

old price per ounce/new price per ounce =

$$\frac{\frac{c}{4}}{\frac{c}{.36}} = \frac{c}{4} \times \frac{3.6}{c} = \frac{3.6}{4} = \frac{9}{10}$$

9. 1%

Let P be the original price. The price increases by 10 percent, or $\frac{1}{10}$: $P + 0.1P = 1.1P$. Then that price decreases by 10 percent: $1.1P - 0.11P = 0.99P$. So the net decrease was $0.01P$, and the percent decrease was $\frac{0.01P}{P} = 0.01 = 1\%$.

10. 5

Harold's age is twice Jack's age; Jack's age is 3 more than Dan's; and Harold's age is 5 times Dan's age. Let H, J, and D stand for the ages of Harold, Jack, and Dan:

$H = 2J$ and $J = D + 3$ and $H = 5D$

Since $H = 2J$, substitute $2J$ for H in the third equation:

$H = 5D$, so $2J = 5D$.

Solve for D:

$2J = 5D$

$D = \frac{2}{5}J$

Now substitute $\frac{2}{5}J$ for D in the equation $J = D + 3$:

$J = \frac{2}{5}J + 3$

$J - \frac{2}{5}J = 3$

$\frac{3}{5}J = 3$

$J = 3\left(\frac{5}{3}\right) = 5$

11. $\frac{T}{X - Y}$

Since water comes in at X gallons per minute and goes out at Y gallons per minute, the net gain is $X - Y$. To find how long it will take to fill the tank, divide the capacity of the tank by the net rate at which the tank is being filled: $T = (X - Y)$, which is $\frac{T}{X - Y}$.

12. $\dfrac{72}{d}$

Divide the available amount by the cost of each pencil. The available amount is 50 cents. Pencils cost d dollars, or $100d$, cents per 144. $50 \div \left(\frac{100d}{144}\right)$ $= 50\left(\frac{144}{100d}\right) = \frac{144}{2d} = \frac{72}{d}$.

13. 3 minutes, 20 seconds. Machine X operates at the rate of w widgets per five minutes. Machines X and Y together operate at the rate of w widgets per two minutes. Take away Machine X's contribution, and you will have the rate at which Machine Y operates.

Rate of X and Y together $-$ Rate of X = Rate of Y

$$\frac{w \text{ widgets}}{2 \text{ minutes}} - \frac{w \text{ widgets}}{5 \text{ minutes}} = \frac{w \text{ widgets}}{x \text{ minutes}}$$

$$\frac{w}{2} - \frac{w}{5} = \frac{w}{x}$$

$$\frac{5w - 2w}{10} = \frac{w}{x}$$

$$\frac{3w}{10} = \frac{w}{x}$$

$x = w\left(\dfrac{10}{3w}\right) = \dfrac{10}{3}$, which is 3 minutes and 20 seconds.

14. $\dfrac{m}{h + 3/4}$

The speed is to be expressed in miles. Miles traveled is m, and time traveled is h hours plus another $\frac{3}{4}$ of an hour, or $h + \frac{3}{4}$. So the speed was $\frac{m}{h} + \frac{3}{4}$.

15. 30

The total number of seesaws less five seesaws is equal to enough seesaws for 50 children.

$$x - 5 = \frac{50}{2}$$

$$x - 5 = 25$$

$$x = 30$$

16. 6

A diagram will show how to set up the equation:

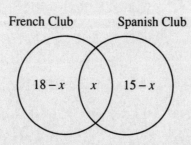

In the diagram above, x represents the number of students who belong to both clubs.

$$(18 - x) + x + (15 - x) = 27$$

$$18 + 15 - x = 27$$

$$33 - x = 27$$

$$x = 6$$

17. 20%

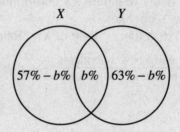

In the diagram above, b represents the percent of the population having both X and Y.

$$(57\% - b\%) + b\% + (63\% - b\%) = 100b\%$$

$$57\% + 63\% - b\% = 100b\%$$

$$120\% - b\% = 100\%$$

$$b = 20\%$$

Problem-Solving: Geometry

✔ Objectives

To review the key principles of geometry frequently tested.

To learn strategies for handling problems involving composite and shaded-area figures.

To learn strategies for solving unusual items.

To learn strategies that avoid the use of geometry formulas altogether.

1. Angles
2. Triangles
3. Rectangles and Squares
4. Circles
5. Solids
6. Coordinate Geometry
7. Complex Figures
8. Nonformulaic Techniques
   - "Guestimating"
   - Measuring
   - "Meastimating"

15

Several problems in each math section will test your knowledge of geometry. You won't be asked to give formal proofs of theorems, but you will need to use logic and your knowledge of basic formulas to do things like finding the size of an angle, the length of a line, or the area of a figure.

Holmes' Attic

In the Holmes stories, Dr. Watson occasionally remarks on the curious imbalance in the detective's learning. Holmes had remarkably detailed knowledge of some areas, such as the geography of London and the effects of exotic poisons, but no knowledge at all of other areas that most people would think important, like literature or politics. To explain this seeming shortcoming, Holmes draws an analogy between the mind and an attic. The mind, like an attic, is a storage facility—with limited space. To make effective use of the space, you have to be sure you don't clutter it up with things you don't need.

Although the term *geometry* covers a lot of knowledge, relatively few principles are tested by the SAT. These are the ones to keep in your "attic."

Angles

THE NUMBER OF DEGREES OF ARC IN A CIRCLE IS 360.

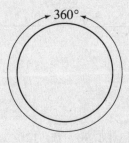

360°

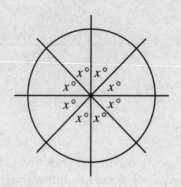

EXAMPLE:

In the figure above, $x =$
(A) 15   **(B)** 30   **(C)** 45   **(D)** 60   **(E)** 75

The answer is (C).

$$x + x + x + x + x + x + x + x = 360$$

$$8x = 360$$

$$x = 45$$

THE MEASURE IN DEGREES OF A STRAIGHT ANGLE IS 180.

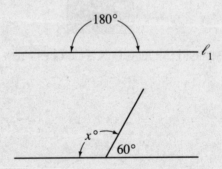

EXAMPLE:

In the figure above, $x =$
(A) 45   **(B)** 60   **(C)** 75   **(D)** 90   **(E)** 120

The answer is (E).

$$x + 60 = 180$$

$$x = 120$$

THE NUMBER OF DEGREES IN A RIGHT ANGLE IS 90.

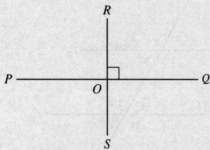

In the figure above, *POR* and angle *ROQ* are both right angles, so each measures 90°. And *RS* is perpendicular to *PQ*.

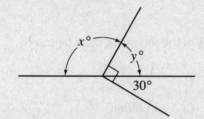

EXAMPLE:

In the figure above, $x =$
(A) 45 (B) 60 (C) 90 (D) 105 (E) 120

The answer is (E).

$$y + 30 = 90$$

$$y = 60$$

$$x + y = 180$$

$$x + 60 = 180$$

$$x = 120$$

WHEN PARALLEL LINES ARE CUT BY A THIRD LINE, THE RESULTING ANGLES
ARE RELATED AS FOLLOWS:

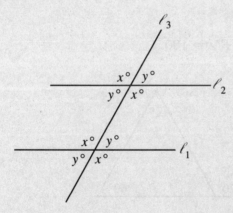

$x = x = x = x$; $y = y = y = y$; and $x + y = 180$. This is the "big angle/little angle" theorem. All the big angles are equal; all the little angles are equal; and any big angle plus any little angle equals 180. (In the event the third line intersects the parallel lines on the perpendicular, then all angles equal 90°.)

15

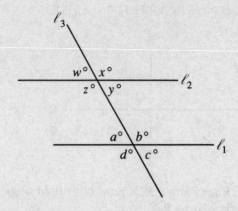

EXAMPLE:

In the figure above, which of the following must be true?
 I. $w = a$
 II. $y + b = 180°$
 III. $x + d = 180°$

(A) I only   (B) II only   (C) I and II only
(D) II and III only   (E) I, II, and III

The answer is (C). w and a are "small" angles, so they are equal, and statement I is true. y is a "small" angle and b is a "large" angle, so their sum is 180°, and II is true. III, however, is not true. x and d are both "large" angles. They would total 180° only in the special case where both are 90°.

THE SUM OF THE MEASURES IN DEGREES OF THE INTERIOR ANGLES OF A TRIANGLE IS 180°.

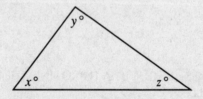

In the figure above, $x + y + z = 180$.

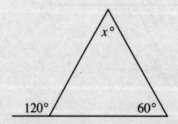

EXAMPLE:

In the figure above, $x =$
(A) 30   (B) 45   (C) 60   (D) 75   (E) 90

The answer is (C). Let y be the measure of the third and unlabeled angle inside the triangle:

$120 + y = 180$

$y = 60$

$x + y + 60 = 180$

$x + 60 + 60 = 180$

$x + 120 = 180$

$x = 60$

THE SUM IN DEGREES OF THE INTERIOR ANGLES OF A POLYGON OF N SIDES IS $180(N - 2)$.

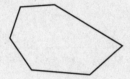 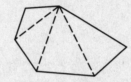

The figure above has six sides, so the sum of the six angles is $180(6 - 2) = 180(4) = 720°$. Instead of memorizing the formula just given, you can reason that the figure is composed of four triangles, each with angles totaling 180°.

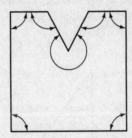

EXAMPLE:

In the figure above, what is the sum of the indicated angles?
(A) 540 **(B)** 720 **(C)** 900 **(D)** 1,080 **(E)** 1,260

The answer is (C). Divide the figure into triangular regions:

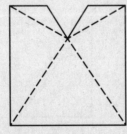

There are five triangles, so the sum of the angles is $5(180) = 900°$.

Note: This principle gives you the sum of the interior angles of the polygon. You might be asked about the average size of the angles. In that case, divide the sum of the angles by the total number of angles inside the figure.

Triangles

WITHIN A TRIANGLE, IF TWO ANGLES ARE EQUAL, THE LENGTHS OF THEIR OPPOSITE SIDES ARE EQUAL, AND VICE VERSA.

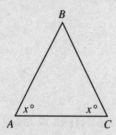

In the figure above, $AB = BC$.

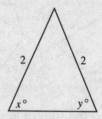

In the figure above, $x = y$.

THE PYTHAGOREAN THEOREM: IN A RIGHT TRIANGLE, THE SQUARE OF THE LONGEST SIDE (THE HYPOTENUSE) IS EQUAL TO THE SUM OF THE SQUARES OF THE OTHER TWO SIDES.

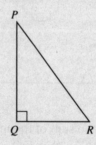

In the figure above, $PR^2 = PQ^2 + QR^2$.

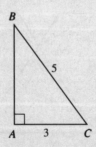

EXAMPLE:

In the figure above, $AB =$
(A) 2   **(B)** $2\sqrt{3}$ **(C)** 4   **(D)** $4\sqrt{2}$ **(E)** 8

The answer is (C).

$$BC^2 = AB^2 + AC^2$$
$$5^2 = AB^2 + 3^2$$
$$25 = AB^2 + 9$$
$$AB^2 = 16$$
$$AB = \sqrt{16} = 4$$

> ANY TRIANGLE WITH SIDES OF 3, 4, AND 5 (OR MULTIPLES THEREOF) IS A
> RIGHT TRIANGLE.

This is a two-edged sword. First, any triangle having sides that fit the Pythagorean Theorem is a right triangle. Since $3^2 + 4^2 = 5^2$, a triangle with those sides must be a right triangle. Additionally, any triangle with sides that are multiples of 3, 4, and 5 is a right triangle. For example, since $6^2 + 8^2 = 10^2$, a triangle with sides of 6, 8, and 10 is a right triangle (as are triangles with sides of 18, 24, and 30; 30, 40, and 50; and so on).

The other edge of the sword gives you an easy method for finding the length of a side in such triangles.

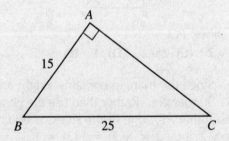

EXAMPLE:

In the figure above, what is the length of *AC*?

(A) 5   (B) 10   (C) 12   (D) 16   (E) 20

The answer is (E). Since *ABC* is a right triangle, you can use the Pythagorean Theorem. Or, you can save time by reasoning that one side is 3×5 and the hypotenuse is 5×5, so the missing length must be $4 \times 5 = 20$.

> IN A TRIANGLE WITH ANGLES OF 45°, 45°, AND 90°, THE LENGTH OF THE
> HYPOTENUSE IS EQUAL TO THE LENGTH OF EITHER SIDE MULTIPLIED BY
> $\sqrt{2}$, AND EACH OF THE SHORTER SIDES IS EQUAL TO $\frac{1}{2}$ TIMES THE LENGTH
> OF THE HYPOTENUSE TIMES $\sqrt{2}$.

15

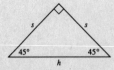

Both of these conclusions follow from the Pythagorean Theorem (coupled with the rule that sides opposite equal angles are equal in length).

$$h^2 = s^2 + s^2$$
$$h^2 = 2s^2$$
$$h = s\sqrt{2}$$

Which is to say, the hypotenuse of the $45-45-90$ triangle is equal to either side times $\sqrt{2}$. Conversely,

$$s^2 + s^2 = h^2$$
$$2s^2 = h^2$$
$$s^2 = \frac{h^2}{2}$$
$$s = \frac{h}{\sqrt{2}} = (\tfrac{1}{2})(h\sqrt{2})$$

Which is to say, either side of the $45-45-90$ triangle is equal to $\frac{1}{2}$ times the hypotenuse times $\sqrt{2}$.

These conversions can save you time.

EXAMPLE:

In the figure above, $PQ =$
(A) 1   (B) $\sqrt{2}$ (C) $2\sqrt{2}$ (D) 4   (E) 5

The answer is (A). Since the triangle contains a right angle and two equal angles, it must be a $45-45-90$ triangle. Rather than use the general form of the Pythagorean Theorem, just reason that PQ, one of the sides, is equal to $\frac{1}{2}$ times the length of the hypotenuse times $\sqrt{2}$: $\frac{1}{2}(\sqrt{2} \times \sqrt{2}) = \frac{1}{2}(2) = 1$.

> IN A TRIANGLE WITH ANGLES OF 30°, 60°, AND 90°, THE LENGTH OF THE SIDE OPPOSITE THE 30° ANGLE IS $\frac{1}{2}$ TIMES THE LENGTH OF THE HYPOTENUSE, AND THE LENGTH OF THE SIDE OPPOSITE THE 60° ANGLE IS $\frac{1}{2}$ TIMES THE LENGTH OF THE HYPOTENUSE TIMES $\sqrt{3}$.

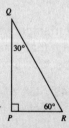

In the figure above, $PR = \frac{1}{2} QR$, and $PQ = \frac{1}{2} QR\sqrt{3}$.

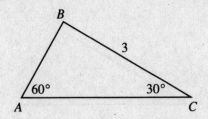

EXAMPLE:

In the triangle above, what is the length of *AC*?

(A) 2   (B) $\sqrt{3}$ (C) $2\sqrt{3}$ (D) $3\sqrt{3}$ (E) 6

The answer is (C). Since two of the angles of the triangle are 30° and 60°, the remaining angle must be 90°. So we have a 30−60−90 triangle, in which the side opposite the 60° angle is equal to $\frac{1}{2}$ times the length of the hypotenuse times $\sqrt{3}$:

$$BC = \frac{1}{2} AC\sqrt{3}$$

$$3 = \frac{1}{2} AC\sqrt{3}$$

$$6 = AC\sqrt{3}$$

$$AC = \frac{6}{\sqrt{3}} = \frac{6\sqrt{3}}{3} = 2\sqrt{3}$$

AN EQUILATERAL TRIANGLE (3 EQUAL SIDES) HAS THREE 60° ANGLES. CONVERSELY, A TRIANGLE WITH THREE EQUAL ANGLES IS EQUILATERAL.

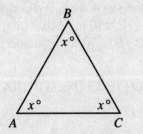
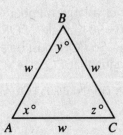

In the figure on the left, $x = 60$, and $AB = BC = AC$. In the figure on the right, since all three sides are equal, $x = y = z = 60$.

THE PERIMETER OF A TRIANGLE IS THE SUM OF THE LENGTHS OF ITS SIDES.

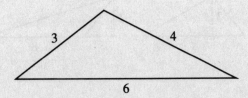

In the figure above, the perimeter is $3 + 4 + 6 = 13$.

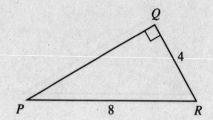

EXAMPLE:

In the figure above, the perimeter of triangle PQR =
(A) $12 + \sqrt{3}$ **(B)** $12 + 2\sqrt{3}$ **(C)** $12 + 4\sqrt{3}$ **(D)** 28
(E) Cannot be determined from the information given.

The answer is (C). To find the perimeter of the triangle, you must first find the length of PQ.

$$PR^2 = PQ^2 + QR^2$$

$$8^2 = PQ^2 + 4^2$$

$$64 = PQ^2 + 16$$

$$PQ^2 = 64 - 16 = 48$$

$$PQ = \sqrt{48} = \sqrt{16 \times 3} = 4\sqrt{3}$$

So the perimeter is $4 + 8 + 4\sqrt{3} = 12 + 4\sqrt{3}$.

You can skip over a large number of the steps we just did if you remember the facts about a 30−60−90 triangle. PQR is a right triangle in which one of the sides is half the hypotenuse. So PQR must be a 30−60−90 triangle and QR is opposite the 30° angle. This means that $PQ = 4\sqrt{3}$.

THE AREA OF A TRIANGLE IS EQUAL TO $\frac{1}{2}$ TIMES THE ALTITUDE TIMES THE BASE.

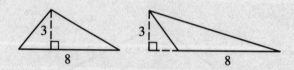

The area of the triangle on the left is $\frac{1}{2} \times 3 \times 8 = 12$. And the area of the triangle on the right is also $\frac{1}{2} \times 3 \times 8 = 12$.

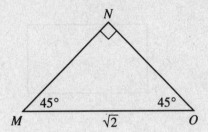

EXAMPLE:

What is the area of triangle *MNO*?

(A) $\frac{1}{2}$ (B) $\frac{\sqrt{2}}{2}$ (C) 1 (D) $\sqrt{2}$ (E) 2

The answer is (A). This is a $45-45-90$ triangle, so each of the two shorter sides is $\frac{1}{2} \times \sqrt{2} \times MO = \frac{1}{2} \times \sqrt{2} \times \sqrt{2} = \frac{1}{2} \times 2 = 1$. Since *MN* and *NO* form a right angle, we can use them as altitude and base:

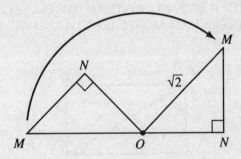

$\frac{1}{2} \times 1 \times 1 = \frac{1}{2} \times 1 = \frac{1}{2}$

Rectangles and Squares

THE PERIMETER OF A RECTANGLE IS EQUAL TO THE SUM OF THE LENGTHS OF THE FOUR SIDES. THE AREA OF A RECTANGLE IS EQUAL TO THE WIDTH MULTIPLIED BY THE LENGTH.

15

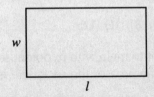

The perimeter of the rectangle above is $w + \ell + w + \ell = 2w + 2\ell$. The area is equal to w times $\ell = w\ell$.

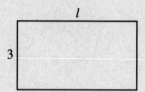

EXAMPLE:

If the area of the rectangle above is 18, what is the perimeter?

(A) 9   **(B)** 12   **(C)** 18   **(D)** 24   **(E)** 30

The answer is (C). The area of a rectangle is $w \times \ell$.

$3 \times \ell = 18$

$\ell = 18 \div 3 = 6$

So the perimeter is $3 + 6 + 3 + 6 = 18$.

THE DIAGONAL OF A RECTANGLE IS THE HYPOTENUSE OF A RIGHT TRIANGLE WITH SIDES THAT ARE THE LENGTH AND WIDTH OF THE RECTANGLE.

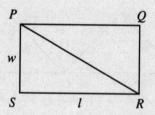

In the figure above, PQRS is a rectangle. PSR and PQR are right triangles, so $PR^2 = w^2 + \ell^2$.

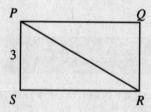

EXAMPLE:

In the figure above, PQRS is a rectangle. If $PR = 5$, then what is the area of the rectangle?

(A) 2   **(B)** 3   **(C)** 4   **(D)** 8   **(E)** 12

The answer is (E). PSR is a right triangle with hypotenuse of 5 and one side of 3, so the missing side must be 4. The area of the rectangle is $3 \times 4 = 12$.

A SQUARE IS A RECTANGLE WITH FOUR EQUAL SIDES. SO THE PERIMETER OF A SQUARE IS 4 TIMES THE LENGTH OF A SIDE, AND THE AREA IS SIDE TIMES SIDE.

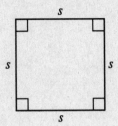

The perimeter of the square is $s + s + s + s = 4s$, and the area of the square is $s \times s = s^2$.

THE SIDE OF A SQUARE IS EQUAL TO $\frac{1}{2}$ TIMES ITS DIAGONAL TIMES $\sqrt{2}$, AND THE DIAGONAL OF A SQUARE IS EQUAL TO ITS SIDE TIMES $\sqrt{2}$.

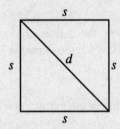

In the square above, $d = s\sqrt{2}$, and $s = \frac{1}{2} \times d\sqrt{2}$. This is just a variation on the Pythagorean Theorem. The two sides of the square and the diagonal create a $45-45-90$ triangle.

GIVEN (1) THE SIDE, (2) THE DIAGONAL, OR (3) THE AREA OF A SQUARE, YOU CAN DEDUCE THE OTHER TWO QUANTITIES.

(1) Given that the side has a length of s, the area is $s \times s = s^2$, and the diagonal $= s\sqrt{2}$.
(2) Given that the diagonal has a length of d, the side is $\frac{1}{2} \times d\sqrt{2}$, and the area is

$$(\tfrac{1}{2} \times d\sqrt{2}) \times (\tfrac{1}{2} \times d\sqrt{2}) = \frac{2d^2}{4}.$$

(3) Given that the area is s^2, the side is s, and the diagonal is $s\sqrt{2}$.

Circles

THE RADIUS OF A CIRCLE IS $\frac{1}{2}$ OF THE DIAMETER, AND THE DIAMETER OF A CIRCLE IS 2 TIMES THE RADIUS.

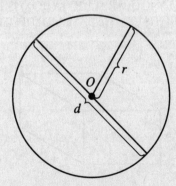

If a circle has a radius of 1, its diameter is 2. Conversely, if a circle has a diameter of 2, its radius is 1.

15

CIRCUMFERENCE $= 2\pi r$

AREA $= \pi r^2$

If a circle has a radius of 3:

CIRCUMFERENCE $= 2\pi(3) = 6\pi$

AREA $= \pi(3^2) = 9\pi$

 GIVEN (1) THE RADIUS, (2) THE DIAMETER, (3) THE CIRCUMFERENCE, OR (4) THE AREA OF A CIRCLE, YOU CAN DEDUCE THE OTHER THREE.

(1) Given a radius of r, the diameter is $2r$, the circumference is $2\pi r$, and the area is πr^2.

(2) Given a diameter of d, the radius is $\frac{1}{2}d$, the circumference is $2\pi\left(\dfrac{d}{2}\right) = \pi d$ and the area is $\pi\left(\dfrac{d}{2}\right)^2 = \dfrac{\pi d^2}{4}$.

(3) Given a circumference of $2\pi r$, the radius is r, the diameter is $2r$, and the area is πr^2.

(4) Given an area of πr^2, the radius is r, the diameter is $2r$, and the circumference is $2\pi r$.

EXAMPLE:

If the area of a circle is 9π, which of the following is (are) true?

I.   The radius is 3.

II. The diameter is 6.

III. The circumference is 6π.

(A) I only   **(B)** II only   **(C)** III only   **(D)** I and II only   **(E)** I, II, and III

The answer is (E). If the area of the circle is 9π, then

$\pi r^2 = 9\pi$

$r^2 = 9$

$r = \sqrt{9} = 3$

So statement I is true. Then if $r = 3$, the diameter is 2×3, so II is also true. Finally, if $r = 3$, then the circumference is $2\pi(3) = 6\pi$.

Solids

THE VOLUME OF A RECTANGULAR SOLID (A BOX) IS THE WIDTH OF THE BASE MULTIPLIED BY THE LENGTH OF THE BASE MULTIPLIED BY THE HEIGHT OF THE SOLID.

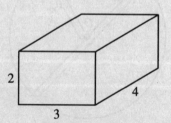

The volume of the rectangular solid above is $2 \times 3 \times 4 = 24$.

THE AREA OF THE FACE OF A RECTANGULAR SOLID (SIDE OF A BOX) IS THE PRODUCT OF THE LENGTH OF ONE EDGE OF THE FACE AND THE LENGTH OF AN ADJACENT EDGE.

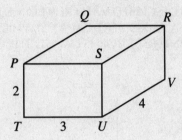

The area of $PTUS = 2 \times 3 = 6$.
The area of $SRVU = 2 \times 4 = 8$.
The area of $PQRS = 3 \times 4 = 12$.

THE TOTAL SURFACE AREA OF A RECTANGULAR SOLID (THE OUTSIDE OF A BOX) IS THE SUM OF THE AREAS OF THE SIX FACES.

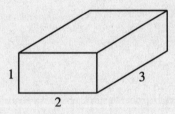

The front has an area of $1 \times 2 = 2$.
The side has an area of $1 \times 3 = 3$.
The bottom has an area of $2 \times 3 = 6$.
Since there are two of each (front = back, side = side, bottom = top), the total surface area is $(2 + 2) + (3 + 3) + (6 + 6) = 22$.

A CUBE IS A RECTANGULAR SOLID WITH THREE EQUAL DIMENSIONS. GIVEN (1) THE LENGTH OF AN EDGE, (2) THE AREA OF A FACE, (3) THE TOTAL SURFACE AREA OF THE CUBE, OR (4) THE VOLUME OF THE CUBE, YOU CAN DEDUCE THE OTHER THREE QUANTITIES.

(1) If the edge is s, then the area of each face is s^2, the total surface area is $6s^2$, and the volume is s^3.

(2) If the area of a face is s^2, then the length of each edge is s, the total surface area is $6s^2$, and the volume is s^3.

(3) If the total surface area is $6s^2$, then the area of each face is s^2, the length of each edge is s, and the volume is s^3.

(4) If the volume is s^3, then the length of each edge is s, the surface area of each face is s^2, and the total surface area is $6s^2$.

15

Coordinate Geometry

A COORDINATE PLANE IS DESCRIBED WITH REFERENCE TO AN *X*-AXIS (HORIZONTAL AXIS) AND A *Y*-AXIS (VERTICAL AXIS) WHICH ARE PERPENDICULAR TO EACH OTHER. THEIR INTERSECTION IS CALLED THE ORIGIN.

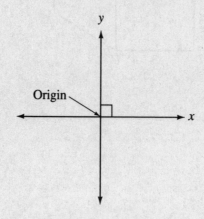

COORDINATE PAIRS ARE USED TO LOCATE POINTS ON THE PLANE. THE GENERAL FORM IS (x,y). THE FIRST ELEMENT GIVES LOCATION WITH REFERENCE TO THE *X*-AXIS, THE SECOND WITH REFERENCE TO THE *Y*-AXIS.

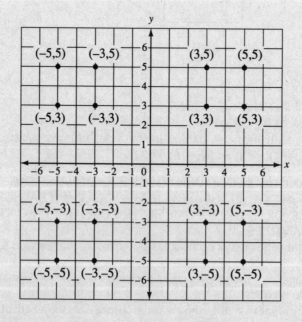

THE LENGTH OF A LINE PARALLEL TO AN AXIS IS THE DIFFERENCE BETWEEN THE
END-POINT COORDINATES FOR THAT AXIS.

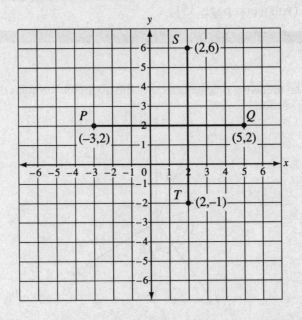

Line *PQ* runs from (−3,2) to (5,2), parallel to the x-axis. So the distance is just the
difference between the x coordinates, 5 and −3: 5 − (−3) = 5 + 3 = 8. Line *ST*
runs from (2,6) to (2,−1), so the length is the difference between the y coordinates:
6 − (−1) = 6 + 1 = 7.

THE LENGTH OF LINES NOT PARALLEL TO EITHER AXIS CAN BE DETERMINED BY
THE PYTHAGOREAN THEOREM.

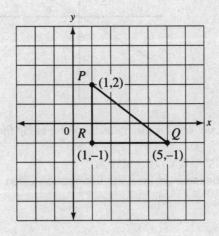

PQR is a right triangle. *PR* = 3, and *RQ* = 4. So *PQ* = 5.

15

Holmes' Attic (Answers, page 351)

Directions: The following problems require the use of the formulas discussed in the preceding section.

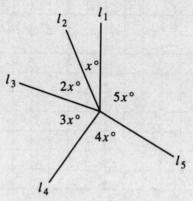

1. In the figure above, $x =$
   (A) 10   (B) 15   (C) 18   (D) 24   (E) 25

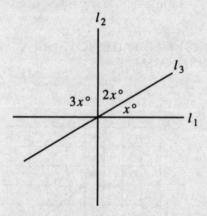

2. In the figure above, what is the measure of the angle formed by the intersection of $\ell 1$ and $\ell 3$?
   (A) 30°   (B) 45°   (C) 60°   (D) 90°
   (E) Cannot be determined from the information given.

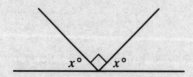

3. In the figure above, $x =$
   (A) 30   (B) 45   (C) 55   (D) 60   (E) 75

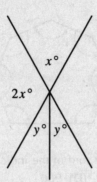

4. In the figure above, y =

(A) 15   (B) 30   (C) 45   (D) 60

(E) Cannot be determined from the information given.

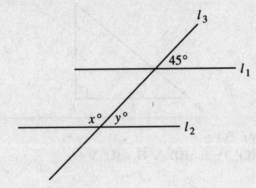

5. In the figure above, x − y =

(A) 0   (B) 45   (C) 60   (D) 90   (E) 135

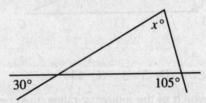

6. In the figure above, x =

(A) 25   (B) 35   (C) 45   (D) 55   (E) 75

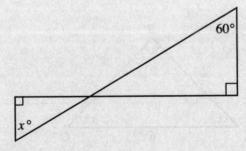

7. In the figure above, x =

(A) 15   (B) 30   (C) 45   (D) 60

(E) Cannot be determined from the information given.

15

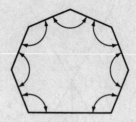

8. In the figure above, what is the sum of the indicated angles?

(A) 360   (B) 540   (C) 720   (D) 900

(E) Cannot be determined from the information given.

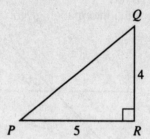

9. In the figure above, $PQ =$

(A) 1   (B) 3   (C) $3\sqrt{2}$ (D) $\sqrt{41}$ (E) $\sqrt{47}$

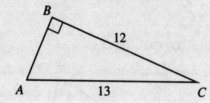

10. In the figure above, $AB =$

(A) 1   (B) 5   (C) $5\sqrt{2}$ (D) $5\sqrt{3}$ (E) 11

11. Triangles with sides in which of the following ratios must be right triangles?

   I. $2:1:\sqrt{3}$

   II. $1:1:\sqrt{2}$

   III. $\sqrt{2}:\sqrt{2}:2$

(A) I only   (B) II only   (C) III only   (D) I and III only   (E) I, II, and III

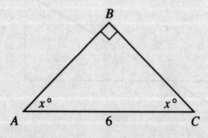

12. In the figure above, $AB =$

(A) 3   (B) $3\sqrt{2}$ (C) $3\sqrt{3}$ (D) 9   (E) $\dfrac{9\sqrt{3}}{2}$

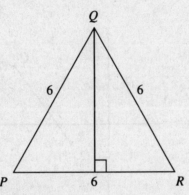

13. In the figure above, *NM* =
   (A) x   **(B)** $\sqrt{3}x$ **(C)** 3x   **(D)** $2\sqrt{3}x$ **(E)** $3\sqrt{3}x$

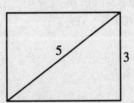

14. What is the area of triangle *PQR*?
   (A) $2\sqrt{3}$ **(B)** 9   **(C)** $9\sqrt{3}$ **(D)** 18   **(E)** $18\sqrt{3}$

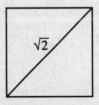

15. What is the area of the rectangle shown above?
   (A) 8   **(B)** 12   **(C)** 15   **(D)** 18   **(E)** 30

16. What is the area of the square shown above?
   (A) 1   **(B)** $\sqrt{2}$ **(C)** 2   **(D)** $2\sqrt{2}$ **(E)** $4\sqrt{2}$

17. If the number of units in the circumference of a circle is equal to the number of square units in the area of the circle, what is the length of the radius of the circle?
   (A) 1   **(B)** $\sqrt{2}$ **(C)** 2   **(D)** π **(E)** 2π

15

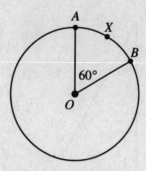

18. If the radius of Circle *O*, shown above, is 3, what is the length of arc *AXB*?

(A) $\frac{1}{6}\pi$ (B) $\frac{1}{3}\pi$ (C) π (D) 3π (E) 6π

19. If a cube has a total surface area of 54, what is the length of the edge of the cube?

(A) 3   (B) $2\sqrt{2}$ (C) $3\sqrt{2}$ (D) 6   (E) 9

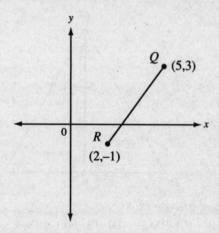

20. In the figure above, what is the length of *PQ*?

(A) 1   (B) $3\sqrt{2}$ (C) 4   (D) 5   (E) 7

Complex Figures

Thus far we have discussed the most commonly used principles of geometry as they apply to simple figures such as intersecting lines, triangles, squares, and circles. Many of the drawings used on the SAT, however, are made up of more than one figure.

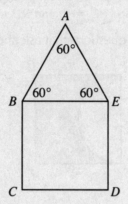

EXAMPLE:

If *BCDE* is a square with an area of 4, what is the perimeter of triangle *ABE*?

(A) 3   (B) 4   (C) 6   (D) 8   (E) 12

The answer is (C). *ABE* has three 60° angles, so it is equilateral. To find the perimeter, you need to find the length of one of the sides. The only information given in the question is the area of the square. To bridge the gap, you must see that one side of the square is also a side of the triangle. If you can find the side of the square, you have everything you need to know.

Since the area of the square is 4, the side of the square is 2:

side × side = area

$s^2 = 4$

$s = \sqrt{4} = 2$

So the perimeter of the triangle is 2 + 2 + 2.

The key to such questions is to see that some line or angle serves two functions. Here is an example of greater difficulty:

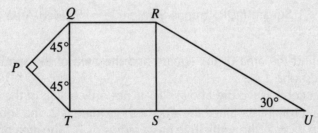

In the figure above, if *QRST* is a square and $PQ = \sqrt{2}$, what is the length of *RU*?

(A) $\sqrt{2}$ (B) $\sqrt{6}$ (C) $2\sqrt{2}$ (D) 4   (E) $4\sqrt{3}$

The question doesn't supply a lot of information—at least not explicitly. So it must be possible to deduce some further conclusions from what is given.

The hypotenuse of PQT is also a side of square $QRST$. And RS is not only a side of the square, it is a side of triangle RSU. If we can find the length of QT, we can deduce the length of RU. Since PQT is a $45-45-90$ triangle and $PQ = \sqrt{2}$, $QT = \sqrt{2} \times \sqrt{2} = 2$. All four sides of a square are equal, so $RS = QT = 2$. RS is also a side in a $30-60-90$ triangle (RS is perpendicular to TU). Since RS is opposite the $30°$ angle, it is $\frac{1}{2}$ the length of RU. So $\frac{1}{2}RU = 2$, and $RU = 4$.

A variation on this theme is questions that ask about shaded portions of a figure.

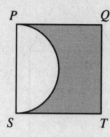

EXAMPLE:

In the figure above, $PQRS$ is a square, and PS is the diameter of a semicircle. If $PQ = 2$, what is the area of the shaded portion of the diagram?

(A) $4 - 2\pi$ **(B)** $4 - \pi$ **(C)** $4 - \dfrac{\pi}{2}$ **(D)** $8 - \pi$ **(E)** $8 - \dfrac{\pi}{2}$

The answer is (C). What makes the problem a little tricky is that you are asked to find the area of a figure that looks like this:

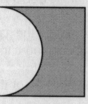

And that is not a figure for which you have a ready-at-hand formula. The key to the solution is to see that the irregular shaded part of the figure is what's left over after you take away the semicircle from the square:

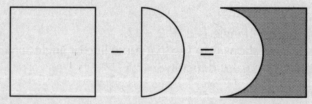

Square $PQRS$ minus Semicircle = Shaded Area

So if you can find the area of the square and the area of the semicircle, you can answer the question.

Now we proceed as we did above. PS is not only a side of the square, it is the diameter of the semicircle. Since the side of the square is 2, the square has an area of 4. And since $PS = 2$, the semicircle has a radius of 1. The area of an entire circle with radius 1 is $\pi r^2 = \pi(1^2) = \pi$. And since this is half a circle, the semicircle has an area of $\frac{\pi}{2}$. So the area of the shaded portion of the figure is $4 - \frac{\pi}{2}$.

Monster Figures (Answers, page 354)

Take a quick glance at the three figures below. They are more complex than anything you should expect to see on your SAT, but they make excellent practice.

The interesting thing about the drawings is that if you know the length of any line or the area of any part of the figure (no matter how weird its shape) you can find the length of every other line in the drawing and the area of every other shape.

Directions: Below each drawing is a table you are to fill in. You are asked to assume values for various aspects of the drawings and to deduce values for other parts of the drawings. In the explanations at the end of the chapter you will find a correctly completed table and an outline of the procedures to follow.

MONSTER DRAWING 1

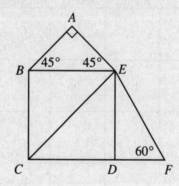

	AB	BC	CE	DF	EF	Area △ ABE	Area BCDE	Area △ EDF
AB = 1	1							
BC = 1		1						
CE = 1			1					
DF = 1				1				
EF = 1					1			

MONSTER DRAWING 2

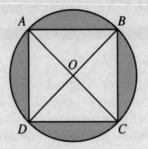

	AB	Radius	Area ABCD	Circum- ference of Circle	Area of Circle	Shaded Area
AB = 1	1					
Radius = 1		1				
Area of ABCD = 4			4			
Circumference of Circle = 2π				2 π		
Area of Circle = 4π					4 π	

MONSTER DRAWING 3

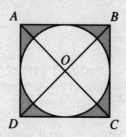

	AB	AO	Radius	Area ABCD	Circum-ference of Circle	Area of Circle	Shaded Area
AB = 1	1						
AO = 1		1					
Radius = 1			1				
Area ABCD = 16				16			
Circumference = 8π					8π		
Area Circle = 9π						9π	

15

IF YOU DON'T SEE WHAT YOU WANT, ASK FOR IT.

This is a strategy we developed for algebra problems, but it applies to some geometry questions as well.

EXAMPLE:

If the width of a rectangle is increased by 10 percent and the length of the rectangle is increased by 20 percent, the area of the rectangle increases by what percent?
(A) 2%   (B) 10%   (C) 15%   (D) 32%   (E) 36%

The answer is (D). Assume that the original width of the rectangle is 10 and the original length is 10. (Yes, the width is equal to the length, but a square is a rectangle too, and 10 is a convenient number.)

On the assumption that $w = 10$ and $\ell = 10$, the original area is 100. Now increase the width by 10 percent from 10 to 11 and the length by 20 percent from 10 to 12. The new area is 11 × 12 = 132. Using the "change-over" formula, the change is 132 − 100 = 32 and the original amount is 100, so the percent change is $\frac{32}{100} = 32\%$.

ONE PICTURE IS WORTH A THOUSAND WORDS.

Some SAT geometry questions do not come equipped with a figure, and this makes them more difficult. When no sketch is provided, make one yourself.

EXAMPLE:

If a circle of radius 1 is inscribed in a square, what is the area of the square?
(A) 1   (B) $\frac{\sqrt{2}}{2}$ (C) $\sqrt{2}$ (D) 2   (E) 4

The answer is (E). This can be seen more easily if you draw the figure:

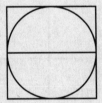

Now you can see that the diameter of the circle is equal to the side of the square. Since the radius of the circle is 1, the diameter is 2. So the side of the square is 2, and the area of the square is 2 × 2 = 4.

Sometimes you may be given a figure that is in some respect incomplete. To see the solution, you may need to add one or more lines to the drawing.

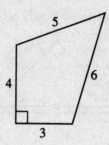

EXAMPLE:

What is the area of the quadrilateral above?
(A) 6   **(B)** $6 + \sqrt{3}$ **(C)** 12   **(D)** 18
(E) Cannot be determined from the information given.

The correct choice is (D), and the numbers 3, 4, and 5 are highly suggestive of one of those famous triangles. Divide the quadrilateral into two triangles:

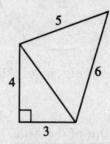

Now the problem turns into a composite figure problem. You have one triangle with an altitude and a base of 3 and 4. So it has an area of $\frac{1}{2} \times 3 \times 4 = 6$. As for the other triangle, it has a base of 6, but you need an altitude. So sketch it in:

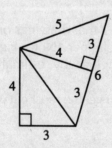

Since the altitude bisects the base (divides it in half), you have created two 3–4–5 triangles. So the area of the second triangle is $\frac{1}{2} \times 4 \times 6 = 12$. And the area of the entire quadrilateral is $6 + 12 = 18$.

EXAMPLE:

An isosceles right triangle is inscribed in a semicircle with radius 1. What is the area of the triangle?

(A) $\frac{1}{2}$ **(B)** $\frac{\sqrt{2}}{2}$ **(C)** 1   **(D)** $\sqrt{2}$ **(E)** $2\sqrt{2}$

15

The correct choice is (C), which is more easily seen if you draw the figure:

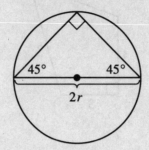

Now you can see that the diameter of the circle is the base of the triangle. But what about an altitude? Sketch that also:

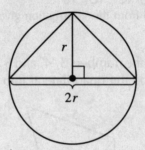

So the altitude is equal to the radius of the circle. And the area of the triangle is $\frac{1}{2} \times 2 \times 1 = 1$.

Out of the Attic

In the story of "The Musgrave Ritual," Holmes steps off the distances provided by a cryptic treasure map to find a family's hidden legacy. A simple, direct, and effective solution. And Holmes would find ample opportunity to use the same tactic on the SAT.

You will recall from Lesson 12 that drawings on the SAT are rendered to scale (unless accompanied by the disclaimer "<u>Note</u>: Figure not drawn to scale"). Take advantage of the accurate drawings by estimating and measuring quantities instead of solving by formulas.

Three techniques will help you get the most out of the drawings: "guestimating," measuring, and "meastimating."

1. "Guestimating"

Sometimes it is possible to arrive at a correct answer just by a rough approximation with the eye.

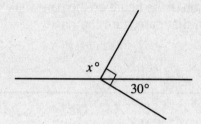

EXAMPLE:

In the figure above, what is the value of x?
(A) 30   **(B)** 65   **(C)** 120   **(D)** 150   **(E)** 170

A glance should show you that angle x is greater than a right angle. This allows you to eliminate both (A) and (B). But x is only 20 or 30 degrees bigger than a right angle, so (D) and (E) can also be eliminated. This leaves only choice (C). And if you do the geometry, you will confirm what we have already deduced.

To develop your skill at "guestimating," study the following angles:

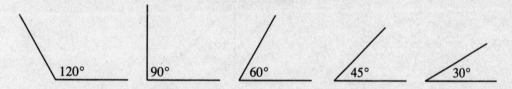

If you can visualize them, you can arrive at a fairly accurate conclusion about the size of almost any angle.

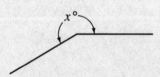

EXAMPLE:

In the figure above, x =
(A) 120   **(B)** 150   **(C)** 180   **(D)** 210   **(E)** 240

The answer is (D). The angle is larger than 180°, so you can eliminate (A), (B), and (C). But what about (D) and (E)? A quick sketch will help you:

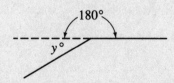

What's your best estimate of the value of y? 30° or 60°. It must be 30°, and 180° + 30° = 210°.

Sometimes the position of the figure on the page makes it difficult to get a feel for the size of the angle. In that case, turn the page.

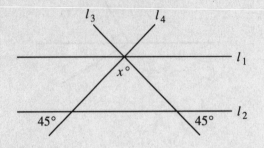

EXAMPLE:

If $\ell1 \parallel \ell2$, then x =
(A) 45 (B) 60 (C) 90 (D) 110 (E) 125

The answer is (C). If you have trouble seeing that x is a right angle, turn your book until x looks like this:

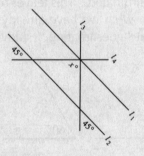

You can also "guestimate" distances.

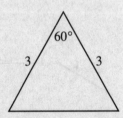

EXAMPLE:

The perimeter of the triangle shown above is
(A) $3\sqrt{2}$ (B) 6 (B) 7.5 (D) 9 (E) 15

The answer is (D). The problem is not that difficult, and you can probably quickly deduce that the third side has a length of 3. But you can also tell that at a glance. It *looks* like it's 3 units long. So the perimeter is 3 + 3 + 3 = 9.

Estimating Angles (Answers, page 355)

Directions: Visualize the following angles.

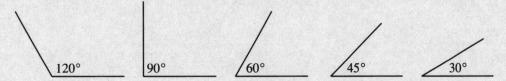

Answer the following questions based solely on your ability to "guestimate." Use the answer choices to guide you. So you won't be tempted to use geometry, all information except the picture has been deleted.

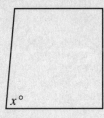

1. In the figure above, $x =$
   (A) 15   **(B)** 30   **(C)** 60   **(D)** 75   **(E)** 85

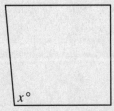

2. In the figure above, $x =$
   (A) 120   **(B)** 95   **(C)** 85   **(D)** 75   **(E)** 60

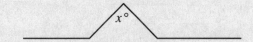

3. In the figure above, $x =$
   (A) 15   **(B)** 30   **(C)** 45   **(D)** 60   **(E)** 90

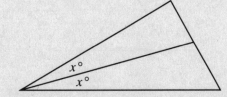

4. In the figure above, $x =$
   (A) 15   **(B)** 30   **(C)** 45   **(D)** 55   **(E)** 70

15

343

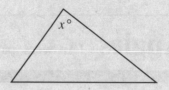

5. In the figure above, x =
   (A) 20   **(B)** 30   **(C)** 45   **(D)** 75   **(E)** 90

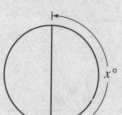

6. In the figure above, x =
   (A) 210   **(B)** 183   **(C)** 175   **(D)** 140   **(E)** 120

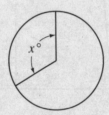

7. In the figure above, x =
   (A) 60   **(B)** 75   **(C)** 90   **(D)** 120   **(E)** 150

8. In the figure above, x =
   (A) 15   **(B)** 30   **(C)** 45   **(D)** 55   **(E)** 60

9. In the figure above, the sum of the indicated angles is
   (A) 180°   **(B)** 360°   **(C)** 540°   **(D)** 680°   **(E)** 720°

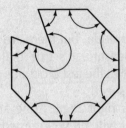

10. What is the average measure of the degrees of the angles indicated above?

(A) 45   (B) 60   (C) 90   (D) 120   (E) 140

15

2. Measuring

"Guestimating" is a useful technique, but there are times when it won't be accurate enough. Then you should measure. It's true that you're not allowed to bring a protractor or a ruler to the test. But the test proctor is going to give you something that does both jobs: your answer sheet!

Your answer sheet has four right angles, one at each corner. You can use the corner for measuring angles. It will tell you immediately whether an angle is larger than, smaller than, or exactly 90°. Additionally, if you have trouble visualizing angles, your answer sheet will help you.

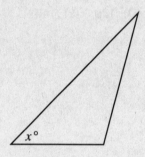

EXAMPLE:

In the figure above, $x =$
(A) 30   (B) 45   (C) 60   (D) 75   (E) 90

If you have trouble seeing that the answer is (B), take a sheet of paper and line up a corner next to the angle in question:

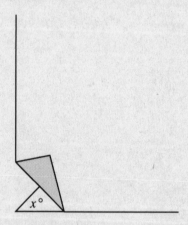

Pull up the edge. The angle seems to be half of the right angle formed by the corner of the page.

There are more ways of using the corner of your answer sheet than can be described in a reasonable space. Just keep your mind open.

The answer sheet can also be used as a ruler. To be sure, it doesn't have inches or centimeters marked on it; but then, you don't need them.

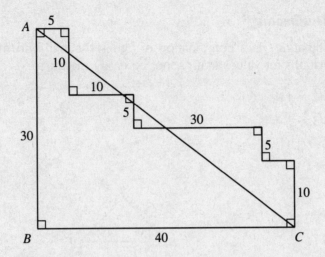

EXAMPLE:

In the figure above, $AC =$
(A) $30\sqrt{2}$ (B) 50 (C) 75 (D) $60\sqrt{2}$ (E) 100

The answer is (B). You can work it out using the Pythagorean Theorem. But you can also use the edge of a sheet of paper to measure it.

Get a piece of notebook paper. Mark off the distance from A to C like this:

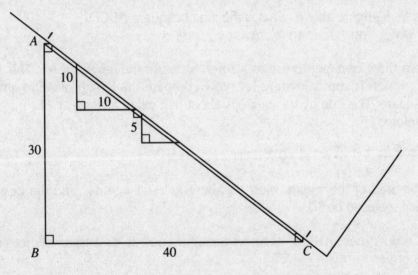

Now measure the distance on the edge of the paper against one of the distances in the problem:

15

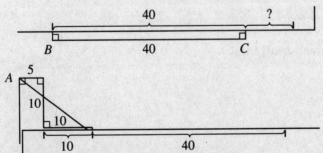

Repeat until you have the full measure of *AC*. It is 50.

3. "Meastimating"

"Meastimating" is a combination of "guestimating" and measuring. It uses approximations for values that cannot be easily measured:

$$\sqrt{2} = 1.4$$
$$\sqrt{3} = 1.7$$
$$\pi = 3.1$$

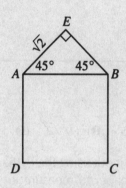

EXAMPLE:

In the figure above, what is the area of square ABCD?
(A) 2 **(B)** $2\sqrt{2}$ **(C)** 4 **(D)** $4\sqrt{2}$ **(E)** 8

Take a sheet of paper to use as a ruler. Measure the length of AE. This length is $\sqrt{2}$, which is approximately 1.4. Now compare the length of AE to any side of the square. The side of the square is about half again as long as AE. Therefore:

$$\text{side} \cong 1.4 + \frac{1}{2}(1.4) = 1.4 + 0.7 = 2.1$$

So the area of the square must be about 2.1x2.1 = 4.41, and the best answer choice seems to be (C).

Is our "mestimation" accurate enough? Look at the answer choices on both sides of (C):

(B) $2\sqrt{2} \cong 2 \times 1.4 = 2.8$

(D) $4\sqrt{2} \cong 4 \times 1.4 = 5.6$

So the best answer must be (C).

The Monster Revisited (Answers, page 356)

Directions: This exercise is based on one of the monster drawings from Exercise 2. Again, you are asked to assume values for various aspects of the drawing and complete a table. This time, however, complete the table by "meastimating." For example, if $AB = 1$, then BE must be about 1.4.

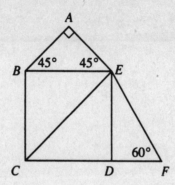

	AB	BC	CE	DF	EF	Area △ABE	Area BCDE	Area △EDF
AB = 1	1							
BC = 1		1						
CE = 1			1					
DF = 1				1				
EF = 1					1			

15

Summary

1. "Holmes' attic" contains all of the geometry principles you need for the SAT.
2. Complex figures can be analyzed as two figures with a common feature.
3. Shaded areas can be analyzed as the difference between two common figures.
4. Instead of working with unknowns, assume values.
5. One picture is worth a thousand words, so draw a sketch if no figure is provided.
6. Unless otherwise noted, all figures are drawn to scale. Take advantage of the accuracy of the drawings by guestimating, measuring, or meastimating.

Explanatory Answers

EXERCISE 1

1. (D)

$x + 2x + 3x + 4x + 5x = 360$

$15x = 360$

$x = 24$

2. (A)

$x + 2x + 3x = 180$

$6x = 180$

$x = 30$

3. (B)

$x + x + 90 = 180$

$2x + 90 = 180$

$2x = 90$

$x = 45$

4. (B)

$2x + x = 180$

$3x = 180$

$x = 60$

$y + y = x$

$y + y = 60$

$2y = 60$

$y = 30$

5. (D) Since $\ell 1 \,/\!/\, \ell 2$, you can use the "big angle/little angle" theorem.

$y = 45$

$x + y = 180$

$x + 45 = 180$

$x = 135$

$x - y = 135 - 45 = 90$

15

6. (E) The angle inside the triangle and opposite the 30° angle is also 30°. The angle inside the triangle and next to the 105° angle is $180 - 105 = 75°$.

$$30 + 75 + x = 180$$
$$105 + x = 180$$
$$x = 75$$

7. (D) The third angle of the larger triangle is 30°. The angle directly opposite it (in the smaller triangle) is also 30°. So:

$$90 + 30 + x = 180$$
$$x = 60$$

8. (D) The figure has seven sides, so the sum of the degree measures of its interior angles is $180(7 - 2) = 900$. (Or, you can divide the polygon into five triangular regions.)

9. (D)

$$PQ^2 = PR^2 + RQ^2$$
$$PQ^2 = 5^2 + 4^2$$
$$PQ^2 = 25 + 16$$
$$PQ^2 = 41$$
$$PQ = \sqrt{41}$$

10. (B)

$$AB^2 + BC^2 = AC^2$$
$$AB^2 = AC^2 - BC^2$$
$$AB^2 = 13^2 - 12^2$$
$$AB^2 = 169 - 144$$
$$AB^2 = 25$$
$$AB = \sqrt{25} = 5$$

11. (E) A 30–60–90 triangle has sides in the ratio $2:1:\sqrt{3}$. A 45–45–90 triangle has sides in the ratio $1:1:\sqrt{2}$. And a triangle with sides of $\sqrt{2}:\sqrt{2}:2$ fits the Pythagorean Theorem:

$$(\sqrt{2})^2 + (\sqrt{2})^2 = 2^2$$

(Also, a triangle with sides in the ratio of $\sqrt{2}:\sqrt{2}:2$ is a 45–45–90 triangle.)

12. (B) AC is the hypotenuse of a 45–45–90 triangle, so AB is equal to $\frac{1}{2}$ times 6 times $\sqrt{2}$:

$$AB = \frac{1}{2}(6)(\sqrt{2}) = 3\sqrt{2}$$

13. (B) *MNO* is a 30–60–90 triangle. *NM* is equal to $\frac{1}{2}$ times *NO* times $\sqrt{3}$:

$$NM = \frac{1}{2}(2x)(\sqrt{3})$$

$$NM = x\sqrt{3} = \sqrt{3}x$$

14. (C) Since *PQR* is equilateral, the altitude creates two 30–60–90 triangles. The altitude is the side opposite the 60° angle, so it is equal to $\frac{1}{2}$ times 6 times $\sqrt{3}$:

$$\text{Altitude} = \frac{1}{2}(6)(\sqrt{3}) = 3\sqrt{3}$$

$$\text{Area } PQR = \frac{1}{2}\,(\text{alt.})(\text{base}) = \frac{1}{2}(3\sqrt{3})(6) = 9\sqrt{3}$$

15. (B) The diagonal creates a right triangle with a hypotenuse of 5 and side of 3. The remaining side, which is the length of the rectangle, is 4.

$$\text{Area} = \text{length} \times \text{width}$$

$$\text{Area} = 4 \times 3 = 12$$

16. (A) The diagonal of the square creates two 45–45–90 triangles. So the side of the square is equal to $\frac{1}{2}$ times the diagonal times $\sqrt{2}$:

$$\text{side} = \frac{1}{2}(\sqrt{2})(\sqrt{2}) = \frac{1}{2}(2) = 1$$

$$\text{Area of square} = \text{side} \times \text{side} = 1 \times 1 = 1$$

17. (C)

$$\text{Area} = \text{Circumference}$$

$$\pi r^2 = 2\pi r$$

$$r^2 = 2r$$

$$r = 2$$

(**Note:** In algebra, $r = +2$ or -2. But r here indicates a distance that can only be positive.)

18. (C) The circumference of Circle *0* is $2\pi r = 2\pi(3) = 6\pi$. Since the entire circle measures 360°, $AXB = \frac{60}{360} = \frac{1}{6}$ of the circle. And $\frac{1}{6}$ of $6\pi = \pi$.

19. (A) Since a cube has six faces, each face has an area of $54 \div 6 = 9$. The area of a face is a function of the length of the edge or side: side $\times$ side $= 9$, $s^2 = 9$, $s = 3$.

20. (D) Drop a line from *Q* parallel to the *Y*-axis. Draw a line through *P* parallel to the *X*-axis. The point where the two intersect (call it *R*) is $(5, -1)$. *PQ* is the hypotenuse of the right triangle you have created. The triangle has sides with lengths of 3 and 4, so the length of *PQ* is 5.

15

EXERCISE 2

	AB	$BE = AB \times \sqrt{2}$ BE	$CE = BE \times \sqrt{2}$ CE	$DF = BE \div \sqrt{3}$ DF	$EF = 2DF$ EF	$\frac{1}{2}(AB)(AE)$ Area ABE	BE^2 Area $BCDE$	$\frac{1}{2}(ED \times DF)$ Area EDF
$AB = 1$	1	$\sqrt{2}$	2	$\frac{\sqrt{2}}{\sqrt{3}} = \frac{\sqrt{6}}{3}$	$\frac{2}{3}\sqrt{6}$	$\frac{1}{2}$	2	$\frac{\sqrt{3}}{3}$
$BE = 1$	$\frac{\sqrt{2}}{2}$	1	$\sqrt{2}$	$\frac{1}{\sqrt{3}} = \frac{\sqrt{3}}{\sqrt{3}}$	$\frac{2}{3}\sqrt{3}$	$\frac{1}{4}$	1	$\frac{\sqrt{3}}{6}$
$CE = 1$	$\frac{1}{2}$	$\frac{\sqrt{2}}{2}$	1	$\frac{\sqrt{2}}{2\sqrt{3}} = \frac{\sqrt{6}}{6}$	$\frac{\sqrt{6}}{3}$	$\frac{1}{8}$	$\frac{1}{2}$	$\frac{\sqrt{3}}{12}$
$DF = 1$	$\frac{\sqrt{6}}{2}$	$\sqrt{3}$	$\sqrt{6}$	1	2	$\frac{3}{4}$	3	$\frac{\sqrt{3}}{2}$
$EF = 1$	$\frac{\sqrt{6}}{4}$	$\frac{\sqrt{3}}{2}$	$\frac{\sqrt{6}}{2}$	$\frac{1}{2}$	1	$\frac{3}{16}$	$\frac{3}{4}$	$\frac{\sqrt{3}}{8}$

	AB	$r = \frac{1}{2} \times AB \times \sqrt{2}$ Radius	AB^2 Area $ABCD$	$2\pi r$ Circumference of Circle	πr^2 Area of Circle	$\pi r^2 - AB^2$ Shaded Area
$AB = 1$	1	$\frac{\sqrt{2}}{2}$	1	$\sqrt{2}\,\pi$	$\frac{\pi}{2}$	$\frac{\pi}{2} - 1$
Radius = 1	$\sqrt{2}$	1	2	2π	π	π
Area of $ABCD = 4$	2	$\sqrt{2}$	4	$2\sqrt{2}\,\pi$	2π	$2\pi - 2$
Circumference of Circle = 2π	$\sqrt{2}$	1	2	2π	π	$\pi - 2$
Area of Circle = 4π	$2\sqrt{2}$	2	8	4π	4π	4π

	AB	AO	Radius	Area ABCD	Circumference of Circle	Area of Circle	Shaded Area
$AB = 1$	1	$\frac{\sqrt{2}}{2}$	$\frac{1}{2}$	1	π	$\frac{\pi}{4}$	$1 - \frac{\pi}{4}$
$AO = 1$	$\sqrt{2}$	1	$\frac{\sqrt{2}}{2}$	2	$\sqrt{2}\,\pi$	$\frac{\pi}{2}$	$2 - \frac{\pi}{2}$
Radius = 1	2	$\sqrt{2}$	1	4	2π	π	$4 - \pi$
Area ABCD = 16	4	$2\sqrt{2}$	2	16	4π	4π	$16 - 4\pi$
Circumference = 8π	8	$4\sqrt{2}$	4	64	8π	16π	$16 - \pi$
Area Circle = 9π	6	$3\sqrt{2}$	3	36	6π	9π	$36 - 9\pi$

EXERCISE 3

1. (E) x is slightly less than a right angle, so the answer must be (E).

2. (B) x is slightly more than a right angle, so the answer must be (B).

3. (E) appears to be a right angle. And no answer is close to 90° except (E). (If you have trouble visualizing the angle, rotate the page.)

4. (A) The entire angle consisting of x and x appears to be about 30°, so x must be 15°.

5. (E) x seems to be a right angle, which is choice (E). No other answer choice is close.

6. (C) The line through the circle seems to be a diameter, so it creates two 180° arcs. x is slightly less than 180, so (C) must be the correct answer. (Notice how this reasoning allows us to distinguish between two numbers that are otherwise very close, 175 and 183.)

7. (D) x appears to take up about $\frac{1}{3}$ of the circle, so x should be $\frac{1}{3}$ of 360 = 120.

8. (B) This question is a bit more difficult than some of the earlier ones, but x seems to be about 30 degrees.

9. (E) Our task here seems difficult, but let's give it a try. Those marked angles could be anywhere from 120° to about 140°. Let's assume they are about 130°. 6 × 130 = 780. Only (E) is in the ballpark.

15

10. (E) At first, it might seem impossible to do this question by visually estimating angles. After all, it's difficult to say whether some of them are 130° or 140° or 150°. Give the problem a try. Assume that the **six** angles that appear to be equal are each about 140°. Then the two acute angles seem to be about 45° each. So far we have (140 × 6) + (2 × 60) = 960. And you still have that large angle, which must be about 300°. (The unmarked angle is about 60°.) So the sum of the angles is about 1,260. Since there are nine angles, the average is 1,260 ÷ 9 = 140, more or less. So (E) is the best bet. (In fact, [E] is correct, as you can prove using the formula for calculating the interior angles of a polygon.)

EXERCISE 4

	$BE \cong AB \times 1.4$	$CE \cong BE \times 1.4$	$DF \cong BE \div 1.7$	$EF = 2DF$	$\frac{1}{2}(AB)(AE)$	BE^2	$\frac{1}{2}(ED \times DF)$
	AB	BE	CE	DF	EF	Area △ ABE	Area BCDE	Area △ EDF
$AB = 1$	1	1.4	2	.8	1.6	$\frac{1}{2}$	about 2	0.5 - 0.6
$BC = 1$	.7	1	1.4	0.5 - 0.6	1.0 - 1.2	about $\frac{1}{4}$	1	0.3
$CE = 1$	about $\frac{1}{2}$	.7	1	0.4	0.8	about $\frac{1}{8}$	about $\frac{1}{2}$	0.14
$DF = 1$	1.2	1.7	2.4	1	2	.7+	2.9+	0.8 - 0.9
$EF = 1$	0.6	0.8 - 0.9	1.2	$\frac{1}{2}$	1	0.18	0.64 - 0.81	0.2

Problem-Solving Drills

✔ Objectives

To do problem-solving items without having to worry about the time pressure.

To practice the special Holmesian strategies for problem-solving items.

1. Walk-Through
2. Drill 1
3. Drill 2
4. Drill 3
5. Drill 4
6. Explanatory Answers

16

This chapter includes five drills. The first drill is a "walk-through." It is set up in the format of a 15-question exercise in which every question is a standard, multiple-choice problem-solving item. In the column facing the questions, you will find answers and discussion so that you can walk through the exercise as you read the explanations.

The remaining four drills each contain ten problem-solving items numbered 1 through 10. Like the test, the questions in each drill are arranged in ascending order of difficulty. The level of difficulty of the first third ranges from easy to just-below-average difficulty; the level of difficulty for the middle third ranges from below average to above average; and the level of difficulty for the final third ranges from above average to very difficult.

The answers and explanations for these drills begin on page 373.

16

Walk-Through

1. What number increased by 6 equals 3 times the number?

    (A) 3   (B) 4   (C) 5   (D) 6   (E) 7

2. If $2x = 5y$, then $10y - 4x =$

    (A) 0   (B) 1   (C) 2   (D) 5
    (E) Cannot be determined from the information given.

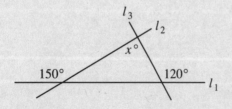

3. In the figure above, $x =$

    (A) 30   (B) 60   (C) 75   (D) 90   (E) 105

1. (A) This is the first question in the section, so it is supposed to be easy. You can solve the problem with an equation:
    A number plus 6 is equal to 3 times the number.

    $$x + 6 = 3 \text{ times } x$$
    $$x + 6 = 3x$$
    $$6 = 3x - x$$
    $$6 = 2x$$
    $$x = 6 \div 2$$
    $$x = 3$$

    But why bother? Just test the test. In this case, start with the smallest number, since it is easiest to work with. Assume the number is 3. 3 increased by 6 is equal to 9, and 9 is how many times greater than 3? 3. So (A) is correct.

2. (A) Here you have one equation with two variables. It isn't possible to solve for either variable individually, and that's not what is required. The question asks for the value of $10y - 4x$. Either $2x = 5y$ can be rewritten as $10y - 4x$, or the answer is (E).
    Multiply both sides of $2x = 5y$ by 2:

    $$(2)2x = (2)5y$$
    $$4x = 10y$$

    And you need $10y - 4x$:

    $$0 = 10y - 4x$$

    So the answer is (A).

3. (D) The task here is to deduce the value of x from the information already given, and there is really only one route to take. Assign the letter y to the angle inside the lower left vertex of the triangle and z to the angle inside the lower right vertex:

    $$150 + y = 180 \text{ and } 120 + z = 180$$

$$y = 30 \qquad\qquad z = 60$$

And $30 + 60 + x = 180$

$x = 90$

This line of reasoning is not that complex, but there is an alternative. The figure is drawn to scale. Either "guestimate" or use the corner of a piece of paper to measure the size of the angle in question. It's 90°.

4. A machine operating at a constant rate without interruption produced 1,200 square yards of fabric in six hours. If the machine continues to operate at the same rate without interruption, how much fabric (in square yards) will it produce in the next four hours?

(A) 800 (B) 900 (C) 1,400
(D) 1,800 (E) 2,000

4. (A) The longer the machine operates, the more fabric it produces. A direct proportion makes this an easy question:

$$\frac{\text{Time } X}{\text{Time } Y} = \frac{\text{Cloth } X}{\text{Cloth } Y}$$

$$\frac{6}{4} = \frac{1,200}{x}$$

Cross-multiply:

$$6x = 4(1,200)$$

$$x = \frac{4(1,200)}{6} = 4(200) = 800$$

5. If the first and last digits are interchanged in each of the following numbers, which number, when changed, will yield the *smallest* result?

(A) 2,453 (B) 4,523 (C) 3,245
(D) 2,345 (E) 5,432

5. (E) There's no real trick to this question. Just transform the numbers in each choice according to the instructions and compare results:

(A) 2,453 becomes 3,452

(B) 4,523 becomes 3,524

(C) 3,245 becomes 5,243

(D) 2,345 becomes 5,342

(E) 5,432 becomes 2,435

And (E) is the smallest.

6. A student must see her dean, her physics professor, and her adviser. If she must visit each person exactly once, in how many different orders can she arrange her appointments?

(A) 3 (B) 4 (C) 6 (D) 9 (E) 12

6. (C) Although this question may seem difficult, it can't really be that difficult, because it's still early in the section. You don't need a formula to solve the problem; just count the number of possibilities (D is for "dean"; P is for "professor"; and A is for "advisor"). DPA, DAP, PDA, PAD, ADP, and APD, or 6.

If this doesn't occur to you, it's better to skip the problem, hoping to come back to it.

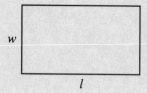

7. The figure above is a rectangle. If the width is increased by 20 percent and the length is decreased by 10 percent, expressed in terms of w and ℓ, what is the new area of the rectangle?

    (A) $.09\ w\ell$ (B) $0.92\ w\ell$ (C) $1.1\ w\ell$
    (D) $1.08\ w\ell$ (E) $1.3\ w\ell$

7. (D) This problem is more difficult than the last one. You might solve it with unknowns. The width of the rectangle increases by 20 percent from w to $1.2\ w$, and the length decreases by 10 percent from ℓ to $0.9\ \ell$. The area of a rectangle is width times length. So the old area was w, and the new area is $1.2\ w \times 0.9\ \ell = 1.08\ w\ell$.

   If working with unknowns is not your cup of tea, then assume some numbers, for example, $w = 1$ and $\ell = 2$. The new dimensions are 1.2 and 1.8, and the new area is $2.16\ w\ell$. Now substitute 1 for w and 2 for ℓ into each answer choice. The correct one will generate the number 2.16:

   (A) $0.09(1)(2) = 1.8$ (Wrong.)

   (B) $0.92(1)(2) = 1.84$ (Wrong.)

   (C) $1.1(1)(2) = 2.2$ (Wrong.)

   (D) $1.08(1)(2) = 2.16$ (Right!)

   (E) $1.3(1)(2) = 2.6$ (Wrong.)

8. If n is an odd integer, all of the following are odd EXCEPT

    (A) $n - 2$
    (B) $2n + n$
    (C) n^2
    (D) $(n + 2)^2$
    (E) $n^2 + n$

8. (E) This question tests properties of numbers. One way of attacking the problem is to reason about each choice in the following way. Since n is odd:

   (A) This is an odd number minus 2, so the result is still odd.

   (B) $2n$ is even and n is odd; so $2n + n$ is odd.

   (C) An odd number times itself is odd.

   (D) n plus 2 is still odd; so this is an odd times an odd, and therefore odd.

   (E) n^2 is odd, and n itself is odd; so this is an odd plus an odd, which is even.

   Or, you could have substituted a number, say 1. If $n = 1$, then

   (A) $n - 1 = 1 - 2 = -1$. An odd number.

(B) $2n + n = 2(1) + 1 = 2 + 1 = 3$. An odd number.

(C) $n^2 = (1)^1 = 1 \times 1 = 1$. An odd number.

(D) $(n + 2)^2 = (1 + 2)^2 = 3^2 = 9$. An odd number.

(E) $n^2 + n = (1)^2 + 1 = 1 + 1 = 2$. An even number!

9. In a game, special cards are printed with one of three symbols, a star, a circle, or a rectangle. A star is worth three points more than a circle, and a circle is worth three points more than a rectangle. If three rectangles are worth x points, a player holding five circles and four stars has how many points?

(A) $3x + 12$
(B) $3x + 39$
(C) $3x + 42$
(D) $7x + 39$
(E) $7x + 42$

9. (B) This question asks you to devise a formula. Use the letters s for star, c for circle, and r for rectangle. The answer choices are expressed in terms of x, so your formula will have to express s and c in terms of r and then in terms of x.

The question stem states that a circle is worth 3 points more than a rectangle, so $c = r + 3$. And a star is worth 3 points more than a circle, which means $s = c + 3$ and so $s = r + 6$. Since $3r = x$, $r = \frac{x}{3}$. Substituting $\frac{x}{3}$ for r: $s = (\frac{x}{3}) + 6$ and $c = (\frac{x}{3}) + 3$. So $5c$ and $4s$ is: $5(\frac{x}{3} + 3) + 4(\frac{x}{3} + 6) = \frac{5x}{3} + 15 + \frac{4x}{3} + 24 = \frac{9x}{3} + 39 = 3x + 39$.

You can also use the principle "it's one of the five suspects." You might assume that $x = 1$, so that a rectangle is equal to $\frac{1}{3}$; but that already involves a fraction. A more convenient assumption is $x = 3$. Then a rectangle is worth 1 point. On that assumption, circles are worth $1 + 3 = 4$, and stars are worth $4 + 3 = 7$. And five circles plus four stars are worth $5(4) + 4(7) = 48$. So on the assumption that $x = 3$, the correct formula yields 48:

(A) $3(3) + 12 = 21$ (Wrong.)
(B) $3(3) + 39 = 48$ (Correct.)
(C) $3(3) + 42 = 52$ (Wrong.)
(D) $7(3) + 39 = 60$ (Wrong.)
(E) $7(3) + 42 = 63$ (Wrong.)

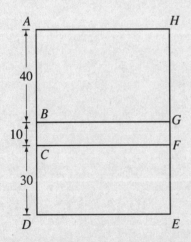

10. The figure above shows three rectangular garden plots which lie side by side. If AE, not shown, is equal to 100 feet, what is the area, in square feet, of plot $BCFG$?

(A) 240   (B) 300   (C) 360
(D) 480   (E) 600

10. (E) The area of a rectangle is equal to its width times its length. The diagram already provides the width, so you'll have to find the length.

An important piece of information, $AE = 100$, is not entered on the diagram. The first thing you should do is draw AE. This creates a right triangle with sides AD and DE and hypotenuse AE. And DE is not only a side of triangle ADE, it is the length of the rectangles. You know the length of *AD* and *AE*, so you can find *DE* with the Pythagorean Theorem:

$$AD^2 + DE^2 = AE^2$$

$$DE^2 = AE^2 - AD^2$$

$$DE^2 = 100^2 - 80^2$$

$$DE^2 = 10,000 - 6,400$$

$$DE^2 = 3,600$$

$$DE = \sqrt{3,600} = 60$$

The area of rectangle *BCFG* is 10 x 60 = 600.

You can save yourself the calculation if you notice that 80 and 100 are multiples of 8 and 10, which are in turn multiples of 4 and 5. This triangle must have sides of 60, 80, and 100.

Or, you can avoid all but the last step of the calculation by measuring to find the length of the rectangle. Using the edge of a sheet of paper (on the test, your answer sheet), mark off the length of *BC*. Since *BC* = 10, the length shown on the edge of the paper is 10 units. Now measure the length of *CF*. Starting at *C*, mark 10 units on *CF*, then another 10, and so on. The final result: *CF* is 60 units long. Finish off the problem by multiplying 10 x 60.

11. At City High School, the marching band has 48 members and the orchestra has 36 members. If a total of 12 students belong to only one of the two groups and all students belong to at least one group, how many students belong to both groups?

(A) 12   (B) 18   (C) 36   (D) 48   (E) 72

11. (C) A diagram can help you understand what's required:

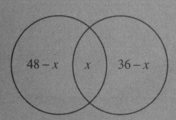

x is the number of students who are members of both groups. Since only 12 students are members of only one group:

$$48 - x + 36 - x = 12$$

$$84 - 12 = 2x$$

$$72 = 2x$$

$$x = 36$$

12. If $x = 2k - 2$ and $y = 4k^2$, what is y in terms of x?

(A) $x + 2$

(B) $(x + 2)^2$

(C) $\dfrac{(x + 2)^2}{2}$

(D) $\dfrac{(x + 2)^2}{4}$

(E) $x^2 + 4$

12. **(B)** Here you are asked to express one variable in terms of another. You have x in terms of k, and y in terms of k^2; so there must be a way of rewriting one equation to correspond to the other. Since it's usually easier to square something than to take the square root of something, work from k towards k^2.

To rewrite the first equation so that x is expressed in terms of k^2, you'll first need to get rid of the -2 on the right side:

$x = 2k - 2$

$x + 2 = 2k$

$k = \dfrac{x + 2}{2}$

Before you square both sides, look at the answer choices to see what form your final result should take. You don't have to multiply $(x + 2)^2$:

$\dfrac{(x + 2)^2}{4} = k^2$

Since y is also equal to $4k^2$,

$y = (x + 2)^2$

You can also attack the question by assuming numbers. Assume a value for k, say 1. If $k = 1$, then $x = 2(1) - 2 = 0$ and $y = 4(1^2) = 4$. When you substitute zero for x into the formulas in the choices, the correct choice will yield the value 4 (which is y).

(A) $0 + 2 = 2$ (Wrong.)

(B) $(0 + 2)^2 = 4$

(C) $\dfrac{(0 + 2)^2}{2} = \dfrac{4}{2} = 2$ (Wrong.)

(D) $\dfrac{(0 + 2)^2}{4} = \dfrac{4}{4} = 1$ (Wrong.)

(E) $0^2 + 4 = 4$

This first substitution eliminated all but (B) and (E).

Try another number, say $k = 2$. If $k = 2$, then $y = 4(2^2) = 16$, and $x = 2(2) - 2 = 2$.

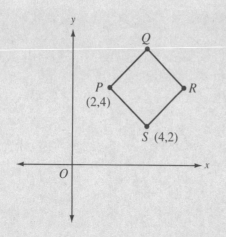

13. What is the area of the square in the figure
     above?
     (A) 4   (B) $4\sqrt{2}$ (C) 8   (D) $8\sqrt{2}$
     (E) 16

So when $x = 2$, the correct formula should generate 16:

(B) $(2 + 2)^2 = 16$ (Correct.)

(E) $2^2 + 4 = 8$ (Wrong.)

13. (C) At the outset, there is one answer choice you can eliminate with confidence. Since this is a difficult question, the correct answer is not likely to be (E).

To find the area of the square, you need only to know the length of its side. And you can find the length of the side with the Pythagorean Theorem. Draw a line from the point (2,4) straight down the page parallel to the y-axis. Draw another line from point (4,2) across the page parallel to the x-axis. The lines intersect at the point (2,2) and form a right angle. The length of each side is 2.

Now you can use the Pythagorean Theorem to find the length of the hypotenuse, which is also the length of the side of the square. Let s be the hypotenuse:

$$s^2 = 2^2 + 2^2$$
$$s^2 = 8$$
$$s = \sqrt{8}$$

So the area of the square is $\sqrt{8} \times \sqrt{8} = 8$.

You can reach the same conclusion by "meastimating." Point (4,2) is 2 units above the x-axis. Mark that distance on the edge of a sheet of paper. Divide that distance in half (by estimating). You now have a little ruler with single units. Measure the side of the square. It's a little less than 3, say 2.8 or so.

Using 2.8 as the length of the side of the square, the area is $2.8 \times 2.8 = 7.84$, or slightly less than 8, which is choice (C). Is that approximation precise enough? (B) is $4\sqrt{2}$, which is approximately $4 \times 1.4 = 5.6$ and not very close to 8. And (D) is $8\sqrt{2}$, which is approximately $8 \times 1.4 = 11.2$ and not very close to 8. So (C) is the correct choice.

14. For all numbers, x, y, and z, the operation $x*y = x - xy$. What is $x*(y*z)$?

   (A) $x - xy + xyz$
   (B) $x - xy - xz - xyz$
   (C) $x + xy - xz + xyz$
   (D) $x^2 - xy^2 - xyz$
   (E) $x^2 - xy^2 - x^2yz$

15. If the cost of x meters of wire is d dollars, what is the cost, in dollars, of y meters of wire at the same rate?

   (A) yd (B) $\dfrac{yd}{x}$ (C) $\dfrac{xd}{y}$ (D) xd (E) $\dfrac{xy}{d}$

14. (A) Here we have a defined function problem. Just take it one step at a time. First, $y*z = y - yz$. Second, $x*(y - yz) = x - x(y - yz) = x - xy + xyz$, which is (A). You can assume values for the three letters, but the arithmetic you would do would exactly parallel what we just did with letters. So there is no real advantage to using numbers

15. (B) This question asks you to devise a formula. The easiest approach is to set up a direct proportion, using k as our unknown:

$$\frac{\text{Length } X}{\text{Length } Y} = \frac{\text{Cost } X}{\text{Cost } Y}$$

$$\frac{x}{y} = \frac{d}{k}$$

$$xk = yd$$

$$k = \frac{yd}{x}$$

You can also assume some values for the three unknowns. Assume that 2 meters of wire costs $4, so 5 meters costs $10. On the assumption that $x = 2$, $d = 4$, and $y = 5$, the correct formula will yield 10:

   (A) $5(4) = 20$ (Wrong.)

   (B) $\dfrac{5(4)}{2} = 10$ (Correct.)

   (C) $\dfrac{2(4)}{5} = \dfrac{8}{5}$ (Wrong.)

   (D) $2(4) = 8$ (Wrong.)

   (E) $\dfrac{2(5)}{4} = \dfrac{10}{4}$ (Wrong.)

Drill 1 (Answers, page 373)

Reference:

Circle: Rectangle: 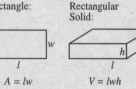   Rectangular Solid: Cylinder: Triangle:

$C = 2\pi r$ $A = lw$ $V = lwh$ $V = \pi r^2 h$ $A = \frac{1}{2}bh$ $a^2 + b^2 = c^2$
$A = \pi r^2$

- The measure in degrees of a straight angle is 180.
- The number of degrees of arc in a circle is 360.
- The sum of the measures of the angles of a triangle is 180.

Notes: The figures accompanying the problems are drawn as accurately as possible unless otherwise stated in specific problems. Again, unless otherwise stated, all figures lie in the same plane. All numbers used in these problems are real numbers. Calculators are permitted for this test.

1. If $\frac{5}{3} + \frac{x}{3} = 2$, then $x =$

   (A) $\frac{2}{9}$ (B) $\frac{3}{5}$ (C) $\frac{5}{9}$ (D) $\frac{5}{6}$ (E) 1

Sales Representative	Sales for May (Units Sold)
Victor	6
Mary	9
Randy	8
Sue	4
Carla	3

2. What was the average of the number of units sold by the sales representatives shown above?

   (A) 4   (B) 5   (C) 6   (D) 9   (E) 30

3. If a machine can produce 50 meters of steel cable every 30 seconds, how many meters of steel cable can the machine produce in an hour?

   (A) 100   (B) 250   (C) 600
   (D) 2,500   (E) 6,000

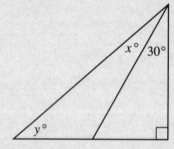

4. In the figure above, $x + y =$
   (A) 15   (B) 30   (C) 60   (D) 90   (E) 120

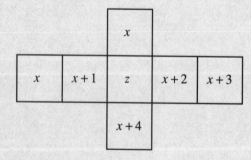

5. If the sum of the three terms arranged vertically in the figure above is equal to the sum of the five terms arranged horizontally, then $x =$

   (A) −2   (B) −1   (C) 0   (D) 1   (E) 2

6. Carl has only $5 bills and $10 bills in his wallet. If he has x $5 bills and ten more $10 bills than $5 bills, in terms of x, how many dollars does Carl have in his wallet?

    (A) $15x$ (B) $15x + 10$ (C) $15x + 15$
    (D) $15x + 100$ (E) $50x + 100$

7. If x and y are positive integers and $\frac{x}{y} < 1$, which of the following is greater than 1?

    (A) $\frac{x}{2y}$ (B) $\sqrt{\frac{x}{y}}$ (C) $\left(\frac{x}{y}\right)^2$

    (D) $x - y$ (E) $\frac{y}{x}$

8. If $p = q + 2$ and $r = 2q^2$, then $r =$

    (A) $(p - 2)^2$ (B) $2(p - 2)^2$ (C) $\frac{p - 2}{2}$

    (D) $\frac{p - 2}{4}$ (E) $\frac{p - 2^2}{4}$

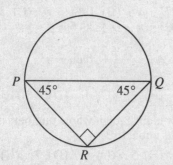

9. In the figure above, PQ is a diameter of the circle and $PR = 2$. What is the area of the circle?

    (A) $\frac{\pi}{2}$ (B) π (C) 2π (D) $2\sqrt{2}\pi$ (E) 4π

10. If a car travels at 40 kilometers per hour, how many *minutes* does it take the car to travel k kilometers?

    (A) $\frac{2}{3}k$ (B) $\frac{3}{2}k$ (C) $\frac{2}{3k}$

    (D) $\frac{3}{2k}$ (E) $40k$

Drill 2 (Answers, page 376)

1. If $\frac{3}{4}x = 1$, then $\frac{2}{3}x =$

   (A) $\frac{1}{3}$ (B) $\frac{1}{2}$ (C) $\frac{2}{3}$ (D) $\frac{8}{9}$ (E) 2

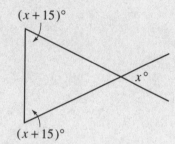

2. In the figure above, $x =$

   (A) 20 (B) 35 (C) 50 (D) 65 (E) 90

3. If $x = \frac{y}{7}$ and $7x = 12$, then $y =$

   (A) 3 (B) 5 (C) 7 (D) 12 (E) 72

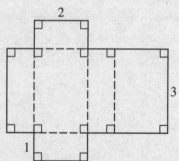

4. A rectangular box with a top is created by folding the figure above along the dotted lines. What is the volume of the box in cubic feet?

   (A) 6 (B) 9 (C) 12 (D) 18 (E) 24

5. What is the difference of the areas of two squares with sides of 5 and 4, respectively?

   (A) 3 (B) 4 (C) 9 (D) 16 (E) 41

6. If the spaces between the lettered points in the figure above are all equal, then $\frac{PT}{2} - \frac{QS}{2}$ is equal to which of the following?

   (A) $PS - QR$ (B) $QR - QS$ (C) PR
   (D) QT (E) ST

7. Exactly three years before the year in which Anna was born, the year was $1980 - x$. In terms of x, on Anna's twentieth birthday, the year will be

   (A) $1977 + x$ (B) $1997 + x$ (C) $2003 - x$
   (D) $2003 + x$ (E) $2006 + x$

8. If $x = k + \frac{1}{2} = \frac{k+3}{2}$, then $x =$

   (A) $\frac{1}{3}$ (B) $\frac{1}{2}$ (C) 1 (D) 2 (E) $\frac{5}{2}$

9. For how many 3-digit whole numbers is the sum of the digits equal to 3?

   (A) 4 (B) 5 (C) 6 (D) 7 (E) 8

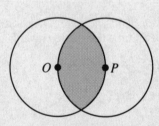

10. In the figure above, if the radius of the circles is 1, then what is the perimeter of the shaded part of the figure?

    (A) $\frac{1}{6}\pi$ (B) $\frac{2}{3}\pi$ (C) $\frac{4}{3}\pi$ (D) $\frac{3}{2}\pi$
    (E) Cannot be determined from the information given.

370

Drill 3 (Answers, page 379)

1. If $7 - x = 0$, then $10 - x =$

   (A) -3 (B) 0 (C) 3 (D) 7 (E) 10

2. A triangle with sides of 3, 6, and 9 has the same perimeter as an equilateral triangle with sides of length

   (A) 2 (B) $\frac{3}{2}$ (C) 3 (D) 6 (E) 8

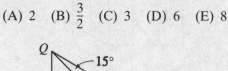
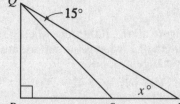

$PQ = PS$

3. In the figure above, $x =$

   (A) 15 (B) 30 (C) 40 (D) 60 (E) 75

4. If x and y are negative numbers, which of the following is negative?

   (A) xy (B) $(xy)^2$ (C) $(x-y)^2$

   (D) $x + y$ (E) $\frac{x}{y}$

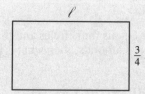

5. If the area of the rectangle shown above is equal to 1, then $\ell =$

   (A) $\frac{4}{9}$ (B) 1 (C) $\frac{4}{3}$ (D) $\frac{9}{4}$

   (E) Cannot be determined from the information given.

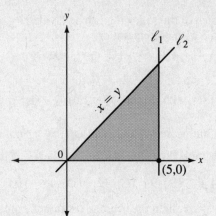

6. In the figure above, if $\ell1$ is parallel to the Y-axis, which of the following points falls within the shaded area?

   (A) $(1,2)$ (B) $(2,3)$ (C) $(3,4)$
   (D) $(4,5)$ (E) $(4,3)$

Questions 7 and 8
For all real numbers, $x*y$ is equal to $2xy - (x + y)$.

7. $2*3 =$

   (A) 3 (B) 5 (C) 7 (D) 11 (E) 15

8. If $5*4 = 4*k$, then $k =$

   (A) 0 (B) 1 (C) 4 (D) 5 (E) 9

9. If $\frac{x}{z} = c$ and $\frac{y}{z} = c - 1$, then x and y are related in which of the following ways?

   (A) $x = y - 1$ (B) $x = y + 1$ (C) $x = z + y$

   (D) $x = z - y$ (E) $x = \frac{y}{1}$

10. A dean must select three students to serve on a committee. If she is considering five students, from how many different possible threesomes must she choose?

   (A) 2 (B) 3 (C) 10 (D) 15 (E) 18

Drill 4 (Answers, page 380)

1. Which of the following can be divided by both 2 and 3 with no remainder?

   (A) 46   (B) 54   (C) 64   (D) 76   (E) 98

2. If $2x = 3$ and $3y + 2x = 6$, then $y =$

   (A) 1   (B) 2   (C) 3   (D) 4   (E) 5

3. If x and y are positive numbers, $xy = 96$, and $\frac{x}{y} = \frac{3}{2}$, what is the value of x?

   (A) 6   (B) 9   (C) 12   (D) 15   (E) 18

4. If $y = 5x$, then the average (arithmetic mean) of x and y, in terms of x, is equal to

   (A) x (B) $2x$ (C) $3x$ (D) $4x$ (E) $5x$

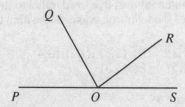

5. If the measure of angle POR is 144° and the measure of angle QOS is 120°, what is the measure in degrees of angle QOR?

   (A) 24   (B) 36   (C) 48   (D) 72   (E) 84

6. A figure has a line of symmetry if the figure can be folded in half so that one half of the figure exactly covers the other half. A square has how many lines of symmetry?

   (A) 1   (B) 2   (C) 3   (D) 4   (E) 5

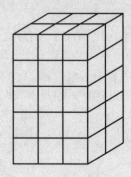

7. In the figure above, if the edge of each small cube has a length of 1, what is the surface area of the entire rectangular solid?

   (A) 84   (B) 62   (C) 42   (D) 31   (E) 18

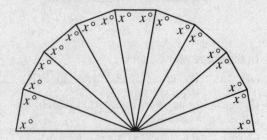

8. In the figure above, what is x?

   (A) 105   (B) 90   (C) 80   (D) 60
   (E) Cannot be determined from the information given.

9. If one star equals four circles and three circles equals four diamonds, then what is the ratio star : diamond?

   (A) $\frac{3}{16}$ (B) $\frac{1}{3}$ (C) $\frac{3}{4}$ (D) $\frac{3}{1}$ (E) $\frac{16}{3}$

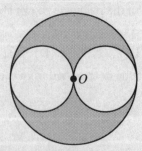

10. In the figure above, O is the center of the large circle. If the radius of Circle O is r, what is the area of the shaded region in terms of r?

    (A) π (B) 3π (C) πr^2
    (D) $\frac{\pi r^2}{2}$ (E) $\frac{3\pi r^2}{2}$

Explanatory Answers

DRILL 1

1. E	**6.** D
2. C	**7.** E
3. E	**8.** B
4. C	**9.** C
5. B	**10.** B

1. (E) Solve for x:

$$\frac{5}{3} + \frac{x}{3} = 2$$

$$\frac{5 + x}{3} = 2$$

$$5 + x = 2(3)$$

$$x = 6 - 5 = 1$$

If you look closely at the equation, you might be able to avoid doing all those steps. What number when added to $\frac{5}{3}$ makes 2, which is $\frac{6}{3}$? The answer is $\frac{1}{3}$. So x must be 1.

You might test the choices. If you do, start with the easiest value to work with, 1.

2. (C) Just calculate the average:

$$\frac{6 + 9 + 8 + 4 + 3}{5} = 6$$

3. (E) If the machine produces 50 meters of cable every 30 seconds, it produces 100 meters every minute. Since 1 hour = 60 minutes, the machine produces $100 \times 60 = 6,000$ meters of cable in an hour.

4. (C)

$$x + y + 30 + 90 = 180$$

$$x + y + 120 = 180$$

$$x + y = 60$$

16

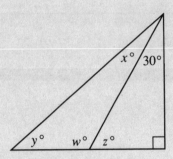

You can arrive at the same conclusion by estimating the size of x and the size of y. x appears to be equal to 30°, so assume x is approximately 30. And y appears to be about 60°. Together they are about 90°. The only choice in the ballpark is (C), so (C) must be correct.

5. (B) Set up an equation:

$(x) + (x + 1) + (z) + (x + 2) + (x + 3) = (x) + (z) + (x + 4)$

$4x + 6 + z = 2x + 4 + z$

$4x + 6 = 2x + 4$

$2x = -2$

$x = -1$

You can also get the correct answer by assuming a value for z, say z = 0, and testing the choices.

6. (D) You can set up the formula. Carl has x $5 bills, or 5x dollars in $5 bills. And he has 10 + x $10 bills, or 10(x + 10) = 10x + 100 dollars in $10 bills. Combine them: 5x + 10x + 100 = 15x + 100.

You can also assume some numbers. To make it easy, assume Carl has one $5 bill, in other words, x = 1. Then he would have 11 $10 bills. The total amount would be 5 + 11(10) = 115. So when x = 1, the correct formula will generate the value 115:

   (A) 15(1) = 15   (Wrong.)

   (B) 15(1) + 10 = 25   (Wrong.)

   (C) 15(1) + 15 = 30   (Wrong.)

   (D) 15(1) + 100 = 115   (Correct.)

   (E) 50(1) + 100 = 150   (Wrong.)

7. (E) This question tests properties of numbers. Since x and y are positive integers such that $\frac{x}{y} > 1$, x must be less than y. Given that x is less than y:

   (A) $\frac{x}{2y}$ is also less than 1, since 2y is a larger denominator than y;

   (B) $\frac{\sqrt{x}}{y}$ is less than 1, since $\sqrt{x}$ is a smaller numerator than x;

(C) $\left(\dfrac{x}{y}\right)^2$ is less than 1, since the square of a fraction is smaller than the original fraction;

(D) $x - y$ is less than 1, since y is larger than x; but

(E) $\dfrac{y}{x}$ is greater than 1, since y is larger than x.

You can also use the technique of assuming some numbers. Assume that $x = 1$ and $y = 2$. Then,

(A) $\dfrac{1}{2(2)} = \dfrac{1}{4}$;

(B) $\sqrt{\dfrac{1}{2}} = \dfrac{1}{2}$;

(C) $\left(\dfrac{1}{2}\right)^2 = \dfrac{1}{4}$;

(D) $1 - 2 = -1$; and

(E) $\dfrac{2}{1} = 2$, which is greater than 1.

8. (B) Rewrite one equation so that its form corresponds to the other. If we are to have r expressed in terms of p, we need to express p in terms of $2q^2$.

$p = q + 2$

$p - 2 = q$

$(p - 2)^2 = q^2$

$2(p - 2)^2 = 2q^2$

So $r = 2(p - 2)^2$.

You can also assume some values. Assume that $q = 1$. On that assumption, $p = (1) + 2 = 3$ and $r = 2(1)^2 = 2$; using the value 3 for p in the correct answer choice will generate the number 2:

(A) $(3 - 2)^2 = 1^2 = 1$ (Wrong.)

(B) $2(3 - 2)^2 = 2(1^2) = 2(1) = 2$ (Correct.)

(C) $\dfrac{2 - 2}{2} = \dfrac{0}{2} = 0$ (Wrong.)

(D) $\dfrac{2 - 2}{4} = \dfrac{0}{4} = 0$ (Wrong.)

(E) $\dfrac{(2 - 2)^2}{4} = \dfrac{0}{4} = 0$ (Wrong.)

9. (C) PQR is an isosceles right triangle. Since $PR = 2$, $PQ = 2\sqrt{2}$. Since the diameter of the circle is $2\sqrt{2}$, the radius is $\sqrt{2}$. And the area of the circle is $\pi r^2 = \pi(\sqrt{2})^2 = 2\pi$.

16

You can also use "meastimation." Mark the length of *PR* on the edge of a sheet of paper. That length is 2 units. Divide that length in half, and you have a ruler 2 units long. Measure the radius of the circle. The radius is longer than 1 unit, but less than 2 units—about $1\frac{1}{2}$, maybe a little less. Assuming the radius to be $1\frac{1}{2}$, or $\frac{3}{2}$, the area of the circle is $\pi(\frac{3}{2})^2 = \frac{9\pi}{4} = 2.25\pi$. That's closest to (C). And when you recall that the actual length of the radius appeared to be slightly less than $1\frac{1}{2}$, you will conclude that the actual area of the circle is slightly less than 2.25π, which really confirms (C) as correct.

10. (B) Create an algebraic formula by using a direct proportion.

$$\frac{\text{Kilometers } X}{\text{Kilometers } Y} = \frac{\text{Time in Minutes}}{\text{Time in Minutes}}$$

$$\frac{40}{k} = \frac{60}{x}$$

Where x is the number of minutes to travel k kilometers:

$$40x = 60k$$

$$x = \frac{60k}{40} = \frac{3k}{2}$$

You can also assume numbers. Assume that k is 40 kilometers. Since the car travels at 40 kilometers per hour, it will need one hour, or 60 minutes, to travel 40 kilometers. So, on the assumption that $k = 40$, the correct choice will generate the number 60:

(A) $\frac{2}{3}(40) = \frac{80}{3}$ (Wrong.)

(B) $\frac{3}{2}(40) = \frac{120}{20} = 60$ (Correct.)

(C) $\frac{2}{3(40)} = \frac{2}{120}$ (Wrong.)

(D) $\frac{3}{2(40)} = \frac{3}{80}$ (Wrong.)

(E) $40(40) = 160$ (Wrong.)

DRILL 2

1. D		**6.** E	
2. C		**7.** C	
3. D		**8.** E	
4. A		**9.** C	
5. C		**10.** C	

1. (D) Solve for x. $\frac{3}{4}x = 1$, so $x = \frac{4}{3}$. Then substitute this for x in the expression $\frac{2}{3x}$. $\frac{2}{3(\frac{4}{3})} = \frac{8}{9}$.

2. (C) Since the unlabeled angle inside the triangle is equal to x:

$(x + 15) + (x + 15) + x = 180$

$3x + 30 = 180$

$3x = 150$

$x = 50$

You can also estimate the size of the angle. It seems to be slightly less than 60°, so the answer must be (C).

3. (D) Treat the two equations as simultaneous equations. You can substitute $\frac{y}{7}$ for x in the second equation. $7(\frac{y}{7}) = 12$, so $y = 12$.

4. (A). The box when assembled looks like this:

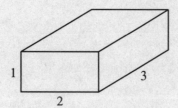

Its volume is $1 \times 2 \times 3 = 6$.

5. (C) The question asks for:
(Area of square with side 5) minus (area of square with side 4) = $(5 \times 5) - (4 \times 4)$
$= 25 - 16 = 9$

6. (E) $\frac{PT}{2}$ is $\frac{1}{2}$ the length of the entire segment. QS is $\frac{1}{2}$ the length of the segment, and $\frac{QS}{2}$ is $\frac{1}{4}$ of the segment. So $\frac{PT}{2} - \frac{QS}{2}$ is $\frac{1}{2}$ of the segment minus $\frac{1}{4}$ of the segment, which is $\frac{1}{4}$ of the length of the segment. Only (E) is $\frac{1}{4}$ the length of the segment.

You can also assign numbers to the lengths. Assume that each segment is equal to 1. Then PT is 4, and $\frac{PT}{2} = 2$. And QS is 2, and $\frac{QS}{2} = 1$. Finally, $2 - 1 = 1$. So the correct answer choice should have a length of 1:

(A) $3 - 1 = 2$ (Wrong.)

(B) $1 - 2 = -1$ (Wrong.)

(C) 2   (Wrong.)

(D) 3   (Wrong.)

(E) 1   (Correct.)

16

7. (C) Create a formula. Anna was born three years after $1980 - x$, so she was born in $1980 - x + 3$. 20 years later the year will be $1980 - x + 3 + 20 = 2003 - x$.

You can also substitute numbers. Assume $x = 1$. And then assume Anna was born three years after $1980 - 1 = 1979$, so she was born in 1982. So she will turn 20 in 2002. Substituting 1 for x in each of the answer choices:

(A) $1977 + 1 = 1978$ (Wrong.)

(B) $1997 + 1 = 1998$ (Wrong.)

(C) $2003 - 1 = 2002$ (Correct.)

(D) $2003 + 1 = 2004$ (Wrong.)

(E) $2006 + 1 = 2007$ (Wrong.)

8. (E) You really have two equations:

$$x = k + \frac{1}{2} \text{ and } k + \frac{1}{2} = \frac{k + 3}{2}$$

Solve for k:

$$k + \frac{1}{2} = \frac{k + 3}{2}$$

$$2\left(k + \frac{1}{2}\right) = k + 3$$

$$2k + 1 = k + 3$$

$$k = 2$$

Now substitute 2 for k:

$$x = k + \frac{1}{2} = 2 + \frac{1}{2} = \frac{5}{2}$$

You can also try testing the choices, but the process is tedious. For example, assume that $x = 1$. On that assumption, the first equation gives the value of k as $\frac{1}{2}$, but when $\frac{1}{2}$ is substituted for k into the second equation, the second equation is false. So (C) is incorrect. (E), however, does work. If $x = \frac{5}{2}$, then the value of k in the first equation is 2. And substituting 2 for both ks in the second equation produces a true statement.

9. (C) They are 102, 111, 120, 201, 210, and 300. The solution is mostly a matter of mental brute force, just counting the possibilities. But that's not too much to do. The only digits that can be used are 0, 1, 2, and 3. You don't have to worry about numbers using digits of 4 or more (4 is already more than 3).

10. (C). This is the last question in the series, and it is very difficult. The solution depends on seeing the following:

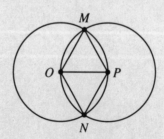

The triangles are equilateral (*OM*, *ON*, *PM*, *PN*, and *OP* are all radii), and angles *MON* and *MPN* are both 120°. So each arc is 120°, or $\frac{1}{3}$ of the circle. Since the radius of the circle is 1, the circumference of each circle is $2\pi(1) = 2\pi$. Therefore each arc is $\frac{1}{3}$ of 2π, or $\frac{2\pi}{3}$. Together, they total $\frac{2\pi}{3} + \frac{2\pi}{3} = \frac{4\pi}{3}$.

This problem can also be attacked by "guestimation." Each arc looks to be $\frac{1}{3}$ of the circle. Use that assumption and you will select (C).

DRILL 3

1. C	**6.** E
2. D	**7.** C
3. B	**8.** D
4. D	**9.** C
5. C	**10.** C

1. (C) Solve for *x*: $7 - x = 0$, so $7 = x$. Then substitute 7 for *x* in the expression $10 - x$: $10 - 7 = 3$.

2. (D) A triangle with sides of 3, 6, and 9 has a perimeter of $3 + 6 + 9 = 18$. An equilateral triangle with the same perimeter would have a side of $18 \div 3 = 6$.

3. (B) Since $PQ = PS$, *PQS* is a 45−45−90 triangle. Angle *PQR* is $45° + 15° = 60°$. And $x = 180° - 90° - 60° = 30°$. You should also be able to estimate the angle as 30°.

4. (D) Since *x* and *y* are negative, both (A) and (E) must be positive. As for (B) and (C), so long as neither *x* nor *y* is zero, those expressions must be positive. (Any number other than zero squared gives a positive result.) (D), however, is negative, since it represents the sum of two negative numbers. And you can also test the choices with numbers.

5. (C) Just use the formula for the area of a rectangle: $\ell \times \frac{3}{4} = 1$, so $\ell = \frac{4}{3}$. You can also test choices until you find one that works in the area formula, but you should be able to solve a simple equation like this without needing to substitute.

6. (E) $\ell2$ contains all the points for which $x = y$, such as (1,1) and (2,2). Since $\ell1$ is parallel to the *y*-axis, $\ell1$ and $\ell2$ intersect at (5,5). Once you know this, you just plot points until you find one that falls within the shaded area.

7. (C) This is a defined function question. It's the first of two, and it's not very difficult. Just substitute 2 for *x* and 3 for *y* in the expression $2xy - (x + y)$: $2(2)(3) - (2 + 3) = 12 - 5 = 7$.

8. (D) One way of solving this problem is to recognize that for any two numbers, *x* and *y*, $x*y = y*x$. The operations in * are multiplication (*xy*) and addition ($x + y$). If you miss that, then find the value of 5*4—$5 * 4 = 3\ell$—and start testing choices for *k* until you find a 4*k that is equal to 31.

9. (C) To relate *x* and *y*, you must use the term *c*. Since $\frac{y}{z} = c - 1$, $\frac{y}{z} + 1 = c$. Next:

$$\frac{x}{z} = \frac{y}{z} + 1$$

$$x = \left(\frac{y}{z} + 1\right)z$$

$$x = y + z = z + y$$

16

You can save some steps if you recognize that $\frac{x}{z}$ can be substituted directly for c in the second equation. You can also avoid the algebra entirely by assuming some numbers. Suppose that $z = 2$ and $c = 3$. Then $x = 6$ and $y = 4$. Plug these numbers into the equations in the answer choices:

(A) $6 = 4 - 1$ (False, so [A] is wrong.)

(B) $6 = 4 + 1$ (False, so [B] is wrong.)

(C) $6 = 4 + 2$ (True, so [C] is correct.)

(D) $6 = 2 - 4$ (False, so [D] is wrong.)

(E) $6 = \dfrac{4}{1}$ (False, so [E] is wrong.)

10. (C) For purposes of discussion, let's assume that you reach this question with little time remaining and have no idea how to attack it. There are three choices you can eliminate with a fair degree of confidence: (A), (B), and (D). The correct answer is not going to be as easy as $5 - 2$ or 3×5 or just picking the number 3 out of the question. You would then have only two choices to pick from—a fifty-fifty chance. So guess.

   You can solve the problem by counting the possibilities. Let A, B, C, D, and E be the individuals. The possible committees are: ABC, ABD, ABE, ACD, ACE, ADE, BCD, BCE, BDE, and CDE.

DRILL 4

1. B	**6.** D
2. A	**7.** B
3. C	**8.** C
4. C	**9.** E
5. A	**10.** D

1. (B) To be divisible by both 2 and 3, a number must be divisible by $2 \times 3 = 6$. (B) is the only choice divisible by 6. Additionally, you could try dividing both 2 and 3 into each choice.

2. (A) Two equations and two variables. Approach the problem as an exercise in solving simultaneous equations. You can substitute 3 directly for $2x$ in the second equation:

$$3y + 3 = 6$$
$$3y = 3$$
$$y = 1$$

3. (C) You can treat this as a problem involving simultaneous equations:

$$\frac{x}{y} = \frac{3}{2}$$

$$x = \frac{3y}{2}$$

$$2x = 3y$$

$$y = \frac{2x}{3}$$

$$x\left(\frac{2x}{3}\right) = 96$$

$$\frac{2x^2}{3} = 96$$

$$2x^2 = 288$$

$$x^2 = 144$$

$$x = +\sqrt{144} = 12 \text{ or } -\sqrt{144} = -12$$

Since the problem stipulates that x and y are positive, $x = 12$.

That's a long process. You can also try substituting numbers. Start with (C). If $x = 12$ and $xy = 96$, then $y = 8$, and $\frac{12}{8}$ is $\frac{3}{2}$. So (C) is correct.

4. (C) Just use the method for finding an average:

$$\text{Average} = \frac{x + y}{2}$$

Substitute into that equation $5x$ for y:

$$\text{Average} = \frac{x + (5x)}{2} = \frac{6x}{2} = 3x$$

Or, you can assume some values for x and y. Assume that $x = 1$. Then $y = 5$. And the average of 5 and 1 is 3. If $x = 1$, the correct formula generates the value 3. Only (C) works.

5. (E) Draw a line perpendicular to PS at point O. Label the line TO.

$\angle QOT = \angle QOS - \angle TOS$	$\angle TOR = \angle POR - \angle POT$
$\angle QOT = 120 - 90$	$\angle TOR = 144 - 90$
$\angle QOT = 30$	$\angle TOR = 54$

$$\angle QOR = \angle QOT + \angle TOR = 30 + 54 = 84$$

You can reach the same conclusion just by estimating the size of $\angle QOR$.

6. (D) This question is of average difficulty, so you know it's a little subtle. Two of the lines of symmetry are obvious:

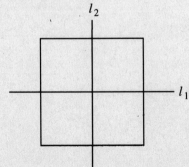

16

But that can't be the whole answer to a question of average difficulty. There is something more to be done. There are two more lines of symmetry:

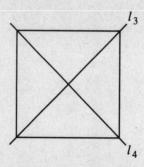

And since this is a question of average difficulty, that's it.

7. (B) Find the area of each face. The "front" of the solid has an area of $3 \times 5 = 15$. The "side" has an area of $2 \times 5 = 10$. And the "top" has an area of $2 \times 3 = 6$. Remember, however, that there are two of each face, a "front" and a "back," two "sides," and a "top" and a "bottom." So the entire surface area is $15 + 15 + 10 + 10 + 6 + 6 = 62$.

8. (C) The sum of all the angles marked as x plus the unmarked angles is the sum of the angles contained in nine triangles: $9(180) = 1620$. The unmarked angles form a straight line, so their sum is 180. The sum of the remaining angles is $1620 - 180 = 1440$. Since there are 18 angles marked x, x is $1440 \div 18 = 80$.

    Or, you might have reasoned that the unmarked angles are equal. Since nine of them form a straight line, each is $180 \div 9 = 20$. In each triangle, you have $x + x + 20 = 180$, so $2x = 160$ and $x = 160 \div 2 = 80$.

    A much simpler solution to this difficult problem is estimation. Those angles look to be slightly less than $90°$. So (A), (B), and (D) are wrong. This is a difficult problem, so (E) is unlikely. And the figure is drawn to scale (there is no warning note).

9. (E) This question is a little tricky. But start by reminding yourself that since it is a difficult question, the correct answer is not going to be $\frac{1}{3}$ or $\frac{3}{1}$, or even $\frac{3}{4}$. This eliminates choices (B), (C), and (D).

    Using the letters s for "star," c for "circle," and d for "diamond," we do the following:

    $1s = 4c$ and $3c = 4d$
    $3s = 12c$ and $12c = 16d$

    So $3s = 12c = 16d$, and $3s = 16d$.

    $$3s = 16d$$
    $$\frac{3s}{d} = \frac{16}{1}$$
    $$\frac{s}{d} = \frac{16}{3}$$

    So the ratio of star:diamond is 16:3.

10. (D) This is a shaded area problem. The shaded area is the area of the larger circle minus the sum of the areas of the two smaller circles.

    The radius of the large circle is also the diameter of each of the smaller circles, so the radius of the two smaller circles is $\frac{r}{2}$. The large circle has an area of πr^2. Each of the smaller circles has an area of $\pi(\frac{r}{2})^2 = \frac{\pi r^2}{4}$. So the shaded area is equal to $\pi r^2 - (\frac{\pi r^2}{4} + \frac{\pi r^2}{4}) = \pi r^2 - \frac{\pi r^2}{2} = \frac{\pi r^2}{2}$.

    Actually, the problem can be solved more easily by estimation. Since the radius of the large circle is r, the area of the large circle is πr^2. The two smaller circles seem to take up about half of the larger circle. So the shaded area should be about half of πr^2. That is (D).

16

Student-Produced Responses

✔ Objectives

To learn to complete the special grid required for student-produced responses.

To practice techniques and strategies for student-produced responses.

1. Using the Grid
   - When Your Answer Is a Whole Number
   - When Your Answer Is a Decimal
   - When Your Answer Is a Fraction
   - When There May Be More Than One Answer

2. Student-Produced Response Drills

17

Research has informed test-makers that math skills can best be tested if they allow test-takers to formulate their own responses. For this reason, some of the questions you meet in the SAT math sections will *not* be multiple-choice. The questions themselves will be problem-solving questions, and you will follow the suggestions in Lessons 12 through 16 in order to solve them. The difference will be that you have no way of using the process of elimination to guide your response; you must come up with an answer on your own.

Using the Grid

When you come to student-produced response questions, you will see a grid like this on your answer sheet:

written response goes here →
fraction bars →
decimal points →

numerals →

As you can see, the grid has limitations, so despite the fact that you are given no answer choices, you can make certain assumptions:

1. Your answer cannot have more than four digits; it cannot be greater than 9999. (Commas between digits are not included in this response format.)

2. If your answer is a decimal, it cannot be less than .001. It cannot be greater than 99.9. (Note that decimal points count as one "digit.")

3. If your answer is a fraction, it cannot be greater than 99/1 or less than 1/99. (Again, the fraction bar counts as one "digit.")

4. There is no accommodation made for negative numbers. Your answer will be positive.

When Your Answer Is a Whole Number

EXAMPLE:

What number increased by
25 equals twice the number?

Solve the problem. Write your answer in the four-digit space on the grid. Then fill in the circles below each digit.

If $x + 25 = 2x$, there is only one possible answer: 25. There are four possible spaces in which to write your two-digit answer, and your answer will be scored correct no matter where you write the digits, as long as they are together. However, it is a good idea to get into the habit of writing answers so that the final digit is on the right. This will allow you to check your response against assumptions 1–4 above. Once you have written the digits, fill in the circles. If you skip that final step, the computer will mark your answer incorrect, *even if you solved the problem correctly.*

When Your Answer Is a Decimal

EXAMPLE:

Dr. Leo's new office is 2.8 yards by 4 yards. She plans to run a decorative border around the perimeter of the office. How many yards of wallpaper border should she purchase?

Solve the problem. Write your answer in the four-digit space on the grid. A decimal point fills one whole space. Then fill in the circles below each digit.

2.8 + 2.8 + 4 + 4 = 13.6. Checking your answer against assumption 2 above, you see that it is both greater than .001 and less than 99.9, so it is viable. Counting the decimal point, your answer has four "digits," so it will fill the entire grid. Remember to fill in the circles, including the one below the decimal point you wrote.

When Your Answer Is a Fraction

EXAMPLE:

At Baldwin State College, one-fourth of the students are from abroad. Of those, one-eighth are from China. What fraction of the student body is Chinese?

Solve the problem. Write your answer in the four-digit space on the grid. The fraction bar fills one whole space. Then fill in the circles below each digit.

$\frac{1}{4} \times \frac{1}{8} = \frac{1}{32}$ This is neither greater than $\frac{99}{1}$ nor less than $\frac{1}{99}$, so you know that it is viable. Including the fraction bar, it contains four "digits," so it will fill the grid completely. You may be used to writing the numerator above the denominator, but when you write your answer here, you will write it like this: 1/32. Remember to fill in the circles, including the one below your written fraction bar.

When There May Be More Than One Answer

In general, the test-makers have tried to remove all ambiguities. Still, when you are dealing with numbers, there is an astonishing potential for subjective responses. You might write 1/32 for the question above, but why couldn't 2/64 serve just as well? It means the same thing. Suppose you have a decimal answer of 3.5. That's the same as 3.50, so why not write 3.50 as long as it fits in the grid?

Following a few rules will help.

1. **Reduce fractions to lowest terms.** Some leeway may be given for fraction answers—the computer may accept more than one response—but to be safe, reduce all your fractions to lowest terms. The lowest-term fraction will *always* be acceptable.

17

2. **Omit unnecessary zeros.** If the zero is not needed as a placeholder, don't write it in.
   Write .35, not 0.35.
   Write 35, not 35.0.

3. **Watch the standard of measure.** If the question asks for yards, give the answer in yards. The computer gives no credit for creative responses.

Summary

1. Realize that student-produced response questions differ from problem-solving questions only in the fact that you are given no answer choices.
2. Count fraction bars and decimal points as "digits." Do not count commas between digits.
3. Remember that your answer cannot have more than four digits; it cannot be greater than 9999 or less than .001. It will be a positive number.
4. Omit ambiguities by reducing fractions to lowest terms, leaving out unnecessary zeros, and watching standards of measure.

Student-Produced Response Drills

Because the questions asked in the student-produced response section of the SAT are just like those in problem-solving, this part will include just two drills. The first drill is a "walk-through," which explains how to fill in the answer grid once you've determined the correct response.

The remaining drill contains ten questions requiring student-produced responses. Answers and explanations for this drill can be found beginning on page 401.

Walk-Through

1. $\dfrac{2}{3} - \dfrac{5}{8} = ?$

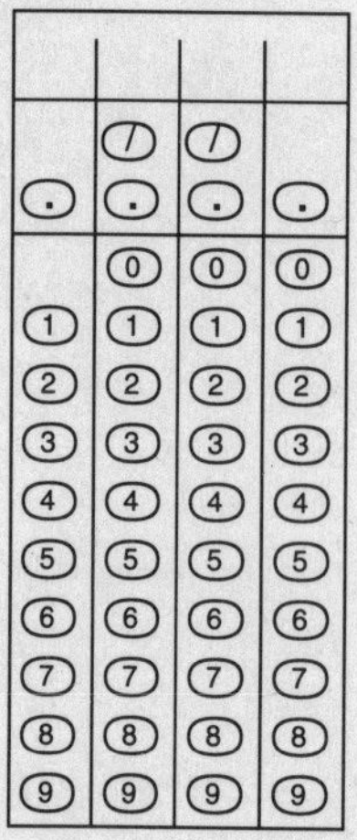

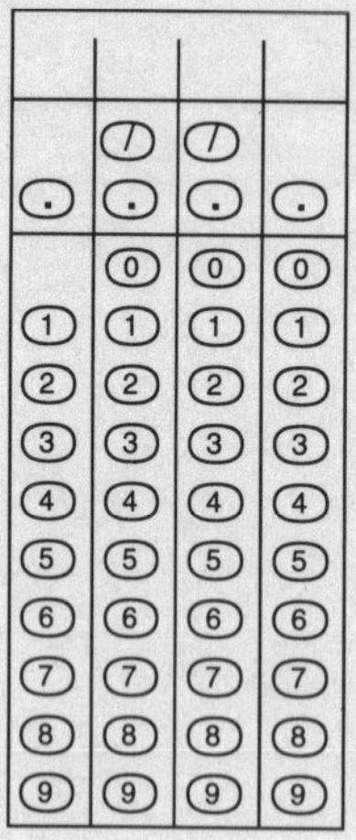

1.   1 / 2 4

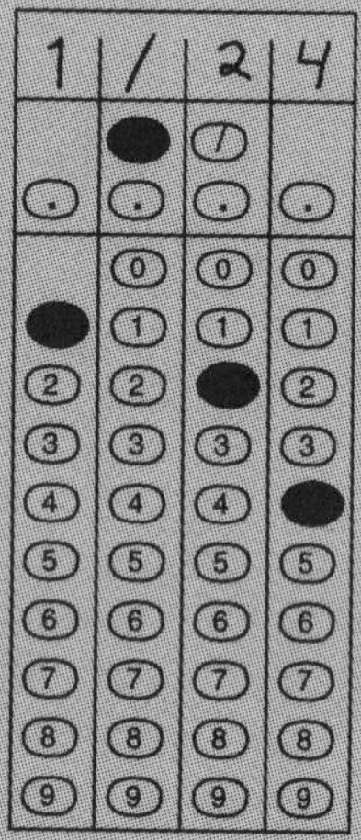

There are no choices, so you must find the answer yourself. Find the lowest common denominator: 24.

$$\frac{2}{3} - \frac{5}{8} = \frac{16 - 15}{24} = \frac{1}{24}$$

For purposes of the grid, you will write this as 1/24 and fill in the circles below 1, /, 2, and 4.

2. $65(1) + 65(2) + 65(3) + 65(4) = ?$

2.   6 5 0

Factor this as $65(1 + 2 + 3 + 4) = 65 \times 10 = 650$
Write the answer in the grid so that the zero is on the right. Fill in the circles below 6, 5, and 0.

3. A jar contains 15 pennies and 25 nickels. Expressed in lowest terms, what fraction of the coins are pennies?

4. Matinee ticket prices are $1.50 for children and $3.50 for adults. Regular ticket prices are $4.50 for children and $6.50 for adults. If three adults and one child attend a matinee, what percentage of the regular price will they pay?

3.

15 + 25 = 40, so the fraction of pennies to coins is $\frac{15}{40}$. Notice, however, that the question asks for the answer *in lowest terms*; you would get no credit for $\frac{15}{40}$, even if it fit into the grid, which it doesn't. Reduce the fraction by dividing numerator and denominator by 5: 3/8. Write this in the grid so that the 8 is on the right, and fill in the circles under 3, /, and 8.

4.

First find the total cost for each possibility:
matinee = 3($3.50) + 1($1.50)
regular = 3($6.50) + 1($4.50)
In other words, the matinee total is $12, and the regular total is $24. The question asks for this difference to be expressed as a percent: $12/$24 = 50%. There is no sign for "percent" in the grid, so 50 is the answer.

5. If the average of 8, 10, 15, 20, and x is 11, what is x?

6. If $x = 14$, what is the value of $2x - (2 + x)$?

7. If $3x + y = 33$ and $x + y = 17$, what is the value of x?

5. The total of the numbers must be $11 \times 5 = 55$. The known quantities add up to 53. The missing number must be $55 - 53 = 2$. Write 2 on the right of the grid, and fill in the 2 circle below it.

6. Simply substitute 14 for x and do the arithmetic:
$2(14) - (2 + 14) = 28 - 16 = 12$
Write the two-digit answer in the last two columns of the grid, and fill in the circles for 1 and 2.

7. Define y in terms of x:
$x + y = 17$, so $y = 17 - x$.
Substitute this new definition for x into the other equation:
$3x + y = 33$
$3x + (17 - x) = 33$
Now solve for x:
$2x + 17 = 33$
$2x = 16$
$x = 8$
Write 8 in the right column of the grid and fill in the 8 circle below it.

8. In this figure, what is the length of *AC*?

$$A$$
24
$$B \quad 18 \quad C$$

9. If the perimeter of this rectangle is 40, what is its area?

15

w

8. | | | 3 | 0 |

ABC is a right triangle. Use the Pythagorean Theorem to solve for *AC*:
$18^2 + 24^2 = 30^2$
AC has a length of 30. Write 30, and fill in the circles for 3 and 0.

9. | | | 7 | 5 |

The perimeter = $2w + 2l$. $2w + 2(15) = 40$, so $2w = 10$, and $w = 5$.
Find the area by multiplying $l \times w$: $15 \times 5 = 75$.
There is no place on the grid to write units of measure, so 75 is the answer. Write 75, and fill in the circles for 7 and 5.

10.   If a circle of radius .25 is inscribed in a square,
      what is the area of the square?

10.   The figure can be drawn thus:

One side of the square is equal in length to 2(.25), or .5. The area of the square, then, is $.5^2$, or .25. Write .25 in the last three columns of the grid, and fill in the circles for ., 2, and 5.

Drill 1 (Answers, page 401)

1. If the price of a book increases from $10.00 to $12.50, what is the percent increase in price?

2. Boys and girls belong to the chess club. There are 36 people in the club, 15 of whom are girls. In lowest terms, what fraction of the club are boys?

3. Jason built a fence around his rectangular garden. The width of the garden is 2.8 yards, and the length is twice that. How many yards of fencing did Jason use?

4. If $x = 9$, what is the value of $x^2 + 2x - 9$?

	/	/	
.	.	.	.
	0	0	0
1	1	1	1
2	2	2	2
3	3	3	3
4	4	4	4
5	5	5	5
6	6	6	6
7	7	7	7
8	8	8	8
9	9	9	9

5. For all numbers, $x * y = 2xy$. What is $1.5 * 2.5$?

	/	/	
.	.	.	.
	0	0	0
1	1	1	1
2	2	2	2
3	3	3	3
4	4	4	4
5	5	5	5
6	6	6	6
7	7	7	7
8	8	8	8
9	9	9	9

6. If $x = 3y - 1$ and $x + y = 15$, what is the value of x?

	/	/	
.	.	.	.
	0	0	0
1	1	1	1
2	2	2	2
3	3	3	3
4	4	4	4
5	5	5	5
6	6	6	6
7	7	7	7
8	8	8	8
9	9	9	9

7. Su Li made \$45 working as a mother's helper. She spent $\frac{1}{5}$ of the money, banked $\frac{1}{3}$ of the remainder, and kept the rest for expenses. What fraction of the original \$45 did she keep?

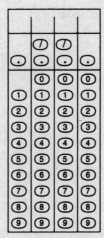

8. What is the area of isosceles triangle *ABC*?

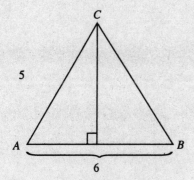

9. If lines 1 and 2 are parallel, what is $x + y$?

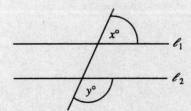

10. In this figure, what is the perimeter of square
    ABCD?

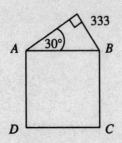

Explanatory Answers

DRILL 1

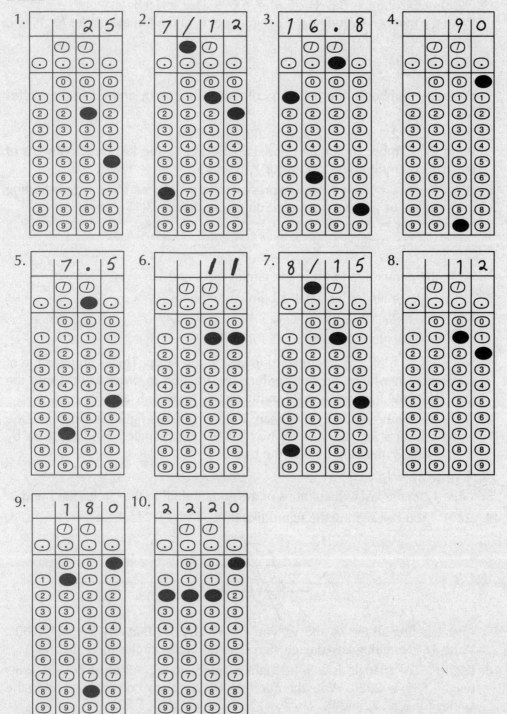

1. (25)   Determine the difference in prices: $12.50 − $10.00 = $2.50
$2.50 is what percent of $10.00?
The answer is 25. Fill in the circles below 2 and 5.

2. (7/12)   There are 36 − 15 boys, or 21 boys. In lowest terms, $\frac{21}{36}$ is $\frac{7}{12}$. Write the fraction, and fill in the circles below 7, /, 1, and 2.

3. (16.8)   The perimeter can be expressed as:
$2(2.8) + 2[2(2.8)] = 5.6 + 2(5.6) = 5.6 + 11.2 = 16.8$
Write the number, including the decimal point, and fill in the circles for 1, 6, ., and 8.

4. (90) $x^2 = 81$, and $2x = 18$.
$81 + 18 − 9 = 90$
Write the number in the last two columns of the grid, and fill in the circles for 9 and 0.

5. (7.5) $1.5 * 2.5 = 2(1.5 \times 2.5) = 2(3.75) = 7.5$
Write the number, including the decimal point, in the last three columns of the grid. Then fill in the circles for 7, ., and 5.

6. (11)   If $x + y = 15$, you can express y in terms of x as $15 − x$. Substituting this in place of y in the first equation gives you $x = 3(15 − x) − 1$.
Solve for x: $x = 45 − 3x − 1$
$$4x = 45 − 1$$
$$x = 11$$
Write the numeral, and fill in the circles for 1 and 1.

7. (8/15)   Pay attention to what is being asked here.
$45 − \frac{1}{5}($45$) = 36

$\frac{1}{3}$ of that goes into the bank: $\frac{1}{3}($36$) = $12.

Su Li has $24 left. $\frac{24}{45}$, reduced to lowest terms, is $\frac{8}{15}$. This is an example of a question in which you *must* reduce the fraction in order to fit it into the grid. Write the fraction, and fill in the circles for 8, /, 1, and 5.

8. (12)   Remember your Pythagorean Theorem. If the figure is isosceles, the altitude bisects leg *AB*, making two 3-4-5 right triangles. Find the area by multiplying $\frac{1}{2}$ the height times the base:
$\frac{1}{2}(6 \times 4) = 12$
Write 12 in the last two columns of the grid, and fill in the circles for 1 and 2.

9. (180)   You can redraw the figure like this:

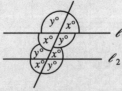

After labeling all the xs and ys, you can clearly see that any $x + y = 180°$. Write 180, omitting any degree sign. The fill in the circles for 1, 8, and 0.

10. (2220)   The triangle is a 3-4-5 right triangle, so leg *AB* must be 555 units long. $4(555) = 2220$. Write the numeral, omitting any comma, and fill in the circles for 2, 2, 2, and 0.

Quantitative Comparisons

✔ **Objectives**

To learn about the special features of the quantitative comparison instructions.

To learn what is tested in quantitative comparisons.

To learn how to use the ladder of difficulty to avoid wrong answers.

To learn to identify patterns of arithmetic, algebra, and geometry peculiar to quantitative comparisons.

To practice techniques and strategies for quantitative comparisons.

1. **The Directions**
   - Illustrations of Choices (A), (B), (C), and (D)

2. **Common Problems**
   - **Arithmetic**
   - **Algebra**
   - **Geometry**

3. **Special Strategies for Quantitative Comparisons**
   - Guessing
   - The "Good Enough" Principle
   - Simplifying the Comparison
   - Substituting Numbers

4. **Quantitative Comparison Drills**

18

Only one of your SAT math sections will contain quantitative comparisons. They should be numbered 1 through 15. Although quantitative comparisons come with a special set of instructions, they still test arithmetic, algebra, and geometry. And many of the strategies presented in the chapters on problem-solving are useful here as well.

Quantitative comparisons are both easy and difficult. They're easy in the sense that they're short, and it usually doesn't take much time to arrive at a solution. But they're also difficult because they can be tricky. In any event, there are only 15 such items on the entire test, making quantitative comparisons less important than problem-solving items.

The Directions

Questions 1-15 each consist of two quantities, one in Column A and one in Column B. You are to compare the two quantities and on the answer sheet fill in oval

  A if the quantity in Column A is greater;
  B if the quantity in Column B is greater;
  C if the two quantities are equal;
  D if the relationship cannot be determined from the information given.

AN E RESPONSE WILL NOT BE SCORED.

	EXAMPLES		
	Column A	Column B	Answers
E1.	2×6	$2 + 6$	● Ⓑ Ⓒ Ⓓ Ⓔ
E2.	$180 - x$	y	Ⓐ Ⓑ ● Ⓓ Ⓔ
E3.	$p - q$	$q - p$	Ⓐ Ⓑ Ⓒ ● Ⓔ

(E2 diagram: two lines with angles $x°$ and $y°$)

Notes:

1. In certain questions, information concerning one or both of the quantities to be compared is centered above the two columns.
2. In a given question, a symbol that appears in both columns represents the same thing in Column A as it does in Column B.
3. Letters such as x, n, and k stand for real numbers.

The only thing you need to memorize here is the meaning of the lettered designations, which should not be difficult. And after you have practiced a few quantitative comparisons you will not even have to think about the letters.

The following questions illustrate the answer choices.

Illustrations of answer choices (A) and (B)

1. Arithmetic

Column A	Column B
2 dozen	23

Column A	Column B
0.5×0.2	$0.5 + 0.2$

The answer to the first question is (A). 2 dozen = $2 \times 12 = 24$, and 24 is larger than 23.

The answer to the second question is (B). $0.5 \times 0.2 = 0.1$, and $0.5 + 0.2 = 0.7$. So Column B is larger.

2. Algebra

Column A	Column B
$x + 1$	x

$$p > 0$$

Column A	Column B
p	$2p$

The answer to the first question is (A). Regardless of the value of x, $x + 1$ is 1 more than x.

The answer to the second question is (B). The centered note states that p is positive. So $2p$ must be twice as large as p.

3. Geometry

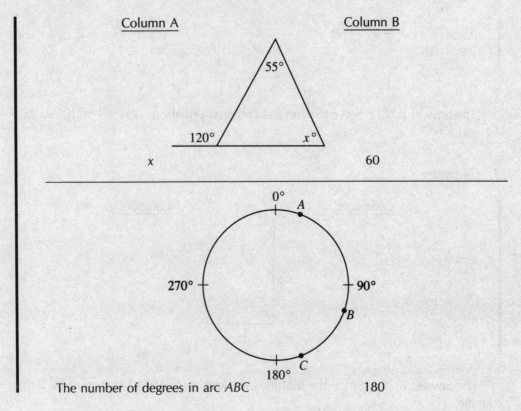

Column A   Column B

55°

120°   x°

x   60

___

0°
A

270°   90°

B

180°   C

The number of degrees in arc *ABC*   180

The answer to the first question is (A). The unlabeled angle must be 60°, and 60 + 55 + x = 180. So x = 65.

The answer to the second question is (B). Point *A* is between 0° and 90°; point *C* is between 90° and 180°. Regardless of the exact locations of the points, arc *ABC* is less than 180°.

Illustrations of answer choice (C)

1. Arithmetic

Column A   Column B
$48^2 + 2(48)(52) + 52^2$ $(100)(100)$

The answer is (C). The expression in Column A can be factored:

$$(48 + 52)(48 + 52) = (100)(100).$$

18

2. Algebra

Column A	Column B
$2x - 4 = 10$	
x	7

The answer is (C). Solve for x in the centered equation. $2x - 4 = 10$, so $2x = 14$ and $x = 7$.

3. Geometry

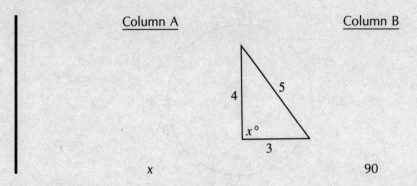

Column A	Column B
x	90

The answer is (C). Since the triangle has sides of 3, 4, and 5, it must be a right triangle.

Illustrations of answer choice (D)

1. Arithmetic

Column A	Column B
n is a positive integer.	
Remainder when $2n + 1$ is divided by 2	Remainder when $3n + 1$ is divided by 2

The answer is (D). As for Column A, $2n + 1$ is odd; and when an odd number is divided by 2 the remainder is 1. So Column A is always 1. As for Column B, if n is even, then $3n$ is even, and $3n + 1$ is odd. And an odd number divided by 2 generates a remainder of 1. But if n is odd, then $3n$ is odd, and $3n + 1$ is even. When divided by 2, an even number leaves no remainder. So Column B could be either 1 or zero. The two columns might both be 1 and equal; but the left-hand column might be larger. Therefore, the relationship is indeterminate.

2. Algebra

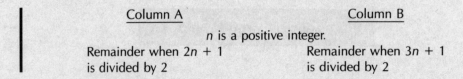

Column A	Column B
x^3	x^4

The answer is (D). You don't know anything about the value of x. x could be negative, or positive, or even zero.

3. Geometry

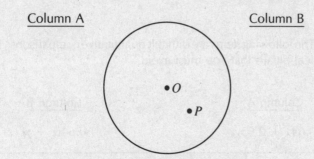

Column A   Column B

O is the center of the circle.

| The distance from P to a point Q (not shown) on the circle | Radius of the circle |

The answer is (D). PQ could be less than, greater than, or even equal to the radius:

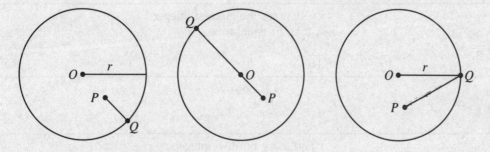

Notice that in each of the examples of a (D) answer choice, we were able to offer a proof of the correctness of (D). The relationship was *indeterminate*. Choice (D) is not a cry of surrender, "I give up. I can't determine it, so I'll mark (D)."

The Ladder of Difficulty

Quantitative comparisons are arranged according to the ladder of difficulty, and the last six or seven items can be fairly tricky. So watch yourself.

Unfortunately, knowing about the ladder of difficulty here is not quite as valuable as it was in the case of problem-solving items. There, you were advised to avoid choices that were numbers in the problem or that could be gotten by a simple operation. Here, however, there are no individual choices—just the (A), (B), (C), and (D) pattern.

Still, it's worth looking at a group of difficult items that would be likely to trip up Watson.

18

Quantitative Comparisons (Answers, page 426)

Directions: The following items are difficult quantitative comparisons. They illustrate the logical pitfalls that you must avoid.

	Column A	Column B
1.	$0.64x + 0.65y$	$0.64(x + y)$

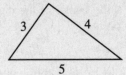

| **2.** | Area of triangle ABC | 6 |

$<x>$ denotes the greatest integer
less than or equal to x.

| **3.** | $<3\frac{1}{16}> + <-3\frac{1}{16}>$ | 0 |

x is positive.

| **4.** | x | x^2 |

x and y are positive integers.

| **5.** | $\dfrac{x}{y}$ | $\dfrac{(x + 1)}{(y + 1)}$ |

$$S_1 = \{1, 3, 5, 7, 9\}$$
$$S_2 = \{2, 4, 6, 8\}$$

| **6.** | The sum of any 3 different numbers from S_1 | The sum of any 2 different numbers from S_2 |

John's birthday is separated
from Pat's birthday by three days
and Pat's birthday is separated
from Ellen's birthday by six days.

| **7.** | The number of days separating John's birthday from Ellen's | 10 |

| **8.** | 0.333 | $\dfrac{1}{3}$ |

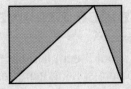

9.   Area of the shaded part   Area of the unshaded part
of the figure   of the figure

PQ and *RS* are diameters of the
same circle.

10.   *PR*   *QS*

Common Problems

Many of the examples so far should seem familiar to you. Quantitative comparisons test the same ideas that problem-solving items test, but they are presented in a different format. Generally, then, you should look for the same things in quantitative comparisons that you look for in problem-solving items.

1. Arithmetic

In quantitative comparisons involving arithmetic, do the operations if they are manageable.

EXAMPLE:

Column A	Column B

Three pounds of Brand X laundry powder costs $12.33.
Four pounds of Brand Y laundry powder costs $16.44.

The average cost per pound of Brand X	The average cost per pound of Brand Y

The answer is (C). You need to divide $12.33 by 3 and $16.44 by 4. The arithmetic is easily managed, so do it.

$12.33 ÷ 3 = $4.11
$16.44 ÷ 4 = $4.11

Of course, if the manipulations would take too long, look for one of the shortcuts (simplifying, factoring, or approximating).

EXAMPLES:

Column A	Column B
$\frac{101}{102} \times \frac{102}{103} \times \frac{103}{104} \times \frac{104}{105} \times \frac{105}{106}$	$\frac{101}{106}$
$25(1) + 25(2) + 25(3) + 25(4)$	250
$\frac{111}{221}$	$\frac{222}{445}$

The answer to the first question is (C). Avoid a lengthy calculation by cancelling. The left-hand column is $\frac{101}{106}$.

The answer to the second question is also (C). Factor the left-hand expression: $25(1 + 2 + 3 + 4) = 25 \times 10 = 250$.

The answer to the third question is (A). Use approximation. $\frac{111}{222}$ would be exactly $\frac{1}{2}$, so $\frac{111}{221}$ must be slightly larger than $\frac{1}{2}$. $\frac{222}{444}$ would be exactly $\frac{1}{2}$, so $\frac{222}{445}$ is slightly less than $\frac{1}{2}$.

For quantitative comparisons testing the properties of numbers, remember that negative numbers and fractions sometimes exhibit peculiar behavior.

EXAMPLES:

Column A	Column B
x	$2x$

x is not equal to 0.

Column A	Column B
x^2	x^3

x is positive.

Column A	Column B
x^2	x^3

$x > 1$

Column A	Column B
x^2	x^3

The answer to the first question is (D). If x is a positive number, $2x$ will be double x. But x is not so restricted. x could be negative, in which case it is larger than $2x$ (the larger the absolute value of a negative number, the smaller the number). Or if x is zero, then $x = 2x$.

The answer to the second question is also (D). x might be negative, in which case x^2 is positive and x^3 is negative.

The answer to the third question is also (D). Even though x is positive, x might be a fraction, in which case x^3 is smaller than x^2. Or x might be equal to 1, in which case $x^2 = x^3$.

The answer to the last question is (B). So long as x is greater than 1, x^3 will be greater than x^2.

When you are analyzing the behavior of a variable, ask yourself whether it can be negative, zero, a fraction, or 1.

2. Algebra

Do whatever algebraic operations are indicated.

EXAMPLES:

Column A	Column B
$3(x + 3)$	$3x + 3$

$xy = 0$

Column A	Column B
$(x + y)^2$	$x^2 + y^2$

$x + 1$ is not equal to 0.

Column A	Column B
$\dfrac{x^2 - 1}{x + 1}$	$x - 1$

The answer to the first question is (A). Do the multiplication indicated in Column A: $3(x + 3) = 3x + 9$. Since $3x$ is a part of both columns, regardless of the value of x, Column A is 6 greater than Column B.

The answer to the second question is (C). Perform the multiplication indicated in Column A:

$$(x + y)^2 = (x + y)(x + y) = x^2 + 2xy + y^2$$

18

Since $xy = 0$, this is equal to $x^2 + y^2$. The two columns are equal.

The answer to the third question is (C). You should recognize $x^2 - 1$ as the difference of two squares. It can be factored into $(x + 1)(x - 1)$. After simplifying, Column A becomes $x + 1$, so the two quantities are equal.

If the problem involves an equation or equations, solve for unknowns using the procedures discussed in Chapter 15.

EXAMPLES:

Column A	Column B
$2x + y = 7$	
$x + y = 4$	
x	y

$$3x = 4y$$

0	$4y - 3x$

The answer to the first question is (A). Two variables and two equations calls for the simultaneous equations treatment. You can solve for x or y in the second equation and substitute the result back into the first. Or, you can simply subtract the second equation from the first (or, more precisely, subtract the left side of the second equation from the left side of the first and the right side of the second from the right side of the first):

$$2x + y = 7$$
$$-(x + y = 4)$$
$$x + 0 = 3$$

So $x = 3$ and $y = 1$.

The answer to the second question is (C). With two variables and only one equation, you cannot solve for x and y individually. But you can turn $3x = 4y$ into something that looks like Column B. $x = 4y$ can be rewritten as $0 = 4y - 3x$.

You may also have occasion to employ the techniques based on the premise "it must be one of the guilty suspects."

EXAMPLES:

Column A		Column B
	$w > 1$	
The number of widgets produced in an hour if the average rate of production is w widgets per one hour		The number of widgets produced in an hour if the average rate of production is 1 widget per w hours

After Diana spent $\frac{1}{2}$ of her allowance on a book and another $3 on lunch, she still had $\frac{1}{6}$ of her allowance.

Diana's allowance $18

The answer to the first question is (A). If you don't see what you need—namely, numbers—then ask for them. Assume that $w = 2$. On that assumption, Column A is 2 and Column B is $\frac{1}{2}$ (one widget every two hours).

The answer to the second question is (B). Work backwards. Assume, for argument's sake, that Diana's allowance is the amount in Column B, $18. On that assumption, Diana had $9 after buying the book and $6 after paying for lunch. And $\frac{6}{18} = \frac{1}{3}$, not $\frac{1}{6}$. So $18 is larger than Diana's allowance.

18

3. *Geometry*

The principles stored in your "attic" are all applicable here.

EXAMPLES:

Column A   Column B

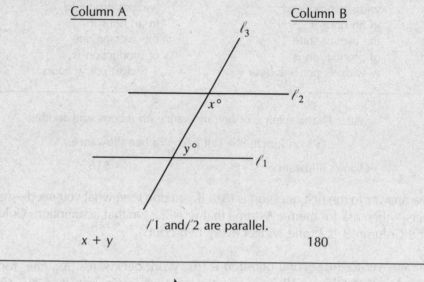

$\ell 1$ and $\ell 2$ are parallel.

$x + y$ 180

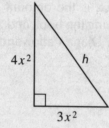

h $5x^2$

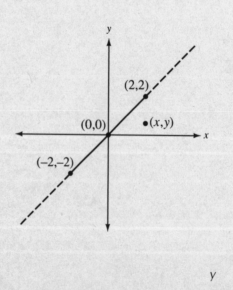

x y

The answer to the first question is (C). Use the "big and little" angle theorem.
$x + y = 180$.

The answer to the second question is (C). You can use the Pythagorean Theorem to calculate the length of the hypotenuse: $5x^2$. Or, better still, just recall that if two sides of a right triangle are 3 and 4, the hypotenuse must be 5. Since $3x^2$ and $4x^2$ are multiples of 3 and 4, the hypotenuse will be the x^2 multiple of 5.

The answer to the third question is (A). Here you need to "pull down from your attic" your knowledge of coordinate geometry. The line consists of all points for which the x coordinate equals the y coordinate. Since point (x,y) falls below that line (and is in the first quadrant), x must be larger than y. (The horizontal distance to the right of the origin is greater than the vertical distance above the origin.)

Quantitative comparisons also employ complex figures and figures with shaded areas.

EXAMPLES:

Column A   Column B

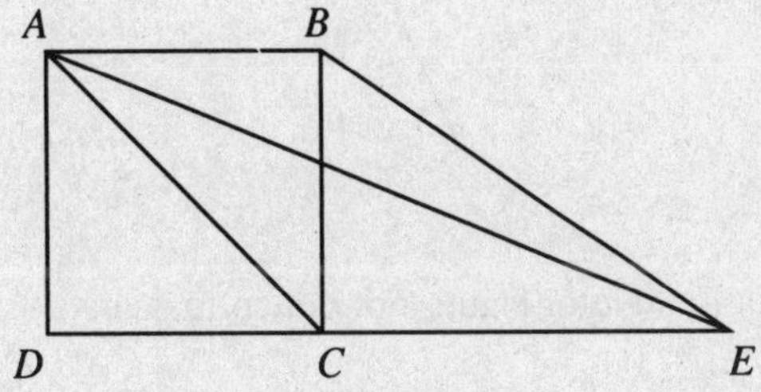

ABCD is a square.

Area of ACE   Area of BCE

_____

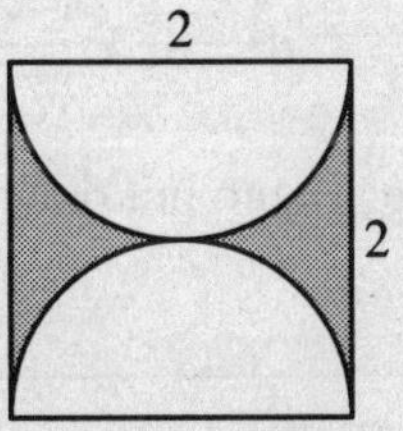

The square above contains two semicircles.

Area of shaded portion $4 - \pi$
of the figure

The answer to the first question is (C). In this composite figure, CE is the base of both triangles. Then, BC is the altitude of triangle BCE and AD is the altitude of triangle ACE. Since ABCD is a square, AD = BC. Both triangles have the same base and equal altitudes, so their areas must be equal.

The answer to the second question is (C). The shaded area is the area of the square minus the area of two semicircles. The area of the square is 4. The radius of the semicircles is $\frac{1}{2}$ the side of the square, or 1. Since there are two semicircles, their area will be equal to that of a complete circle with radius 1: $\pi(1^2) = \pi$. So the unshaded portion of the figure has an area of π. The area of the shaded part of the figure is $4 - \pi$.

18

The one technique that won't work well with quantitative comparisons is measuring. Many of the figures in this part are accompanied by the warning "*Note: Figure not drawn to scale.*" Additionally, the geometry questions in this part are rarely susceptible to this technique anyway.

We have another technique to take the place of measuring: distorting.

EXAMPLES:

<u>Column A</u>   <u>Column B</u>

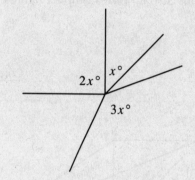

Note: Figure not drawn to scale.

x 45

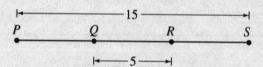

Note: Figure not drawn to scale.

Length of *PR*   Length of *QS*

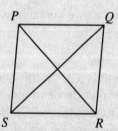

PQRS is a parallelogram.
PR ≠ *SQ*
<u>Note</u>: Figure not drawn to scale.

The measure in degrees   The measure in degrees
of angle *PSR*   of angle *SRQ*

The answer to the first question is (D). Although angle x appears to be 45°, there are two unquantified angles in the figure. You can redraw the figure in different ways:

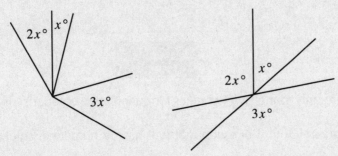

Thus, x might be more or less than 45.

The answer to the second question is (D). The figure is not drawn to scale, so you cannot infer from the fact that *PR appears* to be equal to *QS* that *PR* is really equal to *QS*. You can prove that *PR* is not necessarily equal to *QS* by redrawing the figure:

Now *PR* seems to be bigger than *QS*.

Now *PR* seems to be smaller than *QR*.

The answer to the third question is (D). The note says the figure is not drawn to scale, and the centered information specifically says that *PR* is not equal to *SQ*. If the diagonals of the parallelogram aren't equal to each other, what should the figure look like?

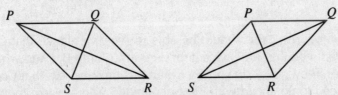

In the one case, it looks as though angle *PSR* is greater than angle *SRQ*, but in the other figure it looks as though *SRQ* is larger.

This does not mean that every problem with a warning note should be answered with (D). Sometimes, the figure is not drawn to scale just to keep you honest, that is, to keep you from measuring to get a solution. On balance, however, if you need to make a guess, it is more likely than not that a problem with a warning note should be answered (D).

18

Special Strategies for Quantitative Comparisons

There are only four answer choices for quantitative comparisons, so never guess (E).

Never guess (D) to a question that will have a numerical solution.

EXAMPLE:

Column A	Column B
5^3	3^5

To a problem like this, you should never guess (D). Even if you lack the time to work out an answer, there is a clear relationship between the two quantities that can be established by multiplication.

The "Good Enough" Principle

Do only as much as you need to do to get the comparison.

EXAMPLE:

Column A	Column B
The average of 7, 8, and 6	The average of 7, 8, 6, and 0

The answer is (A). You should be able to see at a glance that Column A and Column B would be the same except for zero in Column B. And what do zeros do to an average? They pull it down. So Column B must be less that Column A. And there is no need to go ahead with the calculation. You already know Column A is larger, and that's "good enough" for the SAT.

Simplify the Comparison

You can add or subtract the same thing to both sides of the comparison without changing the comparison.

EXAMPLE:

Column A	Column B
$3x + 2$	$2x + 3$

First, subtract 2x from both sides. The comparison becomes:

Column A	Column B
x + 2	3

Next, subtract 2 from both sides. The comparison becomes:

Column A	Column B
x	1

Since there are no restrictions on x, the relationship must be indeterminate. x could be less than, equal to, or greater than 1.

You can also multiply or divide both sides by the same positive number without changing the comparison.

EXAMPLE:

Column A	$m > 1$	Column B
$\dfrac{m + m + m + m}{m \cdot m}$		$\dfrac{4}{m^2}$

Since m^2 must be positive, it is permissible to multiply both sides of the comparison by m^2. The result is:

Column A	$m > 1$	Column B
$m + m + m + m$		4

which is

Column A	$m > 1$	Column B
$4m$		4

And you can divide both sides by 4. The result is:

Column A	$m > 1$	Column B
m		1

Since $m > 1$, Column A must be greater.

Do not, however, multiply or divide by a negative number or by a number that you are not absolutely certain is positive.

EXAMPLE:

Column A	Column B
2x	x

18

First, divide both sides of the comparison by x (a wrong move, as we shall soon see). The result is:

Column A	Column B
2	1

This seems to prove that Column A is greater. In fact, the answer is (D). What happened?

You cannot divide across the comparison by x because you don't know whether or not x is positive. Had the problem read:

Column A		Column B
	$x > 0$	
$2x$		x

it would have been permissible to divide both sides by x. And 2x is larger than x when x is positive.

Why does this technique work? It's based on the rules for manipulating inequalities. Just don't multiply or divide across the comparison unless you are certain the number you are using is positive.

Substitute Numbers

If the problem involves an unknown, substitute values. A single substitution will eliminate two choices.

EXAMPLES:

Column A	Column B
The average (arithmetic mean) of 16, 24, x, and y is 10.	
$y > 0$	
x	0

Column A	Column B
x and y are positive integers.	
x is greater than y.	
x^y	y^x

Column A	Column B
$x^2 = y^2$	
x^2	xy

The answer to the first question is (B). Pick a value to substitute for y, say 5. Use the procedure for finding the missing element of an average. If the average of 26, 14, 5, and x is 10, their sum is $4 \times 10 = 40$. $26 + 14 + 5 = 45$. So $x = 40 - 45 = -5$. In this substitution, you eliminate (A) and (C). (x is not always greater than nor always equal to zero.) You might try another substitution, say 1. $26 + 14 + 1 = 41$, so $x = 40 - 41 = -1$.

Since you have two substitutions showing that x is less than zero, you should guess (B). Of course, there is no guarantee that this is always true. The real answer might be (D). But your substitutions have given you reason to select (B). (And substituting may sometimes lead to a conceptual solution. When $y = 5$, $x = -5$;

when $y = 1$, $x = -1$. That should tell you something.)

The answer to the second question is (D). Again, try some values, say $x = 3$ and $y = 2$. Then $x^y = 3^2 = 9$; and $y^x = 2^3 = 8$. Since this shows Column A can be greater than Column B, eliminate (B) and (C) as choices. Then try some other numbers, say $x = 5$ and $y = 3$. Then $x^y = 5^3 = 125$ and $y^x = 3^5 = 243$. Now Column B is larger, so you know the answer must be (D).

Finally, the answer to the third question is also (D). You might try the values $+1$ and $+1$. On this assumption, Column A is 1 and Column B is 1. Since the two columns can be equal, eliminate (A) and (B). Next, you might try 2 and 2. You get the same result. So you might guess (C).

As it turns our, however, the answer is (D). Substitution doesn't guarantee a correct choice; it merely improves your chances of guessing the right choice. (D) is correct since x might be negative. If $x = -1$ and $y = +1$, the columns are no longer equal.

In summary, a single substitution gives you a fifty-fifty chance of getting the right answer.

When substituting, if

Column A is larger, eliminate choices (B) and (C).

Column B is larger, eliminate choices (A) and (C).

the columns are equal, eliminate choices (A) and (B).

18

Special QC Strategies (Answers, page 427)

Directions: The special strategies just discussed are particularly useful in solving the following quantitative comparisons.

	Column A	Column B
1.	$\left(-\dfrac{1}{2}\right)^{23}$	$\left(\dfrac{1}{2}\right)^{23}$
2.	Area of a square with side 2	Area of a circle with diameter 2
3.	$0.123 \div 123$	$123 \div 0.123$

4.

Circle P has a diameter of 10.
Circle O has a circumference of 4π.

	Area of Circle O	Area of Circle P
5.	Volume of a cone with a base of 5π and a height of 5	Volume of a cylinder with a base of 5π and a height of 5
6.	$5 \times 6 \times 7 \times 8 \times 9 \times 10$	$50 \times 54 \times 56$
7.	$\dfrac{13}{14}$	$\dfrac{14}{15}$
8.	$\dfrac{9}{11}$	$\sqrt{\dfrac{9}{11}}$
9.	$10^{11} - 10^{10}$	10^{10}
10.	$\dfrac{1}{\sqrt{3}}$	$\sqrt{3}$

$x > 0$

11.	$\dfrac{x+2}{2}$	$\dfrac{x+4}{5}$

$a > b > 0$

12.	$(60\%\ \text{of}\ a) + (40\%\ \text{of}\ b)$	$50\%(a + b)$

x and y are positive integers.

| 13. | $5^x \bullet 5^y$ | $(5^x)^y$ |

$k > 0$

| 14. | $k^2 + 2k + 2$ | $\sqrt{k^2 + 2k + 2}$ |

$$\frac{x}{y} > 0$$

$$\frac{x}{z} > 0$$

| 15. | yz | 0 |

18

Explanatory Answers

EXERCISE 1

1. (D) Column B is equal to $0.64x + 0.64y$. So at first glance, since $0.65 > 0.64$, Column A seems larger. But for a difficult problem, that's too obvious. The answer is (D). There are no restrictions on x and y. x and y can be positive, but they can also be zero and negative. For example, if x and y are both 0, the two columns are equal.

2. (C) You might at first jump to the conclusion that the answer is (D). You need an altitude, so you draw one:

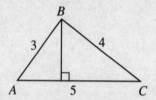

But it doesn't seem possible to find the length of the altitude.

    The answer is (C). Since this triangle has sides of 3, 4, and 5, it is a right triangle. Sides 3 and 4 form a right angle, so you can use them as altitude and base.

3. (B) Here, Watson makes a silly mistake. He sees the symmetry in Column A and concludes that Column A must be zero and answers (C). That's too easy for a difficult item. The answer is (B). $<3\frac{1}{16}>$ is 3, and $<-3\frac{1}{16}>$ is -4. So Column A is -1.

4. (D) Here, Watson immediately jumps to the conclusion that Column B is larger. But x might be a fraction, in which case Column A is larger. (Raising a fraction to a power results in a fraction even smaller than the original.) Or x might be 1, in which case the columns are equal.

5. (D) Here, Watson jumps to the conclusion that Column B is larger, because $x + 1$ is greater than x and $y + 1$ is greater than y. But the answer is (D). If $x = 1$ and $y = 2$, then Column A is $\frac{1}{2}$ and Column B is $\frac{2}{3}$ (and Column B is larger). If $x = 2$ and $y = 1$, then Column A is 2 and Column B is $\frac{3}{2}$ (and Column A is larger).

6. (D) Here, Watson erroneously picks (A). He reasons that the sum of three numbers must be more than the sum of two numbers. It is true that the sum of three numbers from S_1 might be larger than the sum of two numbers from S_2; for example, $5 + 7 + 9 > 2 + 4$. But it is also possible for the sum of two numbers from S_2 to be larger than the sum of three numbers from S_1; for example, $6 + 8 > 1 + 3 + 5$.

7. (D) Here, Watson jumps to the conclusion that the answer is (C). He concludes that Pat's birthday is between those of John and Ellen, so there must be ten days separating the birthdays of John and Ellen. The difficulty is that the phrase "is separated by" doesn't indicate direction (whose birthday is earlier).

There is more than one possibility. The following is the only one Watson sees (because he forgets this is a difficult comparison).

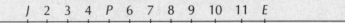

where *P*, *J*, and *E* stand for the birthdays of Pat, John, and Ellen (respectively). But the following is also possible:

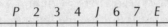

Pat's birthday is still separated from John's by three days and from Ellen's by six days, but now John's and Ellen's birthdays are separated by only two days.

8. (B) Here, Watson sees 0.333 and $\frac{1}{3}$, remembers that $\frac{1}{3}$ is approximately 0.333, then breathes a sigh of relief and calls them equal. It's not that easy. $\frac{1}{3} = 0.333$ ...., a repeating decimal. So $\frac{1}{3}$ is larger than 0.333.

9. (C) Watson looks at this comparison, sees no information other than that the figure is a triangle inside a rectangle, and concludes the answer must be (D). The correct choice is (C). Drop an altitude for the triangle:

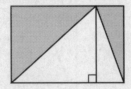

Notice that the figure is divided into two parts. In each part, the shaded area and the unshaded portions are equal. So for the figure as a whole, the area of the unshaded part is equal to the area of the shaded part.

10. (C) Without a figure, you might jump to the wrong conclusion that the answer is (D). Draw the figure:

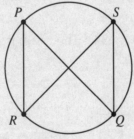

No matter how you draw *PQ* and *RS*, *PR* and *QS* are equal.

EXERCISE 2

1. (B) Apply the "good enough" principle. Column A is negative and Column B is positive. That's all you need to know to establish that Column B is greater.

18

2. (A) Draw a sketch:

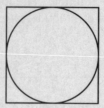

The circle is completely contained within the square. You don't need to do anything more. The square is larger.

3. (B) No need to do the division here. Column A is a decimal fraction divided by a large number; Column B is the same large number divided by the same decimal fraction. And that's "good enough" to prove that Column B is greater.

4. (B) Here, you will need to find the radius of Circle O. Since the circumference of Circle O is 4π, $2\pi r = 4\pi$ and $r = 2$. The radius of Circle O is 2, and the radius of Circle P is $10 \div 2 = 5$. This is "good enough." The longer the radius, the larger the area. Since Circle P has the longer radius, Circle P has the greater area.

5. (B) No need to do a calculation (even if you knew the formulas, which you don't need to know in this case). Just visualize the relationship:

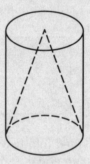

That's "good enough" to prove that Column B is larger.

6. (C) Simplify across the comparison. Divide both sides by 50. The result is:

$6 \times 7 \times 8 \times 9$ 54×56

Then divide both sides by 54. The result is:

7×8 56

And divide both sides of the comparison by 56. The result is:

1 1

So the two quantities are the same.

7. (B) You might reason that Column B must be greater since $\frac{14}{15}$ is closer to 1 than $\frac{13}{14}$ is. An alternative is to "cross-multiply." Multiply both sides of the comparison by 14. The result is:

13 $\frac{14(14)}{15}$

Now multiply both sides by 15. The result is:

| 13(15) | 14(14) |
| 195 | 196 |

So Column B is larger.

8. (B) You might reason as follows. A fraction that is squared is smaller than the original fraction; therefore, taking the square root of a fraction results in a fraction larger than the original. You can also square both sides of the comparison above. (They may not be the same positive numbers, but the procedure cannot upset the *direction* of the inequality if the two sides are not equal.) The result is:

$$\frac{81}{121} \qquad\qquad \frac{9}{11}$$

Now follow the procedure we used above for comparing two fractions. Multiply both sides by 11 and by 121. The result is:

| 81(11) | 9(121) |
| 891 | 1,089 |

And Column B is clearly the larger.

9. (A) Start by factoring Column A:

$$10^{10}(10^1 - 1) \qquad\qquad 10^{10}$$

Then divide both sides of the comparison by 10^{10}. The result is:

$$10^1 - 1 \qquad\qquad 1$$

Or:

$$9 \qquad\qquad 1$$

Which proves that Column A is larger.

10. (B) Multiply both sides by $\sqrt{3}$. The result is:

$$1 \qquad\qquad 3$$

11. (D) Multiply by sides of the comparison by 2 and then by 5. The result is:

$$5(x + 2) \qquad\qquad 2(x + 4)$$

Which is:

$$5x + 10 \qquad\qquad 2x + 8$$

Now subtract 2x and 8 from both sides. The result is:

$$3x + 2 \qquad\qquad 0$$

18

Since there are no restrictions on x, the answer must be (D). If you still have trouble seeing why, subtract 2 from both sides of the comparison. The result is:

$$3x \qquad\qquad\qquad\qquad\qquad -2$$

And divide both sides by 3. The result is:

$$x \qquad\qquad\qquad\qquad\qquad -\frac{2}{3}$$

Since x can be any number whatsoever, the answer must be (D).

12. (A) First, do the operations indicated:

(60% of a) + (40% of b)	(50% of a) + (50% of b)
$.6a + .4b$	$.5a + .5b$

Then simplify the comparison by subtracting $0.5a$ and $0.4b$ from both sides. The result is:

$$0.1a \qquad\qquad\qquad\qquad\qquad 0.1b$$

Since $a > b$, Column A must be greater.

13. (D) Column A is equal to 5^{x+y}, and Column B is equal to $5^{x \cdot y}$. Try substituting numbers. If x and y are both 1 (the centered information does not require that they be different integers), then Column A is 5^2 and Column B is 5^1. Column A is larger. Now try another substitution, say $x = 10$ and $y = 10$. Column A is 5^{20}, while Column B is 5^{100}. And Column B is larger. You have proved by substitution that the relationship between the two columns is indeterminate.

14. (A) Substitute some numbers. If $k = 1$, the value of Column A is 5 and the value of Column B is $\sqrt{5}$. Since $5 > \sqrt{5}$, you eliminate choices (B) and (C). Pick another number for k, say $k = 10$. The value of Column A is 122, and the value of Column B is $\sqrt{122}$. This should prompt you to pick (A). In fact, the answer is (A). Since k is positive, the expression in Column A is always a number greater than 2, and the expression in Column B is always the square root of the number in Column A.

15. (A) Substitute some numbers. If $x = 1$, then y and z could also be 1 ($\frac{1}{1} > 0$). Since $(1)(1) > 0$, eliminate choices (B) and (C). And try another set of numbers. Assume $x = -1$. Then y and z could also be -1 ($\frac{-1}{-1} > 0$). Since $(-1)(-1) = 1$, and $1 > 0$, this suggests that Column A is always larger. In fact, y and z must always have the same sign, so yz is always positive.

Summary

1. Know the meanings of the answer choices:
   (A) means Column A is always greater.
   (B) means Column B is always greater.
   (C) means the two columns are always equal.
   (D) means the relationship is indeterminate.

2. Quantitative comparisons are arranged on a ladder of difficulty. Don't be deceived by a seemingly simple answer to a comparison that, by its position in the section, must be difficult.

3. Use the math principles stored in your "attic" to attack quantitative comparisons.

4. Special strategies for quantitative comparisons:
   A. Never guess (E).
   B. Never guess (D) to a numerical comparison.
   C. Apply the "good enough" principle and do only as much work as is necessary.
   D. Simplify across comparisons by adding or subtracting the same quantity to both sides or by multiplying or dividing both sides by the same *positive* value. (Don't multiply or divide by a quantity unless you are absolutely certain it is positive.)
   E. Substitute numbers. If a substitution shows Column A to be larger, eliminate (B) and (C); Column B to be larger, eliminate (A) and (C); the columns to be equal, eliminate (A) and (B).
   F. If a figure is not drawn to scale, distort the figure.

18

Quantitative Comparison Drills

This part includes five drills. Although the real SAT includes just 15 quantitative comparison questions, each of these untimed drills has 20 questions to give you additional practice.

As on the real SAT, the questions in each drill are arranged in ascending order of difficulty. The first third range in difficulty from easy to just-below-average. The middle third range from below average to above average. The final third range from above average to very difficult.

The first drill is a "walk-through." In the column facing the questions, you will find answers and discussion so that you can walk through the exercise as you read the explanations. Answers and explanations for the remaining four drills begin on page 447.

Walk-Through

Column A	Column B
1. 8×8	7×9

2. Length of the perimeter of an equilateral triangle with sides of 4 | Length of the perimeter of a square with sides of 4

Column A	Column B
3. $n \times \frac{1}{3}$	$n \div 3$

4. The remainder when 13 is divided by 3 | The remainder when 13 is divided by 4

Bill's bank account incorrectly deducted $100 from his savings account when it should have added $200.

5. The correct balance for the account. | $300

---

1. **(A)** The calculation is a simple one, so do the indicated operations. $8 \times 8 = 64$ and $7 \times 9 = 63$, so Column A is larger.

2. **(B)** Again, the calculation is a simple one, so it would not be an error to do the arithmetic. $3 \times 4 = 12$ and $4 \times 4 = 16$, so Column B is larger.

   There is really no need, however, to do even the simple calculation. Since the length of the sides in both figures is the same, the square, which has more sides, has the greater perimeter. Apply the "good enough" principle to the following quantitative comparison:

Column A	Column B
The perimeter of a polygon with 51 equal sides of length 14	The perimeter of a polygon with 50 equal sides of length 14

   There is no need to do the multiplication. Since the length of the sides in both figures is the same, the figure with the greater number of sides has the greater perimeter.

3. **(C)** Just do the operations. $n \times \frac{1}{3} = \frac{n}{3}$, and $n \div 3 = \frac{n}{3}$.

4. **(C)** Do the division. $13 \div 3 = 4$ with a remainder of 1, and $13 \div 4 = 3$ with a remainder of 1.

5. **(D)** Although you can calculate the size of the error, no information is given that will let you find the amount in the account. For that, you would need additional information:

Column A	Column B

   Bill's bank incorrectly deducted $100 from his savings account when it should have added $200. The balance after the error was $1,000.

The correct balance for the account	$1,200

434

$$6x + 6 = 48$$
$$5y + 5 = 40$$

6. x y

$$b > 0$$

7. b^{23} b^{123}

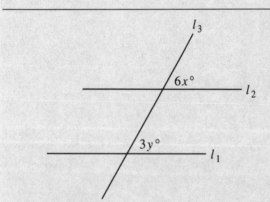

Note: Figure not drawn to scale.

8. x y

Now the answer is (C). If the account shows $900 after the error, then the correct balance is $900 plus the $100 erroneously deducted plus the $200 that should have been credited to the account: $900 + $100 + $200 = $1,200.

6. (C) The comparison here is going to turn on solutions to the center equations. So solve them:

$$6x + 6 = 48 \qquad\qquad 5y + 5 = 40$$
$$6x = 42 \qquad\qquad\quad 5y = 35$$
$$x = 7 \qquad\qquad\qquad y = 7$$

So the two quantities are equal.

7. (D) Remember that certain values exhibit unusual behavior when raised to a power. Negative numbers, when squared, give a positive result; 1 when raised to a power remains itself; and fractions when raised to a power keep getting smaller.

Although b cannot be negative, it can be a fraction, or 1, or a number greater than 1. So the relationship between the two quantities is indeterminate.

If you have trouble seeing this, you can divide both sides by b^{23} since b is a positive number. The result is:

Column A	Column B
1	b^{100}

Since b might be a fraction or 1, the relationship cannot be determined.

8. (D) Observe the warning that the figure is not drawn to scale. Don't try to "guestimate" the sizes of the angles.

The relationship is indeterminate. Since the lines are parallel, you can apply the "big angle/little angle" theorem:

$$6x + 3y = 180$$

But that's one equation with two variables, so there is no way to determine the value of either variable individually.

If Ann had $10 more, she would
have twice as much money as she
actually has. If Dan had $20
less, he would have only half
as much money as he actually has.

9. The amount of money   The amount of money
    Ann actually has   Dan actually has

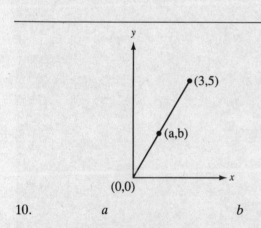

(3,5)

(a,b)

(0,0)

10. a b

$x + y - z = 16$
$x + y + z = 9$

11. $2x + 2y$ 25

9. (B) You can set up equations and solve for the
   amount each person has. As for Ann:

   $x + 10 = 2x$

   $x = 10$

   For Dan:

   $x - 20 = \frac{1}{2}x$

   $x - \frac{1}{2}x = 20$

   $\frac{1}{2}x = 20$

   $x = 40$

   You can reason to the same conclusion without the equations. Since $10 will double Ann's
   holdings, she must have only $10, but Dan has
   more than $20. On the "good enough" prin-
   ciple, the correct choice is (B).

10. (B) Given that the line on the graph includes
    the origin, point (0,0), and the point (3,5), you
    can formulate the equation that describes the
    line: $x = \frac{3y}{5}$. Which means that for every point on
    the line in the first quadrant, x is only $\frac{3}{5}$ of y. So
    Column B is greater.
        But there is no need to devise the equa-
    tion. You can reason to the same conclusion.
    For the point (3,5), you go over three units on
    the x-axis and up five units on the y-axis. And
    for every point on the line (in that quadrant)
    you will go up more than you go over.

11. (C) At first, you might think the answer to this
    question is (D), because you have three vari-
    ables but only two equations. But look at Col-
    umn A. You don't have to solve for the variables
    individually. You need the sum of two of them.
        Just add the centered equations (or, more
    precisely, add the left sides and add the right
    sides):

    $x + \quad y - z = 16$
    $\underline{(x + \quad y + z = \quad 9)}$
    $2x + 2y \quad\quad = 25$

In a certain school, 25 percent of the girls and 18 percent of the boys are enrolled in drivers' education.

12. | The number of girls enrolled in drivers' education | The number of boys enrolled in drivers' education |

For all integers,
$$(x) = x(x - 1)(x + 1)$$

13. $\dfrac{(9)}{(3)}$ 3

$x + y \neq 0$

14. $\dfrac{x^2 + 2xy + y^2}{x + y}$ $x + y + 1$

On a certain test, the average (arithmetic mean) of the scores was 85 for juniors and 89 for seniors.

15.   The average score for all juniors and seniors combined   87

---

12. **(D)** This question requires careful reading. The centered information supplies the percent of each group taking drivers' education, but the question asks for a comparison of the *number* of each taking drivers' education. You cannot assume the two groups are equal in size.

13. **(A)** Here is a defined function problem. Just do the operations indicated.

$(9) = 9(9 - 1)(9 + 1) = 9(8)(10) = 720$

$(3) = 3(3 - 1)(3 + 1) = 3(2)(4) = 24$

And $720 \div 24 = 30$.

So Column A is larger.

The arithmetic isn't that complicated, but here's a little trick to help you avoid some of the calculation. Set the entire calculation up *before* you start multiplying. You can probably cancel:

$$\frac{(9)}{(3)} = \frac{9(8)(10)}{3(2)(4)} = \frac{(3)(2)(5)}{1} = 30$$

14. **(B)** When you see $x^2 + 2xy + y^2$, you should have an irresistible urge to factor:

$$\frac{x^2 + 2xy + y^2}{x + y} = \frac{(x + y)(x + y)}{x + y} = x + y$$

Whatever the value of $x + y$, Column B is 1 larger.

Or, if you wish to pursue the solution, you can subtract x and y from both sides of the comparison. The final comparison, then, is zero in Column A and 1 in Column B.

15. **(D)** This problem is similar to question 12, above. You cannot assume that the groups are of equal size.

If you knew the groups to have the same number of students, then you could just average 85 and 89. Or if the groups were different sizes, but you knew the number of students in each group, you could set up a weighted average. But without this crucial information, the relationship cannot be determined.

16. The area of a triangle with sides of lengths 6, 8, and 10 | The area of a square with sides of length 5

Note: Figure not drawn to scale.

The larger square has sides of length 5.
The smaller square has sides of length 4.

17. Area of the shaded part of the figure | Area of the unshaded part of the figure

Two circles, each with a radius of r, overlap in such a way that the center of each lies within the interior of the other.

18. The distance between the centers of the circles | r

19. $\dfrac{1}{1 - (0.5)^3}$ | 1

---

16. (B) 6, 8, and 10 are multiples of 3, 4, and 5. So the triangle described in Column A is a right triangle. You can use the sides of lengths 6 and 8 as altitude and base:

$$\text{Area} = \frac{1}{2} \times 6 \times 8 = 24$$

The area of the square is $5 \times 5 = 25$.

17. (B) At first glance, you might think the answer to this comparison is (D), since the smaller square is not meaningfully placed with reference to the larger square. It's just floating there in the sea of shaded area. But you do have enough information to find the area of the shaded part of the figure.

The shaded part is the larger square minus the smaller square. The area of the larger square is $5 \times 5 = 25$, and the area of the smaller square is $4 \times 4 = 16$. So the shaded part has an area of $25 - 16 = 9$, which is smaller than the area of the unshaded square.

18. (B) For this one you need a diagram:

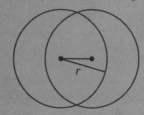

Since the center of each circle is inside the other circle, the distance between their centers must be less than the radius of the circles.

19. (A) Suppose you get to this comparison just as time is running out, so you can only make a guess at the correct answer. What should you do? Guess anything but (D). This comparison involves only numbers, so the relationship is a determinate one. Eliminate (D) and select from the other three remaining choices.

The correct choice is (A), and you don't have to do the calculation. You reason to a conclusion. The denominator of the fraction in Column A is less than 1. And when you divide a whole number (such as 1) by a fraction, the result is larger than the original whole number. So Column A is greater than 1.

How much greater? That's a question we don't have to answer to make the comparison.

---

x is a positive number.
$x(x + 1)(x + 2) = 120$

---

20.   4 $x + 1$

---

20. (A) At first, you might try to solve the centered equation:

$$x(x + 1)(x + 2) = 120$$

$$(x^2 + x)(x + 2) = 120$$

$$x^3 + 2x^2 + x^2 + 2x = 120$$

$$x^3 + 3x^2 + 2x = 120$$

This is obviously the wrong way to go about things. Instead, substitute 4 into the equation:

$$4(4 + 1)(4 + 2) = 4(5)(6) = 120$$

So $x = 4$. Column B, which is $x + 1$, is larger.

Drill 1 (Answers, page 447)

Directions for Quantitative Comparison Questions

Questions 1-15 each consist of two quantities, one in Column A and one in Column B. You are to compare the two quantities and on the answer sheet fill in oval

A if the quantity in Column A is greater;
B if the quantity in Column B is greater;
C if the two quantities are equal;
D if the relationship cannot be determined from the information given.

AN E RESPONSE WILL NOT BE SCORED.

EXAMPLES		
Column A	Column B	Answers
E1. 2×6	$2 + 6$	● Ⓑ Ⓒ Ⓓ Ⓔ
E2. $180 - x$	y	Ⓐ Ⓑ ● Ⓓ Ⓔ
E3. $p - q$	$q - p$	Ⓐ Ⓑ Ⓒ ● Ⓔ

In E2 there is a figure with angles $x°$ and $y°$.

Notes:

1. In certain questions, information concerning one or both of the quantities to be compared is centered above the two columns.
2. In a given question, a symbol that appears in both columns represents the same thing in Column A as it does in Column B.
3. Letters such as x, n, and k stand for real numbers.

	Column A	Column B
1.	$\sqrt{9 + 16}$	7

$$7n = 7$$

	Column A	Column B
2.	$\dfrac{7}{n}$	$\dfrac{n}{7}$
3.	$\left(\dfrac{1}{2}\right)^{11}$	$\left(-\dfrac{1}{2}\right)^{11}$

The digit 3 in the numeral 123,456 represents 3×10^3.

	Column A	Column B
4.	n	5
5.	The greatest prime number less than 29	23

Mary has \$5 less than Sam, and Mark has half as much money as Sam.

	Column A	Column B
6.	Amount of money that Mary has	Amount of money that Mark has

Note: Figure not drawn to scale.

	Column A	Column B
7.	x	y
8.	$\dfrac{0.125}{4}$	$\dfrac{0.25}{8}$

$$xy = 25$$

	Column A	Column B
9.	x	y

	Column A	Column B
10.	yz	xz

x and y are positive integers.
$$x < y$$

	Column A	Column B
11.	$\dfrac{x}{y}$	$\sqrt{\dfrac{x}{y}}$

439

Column A	Column B		Column A	Column B

$$x + y \neq 0$$

12. $\dfrac{5x + 5y}{x + y}$ 5

Questions 13 and 14

For all non-zero numbers $a, b, c, d,\ a \underset{d}{\overset{b}{\diamondsuit}} c = ac - bd.$

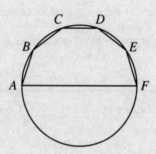

13. $4 \underset{1}{\overset{3}{\diamondsuit}} 2$ 4

14. $x \underset{y}{\overset{y}{\diamondsuit}} x$ $(x + y)(x - y)$

AF is the diameter of the circle.
$$AF = 2$$

15. Area of polygon $\dfrac{\pi}{2}$
 A,B,C,D,E,F

Two unbiased six-sided dice with faces numbered 1 through 6 are to be rolled simultaneously.

16. The probability that the sum of the digits on the top faces will total 6   The probability that the sum of the digits on the top faces will total 9

$P,Q,R,S,$ and T are consecutive integers.
$$P<Q<R<S<T$$

17. The average (arithmetic mean) of $P, Q, R, S,$ and T

18. $y\%$ of x $x\%$ of y

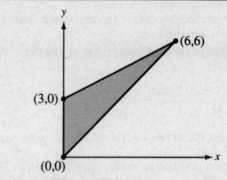

19. Area of the shaded part of the figure   8

20. $(x - y)^2$ $(y - x)^2$

Drill 2 (Answers, page 449)

	Column A	Column B
1.	$\frac{3}{4} \times N$	$3 \times N \times \frac{1}{4}$
2.	Number of minutes in a day	1,400

$$a > c$$
$$b < c$$

| 3. | c | 1 |

The sum of two positive numbers is 30.
The difference between the numbers is 10.

| 4. | The larger of the two numbers | 15 |

| 5. | $5 \times (6 \times 7) \times 8$ | $8 \times (5 \times 6) \times 7$ |

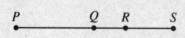

$$PR = 7$$
$$QS = 5$$

Note: Figure not drawn to scale.

| 6. | QR | 2 |

The weight of package x is more than twice the weights of packages y and z combined.

| 7. | The weight of package z | $\frac{1}{3}$ the weight of package x |

$$x + y > 3$$

| 8. | $\frac{x+y}{3}$ | $\frac{x}{3} + y$ |

$$a + 2b = 3$$
$$a - 2b = 3$$

| 9. | a | b |

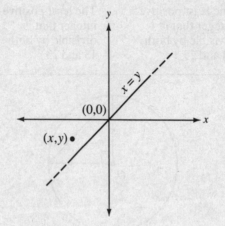

| 10. | x | y |

| 11. | Volume of a rectangular solid with sides of lengths $\frac{1}{2}, \frac{1}{3},$ and $\frac{1}{6}$ | Volume of a rectangular solid with sides of lengths $\frac{1}{6}, \frac{1}{6},$ and 1 |

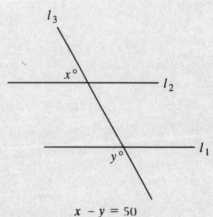

$$x - y = 50$$

| 12. | x | 60 |

One apple costs less than one pear, and one pear costs more than one peach.

| 13. | The cost of one apple | The cost of one peach |

	Column A	Column B		Column A	Column B

For all real numbers,
$$x * y = xy(x + y)$$

| 14. | $2 * 3$ | $3 * 2$ |

| 15. | Peter's age when his mother is twice Peter's age | The age of Peter's mother when Peter was born |

| 16. | The least positive integer that is divisible by both 13 and 19 | The least positive integer that is divisible by both 13 and 23 |

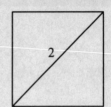

| 18. | Area of the square | 2 |

$$x^2 = y^2$$

| 19. | x | y |

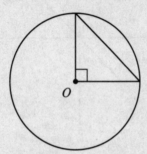

O is the center of the circle.
The area of the triangle is 4.

| 17. | Radius of the circle | 4 |

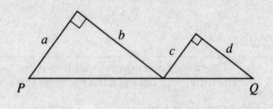

$a + c = 3$
$b + d = 4$

| 20. | Length of PQ | 5 |

Drill 3 (Answers, page 451)

	Column A	Column B
1.	$\dfrac{1}{2} \times \dfrac{2}{3} \times \dfrac{3}{4} \times \dfrac{4}{5}$	$\dfrac{1}{2} + \dfrac{2}{3} + \dfrac{3}{4} + \dfrac{4}{5}$
2.	$\dfrac{1}{3}$ dozen	4

$x \neq 0$

	Column A	Column B
3.	$\dfrac{x + x + x + x + x}{x}$	5
4.	$\sqrt{4.9}$	0.7

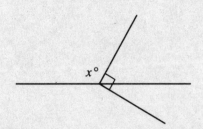

Note: Figure not drawn to scale.

	Column A	Column B
5.	x	120

$\dfrac{x}{y} = -1$

	Column A	Column B
6.	x	y
7.	The ratio 3:7	The ratio 7:15

Note: Figure not drawn to scale.

	Column A	Column B
8.	x^2	$\sqrt{x}$

a and b are positive integers.

	Column A	Column B
9.	The greatest even integer less than ab	The greatest odd integer less than ab

	Column A	Column B

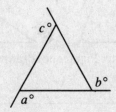

| 10. | $a + b + c$ | 180° |

Questions 11 and 12

For all real numbers such that $xy \neq 0$
$$x * y = \frac{(x + y)}{xy}$$

	Column A	Column B
11.	$2 * 4$	$\dfrac{1}{2}$
12.	$47 * 39$	$39 * 47$

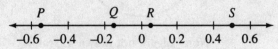

Note: Figure not drawn to scale.

	Column A	Column B
13.	Distance from P to R	Distance from Q to S
14.	The value of the units' digit in 6^{34}	The value of the units' digit in 5^{49}

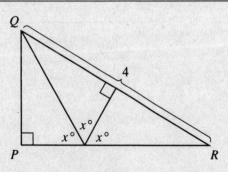

	Column A	Column B
15.	The length of side PQ	2

Column A	Column B

The cost of buying a basketball was originally to be shared by four people. If one more person shares the cost, the cost per person will be $1 less.

16. Cost of the basketball $20

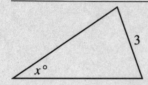 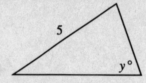

Note: Figures not drawn to scale.

17. x y

18. $\dfrac{\frac{7}{8}}{\frac{8}{7}}$ 1

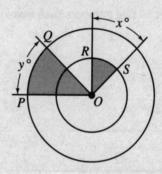

Note: Figure not drawn to scale.

O is the center of both circles.
The area of POQ is equal to the area of ROS.

19. x y

$$x^2 = y^2$$

20. xy y^2

444

Drill 4 (Answers, page 454)

	Column A	Column B
1.	The number of tens in 36	The number of hundreds in 363

$$x \neq 0$$

	Column A	Column B
2.	$1 + x^2$	1

	Column A	Column B
3.	$\frac{1}{4} + \left(\frac{1}{8} + \frac{1}{16}\right) + \frac{1}{32}$	$\left(\frac{1}{4} + \frac{1}{8}\right) + \left(\frac{1}{16} + \frac{1}{32}\right)$

	Column A	Column B
4.	$\frac{1}{10}$ hour	5 minutes

$$\frac{x}{y} = \frac{2}{3}$$

	Column A	Column B
5.	x	y

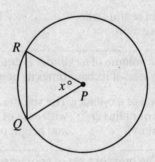

Note: Figure not drawn to scale.

	Column A	Column B
6.	x	y

p, q, and r are consecutive *even* integers, and $p < q < r$.

	Column A	Column B
7.	$p + q + 1$	$p + r - 1$

$$a > 1$$

	Column A	Column B
8.	2^a	a^2

	Column A	Column B
9.	0.2×0.6	$0.2 + 0.4 + 0.6$

	Column A	Column B
10.	Ratio of $\frac{2}{3}$ to $\frac{3}{4}$	Ratio of $\frac{1}{3}$ to $\frac{1}{2}$

P is the center of the circle.

$$RQ < PQ$$

Note: Figure not drawn to scale.

	Column A	Column B
11.	x	60

Circle O has a diameter of 5.
Circle P has a diameter of 4.

	Column A	Column B
12.	The maximum possible number of points of intersection between the circles	2

	Column A	Column B
13.	99% of 100% of 81	81

d is the distance between points $(a + b)$ and $(a + 2b)$.

	Column A	Column B
14.	b	d

	Column A	Column B
15.	The area of a circle with radius $\sqrt{\pi}$	π

	Column A	Column B
16.	The volume of a rectangular solid with sides of x, $2y$, and $3z$	The volume of a rectangular solid with sides of $3x$, y, and $2z$

Column A	Column B

$$x = \frac{1}{y + 1}$$
$$y + 1 \neq 0$$

	Column A	Column B
17.	$\dfrac{1-x}{x}$	y

At a school, out of the total of 120 seniors, 80 seniors took the senior math exam and 64 seniors took the senior spelling exam. Every senior took at least one of the exams.

	Column A	Column B
18.	Number of seniors who took both exams	16

The volume of a cylinder is equal to the area of its base times its height.

	Column A	Column B
19.	The volume of a cylinder with base of radius $2r$ and height of h	The volume of a cylinder with base of radius r and height of $2h$

The price of a set of cookware was reduced by 10 percent for a sale. The sale price is later increased by x percent, so that the new price of the cookware is equal to the original price of the cookware.

	Column A	Column B
20.	x	10

Explanatory Answers

DRILL 1

1.	B	5.	C	9.	D	13.	A	17.	B
2.	A	6.	D	10.	D	14.	C	18.	C
3.	A	7.	D	11.	B	15.	B	19.	A
4.	B	8.	C	12.	C	16.	A	20.	C

1. (B) $\sqrt{9 + 16} = \sqrt{25} = 5$. So Column B is larger.

2. (A) Solve for n in the centered equation: $n = 1$. Then substitute 1 for n in each column. Column A is $\frac{7}{1} = 7$; Column B is $\frac{1}{7}$.

3. (A) Column A is a positive number (a positive number raised to a power is positive). Column B is a negative number (a negative number raised to an odd power is negative).

4. (B) The digit 3 in 123,456 is the thousands digit. It represents 3,000, which is equal to 3×10^3. So $n = 3$.

5. (C) 23 is the greatest prime number less than 29. (24, 25, 26, 27, and 28 are not primes.)

6. (D) You have enough information to conclude that both Mary and Mark have less money than Sam. But you don't have enough information to draw a conclusion about how much each has.

    If you need to, you can assume some numbers. If Sam has $20, then Mary has $15 and Mark has $10. Eliminate (B) and (C). If Sam has $10, then Mary has $5 and Mark also has $5. Eliminate (A) as well. So the correct choice is (D).

7. (D) Heed the warning note. Since the figure is a quadrilateral, the measures of the four interior angles total 360x. So $x + y = 180$. But you cannot draw any conclusion about the size of x or the size of y.

8. (C) The math is easy enough that it would not be a mistake to do the division: $0.125 \div 4 = 0.03125$, and $0.25 \div 8 = 0.03125$.

    Division, however, is not the most elegant solution. Since 4 and 8 are positive numbers, you can multiply both sides of the comparison by both 4 and 8. Column A becomes 8(0.125) and Column B becomes 4(0.25). These operations are easier than division: $8(0.125) = 1$ and $4(0.25) = 1$.

    You can avoid the math altogether by reasoning that the numerator of the fraction in Column A is half the numerator of the fraction in Column B, and the denominator in Column A is half the denominator in Column B. So the two fractions are equivalent (like $\frac{1}{2}$ and $\frac{4}{8}$).

9. (D) x and y might be 5 and 5. But they might also be 1 and 25, or -1 and -25.

10. (D) Don't make the mistake of dividing both sides of the comparison by z. You can't be sure that z is positive.

    The relationship is indeterminate, because you don't know the signs of the numbers. If y and z are both negative, while x is positive, then yz is positive and xz is negative (and Column A is larger). If y is negative but x and z are

18

positive, then yz is negative and xz is positive (and Column B is larger). If z happens to be zero, then yz and xz are equal.

11. (B) There are several ways to attack this comparison. The most sophisticated is to reason that since $x < y$ (and both are positive integers), $\frac{x}{y}$ is a fraction. And the square root of a fraction is larger than the fraction itself. (For example, $\sqrt{\frac{1}{4}} = \frac{1}{2}$, and $\frac{1}{2} > \frac{1}{4}$).

    You can also grind out a solution by manipulating both sides of the comparison. Start by squaring both sides. Column A becomes $\frac{x^2}{y^2}$ and Column B becomes $\frac{x}{y}$. Since x and y are both positive, you can then divide both sides by x and multiply both sides by y. Column A becomes $\frac{x}{y}$ and Column B becomes 1. At this point, you should be able to see that $\frac{x}{y}$ is less than y. But if you are still not sure, multiply both sides by y again. Column A becomes simply x and Column B simply y. And the centered information states specifically that $x < y$.

    Finally, you could substitute some numbers: $x + y \neq 0$.

12. (C) Factor the numerator of the expression in Column A: $5x + 5y = 5(x + y)$. Then $\frac{x+y}{x+y} = 1$, so Column A is just 5. And, of course, if you didn't see the possibility of factoring, you could have substituted a few simple numbers. The fact that one or two substitutions show the columns to be equal is not proof that the answer is (C), but substitution allows you to eliminate (A) and (B) and strongly suggests that the answer is (C) rather than (D).

13. (A) Do the indicated operations. $(4)(2) - (3)(1) = 8 - 3 = 5$. So Column A is larger.

14. (C) Set up the operation: $(x)(x) - (y)(y) = x^2 - y^2$. By now you should recognize that this can be factored: $x^2 - y^2 = (x + y)(x - y)$. So the two columns are equal.

15. (B) The "good enough" principle is the key to this comparison. First, since the circle has a diameter of 2, it has a radius of 1 and an area of $\pi(1^2) = \pi$. Whatever the area of the polygon really is, it is less than that of the semicircle. So the area of the polygon is less than $\frac{\pi}{2}$.

16. (A) This is a difficult question, but it doesn't require any advanced mathematics. What combinations of numbers on the dice will total 6? 1 and 5, 2 and 4, 3 and 3, 4 and 2, and 5 and 1. And for 9? 3 and 6, 4 and 5, 5 and 4, and 6 and 3. So there are five ways to roll a 6 but only four ways to roll a 9. So the chances of rolling a 6 are better. How much better? For games of chance you may want to know, but you don't need to know that to make the comparison.

17. (B) You could create equations for each column. Using P to represent the smallest integer:

$$Q = P + 1; R = P + 2; S = P + 3; T = P + 4$$

The average of all the numbers is:

$$\frac{P + (P + 1) + (P + 2) + (P + 3) + (P + 4)}{5} = \frac{5P + 10}{5} = P + 2$$

The average of Q, S, and T is:

$$\frac{(P + 1) + (P + 3) + (P + 4)}{3} = \frac{3P + 8}{3} = P + \frac{8}{3}$$

So Column B is larger.

That's an awful lot of work. You would be better off just assuming numbers. Take five consecutive integers, say 0, 1, 2, 3, and 4. The average of the five integers is 2; the average of 1, 3, and 4 is $\frac{8}{3}$.

Better still is just to reason your way to the conclusion that Column B is larger. For Column A, the average of five consecutive integers is the middle value, R. For Column B, the average of Q and S alone would also be R, so the average of Q, S, and T must be greater than R.

18. (C) Remember that % just means "per 100." You can replace the percent sign with "$\frac{1}{100}$." So Column A is $(\frac{y}{100})(x) = \frac{yx}{100}$, and Column B is $(\frac{x}{100})(y) = \frac{xy}{100}$. So the columns are equal.

19. (A) The figure in question is a triangle. If you draw a line from point (6,6) across the page and parallel to the x-axis until the line intersects the y-axis, you will have created an altitude for the triangle. (Turn the page 90° in a counterclockwise direction.) The length of the altitude is 6; the length of the base of the triangle is 3; so the area of the triangle is $\frac{1}{2} \times 3 \times 6 = 9$.

20. (C) Don't make a Watson-style mistake here. Don't automatically leap to the conclusion that the answer is (D) just because the expressions are complex.

One way of making the comparison is to do the indicated operations.

$$(x - y)^2 = (x - y)(x - y) = x^2 - 2xy + y^2$$

$$(y - x)^2 = (y - x)(y - x) = y^2 - 2xy + x^2$$

The expressions are the same.

A more elegant solution is to reason that $x - y$ and $y - x$ are both the difference of x and y, one positive, the other negative. When they are squared, they both become positive.

DRILL 2

1. C	**5.** C	**9.** A	**13.** D	**17.** B
2. A	**6.** D	**10.** B	**14.** C	**18.** C
3. D	**7.** D	**11.** C	**15.** C	**19.** D
4. A	**8.** A	**12.** A	**16.** B	**20.** C

1. (C) Do the operations. Column A is $\frac{3N}{4}$ and Column B is $\frac{3N}{4}$.

2. (A) Do the indicated operation. The number of minutes in a day is $60 \times 24 = 1,440$.

3. (D) No information is given to support any conclusion about the value of c.

4. (A) You can make the comparison by setting up two equations: $x + y = 30$ and $x - y = 10$. Solve for x:

$$x + y = 30$$
$$- (x - y = 10)$$
$$\overline{2x = 40}$$

So $2x = 40$, and $x = 20$. The other number is 10.

18

5. (C) No need even to do the multiplication. Since the order of multiplication is irrelevant, the two columns are equal.

6. (D) Use the technique of distorting the figure:

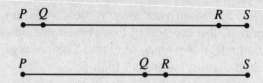

7. (D) No information is supplied about the actual weights of the packages. Assume some numbers. If $x = 100$, $y = 1$, and $z = 1$, then $\frac{1}{3}x > z$. If $x = 100$, $y = 1$, and $z = 48$, then $\frac{1}{3}x < z$. $x + y > 3$.

8. (A) You can simplify across the comparison. Multiply both sides by 3 and both sides by $(x + y)$ (you know $x + y$ is positive). Column A becomes $(x + y)^2$ and Column B becomes 3^2. Then take the square root of both sides. Column A becomes $x + y$; Column B becomes 3. Since $x + y > 3$, Column A is larger.

   You can reason to the same conclusion. Since $x + y$ is greater than 3, Column A is greater than $\frac{3}{3}$, while Column B is less than $\frac{3}{3}$. In other words, Column A is greater than 1 and Column B is a fraction.

9. (A) Solve the centered equations by adding them together. $2a = 6$, so $a = 3$. And b must be zero.

10. (B) Since the point (x,y) is above the line $x = y$, the absolute value of x is greater than the absolute value of y. But both coordinates are negative. So x is smaller than y. For example, (x,y) might be $(-3, -2)$.

11. (C) The calculations are simple, so do them. $\frac{1}{2} \times \frac{1}{3} \times \frac{1}{6} = \frac{1}{36}$. And $\frac{1}{6} \times \frac{1}{6} \times 1 = \frac{1}{36}$. The volumes are equal.

12. (A) Use the "big angle/little angle" theorem: $x + y = 180$. Now you have two equations:

$$
\begin{aligned}
y + x &= 180 \\
-(y - x &= 50) \\
\hline
2x &= 130 \\
x &= 65
\end{aligned}
$$

13. (D) The centered information establishes:

apple < pear

peach < pear

But that is not enough information to permit a comparison of the cost of apples with the cost of peaches.

14. (C) Here we have a defined function. You can do the operations:

$2 * 3 = (2 \times 3)(2 + 3) = (6)(5) = 30$

$3 * 2 = (3 \times 2)(3 + 2) = (6)(5) = 30$

Or, you might have recognized that the function is symmetrical. Since it involves only multiplication and addition, for all numbers $x * y = y * x$.

15. (C) This question is a little tricky, but you can reason to the conclusion as follows. Whatever age Peter's mother was when Peter was born, when she is twice that age, she will have lived a time equal to the time she lived before Peter's birth. But Peter, too, will have lived the same amount of time. So his age will equal the age of his mother at the time of birth.

Or, you can assume some numbers. Assume Peter's mother was 30 when Peter was born. 30 years later, when she is 60, Peter will be 30.

16. (B) Since 13 and 19 are both primes, the least positive integer divisible by both is $13 \times 19 = 247$. And 23 is prime, so the least possible integer divisible by both is $13 \times 23 = 416$. But you don't even need to do the multiplication. 13×23 is larger than 13×19.

17. (B) The two sides of the triangle that form a right angle can be treated as altitude and base. Since they are both radii of the circle, they are equal. Using r to represent their length:

$$\frac{1}{2}(r)(r) = 4$$

$$r^2 = 8$$

$$r = 2\sqrt{2}$$

18 (C) Given the length of the diagonal of a square, you can find the length of its side. The length of the side is equal to $\frac{1}{2}$ times the diagonal times $\sqrt{2}$. So the side of the square is $\frac{1}{2}(2)(\sqrt{2}) = \sqrt{2}$, and the area of the square is $\sqrt{2} \times \sqrt{2} = 2$.

19. (D) Watch out for negative numbers! x could be -1, and y could be 1. So the answer is not (C).

20. (C) The numbers 3, 4, and 5 should suggest the Pythagorean Theorem:

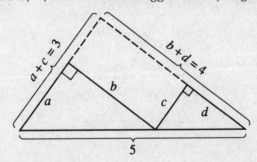

DRILL 3

1. B	**5.** D	**9.** D	**13.** D	**17.** D
2. C	**6.** D	**10.** A	**14.** A	**18.** B
3. C	**7.** B	**11.** A	**15.** C	**19.** A
4. A	**8.** B	**12.** C	**16.** C	**20.** D

1. (B) Don't even do the calculations. Column A contains fractions multiplied by fractions, so the result is smaller than any one of the fractions. Column B indicates the addition of fractions, so the final result will be larger than any one of the fractions.

2. (C) $\frac{1}{3}$ of 12 = 4.

3. (C) Column A is $\frac{5x}{x} = 5$.

18

4. (A) Since $4.9 > 4$, $\sqrt{4.9} > 2$. Column A is greater. Or, you can square both sides of the comparison. Column A becomes 4.9, while Column B becomes 0.49.

5. (D) Heed the warning and distort the figure.

6. (D) The centered equation can be rewritten as $x = -y$. But this doesn't give you enough information to make a comparison of x and y. If x is 1, $y = -1$, and vice versa.

7. (B) Since the ratio is a fraction, you can use any of the techniques for comparing fractions. You can convert $\frac{3}{7}$ and $\frac{7}{15}$ to decimal fractions. $3 \div 7 = 0.428...$ and $7 \div 15 = .4666....$ Or, you can multiply both sides of the comparison by 7 and 15. Column A becomes $3 \times 15 = 45$, and Column B becomes $7 \times 7 = 49$. So Column B is larger.

8. (B) Although x may not be exactly $\frac{1}{2}$ (the figure is not drawn to scale), it is a fraction. As we have seen before, a fraction when raised to a power is smaller than the original fraction. And for the same reason, the square root of a fraction is larger than the fraction itself.

9. (D) Since you don't know whether a and b are odd or even, you don't know whether their product is odd or even. If a and b are both odd, their product is odd, in which case the greatest even integer less than ab is 1 less than ab and the greatest odd integer less than ab is 2 less than ab. For example, if a and b are 3 and 5, their product is 15. The greatest even integer less than 15 is 14, and the greatest odd integer less than 15 is 13. On the other hand, if either a or b or both are even, then ab is even. The greatest odd integer less than ab will be only 1 less than ab, while the greatest even integer less than ab will be 2 less than ab. For example, if a and b are 4 and 5, their product is 20. The greatest odd integer less than 20 is 19, while the greatest even integer less than 20 is 18.

10. (A) Label the interior angles of the triangle:

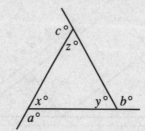

$a + x = 180$

$b + y = 180$

$c + z = 180$

$a + x + b + y + c + z = 3(180)$

Since $x + y + z = 180$,
$a + b + c = 2(180)$.

11. (A) Just perform the indicated operation. $2 * 4 = \frac{(2+4)}{8} = \frac{3}{4}$

12. (C) The numbers are so large that the operations become unmanageable. So you should look for an escape route. In this case, you should see that $x + y = y + x$ and $xy = yx$. So for all real numbers, $x * y = y * x$.

13. (D) Heed the warning and distort the drawing:

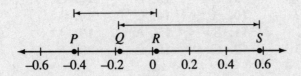

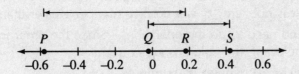

14. (A) There is no way in the world you could hope to do these calculations, so don't even try. And don't even think about guessing (D) here. Whatever the relationship is, it is not indeterminate.

    The answer is (A). $6 \times 6 = 36$, and the units digit is 6. And when you multiply 36×6, the units digit will also be 6. This never changes. The same is true for 5; the final digit of any power of 5 is 5.

15. (C) This is a composite figure, so see what further conclusions can be drawn. First, $x + x + x = 180$, so $x = 60$. Since $x = 60$, angle $PRQ = 30°$. This makes PQR a $30°–60°–90°$ triangle. Since PQ is opposite the $30°$ angle, PQ is $\frac{1}{2}$ of QR, or 2.

16. (C) Work backwards. Assume that the cost of the basketball is $20. If four people share the cost equally, the cost per person is $5. If five people share the cost equally, the cost is $4 per person. Since $20 works, the cost of the basketball must be $20.

17. (D) Heed the warning and distort the figures:

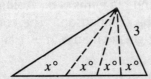 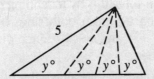

18. (B) If you answered (C), you pulled a Watson trick. This is a difficult question. You won't be able to find the solution just by glancing at two fractions and saying "1."

    Do the indicated operation: $\frac{7}{8} \div \frac{8}{7} = \frac{7}{8} \times \frac{7}{8} = \frac{49}{64}$.

19. (A) This is a difficult question. If the areas of POQ and ROS are equal, even though POQ is part of a larger circle, it must be because ROS is a larger portion of its circle than POQ is of its circle. This means that angle x is larger than angle y.

20. (D) Remember that x and y might have different signs. If x and y are both 1, then the two columns are equal. But if $x = 1$ and $y = -1$, Column A is negative while Column B is positive.

18

DRILL 4

1. C	**5.** D	**9.** B	**13.** B	**17.** C
2. A	**6.** D	**10.** A	**14.** C	**18.** A
3. C	**7.** C	**11.** B	**15.** A	**19.** A
4. A	**8.** D	**12.** C	**16.** C	**20.** A

1. (C) The number of tens in 36 is 3. The number of hundreds in 363 is 3.

2. (A) Subtract 1 from both sides of the equation. You are now comparing x^2 and zero. Since x is not zero, x^2 is a positive number greater than zero.

3. (C) There is no need to do the operations. Since the order in which you do addition is irrelevant, the columns are equal.

4. (A) One-tenth of 60 minutes is six minutes.

5. (D) Remember to watch out for negative numbers. So long as x and y are positive, say $x = 2$ and $y = 3$, y is greater than x. But if x and y are negative, say $x = -2$ and $y = -3$, then x is greater.

6. (D) Heed the warning and distort the figure:

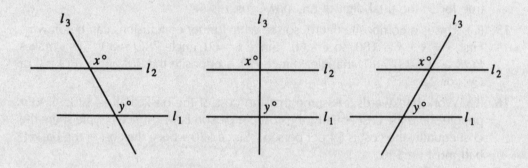

7. (C) You can solve this by redefining q and r in terms of p. A simpler solution is just to subtract p from both sides of the comparison. The comparison then becomes $q + 1$ and $r - 1$. Since r is 2 greater than q, $q + 1$ and $r - 1$ are the same number.

8. (D) The easiest way to attack the question is to test some numbers. If $a = 2$, then the two columns are equal. Eliminate choices (A) and (B). If $a = 3$, then Column A is 8 and Column B is 9. Since there is a case in which the columns are not equal, eliminate (C) as well. By the process of elimination, (D) must be correct.

9. (B) Perform the indicated operations. $0.2 \times 0.6 = 0.12$, and $0.2 + 0.4 + 0.6 = 1.2$.

10. (A) Ratios are just fractions written in a different style. So $\dfrac{\frac{2}{3}}{\frac{3}{4}} = \frac{2}{3} \times \frac{4}{3} = \frac{8}{9}$, and $\dfrac{\frac{1}{3}}{\frac{1}{2}} = \frac{1}{3} \times \frac{2}{1} = \frac{2}{3}$.

11. (B) The triangle consists of two radii and RQ. If RQ were equal to PQ, the triangle would be equilateral and have three 60° angles. But RQ is less than PQ. And within the same triangle, the longer the side, the larger the opposite angle and vice versa. Since RQ is less than PQ, x must be less than 60.

12. (C) Just draw the circles.

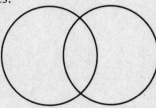

13. (B) Column A is $0.99 \times 1.00 \times 81 = 0.99 \times 81$, which is less than 81.

14. (C) To find d, subtract: $(a + 2b) - (a + b) = b$.

15. (A) The area of a circle with radius $\sqrt{\pi}$ is $\pi(\sqrt{\pi})^2 = \pi(\pi) = \pi^2$. And π^2 is larger than π.

16. (C) The volume of solid A is $(x)(2y)(3z) = 6xyz$, and the volume of solid B is $(3x)(y)(2z) = 6xyz$.

17. (C) Rewrite the centered equation.

$$x = \frac{1}{y + 1}$$

$$x(y + 1) = 1$$

$$xy + x = 1$$

$$xy = 1 - x$$

$$y = \frac{1 - x}{x}$$

18. (A) A diagram may help you see the solution:

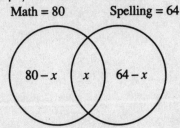

$$(80 - x) + x + (64 - x) = 120$$

$$80 + 64 - x = 120$$

$$144 - x = 120$$

$$144 - 120 = x = 24$$

19. (A) This is a difficult problem. Don't imagine that it can be solved as easily as seeing $2r$ and h in one column and $2h$ and r in the other. The correct solution is not $2hr = 2hr$.

   The volume of the cylinder described in Column A is $h \times \pi(2r)^2 = 4\pi hr^2$. The volume of the cylinder in Column B is $2h \times \pi(r)^2 = 2\pi hr^2$. So Column A is larger.

20. (A) Assume a price for the cookware, say $10. A 10-percent discount reduces the price to $9. But an increase equal to 10 percent of $9 is only $0.90. So if the final price equals the original price, the percent increase was more than 10 percent.

18

Math Warm-Up Exercises

✔ **Objectives**

To practice, under timed conditions, the techniques and strategies learned in chapters 11 through 18.

To reinforce the material learned in lessons 11 through 18 by studying practice items.

To learn to answer questions within the time limits of the actual test.

1. Section 1, 25 Questions, Time—30 minutes
2. Section 2, 25 Questions, Time—30 minutes
3. Explanatory Answers

Use a No. 2 pencil only. Be sure each mark is dark and completely fills the intended oval. Completely erase any errors or stray marks.

A R C O

Start with number 1 for each new section. If a section has fewer than 40 questions, leave the extra answer spaces blank.

SECTION 1

1	Ⓐ Ⓑ Ⓒ Ⓓ Ⓔ	11	Ⓐ Ⓑ Ⓒ Ⓓ Ⓔ	21	Ⓐ Ⓑ Ⓒ Ⓓ Ⓔ	31	Ⓐ Ⓑ Ⓒ Ⓓ Ⓔ
2	Ⓐ Ⓑ Ⓒ Ⓓ Ⓔ	12	Ⓐ Ⓑ Ⓒ Ⓓ Ⓔ	22	Ⓐ Ⓑ Ⓒ Ⓓ Ⓔ	32	Ⓐ Ⓑ Ⓒ Ⓓ Ⓔ
3	Ⓐ Ⓑ Ⓒ Ⓓ Ⓔ	13	Ⓐ Ⓑ Ⓒ Ⓓ Ⓔ	23	Ⓐ Ⓑ Ⓒ Ⓓ Ⓔ	33	Ⓐ Ⓑ Ⓒ Ⓓ Ⓔ
4	Ⓐ Ⓑ Ⓒ Ⓓ Ⓔ	14	Ⓐ Ⓑ Ⓒ Ⓓ Ⓔ	24	Ⓐ Ⓑ Ⓒ Ⓓ Ⓔ	34	Ⓐ Ⓑ Ⓒ Ⓓ Ⓔ
5	Ⓐ Ⓑ Ⓒ Ⓓ Ⓔ	15	Ⓐ Ⓑ Ⓒ Ⓓ Ⓔ	25	Ⓐ Ⓑ Ⓒ Ⓓ Ⓔ	35	Ⓐ Ⓑ Ⓒ Ⓓ Ⓔ
6	Ⓐ Ⓑ Ⓒ Ⓓ Ⓔ	16	Ⓐ Ⓑ Ⓒ Ⓓ Ⓔ	26	Ⓐ Ⓑ Ⓒ Ⓓ Ⓔ	36	Ⓐ Ⓑ Ⓒ Ⓓ Ⓔ
7	Ⓐ Ⓑ Ⓒ Ⓓ Ⓔ	17	Ⓐ Ⓑ Ⓒ Ⓓ Ⓔ	27	Ⓐ Ⓑ Ⓒ Ⓓ Ⓔ	37	Ⓐ Ⓑ Ⓒ Ⓓ Ⓔ
8	Ⓐ Ⓑ Ⓒ Ⓓ Ⓔ	18	Ⓐ Ⓑ Ⓒ Ⓓ Ⓔ	28	Ⓐ Ⓑ Ⓒ Ⓓ Ⓔ	38	Ⓐ Ⓑ Ⓒ Ⓓ Ⓔ
9	Ⓐ Ⓑ Ⓒ Ⓓ Ⓔ	19	Ⓐ Ⓑ Ⓒ Ⓓ Ⓔ	29	Ⓐ Ⓑ Ⓒ Ⓓ Ⓔ	39	Ⓐ Ⓑ Ⓒ Ⓓ Ⓔ
10	Ⓐ Ⓑ Ⓒ Ⓓ Ⓔ	20	Ⓐ Ⓑ Ⓒ Ⓓ Ⓔ	30	Ⓐ Ⓑ Ⓒ Ⓓ Ⓔ	40	Ⓐ Ⓑ Ⓒ Ⓓ Ⓔ

SECTION 2

1	Ⓐ Ⓑ Ⓒ Ⓓ Ⓔ	6	Ⓐ Ⓑ Ⓒ Ⓓ Ⓔ	11	Ⓐ Ⓑ Ⓒ Ⓓ Ⓔ
2	Ⓐ Ⓑ Ⓒ Ⓓ Ⓔ	7	Ⓐ Ⓑ Ⓒ Ⓓ Ⓔ	12	Ⓐ Ⓑ Ⓒ Ⓓ Ⓔ
3	Ⓐ Ⓑ Ⓒ Ⓓ Ⓔ	8	Ⓐ Ⓑ Ⓒ Ⓓ Ⓔ	13	Ⓐ Ⓑ Ⓒ Ⓓ Ⓔ
4	Ⓐ Ⓑ Ⓒ Ⓓ Ⓔ	9	Ⓐ Ⓑ Ⓒ Ⓓ Ⓔ	14	Ⓐ Ⓑ Ⓒ Ⓓ Ⓔ
5	Ⓐ Ⓑ Ⓒ Ⓓ Ⓔ	10	Ⓐ Ⓑ Ⓒ Ⓓ Ⓔ	15	Ⓐ Ⓑ Ⓒ Ⓓ Ⓔ

Note: ONLY the answers entered on the grid are scored.
Handwritten answers at the top of the column are NOT scored.

16. 17. 18. 19. 20.

21. 22. 23. 24. 25.

459

□ A R C O □

Start with number 1 for each new section. If a section has fewer than 40 questions, leave the extra answer spaces blank.

SECTION 1

#						#						#						#					
1	Ⓐ	Ⓑ	Ⓒ	Ⓓ	Ⓔ	11	Ⓐ	Ⓑ	Ⓒ	Ⓓ	Ⓔ	21	Ⓐ	Ⓑ	Ⓒ	Ⓓ	Ⓔ	31	Ⓐ	Ⓑ	Ⓒ	Ⓓ	Ⓔ
2	Ⓐ	Ⓑ	Ⓒ	Ⓓ	Ⓔ	12	Ⓐ	Ⓑ	Ⓒ	Ⓓ	Ⓔ	22	Ⓐ	Ⓑ	Ⓒ	Ⓓ	Ⓔ	32	Ⓐ	Ⓑ	Ⓒ	Ⓓ	Ⓔ
3	Ⓐ	Ⓑ	Ⓒ	Ⓓ	Ⓔ	13	Ⓐ	Ⓑ	Ⓒ	Ⓓ	Ⓔ	23	Ⓐ	Ⓑ	Ⓒ	Ⓓ	Ⓔ	33	Ⓐ	Ⓑ	Ⓒ	Ⓓ	Ⓔ
4	Ⓐ	Ⓑ	Ⓒ	Ⓓ	Ⓔ	14	Ⓐ	Ⓑ	Ⓒ	Ⓓ	Ⓔ	24	Ⓐ	Ⓑ	Ⓒ	Ⓓ	Ⓔ	34	Ⓐ	Ⓑ	Ⓒ	Ⓓ	Ⓔ
5	Ⓐ	Ⓑ	Ⓒ	Ⓓ	Ⓔ	15	Ⓐ	Ⓑ	Ⓒ	Ⓓ	Ⓔ	25	Ⓐ	Ⓑ	Ⓒ	Ⓓ	Ⓔ	35	Ⓐ	Ⓑ	Ⓒ	Ⓓ	Ⓔ
6	Ⓐ	Ⓑ	Ⓒ	Ⓓ	Ⓔ	16	Ⓐ	Ⓑ	Ⓒ	Ⓓ	Ⓔ	26	Ⓐ	Ⓑ	Ⓒ	Ⓓ	Ⓔ	36	Ⓐ	Ⓑ	Ⓒ	Ⓓ	Ⓔ
7	Ⓐ	Ⓑ	Ⓒ	Ⓓ	Ⓔ	17	Ⓐ	Ⓑ	Ⓒ	Ⓓ	Ⓔ	27	Ⓐ	Ⓑ	Ⓒ	Ⓓ	Ⓔ	37	Ⓐ	Ⓑ	Ⓒ	Ⓓ	Ⓔ
8	Ⓐ	Ⓑ	Ⓒ	Ⓓ	Ⓔ	18	Ⓐ	Ⓑ	Ⓒ	Ⓓ	Ⓔ	28	Ⓐ	Ⓑ	Ⓒ	Ⓓ	Ⓔ	38	Ⓐ	Ⓑ	Ⓒ	Ⓓ	Ⓔ
9	Ⓐ	Ⓑ	Ⓒ	Ⓓ	Ⓔ	19	Ⓐ	Ⓑ	Ⓒ	Ⓓ	Ⓔ	29	Ⓐ	Ⓑ	Ⓒ	Ⓓ	Ⓔ	39	Ⓐ	Ⓑ	Ⓒ	Ⓓ	Ⓔ
10	Ⓐ	Ⓑ	Ⓒ	Ⓓ	Ⓔ	20	Ⓐ	Ⓑ	Ⓒ	Ⓓ	Ⓔ	30	Ⓐ	Ⓑ	Ⓒ	Ⓓ	Ⓔ	40	Ⓐ	Ⓑ	Ⓒ	Ⓓ	Ⓔ

SECTION 2

#						#						#					
1	Ⓐ	Ⓑ	Ⓒ	Ⓓ	Ⓔ	6	Ⓐ	Ⓑ	Ⓒ	Ⓓ	Ⓔ	11	Ⓐ	Ⓑ	Ⓒ	Ⓓ	Ⓔ
2	Ⓐ	Ⓑ	Ⓒ	Ⓓ	Ⓔ	7	Ⓐ	Ⓑ	Ⓒ	Ⓓ	Ⓔ	12	Ⓐ	Ⓑ	Ⓒ	Ⓓ	Ⓔ
3	Ⓐ	Ⓑ	Ⓒ	Ⓓ	Ⓔ	8	Ⓐ	Ⓑ	Ⓒ	Ⓓ	Ⓔ	13	Ⓐ	Ⓑ	Ⓒ	Ⓓ	Ⓔ
4	Ⓐ	Ⓑ	Ⓒ	Ⓓ	Ⓔ	9	Ⓐ	Ⓑ	Ⓒ	Ⓓ	Ⓔ	14	Ⓐ	Ⓑ	Ⓒ	Ⓓ	Ⓔ
5	Ⓐ	Ⓑ	Ⓒ	Ⓓ	Ⓔ	10	Ⓐ	Ⓑ	Ⓒ	Ⓓ	Ⓔ	15	Ⓐ	Ⓑ	Ⓒ	Ⓓ	Ⓔ

Note: ONLY the answers entered on the grid are scored.
Handwritten answers at the top of the column are NOT scored.

16. 17. 18. 19. 20.

21. 22. 23. 24. 25.

Now that you have studied each of the two types of math questions and done drills on each, it is time to do some practice under the same time constraints you will have to work within on the SAT.

In this chapter, you will find two math sections, each with a 30-minute time limit. It is recommended that you work one of them and review it and do the other at a later time.

Set aside a half hour during which you won't be interrupted. Use a watch or a clock to time yourself. Enter your answers on the answer sheet provided. Stop working when time is up.

After you have done as much as you can in 30 minutes, go back and review your work. Finish any questions your did not have time to finish. Then study the explanations that begin on page 469. If anything is not clear to you, return to the appropriate chapter and review the material.

Reference:

Circle:

$C = 2\pi r$
$A = \pi r^2$

Rectangle:

$A = lw$

Rectangular Solid:

$V = lwh$

Cylinder:

$V = \pi r^2 h$

Triangle:

$A = \frac{1}{2}bh$

$a^2 + b^2 = c^2$

- The measure in degrees of a straight angle is 180.
- The number of degrees of arc in a circle is 360.
- The sum of the measures of the angles of a triangle is 180.

Notes: The figures accompanying the problems are drawn as accurately as possible unless otherwise stated in specific problems. Again, unless otherwise stated, all figures lie in the same plane. All numbers used in these problems are real numbers. Calculators are permitted for this test.

1. If $y + x^3 = 7 + x^3$, then $y =$
   (A) 7^3 (B) 7 (C) $3\sqrt{7}$ (D) -3^7 (E) -7

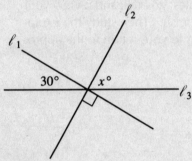

2. In the figure above, $x =$
   (A) 180 (B) 120 (C) 90 (D) 60 (E) 30

3. If $x = -2$ and $y = -1$, then $x^3 - y =$
   (A) -9 (B) -8 (C) -7 (D) 0 (E) 8

4. If $n > 1$ and the remainder when 12 and 17 are divided by n is 2, then $n =$
   (A) 3 (B) 4 (C) 5 (D) 6 (E) 7

5. If the product of the digits of a two-digit number is odd, then the sum of those two digits must be
   (A) even
   (B) odd
   (C) greater than or equal to 3
   (D) less than or equal to 17
   (E) equal to 18

6. $4^2 \times 4^3 =$
   (A) $\frac{1}{4}$ (B) 4 (C) 4^5 (D) 4^6 (E) 8^6

7. If the perimeter of a triangle PQR is 30 units and if side PQ is five units longer than side QR, then what is the length of side PR?
   (A) 5 (B) 10 (C) 15 (D) 20
   (E) Cannot be determined from the information given.

8. In the figure above, $x =$
   (A) 70 (B) 55 (C) 40 (D) 30 (E) 20

9. If $\sqrt{n}$ is a whole number, then which of the following is NOT necessarily a whole number?
   (A) $\frac{n}{2}$ (B) n (C) $\sqrt{4n}$ (D) $4\sqrt{n}$ (E) n^3

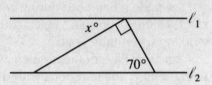

Names	Number of students
A through F	65
G through K	43
L through O	69
P through T	x
U through Z	y

10. The table above shows the number of students in a senior class with the last names beginning with the letters indicated. If a total of 300 students are in the class, what is the maximum number of students whose names could begin with the letters *P* through *T*?
    (A) 60 (B) 123 (C) 177 (D) 223 (E) 300

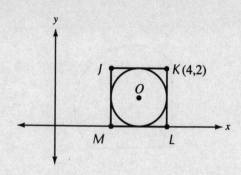

11. In the figure above, point O is the center of the circle. If $JKLM$ is a square, what are the coordinates of point O?

(A) $(2,1)$ (B) $(2,2)$ (C) $(3,0)$
(D) $(3,1)$ (E) $(3,2)$

12. Which of the following fractions is the least?

(A) $\frac{12}{13}$ (B) $\frac{4}{5}$ (C) $\frac{7}{8}$ (D) $\frac{19}{20}$ (E) $\frac{14}{15}$

13. If $30 \times 2{,}000 = 6 \times 10^x$, then $x =$

(A) 2   (B) 3   (C) 4   (D) 5   (E) 6

14. If $n = \frac{x}{15} + \frac{x}{15} + \frac{x}{15} + \frac{x}{15} + \frac{x}{15}$, then what is the least positive integer x for which n is an integer?

(A) 3   (B) 5   (C) 12   (D) 15   (E) 20

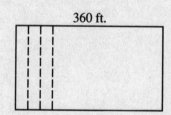

360 ft.

15. The figure above shows a rectangular parcel of land divided into lots of equal size, as shown by the dotted lines. If the area of three of the lots is equal to one-fourth of the total area in the parcel, then how wide, expressed in feet, is each lot?

(A) 30   (B) 40   (C) 60   (D) 90   (E) 120

16. If the product of five consecutive integers is zero, what is the greatest possible sum of these integers?

(A) -2 (B) -1 (C) 0   (D) 4   (E) 10

17. On a certain production line, the ratio of parts produced that are inspected to those that are not inspected is 1:3. What fraction of the parts that are produced are inspected?

(A) $\frac{2}{3}$ (B) $\frac{1}{2}$ (C) $\frac{1}{3}$ (D) $\frac{1}{4}$ (E) $\frac{1}{5}$

18. If 50 equally priced tickets cost a total of d dollars, then, in terms of d, ten of these tickets cost how much?

(A) $5d$ (B) $10d$ (C) $\frac{5}{d}$ (D) $\frac{10}{d}$ (E) $\frac{d}{5}$

19. Bob and Mary together have \$8.00. If the amount that Mary has is $\frac{1}{3}$ of the amount that Bob has, how much money does Mary have?

(A) \$2.00   (B) \$3.60   (C) \$4.80
(D) \$5.60   (E) \$6.00

20. If $\frac{x}{y} - 1 = 0$, then $\frac{x}{y} - \frac{y}{x} =$

(A) -2 (B) -1 (C) 0   (D) 2
(E) Cannot be determined from the information given.

21. If n is an integer, which of the following represents the product of $2n + 1$ and the next greater integer?

(A) $4n + 2$
(B) $4n^2 + 2$
(C) $4n^2 + 2n + 1$
(D) $4n^2 + 2n + 2$
(E) $4n^2 + 6n + 2$

22. If $\frac{x}{y} = \frac{4}{5}$ and $\frac{z}{y} = \frac{2}{5}$, then $\frac{x}{z} =$

(A) $\frac{2}{5}$ (B) $\frac{1}{2}$ (C) $\frac{8}{25}$ (D) 2   (E) $\frac{5}{2}$

23. If $4 < x < 8$ and $0 < y < \frac{3}{2}$, which of the following gives all possible values of xy?

(A) $0 < xy < 6$
(B) $0 < xy < 12$
(C) $\frac{3}{2} < xy < 4$
(D) $\frac{3}{2} < xy < 8$
(E) $4 < xy < 8$

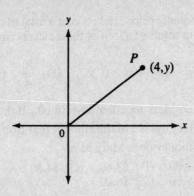

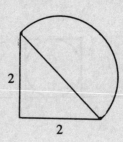

24. In the figure above, if the *x* coordinate of point *P* is 4 and the length of *OP* is 5, what is the *y* coordinate of point *P*?

(A) 4   (B) $3\sqrt{3}$ (C) 3   (D) $\sqrt{3}$
(E) Cannot be determined from the information given.

25. If the figure above is composed of a semicircle and a right triangle, what is the area of the composite figure?

(A) $\pi + \sqrt{2}$ (B) $\pi + 2$ (C) $2\pi + 1$
(D) $\sqrt{2}\pi + 1$ (E) $\sqrt{2}\pi + \sqrt{2}$

For each question in this section, choose the best answer and blacken the corresponding space on the answer sheet.

Reference:

Circle:

$C = 2\pi r$
$A = \pi r^2$

Rectangle:

$A = lw$

Rectangular Solid:

$V = lwh$

Cylinder:

$V = \pi r^2 h$

Triangle:

$A = \frac{1}{2}bh$

$a^2 + b^2 = c^2$

- The measure in degrees of a straight angle is 180.
- The number of degrees of arc in a circle is 360.
- The sum of the measures of the angles of a triangle is 180.

Notes: The figures accompanying the problems are drawn as accurately as possible unless otherwise stated in specific problems. Again, unless otherwise stated, all figures lie in the same plane. All numbers used in these problems are real numbers. Calculators are permitted for this test.

Directions for Quantitative Comparison Questions

Questions 1–15 each consist of two quantities, one in Column A and one in Column B. You are to compare the two quantities and on the answer sheet fill in oval

A if the quantity in Column A is greater;
B if the quantity in Column B is greater;
C if the two quantities are equal;
D if the relationship cannot be determined from the information given.

AN E RESPONSE WILL NOT BE SCORED.

	EXAMPLES		
	Column A	Column B	Answers
E1.	2×6	$2 + 6$	● Ⓑ Ⓒ Ⓓ Ⓔ
E2.	$180 - x$	y	Ⓐ Ⓑ ● Ⓓ Ⓔ
E3.	$p - q$	$q - p$	Ⓐ Ⓑ Ⓒ ● Ⓔ

(For E2: $x°$ / $y°$ diagram shown)

Notes:

1. In certain questions, information concerning one or both of the quantities to be compared is centered above the two columns.
2. In a given question, a symbol that appears in both columns represents the same thing in Column A as it does in Column B.
3. Letters such as *x*, *n*, and *k* stand for real numbers.

	Column A	Column B		Column A	Column B
1.	$\left(\dfrac{1}{3}\right)^2$	$\left(\dfrac{1}{4}\right)^2$	3.	$\dfrac{2}{3} + \dfrac{3}{13} + \dfrac{1}{4}$	$\dfrac{3}{13} + \dfrac{1}{4} + \dfrac{1}{2}$
2.	Number of interior angles of a triangle	Number of interior angles of a quadrilateral	4.	Average (arithmetic mean) of $-11, 8, -8,$ and 11	Average (arithmetic mean) of $1, 2, -1, -2,$ and 0

465

Column A	Column B		Column A	Column B

$$x + 3 = y$$

$$x = \frac{1}{3}$$

$$y = \frac{1}{4}$$

10. x $y - 4$

5. $\dfrac{x}{y}$ $\dfrac{y}{x}$

$$\frac{\sqrt{x}}{4} = \frac{1}{2}$$

11. x 2

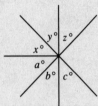

Note: Figure not drawn to scale.

x, y, and z are consecutive integers.
$$x < y < z$$
$$xyz = 0$$

12. y 0

6. $x + y + z$ $a + b + c$

13. The total surface area of 1
a cube having an edge
of $\dfrac{1}{3}$.

Al is twice as old as Charles.
Marsha is ten years older than Charles.

7.   Marsha's age   Al's age

Point P has coordinates $(0, -2)$.
Point Q has coordinates $(-2, 2)$.

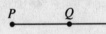

Note: Figure not drawn to scale.

$$PQ = QR = RT$$
S is the midpoint of RT.

14. The distance from P The distance from Q
to the origin.   to the origin.

8. $\dfrac{ST}{PT}$ $\dfrac{1}{5}$

Note: Figure not drawn to scale.

$$r > s$$

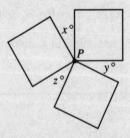

Three squares have a common vertex P.

15. x y

9. $x + y + z$ 90

Part 2: Student-Produced Response Questions

Directions:

Solve each of these problems. Write the answer in the corresponding grid on the answer sheet and fill in the ovals beneath each answer you write. Here are some examples.

Answer: 3/4 (= .75; show answer either way)

Answer: 325

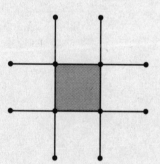

Note: A mixed number such as 3½ must be gridded as 7/2 or as 3.5. If gridded as "31/2," it will be read as "thirty-one halves."

Note: Either position is correct.

16. In the figure above, equally spaced points are joined by line segments that intersect each other at 90 degrees. If the total length of all line segments in the figure is 24, what is the area of the shaded part?

17. Jane and Hector have the same birthday. When Hector was 36, Jane was 30. How many years old was Jane when Hector was twice her age?

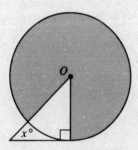

18. In the figure above, the circle with center *O* has a radius of 4. If the area of the shaded region is 14 π, what is the value of *x*?

Day	Mon.	Tues.	Wed.	Thurs.	Fri.
Sales	$40	$60	$80	$20	$50

19. What is the average (arithmetic mean) daily sales in dollars for the week shown above?

467

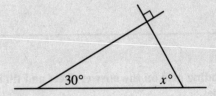

20. In the figure above, $x =$

21. If the sum of two consecutive integers is 29, what is the least of these integers?

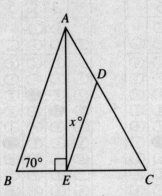

22. In *ABC* above, if $AB \parallel ED$, then $x =$

23. If $x - y = 1.5$ and $2x = 14$, what is the value of xy?

24. If a jar of 300 black and white marbles contains 156 white marbles, what percent of the marbles are black?

25. Mr. Wahl spends $\frac{1}{3}$ of his workday in meetings, $\frac{1}{6}$ on the phone, and $\frac{1}{8}$ answering questions. What fraction of his workday can be devoted to other things?

Explanatory Answers

SECTION 1

1. B	**10.** B	**19.** A
2. D	**11.** D	**20.** C
3. C	**12.** B	**21.** E
4. C	**13.** C	**22.** D
5. A	**14.** A	**23.** B
6. C	**15.** A	**24.** C
7. E	**16.** E	**25.** B
8. E	**17.** D	
9. A	**18.** E	

1. **(B)** This question asks that you solve for y. It is the first question in the section, so it can't be very hard. Once you eliminate the x^3 terms from both sides of the equation, you have $y = 7$.

2. **(D)** You can use the principles of geometry to deduce the value of x. The angle vertically opposite the right angle is also a 90° angle. So:

$$30 + 90 + x = 180$$
$$120 + x = 180$$
$$x = 60$$

You can also "guestimate" the size of x. The angle seems to be about 60°.

3. **(C)** This question asks you to evaluate an expression. Just substitute the given values into the expression:

$$(-2)^3 - (-1) =$$
$$-8 + 1 = -7$$

4. **(C)** One of the five suspects is guilty. Just test answer choices. Divide 12 and 17 by each until you find the one that leaves a remainder of 2 in both cases. $12 \div 5 = 2$ with a remainder of 2, and $17 \div 5 = 3$ with a remainder of 2.

5. **(A)** This question tests properties of numbers. You can get the correct answer by reasoning as follows: If the product of the two digits is odd, then both of the digits themselves must be odd. (If one or more of the digits of the number are even, then the product of the digits is even.) Since both digits are odd, the sum of the digits must be even.

6. **(C)** This question tests your knowledge of the rules of exponents. And no tricks will get you around the need for that information. You have to know that when you multiply powers of like bases, you add exponents:

$$4^2 \times 4^3 = 4^{2+3} = 4^5$$

19

7. (E) Start by sketching a figure:

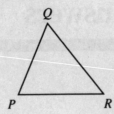

You can prove that the answer is (E) algebraically. The perimeter of the triangle is the sum of the lengths of the three sides:

$PQ + QR + PR = 30$

and

$PQ = QR + 5$

That's three variables with only two equations, so it's not possible to find the length of any one side.

You can also reach this conclusion by playing around with different values for the sides. PQ might be 10, in which case QR is 5 and PR is 15. Or PQ might be 15, in which case QR is 10 and PR is 5.

8. (E) Since $\ell 1$ is parallel to $\ell 2$, the "big angle/little angle" theorem establishes that x is equal to the third and unlabeled angle of the triangle. Find the size of that angle and you have the size of x. Let the unlabeled angle be $y°$:

$y + 90 + 70 = 180$

$y + 160 = 180$

$y = 20$

So $x = 20$ as well.

9. (A) This question tests properties of numbers. You might reason as follows: If $\sqrt{n}$ is a whole number, then

  (A) $\frac{n}{2}$ might or might not be a whole number. The square root of a whole number might be odd, for example, $\sqrt{9}$, in which case $\frac{n}{2}$ is not a whole number;

  (B) n must be a whole number, for n is the product of $\sqrt{n} \times \sqrt{n}$, and a whole number times a whole number generates a whole number;

  (C) $\sqrt{4n}$ must be a whole number, for $\sqrt{4n} = \sqrt{4} \times \sqrt{n} = 2\sqrt{n}$;

  (D) $4\sqrt{n}$ must be a whole number, as it's just a whole number, 4, times another whole number; and

  (E) n^3 must be a whole number, since n is a whole number (see [B] above).

10. (B) First, find the total number of students whose last names begin with the letters A through O:

$65 + 43 + 69 = 177$

Assume for the purpose of argument that $y = 0$, that is, that no students have names beginning with letters U through Z. The maximum number of students whose names could begin with letters P through T is:

$$300 - 177 = 123$$

11. **(D)** This question tests your knowledge of coordinate geometry. To deduce the coordinates of point O, you need to know the length of the sides of the square. Given that K has coordinates of $(4,2)$, L has coordinates of $(4,0)$. (Since $JKLM$ is a square, KL is parallel to the y-axis.) The length of KL is 2. (The difference of the y-coordinates of K and L is 2.)

    Since the circle is inscribed in a square with side 2, the radius of the circle is 1. Point O, therefore, is located 1 unit above the x-axis (so its y coordinate is 1) and 1 unit closer to the origin on the x-axis than K and L. (So its x coordinate is 3.) Therefore, the coordinates of point O are $(3,1)$.

12. **(B)** You know that it would take too long to convert each of these fractions to a decimal for purposes of comparing them. So you look for a benchmark. There is a pattern to the choices. The numerator of each is one less than its denominator. At this point, you should conclude that the correct choice must be either (B) or (D)—those are the choices with the smallest and the largest numbers.

    The answer is (B), and you can reach that conclusion in several ways. One, you might convert both (B) and (D) to decimal fractions. (B) is $\frac{4}{5}$ and $\frac{4}{5} = 0.8$; (D) is $\frac{19}{20}$ and $\frac{19}{20} = 0.95$. Or, you might conclude that $\frac{4}{5} = \frac{16}{20}$, so (B) is smaller than (D).

13. **(C)** Perform the indicated operation. $30 \times 2{,}000 = 60{,}000$. And $60{,}000 = 6 \times 10^4$. (One power of ten for each of the zeros.)

14. **(A)** There is no reason to try to devise a mathematical approach to this question. Just test the answer choices:

    (A) $\frac{3}{15} + \frac{3}{15} + \frac{3}{15} + \frac{3}{15} + \frac{3}{15} = \frac{1}{5} + \frac{1}{5} + \frac{1}{5} + \frac{1}{5} + \frac{1}{5} = \frac{5}{5} = 1.$

    At this point, stop. Since the choices are arranged in order, 3 must be the *smallest* integer that works. (Yes, 15 will also work, but it is not the smallest integer that will work.)

15. **(A)** The question stem doesn't give you the depth of each lot, but you don't need it. It's the same for all of the lots.

    Since the area of three of the lots is $\frac{1}{4}$ the area of the entire rectangle, three lots together must have a width of 90. And since they are all equal, each has a width of 30.

    It is also possible to measure the widths of the lots. The problem is that the widths are fairly small in comparison to the entire length of 360 of the large rectangle. You can, however, play around with the measurements; but in doing so, you will wind up following the same line of thought outlined above.

16. **(E)** This question asks about properties of numbers. If the product of five consecutive integers is zero, then one of the integers must be zero. The greatest possible sum for five consecutive integers, one of which is zero, occurs when the least of the integers is zero: 0, 1, 2, 3, and 4. $0 + 1 + 2 + 3 + 4 = 10$.

19

472   MATH WARM-UP EXERCISES

17. (D) Given the position of this question, it must be of above-average difficulty. The correct answer cannot be as easy as putting 1 over 3, so don't make that mistake.

   The answer is (D). The total number of ratio parts is $3 + 1 = 4$, of which one part is "inspected parts." So the fraction of the parts produced that are inspected is $\frac{1}{4}$.

18. (E) You can solve the problem in one of three ways. One, you can reason that ten tickets is $\frac{1}{5}$ of 50 tickets, so the cost should be $\frac{1}{5}$ of the cost of 50 tickets. And $\frac{1}{5}$ of d is $\frac{d}{5}$. If you are a little squeamish about working things out in your head, you can create a formula by using a direct proportion. The more tickets, the greater the cost:

$$\frac{\text{Tickets } X}{\text{Tickets } Y} = \frac{\text{Cost } X}{\text{Cost } Y}$$

$$\frac{50}{10} = \frac{d}{x}$$

Cross-multiply:

$$50x = 10d$$

$$x = \frac{10d}{50} = \frac{d}{5}$$

   Finally, you can assume some numbers. Assume tickets cost $1 each. The cost of 50 tickets is $50 ($d=50$). The cost of ten tickets is $10. So when $d = 50$, the correct formula will yield ten. Only (E) works.

19. (A) You might attack this problem with simultaneous equations. Let B stand for the amount Bob has and M for the amount Mary has. Then:

$$B + M = 8$$

$$M = \frac{1}{3} B$$

Substitute $\frac{1}{3} B$ for M into the first equation:

$$B + \frac{1}{3} B = 8$$

$$\frac{4}{3} B = 8$$

$$B = 8\left(\frac{3}{4}\right) = 6$$

So Mary has $2.

   Or, you can simply test answer choices, starting with (C). Assume that Mary has $4.80. Then Bob has three times that much, which is much more than $8 (the sum they have together). So (C) is wrong and too large. Try the next smaller number, (B). Again, $3.60 × 3 is more than $8. So the correct choice must be $2.00. And $2.00 × 3 = $6.00, and $6.00 + $2.00 = $8.00.

20. (C) Use the equation to find what x is in terms of y:

$$\frac{x}{y} - 1 = 0$$

$$\frac{x}{y} = 1$$

$$x = y$$

Since $x = y$, $\frac{x}{y}$ and $\frac{y}{x}$ are equal, and $\frac{x}{y}$ minus $\frac{y}{x}$ is zero.

Or, you can assume numbers. Let $x = 1$. Then, to ensure that $\frac{x}{y} - 1 = 0$, y must also be equal to 1. On that assumption, $\frac{x}{y} - \frac{y}{x} = \frac{1}{1} - \frac{1}{1} = 0$.

21. (E) You can attack by using the expression $2n + 1$. The next integer larger than $2n + 1$ is one larger, or $2n + 2$. And their product is:

$$(2n + 1)(2n + 2) = 4n^2 + 6n + 2$$

Or, you can assume some numbers. Let n be 2. Then the number $2n + 1$ is 5. The next larger integer is 6, and the product of the two integers is $5 \times 6 = 30$. So, on the assumption that $n = 2$, the correct answer choice is 30.

(A) $4(2) + 2 = 10$ (Wrong.)

(B) $4(2^2) + 2 = 4(4) + 2 = 18$ (Wrong.)

(C) $4(2^2) + 2(2) + 1 = 16 + 4 + 1 = 21$ (Wrong.)

(D) $4(2^2) + 2(2) + 2 = 22$ (Wrong.)

(E) $4(2^2) + 6(2) + 2 = 16 + 12 + 2 = 30$ (Correct.)

22. (D) There are at least three ways to attack this problem. One, you can see that the first equation has x and y in it and that the second equation has z and y in it. If you rewrite the first equation so that y is defined in terms of x, and rewrite the second equation so that y is defined in terms of z, then you can create an equation between x and z:

$$\frac{x}{y} = \frac{4}{5} \qquad x = \frac{4y}{5} \qquad 5x = 4y \qquad y = \frac{5x}{4}$$

$$\frac{z}{y} = \frac{2}{5} \qquad z = \frac{2y}{5} \qquad 5z = 2y \qquad y = \frac{5z}{2}$$

So $\frac{5x}{4} = \frac{5z}{2}$:

$$\frac{5x}{4} = \frac{5z}{2}$$

$$(4)\frac{5x}{4} = \frac{5z}{2}(4)$$

$$5x = 5z(2)$$

$$x = 2z$$

$$\frac{x}{z} = 2$$

19

This solution is lengthy and tedious, but it is effective.

There is a simpler solution, and you should be looking for it. $\frac{z}{y}$ is exactly half of $\frac{x}{y}$ ($\frac{2}{5}$ is half of $\frac{4}{5}$), so x must be twice z, and $\frac{x}{z}$ must be 2.

Finally, it is also possible to substitute numbers. Assume that $y = 5$. On that assumption, $x = 4$ and $z = 2$, so $\frac{x}{z} = \frac{4}{2} = 2$.

23. (B) Work through the problem step by step. First, if x could be 4 and y could be zero, then xy would be zero. y cannot be zero, but zero marks the lower limit of xy. This eliminates choices (C), (D), and (E).

Next, if x and y could be 8 and $\frac{3}{2}$, their product would be $8 \times \frac{3}{2} = 12$. So 12 marks the upper limit of their product. And the correct choice is (B).

24. (C) First, since this is a difficult question (as indicated by its position in the section), the answer is not likely to be (E). Having eliminated (E), start to work on the assumption that there must be a way to find the x coordinates of P.

Draw a line from point P down the page parallel to the y-axis.

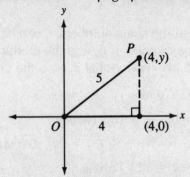

This creates a right triangle, the hypotenuse of which is OP. And the newly drawn line intersects the x-axis at 4. This means that the side of the triangle that lies on the x-axis has a length of 4.

So you have a right triangle with sides of 5 and 4; the remaining side is 3. This means that the y-coordinate of point P is 3.

You can also answer the question by measuring. The length of OP is given as 5. Mark that length on a sheet of paper. Then compare that distance with the vertical distance of point P above the x-axis. It should look to you like P is a bit more than $\frac{1}{2}$ of the distance, say $2\frac{1}{2}$ or 3. That must be (C).

25. (B) This is a composite figure: a 45°−45°−90° triangle plus a semicircle. The area of the composite figure is the sum of the area of the triangle and the semicircle.

First, calculate the area of the triangle. Since this is a right triangle, you can use the two sides forming the right angle as altitude and base:

Area of triangle $= \frac{1}{2} \times 2 \times 2 = \frac{1}{2} \times 4 = 2$

The diameter of the circle is the hypotenuse of that triangle, and the hypotenuse of a 45°−45°−90° triangle is equal to the length of the side times $\sqrt{2}$. So the hypotenuse is equal to $2 \times \sqrt{2} = 2\sqrt{2}$. The diameter of the semicircle is $2\sqrt{2}$, so the radius is $\sqrt{2}$. The area of an entire circle with that radius is $\pi(\sqrt{2})^2 = 2\pi$. But the figure is a semicircle with an area only half that of a full circle: $2\pi \div 2 = \pi$.

So the area of the composite figure is $\pi + 2$.

There are also ways of "meastimating" the answer. You can use the value 2 to "meastimate" the length of the radius of the semicircle. And here's an even neater trick. The semicircle must have an area slightly larger than that of the triangle:

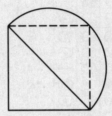

Which means that the composite figure has an area somewhat more than 4, say around 5. That has to be choice (B).

SECTION 2

1. A	10. A
2. B	11. A
3. A	12. D
4. C	13. B
5. A	14. B
6. D	15. B
7. D	
8. B	
9. C	

16. **4**

17. **6**

18. **45**

19. **50**

20. **60**

21. **14**

22. **20**

23. **38.5**

24. [grid-in answer: 4 8]

25. [grid-in answer: 3 / 8]

1. (A) Perform the indicated operations.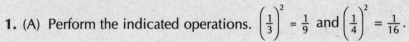

2. (B) A triangle has three sides and three interior angles; a quadrilateral has four sides and four interior angles.

3. (A) Simplify across the comparison. Subtract $\frac{3}{13}$ and $\frac{1}{4}$ from both sides of the comparison. The result is $\frac{2}{3}$ compared with $\frac{1}{2}$, and $\frac{2}{3}$ is obviously larger.

4. (C) You can solve the problem by "brute force" just by calculating the average on each side. The average of the numbers in Column A is zero, and the average of the numbers in Column B is zero.

Or, you might see that the numbers in Column A total zero, so their average must be zero. Also, the numbers in Column B total zero, so their average must be zero.

5. (A) One way to solve the comparison is to substitute the values given for x and y. Column A turns out to be $\frac{\frac{1}{3}}{\frac{1}{4}}=\frac{4}{3}$ and Column B is $\frac{\frac{1}{4}}{\frac{1}{3}}=\frac{3}{4}$. Or, you might reason that since x is larger than y, Column A has the larger numerator and the smaller denominator, while Column B has the smaller numerator and the larger denominator, so the fraction in Column A must be larger.

6. (D) The diagram is not drawn to scale, so you cannot measure. Instead, use our replacement technique: $b = z$ and $c = y$, but watch what happens with x and a:

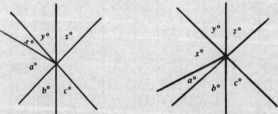

7. (D) You can prove that the relationship is indeterminate by setting up equations. Let A be Al's age, M Marsha's age, and C Charles' age:

$A = 2C$ and $M = C + 10$

There are two equations and three variables, so you won't be able to solve for any one variable.

You can arrive at the same conclusion more quickly by assuming some numbers. Assume that Charles is one year old. Then Al would be two and Marsha would be 12, so Column A would be greater. (Eliminate choices [B] and [D].) Next, assume that Charles is ten years old. Then Al would be 20 and Marsha would be 20. So you can eliminate (A). The correct choice must be (D).

8. (B) PQ, QR, and RT are each $\frac{1}{3}$ of PT. Since S is the midpoint of RT, ST is $\frac{1}{2}$ of $\frac{1}{3}$ of the entire segment, or $\frac{1}{6}$ of the entire segment. So $\frac{ST}{PT}=\frac{1}{6}$.

You could also attack this question by assuming numbers. Assume that PQ, QR, and RT are each 1, so the entire segment is 3. $ST = \frac{1}{2}$. So $\frac{ST}{PT}=\frac{\frac{1}{2}}{3}=\frac{1}{6}$.

9. (C) The sum of the measures of the three interior angles of the squares plus the sum of x, y, and z is 360°. Each of the three interior angles of the squares measures 90°. So:

$$90 + 90 + 90 + x + y + z = 360$$

$$x + y + z = 90$$

10. (A) You can rewrite the centered equation: $x = y - 3$. So Column A is equal to $y - 3$, which is larger than $y - 4$. You can also assume some numbers. If $x = 1$, then $y = 4$. And Column A is 1, while Column B is zero. That doesn't prove that Column A is larger, but it does suggest that.

11. (A) Solve for x in the centered equation:

$$\frac{\sqrt{x}}{4} = \frac{1}{2}$$
$$\sqrt{x} = \frac{4}{2}$$
$$\sqrt{x} = 2$$
$$(\sqrt{x})^2 = 2^2$$
$$x = 4$$

12. (D) Since $xyz = 0$, one of the three consecutive integers must be equal to zero, but you don't know which one it is. The three could be -2, -1, and 0, or -1, 0, and 1, or 0, 1, and 2.

13. (B) The area of each face of the cube is $\frac{1}{3} \times \frac{1}{3} = \frac{1}{9}$. And there are six faces, so the total surface area is $6 \times \frac{1}{9} = \frac{2}{3}$.

14. (B) Draw a sketch of the coordinate system:

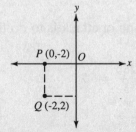

Now you can see that OQ is greater than OP.

19

15. (B) The figure is not drawn to scale, so distort it to see what happens to the angles:

Because $r > s$, $x < y$.

16. (4) Since the four segments total 24, each segment is 24 ÷ 4 = 6 units long. And each segment is divided into three equal parts, so each part is 6 ÷ 3 = 2 units long. The shaded area is bounded by a square with sides of 2. So the area of the shaded part of the figure is 2 × 2 = 4.

Since the figure is drawn to scale, you can also solve the problem by using the lengths shown in the figure. But your solution will have to be a combination of deduction and "guesstimating." For example, once you realize that each segment is 6 units long, you can see that the shaded area is bounded by segments $\frac{1}{3}$ of 6, or 2 units long.

17. (6) You can solve the problem by setting up simultaneous equations. Hector is six years older than Jane, so using H for Hector's age and J for Jane's age, $H = J + 6$. And you are trying to find the values of H and J when $H = 2J$:

$H = J + 6$

$H = 2J$

Substitute the value $2J$ for H in the first equation:

$2J = J + 6$

$J = 6$

So Jane was six when Hector was exactly twice her age.

18. (45) The question stem supplies the area of the shaded part of the figure, which is a portion of the circle. Find what fraction of the circle is shaded, and you can find the value of the unshaded angle at the center of the circle. The area of the entire circle is $\pi r^2 = \pi(4^2) = 16\pi$. So $\frac{14\pi}{16\pi} = \frac{7}{8}$ of the circle is shaded. $\frac{1}{8}$ is unshaded. So the unshaded angle at the circle's center is $\frac{1}{8}$ of 360° = 45°. Now find x:

$x + 45 + 90 = 180$

$x + 135 = 180$

$x = 45$

19. (50) The direct and best line of attack is to do the simple calculation to find the average:

$$\frac{40 + 60 + 80 + 20 + 50}{5} = \frac{250}{5} = 50$$

20. (60) You can deduce the value of x. The angle vertically opposite the right angle is also 90°. Then $30 + 90 + x = 180$, so $x = 60$.

You can also "guesstimate" the angle. It looks to be 60°.

21. (14) You can attack this question by setting up an equation. Let x be the smaller of the two numbers. The other number is $x + 1$. And:

$x + (x + 1) = 29$

$2x + 1 = 29$

$2x = 28$

$x = 14$

Or you can just test the test. Start with choice (C). 12 plus the next larger integer is $12 + 13 = 25$. That's not enough, so try the next larger choice, (D). 13 plus the next larger choice is $13 + 14 = 27$. So (E) must be correct.

22. (20) First, let's label one of the unlabeled angles:

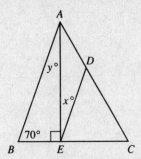

Since AB is parallel to DE, the "big angle/little angle" theorem establishes that $x = y$. So we find the size of y:

$y + 70 + 90 = 180$

$y + 160 = 180$

$y = 20$

So $x = 20$.

23. (38.5) Find x: $2(x) = 14$, so $x = 7$.

Find y: $7 - y = 1.5$, so $y = 5.5$.

Now multiply $7(5.5) = 38.5$.

24. (48) If 156 marbles are white, $300 - 156$ are black.

$300 - 156 = 144$. $\frac{144}{300} = .48$, or 48%.

25. (3/8) Find the common denominator: 24. Do the addition to find out how much time is devoted to the three chores listed: $\frac{8}{24} + \frac{4}{24} + \frac{3}{24} = \frac{15}{24}$. Subtract from 1 to determine how much time is left in the workday: $\frac{24}{24} - \frac{15}{24} = \frac{9}{24}$. Reduce this to lowest terms: $\frac{3}{8}$.

19

PART THREE
Practice Tests

Practice Test 1

Practice Test 1

ANSWER SHEET
PRACTICE TEST 1

If a section has fewer questions than answer ovals, leave the extra ovals blank.

SECTION 1

1 Ⓐ Ⓑ Ⓒ Ⓓ Ⓔ   11 Ⓐ Ⓑ Ⓒ Ⓓ Ⓔ   21 Ⓐ Ⓑ Ⓒ Ⓓ Ⓔ   31 Ⓐ Ⓑ Ⓒ Ⓓ Ⓔ
2 Ⓐ Ⓑ Ⓒ Ⓓ Ⓔ   12 Ⓐ Ⓑ Ⓒ Ⓓ Ⓔ   22 Ⓐ Ⓑ Ⓒ Ⓓ Ⓔ   32 Ⓐ Ⓑ Ⓒ Ⓓ Ⓔ
3 Ⓐ Ⓑ Ⓒ Ⓓ Ⓔ   13 Ⓐ Ⓑ Ⓒ Ⓓ Ⓔ   23 Ⓐ Ⓑ Ⓒ Ⓓ Ⓔ   33 Ⓐ Ⓑ Ⓒ Ⓓ Ⓔ
4 Ⓐ Ⓑ Ⓒ Ⓓ Ⓔ   14 Ⓐ Ⓑ Ⓒ Ⓓ Ⓔ   24 Ⓐ Ⓑ Ⓒ Ⓓ Ⓔ   34 Ⓐ Ⓑ Ⓒ Ⓓ Ⓔ
5 Ⓐ Ⓑ Ⓒ Ⓓ Ⓔ   15 Ⓐ Ⓑ Ⓒ Ⓓ Ⓔ   25 Ⓐ Ⓑ Ⓒ Ⓓ Ⓔ   35 Ⓐ Ⓑ Ⓒ Ⓓ Ⓔ
6 Ⓐ Ⓑ Ⓒ Ⓓ Ⓔ   16 Ⓐ Ⓑ Ⓒ Ⓓ Ⓔ   26 Ⓐ Ⓑ Ⓒ Ⓓ Ⓔ   36 Ⓐ Ⓑ Ⓒ Ⓓ Ⓔ
7 Ⓐ Ⓑ Ⓒ Ⓓ Ⓔ   17 Ⓐ Ⓑ Ⓒ Ⓓ Ⓔ   27 Ⓐ Ⓑ Ⓒ Ⓓ Ⓔ   37 Ⓐ Ⓑ Ⓒ Ⓓ Ⓔ
8 Ⓐ Ⓑ Ⓒ Ⓓ Ⓔ   18 Ⓐ Ⓑ Ⓒ Ⓓ Ⓔ   28 Ⓐ Ⓑ Ⓒ Ⓓ Ⓔ   38 Ⓐ Ⓑ Ⓒ Ⓓ Ⓔ
9 Ⓐ Ⓑ Ⓒ Ⓓ Ⓔ   19 Ⓐ Ⓑ Ⓒ Ⓓ Ⓔ   29 Ⓐ Ⓑ Ⓒ Ⓓ Ⓔ   39 Ⓐ Ⓑ Ⓒ Ⓓ Ⓔ
10 Ⓐ Ⓑ Ⓒ Ⓓ Ⓔ   20 Ⓐ Ⓑ Ⓒ Ⓓ Ⓔ   30 Ⓐ Ⓑ Ⓒ Ⓓ Ⓔ   40 Ⓐ Ⓑ Ⓒ Ⓓ Ⓔ

SECTION 2

1 Ⓐ Ⓑ Ⓒ Ⓓ Ⓔ   11 Ⓐ Ⓑ Ⓒ Ⓓ Ⓔ   21 Ⓐ Ⓑ Ⓒ Ⓓ Ⓔ   31 Ⓐ Ⓑ Ⓒ Ⓓ Ⓔ
2 Ⓐ Ⓑ Ⓒ Ⓓ Ⓔ   12 Ⓐ Ⓑ Ⓒ Ⓓ Ⓔ   22 Ⓐ Ⓑ Ⓒ Ⓓ Ⓔ   32 Ⓐ Ⓑ Ⓒ Ⓓ Ⓔ
3 Ⓐ Ⓑ Ⓒ Ⓓ Ⓔ   13 Ⓐ Ⓑ Ⓒ Ⓓ Ⓔ   23 Ⓐ Ⓑ Ⓒ Ⓓ Ⓔ   33 Ⓐ Ⓑ Ⓒ Ⓓ Ⓔ
4 Ⓐ Ⓑ Ⓒ Ⓓ Ⓔ   14 Ⓐ Ⓑ Ⓒ Ⓓ Ⓔ   24 Ⓐ Ⓑ Ⓒ Ⓓ Ⓔ   34 Ⓐ Ⓑ Ⓒ Ⓓ Ⓔ
5 Ⓐ Ⓑ Ⓒ Ⓓ Ⓔ   15 Ⓐ Ⓑ Ⓒ Ⓓ Ⓔ   25 Ⓐ Ⓑ Ⓒ Ⓓ Ⓔ   35 Ⓐ Ⓑ Ⓒ Ⓓ Ⓔ
6 Ⓐ Ⓑ Ⓒ Ⓓ Ⓔ   16 Ⓐ Ⓑ Ⓒ Ⓓ Ⓔ   26 Ⓐ Ⓑ Ⓒ Ⓓ Ⓔ   36 Ⓐ Ⓑ Ⓒ Ⓓ Ⓔ
7 Ⓐ Ⓑ Ⓒ Ⓓ Ⓔ   17 Ⓐ Ⓑ Ⓒ Ⓓ Ⓔ   27 Ⓐ Ⓑ Ⓒ Ⓓ Ⓔ   37 Ⓐ Ⓑ Ⓒ Ⓓ Ⓔ
8 Ⓐ Ⓑ Ⓒ Ⓓ Ⓔ   18 Ⓐ Ⓑ Ⓒ Ⓓ Ⓔ   28 Ⓐ Ⓑ Ⓒ Ⓓ Ⓔ   38 Ⓐ Ⓑ Ⓒ Ⓓ Ⓔ
9 Ⓐ Ⓑ Ⓒ Ⓓ Ⓔ   19 Ⓐ Ⓑ Ⓒ Ⓓ Ⓔ   29 Ⓐ Ⓑ Ⓒ Ⓓ Ⓔ   39 Ⓐ Ⓑ Ⓒ Ⓓ Ⓔ
10 Ⓐ Ⓑ Ⓒ Ⓓ Ⓔ   20 Ⓐ Ⓑ Ⓒ Ⓓ Ⓔ   30 Ⓐ Ⓑ Ⓒ Ⓓ Ⓔ   40 Ⓐ Ⓑ Ⓒ Ⓓ Ⓔ

SECTION 3

1 Ⓐ Ⓑ Ⓒ Ⓓ Ⓔ   6 Ⓐ Ⓑ Ⓒ Ⓓ Ⓔ   11 Ⓐ Ⓑ Ⓒ Ⓓ Ⓔ   16 Ⓐ Ⓑ Ⓒ Ⓓ Ⓔ
2 Ⓐ Ⓑ Ⓒ Ⓓ Ⓔ   7 Ⓐ Ⓑ Ⓒ Ⓓ Ⓔ   12 Ⓐ Ⓑ Ⓒ Ⓓ Ⓔ   17 Ⓐ Ⓑ Ⓒ Ⓓ Ⓔ
3 Ⓐ Ⓑ Ⓒ Ⓓ Ⓔ   8 Ⓐ Ⓑ Ⓒ Ⓓ Ⓔ   13 Ⓐ Ⓑ Ⓒ Ⓓ Ⓔ   18 Ⓐ Ⓑ Ⓒ Ⓓ Ⓔ
4 Ⓐ Ⓑ Ⓒ Ⓓ Ⓔ   9 Ⓐ Ⓑ Ⓒ Ⓓ Ⓔ   14 Ⓐ Ⓑ Ⓒ Ⓓ Ⓔ   19 Ⓐ Ⓑ Ⓒ Ⓓ Ⓔ
5 Ⓐ Ⓑ Ⓒ Ⓓ Ⓔ   10 Ⓐ Ⓑ Ⓒ Ⓓ Ⓔ   15 Ⓐ Ⓑ Ⓒ Ⓓ Ⓔ   20 Ⓐ Ⓑ Ⓒ Ⓓ Ⓔ

SECTION 4

1 Ⓐ Ⓑ Ⓒ Ⓓ Ⓔ   6 Ⓐ Ⓑ Ⓒ Ⓓ Ⓔ   11 Ⓐ Ⓑ Ⓒ Ⓓ Ⓔ   16 Ⓐ Ⓑ Ⓒ Ⓓ Ⓔ
2 Ⓐ Ⓑ Ⓒ Ⓓ Ⓔ   7 Ⓐ Ⓑ Ⓒ Ⓓ Ⓔ   12 Ⓐ Ⓑ Ⓒ Ⓓ Ⓔ   17 Ⓐ Ⓑ Ⓒ Ⓓ Ⓔ
3 Ⓐ Ⓑ Ⓒ Ⓓ Ⓔ   8 Ⓐ Ⓑ Ⓒ Ⓓ Ⓔ   13 Ⓐ Ⓑ Ⓒ Ⓓ Ⓔ   18 Ⓐ Ⓑ Ⓒ Ⓓ Ⓔ
4 Ⓐ Ⓑ Ⓒ Ⓓ Ⓔ   9 Ⓐ Ⓑ Ⓒ Ⓓ Ⓔ   14 Ⓐ Ⓑ Ⓒ Ⓓ Ⓔ   19 Ⓐ Ⓑ Ⓒ Ⓓ Ⓔ
5 Ⓐ Ⓑ Ⓒ Ⓓ Ⓔ   10 Ⓐ Ⓑ Ⓒ Ⓓ Ⓔ   15 Ⓐ Ⓑ Ⓒ Ⓓ Ⓔ   20 Ⓐ Ⓑ Ⓒ Ⓓ Ⓔ

SECTION 5

1 Ⓐ Ⓑ Ⓒ Ⓓ Ⓔ   11 Ⓐ Ⓑ Ⓒ Ⓓ Ⓔ   21 Ⓐ Ⓑ Ⓒ Ⓓ Ⓔ   31 Ⓐ Ⓑ Ⓒ Ⓓ Ⓔ
2 Ⓐ Ⓑ Ⓒ Ⓓ Ⓔ   12 Ⓐ Ⓑ Ⓒ Ⓓ Ⓔ   22 Ⓐ Ⓑ Ⓒ Ⓓ Ⓔ   32 Ⓐ Ⓑ Ⓒ Ⓓ Ⓔ
3 Ⓐ Ⓑ Ⓒ Ⓓ Ⓔ   13 Ⓐ Ⓑ Ⓒ Ⓓ Ⓔ   23 Ⓐ Ⓑ Ⓒ Ⓓ Ⓔ   33 Ⓐ Ⓑ Ⓒ Ⓓ Ⓔ
4 Ⓐ Ⓑ Ⓒ Ⓓ Ⓔ   14 Ⓐ Ⓑ Ⓒ Ⓓ Ⓔ   24 Ⓐ Ⓑ Ⓒ Ⓓ Ⓔ   34 Ⓐ Ⓑ Ⓒ Ⓓ Ⓔ
5 Ⓐ Ⓑ Ⓒ Ⓓ Ⓔ   15 Ⓐ Ⓑ Ⓒ Ⓓ Ⓔ   25 Ⓐ Ⓑ Ⓒ Ⓓ Ⓔ   35 Ⓐ Ⓑ Ⓒ Ⓓ Ⓔ
6 Ⓐ Ⓑ Ⓒ Ⓓ Ⓔ   16 Ⓐ Ⓑ Ⓒ Ⓓ Ⓔ   26 Ⓐ Ⓑ Ⓒ Ⓓ Ⓔ   36 Ⓐ Ⓑ Ⓒ Ⓓ Ⓔ
7 Ⓐ Ⓑ Ⓒ Ⓓ Ⓔ   17 Ⓐ Ⓑ Ⓒ Ⓓ Ⓔ   27 Ⓐ Ⓑ Ⓒ Ⓓ Ⓔ   37 Ⓐ Ⓑ Ⓒ Ⓓ Ⓔ
8 Ⓐ Ⓑ Ⓒ Ⓓ Ⓔ   18 Ⓐ Ⓑ Ⓒ Ⓓ Ⓔ   28 Ⓐ Ⓑ Ⓒ Ⓓ Ⓔ   38 Ⓐ Ⓑ Ⓒ Ⓓ Ⓔ
9 Ⓐ Ⓑ Ⓒ Ⓓ Ⓔ   19 Ⓐ Ⓑ Ⓒ Ⓓ Ⓔ   29 Ⓐ Ⓑ Ⓒ Ⓓ Ⓔ   39 Ⓐ Ⓑ Ⓒ Ⓓ Ⓔ
10 Ⓐ Ⓑ Ⓒ Ⓓ Ⓔ   20 Ⓐ Ⓑ Ⓒ Ⓓ Ⓔ   30 Ⓐ Ⓑ Ⓒ Ⓓ Ⓔ   40 Ⓐ Ⓑ Ⓒ Ⓓ Ⓔ

SECTION

6

1 Ⓐ Ⓑ Ⓒ Ⓓ Ⓔ   6 Ⓐ Ⓑ Ⓒ Ⓓ Ⓔ   11 Ⓐ Ⓑ Ⓒ Ⓓ Ⓔ
2 Ⓐ Ⓑ Ⓒ Ⓓ Ⓔ   7 Ⓐ Ⓑ Ⓒ Ⓓ Ⓔ   12 Ⓐ Ⓑ Ⓒ Ⓓ Ⓔ
3 Ⓐ Ⓑ Ⓒ Ⓓ Ⓔ   8 Ⓐ Ⓑ Ⓒ Ⓓ Ⓔ   13 Ⓐ Ⓑ Ⓒ Ⓓ Ⓔ
4 Ⓐ Ⓑ Ⓒ Ⓓ Ⓔ   9 Ⓐ Ⓑ Ⓒ Ⓓ Ⓔ   14 Ⓐ Ⓑ Ⓒ Ⓓ Ⓔ
5 Ⓐ Ⓑ Ⓒ Ⓓ Ⓔ   10 Ⓐ Ⓑ Ⓒ Ⓓ Ⓔ   15 Ⓐ Ⓑ Ⓒ Ⓓ Ⓔ

Note: ONLY the answers entered on the grid are scored.
Handwritten answers at the top of the column are NOT scored.

16.   17.   18.   19.   20.

21.   22.   23.   24.   25.

SECTION 1 Time—30 Minutes
35 Questions

For each question in this section, choose the best answer and blacken the corresponding space on the answer sheet.

The passage below is followed by questions based on its content. Answer all questions following the passage on the basis of what is stated or implied in the passage.

Questions 1–12 are based on the following passage.

Charles Darwin (1809–1882) served as a naturalist aboard the world voyage of the H.M.S. Beagle. *His observations on this and later journeys led to his theories of evolution and natural selection. Here, the* Beagle *has arrived on the Galapagos Islands, a rich breeding ground for all kinds of unusual fauna.*

The natural history of these islands is eminently curious, and well deserves attention. Most of the organic productions are aboriginal creations, found nowhere else; there is
(5) even a difference between the inhabitants of the different islands; yet all show a marked relationship with those of America, though separated from that continent by an open space of ocean, between 500 and 600 miles in width. . . .

Of terrestrial mammals, there is only one which must be considered as indigenous, namely, a mouse (*Mus gala-*
(10) *pagoensis*), and this is confined, as far as I could ascertain, to Chatham Island, the most easterly island of the group. It belongs, as I am informed by Mr. Waterhouse, to a division of the family of mice characteristic of America. At James Island, there is a rat sufficiently distinct from the
(15) common kind to have been named and described by Mr. Waterhouse; but as it belongs to the old-world division of the family, and as this island has been frequented by ships for the last hundred and fifty years, I can hardly doubt that this rat is merely a variety, produced by the new and pecu-
(20) liar climate, food, and soil, to which it has been subjected. Although no one has a right to speculate without distinct facts, yet even with respect to the Chatham Island mouse, it should be borne in mind, that it may possibly be an American species imported here; for I have seen, in a
(25) most unfrequented part of the Pampas, a native mouse living in the roof of a newly-built hovel, and therefore its transportation in a vessel is not improbable: analogous facts have been observed by Dr. Richardson in North America. . . .

(30) We will now turn to the order of reptiles, which gives the most striking character to the zoology of these islands. The species are not numerous, but the numbers of individuals of each species are extraordinarily great. There is one small lizard belonging to a South American genus, and
(35) two species (and probably more) of . . . a genus confined to the Galapagos islands. There is one snake which is numerous; it is identical, as I am informed by M. Bibron, with the *Psammophis temminckii* from Chile. Of sea-turtle, I believe there is more than one species, and of tortoises
(40) there are, as we shall presently show, two or three species or races. Of toads and frogs there are none: I was surprised at this, considering how well suited for them the temperate and damp upper woods appear to be. It recalled to my

mind the remark made by Bory St. Vincent, namely, that
(45) none of this family are found on any of the volcanic islands in the great oceans. As far as I can ascertain from various works, this seems to hold good throughout the Pacific, and even in the large islands of the Sandwich archipelago. Mauritius offers an apparent exception, where
(50) I saw the *Rana mascariensis* in abundance: this frog is said now to inhabit the Seychelles, Madagascar, and Bourbon; but on the other hand, Du Bois, in his voyage of 1669, states that there were no reptiles on Bourbon except tortoises; and the Officier du Roi asserts that before 1768
(55) it had been attempted, without success, to introduce frogs into Mauritius—I presume, for the purpose of eating: hence it may well be doubted whether this frog is an aboriginal of these islands. The absence of the frog family in the oceanic islands is the more remarkable, when con-
(60) trasted with the case of lizards, which swarm on most of the smallest islands. May this difference not be caused, by the greater facility with which the eggs of lizards, protected by calcareous shells, might be transported through sea-water, than could the slimy spawn of frogs?

1. The word *aboriginal* (line 3) is used to mean

(A) ancient
(B) primitive
(C) living
(D) elementary
(E) native

2. Why does Darwin mention the distance between the islands and the mainland (line 7)?

(A) They are not far apart, and may once have been connected.
(B) They are far apart, but their animals seem related.
(C) They are close enough to swim between.
(D) They are far apart, but they look very similar.
(E) They are too distant ever to have been connected.

3. Darwin mentions a native mouse in the Pampas (line 25) to

(A) explain his theory of natural selection
(B) prove that mice are indigenous to all islands
(C) support the idea that mice may be transported
(D) show how many species are found in South America
(E) report on an unusual indigenous species

GO ON TO THE NEXT PAGE

487

4. What does the word *analogous* in line 27 mean?

    (A) divergent
    (B) comparable
    (C) disparate
    (D) conventional
    (E) unique

5. When Darwin says that reptiles give "striking character" to the islands, he means that

    (A) they are unusual
    (B) they are dangerous
    (C) they are beautiful
    (D) both A and B
    (E) both B and C

6. How does Darwin feel about the lack of frogs?

    (A) He is worried.
    (B) He is unsurprised.
    (C) He finds it curious.
    (D) He is doubtful.
    (E) He finds it unexplainable.

7. How do lines 33–36 support Darwin's opening paragraph?

    (A) They explain why the creatures of the Galapagos deserve attention.
    (B) They refer to some animals that are aboriginal and others that are found in South America.
    (C) They refer to the distance between the islands and the mainland.
    (D) They show how the inhabitants of different islands differ.
    (E) They do not support the opening paragraph.

8. When Darwin says "none of this family" (line 45), he is referring to

    (A) the Darwins
    (B) reptiles
    (C) *Psammophis temminckii*
    (D) toads and frogs
    (E) none of the above

9. An *archipelago* (line 49) is

    (A) a stream
    (B) a continent
    (C) an ice cap
    (D) a small bay
    (E) an island chain

10. Why does Darwin mention Mauritius (line 49)?

    (A) to show that frogs appear on the mainland
    (B) to show that frogs turn up on some islands
    (C) to show that toads prefer temperate climates
    (D) both A and B
    (E) both B and C

11. In the last sentence, Darwin intends to

    (A) reveal a fact
    (B) recall a detail
    (C) express an emotion
    (D) propose a theory
    (E) relate an event

12. You would expect the next few paragraphs of this essay to deal with

    (A) birds of the Galapagos
    (B) other islands
    (C) details about reptiles
    (D) details of the voyage
    (E) facts about mice

Each sentence below has one or two blanks, each blank indicating that something has been omitted. Beneath the sentence are five lettered words or sets of words. Choose the word or set of words that best fits the meaning of the sentence as a whole.

Example:

Although its publicity has been ----, the film itself is intelligent, well-acted, handsomely produced, and altogether ----.

(A) tasteless..respectable
(B) extensive..moderate
(C) sophisticated..amateur
(D) risqué..crude
(E) perfect..spectacular

---

13. Portraits painted in Colonial America are quite charming but ---- and demonstrate the isolation of the American painter; they show little or no ---- of the development of painting in Europe.

    (A) grotesque..concern
    (B) frivolous..affirmation
    (C) deliberate..domination
    (D) sophisticated..consideration
    (E) primitive..knowledge

14. Although leprosy is not a highly contagious disease, those who have contracted it have always been pariahs and ---- by others.

    (A) ostracized   (B) accepted   (C) sheltered
    (D) admonished   (E) lauded

15. Although the novel was generally boring and awkwardly written, there were ---- passages of power and lyricism which hinted at the author's ----.

    (A) occasional..potential
    (B) frequent..malevolence
    (C) static..style
    (D) ill-conceived..superficiality
    (E) contrived..ignorance

16. Since the doctor could not find anything physically wrong with his patient, he decided to administer a ---- as a way to ---- him.

    (A) remedy..controvert   (B) placebo..placate
    (C) warning..mortify   (D) dictum..provoke
    (E) malady..supervise

17. Although some evidence ---- that *The Iliad* and *The Odyssey* were not written by a single person, the unity of artistic vision and general ---- of the epics prove otherwise.

(A) suggests..coherence
(B) indicates..magnitude
(C) proclaims..demeanor
(D) implies..torpor
(E) hints..lassitude

Each question below consists of a related pair of words or phrases, followed by five lettered pairs of words or phrases. Select the lettered pair that best expresses a relationship similar to that expressed in the original pair

Example:

YAWN : BOREDOM::
(A) dream : sleep
(B) anger : madness
(C) smile : amusement
(D) face : expression
(E) impatience : rebellion

---

18. PAINTER : STUDIO::

(A) composer : piano
(B) teacher : faculty
(C) judge : courtroom
(D) golfer : club
(E) stage : theater

19. SIGH : LONGING::

(A) anger : impatience
(B) laughter : joy
(C) boredom : hostility
(D) grimace : face
(E) stare : eyes

20. MARCHING : HALT::

(A) eating : swallow
(B) driving : turn
(C) humming : shout
(D) flying : land
(E) tracking : ensnare

21. RUTHLESS : COMPASSION::

(A) verbose : conversation
(B) mature : offspring
(C) animated : interest
(D) sublime : perfection
(E) lethargic : energy

22. LEOPARD : CAT::

(A) zebra : zoo
(B) hawk : prey
(C) parrot : jungle
(D) monkey : chimpanzee
(E) chameleon : lizard

23. ANGER : RABID::

(A) hunger : ravenous
(B) concern : careless
(C) modernity : contemporary
(D) petulance : mournful
(E) wisdom : hoary

24. BLAMEWORTHY : REPROACH::

(A) recalcitrant : praise
(B) humorous : approval
(C) sympathetic : rejection
(D) meritorious : reward
(E) noxious : censure

25. PEDESTRIAN : ORIGINALITY::

(A) monotonous : compulsion
(B) ethereal : mysticism
(C) reclusive : misanthropy
(D) indulgent : forbearance
(E) timorous : cowardice

The passage below is followed by questions based on its content. Answer all questions following the passage on the basis of what is stated or implied in the passage.

Questions 26–35 are based on the following passage.

In this 1884 letter to the French author Guy de Maupassant, his fan Marie Bashkirtseff expresses feelings that go beyond mere admiration. A member of the naturalist school, Maupassant is today best remembered for his short stories, including the often-anthologized tale "The Necklace."

Monsieur:

I read your works, I might almost say, with delight. In truth to nature, which you copy with religious fidelity, you find an inspiration that is truly sublime, while you move
Line your readers by touches of feeling so profoundly human,
(5) that we fancy we see ourselves depicted in your pages, and love you with an egotistical love. Is this an unmeaning compliment? Be indulgent, it is sincere in the main.

You will understand that I should like to say many fine and striking things to you, but it is rather difficult, all
Line at once, in this way. I regret this all the more as you are
(10) sufficiently great to inspire one with romantic dreams of becoming the confidant of your beautiful soul, always supposing your soul to be beautiful.

If your soul is not beautiful, and if those things are not
in your line, I shall regret it for your sake, in the first
(15) place; and in the next I shall set you down in my mind as a maker of literature, and dismiss the matter from my thoughts.

GO ON TO THE NEXT PAGE →

(20) For a year past I have had the wish to write to you
and was many times on the point of doing so, but—sometimes I thought I exaggerated your merits and that it was
not worth while. Two days ago, however, I saw suddenly,
in the *Gaulois*, that some one had honoured you with a
flattering epistle and that you had inquired the address of
(25) this amiable person in order to answer him. I at once
became jealous, your literary merits dazzled me anew and—
here is my letter.

And now let me say that I shall always preserve my
incognito for you. I do not even desire to see you from a
(30) distance—your countenance might not please me—who
can tell? All I know of you now is that you are young and
that you are not married, two essential points, even for a
distant adoration.

But I must tell you that I am charming; this sweet
(35) reflection will stimulate you to answer my letter. It seems
to me that if I were a man I should wish to hold no communication, not even an epistolary one, with an old fright
of an Englishwoman, whatever may be thought by

Miss Hastings
(40) P.O. Station of the Madeleine

May I venture to ask you which are your favorite
musicians and painters?

And how if I were a man?

26. What does Bashkirtseff mean by "truth to nature"
(line 2)?

(A) fidelity
(B) ecology
(C) drama
(D) realism
(E) instinct

27. How does Bashkirtseff feel about Maupassant's
work?

(A) It is remarkably true to life.
(B) It reveals human feelings wonderfully.
(C) It inspires religious fervor.
(D) both A and B
(E) both B and C

28. The phrase "in the main" (line 7) means

(A) strongly
(B) at sea
(C) essentially
(D) part time
(E) authoritatively

29. The word *confidant* (line 12) most closely means

(A) friend
(B) confessor
(C) trust
(D) adversary
(E) secret

30. Why does Bashkirtseff mention the *Gaulois*?

(A) to explain her decision to write
(B) to show that she is well-read
(C) to amuse her reader
(D) to compare herself to other admirers
(E) to report on a review she disliked

31. The word *countenance* (line 30) means

(A) air
(B) restraint
(C) appearance
(D) purity
(E) endorsement

32. By "sweet reflection" (line 34), Bashkirtseff means

(A) religious meditation
(B) novel idea
(C) innocent dream
(D) pleasing image
(E) pool of tears

33. The word *epistolary* (line 37) is used to mean

(A) violent
(B) remote
(C) written
(D) imaginary
(E) clinical

34. Why does Bashkirtseff sign the name
"Miss Hastings"?

(A) It is her real name.
(B) Maupassant loves Englishwomen.
(C) She is writing in haste.
(D) Maupassant knows a Miss Hastings.
(E) She wishes to remain anonymous.

35. The general tone of the letter is

(A) awestruck
(B) respectful
(C) somber
(D) breezy
(E) curt

SECTION **2** Time—30 Minutes 25 Questions

In this section, solve each problem, using any available space on the page for scratchwork. Then decide which is the best of the choices given and fill in the corresponding oval on the answer sheet.

Reference:

Circle:

$C = 2\pi r$
$A = \pi r^2$

Rectangle:

$A = lw$

Rectangular Solid:

$V = lwh$

Cylinder:

$V = \pi r^2 h$

Triangle:

$A = \frac{1}{2}bh$

$a^2 + b^2 = c^2$

- The measure in degrees of a straight angle is 180.
- The number of degrees of arc in a circle is 360.
- The sum of the measures of the angles of a triangle is 180.

Notes: The figures accompanying the problems are drawn as accurately as possible unless otherwise stated in specific problems. Again, unless otherwise stated, all figures lie in the same plane. All numbers used in these problems are real numbers. Calculators are permitted for this test.

1. If $\dfrac{1}{x} + \dfrac{1}{x} = 8$, then $x =$

   (A) $\dfrac{1}{4}$ (B) $\dfrac{1}{2}$ (C) 1 (D) 2 (E) 4

2. If $x = 2$ and $y = -1$, then $3x - 4y =$
   (A) -5 (B) -1 (C) 0 (D) 2 (E) 10

3. In a certain school, there are 600 boys and 400 girls. If 20 percent of the boys and 30 percent of the girls are on the honor roll, how many of the students are on the honor roll?

   (A) 120 (B) 175 (C) 240
   (D) 250 (E) 280

4. If $p, q, r, s,$ and t are whole numbers, the expression $t(r(p + q) + s))$ *must* be an even number when which of the five numbers is even?

   (A) p (B) q (C) r (D) s (E) t

RESULTS OF BIOLOGY PROJECT CONDUCTED BY STUDENT X

Week	1	2	3	4	5
Number of flies in bottle	3	12	48	192	

5. A student conducting a lab experiment finds that the population of flies in a bottle increases by a certain multiple from week to week. If the pattern shown in the table continues, how many flies can the student expect to find in the bottle in week 5?

   (A) 195 (B) 240 (C) 384 (D) 448 (E) 768

6. Three students are each scheduled to give a short speech at an assembly. In how many different orders can the speeches by scheduled?

   (A) 12 (B) 9 (C) 6 (D) 4 (E) 3

GO ON TO THE NEXT PAGE

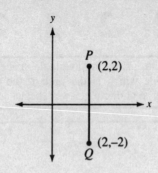

7. If points P and Q lie in the xy-plane and have the coordinates shown above, what is the midpoint of PQ?

(A) $(-2,0)$ (B) $(-2,2)$ (C) $(0,2)$
(D) $(2,0)$ (E) $(2,2)$

8. If xy is positive, which of the following CANNOT be true?

(A) $x > y > 0$
(B) $y > x > 0$
(C) $x > 0 > y$
(D) $0 > x > y$
(E) $0 > y > x$

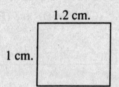

9. In the scale drawing of the floor of a rectangular room shown above, the scale used was 1 centimeter = 4 meters. What is the actual area, in square meters, of the floor of the room?

(A) 9.6   (B) 13.6   (C) 15
(D) 19.2   (E) 38.4

10. If $30,000 \times 20 = 6 \times 10n$, then $n =$

(A) 4   (B) 5   (C) 6   (D) 7   (E) 8

11. Karen purchased a total of 4 pounds of candy, some of which was chocolates and some of which was caramels. If chocolates cost \$3 per pound and caramels cost \$2 per pound, and Karen spent a total of \$10, how many pounds of chocolates did she buy?

(A) 1   (B) 2   (C) 2.5   (D) 3   (E) 3.5

12. The average (arithmetic mean) of Al's scores on three tests was 80. If the average of his scores on the first two tests was also 80, what was his score on the third test?

(A) 90
(B) 85
(C) 80
(D) 75
(E) Cannot be determined from the information given.

13. A book contains ten photographs, some in color and some in black-and-white. Each of the following could be the ratio of color to black-and-white photographs EXCEPT

(A) 9:1   (B) 4:1   (C) 5:2   (D) 3:2   (E) 1:1

14. If $\dfrac{4}{5} = \dfrac{x}{4}$, then $x =$

(A) 5   (B) $\dfrac{16}{5}$ (C) $\dfrac{5}{4}$ (D) $\dfrac{4}{5}$ (E) $\dfrac{5}{16}$

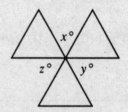

15. In the figure above, three equilateral triangles have a common vertex. $x + y + z =$

(A) 60   (B) 90   (C) 120   (D) 180   (E) 240

16. Peter spent $\dfrac{1}{4}$ of his allowance on Monday and $\dfrac{1}{3}$ of the *remainder* on Tuesday. What part of the allowance does Peter still have?

(A) $\dfrac{1}{12}$ (B) $\dfrac{1}{4}$ (C) $\dfrac{1}{2}$ (D) $\dfrac{3}{4}$ (E) $\dfrac{11}{12}$

17. If 100 identical bricks weigh p pounds, then in terms of p, 20 of these bricks weigh how many pounds?

(A) $\dfrac{p}{20}$ (B) $\dfrac{p}{5}$ (C) $20p$ (D) $\dfrac{5}{p}$ (E) $\dfrac{20}{p}$

18. If the distances between points P, Q, and R are equal, which of the following could be true?

 I. P, Q, and R are points on a circle with center O.
 II. P and Q are points on a circle with center R.
 III. P, Q, and R are vertices on an equilateral triangle.

(A) I only (B) I and II only (C) I and III only
(C) II and III only (E) I, II, and III

	Year					
	1950	1955	1960	1965	1970	1975
Price of a certain item	$2	$4	$7	$12	$20	$30

19. In the table above, the percent increase in the price of the item was greatest during which of the following periods?

(A) 1950–1955 (B) 1955–1960 (C) 1960–1965
(D) 1965–1970 (E) 1970–1975

20. For any integer n, which of the following represents three consecutive odd integers?

(A) $n, n + 1, n + 2$
(B) $n, n + 1, n + 3$
(C) $n, n + 2, n + 4$
(D) $2n + 1, 2n + 2, 2n + 3$
(E) $2n + 1, 2n + 3, 2n + 5$

21. Two cartons weigh $3x - 2$ and $2x - 3$. If the average weight of the cartons is 10, the heavier carton weighs how much more than the lighter carton?

(A) 2 (B) 4 (C) 5 (D) 6 (E) 10

22. A group of 15 students took a test that was scored from zero to 100. If exactly ten students scored 75 or more on the test, what is the *lowest* possible value for the average of the scores of all 15 students?

(A) 25 (B) 50 (C) 70 (D) 75 (E) 90

23. If a machine produces x units in t minutes and 30 seconds, what is its average operating speed in units per minute?

(A) $\dfrac{t + 30}{x}$ (B) $\dfrac{x}{t + 30}$ (C) $tx + \dfrac{1x}{2}$

(D) $\dfrac{t}{x} + \dfrac{1}{2}$ (E) $\dfrac{x}{t + \dfrac{1}{2}}$

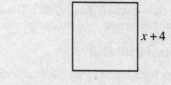

24. If the figure above is a square, what is the perimeter of the figure?

(A) 28
(B) 16
(C) 9
(D) 3
(E) Cannot be determined from the information given.

25. If a certain rectangle has a length that is twice its width, what is the ratio of the area of the rectangle to the area of an isosceles right triangle with hypotenuse equal to the width of the rectangle?

(A) $\dfrac{1}{8}$ (B) $\dfrac{1}{4}$ (C) $\dfrac{1}{2}$ (D) $\dfrac{4}{1}$ (E) $\dfrac{8}{1}$

IF YOU FINISH BEFORE TIME IS CALLED, YOU MAY CHECK YOUR WORK ON THIS SECTION ONLY. DO NOT WORK ON ANY OTHER SECTION IN THE TEST. **S T O P**

SECTION 3   Time—15 Minutes   For each question in this section, choose the best answer and
            10 Questions   blacken the corresponding space on the answer sheet.

The passages below are followed by questions based on their content. Answer all questions following the passages on
the basis of what is <u>stated</u> or <u>implied</u> in the passages.

Questions 1–10 are based on the following passages.

In these excerpts from Captain Basil Hall's The Lieutenant and the Commander *and R. H. Dana's* Two Years Before the
Mast, *the writers, well versed in seamanship, discuss a not-uncommon disaster at sea.*

Passage 1—Captain Basil Hall

Everyone who has been much at sea must remember the
peculiar sounds which pervade a ship when a man is
known to have fallen overboard. The course steered is so
suddenly altered, that as she rounds-to the effect of the
(5) sails is doubled; the creaking of the tiller-ropes and rudder
next strike the ear; then follows the pitter-patter of several
hundred feet in rapid motion, producing a singular tremor,
fore and aft. In the midst of these ominous noises may be
heard, over all, the shrill startling voice of the officer of
(10) the watch, generally betraying in its tone more or less
uncertainty of purpose. Then the violent flapping of the
sails, and the mingled cries of 'Clear away the boats!' 'Is
the lifebuoy gone?' 'Heave that grating after him!' 'Throw
that hencoop over the stern!' 'Who is it, do you know?'
(15) 'Where did he fall from?' 'Can he swim?' 'Silence!' An
impetuous, and too often an ill-regulated rush now succeeds to gain the boats, which are generally so crowded
that it becomes dangerous to lower them down, and more
time is lost in getting the people out again than would
(20) have manned them twice over, if any regular system had
been prepared, and rendered familiar and easy by practice
beforehand.

     I could give a pretty long list of cases which I have
myself seen, or have heard others relate, where men have
(25) been drowned while their shipmates were thus struggling
on board who should be first to save them, but who,
instead of aiding, were actually impeding one another by
their hurry-skurry and general ignorance of what really
ought to be done. I remember, for example, hearing of a
(30) line-of-battle-ship, in the Baltic, from which two men fell
one evening, when the ship's company were at quarters.
The weather was fine, the water smooth, and the ship
going about seven knots. The two lads in question who
were furling the fore-royal at the time, lost their hold, and
(35) were jerked far in the sea. At least a dozen men, leaving
their guns, leaped overboard from different parts of the
ship, some dressed as they were, and others stripped. Of
course, the ship was in a wretched state of discipline
where such frantic proceedings could take place. The con-
(40) fusion soon became worst confounded; but the ship was
hove aback, and several boats lowered down. Had it not
been smooth water, daylight, and fine weather, many of
these absurd volunteers must have perished. I call them
absurd, because there is no sense in merely incurring a
(45) great hazard, without some useful purpose to guide the

exercise of courage. These intrepid fellows merely knew
that a man had fallen overboard, and that was all; so away
they leapt out of the ports and over the hammock-nettings,
without knowing whereabouts the object of their Quixotic
(50) heroism might be. The boats were obliged to pick up the
first that presented themselves, for they were all in a
drowning condition; but the two unhappy men who had
been flung from aloft, being furthest off, went to the bottom before their turn came.

Passage 2—R. H. Dana

(55) This was a black day in our calendar. At seven o'clock in
the morning, it being our watch below, we were aroused
from a sound sleep by the cry of 'All hands ahoy! A man
overboard!' This unwonted cry sent a thrill through the
heart of everyone, and hurrying on deck we found the ves-
(60) sel flat aback, with all the studding-sails set; for the boy
who was at the helm left it to throw something overboard,
and the carpenter, who was an old sailor, knowing that the
wind was light, put the helm down and hove her aback.
The watch on deck were lowering away the quarter-boat,
(65) and I got on deck just in time to heave myself into her as
she was leaving the side; but it was not until out upon the
wide Pacific, in our little boat, that I knew whom we had
lost. It was George Bolemer, a young English sailor, who
was prized by the officers as a lively, hearty fellow, and a
(70) good shipmate. He was going aloft to fit a strap round the
main topmast head, for ringtail halyards, and had the strap
and block, a coil of halyards and a marline-spike about his
neck. He fell from the starboard futtock shrouds, and not
knowing how to swim, and being heavily dressed, with all
(75) those things round his neck, he probably sank immediately. We pulled astern, in the direction in which he fell,
and though we knew that there was no hope of saving him,
yet no-one wished to speak of returning, and we rowed
about for nearly an hour, without the hope of doing any-
(80) thing, but unwilling to acknowledge to ourselves that we
must give him up. At length we turned the boat's head and
made toward the vessel.

1. The sense appealed to in paragraph 1 of Hall's essay
    is that of

    (A) sight
    (B) smell
    (C) hearing
    (D) both A and B
    (E) both B and C

2. Hall uses the word *succeeds* in lines 16–17 to mean

    (A) supplants
    (B) accomplishes
    (C) prospers
    (D) replaces
    (E) ensues

3. What is Hall's opinion of the ship in the Baltic disaster?

    (A) It was overstaffed.
    (B) The ship was too old and in ill-repair.
    (C) Discipline was sorely lacking.
    (D) both A and B
    (E) both B and C

4. What does Hall think about taking risks?

    (A) It is never justified.
    (B) It is always justified.
    (C) It requires a practical goal.
    (D) It should only be done in life-or-death emergencies.
    (E) It separates men from boys.

5. Dana's use of the word *unwonted* (line 58) means

    (A) unusual
    (B) unjustified
    (C) arid
    (D) undesired
    (E) uninformed

6. The term *hove aback*, found in Hall's piece in line 41 and Dana's in line 63, probably means

    (A) taken unawares
    (B) shocked
    (C) living badly
    (D) set to catch the wind
    (E) under steam power

7. In line 65, Dana's narrator proves himself to be

    (A) a good sailor
    (B) inept and uncoordinated
    (C) practical but brave
    (D) the kind of sailor Hall disparages
    (E) the kind of sailor Hall prefers

8. Why does Dana list the materials Bolemer was carrying?

    (A) to suggest his position on the ship
    (B) to show that he was a sailor
    (C) to justify the crew's actions
    (D) to reveal his helpful nature
    (E) to explain why he quickly sank

9. Dana's intent in this passage is to

    (A) argue for better regulations
    (B) show the many forms of death
    (C) demonstrate the perils of poor seamanship
    (D) caution those who would go to sea
    (E) relate a sad tale

10. These two passages might be anthologized with the heading

    (A) "Man Overboard!"
    (B) "Storms on the Water"
    (C) "The Unforgiving Landscape"
    (D) "Funeral at Sea"
    (E) "Disasters I Have Known"

IF YOU FINISH BEFORE TIME IS CALLED, YOU MAY CHECK YOUR WORK ON **S T O P**
THIS SECTION ONLY. DO NOT WORK ON ANY OTHER SECTION IN THE TEST.

SECTION 4	Time—15 Minutes 10 Questions	In this section, solve each problem, using any available space on the page for scratchwork. Then decide which is the best of the choices given and fill in the corresponding oval on the answer sheet.

Reference:

Circle:　Rectangle:　Rectangular Solid:　Cylinder:　Triangle:

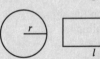   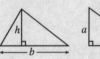

$C = 2\pi r$ 　 $A = lw$ 　 $V = lwh$ 　 $V = \pi r^2 h$ 　 $A = \frac{1}{2}bh$ 　 $a^2 + b^2 = c^2$
$A = \pi r^2$

- The measure in degrees of a straight angle is 180.
- The number of degrees of arc in a circle is 360.
- The sum of the measures of the angles of a triangle is 180.

Notes: The figures accompanying the problems are drawn as accurately as possible unless otherwise stated in specific problems. Again, unless otherwise stated, all figures lie in the same plane. All numbers used in these problems are real numbers. Calculators are permitted for this test.

1. If the perimeter of a rectangular playing field is 120 meters, then which of the following could be the length of one of its sides?

　I. 20
　II. 40
　III. 60

(A) I only　(B) I and II only　(C) I and III only
(D) II and III only　(E) I, II, and III

2. If a six-sided polygon has two sides of length $x - 2y$ each and four sides of length $2x + y$ each, what is its perimeter?

(A) $6x - 6y$　(B) $6x - y$　(C) $5x$
(D) $6x$　(E) $10x$

3. If m and n are negative numbers, which of the following must always be positive?

　I. $m - n$
　II. $m \times n$
　III. $m \div n$

(A) I only　　(B) II only　　(C) I and III only
(D) II and III only　(E) I, II, and III

4. $\dfrac{1}{1 + \frac{1}{x}}$ is equal to which of the following?

(A) $x + 1$　(B) $\dfrac{1}{x + 1}$　(C) $\dfrac{x}{x + 1}$

(D) $\dfrac{x + 1}{x}$　(E) $x^2 + x$

5. If the cost of b books is d dollars, what is the cost, in dollars, of x books at the same rate?

(A) xd　　(B) $\dfrac{xd}{b}$　　(C) $\dfrac{bd}{x}$

(D) bx　　(E) $\dfrac{bx}{d}$

6. If $y = 7x$, then the average (arithmetic mean) of x and y, in terms of x, is equal to

(A) x　(B) $2x$　(C) $3x$　(D) $4x$　(E) $5x$

7. If one * equals two !, and four ! equals five ♥, then what is the ratio * : ♥?

(A) $\frac{1}{4}$ (B) $\frac{1}{2}$ (C) $\frac{4}{1}$ (D) $\frac{5}{4}$ (E) $\frac{5}{2}$

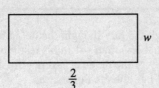

$\frac{2}{3}$

8. If the area of the rectangle above is equal to $\frac{1}{3}$, then $w =$

(A) $\frac{1}{2}$ (B) $\frac{2}{3}$ (C) 1   (D) $\frac{1}{3}$

(E) Cannot be determined from the information given.

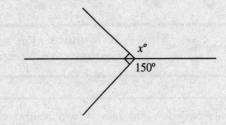

9. In the figure above, what is the value of x?

(A) 60   (B) 90   (C) 120   (D) 150   (E) 180

10. A cabin in the Catskills burns n gallons of oil each month in the winter. At this rate, g gallons of oil will supply c cabins for how many months?

(A) $\frac{g}{nc}$ (B) gnc (C) $\frac{nc}{g}$ (D) $\frac{ng}{c}$ (E) $\frac{n}{gc}$

IF YOU FINISH BEFORE TIME IS CALLED, YOU MAY CHECK YOUR WORK ON THIS SECTION ONLY. DO NOT WORK ON ANY OTHER SECTION IN THE TEST.   **S T O P**

497

Each sentence below has one or two blanks, each
blank indicating that something has been omitted.
Beneath the sentence are five lettered words or sets of
words. Choose the word or set of words that best fits
the meaning of the sentence as a whole.

Example:

Although its publicity has been ----, the film itself
is intelligent, well-acted, handsomely produced, and
altogether ----.

(A) tasteless..respectable
(B) extensive..moderate
(C) sophisticated..amateur
(D) risqué..crude
(E) perfect..spectacular

1. Although his dress is ----, in all other ways he seems
to be a perfectly normal man.

(A) ordinary   (B) mellifluous   (C) eccentric
(D) nondescript   (E) recalcitrant

2. In his private life he was quite ----; but he gave large
sums of money to charities, so most people thought
of him as a ----.

(A) pusillanimous..charlatan
(B) immodest..chauvinist
(C) flamboyant..savant
(D) sinister..mercenary
(E) miserly..philanthropist

3. The term *Indian* is a misnomer for the Native
American, introduced by Columbus and ---- by
historians.

(A) eradicated   (B) arbitrated   (C) infiltrated
(D) perpetuated   (E) coerced

4. She accepted her own misfortune with perfect ----, but
was outraged at any abuse or mistreatment of others.

(A) equanimity   (B) reluctance   (C) sincerity
(D) rabidity   (E) pulchritude

5. Although Mozart's music suggests a composer of
great ---- and seriousness, his letters imply that he
was naïve and ----.

(A) erudition..grave
(B) sophistication..uncouth
(C) fortitude..macabre
(D) levity..sanctimonious
(E) fragility..pensive

6. Although the jury thought the defendant had been
somewhat less than ---- in his testimony, the ----
summary of the defense attorney finally convinced
them of her client's innocence.

(A) interesting..lackluster
(B) candid..persuasive
(C) convincing..inordinate
(D) honest..confusing
(E) forthright..irrational

7. Conditions in the mine were ----, so the mine workers
refused to return to their jobs until the dangers were
----.

(A) hazardous..eliminated
(B) filthy..disbanded
(C) deplorable..collated
(D) conducive..ameliorated
(E) illegal..enhanced

8. Since the actor who played the lead was somewhat
----, the property manager had to let out the costumes and have the furniture used in the production
reinforced.

(A) winsome   (B) virulent   (C) fragile
(D) corpulent   (E) flirtatious

9. The guests invited to meet the famous critic were
---- by a charm which contrasted sharply with the
---- of his writing.

(A) appalled..inadequacy
(B) frustrated..wittiness
(C) deceived..elegance
(D) delighted..venom
(E) enthralled..lucidity

10. Many hours of practice are required of a successful
musician, so it is often not so much ---- as ---- which
distinguishes the professional from the amateur.

(A) talent..discipline
(B) money..education
(C) genius..understanding
(D) fortitude..mediocrity
(E) technique..pomposity

11. The statue was so ---- we found it ---- to view.

(A) repulsive..amusing
(B) delightful..burdensome
(C) grotesque..distressing
(D) warped..captivating
(E) precarious..shocking

12. My aunt is so ---- that you cannot have a short conversation with her; she prates on and on until your ears fall asleep.

    (A) garrulous
    (B) engaging
    (C) brusque
    (D) lilting
    (E) impaired

13. We were less impressed by the play's intricate ---- than we were by its difficult ----.

    (A) length..cast
    (B) theme..setting
    (C) authorship..performance
    (D) meaning..sense
    (E) plot..language

14. It seems ---- to us to dismiss the custodian without a ----.

    (A) obligatory..reason
    (B) reactionary..cause
    (C) formidable..worry
    (D) unethical..hearing
    (E) discourteous..demonstration

15. Without a good ----, fishing becomes an exercise in ----.

    (A) bait..sorrow
    (B) reason..futility
    (C) rod..frustration
    (D) prey..waiting
    (E) weather..dampness

Each question below consists of a related pair of words or phrases, followed by five lettered pairs of words or phrases. Select the lettered pair that best expresses a relationship similar to that expressed in the original pair

Example:

YAWN : BOREDOM::

(A) dream : sleep
(B) anger : madness
(C) smile : amusement
(D) face : expression
(E) impatience : rebellion

---

16. HONE : KNIFE::

    (A) tune : instrument
    (B) count : money
    (C) waste : energy
    (D) paint : brush
    (E) polish : glint

17. DETOUR : IMPASSE::

    (A) remove : residue
    (B) frequent : location
    (C) circumvent : obstacle
    (D) follow : leader
    (E) navigate : ship

18. CLOTH : THREADS::

    (A) wood : furniture
    (B) basket : reeds
    (C) cup : liquids
    (D) china : saucer
    (E) garden : walls

19. DOODLE : AIMLESSNESS::

    (A) revive : substantial
    (B) inform : success
    (C) blurt : planning
    (D) exile : competition
    (E) waver : indecision

20. SLANDER : PEJORATIVE::

    (A) ingratiate : miraculous
    (B) revere : condemning
    (C) extol : laudatory
    (D) ruminate : superficial
    (E) reward : grateful

21. JOURNEYMAN : APPRENTICE::

    (A) colleague : pedagogue
    (B) salesclerk : merchandise
    (C) veteran : rookie
    (D) voter : registration
    (E) champion : practice

22. UNFATHOMABLE : COMPREHEND::

    (A) gullible : distract
    (B) discreet : falsify
    (C) desired : obtain
    (D) untenable : maintain
    (E) secure : revolt

23. IMPULSIVE : SPONTANEITY::

    (A) overwrought : procrastination
    (B) succinct : brevity
    (C) ignoble : simultaneity
    (D) pretentious : modesty
    (E) fallow : fecundity

24. MAELSTROM : WHIRLPOOL::

    (A) catastrophe : reminder
    (B) horizon : crepuscule
    (C) tempest : delight
    (D) inferno : fire
    (E) explosion : concentration

25. AMBULATORY : MOBILITY::

    (A) cantankerous : foolishness
    (B) frolicsome : insight
    (C) venial : goodness
    (D) salubrious : decay
    (E) loquacious : speech

The passage below is followed by questions based on its content. Answer all questions following the passage on the basis of what is stated or implied in the passage.

Questions 26–35 are based on the following passage.

Frederick Douglass was born in slavery in 1817. He became one of the foremost leaders of the antislavery movement and one of the great philosophers of the nineteenth century. He wrote three autobiographies. This passage, depicting a character on the plantation where he once worked, is from My Bondage and My Freedom *(1855).*

Aunt Katy was a woman who never allowed herself to act greatly within the margin of power granted to her, no matter how broad that authority might be. Ambitious, ill-
Line tempered and cruel, she found in her present position an
(5) ample field for the exercise of her ill-omened qualities. She had a strong hold on old master—she was considered a first rate cook, and she really was very industrious. She was, therefore, greatly favored by old master, and as one mark of his favor, she was the only mother who was per-
(10) mitted to retain her children around her. Even to these children she was often fiendish in her brutality. She pursued her son Phil, one day, in my presence, with a huge butcher knife, and dealt a blow with its edge which left a shocking gash on his arm, near the wrist. For this, old
(15) master did sharply rebuke her, and threatened that if she ever should do the like again, he would take the skin off her back. Cruel, however, as Aunt Katy was to her own children, at times she was not destitute of maternal feeling, as I often had occasion to know, in the bitter pinches of
(20) hunger I had to endure. Differing from the practice of Col. Lloyd, old master, instead of allowing so much for each slave, committed the allowance for all to the care of Aunt Katy, to be divided after cooking it, amongst us. The allowance, consisting of coarse corn-meal, was not very
(25) abundant—indeed, it was very slender; and in passing through Aunt Katy's hands, it was made more slender still, for some of us. William, Phil and Jerry were her children, and it is not to accuse her too severely, to allege that she was often guilty of starving myself and the other children,
(30) while she was literally cramming her own. Want of food was my chief trouble the first summer at my old master's. Oysters and clams would do very well, with an occasional supply of bread, but they soon failed in the absence of bread. I speak but the simple truth when I say, I have often
(35) been so pinched with hunger, that I have fought with the dog—"Old Nep"—for the smallest crumbs that fell from the kitchen table, and have been glad when I won a single crumb in the combat. Many times have I followed, with eager step, the waiting-girl when she went out to shake the
(40) table cloth, to get the crumbs and small bones flung out for the cats. The water, in which meat had been boiled, was as eagerly sought for by me. It was a great thing to get the privilege of dipping a piece of bread in such water; and the skin from rusty bacon, was a positive luxury.
(45) Nevertheless, I sometimes got full meals and kind words from sympathizing old slaves, who knew my sufferings, and received the comforting assurance that I should be a man someday. "Never mind, honey—better day comin'," was even then a solace, a cheering consolation to me in
(50) my troubles.

26. The phrase "mark of his favor" (line 9) means
(A) scar from his whip
(B) remembrance
(C) prized token
(D) symbol of his power
(E) sign of his support

27. The phrase "take the skin off her back" (lines 16–17) means
(A) whip her
(B) remove her from the kitchen
(C) fire her
(D) send her out into the night
(E) take away her clothing

28. When Douglass says that Katy "was not destitute of maternal feeling" (line 18), he is being
(A) sympathetic
(B) ironic
(C) deliberately obtuse
(D) kind
(E) reflective

29. The word *committed* (line 22) is used to mean
(A) confined
(B) devoted
(C) swore
(D) promised
(E) assigned

30. How does Douglass feel about old master's practice of dividing food?
(A) It is fairer than the practice of Col. Lloyd.
(B) It is less fair than the practice of Col. Lloyd.
(C) It is fair only to adults.
(D) It is fair if one is careful.
(E) It is the only possible way to divide fairly.

31. When Douglass says "it is not to accuse her too severely" (line 28), he means
(A) he does not wish to accuse her
(B) the accusation is unfair
(C) he simply wants to chastise her gently
(D) she deserves no accusation
(E) the accusation is true

32. What is the purpose of Douglass's lists in lines 32–44?
(A) to express his hatred for Aunt Katy
(B) to illustrate his constant quest for food
(C) to show the poverty of the rural South
(D) to reveal his personal feelings about slavery
(E) to depict the life of a typical slave

500

33. In line 49, what is the best definition of *solace*?

    (A) distress
    (B) relief
    (C) comfort
    (D) calm
    (E) serenity

34. Why does Douglass include the words of the sympathizing slaves?

    (A) to prove that he was constantly misunderstood
    (B) to show that not all slaves were like Aunt Katy
    (C) to demonstrate that his life was not all misery
    (D) both A and B
    (E) both B and C

35. Which of the following would be a good title for this passage?

    (A) "Life on the Plantation"
    (B) "Old Master and Me"
    (C) "Aunt Katy Gets Her Revenge"
    (D) "The Power of Aunt Katy"
    (E) "A Dog's Life"

IF YOU FINISH BEFORE TIME IS CALLED, YOU MAY CHECK YOUR WORK ON THIS SECTION ONLY. DO NOT WORK ON ANY OTHER SECTION IN THE TEST. **STOP**

6 6 6 6 6 6 6 6 6 6 6 6 6

Reference:

Circle: Rectangle: Rectangular Solid: Cylinder: Triangle:

$C = 2\pi r$
$A = \pi r^2$

$A = lw$

$V = lwh$

$V = \pi r^2 h$

$A = \frac{1}{2}bh$

$a^2 + b^2 = c^2$

- The measure in degrees of a straight angle is 180.
- The number of degrees of arc in a circle is 360.
- The sum of the measures of the angles of a triangle is 180.

Notes: The figures accompanying the problems are drawn as accurately as possible unless otherwise stated in specific problems. Again, unless otherwise stated, all figures lie in the same plane. All numbers used in these problems are real numbers. Calculators are permitted for this test.

Directions for Quantitative Comparison Questions

Questions 1–15 each consist of two quantities, one in Column A and one in Column B. You are to compare the two quantities and on the answer sheet fill in oval

- A if the quantity in Column A is greater;
- B if the quantity in Column B is greater;
- C if the two quantities are equal;
- D if the relationship cannot be determined from the information given.

AN E RESPONSE WILL NOT BE SCORED.

	EXAMPLES		
	Column A	Column B	Answers
E1.	2×6	$2 + 6$	● Ⓑ Ⓒ Ⓓ Ⓔ
E2.	$180 - x$	y	Ⓐ Ⓑ ● Ⓓ Ⓔ
E3.	$p - q$	$q - p$	Ⓐ Ⓑ Ⓒ ● Ⓔ

Notes:

1. In certain questions, information concerning one or both of the quantities to be compared is centered above the two columns.
2. In a given question, a symbol that appears in both columns represents the same thing in Column A as it does in Column B.
3. Letters such as x, n, and k stand for real numbers.

GO ON TO THE NEXT PAGE

	Column A	Column B

1. $\dfrac{1}{7} - \dfrac{1}{8}$ | $\dfrac{1}{56}$

---

n is a negative integer.

2. $n + n + n + n$ | $n \times n \times n \times n$

$$x = \dfrac{1}{3}$$
$$y = \dfrac{1}{6}$$

3. $\dfrac{x}{y}$ | $\dfrac{y}{x}$

The cost of three apples and two pears is $2.50.

4. The cost of one apple | The cost of one pear

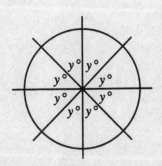

5. The value of x | The value of y

Cheese costs $2.00 per pound.

6. The amount of cheese that can be purchased for $1.50 | $\dfrac{3}{5}$ pound

---

Rectangular solid x has a volume of 24.
Rectangular solid y has a volume of 20.

7. Area of the base of x | Area of the base of y

---

8. $\sqrt{9}$ | $\sqrt{6} + \sqrt{3}$

---

9. Surface area of a sphere with radius 1 | Area of a circle with radius 1

$$2x^2 + 4x + 3 = 0$$

10. $2x^2 + 4x$ | -3

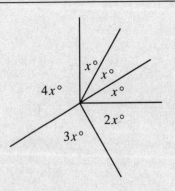

11. 30 | x

GO ON TO THE NEXT PAGE

503

	Column A	Column B		Column A	Column B

Questions 12–13

For $n \neq 0$, $\boxed{n} = n - \dfrac{2}{n}$

| 12. | $\boxed{-3}$ | -3 |

| 13. | $\boxed{2}$ | $-\dfrac{1}{2}$ |

14.

| $(a - b)(a + c)$ | $a(a + c) - b(a + c)$ |

$S_1 = \{3, 6, 9, 12, 15, 18\}$

$S_2 = \{4, 8, 12, 16, 20, 24\}$

15.

| The sum of any three different numbers from S_1 | The sum of any three different numbers from S_2 |

GO ON TO THE NEXT PAGE

Directions for Student-Produced Response Questions

Questions 16–25 each require you to solve a problem and mark your answer on a special answer grid. For each question, you should write your answer in the boxes at the top of each column and then fill in the ovals beneath each answer you write. Here are some examples.

Answer: 3/4 (= .75; show answer either way)

Answer: 325

Note: A mixed number such as 3½ must be gridded as 7/2 or as 3.5. If gridded as "31/2," it will be read as "thirty-one halves."

Note: Either position is correct.

16. If $n + 1 + n + 2 + n + 3 = 1 + 2 + 3$, then $n = ?$

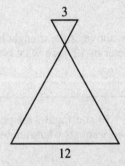

18. If the two triangles above are equilateral, what is the ratio of the perimeter of the smaller to that of the larger?

17. If 5 pounds of coffee cost $12, how much coffee can be purchased for $30?

19. If x and y are positive integers such that $x^2 + y^2 = 10$, then $xy = ?$

GO ON TO THE NEXT PAGE

20. If $\frac{1}{3}$ of a number is 2 more than $\frac{1}{5}$ of the number, then what is the number?

23. At the first stop on her route, a driver unloaded $\frac{2}{5}$ of the packages in her van. After she unloaded another three packages at her next stop, $\frac{1}{2}$ of the original number of packages in the van remained. How many packages were in the van before the first delivery?

24. If S is 150 percent of T, then T is what percent of $S + T$?

21. In the figure above, if the triangle is equilateral and has a perimeter of 12, then what is the perimeter of the square?

22. If $5x + 3y = 19$ and x and y are positive whole numbers, then y equals what number?

25. The large wooden cube above is composed of 27 smaller cubes. If the entire surface of the large cube is painted red, then how many of the smaller cubes will have exactly two red faces?

IF YOU FINISH BEFORE TIME IS CALLED, YOU MAY CHECK YOUR WORK ON THIS SECTION ONLY. DO NOT WORK ON ANY OTHER SECTION IN THE TEST. **S T O P**

Answer Key

SECTION 1

1. E	11. D	21. E	31. C
2. B	12. C	22. E	32. D
3. C	13. E	23. A	33. C
4. B	14. A	24. D	34. E
5. A	15. A	25. D	35. D
6. C	16. B	26. D	
7. B	17. A	27. D	
8. D	18. C	28. C	
9. E	19. B	29. A	
10. B	20. D	30. A	

SECTION 2

1. A	11. B	21. D
2. E	12. C	22. B
3. C	13. C	23. E
4. E	14. B	24. A
5. E	15. D	25. E
6. C	16. C	
7. D	17. B	
8. C	18. E	
9. D	19. A	
10. B	20. E	

SECTION 3

1. C
2. E
3. C
4. C
5. A
6. D
7. D
8. E
9. E
10. A

SECTION 4

1. B
2. E
3. D
4. C
5. B
6. D
7. E
8. A
9. C
10. A

SECTION 5

1. C	11. C	21. C	31. E
2. E	12. A	22. D	32. B
3. D	13. E	23. B	33. C
4. A	14. D	24. D	34. E
5. B	15. C	25. E	35. D
6. B	16. A	26. E	
7. A	17. C	27. A	
8. D	18. B	28. B	
9. D	19. E	29. E	
10. A	20. C	30. B	

SECTION 6

1. C	11. C	21. 16
2. B	12. A	22. 3
3. A	13. B	23. 30
4. D	14. C	24. 40
5. A	15. D	25. 12
6. A	16. 0	
7. D	17. 12.5	
8. B	18. 1/4	
9. A	19. 3	
10. C	20. 15	

Explanatory Answers

SECTION 1

CRITICAL READING

1. The word *aboriginal* (line 3) is used to mean

   (A) ancient
   (B) primitive
   (C) living
   (D) elementary
   (E) native

   (E) This is a vocabulary-in-context question. Take the five suggested responses and plug them into line 3. (A), (B), and even (D) might be considered synonyms for *aboriginal*, but only (E) is a synonym that makes sense.

2. Why does Darwin mention the distance between the islands and the mainland (line 7)?

   (A) They are not far apart, and may once have been connected.
   (B) They are far apart, but their animals seem related.
   (C) They are close enough to swim between.
   (D) They are far apart, but they look very similar.
   (E) They are too distant ever to have been connected.

   (B) This is a main idea of the essay: The Galapagos contain some animals that are native and others that seem very like those on the mainland—despite the fact that the mainland is hundreds of miles away. No suggestion of connection (A or E) is made, nor are the appearances compared (D). Nobody can swim 500 or 600 miles (C).

3. Darwin mentions a native mouse in the Pampas (line 25) to

   (A) explain his theory of natural selection
   (B) prove that mice are indigenous to all islands
   (C) support the idea that mice may be transported
   (D) show how many species are found in South America
   (E) report on an unusual indigenous species

   (C) Since mice can clearly be found anywhere, even in the roof of a hovel miles from anywhere, they might easily find their way onto ships and be transported.

4. What does the word *analogous* in line 27 mean?

   (A) divergent
   (B) comparable
   (C) disparate
   (D) conventional
   (E) unique

   (B) Answers (A), (C), and (E) are antonyms for *analogous*. Plugging *comparable* into line 27, you see that Dr. Richardson has seen comparable things, and, therefore, Darwin's observations are supported.

5. When Darwin says that reptiles give "striking character" to the islands, he means that

   (A) they are unusual
   (B) they are dangerous
   (C) they are beautiful
   (D) both A and B
   (E) both B and C

   (A) For all interpretation questions that are posed in this format, it is wise to look at all the choices before selecting a response. Darwin speaks of the unusual nature of the fauna (A), but never refers to their beauty (C). He certainly never says that the reptiles are dangerous (B). Since (B) and (C) are knocked out, only (A) fits.

6. How does Darwin feel about the lack of frogs?

   (A) He is worried.
   (B) He is unsurprised.
   (C) He finds it curious.
   (D) He is doubtful.
   (E) He finds it unexplainable.

   (C) This evaluation question can be answered easily if you quickly review lines 41–64, where Darwin speaks of the lack of frogs. He says outright that he is surprised (line 41), and goes on to speculate on the reasons. Since he gives some possible reasons, we cannot say that he finds the lack *unexplainable* (E); *curious* (C) is as far as we can go.

7. How do lines 33–36 support Darwin's opening paragraph?

   (A) They explain why the creatures of the Galapagos deserve attention.
   (B) They refer to some animals that are aboriginal and others that are found in South America.
   (C) They refer to the distance between the islands and the mainland.
   (D) They show how the inhabitants of different islands differ.
   (E) They do not support the opening paragraph.

   (B) Reread lines 33–36, and then compare them to the opening paragraph. Lines 33–36 refer to lizards, two of which are aboriginal and one of which is a South American genus. This compares nicely to Darwin's opening observation that many species are indigenous, but many resemble those found on the mainland.

8. When Darwin says "none of this family" (line 45), he is referring to

   (A) the Darwins
   (B) reptiles
   (C) *Psammophis temminckii*
   (D) toads and frogs
   (E) none of the above

   (D) Toads and frogs are, of course, not precisely in the same "family" as we understand the scientific term—to be honest, toads are not even reptiles. Nevertheless, it is to frogs and toads that Darwin refers in line 41, and to which he again refers when he cites Bory St. Vincent a few lines later.

9. An *archipelago* (line 49) is

   (A) a stream
   (B) a continent
   (C) an ice cap
   (D) a small bay
   (E) an island chain

   (E) If you do not know the term, use trial and error to test each response. Neither a stream (A) nor a small bay (D) could support "large islands." You know that there is no continent (B) named "Sandwich," and *ice cap* (C) makes no sense. Only (E) works in context.

10. Why does Darwin mention Mauritius (line 49)?

    (A) to show that frogs appear on the mainland
    (B) to show that frogs turn up on some islands
    (C) to show that toads prefer temperate climates
    (D) both A and B
    (E) both B and C

    (B) This synthesis/analysis question asks you to understand the author's reasoning and structure. Darwin introduces Mauritius as "an apparent exception" to his previous remarks on the lack of frogs; in other words, he uses that island to show that frogs do indeed turn up on some islands. Nothing is said about Mauritius's climate (C), and if it were part of the mainland (A), Mauritius could not be considered an exception to the lack-of-frogs-on-islands rule.

11. In the last sentence, Darwin intends to

    (A) reveal a fact
    (B) recall a detail
    (C) express an emotion
    (D) propose a theory
    (E) relate an event

    (D) Darwin asks a question of his readers in the last sentence: Could the fact that lizards are everywhere but frogs are not be caused by a difference in the transportability of their eggs? This is clearly a theory that has yet to be tested. It cannot be considered a fact (A).

12. You would expect the next few paragraphs of this essay to deal with

    (A) birds of the Galapagos
    (B) other islands
    (C) details about reptiles
    (D) details of the voyage
    (E) facts about mice

    (C) This synthesis/analysis question requires you to look at the whole excerpt and make a prediction. (B) is unlikely, since the piece is primarily about the Galapagos. (D) seems off the track, and (E) has already been covered. You might guess (A) if it were not for a big clue in line 40: Darwin says that there are two or three species of tortoises, "as we shall presently show." Apparently, he will go on discussing reptiles.

SENTENCE COMPLETIONS

13. Portraits painted in Colonial America are quite charming but ---- and demonstrate the isolation of the American painter; they show little or no ---- of the development of painting in Europe.

    (A) grotesque..concern
    (B) frivolous..affirmation
    (C) deliberate..domination
    (D) sophisticated..consideration
    (E) primitive..knowledge

(E) There are two logical clues in the sentence. In the first clause, we have a reversal: "charming but ——." So the first word of the correct choice will complete a contrast. Then the entire second clause extends and explains the idea presented in the first clause. You can eliminate (C) and (D) because they do not provide a contrast with *charming*. The first words of the other choices are possibilities, so we examine their second elements.

You can eliminate (B) because "affirmation of the development of painting" is not a meaningful phrase. As for (A), although *grotesque* contrasts with "charming," the idea of grotesqueness does not set up a thought to be explained by the second clause. The fact that American painters were not concerned with European painting doesn't explain why American painting might have been grotesque. This is why (E) is correct. American painting was primitive because American painters were ignorant of European painting.

14. Although leprosy is not a highly contagious disease, those who have contracted it have always been pariahs and ---- by others.

   (A) ostracized   (B) accepted   (C) sheltered
   (D) admonished   (E) lauded

   (A) This question is pretty much a test of vocabulary. The last part of the sentence (including the blank) is an explanation of what it means to be a pariah. A pariah is an outcast, so (A) must be the correct choice.

15. Although the novel was generally boring and awkwardly written, there were ---- passages of power and lyricism which hinted at the author's ----.

   (A) occasional..potential
   (B) frequent..malevolence
   (C) static..style
   (D) ill-conceived..superficiality
   (E) contrived..ignorance

   (A) There are several ways to attack this question. You can eliminate both (C) and (E) on the grounds that their first elements, when substituted into the passage, don't create meaningful phrases. Next, the *although* sets up a contrast between "generally boring and awkwardly written" and "---- passages of power and lyricism," the former a negative judgment and the latter a positive judgment. On this ground, you can eliminate (B). To create a contrast, the good parts must have been relatively few. (D) also fails to provide a contrast. If the passage were ill-conceived, then the second idea would reinforce the first, rather than contrast with it.

16. Since the doctor could not find anything physically wrong with his patient, he decided to administer a ---- as a way to ---- him.

   (A) remedy..controvert
   (B) placebo..placate
   (C) warning..mortify
   (D) dictum..provoke
   (E) malady..supervise

   (B) If you attack this question at the level of idiom, you can probably eliminate (A), (C), (D), and (E) as unlikely choices. None of the four creates a meaningful phrase when its first element is substituted into the sentence. Beyond that, there are two keys to this question. One, *although*, signals a thought-reversal. The first blank must create a contrast with the doctor's inability to find a physical ailment. And only (B) provides the needed contrast. Two, the second blank must create a phrase that will reinforce the idea introduced by the first blank, which (B) does.

17. Although some evidence ---- that *The Iliad* and *The Odyssey* were not written by a single person, the unity of artistic vision and general ---- of the epics prove otherwise.

   (A) suggests..coherence
   (B) indicates..magnitude
   (C) proclaims..demeanor
   (D) implies..torpor
   (E) hints..lassitude

   (A) At the level of word usage, if you know the vocabulary, you can eliminate (C), (D), and (E). An epic, which is a work of literature, is not going to have demeanor or torpor or lassitude. Beyond that, the *although* introduces a contrast. The evidence suggests or indicates something, but that conclusion is contradicted by the unity and "——" of the works. The size of the work might have some bearing on the issue, but *coherence* is a better choice because it reinforces the idea of "unity."

ANALOGIES

18. PAINTER : STUDIO::

   (A) composer : piano
   (B) teacher : faculty
   (C) judge : courtroom
   (D) golfer : club
   (E) stage : theater

   (C) This analogy is based on a "place" connection. Your sentence might read "A PAINTER'S place of work is a STUDIO, and a *judge's* place of work is a *courtroom*." (A) is perhaps the most troubling wrong answer. It is true that a *composer* might use a *piano*, but there is no necessity to the relationship. It is not part of the definition of *piano* that it is an instrument used for *composing*, but it is a part of the definition of STUDIO that it is a room used for things like *painting*. Additionally, there is a confirming secondary relationship between STUDIO and *courtroom*; both are rooms.

19. SIGH : LONGING::

(A) anger : impatience
(B) laughter : joy
(C) boredom : hostility
(D) grimace : face
(E) stare : eyes

(B) This analogy is based on the "sign of" relationship. A SIGH is a sign of LONGING, and *laughter* is a sign of *joy*. None of the other pairs makes sense in this diagnostic sentence.

20. MARCHING : HALT::

(A) eating : swallow
(B) driving : turn
(C) humming : shout
(D) flying : land
(E) tracking : ensnare

(D) This analogy is based on an "interruption of a process" connection. Adjusting the parts of speech to make the analogy easier to describe, your DXS might say "A HALT interrupts MARCHING, and a *landing* interrupts *flying*." Two of the wrong choices are a bit troubling. First, (E). The problem with (E) is that *ensnaring* is not the interruption of *tracking* but the outcome of *tracking*. Second, (A). *Swallowing* is part of *eating*, not an interruption of eating. And you might try the technique of improving answers to eliminate (A). (A) would be more nearly correct if it were "chewing : swallow."

21. RUTHLESS : COMPASSION::

(A) verbose : conversation
(B) mature : offspring
(C) animated : interest
(D) sublime : perfection
(E) lethargic : energy

(E) This analogy is based on the "lack of" connection. Adjusting the parts of speech to make our DXS read more smoothly, we might say that RUTHLESSNESS is characterized by a lack of COMPASSION and *lethargy* is characterized by a lack of *energy*.

22. LEOPARD : CAT::

(A) zebra : zoo
(B) hawk : prey
(C) parrot : jungle
(D) monkey : chimpanzee
(E) chameleon : lizard

(E) This analogy is based on the "is a type of" connection. A LEOPARD is a type of CAT, and a *chameleon* is a type of *lizard*.

23. ANGER : RABID::

(A) hunger : ravenous
(B) concern : careless
(C) modernity : contemporary
(D) petulance : mournful
(E) wisdom : hoary

(A) This analogy is based on a relationship of degree. To be RABID is to be ANGRY in the extreme, and to be *ravenous* is to be *hungry* in the extreme.

24. BLAMEWORTHY : REPROACH::

(A) recalcitrant : praise
(B) humorous : approval
(C) sympathetic : rejection
(D) meritorious : reward
(E) noxious : censure

(D) This analogy is based on the "defining characteristic" connection, but getting a correctly formulated sentence is a little tricky: Something that is *rewarded* is *meritorious*, and something that is REPROACHED is BLAMEWORTHY.

25. PEDESTRIAN : ORIGINALITY::

(A) monotonous : compulsion
(B) ethereal : mysticism
(C) reclusive : misanthropy
(D) indulgent : forbearance
(E) timorous : cowardice

(D) The analogy relationship here is "lack of"; the analogy itself is fairly simple, but the vocabulary is difficult. PEDESTRIAN means lacking in ORIGINALITY. So something that is pedestrian is lacking in originality, and someone who is *indulgent* is lacking in *forbearance*.

CRITICAL READING

26. What does Bashkirtseff mean by "truth to nature" (line 2)?

(A) fidelity
(B) ecology
(C) drama
(D) realism
(E) instinct

(D) As with any interpretation question, you must test the choices against the cited line. Bashkirtseff is discussing Maupassant's style—he copies "truth to nature" with "religious fidelity"; in other words, he is realistic. Fidelity (A) is not enough; it has too many possible meanings.

27. How does Bashkirtseff feel about Maupassant's work?

(A) It is remarkably true to life.
(B) It reveals human feelings wonderfully.
(C) It inspires religious fervor.
(D) both A and B
(E) both B and C

(D) Any question in this format requires you to look at all the possible answers before choosing one. This is an evaluation question and since Bashkirtseff is fairly open about her opinions, it is not difficult to discern her feelings. Line 2 has to do with Maupassant's fidelity to nature (A); line 4 states that he moves his readers by "touches of feeling so profoundly human" (B). Since both A and B are correct, the answer must be (D). To choose (C) is to misread the first paragraph.

28. The phrase "in the main" (line 7) means

(A) strongly
(B) at sea
(C) essentially
(D) part time
(E) authoritatively

(C) Bashkirtseff is amused at her own compliment, but in her amusement, she wants to make sure that Maupassant understands her sincerity. Test the answer choices in place of the phrase in line 7, and you will see that only (C) makes sense in context.

29. The word *confidant* (line 12) most closely means

(A) friend
(B) confessor
(C) poised
(D) adversary
(E) positive

(A) You might be led astray by the relationship between *confide* and *confidant*, and, in fact, *confidant* implies a friend in whom one can confide. This does not mean a *confessor* (B), who is not necessarily a friend. (D) is an antonym; (C) and (E) are synonyms for *confidence*.

30. Why does Bashkirtseff mention the *Gaulois*?

(A) to explain her decision to write
(B) to show that she is well-read
(C) to amuse her reader
(D) to compare herself to other admirers
(E) to report on a review she disliked

(A) Bashkirtseff was not willing to write until she became jealous on seeing an article in the *Gaulois*. She may well relate this to amuse Maupassant (C), but her *main* purpose is to explain her decision to write to him (A).

31. The word *countenance* (line 30) means

(A) air
(B) restraint
(C) appearance
(D) purity
(E) endorsement

(C) (A) and (E) are also synonyms for *countenance*, but they have meanings that do not fit the context. (B) and (D) are synonyms for *continence*. Bashkirtseff is comically insisting on remaining anonymous because she might not like Maupassant's looks.

32. By "sweet reflection" (line 34), Bashkirtseff means

(A) religious meditation
(B) novel idea
(C) innocent dream
(D) pleasing image
(E) pool of tears

(D) Test the choices to find the answer to this interpretation question. Bashkirtseff announces that she is charming in hopes that this "sweet reflection" will encourage Maupassant to write back. Although the other choices include several meanings of *reflection*, only (D) works in context.

33. The word *epistolary* (line 37) is used to mean

(A) violent
(B) remote
(C) written
(D) imaginary
(E) clinical

(C) *Epistolary* is, of course, based on *epistle*, or "letter." When Bashkirtseff says that she would "wish to hold no communication, not even an epistolary one," she means that she would not even wish to communicate in writing.

34. Why does the writer sign the name "Miss Hastings"?

(A) It is her real name.
(B) Maupassant loves Englishwomen.
(C) She is writing in haste.
(D) Maupassant knows a Miss Hastings.
(E) She wishes to remain anonymous.

(E) Bashkirtseff vows that she will "always preserve my incognito" (line 28)—always remain anonymous. You know from the introduction that (A) is untrue, there is no support for (B) or (D), and (C) is just absurd.

35. The general tone of the letter is

(A) awestruck
(B) respectful
(C) somber
(D) breezy
(E) curt

(D) Considering that it is a cross between a fan letter and a love letter, this letter is remarkable in its carefree wit. Examples of this include line 12 ("always supposing your soul to be beautiful"), line 26 ("your literary merits dazzled me anew"), and line 32 ("two essential points, even for a distant adoration").

SECTION 2

MATH PROBLEM-SOLVING

1. If $\dfrac{1}{x} + \dfrac{1}{x} = 8$, then $x =$

   (A) $\dfrac{1}{4}$ (B) $\dfrac{1}{2}$ (C) 1 (D) 2 (E) 4

   (A) Here you have a single equation with one variable, so you might as well solve for x:

   $$\frac{1}{x} + \frac{1}{x} = 8$$

   $$\frac{2}{x} = 8$$

   $$x = \frac{1}{4}$$

   Or, you might have reasoned that $\frac{1}{x}$ and $\frac{1}{x}$ are equal, and since their sum is 8, $\frac{1}{x}$ must be 4. So the value of x must be $\frac{1}{4}$. And, of course, you could have substituted numbers, but this is such a simple equation, one of the two techniques just described is more effective.

2. If $x = 2$ and $y = -1$, then $3x - 4y =$
   (A) -5 (B) -1 (C) 0 (D) 2 (E) 10

   (E) This question asks that you evaluate the expression $3x - 4y$. It requires only a simple calculation, so the correct approach is just to do it:
   $3x - 4y = 3(2) - 4(-1) = 6 - (-4) = 6 + 4 = 10$

3. In a certain school, there are 600 boys and 400 girls. If 20 percent of the boys and 30 percent of the girls are on the honor roll, how many of the students are on the honor roll?

   (A) 120 (B) 175 (C) 240 (D) 250 (E) 280

   (C) This question asks about percents. You must take a percent of a number:

   20% of 600 boys = 120 boys on the honor roll
   30% of 400 girls = 120 girls on the honor roll
   120 boys + 120 girls = 240 students on the honor roll

4. If $p, q, r, s,$ and t are whole numbers, the expression $t(r(p + q) + s))$ *must* be an even number when which of the five numbers is even?

   (A) p (B) q (C) r (D) s (E) t

   (E) This question tests the even and odd properties of numbers. Since an even number times any other whole number yields an even number, the correct answer is (E). None of the other letters guarantees an even result. If this insight escapes you, you can experiment with some values. For each letter, assume that the letter only is even and that all other numbers are odd. Only t generates an even result under those circumstances.

RESULTS OF BIOLOGY PROJECT CONDUCTED BY STUDENT X					
Week	1	2	3	4	5
Number of Flies in Bottle	3	12	48	192	

5. A student conducting a lab experiment finds that the population of flies in a bottle increases by a certain multiple from week to week. If the pattern shown in the table continues, how many flies can the student expect to find in the bottle in week 5?

   (A) 195 (B) 240 (C) 384 (D) 448 (E) 768

   (E) This is a long question but not that difficult. You must see that the number of flies in each successive week is 4 times the number of the previous week. So the final count should be $4 \times 192 = 768$.

6. Three students are each scheduled to give a short speech at an assembly. In how many different orders can the speeches by scheduled?

   (A) 12 (B) 9 (C) 6 (D) 4 (E) 3

   (C) At first you might think you need a fancy mathematical formula to solve this question. And, in fact, there is a branch of mathematics that studies such problems. (The procedures are called permutations and combinations.) But you don't need any special knowledge to answer this question. Assume that the three speakers are A, B, and C, and count on your fingers the number of possible orders: ABC, ACB, BAC, BCA, CAB, CBA.

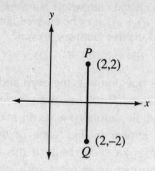

7. If points P and Q lie in the xy-plane and have the coordinates shown above, what is the midpoint of PQ?

(A) $(-2,0)$ (B) $(-2,2)$ (C) $(0,2)$
(D) $(2,0)$ (E) $(2,2)$

(D) This question tests basic coordinate geometry. Since the x coordinate of both points is 2, the line runs parallel to the y axis. The x coordinate of the midpoint will also be 2. As for the y coordinate, the midpoint is halfway between 2 and -2, which is zero.

8. If xy is positive, which of the following CANNOT be true?

(A) $x > y > 0$
(B) $y > x > 0$
(C) $x > 0 > y$
(D) $0 > x > y$
(E) $0 > y > x$

(C) This question tests the positive and negative properties of numbers. If xy is positive, then x and y both have the same sign. They might both be positive, or they might both be negative. And it doesn't make any difference which is larger. So (A), (B), (D), and (E) can all be true. x and y cannot, however, have different signs, because a positive times a negative yields a negative result. And, of course, you could have tried substituting numbers. If $x > 0 > y$, then x could be 1 and y could be -1, and $1 \times -1 = -1$.

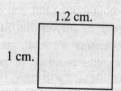

1.2 cm.

1 cm.

9. In the scale drawing of the floor of a rectangular room shown above, the scale used was 1 centimeter = 4 meters. What is the actual area, in square meters, of the floor of the room?

(A) 9.6 (B) 13.6 (C) 15 (D) 19.2 (E) 38.4

(D) Just convert the dimensions shown to real dimensions. Since 1 centimeter is equal to 4 meters, the width of the room is 4 meters, and the length is 4.8. So the area of the room is $4 \times 4.8 = 19.2$.

10. If $30,000 \times 20 = 6 \times 10n$, then $n =$

(A) 4 (B) 5 (C) 6 (D) 7 (E) 8

(B) This question tests powers. $30,000 \times 20 = 600,000 = 6 \times 10^5$. (One power of ten for each zero.)

11. Karen purchased a total of 4 pounds of candy, some of which was chocolates and some of which was caramels. If chocolates cost $3 per pound and caramels cost $2 per pound, and Karen spent a total of $10, how many pounds of chocolates did she buy?

(A) 1 (B) 2 (C) 2.5 (D) 3 (E) 3.5

(B) You can solve this problem with simultaneous equations. Let x be the quantity of chocolates and y the quantity of caramels.

$x + y = 4$ and $3x + 2y = 10$
$y = 4 - x$
$3x + 2(4 - x) = 10$
$3x + 8 - 2x = 10$
$x = 10 - 8 = 2$

Or, you can test the answers starting with (C). If Karen bought 2.5 pounds of chocolates, she bought $4 - 2.5 = 1.5$ pounds of caramels and the total cost would be $(2.5 \times 3) + (1.5 \times 2) = 7.50 + 3 = \$10.50$. Too much money and wrong. Since chocolates are more expensive than caramels, Karen bought less than 2.5 pounds of chocolates. So try (B): 2 pounds of chocolates and 2 pounds of caramels would cost $(2 \times 3) + (2 \times 2) = 10$. (B) is correct.

12. The average (arithmetic mean) of Al's scores on three tests was 80. If the average of his scores on the first two tests was also 80, what was his score on the third test?

(A) 90 (B) 85 (C) 80 (D) 75
(E) Cannot be determined from the information given.

(C) You can use the procedure you learned for finding a missing element of an average. The total of all three numbers is $3 \times 80 = 240$. The total of the two numbers you know is $2 \times 80 = 160$. So the missing number is $240 - 160 = 80$. Or, you might have used the "above and below" method. Since 80 is neither above nor below the average, the first two 80s are equal to the average, so the final number can be neither above nor below the average. It must be 80.

13. A book contains ten photographs, some in color and some in black-and-white. Each of the following could be the ratio of color to black-and-white photographs EXCEPT

(A) 9:1 (B) 4:1 (C) 5:2 (D) 3:2 (E) 1:1

(C) This question tests your understanding of ratio parts. The total number of ratio parts in the ratio 5:2 is 7, and 10 is not evenly divisible by 7.

14. If $\frac{4}{5} = \frac{x}{4}$, then $x =$

(A) 5 (B) $\frac{16}{5}$ (C) $\frac{5}{4}$ (D) $\frac{4}{5}$ (E) $\frac{5}{16}$

(B) You can treat this equation as a proportion. Cross-multiply and solve for x:

$$\frac{4}{5} = \frac{x}{4}$$
$$4(4) = 5x$$
$$x = \frac{16}{5}$$

Yes, you could have substituted numbers here, and it is good to see that as a possibility. But substitution would have taken much more time than simply solving for x.

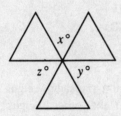

15. In the figure above, three equilateral triangles have a common vertex. $x + y + z =$

(A) 60 (B) 90 (C) 120 (D) 180 (E) 240

(D) Let us label the unlabelled angles:

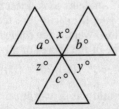

Since the measure of the degrees in a circle is 360, the sum of x, y, and z plus the sum of a, b, and c is 360. What is the value of the angles inside the triangles? Since those are equilateral triangles, each of the angles is 60°.

$$3(60) + x + y + z = 360$$
$$x + y + z = 180$$

Or, you could have guesstimated the size of x, y, and z. Each one appears to be about 60°, so they should total about 180°. (D) is the only choice close to 180, so it must be correct.

16. Peter spent $\frac{1}{4}$ of his allowance on Monday and $\frac{1}{3}$ of the *remainder* on Tuesday. What part of the allowance does Peter still have?

(A) $\frac{1}{12}$ (B) $\frac{1}{4}$ (C) $\frac{1}{2}$ (D) $\frac{3}{4}$ (E) $\frac{11}{12}$

(C) This is just an exercise in multiplying fractions. If Peter spent $\frac{1}{4}$ of his allowance on Monday, he had $\frac{3}{4}$ of his allowance left. Then, he spent $\frac{1}{3}$ of that $\frac{3}{4}$ on Tuesday: $\frac{1}{3}$ of $\frac{3}{4} = \frac{1}{3} \times \frac{3}{4} = \frac{1}{4}$. After spending the additional $\frac{1}{4}$, he has left $\frac{3}{4} - \frac{1}{4} = \frac{1}{2}$ of the original allowance. Of course, you could have substituted numbers, but the arithmetic would have been the same.

17. If 100 identical bricks weigh p pounds, then in terms of p, 20 of these bricks weigh how many pounds?

(A) $\frac{p}{20}$ (B) $\frac{p}{5}$ (C) $20p$ (D) $\frac{5}{p}$ (E) $\frac{20}{p}$

(B) There are three ways of arriving at the solution. The simplest and most direct is to reason that if 100 bricks weigh p pounds, 20 bricks, which is $\frac{1}{5}$ of 100, must weigh $\frac{1}{5}$ of p.

This same reasoning can be expressed using a direct proportion. The more bricks, the greater the weight, so

$$\frac{100}{20} = \frac{p}{x}$$
$$100x = 20p$$
$$x = \frac{20p}{100} = \frac{p}{5}$$

Finally, you could have substituted numbers. Assume that 100 bricks weigh 100 pounds, which is 1 pound apiece. 20 bricks weigh 20 pounds. On the assumption that $p = 100$, the correct formula will generate the number 20.

18. If the distances between points P, Q, and R are equal, which of the following could be true?

    I. P, Q, and R are points on a circle with center O
    II. P and Q are points on a circle with center R
    III. P, Q, and R are vertices on an equilateral triangle.

    (A) I only   (B) I and II only   (C) I and III only
    (C) II and III only   (E) I, II, and III

(E) The following drawings show that I, II, and III are possible.

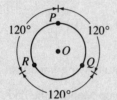 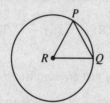

The thing to watch out for here is the Watson blunder. Both I and III are fairly obvious possibilities; II is more subtle. Since this is a problem of above-average difficulty, there must be something more to it than just I and III.

	Year					
	1950	1955	1960	1965	1970	1975
Price of a certain Item	$2	$4	$7	$12	$20	$30

19. In the table above, the percent increase in the price of the item was greatest during which of the following periods?

    (A) 1950–1955   (B) 1955–1960   (C) 1960–1965
    (D) 1965–1970   (E) 1970–1975

(A) This problem can be solved with the "change-over" principle. But, you object, that is five different calculations. True, so look for an escape route: approximation. The percent increase in the period 1950–1955 was $\frac{(4-2)}{2} = 100$ percent. For the next period it was $\frac{3}{4}$, which is less than 100 percent. For the next, $\frac{5}{7}$, which is less than 100 percent. For the next, $\frac{8}{12} = \frac{2}{3}$, which is less than 100 percent. And for the last it was $\frac{10}{20}$, 50 percent less than 100 percent. So the correct answer is (A).

20. For any integer n, which of the following represents three consecutive odd integers?

    (A) $n, n + 1, n + 2$
    (B) $n, n + 1, n + 3$
    (C) $n, n + 2, n + 4$
    (D) $2n + 1, 2n + 2, 2n + 3$
    (E) $2n + 1, 2n + 3, 2n + 5$

(E) This question tests properties of numbers. You can eliminate (A), (B), and (C) because n might or might not be odd (n can be any integer). $2n + 1$, however, must be odd. ($2n$ is even, so $2n + 1$ is odd.) Then the next odd integer will be 2 more, or $2n + 3$, and the next 2 more than that, or $2n + 5$.

Or you could have substituted numbers. Of course, if you pick an odd number for substitution, (C) and (E) both work, in which case you should try another number—hopefully an even number.

21. Two cartons weigh $3x - 2$ and $2x - 3$. If the average weight of the cartons is 10, the heavier carton weighs how much more than the lighter carton?

    (A) 2   (B) 4   (C) 5   (D) 6   (E) 10

(D) The best approach to this question is just to do the algebra. Since the average of $3x - 2$ and $2x - 3$ is 10, their sum is 20:

$3x - 2 + 2x - 3 = 20$
$5x - 5 = 20$
$5x = 25$
$x = 5$

So one of the package weighs $3(5) - 2 = 13$ pounds and the other weighs $2(5) - 3 = 7$ pounds. The difference between their weights is 6.

Testing choices would not be a good strategy for this question, because the question asks for the *difference* between the weights. So the choices are not possible weights of an individual package.

22. A group of 15 students took a test that was scored from zero to 100. If exactly ten students scored 75 or more on the test, what is the *lowest* possible value for the average of the scores of all 15 students?

    (A) 25   (B) 50   (C) 70   (D) 75   (E) 90

(B) This question is a variation on the theme of an average with missing elements. Since ten students have scores of 75 or more, the total of their scores is at minimum $10 \times 75 = 750$. Then, even assuming the other five students each scored zero, the average for the 15 would be at least $750 \div 15 = 50$.

516

23. If a machine produces x units in t minutes and 30 seconds, what is its average operating speed in units per minute?

(A) $\dfrac{t+30}{x}$ (B) $\dfrac{x}{t+30}$ (C) $tx + \dfrac{1x}{2}$

(D) $\dfrac{t}{x} + \dfrac{1}{2}$ (E) $\dfrac{x}{t+\frac{1}{2}}$

(E) The operating speed is expressed in units per minute. The machine produces x units in t minutes plus $\frac{1}{2}$ minute. So the average operating speed is $\dfrac{x}{t+\frac{1}{2}}$. Or, you could have tried substituting some numbers.

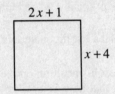

$2x + 1$

$x + 4$

24. If the figure above is a square, what is the perimeter of the figure?

(A) 28
(B) 16
(C) 9
(D) 3
(E) Cannot be determined from the information given.

(A) First, a reminder not to pull a Watson. Since this is a difficult question, most people will not be able to answer it. So it is unlikely that the correct choice is (E).

The correct choice is (A). Since the figure is a square, the two sides are equal:

$2x + 1 = x + 4$
$x = 3$

So each side is $x + 4 = 3 + 4 = 7$, and the perimeter is $4(7) = 28$.

25. If a certain rectangle has a length that is twice its width, what is the ratio of the area of the rectangle to the area of an isosceles right triangle with hypotenuse equal to the width of the rectangle?

(A) $\dfrac{1}{8}$ (B) $\dfrac{1}{4}$ (C) $\dfrac{1}{2}$ (D) $\dfrac{4}{1}$ (E) $\dfrac{8}{1}$

(E) You can work this out algebraically. Let w be the width of the rectangle. The length of the rectangle is twice that or $2w$. So the rectangle has an area of $w \times 2w = 2w^2$. Then, w is also the

length of the hypotenuse of a 45–45–90 triangle. Each of the other two sides (the ones that form the right angle) is $\frac{1}{2} \times w \times \sqrt{2} = \dfrac{\sqrt{2}w}{2}$. (Since the two sides form a right angle they can be the altitude and base.) So the area of the triangle is

$\frac{1}{2} \times$ altitude $\times$ base $= \frac{1}{2}\left(\dfrac{\sqrt{2}w}{2}\right)\left(\dfrac{\sqrt{2}w}{2}\right) = \frac{1}{2}\left(\dfrac{2w^2}{4}\right) = \dfrac{w^2}{4}$.

And the ratio of the area of the rectangle to that of the triangle is $\dfrac{2w^2}{\frac{w^2}{4}} = \dfrac{2}{\frac{1}{4}} = \dfrac{8}{1}$.

It's true the explanation above is difficult to follow without a diagram, which is why you are encouraged to draw figures when one is not provided.

Now the explanation will not only be easier to follow, you can dispense with it altogether.

In the first place, the rectangle is obviously bigger than the triangle, so you can eliminate 3 choices: (A), (B), and (C). Next, a quick addition to the figure shows that the area of the triangle is less than $\frac{1}{4}$ of the area of the rectangle:

By the process of elimination, (E) must be correct.

SECTION 3

CRITICAL READING

1. The sense appealed to in paragraph 1 of Hall's essay is that of

(A) sight
(B) smell
(C) hearing
(D) both A and B
(E) both B and C

(C) This question requires you to summarize the first paragraph in terms of its sensory language. Nearly every sentence deals with sound, so (C) is the best answer. Since no mention of smells is made, (E) cannot be correct.

2. Hall uses the word *succeeds* in lines 16–17 to mean

   (A) supplants
   (B) accomplishes
   (C) prospers
   (D) replaces
   (E) ensues

   (E) Replace *succeeds* in lines 16–17 with each of the choices, and you will find that, of all thee synonyms for *succeeds*, only *ensues* has the appropriate shade of meaning.

3. What is Hall's opinion of the ship in the Baltic disaster?

   (A) It was overstaffed.
   (B) The ship was too old and in ill-repair.
   (C) Discipline was sorely lacking.
   (D) both A and B
   (E) both B and C

   (C) No mention is made of the ship's being crowded or old, but Hall does say that "the ship was in a wretched state of discipline" (line 38). Much of the disaster might have been averted, he implies, had regulations been stricter.

4. What does Hall think about taking risks?

   (A) It is never justified.
   (B) It is always justified.
   (C) It requires a practical goal.
   (D) It should only be done in life-or-death emergencies.
   (E) It separates men from boys.

   (C) This evaluation question requires you to paraphrase lines 43–45, wherein Hall remarks on the "absurd volunteers" who risk their lives "without some useful purpose."

5. Dana's use of the word *unwonted* (line 58) means

   (A) unusual
   (B) unjustified
   (C) arid
   (D) undesired
   (E) uninformed

   (A) Putting the choices in context, you will find that only (A) makes sense. (B) is a synonym for *unwarranted*, (C) for *unwatered*, (D) for *unwanted*, and (E) for *unwarned*.

6. The term *hove aback*, found in Hall's piece in line 41 and Dana's in line 63, probably means

   (A) taken unawares
   (B) shocked
   (C) living badly
   (D) set to catch the wind
   (E) under steam power

   (D) You need know nothing about seamanship to answer this interpretation question. In both cases, the context indicates that the term has to do with sailing, so only (D) will do—(E) refers to a different kind of ship entirely.

7. In line 65, Dana's narrator proves himself to be

   (A) a good sailor
   (B) inept and uncoordinated
   (C) practical but brave
   (D) the kind of sailor Hall disparages
   (E) the kind of sailor Hall prefers

   (D) Just like the "absurd volunteers" in Hall's essay, Dana's narrator heaves himself into a rescue boat without even knowing who is lost at sea. The kind of chaos and futile wandering about that he describes is precisely what Hall disparages.

8. Why does Dana list the materials Bolemer was carrying?

   (A) to suggest his position on the ship
   (B) to show that he was a sailor
   (C) to justify the crew's actions
   (D) to reveal his helpful nature
   (E) to explain why he quickly sank

   (E) Bolemer is certainly a sailor (B), but the objects he is carrying are unnecessary to prove that. He may be helpful (D), but revealing his nature is not Dana's intent. As with any synthesis/analysis question, you must use your understanding of the structure of a passage to analyze a part of it. Dana goes on to describe Bolemer's death by saying ". . . with all those things round his neck, he probably sank immediately" (line 75).

9. Dana's intent in this passage is to

   (A) argue for better regulations
   (B) show the many forms of death
   (C) demonstrate the perils of poor seamanship
   (D) caution those who would go to sea
   (E) relate a sad tale

   (E) Unlike Hall, Dana has no bone to pick with the way rescues are attempted (A). This is not a cautionary tale (D), and only one form of death or peril is noted (B, C). The only purpose here is to tell a story.

10. These two passages might be anthologized with the heading

   (A) "Man Overboard!"
   (B) "Storms on the Water"
   (C) "The Unforgiving Landscape"
   (D) "Funeral at Sea"
   (E) "Disasters I Have Known"

   (A) This kind of evaluation question asks you to choose a title that might apply to both passages;

518

in other words, it asks you to determine their common theme. (B), (C), and (D) are clearly out; none of them applies to either passage. (E) is possible, but it more clearly relates to the Dana piece than to Hall's—Hall is not speaking just of disasters he himself has seen. (A) works for either passage, and so it works for both.

SECTION 4

MATH PROBLEM-SOLVING

1. If the perimeter of a rectangular playing field is 120 meters, then which of the following could be the length of one of its sides?

    I. 20
    II. 40
    III. 60

    (A) I only   (B) I and II only   (C) I and III only
    (D) II and III only   (E) I, II, and III

    (B) Again we have a simple problem that needs only a simple solution: just use numbers. As for item I, a rectangle could have sides of 20 and 40: $20 + 20 + 40 + 40 = 120$. And so it can also have a side of 40, and II is part of the correct answer. But what rectangle can have a side of 60 and a perimeter of only 120? It doesn't exist; $60 + 60$ is equal to 120, so the other sides would be zero.

2. If a six-sided polygon has two sides of length $x - 2y$ each and four sides of length $2x + y$ each, what is its perimeter?

    (A) $6x - 6y$
    (B) $6x - y$
    (C) $5x$
    (D) $6x$
    (E) $10x$

    (E) To find the perimeter of a figure, you add the lengths of the sides:

    $2(x - 2y) + 4(2x + y) =$
    $(2x - 4y) + (8x + 4y) =$
    $2x + 8x - 4y + 4y = 10x$

    You can, if you prefer, substitute numbers. Assume that $x = 3$ and $y = 1$. The two short sides are each $3 - 2(1) = 1$, for a total of 2. And the four long sides are $2(3) + 1 = 7$, for a total of 28. The perimeter is $28 + 2 = 30$. So if $x = 3$ and $y = 1$, the correct formula will generate the number 30. Only (E) produces the correct value.

3. If m and n are negative numbers, which of the following must always be positive?

    I. $m - n$
    II. $m \times n$
    III. $m \div n$

    (A) I only   (B) II only   (C) I and III only
    (D) II and III only   (E) I, II, and III

    (D) This question tests properties of numbers. As for II, $m \times n$ is a negative times a negative, which always generates a positive number. As for III, $m \div n$ is a negative divided by a negative, which always generates a positive number. But $m - n$ (I) may or may not generate a positive number. If m is larger than n, then $m - n$ is positive; but if n is larger than m, $m - n$ is negative. Example: If $m = -2$ and $n = -1$, then $-2 - (-1) = -2 + 1 = -1$.

4. $\dfrac{1}{1 + \dfrac{1}{x}}$ is equal to which of the following?

    (A) $x + 1$ (B) $\dfrac{1}{x + 1}$ (C) $\dfrac{x}{x + 1}$
    (D) $\dfrac{x + 1}{x}$ (E) $x^2 + x$

    (C) This question asks you to rewrite the expression:

    $$\frac{1}{1 + \dfrac{1}{x}} = \frac{1}{\dfrac{x + 1}{x}} = 1\left(\frac{x}{x + 1}\right) = \frac{x}{x + 1}$$

    Or you could have substituted numbers. If $x = 1$, then

    $$\frac{1}{1 + \dfrac{1}{x}} = \frac{1}{1 + \dfrac{1}{1}} = \frac{1}{1 + 1} = \frac{1}{2}$$

    On the assumption that $x = 1$, two answer choices generate the result $\frac{1}{2}$—(B) and (C). So try another number, say $x = 2$. If $x = 2$, the correct answer should generate the value $\frac{2}{3}$. Now you eliminate (B), and (C) must be correct.

5. If the cost of b books is d dollars, what is the cost, in dollars, of x books at the same rate?

    (A) xd (B) $\dfrac{xd}{b}$ (C) $\dfrac{bd}{x}$ (D) bx (E) $\dfrac{bx}{d}$

    (B) You can set up an algebraic formula using a proportion.

519

$$\frac{b}{x} = \frac{d}{?}$$

where ? represents our unknown. Cross-multiply:

$$b(?) = dx$$

Divide by b:

$$? = \frac{dx}{b}$$

Or, you can assume numbers to test answer choices, a procedure you are familiar with by now.

6. If $y = 7x$, then the average (arithmetic mean) of x and y, in terms of x, is equal to

   (A) x (B) $2x$ (C) $3x$ (D) $4x$ (E) $5x$

   (D) The average of x and y would be $\frac{(x+y)}{2}$. The average of x and $7x$ is $\frac{(x+7x)}{2}$, or $\frac{8x}{2}$, or $4x$. You might also solve this by plugging in values for x and y: say, 2 and 14. $\frac{(2+14)}{2} = \frac{16}{2} = 8$, or $4x$.

7. If one * equals two !, and four ! equals five ♥, then what is the ratio * : ♥?

   (A) $\frac{1}{4}$ (B) $\frac{1}{2}$ (C) $\frac{4}{1}$ (D) $\frac{5}{4}$ (E) $\frac{5}{2}$

   (E) $1* = 2!$ and $4! = 5♥$
   $2* = 4! = 5♥$
   $2* = 5♥$, so $\frac{*}{♥} = \frac{5}{2}$

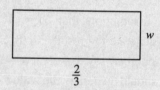

8. If the area of the rectangle above is equal to $\frac{1}{3}$, then $w =$

   (A) $\frac{1}{2}$ (B) $\frac{2}{3}$ (C) 1 (D) $\frac{1}{3}$

   (E) Cannot be determined from the information given.

   (A) The area of a rectangle equals lw. In this case, $\frac{2}{3}w = \frac{1}{3}$. Therefore, $w = \frac{1}{3} \times \frac{3}{2}$, or $\frac{1}{2}$.

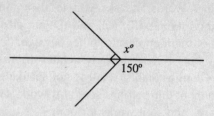

9. In the figure above, what is the value of x?

   (A) 60 (B) 90 (C) 120 (D) 150 (E) 180

   (C) If you redraw the figure and put in all the numbers you can, this answer is easy to find:

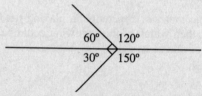

10. A cabin in the Catskills burns n gallons of oil each month in the winter. At this rate, g gallons of oil will supply c cabins for how many months?

    (A) $\frac{g}{nc}$ (B) gnc (C) $\frac{nc}{g}$ (D) $\frac{ng}{c}$ (E) $\frac{n}{gc}$

    (A) The best way to solve this is to make up numbers to use. Suppose one cabin burns 50 gallons of oil a month. At this rate, 500 gallons will supply 5 cabins for how many months? The correct answer would be 2.

    (A) $\frac{g}{nc} = \frac{500}{50(5)} = 2$ (Right answer.)

    You can stop right there, but let's try the other choices.

    (B) $gnc = 500 \times 50 \times 5 = 125,500$ (Way off!)

    (C) $\frac{nc}{g} = \frac{50(5)}{500} = \frac{1}{2}$ (Wrong answer.)

    (D) $\frac{ng}{c} = \frac{50(500)}{5} = 5,000$ (Again, way off!)

    (E) $\frac{n}{gc} = \frac{50}{500(5)} = \frac{1}{50}$ (Way off in the other direction!)

520

SECTION 5

SENTENCE COMPLETIONS

1. Although his dress is ----, in all other ways he seems to be a perfectly normal man.

   (A) ordinary
   (B) mellifluous
   (C) eccentric
   (D) nondescript
   (E) recalcitrant

   (C) At the level of word usage, you can eliminate (B) and (E). Those adjectives cannot be used to describe clothing. Then, the *although*, a thought-reverser, sets up a contrast between the first idea (everything from the beginning of the sentence to the comma) and the second idea (the rest of the sentence). And the entire weight of the contrast rests on the distinction between the word selected for the blank and *normal*. Choices (A) and (D) are parallel to the idea of "normal." Only (C) provides the needed contrast.

2. In his private life he was quite ----; but he gave large sums of money to charities, so most people thought of him as a ----.

   (A) pusillanimous..charlatan
   (B) immodest..chauvinist
   (C) flamboyant..savant
   (D) sinister..mercenary
   (E) miserly..philanthropist

   (E) It doesn't seem to be possible to eliminate any choices at the level of usage. Every substitution, at least when taken in isolation from the rest of the sentence, seems to create a meaningful phrase. So we will analyze the structure of the sentence.

   The *although* creates a contrast between the first idea and the second. Additionally, the last part of the sentence (from the *so* to the end) must extend the idea of giving money to charities. (E) does both jobs. A *philanthropist* is someone who gives to charities, and *miserly* contrasts with *philanthropist*.

3. The term *Indian* is a misnomer for the Native American, introduced by Columbus and ---- by historians.

   (A) eradicated
   (B) arbitrated
   (C) infiltrated
   (D) perpetuated
   (E) coerced

(D) This is primarily a vocabulary question. The logical structure of the second part of the sentence is very simple. The blank, when completed, must somehow extend the idea of "introduction." (D) works nicely. The mistake was made and then perpetuated. No other answer choice makes any sense when coupled with *introduced*.

4. She accepted her own misfortune with perfect ----, but was outraged at any abuse or mistreatment of others.

   (A) equanimity
   (B) reluctance
   (C) sincerity
   (D) rabidity
   (E) pulchritude

   (A) Again, we have a question that is primarily a test of vocabulary. The sentence does contain a contrast; so the blank, when completed, must contrast with *outrage*. (E) can be eliminated because *pulchritude* refers to a physical quality, not a state of mind. Of the remaining choices, (A) provides the best contrast to *outrage*.

5. Although Mozart's music suggests a composer of great ---- and seriousness, his letters imply that he was naïve and ----.

   (A) erudition..grave
   (B) sophistication..uncouth
   (C) fortitude..macabre
   (D) levity..sanctimonious
   (E) fragility..pensive

   (B) There are several ways to approach this question. At the level of word usage, you can eliminate (E). The phrase "great fragility" seems an unlikely construction. Beyond that, there are several logical clues in the sentence. The idea in the first clause must contrast with the idea in the second (*although*). In the first clause, the completion must parallel *seriousness*; in the second, the completion must parallel *naïve*. (B) does the trick. Notice also that when the completions are inserted in the sentence, (B) has the merit of making an additional contrast between *sophistication* and *naïve* and between *seriousness* and *uncouth*.

6. Although the jury thought the defendant had been somewhat less than ---- in his testimony, the ---- summary of the defense attorney finally convinced them of her client's innocence.

   (A) interesting..lackluster
   (B) candid..persuasive
   (C) convincing..inordinate
   (D) honest..confusing
   (E) forthright..irrational

521

(B) The key structural element of this question is the thought-reversal introduced by *although*. The idea of the second clause must contrast with that of the first clause. Only (B) does this. The first words of the other choices do represent possible descriptions of the testimony, but *lackluster, confusing,* and *irrational* do not provide the needed contrast. And (C) can be eliminated because "inordinate summary" is not idiomatic.

7. Conditions in the mine were ----, so the mine workers refused to return to their jobs until the dangers were ----.

    (A) hazardous..eliminated
    (B) filthy..disbanded
    (C) deplorable..collated
    (D) conducive..ameliorated
    (E) illegal..enhanced

(A) The second idea must extend the first idea by explaining what consequences follow from the conditions in the mine. (D) can be eliminated because "conducive conditions" is not idiomatic. The other choices, however, contain first words that might describe conditions in a mine. So you look at the second words. You can eliminate (B) and (C) because "dangers were disbanded" and "dangers were collated" do not create meaningful English phrases. And finally, you eliminate (E) in favor of (A), because (E) does not provide a thought continuation. The conditions at the mine must have changed in the miners' favor.

8. Since the actor who played the lead was somewhat ----, the property manager had to let out the costumes and have the furniture used in the production reinforced.

    (A) winsome
    (B) virulent
    (C) fragile
    (D) corpulent
    (E) flirtatious

(D) The part of the sentence following the comma explains the consequences of the first thought. The property manger had to make the costumes bigger and reinforce the furniture, so the performer must have been overweight. *Corpulent* means "portly or stout."

9. The guests invited to meet the famous critic were ---- by a charm which contrasted sharply with the ---- of his writing.

    (A) appalled..inadequacy
    (B) frustrated..wittiness
    (C) deceived..elegance
    (D) delighted..venom
    (E) enthralled..lucidity

(D) There are two keys to this sentence. The first blank must be completed by a word that describes an appropriate reaction to charm. You can eliminate (A) and (B). One would not be appalled nor frustrated by something like charm. Next, there is a thought-reversal introduced by the word *contrasted.* So the second word must contrast with the idea of charm. Of the remaining choices, only (D) supplies the needed contrast.

10. Many hours of practice are required of a successful musician, so it is often not so much ---- as ---- which distinguishes the professional from the amateur.

    (A) talent..discipline
    (B) money..education
    (C) genius..understanding
    (D) fortitude..mediocrity
    (E) technique..pomposity

(A) The "not so much ---- as ----" sets up a contrast between two ideas. The ideas in (C) seem similar to each other, so (C) can be eliminated. Additionally, the ideas in (D) and (E), while not similar to each other, don't express a clear contrast. This leaves only (A) and (B). The ideas in (B) could express a contrast (he has money but no education), but the ideas are not appropriate in the context; for example, "hours of practice" equals *discipline.*

11. The statue was so ---- we found it ---- to view.

    (A) repulsive..amusing
    (B) delightful..burdensome
    (C) grotesque..distressing
    (D) warped..captivating
    (E) precarious..shocking

(C) The second idea extends the first. Thus, (A) and (B) can be eliminated; one does not lead to the other. (D) is odd, and (E) is not especially logical. It is possible, on the other hand, that viewing a grotesque statue might be *distressing.*

12. My aunt is so ---- that you cannot have a short conversation with her; she prates on and on until your ears fall asleep.

(A) garrulous
(B) engaging
(C) brusque
(D) lilting
(E) impaired

(A) The key words are *short conversation* and *prates*; the aunt is the opposite of *brusque* (curt); she is talkative beyond reason, or *garrulous.* This makes her less than *engaging* (B); you are not engaged if your ears are asleep.

13. We were less impressed by the play's intricate ---- than we were by its difficult ----.

(A) length..cast
(B) theme..setting
(C) authorship..performance
(D) meaning..sense
(E) plot..language

(E) The correct choice must be able to be modified by the words *intricate* and *difficult.* A length cannot be intricate, so (A) is eliminated. A theme might be intricate, but a setting would not be called difficult, so (B) is incorrect. Authorship (C) cannot be intricate. Sense (D) cannot be difficult. Only (E) works.

14. It seems ---- to us to dismiss the custodian without a ----.

(A) obligatory..reason
(B) reactionary..cause
(C) formidable..worry
(D) unethical..hearing
(E) discourteous..demonstration

(D) It might be discourteous to dismiss someone, but why would a demonstration be necessary (E)? If there were no reason, dismissal would not be obligatory (A). *Reactionary* is the wrong word (B), and (C) makes little sense.

15. Without a good ----, fishing becomes an exercise in ----.

(A) bait..sorrow
(B) reason..futility
(C) rod..frustration
(D) prey..waiting
(E) weather..dampness

(C) You would never say "a good bait" (A) or "a good weather" (E). (D) makes no sense, and (B) is not much better. Only (C) is logical: You need a good rod in order to avoid frustration.

ANALOGIES

16. HONE : KNIFE::

(A) tune : instrument
(B) count : money
(C) waste : energy
(D) paint : brush
(E) polish : glint

(A) This analogy is difficult to describe as any one of the common forms. Perhaps, it is closest to the "tool" category. In any event, it can be described as follows: HONING is the process of preparing a KNIFE for use, and *tuning* is the process of preparing an *instrument* for use.

17. DETOUR : IMPASSE::

(A) remove : residue
(B) frequent : location
(C) circumvent : obstacle
(D) follow : leader
(E) navigate : ship

(C) Again, we have an analogy that is difficult to classify. Your diagnostic sentence might read "DETOURING is how to get around an IMPASSE, and *circumventing* is how to get around an *obstacle.*" Once you have screened choices with a sentence, then you can see a very nice confirming secondary relationship between the capitalized words and the words in (C). An IMPASSE is like an *obstacle*, and to DETOUR and to *circumvent* are similar.

18. CLOTH : THREADS::

(A) wood : furniture
(B) basket : reeds
(C) cup : liquids
(D) china : saucer
(E) garden : walls

(B) This analogy is based on the "part of" connection. THREADS are a part of CLOTH, and *reeds* are a part of *basket.* And the analogy is very precise, since the way in which threads are a part of cloth is very similar to the way in which reeds are a part of a basket (woven together).

19. DOODLE : AIMLESSNESS::

(A) revive : substantial
(B) inform : success
(C) blurt : planning
(D) exile : competition
(E) waver : indecision

(E) This analogy is based on the "defining characteristic" connection. Taking some liberty with parts of speech, your sentence might read "AIMLESSNESS is a defining characteristic of DOODLING, and *indecision* is a defining characteristic of *wavering*."

20. SLANDER : PEJORATIVE::

(A) ingratiate : miraculous
(B) revere : condemning
(C) extol : laudatory
(D) ruminate : superficial
(E) reward : grateful

(C) This analogy is based on the "defining characteristic" connection. A defining characteristic of a statement that SLANDERS someone is its PEJORATIVE content, and a defining characteristic of a statement that *extols* something is its *laudatory* content.

21. JOURNEYMAN : APPRENTICE::

(A) colleague : pedagogue
(B) salesclerk : merchandise
(C) veteran : rookie
(D) voter : registration
(E) champion : practice

(C) You might view this analogy as based on process: one begins in a profession as an APPRENTICE and advances to JOURNEYMAN, and one begins an activity as a *rookie* and advances to *veteran*. Or, you might view the connection as one of degree based on the length of time of service. An apprentice has only a little time in the trade, while a journeyman has a great deal; a rookie has participated in the activity only a short time, a veteran longer. Either way you analyze the analogy, there is a very nice secondary relationship to confirm the correctness of (C). Journeymen and veterans are similar; apprentices and rookies are similar.

22. UNFATHOMABLE : COMPREHEND::

(A) gullible : distract
(B) discreet : falsify
(C) desired : obtain
(D) untenable : maintain
(E) secure : revolt

(D) This analogy is based on the "lack of" connection. Taking some liberty with the phrasing, you might say "Something that is UNFATHOMABLE cannot be COMPREHENDED, and something that is *untenable* cannot be *maintained*." The words *lack of* do not appear in this formulation because the *cannot* replaces them, but the basic idea of the analogy is "lack of."

23. IMPULSIVE : SPONTANEITY::

(A) overwrought : procrastination
(B) succinct : brevity
(C) ignoble : simultaneity
(D) pretentious : modesty
(E) fallow : fecundity

(B) This analogy is based on the "defining characteristic" connection. SPONTANEITY is a defining characteristic of IMPULSIVENESS, and *brevity* is a defining characteristic of *succinctness*.

24. MAELSTROM : WHIRLPOOL::

(A) catastrophe : reminder
(B) horizon : crepuscule
(C) tempest : delight
(D) inferno : fire
(E) explosion : concentration

(D) This analogy is based upon the "degree" connection. A MAELSTROM is a large and violent WHIRLPOOL, and an *inferno* is a large and very destructive *fire*.

25. AMBULATORY : MOBILITY::

(A) cantankerous : foolishness
(B) frolicsome : insight
(C) venial : goodness
(D) salubrious : decay
(E) loquacious : speech

(E) This analogy is based on the "defining characteristic" connection. MOBILITY is a defining characteristic of someone who is AMBULATORY, and *speech* is a defining characteristic of someone who is *loquacious*.

CRITICAL READING

26. The phrase "mark of his favor" (line 9) means

(A) scar from his whip
(B) remembrance
(C) prized token
(D) symbol of his power
(E) sign of his support

(E) Test the choices in this interpretation question in place of the phrase in line 9. Old master allows Katy to have her children with her; this boon is a sign of his support of her.

27. The phrase "take the skin off her back" (lines 16–17) means

(A) whip her
(B) remove her from the kitchen
(C) fire her
(D) send her out into the night
(E) take away her clothing

(A) Aunt Katy would clearly receive some kind of punishment; only whipping would result in the kinds of wounds that "take the skin off her back."

28. When Douglass says that Katy "was not destitute of maternal feeling" (line 18), he is being

(A) sympathetic
(B) ironic
(C) deliberately obtuse
(D) kind
(E) reflective

(B) Katy has proved herself a monster; she cut her own son with a knife. However, she overfeeds her children at the expense of others; she is "not destitute of maternal feeling." Since Douglass is deprived of food thanks to her maternal feeling, he can only look on this ironically. In any autobiography, the author is *reflective* (E); in this case, (B) is the better answer.

29. The word *committed* (line 22) is used to mean

(A) confined
(B) devoted
(C) swore
(D) promised
(E) assigned

(E) Read the choices in place of the word in line 22. Of all of the synonyms for *committed*, only *assigned* has the proper shade of meaning. Old master assigns Katy the food allowance.

30. How does Douglass feel about old master's practice of dividing food?

(A) It is fairer than the practice of Col. Lloyd.
(B) It is less fair than the practice of Col. Lloyd.
(C) It is fair only to adults.
(D) It is fair if one is careful.
(E) It is the only possible way to divide fairly.

(B) To determine the answer to this evaluation question, reread the section about dividing food (lines 20–27). The practice of old master differs from that of Col. Lloyd—instead of dividing food evenly among slaves, he gives it all to Aunt Katy to divide. The results are uneven, so the practice is less fair.

31. When Douglass says "it is not to accuse her too severely" (line 28), he means

(A) he does not wish to accuse her
(B) the accusation is unfair
(C) he simply wants to chastise her gently
(D) she deserves no accusation
(E) the accusation is true

(E) This could be tricky; it is an unusual turn of phrase. The key is the phrase that follows: Katy was guilty of starving other children while cramming her own. Douglass means that the accusation is not too severe—it is merely the truth.

32. What is the purpose of Douglass's lists in lines 32–44?

(A) to express his hatred for Aunt Katy
(B) to illustrate his constant quest for food
(C) to show the poverty of the rural South
(D) to reveal his personal feelings about slavery
(E) to depict the life of a typical slave

(B) (A) is not true of this particular part of the passage, and (D) is not true—this is a narrative, not an opinion piece. (C) and (E) are too vague. The list of activities and foods illustrates the hungry young boy's quest.

33. In line 49, what is the best definition of *solace*?

(A) distress
(B) relief
(C) comfort
(D) calm
(E) serenity

(C) All of these are close, with the exception of (A), which is an antonym. In context, though, you would never say "a calm" or "a serenity," so (D) and (E) are out. Of the two remaining choices, the one that best parallels *consolation* is *comfort*.

34. Why does Douglass include the words of the sympathizing slaves?

(A) to prove that he was constantly misunderstood
(B) to show that not all slaves were like Aunt Katy
(C) to demonstrate that his life was not all misery
(D) both A and B
(E) both B and C

(E) Following his saga of despair and unfairness, Douglass feels compelled to end on an uplifting note. His inclusion of this reference does two things: It shows that some slaves were kind (B), and it shows that he could feel comforted (C). Since both (B) and (C) are correct, the answer must be (E).

35. Which of the following would be a good title for this passage?

(A) "Life on the Plantation"
(B) "Old Master and Me"
(C) "Aunt Katy Gets Her Revenge"
(D) "The Power of Aunt Katy"
(E) "A Dog's Life"

(D) This kind of evaluation question asks you to summarize and affix a title to the passage. (A) is too vague. (B) is not applicable. (C) is absurd; there is no talk of revenge. (E) is not particularly descriptive. Much of the passage is about Aunt Katy and her power over the narrator and other children, so (D) is the best choice.

SECTION 6

QUANTITATIVE COMPARISONS

1.

$\dfrac{1}{7} - \dfrac{1}{8}$	$\dfrac{1}{56}$

(C) All that's required here is a simple calculation, so do it. Use the "flying x":

$$\frac{1}{7} - \frac{1}{8} = \frac{(8-7)}{56} = \frac{1}{56}$$

n is a negative integer.

2.

$n + n + n + n$	$n \times n \times n \times n$

(B) If you are comfortable with properties of numbers, you might be able to see in one glance that since n is negative, Column A (which is the sum of negative numbers) is negative and Column B is positive (four negatives multiplied together). At that point, using the "good enough" principle, you would mark (B). You don't need to know anything more.

If the answer is not immediately clear to you, start by doing the operations that are indicated. Column A is $4n$ and Column B is n^4. At this point, you might see that since n is negative, $4n$ is also negative while n^4 is positive. Applying the "good enough" principle, you mark (B). Or if need be, you could substitute numbers.

$$x = \frac{1}{3}$$

$$y = \frac{1}{6}$$

3.

$\dfrac{x}{y}$	$\dfrac{y}{x}$

(A) One way of making the comparison is to recognize that x is greater than y. So Column A has the "big" numerator and the "small" denominator, and Column B has the "small" numerator and the "big" denominator. Column A is larger, so mark choice (A).

If you miss that trick, go ahead and plug in $\frac{1}{3}$ for x and $\frac{1}{6}$ for y. Column A is 2, Column B is $\frac{1}{2}$.

The cost of three apples and two pears is $2.50.

4.

The cost of one apple	The cost of one pear

(D) If you translate the centered information into "algebrese," you immediately see the answer must be (D): $3a + 2p = 2.5$. That's one equation with two variables, and there is no way to solve for either variable individually. You don't need to write down an equation; the equation just summarizes the conclusion that you can reach verbally: "There's nothing here to tell me whether an apple or a pear costs more."

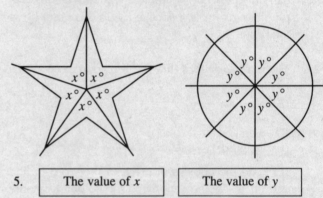

5.

The value of x	The value of y

(A) First, the shapes of the figures are really not important. What is important is the number of equal angles that make up the 360° of arc. For Column A, $5x = 360°$, and for Column B, $8y = 360°$. Now apply the "good enough" principle; there is no need to solve for x. $\frac{360}{5}$ is larger than $\frac{360}{8}$, so Column A is larger.

Cheese costs $2.00 per pound.

6.

The amount of cheese that can be purchased for $1.50	$\dfrac{3}{5}$ pound

(A) The easiest approach to this item is "supermarket math." If cheese costs $2.00 per pound, for $1.50 you can buy $\frac{\$1.50}{\$2.00} = \frac{3}{4}$ of a pound. Since $\frac{3}{4}$ is larger than $\frac{3}{5}$, Column A is greater.

526

Rectangular solid X has a volume of 24.
Rectangular solid Y has a volume of 20.

7.

| Area of the base of x | Area of the base of y |

(D) Expressed in equations, the centered information states:

Volume $X = 24 = $ height of $X \times$ base area of X
Volume $Y = 20 = $ height of $Y \times$ base area of Y

Two different equations, each with two different variables, so there is no way to solve for the base of either. Don't make the error of assuming that the larger volume has the larger base. Solid X could have a base of 1×1 and a height of 24 and Solid Y a base of 5×4 and a height of 1.

8.

| $\sqrt{9}$ | $\sqrt{6} + \sqrt{3}$ |

(B) First, $\sqrt{6} + \sqrt{3}$ is not equal to $\sqrt{9}$. (The radicals don't work that way.) Second, you don't need to try to find an exact value for $\sqrt{6}$, since 6 is more than 4, $\sqrt{6}$ is more than $\sqrt{4}$, and $\sqrt{6}$ is more than 2. And you know that $\sqrt{3}$ is about 1.7, so Column B is more than 3.7, which makes it more than $\sqrt{9}$.

9.

| Surface area of a sphere with radius 1 | Area of a circle with radius 1 |

(A) What? You have forgotten the formula for finding the surface area of a sphere! You don't need it. Just visualize the "disk" and the "ball":

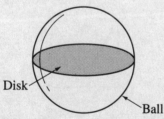

Disk
Ball

$2x^2 + 4x + 3 = 0$

10.

| $2x^2 + 4x$ | -3 |

(C) Look first at what is required by the two columns, then rewrite the centered equation:
$2x^2 + 4x = -3$

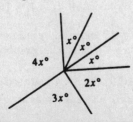

$x°$
$x°$
$4x°$
$x°$
$2x°$
$3x°$

11.

| 30 | x |

(C) $x + x + x + 2x + 3x + 4x = 360$

$12x = 360$
$x = 30$

Questions 12–13

For $n \neq 0$, $\boxed{n} = n - \dfrac{2}{n}$

12.

| $\boxed{-3}$ | -3 |

(A) You know how to handle defined functions.
$\boxed{-3} = -3 - \frac{2}{-3} = -3 + \frac{2}{3}$, which is greater than -3. So Column A is larger.

13.

| $\boxed{2}$ | $-\dfrac{1}{2}$ |

(B) Just perform the indicated operations. Column B is $-\frac{1}{2} - \dfrac{2}{-\frac{1}{2}} = -\frac{1}{2} - (-4) = -\frac{1}{2} + 4 = 3\frac{1}{2}$.

Column A is $2 - \frac{2}{2} = 1$. So Column B is larger.

14.

| $(a - b)(a + c)$ | $a(a + c) - b(a + c)$ |

(C) Do the indicated operations. Column A:

$(a - b)(a + c) = a^2 + ac - ab - bc$

Column B:
$a(a + c) - b(a + c) = a^2 + ac - ab - bc$

$$S_1 = \{3, 6, 9, 12, 15, 18\}$$
$$S_2 = \{4, 8, 12, 16, 20, 24\}$$

15.

| The sum of any three different numbers from S_1 | The sum of any three different numbers from S_2 |

(D) Just try different numbers. The minimum value of Column A is $3 + 6 + 9 = 18$, while the maximum value of Column B is $16 + 20 + 24 = 60$. So Column B could be larger. (Eliminate [A] and [C].) On the other hand, Column A could be as large as $12 + 15 + 18 = 45$, and Column B as small as $4 + 8 + 12 = 24$. So the correct answer is (D).

527

STUDENT-PRODUCED RESPONSES

16. If $n + 1 + n + 2 + n + 3 = 1 + 2 + 3$, then $n = $?

(0) Although the equation is long, it can be solved fairly easily:

$$n + 1 + n + 2 + n + 3 = 1 + 2 + 3$$
$$3n + 6 = 6$$
$$3n = 0$$
$$n = 0$$

Or you might have seen that the values 1, 2, and 3 appear on both sides of the equation. Once those are removed, nothing will remain but n and zero, so n must be equal to zero.

17. If 5 pounds of coffee cost $12, how much coffee can be purchased for $30?

(12.5) This question can be answered using "supermarket math." You find out how much coffee costs per pound: $12 ÷ 5 pounds = $2.40 per pound.

Then you divide $30 by $2.40: $30 ÷ $2.40 = 12.5.

The steps of the process can all be represented in a single proportion:

$$\frac{\text{Cost } X}{\text{Cost } Y} = \frac{\text{Pounds } X}{\text{Pounds } Y}$$
$$\frac{\$12}{\$30} = \frac{5}{x}$$
$$12x = 5(30)$$
$$x = \frac{150}{12} = 12.5$$

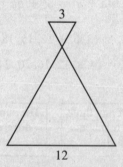

18. If the two triangles above are equilateral, what is the ratio of the perimeter of the smaller to that of the larger?

(1/4) Attack the question directly. Find the perimeter of each triangle. Since the triangles are equilateral, the smaller one has a perimeter of $3 + 3 + 3 = 9$, and the larger one has a perimeter of $12 + 12 + 12 = 36$. And $\frac{9}{36} = \frac{1}{4}$.

You might also have reasoned that since the triangles are equilateral, the ratio of their perimeters is the same as the ratio of their sides. So the ratio of their perimeters will also be $\frac{3}{12}$, or $\frac{1}{4}$.

The second line of reasoning is more elegant (simpler), but who needs elegance when the first line of attack is easily managed anyway?

19. If x and y are positive integers such that $x^2 + y^2 = 10$, then $xy = $?

(3) At first glance, this problem looks as though it requires some sophisticated algebra, but it's actually an easy problem that doesn't require a fancy solution. Just play around with some numbers. The sum of the squares of what two positive integers is 10? (They must be small.) Not 1 and 2; they total $1^2 + 2^2 = 5$. What about 1 and 3? $1^2 + 3^2 = 10$. Bingo! And $1 \times 3 = 3$.

20. If $\frac{1}{3}$ of a number is 2 more than $\frac{1}{5}$ of the number, then what is the number?

(15) You can, if you insist, solve this problem with an equation:

$$\frac{1}{3}x - 2 = \frac{1}{5}x$$
$$\frac{1}{3}x - \frac{1}{5}x = 2$$
$$\frac{2}{15}x = 2$$
$$x = 15$$

21. In the figure above, if the triangle is equilateral and has a perimeter of 12, then the perimeter of the square is what?

(16) This is a composite figure. One side of the equilateral triangle is also a side of the square. The triangle has a perimeter of 12, so each side is 4. If the square has a side of 4, then it has a perimeter of $4 + 4 + 4 + 4 = 16$.

22. If $5x + 3y = 19$ and x and y are positive whole numbers, then y equals what number?

(3) No need to devise a mathematical strategy for this question; just start playing with numbers. If

5x + 3y = 19, then both *x* and *y* have to be small. Say that *y* = 2. Then 5x + 3(2) = 19, 5x = 13, and $x = \frac{13}{5}$ (not an integer). Thus *y* cannot be 2. However, if *y* = 3, then 5x + 3(3) = 19, 5x = 10, and *x* = 2, an integer.

23. At the first stop on her route, a driver unloaded $\frac{2}{5}$ of the packages in her van. After she unloaded another three packages at her next stop, $\frac{1}{2}$ of the original number of packages in the van remained. How many packages were in the van before the first delivery?

(30) This problem should now seem familiar to you. You can solve it with an equation:

$$x - \frac{2}{5}x - 3 = \frac{1}{2}x$$

$$\frac{3}{5}x - 3 = \frac{1}{2}x$$

$$\frac{3}{5}x - \frac{1}{2}x = 3$$

$$\frac{1}{10}x = 3$$

$$x = 30$$

24. If *S* is 150 percent of *T*, then *T* is what percent of *S* + *T*?

(40) You can solve this problem using *S* and *T* as unknowns. Since *S* is 150 percent of *T*, *S* = 1.5*T*. Then the question asks you to express $\frac{T}{S+T}$ as a percent. Just substitute 1.5*T* for *S*:

$\frac{T}{1.5T + T} = \frac{T}{2.5T} = \frac{1}{2.5} = 40\%$. If you don't like working with letters, then pick some numbers. Let *S* be 10 and *T* be 15. Then $\frac{T}{S+T} = \frac{15}{10 + 15} = \frac{10}{25} = 40\%$.

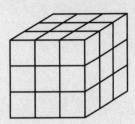

25. The large wooden cube above is composed of 27 smaller cubes. If the entire surface of the large cube is painted red, then how many of the smaller cubes will have exactly two red faces?

(12) You have to figure out which of the smaller cubes will have exactly two red faces.

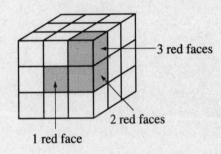

3 red faces

2 red faces

1 red face

And there are 12 of them.

Practice Test 2

Practice Test 2

ANSWER SHEET
PRACTICE TEST 2

If a section has fewer questions than answer ovals, leave the extra ovals blank.

SECTION 1

1 Ⓐ Ⓑ Ⓒ Ⓓ Ⓔ 11 Ⓐ Ⓑ Ⓒ Ⓓ Ⓔ 21 Ⓐ Ⓑ Ⓒ Ⓓ Ⓔ 31 Ⓐ Ⓑ Ⓒ Ⓓ Ⓔ
2 Ⓐ Ⓑ Ⓒ Ⓓ Ⓔ 12 Ⓐ Ⓑ Ⓒ Ⓓ Ⓔ 22 Ⓐ Ⓑ Ⓒ Ⓓ Ⓔ 32 Ⓐ Ⓑ Ⓒ Ⓓ Ⓔ
3 Ⓐ Ⓑ Ⓒ Ⓓ Ⓔ 13 Ⓐ Ⓑ Ⓒ Ⓓ Ⓔ 23 Ⓐ Ⓑ Ⓒ Ⓓ Ⓔ 33 Ⓐ Ⓑ Ⓒ Ⓓ Ⓔ
4 Ⓐ Ⓑ Ⓒ Ⓓ Ⓔ 14 Ⓐ Ⓑ Ⓒ Ⓓ Ⓔ 24 Ⓐ Ⓑ Ⓒ Ⓓ Ⓔ 34 Ⓐ Ⓑ Ⓒ Ⓓ Ⓔ
5 Ⓐ Ⓑ Ⓒ Ⓓ Ⓔ 15 Ⓐ Ⓑ Ⓒ Ⓓ Ⓔ 25 Ⓐ Ⓑ Ⓒ Ⓓ Ⓔ 35 Ⓐ Ⓑ Ⓒ Ⓓ Ⓔ
6 Ⓐ Ⓑ Ⓒ Ⓓ Ⓔ 16 Ⓐ Ⓑ Ⓒ Ⓓ Ⓔ 26 Ⓐ Ⓑ Ⓒ Ⓓ Ⓔ 36 Ⓐ Ⓑ Ⓒ Ⓓ Ⓔ
7 Ⓐ Ⓑ Ⓒ Ⓓ Ⓔ 17 Ⓐ Ⓑ Ⓒ Ⓓ Ⓔ 27 Ⓐ Ⓑ Ⓒ Ⓓ Ⓔ 37 Ⓐ Ⓑ Ⓒ Ⓓ Ⓔ
8 Ⓐ Ⓑ Ⓒ Ⓓ Ⓔ 18 Ⓐ Ⓑ Ⓒ Ⓓ Ⓔ 28 Ⓐ Ⓑ Ⓒ Ⓓ Ⓔ 38 Ⓐ Ⓑ Ⓒ Ⓓ Ⓔ
9 Ⓐ Ⓑ Ⓒ Ⓓ Ⓔ 19 Ⓐ Ⓑ Ⓒ Ⓓ Ⓔ 29 Ⓐ Ⓑ Ⓒ Ⓓ Ⓔ 39 Ⓐ Ⓑ Ⓒ Ⓓ Ⓔ
10 Ⓐ Ⓑ Ⓒ Ⓓ Ⓔ 20 Ⓐ Ⓑ Ⓒ Ⓓ Ⓔ 30 Ⓐ Ⓑ Ⓒ Ⓓ Ⓔ 40 Ⓐ Ⓑ Ⓒ Ⓓ Ⓔ

SECTION 2

1 Ⓐ Ⓑ Ⓒ Ⓓ Ⓔ 11 Ⓐ Ⓑ Ⓒ Ⓓ Ⓔ 21 Ⓐ Ⓑ Ⓒ Ⓓ Ⓔ 31 Ⓐ Ⓑ Ⓒ Ⓓ Ⓔ
2 Ⓐ Ⓑ Ⓒ Ⓓ Ⓔ 12 Ⓐ Ⓑ Ⓒ Ⓓ Ⓔ 22 Ⓐ Ⓑ Ⓒ Ⓓ Ⓔ 32 Ⓐ Ⓑ Ⓒ Ⓓ Ⓔ
3 Ⓐ Ⓑ Ⓒ Ⓓ Ⓔ 13 Ⓐ Ⓑ Ⓒ Ⓓ Ⓔ 23 Ⓐ Ⓑ Ⓒ Ⓓ Ⓔ 33 Ⓐ Ⓑ Ⓒ Ⓓ Ⓔ
4 Ⓐ Ⓑ Ⓒ Ⓓ Ⓔ 14 Ⓐ Ⓑ Ⓒ Ⓓ Ⓔ 24 Ⓐ Ⓑ Ⓒ Ⓓ Ⓔ 34 Ⓐ Ⓑ Ⓒ Ⓓ Ⓔ
5 Ⓐ Ⓑ Ⓒ Ⓓ Ⓔ 15 Ⓐ Ⓑ Ⓒ Ⓓ Ⓔ 25 Ⓐ Ⓑ Ⓒ Ⓓ Ⓔ 35 Ⓐ Ⓑ Ⓒ Ⓓ Ⓔ
6 Ⓐ Ⓑ Ⓒ Ⓓ Ⓔ 16 Ⓐ Ⓑ Ⓒ Ⓓ Ⓔ 26 Ⓐ Ⓑ Ⓒ Ⓓ Ⓔ 36 Ⓐ Ⓑ Ⓒ Ⓓ Ⓔ
7 Ⓐ Ⓑ Ⓒ Ⓓ Ⓔ 17 Ⓐ Ⓑ Ⓒ Ⓓ Ⓔ 27 Ⓐ Ⓑ Ⓒ Ⓓ Ⓔ 37 Ⓐ Ⓑ Ⓒ Ⓓ Ⓔ
8 Ⓐ Ⓑ Ⓒ Ⓓ Ⓔ 18 Ⓐ Ⓑ Ⓒ Ⓓ Ⓔ 28 Ⓐ Ⓑ Ⓒ Ⓓ Ⓔ 38 Ⓐ Ⓑ Ⓒ Ⓓ Ⓔ
9 Ⓐ Ⓑ Ⓒ Ⓓ Ⓔ 19 Ⓐ Ⓑ Ⓒ Ⓓ Ⓔ 29 Ⓐ Ⓑ Ⓒ Ⓓ Ⓔ 39 Ⓐ Ⓑ Ⓒ Ⓓ Ⓔ
10 Ⓐ Ⓑ Ⓒ Ⓓ Ⓔ 20 Ⓐ Ⓑ Ⓒ Ⓓ Ⓔ 30 Ⓐ Ⓑ Ⓒ Ⓓ Ⓔ 40 Ⓐ Ⓑ Ⓒ Ⓓ Ⓔ

SECTION 3

1 Ⓐ Ⓑ Ⓒ Ⓓ Ⓔ 6 Ⓐ Ⓑ Ⓒ Ⓓ Ⓔ 11 Ⓐ Ⓑ Ⓒ Ⓓ Ⓔ 16 Ⓐ Ⓑ Ⓒ Ⓓ Ⓔ
2 Ⓐ Ⓑ Ⓒ Ⓓ Ⓔ 7 Ⓐ Ⓑ Ⓒ Ⓓ Ⓔ 12 Ⓐ Ⓑ Ⓒ Ⓓ Ⓔ 17 Ⓐ Ⓑ Ⓒ Ⓓ Ⓔ
3 Ⓐ Ⓑ Ⓒ Ⓓ Ⓔ 8 Ⓐ Ⓑ Ⓒ Ⓓ Ⓔ 13 Ⓐ Ⓑ Ⓒ Ⓓ Ⓔ 18 Ⓐ Ⓑ Ⓒ Ⓓ Ⓔ
4 Ⓐ Ⓑ Ⓒ Ⓓ Ⓔ 9 Ⓐ Ⓑ Ⓒ Ⓓ Ⓔ 14 Ⓐ Ⓑ Ⓒ Ⓓ Ⓔ 19 Ⓐ Ⓑ Ⓒ Ⓓ Ⓔ
5 Ⓐ Ⓑ Ⓒ Ⓓ Ⓔ 10 Ⓐ Ⓑ Ⓒ Ⓓ Ⓔ 15 Ⓐ Ⓑ Ⓒ Ⓓ Ⓔ 20 Ⓐ Ⓑ Ⓒ Ⓓ Ⓔ

SECTION 4

1 Ⓐ Ⓑ Ⓒ Ⓓ Ⓔ 6 Ⓐ Ⓑ Ⓒ Ⓓ Ⓔ 11 Ⓐ Ⓑ Ⓒ Ⓓ Ⓔ 16 Ⓐ Ⓑ Ⓒ Ⓓ Ⓔ
2 Ⓐ Ⓑ Ⓒ Ⓓ Ⓔ 7 Ⓐ Ⓑ Ⓒ Ⓓ Ⓔ 12 Ⓐ Ⓑ Ⓒ Ⓓ Ⓔ 17 Ⓐ Ⓑ Ⓒ Ⓓ Ⓔ
3 Ⓐ Ⓑ Ⓒ Ⓓ Ⓔ 8 Ⓐ Ⓑ Ⓒ Ⓓ Ⓔ 13 Ⓐ Ⓑ Ⓒ Ⓓ Ⓔ 18 Ⓐ Ⓑ Ⓒ Ⓓ Ⓔ
4 Ⓐ Ⓑ Ⓒ Ⓓ Ⓔ 9 Ⓐ Ⓑ Ⓒ Ⓓ Ⓔ 14 Ⓐ Ⓑ Ⓒ Ⓓ Ⓔ 19 Ⓐ Ⓑ Ⓒ Ⓓ Ⓔ
5 Ⓐ Ⓑ Ⓒ Ⓓ Ⓔ 10 Ⓐ Ⓑ Ⓒ Ⓓ Ⓔ 15 Ⓐ Ⓑ Ⓒ Ⓓ Ⓔ 20 Ⓐ Ⓑ Ⓒ Ⓓ Ⓔ

SECTION 5

1 Ⓐ Ⓑ Ⓒ Ⓓ Ⓔ 11 Ⓐ Ⓑ Ⓒ Ⓓ Ⓔ 21 Ⓐ Ⓑ Ⓒ Ⓓ Ⓔ 31 Ⓐ Ⓑ Ⓒ Ⓓ Ⓔ
2 Ⓐ Ⓑ Ⓒ Ⓓ Ⓔ 12 Ⓐ Ⓑ Ⓒ Ⓓ Ⓔ 22 Ⓐ Ⓑ Ⓒ Ⓓ Ⓔ 32 Ⓐ Ⓑ Ⓒ Ⓓ Ⓔ
3 Ⓐ Ⓑ Ⓒ Ⓓ Ⓔ 13 Ⓐ Ⓑ Ⓒ Ⓓ Ⓔ 23 Ⓐ Ⓑ Ⓒ Ⓓ Ⓔ 33 Ⓐ Ⓑ Ⓒ Ⓓ Ⓔ
4 Ⓐ Ⓑ Ⓒ Ⓓ Ⓔ 14 Ⓐ Ⓑ Ⓒ Ⓓ Ⓔ 24 Ⓐ Ⓑ Ⓒ Ⓓ Ⓔ 34 Ⓐ Ⓑ Ⓒ Ⓓ Ⓔ
5 Ⓐ Ⓑ Ⓒ Ⓓ Ⓔ 15 Ⓐ Ⓑ Ⓒ Ⓓ Ⓔ 25 Ⓐ Ⓑ Ⓒ Ⓓ Ⓔ 35 Ⓐ Ⓑ Ⓒ Ⓓ Ⓔ
6 Ⓐ Ⓑ Ⓒ Ⓓ Ⓔ 16 Ⓐ Ⓑ Ⓒ Ⓓ Ⓔ 26 Ⓐ Ⓑ Ⓒ Ⓓ Ⓔ 36 Ⓐ Ⓑ Ⓒ Ⓓ Ⓔ
7 Ⓐ Ⓑ Ⓒ Ⓓ Ⓔ 17 Ⓐ Ⓑ Ⓒ Ⓓ Ⓔ 27 Ⓐ Ⓑ Ⓒ Ⓓ Ⓔ 37 Ⓐ Ⓑ Ⓒ Ⓓ Ⓔ
8 Ⓐ Ⓑ Ⓒ Ⓓ Ⓔ 18 Ⓐ Ⓑ Ⓒ Ⓓ Ⓔ 28 Ⓐ Ⓑ Ⓒ Ⓓ Ⓔ 38 Ⓐ Ⓑ Ⓒ Ⓓ Ⓔ
9 Ⓐ Ⓑ Ⓒ Ⓓ Ⓔ 19 Ⓐ Ⓑ Ⓒ Ⓓ Ⓔ 29 Ⓐ Ⓑ Ⓒ Ⓓ Ⓔ 39 Ⓐ Ⓑ Ⓒ Ⓓ Ⓔ
10 Ⓐ Ⓑ Ⓒ Ⓓ Ⓔ 20 Ⓐ Ⓑ Ⓒ Ⓓ Ⓔ 30 Ⓐ Ⓑ Ⓒ Ⓓ Ⓔ 40 Ⓐ Ⓑ Ⓒ Ⓓ Ⓔ

SECTION 6

1 (A) (B) (C) (D) (E)   6 (A) (B) (C) (D) (E)   11 (A) (B) (C) (D) (E)
2 (A) (B) (C) (D) (E)   7 (A) (B) (C) (D) (E)   12 (A) (B) (C) (D) (E)
3 (A) (B) (C) (D) (E)   8 (A) (B) (C) (D) (E)   13 (A) (B) (C) (D) (E)
4 (A) (B) (C) (D) (E)   9 (A) (B) (C) (D) (E)   14 (A) (B) (C) (D) (E)
5 (A) (B) (C) (D) (E)   10 (A) (B) (C) (D) (E)   15 (A) (B) (C) (D) (E)

Note: ONLY the answers entered on the grid are scored.
Handwritten answers at the top of the column are NOT scored.

16. [grid]   17. [grid]   18. [grid]   19. [grid]   20. [grid]

21. [grid]   22. [grid]   23. [grid]   24. [grid]   25. [grid]

The passage below is followed by questions based on its content. Answer all questions following the passage on the basis of what is <u>stated</u> or <u>implied</u> in the passage.

Questions 1–12 are based on the following passage.

The Arab writer and philosopher Al-Jahiz (d. 869) developed a new style of didactic but entertaining prose called adab *literature. This piece is from* The Book of Animals. *It reflects Al-Jahiz's interest in nature.*

In the fly there are two good qualities. One of these is the facility with which it may be prevented from causing annoyance and discomfort. For if any person wish to make
(5) the flies quit his house and secure himself from being troubled by them without diminishing the amount of light in the house, he has only to shut the door, and they will hurry forth as fast as they can and try to outstrip each other in seeking the light and fleeing from the darkness. Then no sooner is the curtain let down and the door opened than
(10) the light will return and the people of the house will no longer be harassed by flies. If there be a slit in the door, or if, when it is shut, one of the two folding leaves does not quite close on the other, that will serve them as a means of exit; and the flies often go out through the gap between the
(15) bottom of the door and the lintel. Thus it is easy to get rid of them and escape from their annoyance. With the mosquito it is otherwise, for just as the fly has greater power [for mischief] in the light, so the mosquito is more tormenting and mischievous and bloodthirsty after dark; and
(20) it is not possible for people to let into their houses sufficient light to stop the activity of the mosquito, because for this purpose they would have to admit the beams of the sun, and there are no mosquitoes except in summer when the sun is unendurable. . . . Hence, while it is easily possi-
(25) ble to contrive a remedy against flies, this is difficult in the case of mosquitoes.

The second merit of the fly is that unless it ate the mosquito, which it pursues and seeks after on the walls and in the corners of rooms, people would be unable to
(30) stay in their houses. I am informed by a trustworthy authority that Muhammad son of Jahm said one day to some of his acquaintance, "Do you know the lesson which we have learned with regard to the fly?" They said, "No." "But the fact is," he replied, "that it eats mosquitoes and
(35) chases them and picks them up and destroys them. I will tell you how I learned this. Formerly, when I wanted to take the siesta, I used to give orders that the flies should be cleared out and the curtain drawn and the door shut an hour before noon. On the disappearance of the flies, the
(40) mosquitoes would collect in the house and become exceedingly strong and powerful and bite me violently as soon as I began to rest. Now on a certain day I came in and found the room open and the curtain up. And when I lay down to sleep, there were no mosquitoes and I slept
(45) soundly, although I was very angry with the slaves. Next

day they cleared out the flies and shut the door as usual, and on my coming to take the siesta I saw a multitude of mosquitoes. Then on another day they forgot to shut the door, and when I perceived that it was open I reviled them.
(50) However, when I came for the siesta, I did not find a single mosquito and I said to myself, 'Methinks I have slept on the two days on which my precautions were neglected, and have been hindered from sleeping whenever they were carefully observed. Why should not I try today the effect
(55) of leaving the door open? If I sleep three days with the door open and suffer no annoyance from the mosquitoes, I shall know that the right way is to have the flies and the mosquitoes together, because the flies destroy them, and that our remedy lies in keeping near us what we used to
(60) keep at a distance.' I made the experiment, and now the end of the matter is that whether we desire to remove the flies or destroy the mosquitoes, we can do it with very little trouble."

1. The word *outstrip* (line 7) is used to mean

  (A) trail
  (B) defeat
  (C) expose
  (D) divest
  (E) overtake

2. An adjective Al-Jahiz might use to describe flies is

  (A) preventable
  (B) bothersome
  (C) destructive
  (D) both A and B
  (E) both B and C

3. A *lintel* (line 15) is

  (A) a doorsill
  (B) a gateway
  (C) a window
  (D) a sofa
  (E) an inlet

4. Why does Al-Jahiz say that the fly "has greater power in the light"?

  (A) It sleeps during the day.
  (B) It is active during the day.
  (C) It is more annoying when the lights are on.
  (D) It draws its energy from the sun.
  (E) It lives only one day.

GO ON TO THE NEXT PAGE

5. Why can't people let light in to rid their houses of mosquitoes?

   (A) They have no windows.
   (B) Mosquitoes only appear at night.
   (C) It is too hot.
   (D) Mosquitoes like light.
   (E) The flies will escape.

6. A reasonable summary of Al-Jahiz's discussion of the difficulty of controlling mosquitoes might be

   (A) Mosquitoes appear at night, but no artificial light will repel them.
   (B) Mosquitoes are especially dangerous in summer.
   (C) Mosquitoes prefer the dark, but people cannot get rid of them by letting in light.
   (D) Although mosquitoes like the light, opening doors in summer is not advisable.
   (E) Mosquitoes lie quietly in the sun all day and come into the house only after dark.

7. Unlike paragraph 1, paragraph 2 focuses on

   (A) The good qualities of mosquitoes.
   (B) The good qualities of flies.
   (C) A different virtue of flies.
   (D) Flies and mosquitoes.
   (E) Neither flies nor mosquitoes.

8. Why does Al-Jahiz include the tale of Muhammad son of Jahm?

   (A) to show how flies can be eliminated
   (B) to provide confirmation of his first paragraph
   (C) to demonstrate one method of pest control
   (D) to support his theory that flies eat mosquitoes
   (E) to cheer his readers

9. What does the word *reviled* in line 49 mean?

   (A) scorned
   (B) hated
   (C) screeched
   (D) praised
   (E) berated

10. By "our remedy" (line 59), Muhammad means

    (A) drugs
    (B) relief
    (C) healing
    (D) restoration
    (E) doctoring

11. The phrase "the end of the matter" (line 61) is used to mean

    (A) the boundary
    (B) the goal
    (C) death
    (D) the final exchange
    (E) the conclusion

12. This passage could be entitled

    (A) "Happy the House with Insects"
    (B) "Ridding Your Home of Pests"
    (C) "Flies Eat Household Pests"
    (D) "Why Flies Are Preferable to Mosquitoes"
    (E) "Facts About Insects"

Each sentence below has one or two blanks, each blank indicating that something has been omitted. Beneath the sentence are five lettered words or sets of words. Choose the word or set of words that best fits the meaning of the sentence as a whole.

Example:

   Although its publicity has been ----, the film itself is intelligent, well-acted, handsomely produced, and altogether ----.

   (A) tasteless..respectable
   (B) extensive..moderate
   (C) sophisticated..amateur
   (D) risqué..crude
   (E) perfect..spectacular

13. When the real estate agent finally suggested a property the young couple could ----, they were shocked to see a ---- house that seemed as though it was on the verge of collapse.

    (A) renovate..modern
    (B) purchase..galling
    (C) afford..ramshackle
    (D) diversify..dilapidated
    (E) envision..reserved

14. Psychologists agree that human beings have a strong need to ---- their time; having too much idle time can be as stressful as having none at all.

    (A) threaten
    (B) annihilate
    (C) structure
    (D) punctuate
    (E) remand

15. While scientists continue to make advances in the field of ----, some members of the clergy continue to oppose the research arguing that it is ---- for human beings to tamper with life.

    (A) psychology..imperative
    (B) astronomy..fallacious
    (C) genetics..immoral
    (D) geology..erroneous
    (E) botany..unethical

16. John was bright but lazy and because of his ---- was never promoted to senior partner.

    (A) novelty   (B) perjury   (C) zeal
    (D) indemnity   (E) indolence

17. The film was completely devoid of plot or character development; it was merely a ---- of striking images.

   (A) renouncement   (B) montage
   (C) calumny   (D) carnage   (E) premonition

Each question below consists of a related pair of words or phrases, followed by five lettered pairs of words or phrases. Select the lettered pair that best expresses a relationship similar to that expressed in the original pair

Example:

YAWN : BOREDOM::

(A) dream : sleep
(B) anger : madness
(C) smile : amusement
(D) face : expression
(E) impatience : rebellion   Ⓐ Ⓑ ● Ⓓ Ⓔ

---

18. FLY : WEB::

   (A) cat : milk
   (B) fish : net
   (C) hair : comb
   (D) tennis : racket
   (E) spider : spinning

19. WALK : SCURRY::

   (A) climb : scramble
   (B) write : type
   (C) sing : dance
   (D) anger : calm
   (E) cultivate : nurture

20. CHAPTER : NOVEL::

   (A) piano : orchestra
   (B) diamond : gem
   (C) scene : drama
   (D) poetry : prose
   (E) fraction : portion

21. IMPLY : AVER::

   (A) reject : announce
   (B) hint : proclaim
   (C) encourage : absolve
   (D) remind : contradict
   (E) embolden : accept

22. VERBOSE : WORDS::

   (A) unique : copies
   (B) deafening : sound
   (C) youthful : age
   (D) expressive : sentence
   (E) mournful : joy

23. DETENTION : RELEASE::

   (A) viciousness : attack
   (B) calamity : repair
   (C) qualification : employ
   (D) induction : discharge
   (E) therapy : confuse

24. PONDEROUS : WEIGHT::

   (A) eternity : temporality
   (B) conviction : decision
   (C) gargantuan : size
   (D) ancient : value
   (E) prototypical : affection

25. FEBRILE : ILLNESS::

   (A) tenacious : astonishment
   (B) juvenile : maturity
   (C) classic : cultivation
   (D) eccentric : discrimination
   (E) delusional : insanity

The passage below is followed by questions based on its content. Answer all questions following the passage on the basis of what is stated or implied in the passage.

Questions 26–35 are based on the following passage.

In 1801, Thomas Jefferson commissioned Meriwether Lewis to plan and carry out a western expedition. Choosing his friend William Clark to accompany him, Lewis crossed the continent from the Mississippi to the Pacific, recording data as he went. After Lewis's death in 1809, Clark found an editor, Nicholas Biddle, to edit the numerous journals that described their trip. Here they approach the Rocky Mountains.

The country on each side is high, broken, and rocky; the rock being either a soft brown sandstone, covered with a thin stratum of limestone, or else a hard black rugged granite, both usually in horizontal stratas, and the sandrock overlaying the other. Salts and quartz as well as some coal and pumicestone still appear: the bars of the river are composed primarily of gravel; the river low grounds are narrow, and afford scarcely any timber; nor is there much pine on the hills. The buffalo have now become scarce: we saw a polecat this evening, which was the first for several days: in the course of the day we also saw several herds of the big-horned animals among the steep cliffs on the north, and killed several of them. At the distance of eighteen miles we encamped on the south, and the next morning, *Sunday, 26th*, proceeded on at an early hour by means of the towline, using our oars merely in passing the river, to

Line (5)

(10)

(15)

GO ON TO THE NEXT PAGE ⟶

take advantage of the best banks. There are now scarcely any low grounds on the river, the hills being high and in many places pressing on both sides to the verge of the
(20) water. The black rock has given place to a very soft sandstone, which seems to be washed away fast by the river, and being thrown into the river renders its navigation more difficult than it was yesterday: above this sandstone, and towards the summits of the hills, a hard freestone of a yel-
(25) lowish brown colour shows itself in several stratas of unequal thickness, frequently overlaid or incrusted by a thin stratum of limestone, which seems to be formed of concreted shells. At eight and a quarter miles we came to the mouth of a creek on the north, thirty yards wide, with
(30) some running water and a rocky bed: we called it Windsor creek, after one of the party. Four and three-quarter miles beyond this we came to another creek in a bend to the north, which is twenty yards wide, with a handsome little stream of water: there is however no timber on either side
(35) of the river except a few pines on the hills: Here we saw for the first time since we left the Mandans several soft shelled turtles, though this may be owing more to the season of the year than to any scarcity of the animal.

It was here that after ascending the highest summits of
(40) the hills on the north side of the river, that captain Lewis first caught a distant view of the Rock [Rocky] mountains, the object of all our hopes, and the reward of all our ambition.

26. The word *stratum* (line 3) means

   (A) avenue
   (B) hide
   (C) boulder
   (D) layer
   (E) geology

27. The "bars of the river" (line 6) are apparently

   (A) shoals
   (B) saloons
   (C) poles
   (D) tribunals
   (E) ingots

28. The word *afford* (line 8) is used to mean

   (A) risk
   (B) chance
   (C) buy
   (D) manage
   (E) bear

29. The difference before and after the words *Sunday, 26th,* (line 15) is one of

   (A) writing style
   (B) authorship
   (C) geology
   (D) form of transportation
   (E) season

30. Why did Lewis's group name a stream "Windsor creek"?

   (A) after the Duke of Windsor
   (B) after someone they had met at a party
   (C) after a man of their political leaning
   (D) after a member of their group
   (E) no reason is given

31. "Concreted shells" (line 28) are probably

   (A) shells mixed with cement
   (B) shells imbedded in stone
   (C) shell-lined pavements
   (D) canoes carved in stone
   (E) frameworks of stone buildings

32. Clark suspects that the time of year may be responsible for

   (A) the reappearance of turtles
   (B) the soft shells of turtles
   (C) the scarcity of turtles
   (D) the lack of timber
   (E) the migration of Mandan turtles

33. How does Clark feel about seeing the Rockies?

   (A) frolicsome
   (B) hopeless
   (C) suspicious
   (D) morose
   (E) appreciative

34. The journal entry seems to unfold

   (A) according to the whim of the author
   (B) with a certain amount of backtracking
   (C) in backward chronological order
   (D) in space order tied to the movements of the travelers
   (E) with leaps forward in time

35. The primary goal of the passage is to

   (A) entertain
   (B) persuade
   (C) inform
   (D) preach
   (E) interpret

IF YOU FINISH BEFORE TIME IS CALLED, YOU MAY CHECK YOUR WORK ON THIS SECTION ONLY. DO NOT WORK ON ANY OTHER SECTION IN THE TEST.   **S T O P**

538

| SECTION 2 | Time—30 Minutes 25 Questions | In this section, solve each problem, using any available space on the page for scratchwork. Then decide which is the best of the choices given and fill in the corresponding oval on the answer sheet. |

Reference:

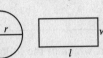

Circle: Rectangle: Rectangular Solid: Cylinder: Triangle:

$C = 2\pi r$
$A = \pi r^2$

$A = lw$

$V = lwh$

$V = \pi r^2 h$

$A = \frac{1}{2}bh$

$a^2 + b^2 = c^2$

- The measure in degrees of a straight angle is 180.
- The number of degrees of arc in a circle is 360.
- The sum of the measures of the angles of a triangle is 180.

Notes: The figures accompanying the problems are drawn as accurately as possible unless otherwise stated in specific problems. Again, unless otherwise stated, all figures lie in the same plane. All numbers used in these problems are real numbers. Calculators are permitted for this test.

1. A barrel contained 5.75 liters of water and 4.5 liters evaporated. How many liters of water remain in the barrel?

   (A) 0.75   (B) 1.25   (C) 1.75
   (D) 2.25   (E) 13.25

2. The expressions "3 less than the product of 4 times x" can be written as

   (A) $4x - 3$ (B) $3x - 4$ (C) $4(x - 3)$

   (D) $3(4x)$ (E) $\frac{4x}{3}$

3. If $\frac{3}{4}$ of x is 36, then $\frac{1}{3}$ of x is

   (A) 9   (B) 12   (C) 16   (D) 24   (E) 42

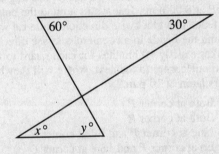

4. In the figure above, what is the value of $x + y$?

   (A) 45   (B) 60   (C) 75   (D) 90
   (E) It cannot be determined from the information given.

5. If n is a multiple of 3, which of the following is also a multiple of 3?

   (A) $2 + n$ (B) $2 - n$ (C) $2n - 1$

   (D) $2n + 1$ (E) $2n + 3$

GO ON TO THE NEXT PAGE

6. Which of the following is NOT equal to the ratio of two whole numbers?

   (A) $\left(\dfrac{1}{5}\right)^2$ (B) $\dfrac{1}{5}$ (C) 0.20 (D) 5%

   (E) $\sqrt{\dfrac{5}{1}}$

7. If the area of a square is 16, what is the perimeter?

   (A) 2 (B) 4 (C) 8 (D) 16 (E) 32

8. If $12 + x = 36 - y$, then $x + y =$

   (A) -48 (B) -24 (C) 3 (D) 24 (E) 48

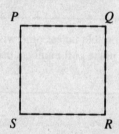

9. Two security guards, Jane and Ed, patrol the perimeter of the square area shown above. Starting at corner P at 8:00 p.m., Jane walks around the outside of the fence in a clockwise direction while Ed walks around the inside in a counterclockwise direction. If it takes exactly 10 minutes for each guard to walk from one corner to the next, where will they be two hours later, at 10 p.m.?

   (A) Both at corner P
   (B) Both at corner R
   (C) Jane at corner P and Ed at corner R
   (D) Ed at corner P and Jane at corner Q
   (E) Ed at corner P and Jane at corner R

10. Depending on the value of k, the expression $3k + 4k + 5k + 6k + 7k$ may or may not be divisible by 7. Which of the terms, when eliminated from the expression, guarantees that the resulting expression is divisible by 7 for every positive integer k?

    (A) $3k$ (B) $4k$ (C) $5k$ (D) $6k$ (E) $7k$

11. If $\dfrac{1}{3} < x < \dfrac{3}{8}$, which of the following is a possible value of x?

    (A) $\dfrac{1}{2}$ (B) $\dfrac{3}{16}$ (C) $\dfrac{17}{48}$ (D) $\dfrac{9}{24}$ (E) $\dfrac{5}{12}$

12. If $x^2 - y^2 = 3$ and $x - y = 3$, then $x + y =$

    (A) 0 (B) 1 (C) 2 (D) 3 (E) 9

13. If n is a positive integer, which of the following must be an even integer?

    (A) $n + 1$ (B) $3n + 1$ (C) $3n + 2$
    (D) $n^2 + 1$ (E) $n^2 + n$

14. If the area of a square inscribed in a circle is 16, what is the area of the circle?

    (A) 2π (B) 4π (C) 8π (D) 16π (E) 32π

15. In a certain group of 36 people, only 18 people are wearing hats and only 24 people are wearing sweaters. If 6 people are wearing neither a hat nor a sweater, how many people are wearing both a hat and a sweater?

    (A) 30 (B) 22 (C) 12 (D) 8 (E) 6

16. A certain mixture of gravel and sand consists of 2.5 kilograms of gravel and 12.5 kilograms of sand. What percent of the mixture, by weight, is gravel?

    (A) 10% (B) $16\dfrac{2}{3}\%$ (C) 20%

    (D) 25% (E) $33\dfrac{1}{3}\%$

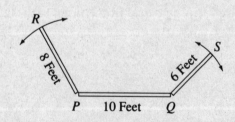

17. The figure above is the top view of a folding room divider, hinged at P and Q. If sections PR and QS are moved as shown until R and S meet, what will be the area, in square feet, enclosed? (Ignore the thickness of the hinges and the screen's sections.)

    (A) 6 (B) 12 (C) 6π (D) 24 (E) 12π

18. Motorcycle *X* averages 40 kilometers per liter of gasoline while Motorcycle *Y* averages 50 kilometers per liter. If the cost of gasoline is $2 per liter, what will be the difference in the cost of operating the two motorcycles for 300 kilometers?

(A) $3   (B) $6   (C) $12   (D) $15   (E) $20

19. If for all positive integers,

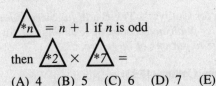

$\boxed{*n} = \frac{1}{2}n$ if *n* is even

$\boxed{*n} = n + 1$ if *n* is odd

then $\boxed{*2} \times \boxed{*7} =$

(A) 4   (B) 5   (C) 6   (D) 7   (E) 8

20. For a positive integer *k*, which of the following equals $6k + 3$?

(A) $\frac{1}{2}(k + 1)$ (B) $\frac{1}{k} + 4$ (C) $2k + 1$

(D) $3(k + 1)$ (E) $3(2k + 1)$

21. To mail a letter costs *x* cents for the first ounce and *y* cents for every additional ounce or fraction of an ounce. What is the cost, *in cents*, to mail a letter weighing a whole number of ounces, *w*?

(A) $w(x + y)$
(B) $x(w - y)$
(C) $x(w - 1) + y(w - 1)$
(D) $x + wy$
(E) $x + y(w - 1)$

22. The figure above shows nine tiles with single-digit numbers painted on them. If *xy* is the product of the value of any two tiles selected at random, how many *different* possible values for *xy* are there?

(A) 4   (B) 7   (C) 10   (D) 12   (E) 16

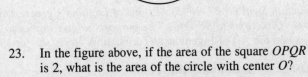

23. In the figure above, if the area of the square *OPQR* is 2, what is the area of the circle with center *O*?

(A) $\frac{\pi}{4}$ (B) $\pi\sqrt{2}$ (C) 2π (D) $2\sqrt{2\pi}$ (E) 4π

24. How many positive integers less than 30 are equal to 3 times an *odd* integer?

(A) 10   (B) 7   (C) 5   (D) 4   (E) 3

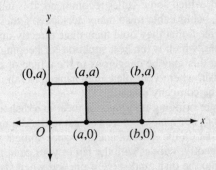

25. What is the area of the shaded portion of the figure above, expressed in terms of *a* and *b*?

(A) $a(b - a)$ (B) $a(a - b)$ (C) $b(a - b)$
(D) $b(b - a)$ (E) ab

IF YOU FINISH BEFORE TIME IS CALLED, YOU MAY CHECK YOUR WORK ON THIS SECTION ONLY. DO NOT WORK ON ANY OTHER SECTION IN THE TEST.   **STOP**

SECTION 3   Time—15 Minutes   For each question in this section, choose the best answer and
             10 Questions   blacken the corresponding space on the answer sheet.

The passage below is followed by questions based on its content. Answer all questions following the passage on the basis of what is stated or implied in the passage.

Questions 1–10 are based on the following passages.

Jonathan Swift (1667–1745) was one of England's greatest satirists, best known for Gulliver's Travels. *In his piece below, from "Directions to Servants," he purports to give advice to footmen. Jane Collier published a book in 1753 entitled* An Essay on the Art of Ingeniously Tormenting. *Here, she too gives advice, this time to parents of large broods.*

Passage 1—Jonathan Swift (1745)

There is a great controversy about the most convenient and genteel way of holding your plate, when you wait on your Master, and his company, at meals; some butlers stick it
Line between the frame of the back of the chair, which is an
(5) excellent expedient, where the make of the chair will allow it: Others, for fear the plate should fall, grasp it so firmly, that their thumb reacheth to the middle of the hollow; which however, if your thumb be dry, is no secure method; and therefore in that case, I advise your wetting
(10) the bowl of it with your tongue: As to that absurd practice of letting the back of the plate lie leaning on the hollow of your hand, which some ladies recommend, it is universally exploded, being liable to so many accidents. Others again, are so refined, that they hold their plate directly under the
(15) left arm-pit, which is the best situation for keeping it warm; but this may be dangerous in the article of taking away a dish, where your plate may happen to fall upon some of the company's heads. . . .
   If you are bringing up a joint of meat in a dish and it
(20) falls out of your hands, before you get to the dining room, with the mat on the ground, and the sauce spilled, take up the meat gently, wipe it with the lap of your coat, then put it again into the dish, and serve it up; and when your lady misses the sauce, tell her it is to be sent up in a plate by
(25) itself. When you carry up a dish of meat, dip your fingers in the sauce, or lick it with your tongue, to try whether it be good and fit for your master's table....
   While Grace is saying after meat, do you and your brethren take the chairs from behind the company, so that
(30) when they go to sit again, they may fall backwards, which will make them all merry; but be you so discreet as to hold your laughter till you get to the kitchen, and then divert your fellow-servants....
   Never wear socks when you wait at meals, on the
(35) account of your own health, as well as them who sit at table; because as most ladies like the smell of young mens toes, so it is a sovereign remedy against vapours.

Passage 2—Jane Collier (1753)

Suppose your stock of children too large; and that, by your care for their support, you should be abridged of some of
Line your own luxuries and pleasures. To make away with the
(40) troublesome and expensive brats, I allow, would be the desirable thing: but the question is, how to effect this without subjecting yourself to that punishment which the law has thought proper to affix to such sort of jokes. Whipping and starving, with some caution, might do the business:
(45) but, since a late execution for a fact of that kind may have given a precedent for the magistrates to examine into such affairs, you may, by these means, find your way to the gallows, if you are low enough for such a scrutiny into your conduct: and, if you are too high to have your actions pun-
(50) ished, you may possibly be a little ill spoken of amongst your acquaintance. I think, therefore, it is best not to venture, either your neck, or your reputation, by such a proceeding; especially as you may effect the thing, full as well, by following the directions I have given, of holding
(55) no restraint over them.
   Suffer them to climb, without contradiction, to heights from which they may break their necks: let them eat every thing they like, and at all times; not refusing them the richest meats, and highest sauces, with as great a variety as
(60) possible; because even excess in one dish of plain meat cannot, as I have been told by physicians, do much harm. Suffer them to sit up as late as they please at night, and make hearty meat-suppers; and even in the middle of the night, if they call for it, don't refuse the poor things some
(65) victuals. By this means, nobody can say you starve your children: and if they should chance to die of a surfeit, or of an ill habit of body, contracted from such diet, so far will you be from censure, that your name will be recorded for a kind and indulgent parent.
(70)

1. When Swift says, "it is universally exploded" (line 12), he means

   (A) the practice erupts worldwide
   (B) the practice can blow up in one's face
   (C) the practice is completely discredited
   (D) the practice always ends in disgrace
   (E) the practice makes everyone angry

GO ON TO THE NEXT PAGE →

542

2. Swift's reference to "while Grace is saying after meat" (line 28) has to do with

   (A) after-dinner speeches by the host and hostess
   (B) the lady of the house ringing for dessert
   (C) an important visitor, such as the Bishop, dropping in
   (D) the saying of prayers after the main course
   (E) a parlor game wherein everyone leaves his or her seat

3. The word *divert* in Swift's piece (line 32) means

   (A) distract
   (B) sidetrack
   (C) shift
   (D) occupy
   (E) entertain

4. Swift uses the word *sovereign* (line 37) to mean

   (A) autonomous
   (B) dominant
   (C) lordly
   (D) incomparable
   (E) independent

5. Collier uses the word *abridged* (line 39) to mean

   (A) summarized
   (B) curtailed
   (C) compressed
   (D) abbreviated
   (E) concentrated

6. The words *low* and *high*, as used by Collier in lines 49 and 50, refer to

   (A) class
   (B) religion
   (C) morals
   (D) population
   (E) location

7. Why, in summary, does Collier not recommend starvation?

   (A) It is too difficult to control.
   (B) It is unethical.
   (C) It must be done with caution.
   (D) It was recently found illegal.
   (E) It cannot do much harm.

8. The word *surfeit*, used by Collier in line 67, means

   (A) default
   (B) forging
   (C) facsimile
   (D) surrender
   (E) overabundance

9. The tone of both passages could be described as

   (A) argumentative
   (B) prosaic
   (C) ironic
   (D) snide
   (E) vengeful

10. These two passages might be anthologized with the heading

    (A) "The Servants' Guidebook"
    (B) "Better Living"
    (C) "Helping Parents in the Home"
    (D) "Ridiculous Recommendations"
    (E) "Don't Ask Me"

IF YOU FINISH BEFORE TIME IS CALLED, YOU MAY CHECK YOUR WORK ON **STOP** THIS SECTION ONLY. DO NOT WORK ON ANY OTHER SECTION IN THE TEST.

SECTION **4**	Time—15 Minutes 10 Questions	In this section, solve each problem, using any available space on the page for scratchwork. Then decide which is the best of the choices given and fill in the corresponding oval on the answer sheet.

Reference:

Circle: Rectangle: Rectangular Solid: Cylinder: Triangle:

$C = 2\pi r$
$A = \pi r^2$

$A = lw$

$V = lwh$

$V = \pi r^2 h$

$A = \frac{1}{2}bh$

$a^2 + b^2 = c^2$

- The measure in degrees of a straight angle is 180.
- The number of degrees of arc in a circle is 360.
- The sum of the measures of the angles of a triangle is 180.

Notes: The figures accompanying the problems are drawn as accurately as possible unless otherwise stated in specific problems. Again, unless otherwise stated, all figures lie in the same plane. All numbers used in these problems are real numbers. Calculators are permitted for this test.

Fabric	Cost
A	3 yards for $8
B	2 yards for $6
C	4 yards for $9
D	5 yards for $7
E	6 yards for $5

1. According to the table above, which fabric costs the *least* per square yard?

   (A) A   (B) B   (C) C   (D) D   (E) E

2. $\dfrac{10^3(10^5 + 10^5)}{10^4} =$

   (A) 10^4 (B) 10^6 (C) $2(10^2)$ (D) $2(10^4)$
   (E) $2(10^9)$

3. If $x = b + 4$ and $y = b - 3$, then in terms of x and y, $b =$

   (A) $x + y - 1$ (B) $x + y + 1$ (C) $x - y - 1$

   (D) $\dfrac{x + y + 1}{2}$ (E) $\dfrac{x + y - 1}{2}$

4. If $5x = 3y = z$, and x, y, and z are positive integers, all of the following must be integers EXCEPT

   (A) $\dfrac{x}{zy}$ (B) $\dfrac{z}{5}$ (C) $\dfrac{z}{3}$ (D) $\dfrac{z}{15}$ (E) $\dfrac{x}{3}$

5. What is the width of a rectangle with area $48x^2$ and a length of $24x$?

   (A) 2   (B) $2x$ (C) $24x$ (D) $2x^2$ (E) $2x^3$

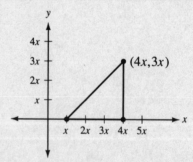

6. In the figure above, if the area of the triangle is 54, then $x =$

   (A) $3\sqrt{3}$ (B) 3   (C) $2\sqrt{3}$ (D) 2
   (E) It cannot be determined from the information given.

GO ON TO THE NEXT PAGE

7. If $x = \dfrac{1}{y+1}$ and $y \neq 1$, then $y =$

(A) $x+1$ (B) x (C) $\dfrac{x+1}{x}$

(D) $\dfrac{x-1}{x}$ (E) $\dfrac{1-x}{x}$

8. If $\blacktriangle(x) = x + 1$ and $\blacktriangledown(x) = x - 1$, then which of the following is equal to $\blacktriangle(3) \times \blacktriangledown(5)$?

(A) $\blacktriangle 8$ (B) $\blacktriangle 12$ (C) $\blacktriangle 14$
(D) $\blacktriangledown 17$ (E) $\blacktriangledown 20$

9. If $x + y = 14$, then $\dfrac{1}{2}x + \dfrac{1}{2}y =$

(A) 4
(B) 5
(C) 6
(D) 7
(E) $\dfrac{1}{2}y$

10. If the average of ten numbers—1, 2, 3, 4, 5, 6, 7, 8, 9, and x—is 6, what is x?

(A) 5
(B) 6
(C) 10
(D) 12
(E) 15

IF YOU FINISH BEFORE TIME IS CALLED, YOU MAY CHECK YOUR WORK ON THIS SECTION ONLY. DO NOT WORK ON ANY OTHER SECTION IN THE TEST.   **S T O P**

545

SECTION 5   Time—30 Minutes   For each question in this section, choose the best answer and
35 Questions   blacken the corresponding space on the answer sheet.

Each sentence below has one or two blanks, each
blank indicating that something has been omitted.
Beneath the sentence are five lettered words or sets of
words. Choose the word or set of words that best fits
the meaning of the sentence as a whole.

Example:

Although its publicity has been ----, the film itself
is intelligent, well-acted, handsomely produced, and
altogether ----.

(A) tasteless..respectable
(B) extensive..moderate
(C) sophisticated..amateur
(D) risqué..crude
(E) perfect..spectacular

1. Although for centuries literature was considered
something which would instruct as well as entertain,
the modern reader has little patience with ---- works
and seeks only to be ----.

(A) epic..demoralized
(B) didactic..distracted
(C) bawdy..absorbed
(D) superficial..enlightened
(E) ambiguous..misled

2. Because the poet was restless and uneasy in society,
he sought a ---- existence and a life of ----.

(A) stable..pleasure
(B) claustrophobic..frivolity
(C) materialistic..urbanity
(D) conservative..squalor
(E) nomadic..solitude

3. Because he was ---- and the life of the party, his
friends thought that he was happy; but his wife was
---- and shy and was thought to be unhappy.

(A) melancholy..sympathetic
(B) philanthropic..conciliatory
(C) vitriolic..sophomoric
(D) garrulous..taciturn
(E) inimical..gregarious

4. His offhand, rather ---- remarks ---- a character that
was really rather serious and not at all superficial.

(A) flippant..masked
(B) pernicious..betrayed
(C) bellicose..belied
(D) controversial..revealed
(E) shallow..enlivened

5. Although the faculty did not always agree with the
chairperson of the department, they ---- her ideas,
mostly in ---- her seniority and out of respect for her
previous achievements.

(A) scoffed at..fear of
(B) harbored..defense of
(C) implemented..deference to
(D) marveled at..lieu of
(E) ignored..honor of

6. Despite the millions of dollars spent on improvements, the telephone system in India remains ---- and
continues to ---- the citizens who depend on it.

(A) primitive..inconvenience
(B) bombastic..upset
(C) suspicious..connect
(D) outdated..elate
(E) impartial..vex

7. Contrary to popular opinion, bats are not generally
aggressive and rabid; most are shy and ----.

(A) turgid
(B) disfigured
(C) punctual
(D) innocuous
(E) depraved

8. The ballet company demonstrated its ---- by putting
both classical and modern works in the repertoire.

(A) versatility
(B) mollification
(C) treachery
(D) dignity
(E) obtrusiveness

9. Unlike the images in symbolist poetry which are
often vague and ----, the images of surrealist poetry
are startlingly ---- and bold.

(A) extraneous..furtive
(B) trivial..inadvertent
(C) obscure..concrete
(D) spectacular..pallid
(E) symmetrical..virulent

GO ON TO THE NEXT PAGE

10. A good trial lawyer will argue only what is central to an issue, eliminating ---- information or anything else that might ---- the client.

    (A) seminal..amuse
    (B) extraneous..jeopardize
    (C) erratic..enhance
    (D) prodigious..extol
    (E) reprehensible..initiate

11. The music was so ---- that we begged for some ----.

    (A) thunderous..relief
    (B) provocative..harmony
    (C) noisome..silence
    (D) lugubrious..upbeat
    (E) fractious..tempo

12. Richard is ---- on many topics; he is a true ----.

    (A) scholarly..renaissance
    (B) erudite..prodigy
    (C) clever..intelligentsia
    (D) versed..aficionado
    (E) familiar..aesthete

13. The novel was long, but the ---- plot kept our interest.

    (A) torpid
    (B) alien
    (C) insipid
    (D) labyrinthine
    (E) humdrum

14. Is he ----, or is he merely ----?

    (A) amusing..witty
    (B) tranquil..mannerly
    (C) divisive..voracious
    (D) timid..unruly
    (E) uncivil..reticent

15. Anyone who works at home needs to be self-disciplined and ----.

    (A) straitlaced
    (B) chronic
    (C) idiosyncratic
    (D) systematic
    (E) extremist

Each question below consists of a related pair of words or phrases, followed by five lettered pairs of words or phrases. Select the lettered pair that best expresses a relationship similar to that expressed in the original pair

Example:

YAWN : BOREDOM::

    (A) dream : sleep
    (B) anger : madness
    (C) smile : amusement
    (D) face : expression
    (E) impatience : rebellion

Ⓐ Ⓑ ● Ⓓ Ⓔ

16. MIRROR : GLASS::

    (A) igloo : ice
    (B) marsh : reed
    (C) grain : wood
    (D) thread : weave
    (E) straw : hay

17. SCULPTOR : STONE::

    (A) poet : sonnet
    (B) lawyer : crime
    (C) carpenter : wood
    (D) doctor : patient
    (E) painter : museum

18. LIAR : MENDACITY::

    (A) swindler : burglary
    (B) glutton : appetite
    (C) philistine : knowledge
    (D) soldier : orders
    (E) diplomat : nationalism

19. WATERFALL : CASCADE::

    (A) snow : freeze
    (B) missile : launch
    (C) tree : exfoliate
    (D) wave : undulate
    (E) monarch : reign

20. INFLATE : MAGNITUDE::

    (A) measure : weight
    (B) extend : duration
    (C) magnify : coin
    (D) limit : speed
    (E) legislate : crime

21. MOCK : DERISION::

    (A) despise : contempt
    (B) reject : account
    (C) repair : corruption
    (D) inspire : muse
    (E) observe : refinement

GO ON TO THE NEXT PAGE

22. WEB : ENTANGLE::

(A) spider : spin
(B) trap : ensnare
(C) treason : betray
(D) ransom : kidnap
(E) grid : delineate

23. LETHARGY : ENERGY::

(A) appetite : hunger
(B) redemption : sacrament
(C) sorrow : pity
(D) merit : remuneration
(E) apathy : interest

24. THWART : ACHIEVE::

(A) retain : submit
(B) couch : conceal
(C) silence : speak
(D) pretend : inherit
(E) permeate : infiltrate

25. APOCRYPHAL : GENUINE::

(A) spurious : authentic
(B) labored : relieved
(C) fragmented : riddled
(D) enigmatic : rambunctious
(E) credulous : flagrant

The passage below is followed by questions based on its content. Answer all questions following the passage on the basis of what is stated or implied in the passage.

Questions 26–35 are based on the following passage.

Susan Brownell Anthony (1820–1906) presided over the National Woman Suffrage Association from 1892 until 1900. In 1884 she was called to testify before the Senate Select Committee on Woman Suffrage. This is part of her statement.

I wish you, gentlemen, would look down there and see the myriads that are there. We want to help them and lift them up. That is exactly the trouble with you, gentlemen; you
Line are forever looking at your own wives, your own mothers,
(5) your own sisters, and your own daughters, and they are well cared for and protected; but only look down to the struggling masses of women who have no one to protect them, neither husband, father, brother, son, with no mortal in all the land to protect them. If you would look down
(10) there the question would be solved; but the difficulty is that you think only of those who are doing well. We are not speaking for ourselves, but for those who can not speak for themselves. We are speaking for the doomed as much as you, Senator Edmunds, used to speak for the
(15) doomed on the plantations of the South. . . .

You ask us why we do not get this right to vote first in the school districts, and on school questions, or the questions of liquor license. It has been shown very clearly why we need something more than that. You have good
(20) enough laws to-day in every State in this Union for the suppression of what are termed the social vices; for the suppression of the grog-shops, the gambling houses, the brothels, the obscene shows. There is plenty of legislation in every State in this Union for their suppression if it could
(25) be executed. Why is the Government, why are the States and the cities, unable to execute those laws? Simply because there is a large balance of power in every city that does not want those laws executed. Consequently both parties must alike cater to that balance of political power. The
(30) party that puts a plank in its platform that the laws against the grog-shops and all the other sinks of iniquity must be executed, is the party that will not get this balance of power to vote for it, and, consequently, the party that can not get into power.

What we ask of you is that you will make of the (35) women of the cities a balance of political power, so that when a mayor, a member of the common council, a supervisor, a justice of the peace, a district attorney, a judge on the bench even, shall go before the people of that city as a candidate for the suffrages of the people he shall not only (40) be compelled to look to the men who frequent the grog-shops, the brothels, and the gambling houses, who will vote for him if he is not in favor of executing the law, but that he shall also have to look to the mothers, the sisters, the wives, and the daughters of those deluded men to see (45) what they will do if he does not execute the law.

We want to make of ourselves a balance of political power. What we need is the power to execute the laws. We have laws enough. Let me give you one little fact in regard to my own city of Rochester. You all know how (50) that wonderful whip called the temperance crusade roused the whisky ring. It caused the whisky force to concentrate itself more strongly at the ballot-box than ever before, so that when the report of the elections in the spring of 1874 went over the country the result was that the whisky ring (55) was triumphant, and that the whisky ticket was elected even more strongly than before. Senator Thurman will remember how it was in his own State of Ohio. Everybody knows that if my friends, Mrs. ex-Governor Wallace, Mrs. Allen, and all the women of the great West could have (60) gone to the ballot-box at those municipal elections and voted for candidates, no such result would have occurred; while you refused by the laws of the State to the women the right to have their opinions counted, every rum-seller, every drunkard, every pauper even from the poor-house, (65) and every criminal outside of the State's prison came out on election day to express his opinion and have it counted.

26. Anthony uses the phrase "the myriads" (line 2) to mean

(A) poor people
(B) the unemployed
(C) all women
(D) women without protection
(E) slaves

27. According to the beginning of paragraph 2, Congress wants women to

(A) vote the way their husbands vote
(B) vote only on "family-centered" issues
(C) stay home on election day
(D) give up the fight for suffrage
(E) put more laws on the books

28. Why does Anthony repeat the words *grog-shops*, *brothels*, and *gambling houses*?

(A) to stress the need for new laws
(B) to remind Congress of the existence of corruption despite laws
(C) to show Congress the vices upheld by men's votes
(D) both A and B
(E) both B and C

29. The word *execute* (line 26) is used to mean

(A) do
(B) render
(C) behead
(D) enforce
(E) dramatize

30. The term "sinks of iniquity" (line 31) is used to mean

(A) dens of vice
(B) figures of fun
(C) signs of freedom
(D) laws fostering injustice
(E) harbingers of doom

31. Anthony urges Congress to give women the vote primarily as a means of

(A) legality
(B) trickery
(C) fairness
(D) balance
(E) appeasement

32. How does Anthony feel about the temperance movement?

(A) approving
(B) critical
(C) superior
(D) amused
(E) exasperated

33. Why does Anthony include the discussion of problems in Rochester?

(A) to show that trouble can occur close to home
(B) to demonstrate the need for temperance
(C) to support her opinion that allowing only men to vote maintains the *status quo*
(D) both A and B
(E) both B and C

34. Anthony probably addresses certain Senators by name to

(A) address their prejudices
(B) embarrass their colleagues
(C) demonstrate her erudition
(D) promote their causes
(E) invoke their sympathies

35. A phrase that summarizes Anthony's speech thus far might be

(A) "Women's votes can rid us of vice."
(B) "Let my people go."
(C) "Clean up our cities now."
(D) "How can we effect change?"
(E) "We must protect all women."

SECTION **6**   Time—30 Minutes   This section contains two types of problems with separate directions for
25 Questions   each. You may use any available space on the page for scratchwork.

Reference:

Circle: Rectangle: Rectangular Solid: Cylinder: Triangle:

$C = 2\pi r$
$A = \pi r^2$ $A = lw$ $V = lwh$ $V = \pi r^2 h$ $A = \frac{1}{2}bh$ $a^2 + b^2 = c^2$

- The measure in degrees of a straight angle is 180.
- The number of degrees of arc in a circle is 360.
- The sum of the measures of the angles of a triangle is 180.

Notes: The figures accompanying the problems are drawn as accurately as possible unless otherwise stated in specific problems. Again, unless otherwise stated, all figures lie in the same plane. All numbers used in these problems are real numbers. Calculators are permitted for this test.

Directions for Quantitative Comparison Questions

Questions 1–15 each consist of two quantities, one in Column A and one in Column B. You are to compare the two quantities and on the answer sheet fill in oval

A if the quantity in Column A is greater;
B if the quantity in Column B is greater;
C if the two quantities are equal;
D if the relationship cannot be determined from the information given.

AN E RESPONSE WILL NOT BE SCORED.

	EXAMPLES		
	Column A	Column B	Answers
E1.	2×6	$2 + 6$	● Ⓑ ⒸⒹⒺ
E2.	$180 - x$	y	ⒶⒷ ● ⒹⒺ
E3.	$p - q$	$q - p$	ⒶⒷⒸ ● Ⓔ

Notes:

1. In certain questions, information concerning one or both of the quantities to be compared is centered above the two columns.
2. In a given question, a symbol that appears in both columns represents the same thing in Column A as it does in Column B.
3. Letters such as x, n, and k stand for real numbers.

GO ON TO THE NEXT PAGE

550

Column A	Column B

$54 - 3n = 6$

1.

n	16

Four faces of a solid cube are red and the others are black.

2.

The number of faces that are black	3

3.

The number of ounces in x pounds	y ounces

4.

$\dfrac{2}{3}$	.66

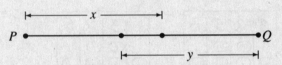

5.

Length of PQ	$x + y$

In a shipment of six packages, five of the packages weigh exactly 25 pounds and the sixth package weighs more than 1 pound but less than 20 pounds.

6.

Average (arithmetic mean) weight, in pounds, of the six packages	22.5

Column A	Column B

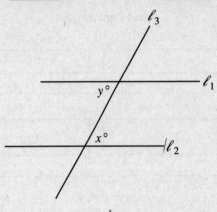

$l1 \parallel l2$

7.

$2x$	$x + y$

Tina has more than twice as many marbles as Chuck and Luis have together.

8.

Number of marbles Tina has	Three times the number of marbles Chuck has

---

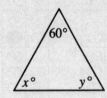 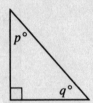

Note: Figures not drawn to scale.

9.

$x + y$	$p + q$

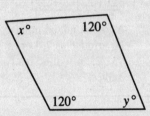

Note: Figure not drawn to scale.

10.

x	y

GO ON TO THE NEXT PAGE

$$-3 > x > -7$$
$$-5 > y > -9$$
x and *y* are integers.

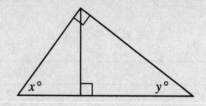

11.
x		*y*

14.
x		*y*

12.
$3\sqrt{3}$		$\dfrac{3}{\sqrt{3}}$

$$
\begin{array}{r}
30\blacksquare \\
\times\ 6 \\
\hline
1{,}85\blacktriangle
\end{array}
$$

$$x < 0 < y$$

13.
$x + y$		*x*

15.
$\blacksquare$		$\blacktriangle$

Directions for Student-Produced Response Questions

Questions 16–25 each require you to solve a problem and mark your answer on a special answer grid. For each question, you should write your answer in the boxes at the top of each column and then fill in the ovals beneath each answer you write. Here are some examples.

Answer: 3/4 (= .75; show answer either way)

Answer: 325

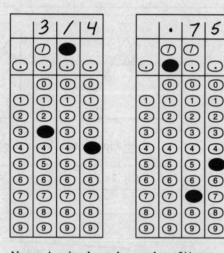

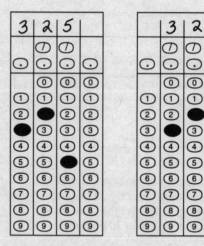

Note: A mixed number such as 3½ must be gridded as 7/2 or as 3.5. If gridded as "31/2," it will be read as "thirty-one halves."

Note: Either position is correct.

16. $\sqrt{(43 - 7)(29 + 7)} = ?$

17. A certain concrete mixture uses 4 cubic yards of cement for every 20 cubic yards of grit. If a contractor orders 50 cubic yards of cement, how much grit (in cubic yards), should he order if he plans to use all of the cement?

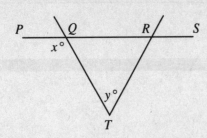

18. In the figure above, $QT = QR$. If $x = 120$, then $y = ?°$

19. If $\dfrac{x}{y} = -1$, then $x + y = ?$

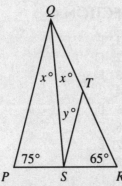

Note: Figure not drawn to scale.

20. In triangle PQR above, if $PQ \parallel$ to ST, then $y = ?°$

21. The average of seven different positive integers is 12. What is the greatest that any one of the integers could be?

22. A drawer contains 4 green socks, 6 blue socks, and 10 white socks. If socks are pulled out of the drawer at random and not replaced, what is the minimum number of socks that must be pulled out of the drawer to *guarantee* that two of every color have been pulled out of the drawer?

23. On a trip, a motorist drove 10 miles at 20 miles per hour, 10 miles at 30 miles per hour, and 10 miles at 60 miles per hour. What fraction of her total driving time was spent driving 60 miles per hour?

24. In Company A, 50% of the employees are women. In Company B, 40% of the employees are women. If Company A has 800 employees, and Company B has half that number, how many more women are employed at Company A than at Company B?

25. In the country of Zzyzyyx, $\dfrac{2}{5}$ of the population have blue eyes. How many people would you have to look at to find 50 with blue eyes?

IF YOU FINISH BEFORE TIME IS CALLED, YOU MAY CHECK YOUR WORK ON THIS SECTION ONLY. DO NOT WORK ON ANY OTHER SECTION IN THE TEST. **S T O P**

Answer Key

SECTION 1

1. E	11. E	21. B	31. B
2. D	12. D	22. B	32. C
3. A	13. C	23. D	33. E
4. B	14. C	24. C	34. D
5. C	15. C	25. E	35. C
6. C	16. E	26. D	
7. C	17. B	27. A	
8. D	18. B	28. E	
9. E	19. A	29. C	
10. B	20. C	30. D	

SECTION 2

1. B	11. C	21. E
2. A	12. B	22. B
3. C	13. E	23. C
4. D	14. C	24. C
5. E	15. C	25. A
6. E	16. B	
7. D	17. D	
8. D	18. A	
9. A	19. E	
10. B	20. E	

SECTION 3

1. C
2. D
3. E
4. D
5. B
6. A
7. D
8. E
9. C
10. D

SECTION 4

1. E
2. D
3. E
4. A
5. B
6. C
7. E
8. D
9. D
10. E

SECTION 5

1. B	11. A	21. A	31. D
2. E	12. B	22. B	32. A
3. D	13. D	23. E	33. C
4. A	14. E	24. C	34. E
5. C	15. D	25. A	35. A
6. A	16. A	26. D	
7. D	17. C	27. B	
8. A	18. B	28. E	
9. C	19. D	29. D	
10. B	20. B	30. A	

SECTION 6

1. C	11. D	21. 63
2. B	12. A	22. 18
3. D	13. B	23. 1/6
4. A	14. D	24. 240
5. B	15. A	25. 125
6. D	16. 36	
7. C	17. 250	
8. D	18. 60	
9. A	19. 0	
10. D	20. 20	

Explanatory Answers

SECTION 1

CRITICAL READING

1. The word *outstrip* (line 7) is used to mean

   (A) trail
   (B) defeat
   (C) expose
   (D) divest
   (E) overtake

   (E) This is a vocabulary-in-context question. Return to the context (lines 6–7) and plug in the answer choices. The flies "hurry" and are "fleeing," which gives you a clue. They are racing to see which will overtake (E) the others.

2. An adjective Al-Jahiz might use to describe flies is

   (A) preventable
   (B) bothersome
   (C) destructive
   (D) both A and B
   (E) both B and C

   (D) In questions of this type, you must read all the answers. In this case, flies are proved by Al-Jahiz to be *preventable* (A); the second sentence of the passage introduces a means of ridding the house of them. At the same time, flies are surely *bothersome* (B); that is why one wants to get rid of them. Nowhere are they accused of being *destructive* (C). Since (A) and (B) are true, the answer must be (D).

3. A *lintel* (line 15) is

   (A) a doorsill
   (B) a gateway
   (C) a window
   (D) a sofa
   (E) an inlet

   (A) Even if you have never seen this word before, you can determine its meaning by eliminating obvious incorrect choices and plugging in the remaining choices in context. There is apparently a "gap between the bottom of the door and the lintel" (line 15) through which flies can escape. This eliminates (B), (D), and (E) as logical choices. Of the other two, the most likely is (A).

4. Why does Al-Jahiz say that the fly "has greater power in the light"?

   (A) It sleeps during the day.
   (B) It is active during the day.
   (C) It is more annoying when the lights are on.
   (D) It draws its energy from the sun.
   (E) It lives only one day.

   (B) It is clear from the passage, even if you did not know the date when it was written, that no electric lights exist here, so (C) cannot be a correct choice. There is no support for (A), (D), or (E), so the answer must be (B).

5. Why can't people let light in to rid their houses of mosquitoes?

   (A) They have no windows.
   (B) Mosquitoes appear only at night.
   (C) It is too hot.
   (D) Mosquitoes like light.
   (E) The flies will escape.

   (C) Even if they had no windows (A), they could still open their doors, but they must not do so during the summer daylight hours, because "the sun is unendurable" (line 24). (D) is directly contradicted by the text, (E) is irrelevant, and (B) is indirectly contradicted—there would be no mosquitoes during siesta time if they appeared only at night.

6. A reasonable summary of Al-Jahiz's discussion of the difficulty of controlling mosquitoes might be

   (A) Mosquitoes appear at night, but no artificial light will repel them.
   (B) Mosquitoes are especially dangerous in summer.
   (C) Mosquitoes prefer the dark, but people cannot get rid of them by letting in light.
   (D) Although mosquitoes like the light, opening doors in summer is not advisable.
   (E) Mosquitoes lie quietly in the sun all day and come into the house only after dark.

   (C) An evaluation question of this type requires you to summarize facts and details and compare your summation to the answer choices. In this case, no support is given for (A) (artificial light is not mentioned), (B) (mosquitoes are not called "dangerous"), (D) (mosquitoes, it is said, prefer the dark), or (E). Through a process of elimination, then, the only logical choice is (C).

7. Unlike paragraph 1, paragraph 2 focuses on

   (A) The good qualities of mosquitoes.
   (B) The good qualities of flies.
   (C) A different virtue of flies.
   (D) Flies and mosquitoes.
   (E) Neither flies nor mosquitoes.

   (C) An understanding of the structure of the passage as a whole is needed to answer this synthesis/analysis question. The passage begins: "In the fly there are two good qualities." Paragraph 1 deals with one good quality, and paragraph 2 with the other. (B) is true, but too general.

8. Why does Al-Jahiz include the tale of Muhammad son of Jahm?

   (A) to show how flies can be eliminated
   (B) to provide confirmation of his first paragraph
   (C) to demonstrate one method of pest control
   (D) to support his theory that flies eat mosquitoes
   (E) to cheer his readers

   (D) This is another type of synthesis/analysis question. You must summarize the tale in your head to determine its function in the passage as a whole. The tale is about flies eating mosquitoes, so it must be used to support Al-Jahiz's contention that this takes place.

9. What does the word *reviled* in line 49 mean?

   (A) scorned
   (B) hated
   (C) screeched
   (D) praised
   (E) berated

   (E) Testing the choices in context will prove that only *berated*, or "scolded," is a sensible replacement for *reviled*.

10. By "our remedy" (line 59), Muhammad means

    (A) drugs
    (B) relief
    (C) healing
    (D) restoration
    (E) doctoring

    (B) Each of these choices might replace the word *remedy*, but this interpretation question requires you to understand *how* the phrase is used. Only (B) makes sense in context.

11. The phrase "the end of the matter" (line 61) is used to mean

    (A) the boundary
    (B) the goal
    (C) death
    (D) the final exchange
    (E) the conclusion

    (E) Again, this is an interpretation question. Try out the various answer choices in place of the excerpted phrase: "I made the experiment, and now . . . is that . . . we can do it with very little trouble." Only (E) makes sense.

12. This passage could be entitled

    (A) "Happy the House with Insects"
    (B) "Ridding Your Home of Pests"
    (C) "Flies Eat Household Pests"
    (D) "Why Flies Are Preferable to Mosquitoes"
    (E) "Facts About Insects"

    (D) Evaluation questions like this one ask you to summarize the entire passage and choose an appropriate title. In this case, (A) is clearly wrong, (B) and (E) are too vague, and (C) is too specific. The best choice is (D), which applies to the whole passage.

SENTENCE COMPLETIONS

13. When the real estate agent finally suggested a property the young couple could ----, they were shocked to see a ---- house that seemed as though it was on the verge of collapse.

    (A) renovate..modern   (B) purchase..galling
    (C) afford..ramshackle   (D) diversify..dilapidated
    (E) envision..reserved

    (C) This question is basically a matter of vocabulary. We can eliminate (D) on the basis of usage because one does not *diversify* a house. The other four choices are possibilities. The blank, however, must be filled by an adjective which might describe a house about to collapse. The second element of (A) disqualifies that answer. A *modern* house would not look as if it were about to collapse. A house can be neither *galling* nor *reserved*, so that eliminates (B) and (E). *Ramshackle*, the second word of choice (C), means broken down or about to collapse and completes the sentence perfectly.

14. Psychologists agree that human beings have a strong need to ---- their time; having too much idle time can be as stressful as having none at all.

    (A) threaten
    (B) annihilate
    (C) structure
    (D) punctuate
    (E) remand

    (C) This question contains a type of thought-reverser. Before looking at the choices, you already know that you need a word which describes something you can do with time so that it is not *idle*. All choices except (C) can be eliminated because they not only say nothing useful about time, they create meaningless sentences.

15. While scientists continue to make advances in the field of ----, some members of the clergy continue to oppose the research, arguing that it is ---- for human beings to tamper with life.

    (A) psychology..imperative
    (B) astronomy..fallacious
    (C) genetics..immoral
    (D) geology..erroneous
    (E) botany..unethical

    (C) You cannot eliminate any of the choices on the grounds of usage, since each when substituted into the sentence will create meaningful idiomatic phrases. The key to the sentence is the word "life." The field of study which completes the first blank must be a science which not only studies but directs the course of life, as indicated by the word "tamper." This eliminates (B), (D), and (E). Although one might say that psychology "tampers" with life, it makes no sense to say that the clergy oppose it and think that it is imperative. By the process of elimination this leaves only (C).

16. John was bright but lazy and because of his ---- was never promoted to senior partner.

    (A) novelty   (B) perjury   (C) zeal
    (D) indemnity   (E) indolence

    (E) This is a straightforward vocabulary question. The word substituted in the blank must continue the idea of *lazy*; in fact, since the blank refers to *lazy* it will be a synonym. Only (E), which means slothfulness or laziness, does the job.

17. The film was completely devoid of plot or character development; it was merely a ---- of striking images.

    (A) renouncement   (B) montage
    (C) calumny   (D) carnage   (E) premonition

    (B) This is also primarily a vocabulary question. You can eliminate (A), (C), (D), and (E) because they are not things that could be said of images and therefore fail on the grounds of usage. This leaves you with the correct answer (B). A *montage* is a series of rapid images in film. The structure of this question doesn't help you at all, so if you are unfamiliar with the vocabulary it would be difficult to answer.

ANALOGIES

18. FLY : WEB::

    (A) cat : milk
    (B) fish : net
    (C) hair : comb
    (D) tennis : racket
    (E) spider : spinning

    (B) This analogy does not fit one of our categories, but you might formulate a diagnostic sentence such as "the purpose of the web is to catch a fly" and "the purpose of a net is to catch fish."

    Don't be distracted by the superficial similarity between spider and web!

19. WALK : SCURRY::

    (A) climb : scramble
    (B) write : type
    (C) sing : dance
    (D) anger : calm
    (E) cultivate : nurture

    (A) This analogy may be analyzed as one of "type" or "degree." SCURRYING is a type of WALKING—it means "to walk quickly," so you might say either that scurrying is a type of walking or that scurrying is more intense than walking. *Scramble* means "to *climb* quickly"; so you could say either that scrambling is a type of climbing or that scrambling is more intense than climbing.

20. CHAPTER : NOVEL::

    (A) piano : orchestra
    (B) diamond : gem
    (C) scene : drama
    (D) poetry : prose
    (E) fraction : portion

    (C) This is clearly a part to whole analogy. A CHAPTER is part of a NOVEL and a *scene* is part of a *drama*. Don't be deceived by the mention of other literary terms such as *poetry* and *prose* or by other words such as *fraction* and *portion*; which mean "part."

21. IMPLY : AVER::
    (A) reject : announce
    (B) hint : proclaim
    (C) encourage : absolve
    (D) remind : contradict
    (E) embolden : accept

    (B) This analogy is one of degree. To AVER is to affirm with confidence. There is a strong secondary relationship here, because *hint* is like IMPLY and AVER is like *proclaim*.

22. VERBOSE : WORDS::
    (A) unique : copies
    (B) deafening : sound
    (C) youthful : age
    (D) expressive : sentence
    (E) mournful : joy

    (B) This is a difficult analogy to categorize, but you might use the following diagnostic sentences: "VERBOSE describes that which is characterized by excessive WORDS" and "*deafening* describes that which is characterized by an excess of *sound* or noise."

23. DETENTION : RELEASE::
    (A) viciousness : attack
    (B) calamity : repair
    (C) qualification : employ
    (D) induction : discharge
    (E) therapy : confuse

    (D) This is an analogy based on sequence of events. After DETENTION one may be RELEASED, and after *induction* one may be *discharged*. Notice how DETENTION and *induction*, and RELEASE and *discharge*, echo each other.

24. PONDEROUS : WEIGHT::
    (A) eternity : temporality
    (B) conviction : decision
    (C) gargantuan : size
    (D) ancient : value
    (E) prototypical : affection

    (C) This analogy is based on a defining characteristic. By definition, something that is PONDEROUS has a lot of WEIGHT, and something *gargantuan* is large or *sizable*.

25. FEBRILE : ILLNESS::
    (A) tenacious : astonishment
    (B) juvenile : maturity
    (C) classic : cultivation
    (D) eccentric : discrimination
    (E) delusional : insanity

    (E) This analogy is based on the "sign of" relationship. To be FEBRILE is a sign of ILLNESS and to be *delusional* is a sign of *insanity*.

CRITICAL READING

26. The word *stratum* (line 3) means
    (A) avenue
    (B) hide
    (C) boulder
    (D) layer
    (E) geology

    (D) In context, it is clear that the word has to do with the rocks being described. This eliminates (A) and (B) as possible answers. Neither (C) nor (E) makes sense in context, so the answer must be (D).

27. The "bars of the river" (line 6) are apparently
    (A) shoals
    (B) saloons
    (C) poles
    (D) tribunals
    (E) ingots

    (A) If you do not know the word *shoals*, you are at a disadvantage, but it is one you can make up for by using the process of elimination. Every one of the choices for this interpretation question is a synonym for *bar*, but only (A) and (C) have any connection to a river. Even if you thought *poles* might be correct, the fact that they are supposed to be "composed primarily of gravel" would dissuade you.

28. The word *afford* (line 8) is used to mean
    (A) risk
    (B) chance
    (C) buy
    (D) manage
    (E) bear

    (E) Each choice in this vocabulary-in-context question is a synonym for *afford*, but only (E) makes sense when substituted for *afford* in context.

29. The difference before and after the words *Sunday, 26th,* (line 15) is one of
    (A) writing style
    (B) authorship
    (C) geology
    (D) form of transportation
    (E) season

    (C) This is a synthesis/analysis question. It asks you to look at the structure of the passage before and after a particular point. You must summarize what happens before and after that point and compare your summary with the choices. Writing style (A) does not change, and there is no indication that authorship (B) does, either. There would be no change of seasons (E) between the 25th and 26th of a month, and the company appears to be boating down a river throughout (D). However, the geology they are seeing does change, and the passage is quite specific in recording that difference.

30. Why did Lewis's group name a stream "Windsor creek"?

 (A) after the Duke of Windsor
 (B) after someone they had met at a party
 (C) after a man of their political leaning
 (D) after a member of their group
 (E) no reason is given

 (D) This is really an interpretation question; it asks you to interpret the phrase "We called it Windsor creek, after one of the party." Only (D) is a logical choice.

31. "Concreted shells" (line 28) are probably

 (A) shells mixed with cement
 (B) shells imbedded in stone
 (C) shell-lined pavements
 (D) canoes carved in stone
 (E) frameworks of stone buildings

 (B) This can be answered through a process of elimination. No cement (A) or pavement (C) would be found in a wilderness, and it is "a thin stratum of limestone" that is formed of the "concreted shells," so that eliminates (D) and (E) as well.

32. Clark suspects that the time of year may be responsible for
 (A) the reappearance of turtles
 (B) the soft shells of turtles
 (C) the scarcity of turtles
 (D) the lack of timber
 (E) the migration of Mandan turtles

 (C) This is an interpretation question. Reread the section of the passage that tells about turtles, and you will see that they were seen for the first time in a long time, but that the fact that they have been rarely seen may be due to the season.

33. How does Clark feel about seeing the Rockies?
 (A) frolicsome
 (B) hopeless
 (C) suspicious
 (D) morose
 (E) appreciative

 (E) Evaluation questions of this kind ask you to look inside the writer's head and determine his or her opinions or feelings. (E) is the only possible translation of the final sentence of the journal entry.

34. The journal entry seems to unfold
 (A) according to the whim of the author
 (B) with a certain amount of backtracking
 (C) in backward chronological order
 (D) in space order tied to the movements of the travelers
 (E) with leaps forward in time

 (D) This synthesis/analysis question asks you to determine the order of the passage—is it step by step in order of events, or is there some twist to it? The passage seems to move along the river just as the passengers do, with no shifts in time or space.

35. The primary goal of the passage is to
 (A) entertain
 (B) persuade
 (C) inform
 (D) preach
 (E) interpret

 (C) Every writer has a purpose, and the purpose of Lewis and Clark is to describe and inform. There is no support in the text for any of the other choices.

SECTION 2

MATH PROBLEM-SOLVING

1. A barrel contained 5.75 liters of water and 4.5 liters evaporated. How many liters of water remain in the barrel?
 (A) 0.75   (B) 1.25   (C) 1.75
 (D) 2.25   (E) 13.25

 (B) Perform the indicated operation: $5.75 - 4.5 = 1.25$.

2. The expression "3 less than the product of 4 times x" can be written as
 (A) $4x - 3$ (B) $3x - 4$ (C) $4(x - 3)$
 (D) $3(4x)$ (E) $\dfrac{4x}{3}$

 (A) Translate the expression into "algebrese." The product of 4 times x is written as $4x$. And 3 less than that would be $4x - 3$.

3. If $\dfrac{3}{4}$ of x is 36, then $\dfrac{1}{3}$ of x is

 (A) 9   (B) 12   (C) 16   (D) 24   (E) 42

(C) This question really just tests fractions. If $\frac{3}{4}$ of x is 36, then:

$$\left(\frac{3}{4}\right)(x) = 36$$

$$x = 36\left(\frac{4}{3}\right) = 48.$$

and $\frac{1}{3}$ of 48 is 16.

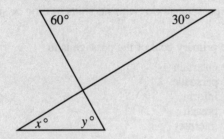

4. In the figure above, what is the value of $x + y$?
   (A) 45   (B) 60   (C) 75   (D) 90
   (E) It cannot be determined from the information given.

(D) The measure of the unlabeled angle in the triangle on the right is 90°. The angle vertically opposite it in the triangle on the left is also equal to 90°. Therefore,

$$x + y + 90 = 180$$
$$x + y = 90$$

5. If n is a multiple of 3, which of the following is also a multiple of 3?
   (A) $2 + n$ (B) $2 - n$ (C) $2n - 1$
   (D) $2n + 1$ (E) $2n + 3$

(E) There are two ways to attack this question. One is to reason that
(A) $2 + n$ cannot be a multiple of 3. Since n is a multiple of 3, when $2 + n$ is divided by 3, there will be a remainder of 2;
(B) $2 - n$ cannot be a multiple of 3 for the same reason that $2 + n$ cannot be a multiple of 3;
(C) $2n - 1$ cannot be a multiple of 3. Since n is a multiple of 3, $2n$ will also be a multiple of 3, and $2n - 1$ cannot be a multiple of 3.
(D) $2n + 1$ cannot be a multiple for the same reason that $2n - 1$ cannot be a multiple of 3; and finally
(E) $2n + 3$ is a multiple of 3. $2n$ is a multiple of 3; 3 is a multiple of 3; so $2n + 3$ is a multiple of 3.

You can reach the same conclusion just by substituting an assumed value into the choices. Assume that $n = 3$.

(A) $2 + n = 2 + 3 = 5$, not a multiple of 3.

(B) $2 - n = 2 - 3 = -1$, not a multiple of 3.

(C) $2n - 1 = 2(3) - 1 = 6 - 1 = 5$, not a multiple of 3.

(D) $2n + 1 = 2(3) + 1 = 6 + 1 = 7$, not a multiple of 3.

(E) $2n + 3 = 2(3) + 3 = 6 + 3 = 9$, a multiple of 3.

6. Which of the following is NOT equal to the ratio of two whole numbers?

   (A) $\left(\frac{1}{5}\right)^2$ (B) $\frac{1}{5}$ (C) 0.20   (D) 5%

   (E) $\sqrt{\frac{5}{1}}$

(E) Remember that a ratio is just another way of writing a fraction. So just inspect each of the answer choices. As for (A), $\left(\frac{1}{5}\right)^2$ is equal to $\frac{1}{25}$, and both 1 and 25 are whole numbers. As for (B), $\frac{1}{5}$ is the ratio of 1 to 5, so (B) is not the correct choice. As for (C), 0.20 is equal to $\frac{1}{5}$, the ratio of two whole numbers. And 5% can be written as $\frac{5}{100}$ or $\frac{1}{20}$. Finally, $\sqrt{5}$ is not a whole number, so the expression in (E) is not the ratio of two whole numbers.

7. If the area of a square is 16, what is the perimeter?
   (A) 2   (B) 4   (C) 8   (D) 16   (E) 32

(D) If you know the area of a square, you can find its perimeter, and vice versa.

Area = side × side
side × side = 16
$s^2 = 16$
$s = 4$ (Remember distances are always positive, never negative.)
Then the perimeter is equal to $4s$, or $4 \times 4 = 16$.

8. If $12 + x = 36 - y$, then $x + y =$
   (A) -48 (B) -24 (C) 3   (D) 24   (E) 48

(D) Here you have one equation with two variables. It's not possible to solve for x or y individually, but you don't need to. Just rewrite the equation so that you have it in the form $x + y$.

$12 + x = 36 - y$
$x + y = 36 - 12 = 24$

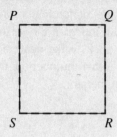

P   Q

S   R

9. Two security guards, Jane and Ed, patrol the perimeter of the square area shown above. Starting at corner P at 8:00 p.m., Jane walks around the outside of the fence in a clockwise direction while Ed walks around the inside in a counterclockwise direction. If it takes exactly 10 minutes for each guard to walk from one corner to the next, where will they be two hours later, at 10 p.m.?

(A) Both at corner P
(B) Both at corner R
(C) Jane at corner P and Ed at corner R
(D) Ed at corner P and Jane at corner Q
(E) Ed at corner P and Jane at corner R

(A) One way of analyzing this question is to reason that the square has four sides and each guard requires ten minutes to walk the distance of a side. In two hours, or 120 minutes, each guard will walk $120 \div 10 = 12$ sides. So each guard will make three complete trips around the lot ($12 \div 4 = 3$), bringing each back to his or her original starting point.

That's a big explanation for something that is not really that complicated. Why not just let your finger do the walking? Trace the route each guard will follow. At 8:10 Jane is at point Q; at 8:20 she is at point R; at 8:30 she is at point S; and so on. Not very elegant, but effective.

10. Depending on the value of k, the expression $3k + 4k + 5k + 6k + 7k$ may or may not be divisible by 7. Which of the terms, when eliminated from the expression, guarantees that the resulting expression is divisible by 7 for every positive integer k?

(A) $3k$ (B) $4k$ (C) $5k$ (D) $6k$ (E) $7k$

(B) Again, here is a problem for which there is a standard math approach and a Holmesian approach. You can analyze the problem as follows. The sum of $3k$, $4k$, $5k$, $6k$, and $7k$ is $25k$, a number that will be divisible by 7 only if k is divisible by 7. If, however, the coefficient of k were divisible by 7, then that number would be divisible by 7 regardless of value of k. If we drop the term $4k$ from the group, the sum of the remaining terms is $21k$. Since 21 is divisible by 7, $21k$ will be divisible by 7 regardless of the value of k.

What would Holmes do? Assume a value for k,

say $k = 1$. Then the total of the five terms is $3 + 4 + 5 + 6 + 7 = 25$. Getting rid of which one will yield a number divisible by 7? The answer is to get rid of the 4, because 21 is divisible by 7.

11. If $\frac{1}{3} < x < \frac{3}{8}$, which of the following is a possible value of x?

(A) $\frac{1}{2}$ (B) $\frac{3}{16}$ (C) $\frac{17}{48}$ (D) $\frac{9}{24}$ (E) $\frac{5}{12}$

(C) It would be a mistake to try to convert each of these fractions to decimals to find the value that lies between $\frac{1}{3}$ and $\frac{3}{8}$. Instead, find an escape route. Use a benchmark, approximate, or whatever else is available.

First, eliminate (A), because $\frac{1}{2}$ is more than $\frac{3}{8}$. Next eliminate (B). $\frac{3}{15}$ is equal to $\frac{1}{3}$, so $\frac{3}{16}$ is smaller than $\frac{1}{3}$ (a larger denominator makes for a smaller fraction, given the same numerator). (C) is close to and slightly less than $\frac{18}{48}$ which is $\frac{3}{8}$. So (C) is the correct choice. But let's finish the line of reasoning. As for (D), $\frac{9}{24}$ is equal to $\frac{3}{8}$, not less than $\frac{3}{8}$. Finally, $\frac{5}{12}$ is equal to $\frac{10}{24}$, and $\frac{3}{8}$ is equal to $\frac{9}{24}$.

12. If $x^2 - y^2 = 3$ and $x - y = 3$, then $x + y =$
(A) 0   (B) 1   (C) 2   (D) 3   (E) 9

(B) By this point in your study you should almost automatically factor the expression $x^2 - y^2$ into $(x + y)(x - y)$. Since $(x - y) = 3$, $(x + y)3 = 3$, so $x + y = 1$

13. If n is a positive integer, which of the following must be an even integer?

(A) $n + 1$ (B) $3n + 1$ (C) $3n + 2$
(D) $n^2 + 1$ (E) $n^2 + n$

(E) You can reason this out mathematically. As for (A), whether $n + 1$ is odd or even will depend on whether n is odd or even. The same is true for (B) and (C), because whether $3n$ is odd or even will depend on whether n is odd or even. As for (D), n^2 will be odd or even depending on whether n is odd or even. But (E) is even regardless of whether n is odd or even. If n is even, then the expression $n^2 + n$ is equal to an even number times itelf plus itself, which is an even number. And if n is odd, the expression is equal to an odd number times an odd number, which is an odd number, plus an odd number, and the sum of two odd numbers is even. Or you can just assume some numbers.

561

14. If the area of a square inscribed in a circle is 16, what is the area of the circle?

(A) 2π (B) 4π (C) 8π (D) 16π (E) 32π

(C) No figure is provided, so sketch one:

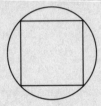

Since the square has an area of 16, it has a side of 4 and a diagonal $4\sqrt{2}$. The diagonal of the square is also the diameter of the circle. So the circle has a diameter of $4\sqrt{2}$ and a radius of $2\sqrt{2}$. Finally, a circle with a radius of length $2\sqrt{2}$ has an area of $\pi(2\sqrt{2})^2 = \pi(8) = 8\pi$.

15. In a certain group of 36 people, only 18 people are wearing hats and only 24 people are wearing sweaters. If 6 people are wearing neither a hat nor a sweater, how many people are wearing both a hat and a sweater?

(A) 30   (B) 22   (C) 12   (D) 8   (E) 6

(C) Here we can use the overlapping circles diagram we have used before:

Hats = 18   Sweaters = 24

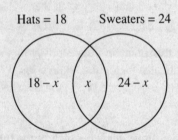

The twist here is that the diagram is not intended to represent all 36 people in the group. 6 of the 36 are wearing neither a hat nor a sweater. So the total represented by the diagram is $36 - 6 = 30$.

$18 - x + x + 24 - x = 30$
$-x + x - x + 18 + 24 = 30$
$-x + 42 = 30$
$-x = -12$
$x = 12$

16. A certain mixture of gravel and sand consists of 2.5 kilograms of gravel and 12.5 kilograms of sand. What percent of the mixture, by weight, is gravel?

(A) 10%   (B) $16\frac{2}{3}\%$ (C) 20%

(D) 25%   (E) $33\frac{1}{3}\%$

(B) Use the "this-of-that" formula. The "of that" which forms the denominator of the fraction, is "mixture." How much of the mixture is there? 2.5 + 12.5 = 15. So 15 is the denominator of the fraction, and the other number in the problem (the "this") is the numerator:

$$\frac{2.5}{15} = \frac{1}{6}$$

And $\frac{1}{6}$ is one of the common fraction/decimal equivalents you were encouraged to memorize. Don't divide; just convert by memory:

$$\frac{1}{6} = 0.16\frac{2}{3} = 16\frac{2}{3}\%$$

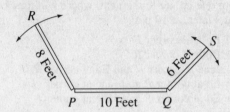

17. The figure above is the top view of a folding room divider, hinged at P and Q. If sections PR and QS are moved as shown until R and S meet, what will be the area, in square feet, enclosed? (Ignore the thickness of the hinges and the screen's sections.)

(A) 6   (B) 12   (C) 6π (D) 24   (E) 12π

(D) Complete the sketch:

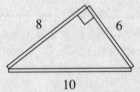

The triangle has sides of 6, 8, and 10, which you should recognize as multiples of 3, 4, and 5. So the triangle is a right triangle. The sides of 6 and 8 form the right angle, so they can be used as altitude and base for finding the area:

$$\text{Area} = \frac{1}{2} \times \text{altitude} \times \text{base} = \frac{1}{2} \times 6 \times 8 = 24$$

18. Motorcycle X averages 40 kilometers per liter of gasoline while Motorcycle Y averages 50 kilometers per liter. If the cost of gasoline is $2 per liter, what will be the difference in the cost of operating the two motorcycles for 300 kilometers?

(A) $3   (B) $6   (C) $12   (D) $15   (E) $20

(A) Proportions make this calculation easy. First do the calculation for Motorcycle X.

$$\frac{\text{Fuel Used } X}{\text{Fuel Used } Y} = \frac{\text{Miles Driven } X}{\text{Miles Driven } Y}$$

(The X and Y here refer to the two different situations, not the motorcycles.)

$$\frac{1}{x} = \frac{40}{300}$$

Cross-multiply and solve for x:

$300 = 40x$
$40x = 300$
$x = 7.5$

So Motorcycle X uses 7.5 liters of fuel for the 300-mile trip. Now do the same for Motorcycle Y:

$$\frac{1}{x} = \frac{50}{300}$$

$300 = 50x$
$50x = 300$
$x = 6$

So Motorcycle Y uses 6 liters of fuel for the trip. Since Motorcycle X uses $7.5 - 6 = 1.5$ liters more than Motorcycle Y, the fuel for Motorcycle X costs $1.5 \times \$2 = \$3$ more.

19. If for all positive integers,

$$\triangle{*n} = \frac{1}{2}n \text{ if } n \text{ is even}$$

$$\triangle{*n} = n + 1 \text{ if } n \text{ is odd}$$

then $\triangle{*2} \times \triangle{*7} =$
(A) 4   (B) 5   (C) 6   (D) 7   (E) 8

(E) Here we have a defined function problem. Just do the indicated operations.

$$\triangle{*2} = \frac{1}{2}(2) = 1;$$

$$\triangle{*7} = 7 + 1 = 8, \text{ and } 1 \times 8 = 8.$$

20. For a positive integer k, which of the following equals $6k + 3$?

(A) $\frac{1}{2}(k + 1)$ (B) $\frac{1}{k} + 4$ (C) $2k + 1$

(D) $3(k + 1)$ (E) $3(2k + 1)$

(E) You can factor $6k + 3$: $6k + 3 = 3(2k + 1)$ which is choice (E). If you miss that insight, you can assume some numbers to substitute into the choices. Assume $k = 1$. Then $6k + 3 = 6(1) + 3 = 6 + 3 = 9$. Now substitute 1 for k into the choices. The correct one will yield the value 9.

21. To mail a letter costs x cents for the first ounce and y cents for every additional ounce or fraction of an ounce. What is the cost, *in cents*, to mail a letter weighing a whole number of ounces, w?

(A) $w(x + y)$
(B) $x(w - y)$
(C) $x(w - 1) + y(w - 1)$
(D) $x + wy$
(E) $x + y(w - 1)$

(E) You can devise the formula as follows. The formula will be x, the cost for the first ounce, plus some expression to represent the additional postage for weight over x ounces. The postage for the additional weight is y cents per ounce, and the additional weight is w minus the first ounce, or $w - 1$. So the additional postage is $y(w - 1)$, and the total postage is $x + y(w - 1)$.

You can reach the same conclusion by assuming some numbers to be substituted into the answer choices. Make the ridiculous assumption that the first ounce costs 1 cent and every additional ounce is free. If $x = 1$ and $y = 0$, then a letter of say 10 ounces ($w = 10$) will cost 1 cent. Substitute 1 for x, 0 for y, and 10 for w into the choices. The correct formula will generate the value 1. Even on these silly assumptions, you can eliminate every choice but (D) and (E). Make another set of assumptions, and you'll have the correct answer.

22. The figure above shows nine tiles with single-digit numbers painted on them. If xy is the product of the value of any two tiles selected at random, how many *different* possible values for xy are there?

(A) 4   (B) 7   (C) 10   (D) 12   (E) 16

(B) This problem is number 22 out of 25, so it must be fairly difficult. We can assume that the correct solution is not so easy as $4 + 4 = 8$ or $4 \times 4 = 16$. In fact the best way to solve the problem is just to test for the different values. The seven possibilities are 0, 2, 3, 4, 6, 8, and 12.

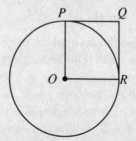

23. In the figure above, if the area of the square $OPQR$ is 2, what is the area of the circle with center O?

(A) $\frac{\pi}{4}$　(B) $\pi\sqrt{2}$　(C) 2π　(D) $2\sqrt{2\pi}$　(E) 4π

(C) Here we have another composite figure. The side of the square is also the radius of the circle. Since the square has an area of 2, its side is:

$$s \times s = 2$$
$$s^2 = 2$$
$$s = \sqrt{2}$$

And $\sqrt{2}$ is the radius of the circle. So the area of the circle is $\pi r^2 = \pi(\sqrt{2})^2 = 2\pi$.

24. How many positive integers less than 30 are equal to 3 times an *odd* integer?

    (A) 10　(B) 7　(C) 5　(D) 4　(E) 3

    (C) You can solve this problem mathematically by reasoning that the eligible integers must meet two requirements. They must be between 0 and 30, and they must equal 3 times an odd integer. So the eligible numbers are 3 multiplied by the sequence of odd numbers, with the last eligible number being the one before the one which, when multiplied by 3, generates a product greater than 30.

    But why reason in that way? Just start counting. The first such number is 3 ($3 \times 1 = 3$). Then you skip 6 ($3 \times 2 = 6$, but 2 is even). The next eligible number is 9 ($3 \times 3 = 9$). The next is 15 ($3 \times 5 = 15$). The next is 21 ($3 \times 7 = 21$). And the last is 27 ($3 \times 9 = 27$). So there are 5 of them.

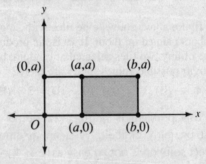

25. What is the area of the shaded portion of the figure above, expressed in terms of a and b?

    (A) $a(b - a)$　(B) $a(a - b)$　(C) $b(a - b)$

    (D) $b(b - a)$　(E) ab

    (A) The coordinates establish that this figure is a rectangle. The width of the rectangle is a, and the length is $b - a$. So the area is $a(b - a)$. You can also assume values and get the same result. Assume that $a = 2$ and $b = 4$. The rectangle has a width of 2, and a length of $4 - 2 = 2$, and an area of $2 \times 2 = 4$. Substitute 2 for a and 4 for b into the formulas in the answer choices and the correct formula will yield 4.

SECTION 3

CRITICAL READING

1. When Swift says, "it is universally exploded" (lines 13–14), he means

    (A) the practice erupts worldwide
    (B) the practice can blow up in one's face
    (C) the practice is completely discredited
    (D) the practice always ends in disgrace
    (E) the practice makes everyone angry

    (C) As with any interpretation question, you should test the choices in context. Ignore the dramatic implications of the word *exploded*; Swift here uses it in a very particular connotation: "discredited." None of the other synonymous choices for *exploded* fits the context.

2. Swift's reference to "while Grace is saying after meat" (line 28) has to do with

    (A) after-dinner speeches by the host and hostess
    (B) the lady of the house ringing for dessert
    (C) an important visitor, such as the Bishop, dropping in
    (D) the saying of prayers after the main course
    (E) a parlor game wherein everyone leaves his or her seat

    (D) You would be wise to go with your first instincts here and ignore the archaic phrasing. Of course, "Grace" at table refers to the saying of a prayer and not to a person.

3. The word *divert* in Swift's piece (line 33) means

    (A) distract
    (B) sidetrack
    (C) shift
    (D) occupy
    (E) entertain

    (E) *Divert* has many meanings, but only one of the choices is a logical replacement in this vocabulary-in-context question. The footman will not "distract," "sidetrack," "shift," nor "occupy" his fellow-servants with the tale of slipping the chairs out from under the guests (A through D); he will certainly "entertain" them, however.

4. Swift uses the word *sovereign* (line 37) to mean

    (A) autonomous
    (B) dominant
    (C) lordly
    (D) incomparable
    (E) independent

    (D) This vocabulary question is a little harder, because the synonyms for *sovereign* are closely related. Of the choices, however, only (B) and (D) seem sensible, and (D) is the better choice.

5. Collier uses the word *abridged* (line 39) to mean

   (A) summarized
   (B) curtailed
   (C) compressed
   (D) abbreviated
   (E) concentrated

   (B) Each of the choices is a synonym for *abridged*, but the context in which Collier uses the word is very specific, and only "curtailed," or "diminished," supplies the appropriate shade of meaning.

6. The words *low* and *high*, as used by Collier in lines 49 and 50, refer to

   (A) class
   (B) religion
   (C) morals
   (D) population
   (E) location

   (A) This is an interpretation question. It requires that you look closely at the context in which the words are used. Collier refers to being "too high" to have actions punished or "low enough" for scrutiny. (D) and (E) make no sense. (B) is dubious, and (C) is absurd in the context of the passage as a whole.

7. Why, in summary, does Collier not recommend starvation?

   (A) It is too difficult to control.
   (B) It is unethical.
   (C) It must be done with caution.
   (D) It was recently found illegal.
   (E) It cannot do much harm.

   (D) This is a kind of evaluation question that asks you to summarize one of the author's points. Neither (A) nor (E) is supported, and (B) is clearly not an issue to Collier. She does say (C), but this is not a reason to refrain from starvation. Lines 46-48, on the other hand, point out that a "late [recent] execution" for just such a crime may have set a legal precedent.

8. The word *surfeit*, used by Collier in line 67, means

   (A) default
   (B) forging
   (C) facsimile
   (D) surrender
   (E) overabundance

   (E) Only (E) is a synonym for *surfeit*, and only (E) could be a cause of death. (A) and (D) are synonyms for *forfeit*, and (B) and (C) are synonyms for *counterfeit*.

9. The tone of both passages could be described as

   (A) argumentative
   (B) prosaic
   (C) ironic
   (D) snide
   (E) vengeful

   (C) Most double-passage tests will ask a few questions comparing or contrasting the passages. In this case, the word *both* alerts you to a comparison. You must find an answer that applies to both passages, and (C) is that answer.

10. These two passages might be anthologized with the heading

    (A) "The Servants' Guidebook"
    (B) "Better Living"
    (C) "Helping Parents in the Home"
    (D) "Ridiculous Recommendations"
    (E) "Don't Ask Me"

    (D) This is an evaluation question that asks you for a comparison. You must determine how the passages are alike in order to choose a title that works for both. (A) works only for Passage A, and (C) fits Passage B only. (B) and (E) apply to neither. Only (D) could apply to either, and so, to both.

SECTION 4

MATH PROBLEM SOLVING

Fabric	Cost
A	3 yards for $8
B	2 yards for $6
C	4 yards for $9
D	5 yards for $7
E	6 yards for $5

1. According to the table above, which fabric costs the *least* per square yard?

   (A) A   (B) B   (C) C   (D) D   (E) E

   (E) Don't do lengthy calculations. Set up the cost of each fabric as a fraction and compare the fractions directly using a benchmark.

(A) $= \dfrac{8}{3}$

(B) $= \dfrac{6}{2} = 2$

(C) $= \dfrac{9}{4}$

(D) $= \dfrac{7}{5}$

(E) $= \dfrac{5}{6}$

(E) $\dfrac{5}{6}$ is less than 1. The other fractions are greater than 1. So (E) is the smallest.

2. $\dfrac{10^3\left(10^5 + 10^5\right)}{10^4} =$

(A) 10^4 (B) 10^6 (C) $2(10^2)$ (D) $2(10^4)$
(E) $2(10^9)$

(D) Obviously, you can't do the calculation, so look for an escape route. Cancel and factor!

$$\dfrac{10^3\left(10^5 + 10^5\right)}{10^4} = \dfrac{\left(10^5 + 10^5\right)}{10} = \dfrac{10\left(10^4 + 10^4\right)}{10} = 2\left(10^4\right)$$

3. If $x = b + 4$ and $y = b - 3$, then in terms of x and y, $b =$

(A) $x + y - 1$ (B) $x + y + 1$ (C) $x - y - 1$
(D) $\dfrac{x + y + 1}{2}$ (E) $\dfrac{x + y - 1}{2}$

(E) To find b in terms of x and y, you will first need to set b equal to x and equal to y:

$x = b + 4$ $y = b - 3$
$x - 4 = b$ $y + 3 = b$

Now combine the two equations by adding:

$b = x - 4$
$+ (b = y + 3)$
$\overline{}$
$2b = x + y - 1$

So $b = \dfrac{(x+y-1)}{2}$

You can arrive at the same conclusion by substituting some numbers. Let $b = 1$. Then $x = 1 + 4 = 5$, and $y = 1 - 3 = -2$. Substitute 5 for x and -2 for y into the answer choices. The correct choice will yield the value 1.

4. If $5x = 3y = z$, and x, y, and z are positive integers, all of the following must be integers EXCEPT

(A) $\dfrac{x}{zy}$ (B) $\dfrac{z}{5}$ (C) $\dfrac{z}{3}$ (D) $\dfrac{z}{15}$ (E) $\dfrac{x}{3}$

(A) Since $z = 5x = 3y$, and x, y, and z are integers, z is a multiple of both 3 and 5, so z is evenly divisible by 5, 3, and 15. And z is divisible by both x and y individually, but z is not necessarily divisible by the product of x and y. Finally, since $5x = 3y$, and x and y are integers, x is a multiple of 3 (and evenly divisible by 3).

You can reach the same conclusion by substituting some numbers. The most natural assumption is to let $z = 15$, so $x = 3$ and $y = 5$. But on that assumption, every answer choice is an integer. So try the next multiple of 15. Let $z = 30$, so $x = 6$ and $y = 10$. Now (A) is no longer an integer: $30 \div (6 \times 10) = \dfrac{1}{2}$.

5. What is the width of a rectangle with area $48x^2$ and a length of $24x$?

(A) 2   (B) $2x$ (C) $24x$ (D) $2x^2$ (E) $2x^3$

(B) You can solve the problem by using the formula for finding the area of a rectangle:

Area of rectangle = width $\times$ length

$48x^2 = w(24x)$

$w = \dfrac{48x^2}{24x} = 2x$

You can reach the same conclusion by substituting numbers. Assume that $x = 2$. Then the area of the rectangle is $48(2^2) = 48(4) = 192$, and the length is 48. So 48 times the width is equal to 192, and the width is $192 \div 48 = 4$. So if $x = 2$, the correct choice will yield the value 4. Only choice (B) works.

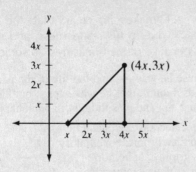

6. In the figure above, if the area of the triangle is 54, then $x =$

(A) $3\sqrt{3}$ (B) 3   (C) $2\sqrt{3}$ (D) 2
(E) It cannot be determined from the information given.

(C) Given that this is a difficult question, the correct answer is not likely to be (E). Operate on the assumption that it is possible to find a value for x.

You can deduce the value for x in the following way. The length of the base of the triangle is $4x - x = 3x$, and the length of the altitude is $3x - 0 = 3x$ (the difference in the y coordinates). Now use the formula for finding the area of a triangle:

$\frac{1}{2}(3x)(3x) = 54$

$(3x)(3x) = 108$

$9x^2 = 108$

$x^2 = 12$

$x = \sqrt{12} = 2\sqrt{3}$ (x is a distance, so x must be positive.)

7. If $x = \dfrac{1}{y+1}$ and $y \neq 1$, then $y =$

(A) $x + 1$ (B) x (C) $\dfrac{x+1}{x}$

(D) $\dfrac{x-1}{x}$ (E) $\dfrac{1-x}{x}$

(E) Rewrite the equation:

$x = \frac{1}{y+1}$

$x(y + 1) = 1$

$y + 1 = \frac{1}{x}$

$y = \frac{1}{x} - 1$

$y = \frac{1-x}{x}$

You can arrive at the same conclusion by assuming some numbers. Assume that $y = 1$. On that assumption $x = \frac{1}{2}$. Then substitute $\frac{1}{2}$ for x in the formulas in the answer choices; the correct choice will yield the value 1.

8. If $\blacktriangle(x) = x + 1$ and $\blacktriangledown(x) = x - 1$, then which of the following is equal to $\blacktriangle(3) \times \blacktriangledown(5)$?

(A) $\blacktriangle 8$ (B) $\blacktriangle 12$ (C) $\blacktriangle 14$
(D) $\blacktriangledown 17$ (E) $\blacktriangledown 20$

(D) Here we have a defined function. First, do $\blacktriangle$ to 3 and $\blacktriangledown$ to 5:

$\blacktriangle(3) = 3 + 1 = 4$

$\blacktriangledown(5) = 5 - 1 = 4$

So $\blacktriangle(3) \times \blacktriangledown(4) = 16$. Now test the test. Work backwards from the choices:

(A) $\blacktriangle(8) = 8 + 1 = 9$ (Wrong.)

(B) $\blacktriangle(12) = 12 + 1 = 13$ (Wrong.)

(C) $\blacktriangle(14) = 14 + 1 = 15$ (Wrong.)

(D) $\blacktriangle(17) = 17 - 1 = 16$ (Correct.)

(E) $\blacktriangle(20) = 20 - 1 = 19$ (Wrong.)

9. If $x + y = 14$, then $\dfrac{1}{2}x + \dfrac{1}{2}y =$

(A) 4
(B) 5
(C) 6
(D) 7
(E) $\dfrac{1}{2}y$

(D) You may be able to figure this out without doing any arithmetic by thinking, $\frac{1}{2}x + \frac{1}{2}y = 1/2(14)$. Another easy way is to try any numbers that fit in place of x and y.

$4 + 10 = 14$ $\frac{1}{2}(4) + \frac{1}{2}(10) = 7$

$6 + 8 = 14$ $\frac{1}{2}(6) + \frac{1}{2}(8) = 7$

10. If the average of ten numbers—1, 2, 3, 4, 5, 6, 7, 8, 9, and x—is 6, what is x?

(A) 5
(B) 6
(C) 10
(D) 12
(E) 15

(E) If the average of ten numbers is 6, then the total

of the numbers must be $60 - 60 \div 10 = 6$.

$$1 + 2 + 3 + 4 + 5 + 6 + 7 + 8 + 9 = 45$$

$60 - 45 = 15$, so x must equal 15.

SECTION 5

SENTENCE COMPLETIONS

1. Although for centuries literature was considered something which would instruct as well as entertain, the modern reader has little patience with ---- works and seeks only to be ----.

   (A) epic..demoralized   (B) didactic..distracted
   (C) bawdy..absorbed   (D) superficial..enlightened
   (E) ambiguous..misled

   (B) The logical key to this question is a double reversal. *Although* sets up a contrast between the idea in the first clause and the idea in the second clause. But the second clause contains the word "little" which functions as a negative. So the blanks will actually extend the thought expressed in the first clause. The first blank is an extender of the concept of literature that instructs as well as entertains, so you should look for an adjective that describes this type of literature. All of the first choices might describe literature, so you must know that didactic means instructive. The *only* sets up a contrast between the second blank and the first. You are now looking for something more or less opposite to instructive. Again, all of the second elements make some sense when substituted into the blanks, but only one reverses the idea of instruction, and that is pleasure, or entertainment. Therefore, *distracted* is the best choice.

2. Because the poet was restless and uneasy in society, he sought a ---- existence and a life of ----.

   (A) stable..pleasure
   (B) claustrophobic..frivolity
   (C) materialistic..urbanity
   (D) conservative..squalor
   (E) nomadic..solitude

   (E) This question is basically a thought-extender. The blanks are further indications of the poet's restlessness and uneasiness in society. You can eliminate (B) on the grounds of usage, because it makes no sense to say that someone seeks a *claustrophobic* existence. You can eliminate (C) because someone who is uneasy in society would hardly seek a life of *urbanity*. Although (A) and (D) create meaningful English sentences, they do not extend the logic of the first part of the sentence. The poet would not seek a *conservative* nor a *stable* existence as a result of his restlessness, nor would he seek a life of *pleasure* or *squalor* as a result of his uneasiness in society.

   Only (E) makes it clear that the poet was *nomadic* due to his restlessness, and sought *solitude* because of his uneasiness in society.

3. Because he was ---- and the life of the party, his friends thought that he was happy; but his wife was ---- and shy and was thought to be unhappy.

   (A) melancholy..sympathetic
   (B) philanthropic..conciliatory
   (C) vitriolic..sophomoric
   (D) garrulous..taciturn
   (E) inimical..gregarious

   (D) This question contains a thought-extender and a thought-reverser as its logical elements. The first blank must parallel the idea that someone was the life of the party. We can immediately eliminate (A), because someone who is *melancholy* is not likely to be the life of a party. (B) makes no logical sense. You can eliminate (C) and (E) on the same grounds. This is largely a matter of vocabulary, since you must know that *garrulous* means "talkative," *inimical* means "hostile," and *vitriolic* means "nasty." Only (D) makes any sense. His wife must be the opposite of "fun and talkative." The second element of (D), *taciturn*, which means "silent," works very nicely.

4. His offhand, rather ---- remarks ---- a character that was really rather serious and not at all superficial.

   (A) flippant..masked
   (B) pernicious..betrayed
   (C) bellicose..belied
   (D) controversial..revealed
   (E) shallow..enlivened

   (A) This sentence begins with a thought-extender and then reverses the idea. The first blank needs an adjective related to offhand that could be applied to remarks. This becomes a vocabulary question because you must know the meanings of all five of the first elements. All five answers make some sense, so it is a matter of substituting each pair to make sure that the logic of the sentence is maintained. If you know the meaning of *flippant*, you don't have to look any further. He was *flippant*, but this attitude masked a serious nature. This works very well. The logic of "he seemed x but was really y" is maintained.

5. Although the faculty did not always agree with the chairperson of the department, they ---- her ideas, mostly in ---- her seniority and out of respect for her previous achievements.

   (A) scoffed at..fear of
   (B) harbored..defense of
   (C) implemented..deference to
   (D) marveled at..lieu of
   (E) ignored..honor of

(C) This question starts with a thought-reverser, *although.* (A) does not reverse the idea. The same is true of (D) and (E). (B) and (C) remain possibilities, so test the second elements. The faculty might *harbor* her ideas, but they can't be doing it in *defense of* her seniority. That makes no sense. (C) works well. The faculty *implements* her ideas although they do not agree with her. This makes a perfectly logical and idiomatic sentence.

6. Despite the millions of dollars spent on improvements, the telephone system in India remains ---- and continues to ---- the citizens who depend on it.

   (A) primitive..inconvenience
   (B) bombastic..upset
   (C) suspicious..connect
   (D) outdated..elate
   (E) impartial..vex

   (A) The sentence starts with a thought-reverser, so we know that the correct choice will describe something unexpected given the amount of money invested. The second blank will be a logical continuation of the first blank as the verb *continues* indicates. (B), (C), and (E) can be eliminated immediately because they do not create meaningful phrases when substituted into the first blank. (A) and (D) are possibilities because a phone system can be both *primitive* and *outdated.* Next, we eliminate (D) because an *outdated* phone system would hardly *elate* those who depend on it. (A) creates a logical sentence. The system is *primitive,* despite the money spent on it, and it continues to *inconvenience* those who use it.

7. Contrary to popular opinion, bats are not generally aggressive and rabid; most are shy and ----.

   (A) turgid
   (B) disfigured
   (C) punctual
   (D) innocuous
   (E) depraved

   (D) This sentence starts with a thought-reverser, so we know that bats are going to be something which is the opposite of *aggressive* and *rabid.* The item is basically a vocabulary question. We can eliminate (A), (B), and (C) because they are not things one could say about bats and are not opposites for *aggressive* and *rabid.* We can also eliminate (E) because a bat would probably not be described as *depraved.* (D) *innocuous,* which means "harmless," is the opposite of *rabid* and goes nicely with *shy.*

8. The ballet company demonstrated its ---- by putting both classical and modern works in the repertoire.

   (A) versatility
   (B) mollification
   (C) treachery
   (D) dignity
   (E) obtrusiveness

   (A) This is basically a vocabulary question. You need to know what noun means "the ability to do more than one thing well." Only *versatility* completes the sentence. (B), (C), (D) and (E) create meaningless sentences.

9. Unlike the images in symbolist poetry which are often vague, and —, the images of surrealist poetry are startlingly — and bold.

   (A) extraneous..furtive
   (B) trivial..inadvertent
   (C) obscure..concrete
   (D) spectacular..pallid
   (E) symmetrical..virulent

   (C) In this sentence, a thought-extender and a thought-reverser are the logical keys. The first blank needs a word which continues the idea of *vagueness;* the second blank is *unlike* the first and must therefore be something close to an opposite. All of the choices make sense since they can all be used to describe images, but only one parallels *vague* and that is *obscure.* The second element, *concrete,* is an opposite of *obscure* and completes the sentence nicely. The second elements of (A), (B), (D), and (E) are not things that could be said of images and make no sense when substituted in the sentence.

10. A good trial lawyer will argue only what is central to an issue, eliminating ---- information or anything else which might ---- the client.

    (A) seminal..amuse
    (B) extraneous..jeopardize
    (C) erratic..enhance
    (D) prodigious..extol
    (E) reprehensible..initiate

    (B) This sentence has a thought-reverser and a thought-extender as its logical structure. The sentence says that the lawyer argues only what is central, eliminating something. Logically, what is eliminated is what is not central, so you should look for a word that means not central. (A) and (B) are both possibilities. We can eliminate (C), (D), and (E) because they do not make sense in this context. The second element is the deciding factor here. The lawyer would not want to *jeopardize* her client, therefore (B) is the best answer. It makes no sense to say that the lawyer would not want to *amuse* her client.

11. The music was so ---- that we begged for some ----.

    (A) thunderous..relief
    (B) provocative..harmony
    (C) noisome..silence
    (D) lugubrious..upbeat
    (E) fractious..tempo

    (A) The second idea extends the first. Neither (B) nor (E) provides this connection. (C) tries to trick you by using the word *noisome*, which relates to odor rather than to sound. You would never "beg for some *upbeat*" (D), so the answer is (A).

12. Richard is ---- on many topics; he is a true ----.

    (A) scholarly..renaissance
    (B) erudite..prodigy
    (C) clever..intelligentsia
    (D) versed..aficionado
    (E) familiar..aesthete

    (B) One is not "scholarly on," "clever on," "versed on," or "familiar on," so the use of that preposition eliminates all choices but one.

13. The novel was long, but the ---- plot kept our interest.

    (A) torpid
    (B) alien
    (C) insipid
    (D) labyrinthine
    (E) humdrum

    (D) A plot that was *torpid* (inert), *insipid* (pointless), or *humdrum* (routine) would not keep anyone's interest. *Alien* is an odd word to describe a plot. A *labyrinthine* (intricate) plot might indeed be interesting.

14. Is he ----, or is he merely ----?

    (A) amusing..witty
    (B) tranquil..mannerly
    (C) divisive..voracious
    (D) timid..unruly
    (E) uncivil..reticent

    (E) One part of the sentence both extends and negates the other. The choices cannot be synonymous (A), nor can they be completely opposed (D). (B) and (C) are silly, but one could easily be thought *uncivil* (rude) when one is merely *reticent* (shy).

15. Anyone who works at home needs to be self-disciplined and ----.

    (A) straitlaced
    (B) chronic
    (C) idiosyncratic
    (D) systematic
    (E) extremist

    (D) The clue is "needs to be"; nobody needs to be (A), (B), (C), or (E); although people who work at home may well be any of these. The only word that applies to a possible need is (D), meaning "orderly."

ANALOGIES

16. MIRROR : GLASS ::

    (A) igloo : ice
    (B) marsh : reed
    (C) grain : wood
    (D) thread : weave
    (E) straw : hay

    (A) This analogy is quite simple and your diagnostic sentence might read "a MIRROR is made of GLASS" and "an *igloo* is made of *ice.*"

17. SCULPTOR : STONE ::

    (A) poet : sonnet
    (B) lawyer : crime
    (C) carpenter : wood
    (D) doctor : patient
    (E) painter : museum

    (C) Although this doesn't fit precisely into a category, the relationship is fairly obvious. A SCULPTOR works in STONE and a *carpenter* works with *wood*. Do not be distracted by (A). A *sonnet* is not the material of a *poet*. (A) would be more nearly correct if it read *poet : words*.

18. LIAR : MENDACITY ::

    (A) swindler : burglary
    (B) glutton : appetite
    (C) philistine : knowledge
    (D) soldier : orders
    (E) diplomat : nationalism

    (B) This analogy is one of "defining characteristic." MENDACITY, or untruthfulness, is the defining characteristic of a LIAR, and an *appetite* is the defining characteristic of a *glutton*. Do not be deceived by (E). Although the words are related, a *diplomat* is not necessarily a *nationalist*.

19. WATERFALL : CASCADE ::

    (A) snow : freeze
    (B) missile : launch
    (C) tree : exfoliate
    (D) wave : undulate
    (E) monarch : reign

    (D) This analogy is one of "defining characteristic." By its nature, a WATERFALL CASCADES and a *wave undulates*. You might be attracted to answer choice (A). But you can eliminate it by trying to improve it. (A) would be more nearly correct if it were snow:fall. Finally, notice how both CASCADE and *undulate* refer to movement.

20. INFLATE : MAGNITUDE ::

(A) measure : weight
(B) extend : duration
(C) magnify : coin
(D) limit : speed
(E) legislate : crime

(B) Although this does not fit into any category, the relationship is clear. To INFLATE something means to increase its MAGNITUDE, and to *extend* something means to increase its *duration*. Notice that the original pair refers to space, and the correct answer echoes the relationship with reference to time.

21. MOCK : DERISION ::

(A) despise : contempt
(B) reject : account
(C) repair : corruption
(D) inspire : muse
(E) observe : refinement

(A) This analogy is a "defining characteristic." MOCKING must be, by definition, DERISIVE, and *despising* must involve *contempt*.

22. WEB : ENTANGLE ::

(A) spider : spin
(B) trap : ensnare
(C) treason : betray
(D) ransom : kidnap
(E) grid : delineate

(B) A WEB may be used to ENTANGLE and a *trap* is used to *ensnare*. Do not be distracted by (A) because *spider* and *spin* seem related to WEB.

23. LETHARGY : ENERGY ::

(A) appetite : hunger
(B) redemption : sacrament
(C) sorrow : pity
(D) merit : remuneration
(E) apathy : interest

(E) This analogy is based on a "lack of" relationship. LETHARGY is a lack of ENERGY and *apathy* is a lack of *interest*.

24. THWART : ACHIEVE::

(A) retain : submit
(B) couch : conceal
(C) silence : speak
(D) pretend : inherit
(E) permeate : infiltrate

(C) This analogy is a twist on the defining characteristic analogy. It is characteristic of the word THWART that one does not ACHIEVE, and of *silence* that one does not *speak*.

25. APOCRYPHAL : GENUINE ::

(A) spurious : authentic
(B) labored : relieved
(C) fragmented : riddled
(D) enigmatic : rambunctious
(E) credulous : flagrant

(A) This is a type of "lack of" analogy. Something which is APOCRYPHAL is not GENUINE and what is *spurious* is not *authentic*.

CRITICAL READING

26. Anthony uses the phrase "the myriads" (line 2) to mean

(A) poor people
(B) the unemployed
(C) all women
(D) women without protection
(E) slaves

(D) This interpretation question requires you to look at the entire paragraph in which the citation is found. Anthony declares her wish to "lift up" the myriads, and she asks Congress to "look down to the struggling masses of women who have no one to protect them." The two phrases are parallel; the myriads *are* the masses of women.

27. According to the beginning of paragraph 2, Congress wants women to

(A) vote the way their husbands vote
(B) vote only on "family-centered" issues
(C) stay home on election day
(D) give up the fight for suffrage
(E) put more laws on the books

(B) This, too, is an interpretation question. Anthony says, "You ask us why we do not get this right to vote . . . on school questions, or the questions of liquor license." In other words, Congress wants women to vote first (if they are to vote at all) on "women's issues" that affect the family.

28. Why does Anthony repeat the words *grog-shops*, *brothels*, and *gambling houses*?

(A) to stress the need for new laws
(B) to remind Congress of the existence of corruption despite laws
(C) to show Congress the vices upheld by men's votes
(D) both A and B
(E) both B and C

(E) Because of the format of this synthesis/analysis question, you must look at all the choices. Anthony is *not* calling for new laws; she says that there are "good enough laws." Both (B) and (C) are possible, though, making (E) the best choice.

29. The word *execute* (line 26) is used to mean

   (A) do
   (B) render
   (C) behead
   (D) enforce
   (E) dramatize

   (D) Any of these words might replace *execute* in some context, but only (D) replaces it in the context of line 26. Anthony's point is that there are laws, but they are not being enforced.

30. The term "sinks of iniquity" (line 31) is used to mean

   (A) dens of vice
   (B) figures of fun
   (C) signs of freedom
   (D) laws fostering injustice
   (E) harbingers of doom

   (A) Test the choices for this interpretation question in place of the phrase in question. "Grog-shops" are listed with "other sinks of iniquity." Only (A) works in context.

31. Anthony urges Congress to give women the vote primarily as a means of

   (A) legality
   (B) trickery
   (C) fairness
   (D) balance
   (E) appeasement

   (D) The first sentences of paragraphs 3 and 4 repeat this notion, and the passage as a whole has this as its major theme. The idea of suffrage as being fair (C) is never mentioned.

32. How does Anthony feel about the temperance movement?

   (A) approving
   (B) critical
   (C) superior
   (D) amused
   (E) exasperated

   (A) When Anthony calls the movement a "wonderful whip" (line 50), she is not being ironic. You can easily evaluate her feelings on the subject by noting that she refers to many members of the movement as her friends.

33. Why does Anthony include the discussion of problems in Rochester?

   (A) to show that trouble can occur close to home
   (B) to demonstrate the need for temperance
   (C) to support her opinion that allowing only men to vote maintains the *status quo*
   (D) both A and B
   (E) both B and C

(C) (A) might be a consideration, but it is hardly a main reason for including this information. Anthony's motive is not (B), either; she is not out to persuade Congress to make laws outlawing liquor. Her purpose is to get the vote for women, and the Rochester story serves to support her in this.

34. Anthony probably addresses certain Senators by name to

   (A) address their prejudices
   (B) embarrass their colleagues
   (C) demonstrate her erudition
   (D) promote their causes
   (E) invoke their sympathies

   (E) She addresses two Senators, both in familiar terms, and in both cases, she refers to problems they have in common. Her only motivation can be to promote her own cause by garnering their support.

35. A phrase that summarizes Anthony's speech thus far might be

   (A) "Women's votes can rid us of vice."
   (B) "Let my people go."
   (C) "Clean up our cities now."
   (D) "How can we effect change?"
   (E) "We must protect all women."

   (A) You must choose a phrase that applies to the passage overall. (B) and (D) are too vague; (C) and (E) are too specific. Only (A) accurately summarizes Anthony's main thesis in this part of her presentation.

SECTION 6

QUANTITATIVE COMPARISON

$$54 - 3n = 6$$

1.

n	16

(C) Solve for n in the centered equation:

$54 - 3n = 6$

$-3n = -48$

$3n = 48$

$n = 16$

Four faces of a solid cube are red
and the others are black.

2.

The number of faces that are black	3

(B) A cube has six faces. If 4 are red, then only 2 can be black. So Column A is equal to 2.

3.

The number of ounces in x pounds	y ounces

(D) No information is given about the value of x or y. So the relationship is indeterminate. For example, if $x = 1$ and $y = 16$, the two columns are equal. But if $x = 1$ and y is anything else, x will be larger or smaller than y.

4.

$\dfrac{2}{3}$	0.66

(A) Don't make a silly mistake and select (C). $\frac{2}{3}$ is a repeating decimal: 0.6666..., which is larger than 0.66.

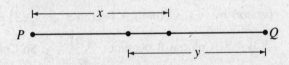

5.

Length of PQ	$x + y$

(B) Use the technique of distorting the figure:

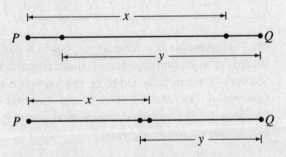

No matter how you draw the figure, there must be some distance between the unlabeled points marking the ends of lengths x and y. So x and y will always be that much longer than PQ.

In a shipment of six packages, five of the packages weigh exactly 25 pounds and the sixth package weighs more than 1 pound but less than 20 pounds.

6.

Average (arithmetic mean) weight, in pounds, of the six packages	22.5

(D) Use the extremes of the weight range for the sixth package to test the range of the average. If the sixth package weighs 1 pound (the lower limit), the average for the six packages is:

$$\frac{5\,(25) + 1}{6} = \frac{126}{6} = 21$$

If the sixth package weighs 20 pounds (the upper limit) the average of the six is:

$$\frac{5\,(25) + 20}{6} = \frac{145}{6} = 24\frac{1}{6}$$

So the relationship between the two columns is indeterminate.

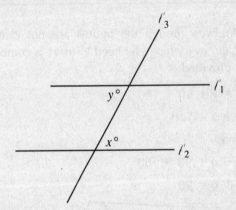

$\ell 1 \parallel \ell 2$

7.

$2x$	$x + y$

(C) Since the lines are parallel, the "big angle/ little angle" theorem establishes that $x = y$. So Column A, which is equivalent to $x + x$, could be written as $x + y$. This shows the two columns are equal.

573

Tina has more than twice as many marbles as Chuck and Luis have together.

8.

| Number of marbles Tina has | Three times the number of marbles Chuck has |

(D) Assume some numbers. For example, if Chuck and Luis each have 1 marble and Tina has 100 marbles, then Column A is larger. If Chuck has 10 marbles, Luis 1, and Tina 25, then Column B is greater.

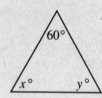 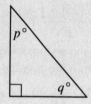

Note: Figures not drawn to scale.

9.

| $x + y$ | $p + q$ |

(A) Even though the figures are not drawn to scale, everything you need to make a comparison is provided:

$x + y + 60 = 180$

$x + y = 120$

And,

$p + q + 90 = 180$

$p + q = 90$

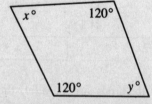

Note: Figure not drawn to scale.

10.

| x | y |

(D) Here the story is different. Since the sum of the measures of the interior angles of a quadrilateral is 360,

$x + y + 120 + 120 = 360$

$x + y + 240 = 360$

$x + y = 120$

You're stuck with one equation and two variables. So there is no way to find a value for x or y individually.

$$-3 > x > -7$$
$$-5 > y > -9$$
$$x \text{ and } y \text{ are integers.}$$

11.

| x | y |

(D) Write down the possible values for x and y.

$-3 > x > -7$, so x is -4, -5, or -6.

$-5 > y > -9$, so y is -6, -7, or -8.

Since the x and y might both be -6, the relationship between x and y is indeterminate.

12.

| $3\sqrt{3}$ | $\dfrac{3}{\sqrt{3}}$ |

(A) Use the technique of simplifying across the comparison. First multiply both sides of the comparison by $\sqrt{3}$. Column A becomes $3\sqrt{3}\left(\sqrt{3}\right) = 3(3) = 9$. Column B becomes $\dfrac{3\left(\sqrt{3}\right)}{\sqrt{3}} = 3$. So Column A is greater.

$$x < 0 < y$$

13.

| $x + y$ | x |

(B) This question is a little tricky, but it is easily solved if you simplify across the comparison. Subtract x from both sides of the comparison. Column A becomes simply y and Column B becomes 0. The centered information states that $0 < y$, so Column A is greater.

574

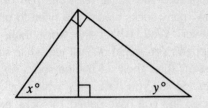

14.

x	y

(D) Use the technique of distorting the drawing:

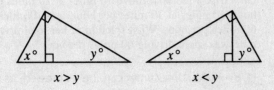

$$\begin{array}{r} 30\blacksquare \\ \times\ 6 \\ \hline 1{,}85\blacktriangle \end{array}$$

15.

■	▲

(A) One way of attacking this comparison is to rewrite the multiplication in the form of an equation:

$6(30\blacksquare) = 185\blacktriangle$

Since $30\blacksquare = 3(100) + 0(10) + \blacksquare$,

and $185 = 1(1000) + 8(100) + 5(10) + \blacktriangle$:

$6(3(100) + 0(10) + \blacksquare) =$
$1(1000) + 8(100) + 5(10) + \blacktriangle$

$6(300 + 0 + \blacksquare) = 1000 + 800 + 50 + \blacktriangle$

$1800 + 6\blacksquare = 1850 + \blacktriangle$

$6\blacksquare = 50 + \blacktriangle$

This is just an equation with two variables, and without additional information you can't solve for either variable individually. But you do have some more information. ■ and ▲ represent digits. And there is only one digit which, when multiplied by 6, yields a number of 50 or greater, and that number is 9. So ■ = 9, and ▲ = 4. So Column (A) is greater.

You can reach the same conclusion without having to use an equation. Since the tens' digit of 30■ is 0, the 5 in the tens' digit of the product came from the multiplication ▲ × 6. Now you are in the same position we were in at our last step above. Only one digit can do the job, 9.

STUDENT-PRODUCED RESPONSES

16. $\sqrt{(43 - 7)(29 + 7)} = ?$

(36) This is an easy problem; do the operations:

$$\sqrt{(43 - 7)(29 + 7)} = \sqrt{(36)(36)} = 36$$

17. A certain concrete mixture uses 4 cubic yards of cement for every 20 cubic yards of grit. If a contractor orders 50 cubic yards of cement, how much grit (in cubic yards), should he order if he plans to use all of the cement?

(250) Set up a direct proportion:

$$\frac{\text{Cement } X}{\text{Cement } Y} = \frac{\text{Grit } X}{\text{Grit } Y}$$

$$\frac{4}{50} = \frac{20}{x}$$

Cross-multiply :
$4x = (20)(50)$

$$x = \frac{(20)(50)}{4} = 250$$

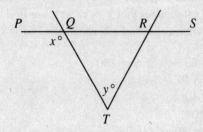

18. In the figure above, $QT = QR$. If $x = 120$, then $y = ?°$

(60) Let's label the other two angles in the triangle:

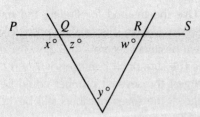

$x + y = 180$

$120 + z = 180$

$z = 60$

Next: $z + w + y = 180$

And since $QT = QR$, $y = w$.

So $60 + y + y = 180$

$2y = 120$

$y = 60$

575

19. If $\frac{x}{y} = -1$, then $x + y = ?$

(0) You have only one equation but two variables, so you cannot solve for x and y individually. Instead look for a way to rewrite the first equation to give you the information you need:

$$\frac{x}{y} = -1$$
$$x = -y$$
$$x + y = 0$$

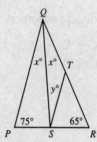

Note: Figure not drawn to scale.

20. In triangle PQR above, if $PQ \parallel$ to ST, then $y = ?°$

(20) Since $PQ \parallel ST$, the "big angle/little angle" theorem establishes that $x = y$. So if we find the value of x, we have found the value of y.

$75 + 65 + x + x = 180$
$2x + 140 = 180$
$2x = 40$
$x = 20$
So $y = 20$.

21. The average of seven different positive integers is 12. What is the greatest that any one of the integers could be?

(63) Use the method for finding the missing element of an average. The smallest possible sum for six different positive integers is $1 + 2 + 3 + 4 + 5 + 6 = 21$. The sum of all 7 integers is $7 \times 12 = 84$. So the largest the seventh number could be (and the average of the seven numbers still be 12) is $84 - 21 = 63$.

22. A drawer contains four green socks, six blue socks, and ten white socks. If socks are pulled out of the drawer at random and not replaced, what is the minimum number of socks that must be pulled out of the drawer to *guarantee* that two of every color have been pulled out of the drawer?

(18) This question is a little tricky, but it doesn't require any advanced mathematics. If the room were completely dark and you were in a hurry to make sure you got at least one pair of each color how many socks would you need to pull from the drawer? Well, what's the worst thing that might happen? You might pull all ten white socks on the first 10 tries, then all 6 blue socks on the next 6 tries. So far you have only white socks and blue socks, and you have pulled 16 socks. Now there is nothing left in the drawer but green socks. Two more picks and you'd have two green socks. So on the worst assumption, 18 picks will guarantee you a pair of each color.

23. On a trip, a motorist drove 10 miles at 20 miles per hour, 10 miles at 30 miles per hour, and 10 miles at 60 miles per hour. What fraction of her total driving time was spent driving 60 miles per hour?

(1/6) Recall that time can be expressed as distance/rate. In this case, then, time $= \frac{10}{20} + \frac{10}{30} + \frac{10}{60}$. Giving the fractions a common denominator, you find that

$$\text{time} = \frac{3}{6} + \frac{2}{6} + \frac{1}{6}, \text{ or } \frac{6}{6}$$

She spent $\frac{1}{6}$ of $\frac{6}{6}$ time driving 60 miles per hour, so $\frac{1}{6}$ of her total driving time was spent at that rate.

24. In Company A, 50% of the employees are women. In Company B, 40% of the employees are women. If Company A has 800 employees, and Company B has half that number, how many more women are employed at Company A than at Company B?

(240) This is a simple problem with multiple steps. You know that Company A has 800 employees, and Company B has half that, or 400 employees. Of those at Company A, 50% are women. At Company B, 40% are women.

Company A: 0.50(800) = 400 women
Company B: 0.40(400) = 160 women

Company A has 400 − 160 more women than Company B, or 240 more women.

25. In the country of Zzyzyyx, $\frac{2}{5}$ of the population have blue eyes. How many people would you have to look at to find 50 with blue eyes?

(125) Use a direct proportion to solve:
$$\frac{2}{5} = \frac{50}{x}$$

Cross multiply: $2x = 250$

$x = 125$

Practice Test 3

ANSWER SHEET
PRACTICE TEST 3

If a section has fewer questions than answer ovals, leave the extra ovals blank.

SECTION 1

1 Ⓐ Ⓑ Ⓒ Ⓓ Ⓔ	11 Ⓐ Ⓑ Ⓒ Ⓓ Ⓔ	21 Ⓐ Ⓑ Ⓒ Ⓓ Ⓔ	31 Ⓐ Ⓑ Ⓒ Ⓓ Ⓔ
2 Ⓐ Ⓑ Ⓒ Ⓓ Ⓔ	12 Ⓐ Ⓑ Ⓒ Ⓓ Ⓔ	22 Ⓐ Ⓑ Ⓒ Ⓓ Ⓔ	32 Ⓐ Ⓑ Ⓒ Ⓓ Ⓔ
3 Ⓐ Ⓑ Ⓒ Ⓓ Ⓔ	13 Ⓐ Ⓑ Ⓒ Ⓓ Ⓔ	23 Ⓐ Ⓑ Ⓒ Ⓓ Ⓔ	33 Ⓐ Ⓑ Ⓒ Ⓓ Ⓔ
4 Ⓐ Ⓑ Ⓒ Ⓓ Ⓔ	14 Ⓐ Ⓑ Ⓒ Ⓓ Ⓔ	24 Ⓐ Ⓑ Ⓒ Ⓓ Ⓔ	34 Ⓐ Ⓑ Ⓒ Ⓓ Ⓔ
5 Ⓐ Ⓑ Ⓒ Ⓓ Ⓔ	15 Ⓐ Ⓑ Ⓒ Ⓓ Ⓔ	25 Ⓐ Ⓑ Ⓒ Ⓓ Ⓔ	35 Ⓐ Ⓑ Ⓒ Ⓓ Ⓔ
6 Ⓐ Ⓑ Ⓒ Ⓓ Ⓔ	16 Ⓐ Ⓑ Ⓒ Ⓓ Ⓔ	26 Ⓐ Ⓑ Ⓒ Ⓓ Ⓔ	36 Ⓐ Ⓑ Ⓒ Ⓓ Ⓔ
7 Ⓐ Ⓑ Ⓒ Ⓓ Ⓔ	17 Ⓐ Ⓑ Ⓒ Ⓓ Ⓔ	27 Ⓐ Ⓑ Ⓒ Ⓓ Ⓔ	37 Ⓐ Ⓑ Ⓒ Ⓓ Ⓔ
8 Ⓐ Ⓑ Ⓒ Ⓓ Ⓔ	18 Ⓐ Ⓑ Ⓒ Ⓓ Ⓔ	28 Ⓐ Ⓑ Ⓒ Ⓓ Ⓔ	38 Ⓐ Ⓑ Ⓒ Ⓓ Ⓔ
9 Ⓐ Ⓑ Ⓒ Ⓓ Ⓔ	19 Ⓐ Ⓑ Ⓒ Ⓓ Ⓔ	29 Ⓐ Ⓑ Ⓒ Ⓓ Ⓔ	39 Ⓐ Ⓑ Ⓒ Ⓓ Ⓔ
10 Ⓐ Ⓑ Ⓒ Ⓓ Ⓔ	20 Ⓐ Ⓑ Ⓒ Ⓓ Ⓔ	30 Ⓐ Ⓑ Ⓒ Ⓓ Ⓔ	40 Ⓐ Ⓑ Ⓒ Ⓓ Ⓔ

SECTION 2

1 Ⓐ Ⓑ Ⓒ Ⓓ Ⓔ	11 Ⓐ Ⓑ Ⓒ Ⓓ Ⓔ	21 Ⓐ Ⓑ Ⓒ Ⓓ Ⓔ	31 Ⓐ Ⓑ Ⓒ Ⓓ Ⓔ
2 Ⓐ Ⓑ Ⓒ Ⓓ Ⓔ	12 Ⓐ Ⓑ Ⓒ Ⓓ Ⓔ	22 Ⓐ Ⓑ Ⓒ Ⓓ Ⓔ	32 Ⓐ Ⓑ Ⓒ Ⓓ Ⓔ
3 Ⓐ Ⓑ Ⓒ Ⓓ Ⓔ	13 Ⓐ Ⓑ Ⓒ Ⓓ Ⓔ	23 Ⓐ Ⓑ Ⓒ Ⓓ Ⓔ	33 Ⓐ Ⓑ Ⓒ Ⓓ Ⓔ
4 Ⓐ Ⓑ Ⓒ Ⓓ Ⓔ	14 Ⓐ Ⓑ Ⓒ Ⓓ Ⓔ	24 Ⓐ Ⓑ Ⓒ Ⓓ Ⓔ	34 Ⓐ Ⓑ Ⓒ Ⓓ Ⓔ
5 Ⓐ Ⓑ Ⓒ Ⓓ Ⓔ	15 Ⓐ Ⓑ Ⓒ Ⓓ Ⓔ	25 Ⓐ Ⓑ Ⓒ Ⓓ Ⓔ	35 Ⓐ Ⓑ Ⓒ Ⓓ Ⓔ
6 Ⓐ Ⓑ Ⓒ Ⓓ Ⓔ	16 Ⓐ Ⓑ Ⓒ Ⓓ Ⓔ	26 Ⓐ Ⓑ Ⓒ Ⓓ Ⓔ	36 Ⓐ Ⓑ Ⓒ Ⓓ Ⓔ
7 Ⓐ Ⓑ Ⓒ Ⓓ Ⓔ	17 Ⓐ Ⓑ Ⓒ Ⓓ Ⓔ	27 Ⓐ Ⓑ Ⓒ Ⓓ Ⓔ	37 Ⓐ Ⓑ Ⓒ Ⓓ Ⓔ
8 Ⓐ Ⓑ Ⓒ Ⓓ Ⓔ	18 Ⓐ Ⓑ Ⓒ Ⓓ Ⓔ	28 Ⓐ Ⓑ Ⓒ Ⓓ Ⓔ	38 Ⓐ Ⓑ Ⓒ Ⓓ Ⓔ
9 Ⓐ Ⓑ Ⓒ Ⓓ Ⓔ	19 Ⓐ Ⓑ Ⓒ Ⓓ Ⓔ	29 Ⓐ Ⓑ Ⓒ Ⓓ Ⓔ	39 Ⓐ Ⓑ Ⓒ Ⓓ Ⓔ
10 Ⓐ Ⓑ Ⓒ Ⓓ Ⓔ	20 Ⓐ Ⓑ Ⓒ Ⓓ Ⓔ	30 Ⓐ Ⓑ Ⓒ Ⓓ Ⓔ	40 Ⓐ Ⓑ Ⓒ Ⓓ Ⓔ

SECTION 3

1 Ⓐ Ⓑ Ⓒ Ⓓ Ⓔ	6 Ⓐ Ⓑ Ⓒ Ⓓ Ⓔ	11 Ⓐ Ⓑ Ⓒ Ⓓ Ⓔ	16 Ⓐ Ⓑ Ⓒ Ⓓ Ⓔ
2 Ⓐ Ⓑ Ⓒ Ⓓ Ⓔ	7 Ⓐ Ⓑ Ⓒ Ⓓ Ⓔ	12 Ⓐ Ⓑ Ⓒ Ⓓ Ⓔ	17 Ⓐ Ⓑ Ⓒ Ⓓ Ⓔ
3 Ⓐ Ⓑ Ⓒ Ⓓ Ⓔ	8 Ⓐ Ⓑ Ⓒ Ⓓ Ⓔ	13 Ⓐ Ⓑ Ⓒ Ⓓ Ⓔ	18 Ⓐ Ⓑ Ⓒ Ⓓ Ⓔ
4 Ⓐ Ⓑ Ⓒ Ⓓ Ⓔ	9 Ⓐ Ⓑ Ⓒ Ⓓ Ⓔ	14 Ⓐ Ⓑ Ⓒ Ⓓ Ⓔ	19 Ⓐ Ⓑ Ⓒ Ⓓ Ⓔ
5 Ⓐ Ⓑ Ⓒ Ⓓ Ⓔ	10 Ⓐ Ⓑ Ⓒ Ⓓ Ⓔ	15 Ⓐ Ⓑ Ⓒ Ⓓ Ⓔ	20 Ⓐ Ⓑ Ⓒ Ⓓ Ⓔ

SECTION 4

1 Ⓐ Ⓑ Ⓒ Ⓓ Ⓔ	6 Ⓐ Ⓑ Ⓒ Ⓓ Ⓔ	11 Ⓐ Ⓑ Ⓒ Ⓓ Ⓔ	16 Ⓐ Ⓑ Ⓒ Ⓓ Ⓔ
2 Ⓐ Ⓑ Ⓒ Ⓓ Ⓔ	7 Ⓐ Ⓑ Ⓒ Ⓓ Ⓔ	12 Ⓐ Ⓑ Ⓒ Ⓓ Ⓔ	17 Ⓐ Ⓑ Ⓒ Ⓓ Ⓔ
3 Ⓐ Ⓑ Ⓒ Ⓓ Ⓔ	8 Ⓐ Ⓑ Ⓒ Ⓓ Ⓔ	13 Ⓐ Ⓑ Ⓒ Ⓓ Ⓔ	18 Ⓐ Ⓑ Ⓒ Ⓓ Ⓔ
4 Ⓐ Ⓑ Ⓒ Ⓓ Ⓔ	9 Ⓐ Ⓑ Ⓒ Ⓓ Ⓔ	14 Ⓐ Ⓑ Ⓒ Ⓓ Ⓔ	19 Ⓐ Ⓑ Ⓒ Ⓓ Ⓔ
5 Ⓐ Ⓑ Ⓒ Ⓓ Ⓔ	10 Ⓐ Ⓑ Ⓒ Ⓓ Ⓔ	15 Ⓐ Ⓑ Ⓒ Ⓓ Ⓔ	20 Ⓐ Ⓑ Ⓒ Ⓓ Ⓔ

SECTION 5

1 Ⓐ Ⓑ Ⓒ Ⓓ Ⓔ	11 Ⓐ Ⓑ Ⓒ Ⓓ Ⓔ	21 Ⓐ Ⓑ Ⓒ Ⓓ Ⓔ	31 Ⓐ Ⓑ Ⓒ Ⓓ Ⓔ
2 Ⓐ Ⓑ Ⓒ Ⓓ Ⓔ	12 Ⓐ Ⓑ Ⓒ Ⓓ Ⓔ	22 Ⓐ Ⓑ Ⓒ Ⓓ Ⓔ	32 Ⓐ Ⓑ Ⓒ Ⓓ Ⓔ
3 Ⓐ Ⓑ Ⓒ Ⓓ Ⓔ	13 Ⓐ Ⓑ Ⓒ Ⓓ Ⓔ	23 Ⓐ Ⓑ Ⓒ Ⓓ Ⓔ	33 Ⓐ Ⓑ Ⓒ Ⓓ Ⓔ
4 Ⓐ Ⓑ Ⓒ Ⓓ Ⓔ	14 Ⓐ Ⓑ Ⓒ Ⓓ Ⓔ	24 Ⓐ Ⓑ Ⓒ Ⓓ Ⓔ	34 Ⓐ Ⓑ Ⓒ Ⓓ Ⓔ
5 Ⓐ Ⓑ Ⓒ Ⓓ Ⓔ	15 Ⓐ Ⓑ Ⓒ Ⓓ Ⓔ	25 Ⓐ Ⓑ Ⓒ Ⓓ Ⓔ	35 Ⓐ Ⓑ Ⓒ Ⓓ Ⓔ
6 Ⓐ Ⓑ Ⓒ Ⓓ Ⓔ	16 Ⓐ Ⓑ Ⓒ Ⓓ Ⓔ	26 Ⓐ Ⓑ Ⓒ Ⓓ Ⓔ	36 Ⓐ Ⓑ Ⓒ Ⓓ Ⓔ
7 Ⓐ Ⓑ Ⓒ Ⓓ Ⓔ	17 Ⓐ Ⓑ Ⓒ Ⓓ Ⓔ	27 Ⓐ Ⓑ Ⓒ Ⓓ Ⓔ	37 Ⓐ Ⓑ Ⓒ Ⓓ Ⓔ
8 Ⓐ Ⓑ Ⓒ Ⓓ Ⓔ	18 Ⓐ Ⓑ Ⓒ Ⓓ Ⓔ	28 Ⓐ Ⓑ Ⓒ Ⓓ Ⓔ	38 Ⓐ Ⓑ Ⓒ Ⓓ Ⓔ
9 Ⓐ Ⓑ Ⓒ Ⓓ Ⓔ	19 Ⓐ Ⓑ Ⓒ Ⓓ Ⓔ	29 Ⓐ Ⓑ Ⓒ Ⓓ Ⓔ	39 Ⓐ Ⓑ Ⓒ Ⓓ Ⓔ
10 Ⓐ Ⓑ Ⓒ Ⓓ Ⓔ	20 Ⓐ Ⓑ Ⓒ Ⓓ Ⓔ	30 Ⓐ Ⓑ Ⓒ Ⓓ Ⓔ	40 Ⓐ Ⓑ Ⓒ Ⓓ Ⓔ

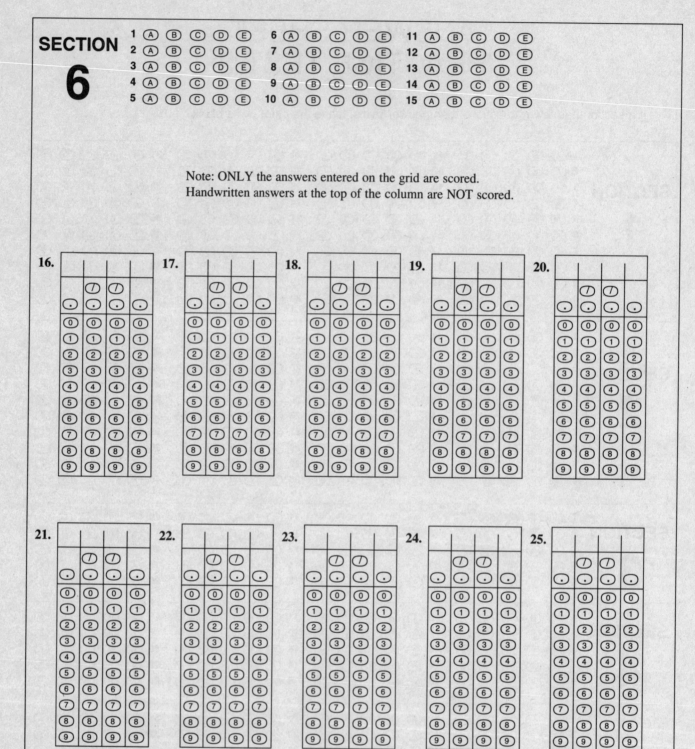

SECTION 6

1 Ⓐ Ⓑ Ⓒ Ⓓ Ⓔ   6 Ⓐ Ⓑ Ⓒ Ⓓ Ⓔ   11 Ⓐ Ⓑ Ⓒ Ⓓ Ⓔ
2 Ⓐ Ⓑ Ⓒ Ⓓ Ⓔ   7 Ⓐ Ⓑ Ⓒ Ⓓ Ⓔ   12 Ⓐ Ⓑ Ⓒ Ⓓ Ⓔ
3 Ⓐ Ⓑ Ⓒ Ⓓ Ⓔ   8 Ⓐ Ⓑ Ⓒ Ⓓ Ⓔ   13 Ⓐ Ⓑ Ⓒ Ⓓ Ⓔ
4 Ⓐ Ⓑ Ⓒ Ⓓ Ⓔ   9 Ⓐ Ⓑ Ⓒ Ⓓ Ⓔ   14 Ⓐ Ⓑ Ⓒ Ⓓ Ⓔ
5 Ⓐ Ⓑ Ⓒ Ⓓ Ⓔ   10 Ⓐ Ⓑ Ⓒ Ⓓ Ⓔ   15 Ⓐ Ⓑ Ⓒ Ⓓ Ⓔ

Note: ONLY the answers entered on the grid are scored.
Handwritten answers at the top of the column are NOT scored.

16. 17. 18. 19. 20.

21. 22. 23. 24. 25.

580

The passage below is followed by questions based on its content. Answer the questions following the passage on the basis of what is <u>stated</u> or <u>implied</u> in the passage.

Questions 1–12 are based on the following passage.

John Muir (1838–1914) was a naturalist and nature writer, a conservationist and supporter of national parks. This excerpt is from an essay entitled "The New Sequoia Forests of California," first published in 1878.

Next morning shortly after sunrise, just as the light was beginning to come streaming through the trees, while I lay leaning on my elbow taking my bread and tea, and looking
Line down across the canyon, tracing the dip of the granite
(5) headlands, and trying to plan a way to the river at a point likely to be fordable, suddenly I caught the big bright eyes of a deer gazing at me through the garden hedge. The expressive eyes, the slim black-tipped muzzle, and the large ears were as perfectly visible as if placed there at just
(10) the right distance to be seen, like a picture on a wall. She continued to gaze, while I gazed back with equal steadiness, motionless as a rock. In a few minutes she ventured forward a step, exposing her fine arching neck and forelegs, then snorted and withdrew.
(15)   This alone was a fine picture—the beautiful eyes framed in colored cherry leaves, the topmost sprays lightly atremble, and just glanced by the level sunrays, all the rest in shadow.
      But more anon. Gaining confidence, and evidently
(20) piqued by curiosity, the trembling sprays indicated her return, and her head came into view; then another and another step, and she stood wholly exposed inside the garden hedge, gazed eagerly around, and again withdrew, but returned a moment afterward, this time advancing into the
(25) middle of the garden; and behind her I noticed a second pair of eyes, not fixed on me, but on her companion in front, as if eagerly questioning, "What in the world do you see?" . . .
      It then occurred to me that I might possibly steal up to
(30) one of them and catch it, not with any intention of killing it, for that was far indeed from my thoughts. I only wanted to run my hand along its beautiful curving limbs. But no sooner had I made a little advance on this line than, giving a searching look, they seemed to penetrate my conceit,
(35) and bounded off with loud shrill snorts, vanishing in the forest. . . .
      I have often tried to understand how so many deer, and wild sheep, and bears, and flocks of grouse—nature's cattle and poultry—could be allowed to run at large
(40) through the mountain gardens without in any way marring their beauty. I was therefore all the more watchful of this feeding flock, and carefully examined the garden after they left, to see what flowers had suffered; but I could not detect the slightest disorder, much less destruction. It
(45) seemed rather that, like gardeners, they had been keeping

it in order. At least I could not see a crushed flower, nor a single grass stem that was misbent or broken down. Nor among the daisy, gentian, bryanthus gardens of the Alps,
Line where the wild sheep roam at will, have I ever noticed the
(50) effects of destructive feeding or trampling. Even the burly shuffling bears beautify the ground on which they walk, picturing it with their awe-inspiring tracks, and also writing poetry on the soft sequoia bark in boldly drawn hieroglyphics. But, strange to say, man, the crown, the sequoia
(55) of nature, brings confusion with all his best gifts, and, with the overabundant, misbegotten animals that he breeds, sweeps away the beauty of wildness like a fire.

1. The word *fordable* (line 6) means

    (A) provided
    (B) sustainable
    (C) traversable
    (D) paid for
    (E) sluggish

2. The word *sprays* (line 16) is used to mean

    (A) droplets
    (B) weeds
    (C) ferns
    (D) showers
    (E) sprigs

3. Muir uses the word *glanced* in line 17 to mean

    (A) viewed
    (B) skipped over
    (C) observed
    (D) scanned
    (E) blinked

4. Paragraph 2 extends Muir's intention to

    (A) tell a story
    (B) paint a picture
    (C) teach a lesson
    (D) express an opinion
    (E) inspire good works

5. The "second pair of eyes" (lines 25–26) belongs to

    (A) a second deer
    (B) Muir
    (C) the gardener
    (D) a sheep
    (E) none of the above

GO ON TO THE NEXT PAGE →

6. The response Muir has to the deer might be summarized as one of

(A) envy
(B) scorn
(C) amusement
(D) reverence
(E) disbelief

7. The phrase "they seemed to penetrate my conceit" (line 34) means

(A) "They invaded my narcissism."
(B) "They filled my thoughts."
(C) "They punctured my pride."
(D) "They entered my fantasy."
(E) "They guessed my intentions."

8. Unlike the first paragraph, the last paragraph is

(A) descriptive
(B) didactic
(C) humorous
(D) fictional
(E) expressive

9. Muir compares deer to gardeners in terms of their

(A) use of tools
(B) enjoyment of the outdoors
(C) tending of nature
(D) both A and B
(E) both B and C

10. Why does Muir refer to the Alps in line 48?

(A) to contrast their vegetation with California's
(B) to contrast sheep's destructiveness with deer's preservation
(C) to compare deer and sheep in terms of conservation
(D) to contrast European conservation movements with ours
(E) to show that deer are found around the world

11. The "boldly drawn hieroglyphics" referred to in lines 53–54 are probably

(A) claw marks
(B) ancient runes
(C) prehistoric paintings
(D) pawprints in the dirt
(E) graffiti

12. The purpose of the last sentence seems to be to

(A) sound an alarm
(B) offer praise
(C) make concessions
(D) prejudge
(E) make a recommendation

Each sentence below has one or two blanks, each blank indicating that something has been omitted. Beneath the sentence are five lettered words or sets of words. Choose the word or set of words that best fits the meaning of the sentence as a whole.

Example:

Although its publicity has been ----, the film itself is intelligent, well-acted, handsomely produced, and altogether ----.

(A) tasteless..respectable
(B) extensive..moderate
(C) sophisticated..amateur
(D) risqué..crude
(E) perfect..spectacular

13. Although some critics interpret *The Aeneid* as a Christian epic, this interpretation is totally ----, since the epic predates Christianity.

(A) infallible   (B) acceptable   (C) convincing
(D) anachronistic   (E) conventional

14. Black comedy is the combination of that which is humorous with that which would seem ---- to humor: the ----.

(A apathetic..ignoble
(B) heretical..salacious
(C) inferior..grandiose
(D) extraneous..innocuous
(E) antithetical..macabre

15. The original British cast was talented and energetic, while the Broadway cast lacks the ---- of the original players; in fact, the performance is ----.

(A) calmness..scintillating
(B) splendor..fallow
(C) verve..insipid
(D) flexibility..meticulous
(E) intractability..quaint

16. The press conference did not clarify many issues since the President responded with ---- and ---- rather than clarity and precision.

(A) sincerity..humor
(B) incongruity..candor
(C) fervor..lucidity
(D) animation..formality
(E) obfuscation..vagueness

17. Although the novel was not well written, it was such an exciting story that I was completely ---- and could not put it down.

(A) disenchanted   (B) enthralled   (C) indecisive
(D) disgruntled   (E) skeptical

18. SINGER : CHORUS::

    (A) architect : blueprint
    (B) teacher : student
    (C) author : publisher
    (D) driver : highway
    (E) actor : cast

19. INCISION : SCALPEL::

    (A) hospital : patient
    (B) playground : swing
    (C) kitchen : knife
    (D) electricity : wire
    (E) cut : saw

20. TRANQUILITY : PEACE::

    (A) chaos : disorder
    (B) retraction : indictment
    (C) combustion : ignition
    (D) portability : permanence
    (E) tension : release

21. ALTIMETER : HEIGHT::

    (A) speedometer : velocity
    (B) frustration : vexation
    (C) racetrack : furlong
    (D) vessel : knots
    (E) compass : map

22. CARAVAN : PROCESSION::

    (A) merchant : commerce
    (B) wedding : ceremony
    (C) menagerie : animal
    (D) hunter : prey
    (E) forum : argument

23. SLANDER : PEJORATIVE::

    (A) ingratiate : miraculous
    (B) revere : condemnatory
    (C) extol : laudatory
    (D) ruminate : unexpected
    (E) inculcate : plaintive

24. UNGAINLY : ELEGANCE::

    (A) stately : majesty
    (B) suitable : propriety
    (C) vacuous : temerity
    (D) feckless : sobriety
    (E) perfunctory : attention

25. GUARDIAN : PROTECTION::

    (A) sentinel : vigilance
    (B) monarch : subject
    (C) demagogue : benevolence
    (D) chaperon : transgression
    (E) minister : profanity

The passage below is followed by questions based on its content. Answer the questions following the passage on the basis of what is stated or implied in the passage.

Questions 26–35 are based on the following passage.

Charles Eastman was born in 1858 to a Wahpeton Sioux father and a mother who was part Indian. He was raised in the Sioux tradition until he was a teenager, when he was enrolled in a mission school. After that, he attended Beloit College, Dartmouth, and Boston University School of Medicine. He worked as a government physician, a field secretary for the YMCA, and an author and lecturer. This excerpt is from a story entitled "The Singing Spirit," about the adventures of a Bois Brulé Indian.

It was now dark. The night was well-nigh intolerable for Antoine. The buffalo were about him in countless numbers, regarding him with vicious glances. It was only by
(5) reason of the natural offensiveness of man that they gave him any space. The bellowing of the bulls became general, and there was a marked uneasiness on the part of the herd. This was a sign of approaching storm, therefore the unfortunate hunter had additional cause for anxiety. Upon the western horizon were seen flashes of lightning.

The cloud which had been a mere speck upon the (10) horizon had now increased to large proportions. Suddenly the wind came, and lightning flashes became more frequent, showing the ungainly forms of the animals like strange monsters in the white light. The colossal herd was again in violent motion. It was a blind rush for shelter, and (15) no heed was paid to buffalo wallows or even deep gulches. All was in the deepest of darkness. There seemed to be groaning in heaven and earth—millions of hoofs and throats roaring in unison.

As a shipwrecked man clings to a mere fragment of (20) wood, so Antoine, although almost exhausted with fatigue, still stuck to the saddle of his equally plucky pony. As the mad rush continued, every flash displayed heaps of bison in death struggle under the hoofs of their companions. . . .

When he awoke and looked around him again it was (25) morning. The herd had entered the strip of timber which

GO ON TO THE NEXT PAGE

lay on both sides of the river, and it was here that Antoine conceived his first distinct hope of saving himself.

(Line 30) "Waw, waw, waw!" was the hoarse cry that came to his ears, apparently from a human being in distress. Antoine strained his eyes and craned his neck to see who it could be. Through an opening in the branches ahead he perceived a large grizzly bear lying along an inclined limb and hugging it desperately to maintain his position. The (35) herd had now thoroughly pervaded the timber, and the bear was likewise hemmed in. He had taken his unaccustomed refuge after making a brave stand against several bulls, one of which lay dead near by, while he himself was bleeding from several wounds.

(40) Antoine had been assiduously looking for a friendly tree, by means of which he hoped to effect his escape from captivity by the army of bison. His horse, by chance, made his way directly under the very box-elder that was sustaining the bear and there was a convenient branch just within (45) his reach. . . . he saw at a glance that the occupant of the tree would not interfere with him. They were, in fact, companions in distress. Antoine tried to give a war-whoop as he sprang desperately from the pony's back and seized the cross-limb with both his hands. . . .

(50) By the middle of the afternoon the main body of the herd had passed, and Antoine was sure that his captivity had at last come to an end. Then he swung himself from his limb to the ground, and walked stiffly to the carcass of the nearest cow, which he dressed, and prepared himself a (55) meal. But first he took a piece of liver on a long pole to the bear!

26. By "the natural offensiveness of man" (line 4), Eastman probably refers to man's

(A) rudeness
(B) odor
(C) aggression
(D) distasteful behavior
(E) primitive nature

27. The word *ungainly* (line 13) means

(A) difficult
(B) enlarging
(C) awkward
(D) decreased
(E) tall

28. Eastman makes the buffalo seem

(A) cunning
(B) terrifying
(C) menacing
(D) both A and B
(E) both B and C

29. The tone of the first two paragraphs is

(A) frivolous
(B) suspenseful
(C) animated
(D) reserved
(E) lighthearted

30. The word *pervaded* (line 35) means

(A) saturated
(B) marched
(C) diffused
(D) corrupted
(E) penetrated

31. By "unaccustomed refuge" (lines 36–37), the author means that

(A) bears never need shelter
(B) bears live in caves
(C) bears prefer the open range
(D) bears rarely climb trees
(E) bears never retreat

32. The word *assiduously* (line 40) means

(A) constantly
(B) erratically
(C) unsteadily
(D) irresolutely
(E) reluctantly

33. The bear and the Indian are "companions in distress" (lines 46–47); in other words, they are

(A) friends for life
(B) stuck with each other
(C) fair-weather friends
(D) in the same danger
(E) alike under the skin

34. The word *dressed* (line 54) is used to mean

(A) adorned
(B) clothed
(C) bound
(D) embellished
(E) prepared

35. The mood of the passage moves from

(A) joy to despair
(B) hopelessness to hope
(C) happiness to gloom
(D) excitement to torpor
(E) apprehension to courageousness

IF YOU FINISH BEFORE TIME IS CALLED, YOU MAY CHECK YOUR WORK ON THIS SECTION ONLY. DO NOT WORK ON ANY OTHER SECTION IN THE TEST. **S T O P**

SECTION 2	Time—30 Minutes 25 Questions	In this section, solve each problem, using any available space on the page for scratchwork. Then decide which is the best of the choices given and fill in the corresponding oval on the answer sheet.

Reference:

Circle: Rectangle: Rectangular Solid: Cylinder: Triangle:

$C = 2\pi r$ $A = lw$ $V = lwh$ $V = \pi r^2 h$ $A = \frac{1}{2}bh$ $a^2 + b^2 = c^2$
$A = \pi r^2$

- The measure in degrees of a straight angle is 180.
- The number of degrees of arc in a circle is 360.
- The sum of the measures of the angles of a triangle is 180.

Notes: The figures accompanying the problems are drawn as accurately as possible unless otherwise stated in specific problems. Again, unless otherwise stated, all figures lie in the same plane. All numbers used in these problems are real numbers. Calculators are permitted for this test.

---

1. $121,212 + (2 \times 10^4) =$

    (A) 321,212   (B) 141,212   (C) 123,212
    (D) 121,412   (E) 121,232

2. If $6x + 3 = 21$, then $2x + 1 =$

    (A) 2   (B) 3   (C) 8   (D) 6   (E) 7

3. At a recreation center, it cost $3 per hour to rent a Ping-Pong table and $12 per hour to rent a lane for bowling. For the cost of renting a bowling lane for two hours, it is possible to rent a Ping-Pong table for how many hours?

    (A) 4   (B) 6   (C) 8   (D) 18   (E) 36

4. Jack, Ken, Larry, and Mike are j, k, l. and m years old, respectively. If $j < k < l < m$, which of the following *could* be true?

    (A) $k = j + l$
    (B) $j = k + l$
    (C) $j + k = l + m$
    (D) $j + k + m = l$
    (E) $j + m = k + l$

5. Of the following, which is greater than $\frac{1}{2}$?

    (A) $\frac{9}{19}$ (B) $\frac{7}{15}$ (C) $\frac{4}{9}$ (D) $\frac{6}{11}$ (E) $\frac{3}{7}$

6. Out of a group of 360 students, exactly 18 are on the track team. What pecent of the students are on the track team?

    (A) 5%   (B) 10%   (C) 12%   (D) 20%   (E) 25%

GO ON TO THE NEXT PAGE

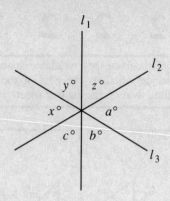

7. In the figure above, three lines intersect as shown. Which of the following must be true?

   I. $a = x$
   II. $y + z = b + c$
   III. $x + a = y + b$

(A) I only   (B) II only   (C) I and II only
(D) I and III only   (E) I, II, and III

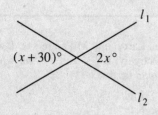

8. In the figure above, $x =$
(A) 15   (B) 30   (C) 45   (D) 60
(E) Cannot be determined from the information given.

9. The sum of the digits of a three-digit number is 11. If the hundreds' digit is 3 times the units' digit and 2 times the tens' digit, what is the number?

(A) 168 (B) 361 (C) 632 (D) 641 (E) 921

10. The **average (arithmetic** mean) height of four buildings is 20 meters. If three of the buildings have a height of 16 meters, what is the height, in meters, of the fourth building?

(A) 32 (B) 28 (C) 24 (D) 22 (E) 18

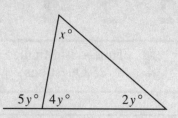

11. In the figure above, what is the value of x?
(A) 15 (B) 20 (C) 30 (D) 45 (E) 60

12. In the figure above, what is the length of PQ?
(A) 0.12 (B) 0.16 (C) 0.13 (D) 0.11 (E) 0.09

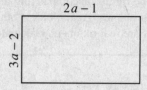

13. What is the perimeter of the rectangle shown above?
(A) $10a - 6$ (B) $10a - 3$ (C) $6a - 2$
(D) $5a - 6$ (E) $5a - 3$

14. If the average (arithmetic mean) of x, x, x, 56, and 58 is 51, then $x =$
(A) 43 (B) 47 (C) 49 (D) 51 (E) 53

15. For how many integers x is $-2 \le 2x \le 2$?
(A) 1   (B) 2   (C) 3   (D) 4   (E) 5

16. If x is an odd integer, all of the following are odd EXCEPT
(A) $x + 2$ (B) $3x + 2$ (C) $2x^2 + x$
(D) $2x^3 + x$ (E) $3x^3 + x$

17. What is the sum of the areas of two squares with sides of 2 and 3 respectively?
(A) 1   (B) 5   (C) 13   (D) 25   (E) 36

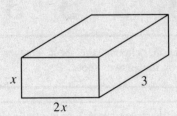

Note: Figure not drawn to scale

18. If the rectangular solid shown above has a volume of 54, then $x =$

(A) 2   (B) 3   (C) 6   (D) 9   (E) 12

---

19. If x is 80 percent of y, then y is what percent of x?

(A) $133\frac{1}{3}\%$ (B) 125%   (C) 120%

(D) 90%   (E) 80%

---

20. From which of the following statements can it be deduced that $m > n$?

(A) $m + 1 = n$
(B) $2m = n$
(C) $m + n > 0$
(D) $m - n > 0$
(E) $mn > 0$

---

21. If for any number n, is defined as the least integer that is greater than or equal to n^2, then

$$\boxed{-1.1} =$$

(A) -2 (B) -1 (C) 0   (D) 1   (E) 2

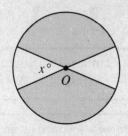

22. The circle with center O has a radius of length 2. If the total area of the shaded regions is 3π, then $x =$

(A) 270   (B) 180   (C) 120   (D) 90   (E) 45

---

23. If a bar of metal alloy consists of 100 grams of tin and 150 grams of lead, what percent of the entire bar, by weight, is tin?

(A) 10%   (B) 15%   (C) $33\frac{1}{3}\%$ (D) 40%

(E) $66\frac{2}{3}\%$

---

24. If $\dfrac{1}{x} + \dfrac{1}{y} = \dfrac{1}{z}$, then $z =$

(A) $\dfrac{1}{xy}$ (B) xy (C) $\dfrac{x+y}{xy}$

(D) $\dfrac{xy}{x+y}$ (E) $\dfrac{2xy}{x+y}$

---

25. In a certain clothing store, 60 percent of all the articles are imported and 20 percent of all the articles are priced at $100 or more. If 40 percent of the articles priced at $100 or more are imported, what percent of the articles priced *under* $100 are *not* imported?

(A) 28%   (B) 12%   (C) 8%   (D) 4.8%   (E) 2%

IF YOU FINISH BEFORE TIME IS CALLED, YOU MAY CHECK YOUR WORK ON THIS SECTION ONLY. DO NOT WORK ON ANY OTHER SECTION IN THE TEST.

STOP

The passages below are followed by questions based on their content. Answer the questions following the passages on the basis of what is stated or implied in the passages.

Questions 1–10 are based on the following passages.

Fanny Burney and Jane Austen were contemporaries, although Austen is justly more famous. Both wrote novels of manners, giving glimpses into a society long since departed. Each used humor to good effect in her work. Austen certainly read Burney; her title Pride and Prejudice *comes from a line in a Burney novel.*

Passage 1—Fanny Burney, from *Evelina* (1778)

I was saved from the importunities of Mr Smith, the beginning of the evening, by Madame Duval's declaring her intention to dance the first two dances with him herself. Mr Smith's chagrin was very evident, but as she paid
(5) no regard to it, he was necessitated to lead her out. . . .

For a few moments I very much rejoiced at being relieved from this troublesome man; but scarce had I time to congratulate myself, before I was accosted by another. . . .

I knew not whether to be glad or sorry, when Madame
(10) Duval and Mr Smith returned. The latter instantly resumed his tiresome entreaties, and Madame Duval said she would go to the card table; and as soon as she was accommodated, she desired us to join the dancers. . . .

In short time . . . he contrived to draw my attention to
(15) himself, by his extreme impertinence; for he chose to express what he called his *admiration* of me, in terms so open and familiar, that he forced me to express my displeasure with equal plainness.

But how was I surprised, when I found he had the
(20) temerity—what else can I call it?—to impute my resentment to doubts of his honour; for he said, 'My dear Ma'am, you must be a little patient; I assure you I have no bad designs, I have not upon my word; but, really, there is no resolving on such a thing as matrimony all at once;
(25) what with the loss of one's liberty, and what with the ridicule of all one's acquaintance, —I assure you, Ma'am, you are the first lady who ever made me even demur on this subject; for, after all, my dear Ma'am, marriage is the devil!'

(30) 'Your opinion, Sir,' answered I, 'of either the married or the single life, can be of no manner of consequence to me, and therefore I would by no means trouble you to discuss their different merits.'

'Why, really, Ma'am, as to your being a little out of sorts,
(35) I must own I can't wonder at it, for, to be sure, marriage is all in all with the ladies; but with us gentlemen it's quite another thing! Now only put yourself in my place,—suppose you had such a large acquaintance of gentlemen as I have,—and that you had already been used to appear a lit-
(40) tle—a little smart among them,—why now, how should you like to let yourself down all at once into a married man?'

I could not tell what to answer; so much conceit, and so much ignorance, both astonished and silenced me.

Passage 2—Jane Austen, from *Northanger Abbey* (1818)

'For Heaven's sake, let us move away from this end of the room.' [said Isabella] 'Do you know, there are two odious
(45) young men who have been staring at me this half-hour. They really put me quite out of countenance. Let us go and look at the arrivals. They will hardly follow us there.'

Away they walked to the book; and while Isabella examined the names, it was Catherine's employment to
(50) watch the proceedings of these alarming young men.

'They are not coming this way, are they? I hope they are not so impertinent as to follow us. Pray let me know if they are coming. I am determined I will not look up.'

In a few moments Catherine, with unaffected pleasure,
(55) assured her that she need not be longer uneasy, as the gentlemen had just left the Pump Room.

'And which way are they gone?' said Isabella, turning hastily round. 'One was a very good-looking young man.'

'They went toward the churchyard.'
(60)

'Well, I am amazingly glad to have got rid of them! And now, what say you to going to Edgar's Buildings with me, and looking at my new hat? You said you should like to see it.'

Catherine readily agreed. 'Only,' she added, 'perhaps
(65) we may overtake the young men.'

'Oh! never mind that. If we make haste we shall pass by them presently, and I am dying to show you my hat.'

'But if we only wait a few minutes, there will be no danger of our seeing them at all.'
(70)

'I shall not pay them any such compliment, I assure you. I have no notion of treating men with such respect. *That* is the way to spoil them.'

Catherine had nothing to oppose against such reasoning; and therefore, to show the independence of Miss Thorpe,
(75) and her resolution of humbling the sex, they set off immediately as fast as they could walk, in pursuit of the two young men.

1. Burney uses the word *importunities* (line 1) to mean

(A) cruelties
(B) refusals
(C) entreaties
(D) chances
(E) openings

2. By "terms so open and familiar" (lines 16–17), Burney means

   (A) commonly used phrases
   (B) friendly behavior
   (C) brotherly conversation
   (D) truthful and kind words
   (E) intimate and revealing language

3. The word *demur* (line 27) is used by Burney to mean

   (A) object
   (B) debate
   (C) have misgiving
   (D) protest
   (E) reject

4. How does Burney feel about the character of Mr. Smith?

   (A) He is well-meaning and kind.
   (B) He is a good catch.
   (C) He is shy and diffident.
   (D) He is boorish and absurd.
   (E) He is independent and haughty.

5. The phrase "how should you like to let yourself down all at once into a married man" (lines 40–41) implies that Smith

   (A) finds adultery repugnant
   (B) is insulting toward women
   (C) thinks marriage is a come-down
   (D) both A and B
   (E) both B and C

6. The word *odious* is used by Austen in line 45 to mean

   (A) attractive
   (B) appealing
   (C) admirable
   (D) burdensome
   (E) loathsome

7. By the phrase "unaffected pleasure" (line 55), Austen implies Catherine's

   (A) naïveté
   (B) affectionate nature
   (C) pretentiousness
   (D) self-satisfaction
   (E) recklessness

8. Catherine is used by Austen in this scene as a

   (A) foil to Isabella's calculations
   (B) mimic of Isabella's speech
   (C) facsimile of Isabella
   (D) watchdog over Isabella
   (E) miniature version of Isabella

9. In contrast to Burney's narrator, Isabella

   (A) treats her admirers scornfully
   (B) feigns lack of interest in her admirers
   (C) does not like men
   (D) both A and B
   (E) both B and C

10. The passages have in common

   (A) a light tone
   (B) a sense of irony
   (C) moralistic undertones
   (D) both A and B
   (E) both B and C

SECTION **4**   Time—15 Minutes
10 Questions

In this section, solve each problem, using any available space on the page for scratchwork. Then decide which is the best of the choices given and fill in the corresponding oval on the answer sheet.

Reference:

Circle: Rectangle: Rectangular Solid: Cylinder: Triangle:

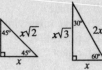

$C = 2\pi r$
$A = \pi r^2$

$A = lw$

$V = lwh$

$V = \pi r^2 h$

$A = \frac{1}{2}bh$

$a^2 + b^2 = c^2$

- The measure in degrees of a straight angle is 180.
- The number of degrees of arc in a circle is 360.
- The sum of the measures of the angles of a triangle is 180.

Notes: The figures accompanying the problems are drawn as accurately as possible unless otherwise stated in specific problems. Again, unless otherwise stated, all figures lie in the same plane. All numbers used in these problems are real numbers. Calculators are permitted for this test.

1. If p, q, r, s, and t are whole numbers and the expression $2(p(q + r) + s) + t$ is even, which of the numbers *must* be even?

   (A) p (B) q (C) r (D) s (E) t

2. If the area of a square is $9x^2$, what is the length of its side expressed in terms of x?

   (A) $\frac{x}{3}$ (B) $3x$ (C) $9x$ (D) $\frac{x^2}{3}$ (E) $3x^2$

3. The sum, the product, and the average (arithmetic mean) of three different integers are equal. If two of the integers are x and $-x$, the third integer is

   (A) $\frac{x}{2}$ (B) $2x$ (C) 1   (D) 0

   (E) It cannot be determined from the information given.

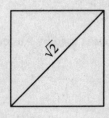

4. The perimeter of the square above is

   (A) 1   (B) $\sqrt{2}$ (C) 4   (D) $4\sqrt{2}$ (E) 8

5. A triangle has one side of length 4 and another side of length 11. What are the greatest and least possible *integer* values for the length of the remaining side?

   (A) 7 and 4   (B) 11 and 4   (C) 14 and 8
   (D) 15 and 7   (E) 16 and 7

6. If $2x + 3y = 19$, and x and y are positive integers, then x could be equal to which of the following?

   (A) 3   (B) 4   (C) 5   (D) 6   (E) 7

7. If the cost of N nails is C cents, what is the cost, *in dollars*, of X nails?

(A) $100CX$ (B) $\dfrac{100CX}{N}$ (C) $\dfrac{100NX}{C}$

(D) $\dfrac{NX}{100C}$ (E) $\dfrac{CX}{100N}$

---

8. If $a^2b^3c < 0$, then which of the following must be true?

(A) $b^3 < 0$ (B) $b^2 < 0$ (C) $b < 0$

(D) $c < 0$ (E) $bc < 0$

---

9. If the figure above is an equilateral triangle, what is its perimeter?

(A) 1   (B) 3   (C) 9   (D) 12

(E) It cannot be determined from the information given.

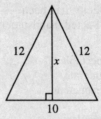

10. In the figure above, what is x?

(A) 5   (B) 7.5   (C) 13   (D) $\sqrt{119}$

(E) Cannot be determined from the information given

IF YOU FINISH BEFORE TIME IS CALLED, YOU MAY CHECK YOUR WORK ON THIS SECTION ONLY. DO NOT WORK ON ANY OTHER SECTION IN THE TEST.   **S T O P**

Each sentence below has one or two blanks, each blank indicating that something has been omitted. Beneath the sentence are five lettered words or sets of words. Choose the word or set of words that best fits the meaning of the sentence as a whole.

Example:

Although its publicity has been ----, the film itself is intelligent, well-acted, handsomely produced, and altogether ----.

(A) tasteless..respectable
(B) extensive..moderate
(C) sophisticated..amateur
(D) risqué..crude
(E) perfect..spectacular

1. The history book, written in 1880, was tremendously ----, unfairly blaming the South for the Civil War.

(A) biased   (B) objective   (C) suppressed
(D) questionable   (E) complicated

2. In the Middle Ages, scientists and clergymen thought the universe was well-ordered and ----; today scientists are more likely to see the world as ----.

(A) baffling..dogmatic
(B) harmonious..chaotic
(C) transient..predictable
(D) emancipated..intriguing
(E) divergent..galling

3. Hot milk has long been a standard cure for insomnia because of its ---- quality.

(A) malevolent   (B) amorphous   (C) soporific
(D) plaintive   (E) desultory

4. Since the results of the experiment were ---- the body of research already completed, the committee considered the results to be ----.

(A) similar to..speculative
(B) inconsistent with..anomalous
(C) compounded by..heretical
(D) dispelled by..convincing
(E) contradicted by..redundant

5. Psychologists believe that modern life ---- neurosis because of the ---- of traditional values which define acceptable behavior.

(A) copes with..inundation
(B) strives for..condoning
(C) concentrates on..plethora
(D) fosters..disappearance
(E) corroborates..dispelling

6. The millionaire was such a ---- that any appearance he made in public was ----.

(A) philistine..negligible
(B) recluse..noteworthy
(C) gourmand..distorted
(D) lecher..unexpected
(E) traitor..protracted

7. Because of the ---- of acupuncture therapy in China, Western physicians are starting to learn the procedure.

(A) veracity   (B) manipulation   (C) liquidity
(D) effectiveness   (E) inflation

8. Being a celebrity has its ----, one of which is the almost complete lack of ----.

(A) delusions..repression
(B) presumptions..income
(C) drawbacks..privacy
(D) frustrations..notoriety
(E) confrontations..intimacy

9. The program concluded with a modern symphony that contained chords so ---- that the piece produced sounds similar to the ---- one hears as the individual orchestra members tune their instruments before a concert.

(A) superfluous..melody
(B) pretentious..roar
(C) melodious..applause
(D) versatile..harmony
(E) discordant..cacophony

10. The king was a haughty aristocrat, but he was not a ----; he ruled his country ---- with genuine affection for his people.

(A) sycophant..benevolently
(B) diplomat..complacently
(C) monarch..stringently
(D) despot..magnanimously
(E) tyrant..superciliously

11. There is a ---- of verbiage in your writing; try not to be so ----.

(A) dearth..pompous
(B) preponderance..verbose
(C) predilection..long-winded
(D) element..prolix
(E) fraction..detrimental

12. My dog is a rare breed found ---- in the Arctic.

    (A) ultimately
    (B) comprehensively
    (C) exclusively
    (D) vitally
    (E) extensively

13. Great minds think alike: This old ---- is a favorite of mine.

    (A) draft
    (B) opus
    (C) term
    (D) maxim
    (E) logo

14. Most sitcoms are ----, but this new one is actually ----.

    (A) banal..engaging
    (B) vapid..ordinary
    (C) profound..solemn
    (D) unsightly..atrocious
    (E) passionate..repugnant

15. Paul is ---- and ----; he volunteers for everything.

    (A) saintly..appreciative
    (B) flighty..moody
    (C) unappreciated..misunderstood
    (D) generous..altruistic
    (E) underpaid..insignificant

Each question below consists of a related pair of words or phrases, followed by five lettered pairs of words or phrases. Select the lettered pair that best expresses a relationship similar to that expressed in the original pair.

Example:

YAWN : BOREDOM::
(A) dream : sleep
(B) anger : madness
(C) smile : amusement
(D) face : expression
(E) impatience : rebellion

---

16. BALLAD : SONG::

    (A) spire : church
    (B) ode : poem
    (C) novel : chapter
    (D) envelope : letter
    (E) leopard : jaguar

17. TEACHER : CLASSROOM::

    (A) student : library
    (B) minister : church
    (C) horse : carriage
    (D) desert : heat
    (E) curb : highway

18. UNIFORM : SOLDIER::

    (A) silks : jockey
    (B) leash : dog
    (C) pasture : cow
    (D) farmer : tractor
    (E) costume : scenery

19. MURAL : WALL::

    (A) pen : letter
    (B) tree : forest
    (C) painting : canvas
    (D) tobacco : smoke
    (E) museum : curator

20. BEGIN : PROCRASTINATION::

    (A) terminate : prolongation
    (B) show : demonstration
    (C) frighten : terror
    (D) guarantee : refund
    (E) capture : torture

21. LUBRICANT : FRICTION::

    (A) machine : operator
    (B) spasm : muscle
    (C) dessert : sugar
    (D) balm : pain
    (E) drawer : chest

22. REGRETTABLE : LAMENT::

    (A) praiseworthy : applaud
    (B) verbose : rejoice
    (C) incongruous : detect
    (D) reliable : defend
    (E) obnoxious : boast

23. FASTIDIOUS : CLEANLINESS::

    (A) pliant : fabrication
    (B) meticulous : detail
    (C) timorous : hostility
    (D) bereft : animosity
    (E) enervated : activity

24. DISAPPROBATION : CONDEMN::

    (A) solvency : deploy
    (B) calumny : laud
    (C) enigma : enlighten
    (D) fallacy : disseminate
    (E) exhortation : urge

25. AMBIVALENCE : COMMITMENT::

    (A) perfidy : profitability
    (B) gullibility : discernment
    (C) travesty : justice
    (D) enthusiasm : predicament
    (E) conundrum : epigram

GO ON TO THE NEXT PAGE

Questions 26–35 are based on the following passage.

Alain Locke (1886–1954) taught philosophy at Howard University for over 40 years. He wrote prolifically on topics involving African–American culture and aesthetics. Like Du Bois and Garvey, Locke encouraged African–Americans to identify with Africa. This excerpt is from a 1924 essay entitled "Apropos of Africa."

The great reason for this unfortunate apathy of interests is the lack of widespread and matter of fact information about Africa. Our interests are fed on sentiment, and not with knowledge. Our first duty is to cultivate every oppor-
(5) tunity for diffusion among us of the knowledge of Africa both of today and of the past. Travel, exchange of students, the spread of journalistic and academic information are for the moment of paramount importance. In a decade in which the study of African art and archeology has come
(10) to the very forefront of scholarship, it is both a reproach and a handicap to have no recognized experts of our own in these fields. Instead of being reluctant, our Negro colleges should be eager to develop special scholarship in these directions; in the cultural field, here is their special
(15) and peculiar chance to enter the academic arena and justify themselves. The pioneer work of the *Journal of Negro History*, under Dr. Carter G. Woodson, and of Howard University in the courses of the history of African civilizations, under Mr. Leo Hansberry, deserve not mere passing
(20) interest and praise but the financial support of the people and the active participation of the talented tenth. And both must eventually culminate, the sooner, the better, for the present is a very psychological moment in African studies, in well-planned and well-supported research investigation
(25) in Africa. Later I shall write more specifically about the problems and opportunities of research in this field as they have come under observation in the *reconnaisance* trip I have been able to undertake; for the moment it will suffice to quote, by permission, the following representative opin-
(30) ion from a letter of Mr. Arthur Weigall, former Chief Inspector of Antiquities for Upper Egypt, to that most eminent of archeologists, Sir William Flinders-Petrie: "The study of the history and traditions of the African races by their own students is, I think, most interesting, and I am
(35) sure you will find the idea of an African mind applying itself to ancient African manners and customs a very promising one." Out of over a score of most eminent authorities interviewed on this subject, all save two have substantially concurred in this opinion, and these two were
(40) investigators who strictly relegate ethnological matters to the findings of anthropometry and, naturally enough, consider physical anthropology too scientifically neutral for there to be any advantage or peculiar point to our participation. On the other hand, even they were willing to admit
(45) that in the question of folk-lore and comparative study of customs, psychological *rapport* and *entree* to the groups studied were of paramount importance, and that with respect to the study of African peoples, the employment of trained colored investigators would inaugurate a new era
(50) in this important, but admittedly unsatisfactory, field of research.

As an instance of the effectiveness of an identity of interest of this sort, one might cite the case of the Museum for Coptic Antiquities in Cairo. In ten years, six of them
(55) almost useless to the project because of the war, and with only limited private funds, but with the great intangible capital of group loyalty and cooperation, Murcos Samaika Pasha has assembled in competition with the great endowed museums of Europe and America a collection of
(60) Coptic antiquities which almost rivals the best in any line of special collection and in variety outmatches all. . . . [I]t is really one of the treasures of Cairo, and though quite off the beaten track, its register of prominent public and academic visitors attests to the power of attraction of anything
(65) unique and distinctive. For this people, the martyrs and guardians of Christianity in Africa, and their interesting history and institutions, we should cultivate a very special and intimate interest.

26. The word *diffusion* (line 5) means

    (A) wandering
    (B) redundancy
    (C) concentration
    (D) rambling
    (E) circulation

27. Locke uses the word *peculiar* (line 15) to mean

    (A) outlandish
    (B) quaint
    (C) characteristic
    (D) unique
    (E) odd

28. The *Journal of Negro History* is introduced as an example of

    (A) an analysis of African pioneers
    (B) scholarship on Africa by African–Americans
    (C) work that African–Americans should support
    (D) both A and B
    (E) both B and C

29. Locke's "*reconnaisance* trip" apparently included

    (A) trips to Howard University
    (B) tours of archaeological digs
    (C) talks with Dr. Woodson
    (D) a journey to Cairo
    (E) none of the above

30. Why does Locke include the citation from Arthur Weigall?

    (A) to show the racism inherent in white researchers
    (B) to establish a target for his audience
    (C) to support his goal of African–American participation
    (D) both A and B
    (E) both B and C

31. The phrase "substantially concurred" (line 39) means

    (A) agreed for the most part
    (B) significantly differed
    (C) grossly overrated
    (D) largely preferred
    (E) mostly defeated

32. How does Locke feel toward scientifically neutral studies?

    (A) approving
    (B) derogatory
    (C) tolerant
    (D) frustrated
    (E) infuriated

33. The Museum for Coptic Antiquities is discussed in order to

    (A) show that African studies are overrun by white scholars
    (B) demonstrate the need for more funding of archaeology
    (C) provide an example of important African cultural studies
    (D) both A and B
    (E) both B and C

34. By "the great intangible capital" (lines 56–57), Locke means

    (A) loyalty and cooperation cannot be bought
    (B) loyalty and cooperation are abstract but invaluable
    (C) nothing is worthwhile but loyalty and cooperation
    (D) transient loyalty and cooperation are worthless
    (E) the museum is a headquarters for loyal workers

35. Locke's main goal in this passage is to

    (A) encourage students to expand their horizons
    (B) urge African–Americans to study Africa
    (C) show the difference between African and American art
    (D) demonstrate a way of saving African culture
    (E) convince archaeologists to research African history

IF YOU FINISH BEFORE TIME IS CALLED, YOU MAY CHECK YOUR WORK ON THIS SECTION ONLY. DO NOT WORK ON ANY OTHER SECTION IN THE TEST. **STOP**

595

6 6 6 6 6 6 6 6 6 6 6

<table>
<tr><td>SECTION 6</td><td>Time—30 Minutes
25 Questions</td><td>This section contains two types of problems with separate directions for each. You may use any available space on the page for scratchwork.</td></tr>
</table>

Reference:

Circle: Rectangle: Rectangular Solid: Cylinder: Triangle:

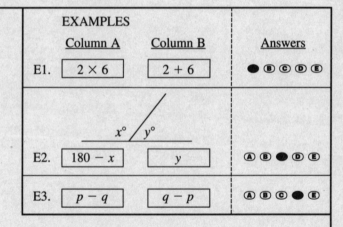

$C = 2\pi r$ $A = lw$ $V = lwh$ $V = \pi r^2 h$ $A = \frac{1}{2}bh$ $a^2 + b^2 = c^2$
$A = \pi r^2$

- The measure in degrees of a straight angle is 180.
- The number of degrees of arc in a circle is 360.
- The sum of the measures of the angles of a triangle is 180.

Notes: The figures accompanying the problems are drawn as accurately as possible unless otherwise stated in specific problems. Again, unless otherwise stated, all figures lie in the same plane. All numbers used in these problems are real numbers. Calculators are permitted for this test.

Directions for Quantitative Comparison Questions

Questions 1–15 each consist of two quantities, one in Column A and one in Column B. You are to compare the two quantities and on the answer sheet fill in oval

A if the quantity in Column A is greater;
B if the quantity in Column B is greater;
C if the two quantities are equal;
D if the relationship cannot be determined from the information given.

AN E RESPONSE WILL NOT BE SCORED.

EXAMPLES

	Column A	Column B	Answers
E1.	2×6	$2 + 6$	● Ⓑ Ⓒ Ⓓ Ⓔ
E2.	$180 - x$	y	Ⓐ Ⓑ ● Ⓓ Ⓔ
E3.	$p - q$	$q - p$	Ⓐ Ⓑ Ⓒ ● Ⓔ

Notes:

1. In certain questions, information concerning one or both of the quantities to be compared is centered above the two columns.
2. In a given question, a symbol that appears in both columns represents the same thing in Column A as it does in Column B.
3. Letters such as x, n, and k stand for real numbers.

GO ON TO THE NEXT PAGE

596

Column A	Column B

$$\frac{x}{2} = 18$$

$$\frac{y}{3} = 18$$

1.

x	y

2.

10% of 50	50% of 10

3.

The sum of the 5 greatest odd integers less than 20	The sum of the 5 least even integers greater than 10

4.

The fraction of a day represented by 8 hours	The fraction of an hour represented by 40 minutes

$$x \cdot 1 = x$$

5.

x	1

6.

70°

$4x°$

110° $2x°$

Note: Figure not drawn to scale.

x	30

7.

$\sqrt{6} \times \sqrt{10}$	$\sqrt{3} \times \sqrt{20}$

Column A	Column B

$$x < 0$$

8.

x^{15}	x^{16}

$$x < 50$$

9.

$50 + x$	100

The average of x, y, and z is y.

10.

x	z

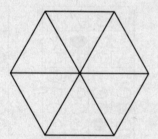

The figure above consists of 6 equilateral triangles, each with a perimeter of 6.

11.

36	The sum of the lengths of all the line segments in the figure

$$\begin{array}{r} 50M \\ \times \quad 7 \\ \hline 3,56N \end{array}$$

M and N represent digits

12.

M	N

GO ON TO THE NEXT PAGE

Smithtown is 20 kilometers from Jamestown.

Jamestown is 50 kilometers from Charlestown.

13.	Distance in kilometers from Smithtown to Charlestown	70

14.	$\dfrac{1}{9}$	0.11

$x < 0$
$y > 0$

15.	$x^2 + y^2$	$(x + y)^2$

Directions for Student-Produced Response Questions

Questions 16–25 each require you to solve a problem and mark your answer on a special answer grid. For each question, you should write your answer in the boxes at the top of each column and then fill in the ovals beneath each answer you write. Here are some examples.

Answer: 3/4 (= .75; show answer either way)

Answer: 325

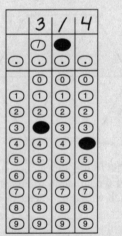

Note: A mixed number such as 3½ must be gridded as 7/2 or as 3.5. If gridded as "31/2," it will be read as "thirty-one halves."

Note: Either position is correct.

16. If $3x + 2 = 8$, then $6x = ?$

17. Members of a civic organization purchase boxes of candy for $1 apiece and sell them for $2 apiece. If no other expenses are incurred, how many boxes of candy must they sell to earn a net profit of $500?

18. In a school with a total enrollment of 360, 90 students are seniors. What percent of all students enrolled in the school are seniors?

22. If the average of six numbers—10, 12, 15.1, 15.2, 28, and x—is 16, what is x?

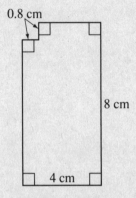

19. The figure above is a scale drawing of the floor of a dining hall. If 1 centimeter on the drawing represents 5 meters, what is the area, in square meters, of the floor?

23. At the zoo, 25% of the animals are birds, 30% are reptiles or amphibians, and the rest are mammals. If there are 12 geese, representing 20% of the birds, how many mammals are there at the zoo?

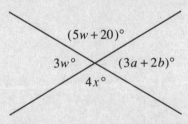

20. If two straight lines intersect as shown, what is the value of x?

24. Jerry grew 5 inches in 1993, and 2 inches more in 1994 before reaching his final height of 5 feet 10 inches. What percentage of his final height did his 1993–1994 growth represent?

21. A school club spent $\frac{2}{5}$ of its budget for one project and $\frac{1}{3}$ of what remained for another project. If the club's entire budget was equal to $300, how much of the budget, in dollars, was left after the two projects?

25. A circle with radius 2 is superimposed upon a square with sides measuring 5 so that the center of the circle and the center of the square are identical. At how many points will the square and circle intersect?

IF YOU FINISH BEFORE TIME IS CALLED, YOU MAY CHECK YOUR WORK ON THIS SECTION ONLY. DO NOT WORK ON ANY OTHER SECTION IN THE TEST. **S T O P**

Answer Key

SECTION 1

1. C	11. A	21. A	31. D
2. E	12. A	22. B	32. A
3. B	13. D	23. C	33. D
4. B	14. E	24. E	34. E
5. A	15. C	25. A	35. B
6. D	16. E	26. B	
7. E	17. B	27. C	
8. B	18. E	28. E	
9. C	19. E	29. B	
10. C	20. A	30. E	

SECTION 2

1. B	11. E	21. E
2. E	12. B	22. E
3. C	13. A	23. D
4. E	14. B	24. D
5. D	15. C	25. A
6. A	16. E	
7. C	17. C	
8. B	18. B	
9. C	19. B	
10. A	20. D	

SECTION 3

1. C
2. E
3. B
4. D
5. E
6. E
7. A
8. A
9. B
10. D

SECTION 4

1. E
2. B
3. D
4. C
5. C
6. C
7. E
8. E
9. C
10. D

SECTION 5

1. A	11. B	21. D	31. A
2. B	12. C	22. A	32. C
3. C	13. D	23. B	33. C
4. B	14. A	24. E	34. B
5. D	15. D	25. B	35. B
6. B	16. B	26. E	
7. D	17. B	27. D	
8. C	18. A	28. E	
9. E	19. C	29. D	
10. D	20. A	30. C	

SECTION 6

1. B	6. C	11. A	16. 12	21. 120
2. C	7. C	12. A	17. 500	22. 15.7
3. B	8. B	13. D	18. 25	23. 108
4. B	9. B	14. A	19. 784	24. 10
5. D	10. D	15. A	20. 30	25. 0

Explanatory Answers

SECTION 1

CRITICAL READING

1. The word *fordable* (line 6) means

    (A) provided
    (B) sustainable
    (C) traversable
    (D) paid for
    (E) sluggish

    (C) The word is used in context to describe a point in a river, so immediately all choices but (C) and (E) may be eliminated. Muir speaks of planning a way to the river at that point; while he might choose a sluggish point, he is more likely to choose one that is easily crossed.

2. The word *sprays* (line 16) is used to mean

    (A) droplets
    (B) weeds
    (C) ferns
    (D) showers
    (E) sprigs

    (E) Test the choices in this vocabulary-in-context question. The deer is walking through cherry trees, and the "topmost sprays" are trembling. Weeds (B) and ferns (C) could tremble, but why would Muir call them "topmost"? Anyway, he is talking about the trees. Don't be fooled by (A) and (D), which refer to an alternate meaning of *sprays*. The movement of a deer would not make droplets or showers tremble. The most likely replacement is (E), meaning the thin sets of leaves at the ends of branches.

3. Muir uses the word *glanced* in line 17 to mean

    (A) viewed
    (B) skipped over
    (C) observed
    (D) scanned
    (E) blinked

    (B) Disregard this word's most common meaning, having to do with sight; sunrays do not have eyes. That eliminates (A), (C), (D), and (E), leaving only (B).

4. Paragraph 2 extends Muir's intention to

    (A) tell a story
    (B) paint a picture
    (C) teach a lesson
    (D) express an opinion
    (E) inspire good works

    (B) Even if you did not recognize Muir's intention, you can answer this synthesis/analysis question easily by referring back to the paragraph in question. Muir pauses to set a scene, to paint a picture. The entire paragraph is merely descriptive, freezing a moment in time.

5. The "second pair of eyes" (line 25) belongs to

    (A) a second deer
    (B) Muir
    (C) the gardener
    (D) a sheep
    (E) none of the above

    (A) Return to the citation to answer this interpretation question. Muir notices "a second pair of eyes, not fixed on me" — clearly not *his* eyes (B). Turning to the next paragraph, you can see that Muir is referring to the two animals as a pair; they must both be deer.

6. The response Muir has to the deer might be summarized as one of

    (A) envy
    (B) scorn
    (C) amusement
    (D) reverence
    (E) disbelief

    (D) Muir wants to run his hand along the deer's bodies. He uses words such as *fine* and *beautiful* to describe them. He is not envious (A), but he is reverent (D), or worshipful.

7. The phrase "they seemed to penetrate my conceit" (line 34) means

    (A) "They invaded my narcissism."
    (B) "They filled my thoughts."
    (C) "They punctured my pride."
    (D) "They entered my fantasy."
    (E) "They guessed my intentions."

    (E) Test the choices in place of the phrase in question, and you will easily find the answer to this interpretation question. Muir makes an advance

601

toward the deer, and they bound away, having guessed his intentions to touch them.

8. Unlike the first paragraph, the last paragraph is
   (A) descriptive
   (B) didactic
   (C) humorous
   (D) fictional
   (E) expressive

   (B) Muir changes gears from a strictly descriptive tone to a somewhat moralizing one. Even if you do not know the term *didactic*, you can find the answer by process of elimination. The first paragraph is both descriptive (A) and expressive (E); the last is neither humorous (C) nor fictional (D).

9. Muir compares deer to gardeners in terms of their
   (A) use of tools
   (B) enjoyment of the outdoors
   (C) tending of nature
   (D) both A and B
   (E) both B and C

   (C) The only thing Muir says about gardeners is that, like gardeners, the deer have left the garden in order. There is no mention of enjoyment of the outdoors (B), so neither (B) nor (E) is an appropriate answer.

10. Why does Muir refer to the Alps in line 48?
    (A) to contrast their vegetation with California's
    (B) to contrast sheep's destructiveness with deer's preservation
    (C) to compare deer and sheep in terms of conservation
    (D) to contrast European conservation movements with those of the United States
    (E) to show that deer are found around the world

    (C) The entire last paragraph deals with animals' abilities to conserve nature, whether they be the deer of Yosemite or the sheep of the Alps. No answer besides (C) is supported by the text.

11. The "boldly drawn hieroglyphics" referred to in lines 53–54 are probably
    (A) claw marks
    (B) ancient runes
    (C) prehistoric paintings
    (D) pawprints in the dirt
    (E) grafitti

    (A) This interpretation question asks you to make a creative leap from Muir's words to picture the kind of marks bears might make on tree bark. (B), (C), and (E) do not correspond to anything a bear might create, and since the marks are on trees, (D) is inappropriate.

12. The purpose of the last sentence seems to be to
    (A) sound an alarm
    (B) offer praise
    (C) make concessions
    (D) prejudge
    (E) make a recommendation

    (A) Muir implies a certain amount of praise for the animals to which he refers in the rest of the paragraph, but in the final sentence, his only purpose is to castigate man for his destructiveness. He does not, however, go so far as to recommend any recourse (E).

SENTENCE COMPLETION

13. Although some critics interpret *The Aeneid* as a Christian epic, this interpretation is totally ----, since the epic predates Christianity.

    (A) infallible   (B) acceptable   (C) convincing
    (D) anachronistic   (E) conventional

    (D) This question is largely a matter of vocabulary. The correct choice must be a word that means that something predates something else. Only (D) has this meaning.

14. Black comedy is the combination of that which is humorous with that which would seem ---- to humor: the ----.

    (A) apathetic..ignoble
    (B) heretical..salacious
    (C) inferior..grandiose
    (D) extraneous..innocuous
    (E) antithetical..macabre

    (E) The best way to attack this question is to substitute each pair until you find one that works. You can immediately eliminate (A) on the grounds of usage as *apathetic to humor* makes no sense. Next, the *salacious* is not heretical to humor, so eliminate (B). The *grandiose* is not *inferior* to *humor*, so eliminate (C). The *innocuous* is not *extraneous* to *humor*, so eliminate (D). You are left with (E), which does make sense. The *macabre* might be *antithetical* to *humor*.

15. The original British cast was talented and energetic, while the Broadway cast lacks the ---- of the original players; in fact, the performance is ----.

    (A) calmness..scintillating
    (B) splendor..fallow
    (C) verve..insipid
    (D) flexibility..meticulous
    (E) intractability..quaint

    (C) This question contains a thought-reverser and a thought-extender. The logical clue in the first part of the sentence is the word "while." This tells you that the *Broadway cast* was the opposite of the *British cast*. The first blank extends the idea of what the British cast was. Look for a word that goes with energy and talent. (B) and (C) are possibilities; the others do not extend the idea. The word in the second blank must be the opposite of the description of the *British cast*. (D), *meticulous*, makes no sense, so you are left with (C).

16. The press conference did not clarify many issues since the President responded with ---- and ---- rather than clarity and precision.

    (A) sincerity..humor
    (B) incongruity..candor
    (C) fervor..lucidity
    (D) animation..formality
    (E) obfuscation..vagueness

    (E) This entire sentence is a thought-reverser. The President responded with something other than *clarity* and *precision*. You should immediately look for opposites of these words for the blanks. (E) *obfuscation* and *vagueness* do the job.

17. Although the novel was not well written, it was such an exciting story that I was completely ---- and could not put it down.

    (A) disenchanted   (B) enthralled   (C) indecisive
    (D) disgruntled   (E) skeptical

    (B) The sentence contains a thought-reverser, although, and a thought-extender. First, the reader's reaction to the novel is opposite to what would be expected if the book were well-written. Also, you must extend the thought of the exciting story, which the reader could not put down. Eliminate (A), (D), and (E) because the reader would have put the book down had he or she been any of those things. (C) makes no sense at all, so you are left with (B), which completes the thought perfectly.

ANALOGIES

18. SINGER : CHORUS::

    (A) architect : blueprint
    (B) teacher : student
    (C) author : publisher
    (D) driver : highway
    (E) actor : cast

    (E) This a part to whole analogy. A SINGER is part of a CHORUS, and an *actor* is part of a *cast*.

19. INCISION : SCALPEL::

    (A) hospital : patient
    (B) playground : swing
    (C) kitchen : knife
    (D) electricity : wire
    (E) cut : saw

    (E) This analogy falls into our "tool" category. An INCISION is made with a SCALPEL, or a SCALPEL is the tool used to make an INCISION. A *cut* is made with a *saw*, or a *saw* is the tool used to *cut*.

20. TRANQUILITY : PEACE::

    (A) chaos : disorder
    (B) retraction : indictment
    (C) combustion : ignition
    (D) portability : permanence
    (E) tension : release

    (A) This is a "defining characteristic" analogy. TRANQUILITY means PEACEFUL, and *chaos* means *disorderly*.

21. ALTIMETER : HEIGHT::

    (A) speedometer : velocity
    (B) frustration : vexation
    (C) racetrack : furlong
    (D) vessel : knots
    (E) compass : map

    (A) This analogy is fairly straightforward. An ALTIMETER measures HEIGHT, and a *speedometer* measures *velocity*.

22. CARAVAN : PROCESSION::

    (A) merchant : commerce
    (B) wedding : ceremony
    (C) menagerie : animal
    (D) hunter : prey
    (E) forum : argument

    (B) This is a "type of" analogy. A CARAVAN is a type of PROCESSION, and a *wedding* is a type of *ceremony*.

23. SLANDER : PEJORATIVE::

    (A) ingratiate : miraculous
    (B) revere : condemnatory
    (C) extol : laudatory
    (D) ruminate : unexpected
    (E) inculcate : plaintive

    (C) This analogy is based on the "defining characteristic" connection. A defining characteristic of speech that SLANDERS is its PEJORATIVE content, and a defining characteristic of speech that *extols* is its *laudatory* content.

24. UNGAINLY : ELEGANCE::

    (A) stately : majesty
    (B) suitable : propriety
    (C) vacuous : temerity
    (D) feckless : sobriety
    (E) perfunctory : attention

    (E) This analogy fits into the "lack of" category. That which is UNGAINLY lacks ELEGANCE, and that which is *perfunctory* lacks *attention*.

25. GUARDIAN : PROTECTION::

    (A) sentinel : vigilance
    (B) monarch : subject
    (C) demagogue : benevolence
    (D) chaperon : transgression
    (E) minister : profanity

    (A) This is a "defining characteristic" analogy. By definition, a GUARDIAN must PROTECT, and a *sentinel* must be *vigilant*.

CRITICAL READING

26. By "the natural offensiveness of man" (line 4), Eastman probably refers to man's

    (A) rudeness
    (B) odor
    (C) aggression
    (D) distasteful behavior
    (E) primitive nature

    (B) Think about what you know about the phrase as it is used in context; whatever it is, it keeps the buffalo from moving toward the hunter. (A), (D), and (E) are then probably not logical choices. There is no sign that the Indian is acting aggressively (C), even if you read no further than the first paragraph. Only (B) works in context.

27. The word *ungainly* (line 13) means

    (A) difficult
    (B) enlarging
    (C) awkward
    (D) decreased
    (E) tall

    (C) *Ungainly* can have several shades of meaning, but in context, the "ungainly forms of the animals" look like monsters and move "in violent motion." Only (C) covers both appearance and demeanor.

28. Eastman makes the buffalo seem

    (A) cunning
    (B) terrifying
    (C) menacing
    (D) both A and B
    (E) both B and C

    (E) Throughout the passage, the hunter's life is threatened by these animals, but not because of their cunning (A). He spends a good amount of time in terror (B) because the huge bodies are so menacing (C). Since (B) and (C) are possible, the best answer is (E).

29. The tone of the first two paragraphs is

    (A) frivolous
    (B) suspenseful
    (C) animated
    (D) reserved
    (E) lighthearted

    (B) You can easily eliminate (A) and (E). (D) is an odd way to describe a tone, and *animated* (C) implies an exuberance that is lacking here.

30. The word *pervaded* (line 35) means

    (A) saturated
    (B) marched
    (C) diffused
    (D) corrupted
    (E) penetrated

    (E) Try the choices in context. Although (A) and (C) may be synonyms for *pervaded*, they do not fit this particular use of the word. (B) is a synonym for *paraded*, and (D) is a synonym for *perverted*.

31. By "unaccustomed refuge" (lines 36–37), the author means that

    (A) bears never need shelter
    (B) bears live in caves
    (C) bears prefer the open range
    (D) bears rarely climb trees
    (E) bears never retreat

    (D) Think about where the bear is: up a tree. (B) may be true, but it is unsupported by the text. (A), (C), and (E) are almost certainly untrue. Only (D) follows logically from the text thus far.

32. The word *assiduously* (line 40) means

    (A) constantly
    (B) erratically
    (C) unsteadily
    (D) irresolutely
    (E) reluctantly

    (A) Unlike the choices in question 30, (B), (C), (D), and (E) can really be considered antonyms for *assiduously*, which implies a continual action and a certain determination.

33. The bear and the Indian are "companions in distress" (lines 46–47); in other words, they are

(A) friends for life
(B) stuck with each other
(C) fair-weather friends
(D) in the same danger
(E) alike under the skin

(D) Do not overextend your imagination on this interpretation question; it is quite straightforward. The bear and the Indian, although natural enemies, are in the same boat (or tree, actually); and they share the same danger.

34. The word *dressed* (line 54) is used to mean

(A) adorned
(B) clothed
(C) bound
(D) embellished
(E) prepared

(E) *Dressing*, in this case, refers to a way of preparing meat to be cooked. If you test the choices in context, you will find that, despite the fact all are synonyms, only (E) could possibly be applied to meat.

35. The mood of the passage moves from

(A) joy to despair
(B) hopelessness to hope
(C) happiness to gloom
(D) excitement to torpor
(E) apprehension to courageousness

(B) This synthesis/analysis question asks you to look at the passage as a whole: How does it begin, and how does it end? Neither *joy* (A) nor *happiness* (C) accurately describes the beginning; neither *torpor* (D) nor *courageousness* (E) accurately describes the ending. Only (B) fits.

SECTION 2

MATH PROBLEM-SOLVING

1. $121,212 + (2 \times 10^4) =$

(A) 321,212   (B) 141,212   (C) 123,212
(D) 121,412   (E) 121,232

(B) $2 \times 10^4 = 20,000$, and $121,212 + 20,000 = 141,212$

2. If $6x + 3 = 21$, then $2x + 1 =$

(A) 2   (B) 3   (C) 8   (D) 6   (E) 7

(E) Solve for x:
$6x + 3 = 21$
$6x = 18$
$x = 3$
So $2x + 1 = 2(3) + 1 = 7$

3. At a recreation center, it cost $3 per hour to rent a Ping-Pong table and $12 per hour to rent a lane for bowling. For the cost of renting a bowling lane for two hours, it is possible to rent a Ping-Pong table for how many hours?

(A) 4   (B) 6   (C) 8   (D) 18   (E) 36

(C) There is no trick to this question. Just use "supermarket" math. Find out how much the one thing would cost. Then, using that cost find how much of the other you can buy.

The cost of renting a bowling lane for two hours is $2 \times \$12 = \$24$. And for $24 you can rent a Ping Pong table for $\$24 \div \$3 = 8$ hours.

4. Jack, Ken, Larry, and Mike are j, k, l. and m years old, respectively. If $j < k < l < m$, which of the following *could* be true?

(A) $k = j + l$
(B) $j = k + l$
(C) $j + k = l + m$
(D) $j + k + m = l$
(E) $j + m = k + l$

(E) You can reason in general terms to the correct answer. As for (A), since k is less than l, k cannot be equal to l plus something. The same reasoning applies to (B), (C), and (D). (E), however, could be true. For example, if Jack is 5, and Ken is 10, and Larry is 15, and Mike is 20, then $5 + 20 = 10 + 15$.

5. Of the following, which is greater than $\frac{1}{2}$?

(A) $\frac{9}{19}$ (B) $\frac{7}{15}$ (C) $\frac{4}{9}$ (D) $\frac{6}{11}$ (E) $\frac{3}{7}$

(D) Use $\frac{1}{2}$ as a benchmark. And reason in this way: Eliminate (A), since $\frac{9}{18}$ is $\frac{1}{2}$, $\frac{9}{19}$ is less than $\frac{1}{2}$. Continue eliminating choices until you are left with (D).

6. Out of a group of 360 students, exactly 18 are on the track team. What percent of the students are on the track team?

(A) 5%   (B) 10%   (C) 12%   (D) 20%   (E) 25%

(A) Use the "this-of-that" strategy:
this/of that = student on track team/total students
$= \frac{18}{360} = \frac{1}{20} = 5\%$.

605

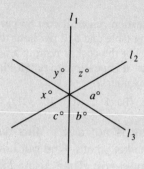

7. In the figure above, three lines intersect as shown. Which of the following must be true?

   I. $a = x$
   II. $y + z = b + c$
   III. $x + a = y + b$

   (A) I only   (B) II only   (C) I and II only
   (D) I and III only   (E) I, II, and III

   (C) I must be true because a and x are vertically opposite each other. Similarly, II must be true because y and b are equal and z and c are equal. III, however, is not necessarily true. x and a are equal, y and b are equal, but you don't have information on which to base a conclusion about the relation between x and y or the relation between z and b.

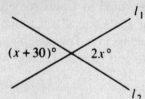

8. In the figure above, $x =$

   (A) 15   (B) 30   (C) 45   (D) 60
   (E) Cannot be determined from the information given.

   (B) You can set up an equation:
   $x + 30 = 2x$
   $x = 30$

   Or you can just guesstimate the size of the right hand angle as being about 60°, so half of that would be about 30°.

9. The sum of the digits of a three-digit number is 11. If the hundreds' digit is 3 times the units' digit and 2 times the tens' digit, what is the number?

   (A) 168   (B) 361   (C) 632   (D) 641   (E) 921

   (C) Here you should just "test the test." Only the number in (C) fits the specified conditions. $6 + 3 + 2 = 11$; $6 = 3 \times 2$; and $6 = 2 \times 3$.

10. The average (arithmetic mean) height of four buildings is 20 meters. If three of the buildings have a height of 16 meters, what is the height, in meters, of the fourth building?

    (A) 32   (B) 28   (C) 24   (D) 22   (E) 18

    (A) Use the method for finding the missing element of an average. Since the average height of all four buildings is 20, the sum of the heights of all four is $4 \times 20 = 80$. The three known heights total $3 \times 16 = 48$. So the missing value is $80 - 48 = 32$.

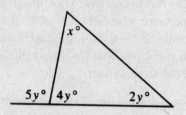

11. In the figure above, what is the value of x?

    (A) 15   (B) 20   (C) 30   (D) 45   (E) 60

    (E) First find the value of y:

    $5y + 4y = 180$
    $9y = 180$
    $y = 20$

    Next find the value of x:

    $4y + 2y + x = 180$
    $6y + x = 180$
    $6(20) + x = 180$
    $120 + x = 180$
    $x = 60$

12. In the figure above, what is the length of PQ?

    (A) 0.12   (B) 0.16   (C) 0.13
    (D) 0.11   (E) 0.09

    (B) The trick here is to recognize that each of the marks between the numbered marks is $\frac{1}{5}$ of the distance between the numbered marks. The distance between each numbered mark is 0.1, so each of the others is worth $0.1 \div 5 = 0.02$, So $PQ = 0.02 + 0.1 + 2(0.02) = 0.16$.

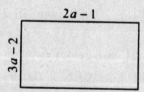

13. What is the perimeter of the rectangle shown above?

    (A) $10a - 6$ (B) $10a - 3$ (C) $6a - 2$
    (D) $5a - 6$ (E) $5a - 3$

606

(A) The perimeter is:

$2(3a - 2) + 2(2a - 1) = 6a - 4 + 4a - 2 = 10a - 6$

That's a fairly simple algebraic manipulation, but if you insist on avoiding algebra altogether, you could assume a value for a. For example, if $a = 2$ then the length of the figure is $3(2) - 2 = 4$, and the width of the figure is $2(2) - 1 = 3$. The perimeter would be $4 + 4 + 3 + 3 = 14$. Substituting 2 for a into the correct formula yields the value 14. And only (A) does that.

14. If the average (arithmetic mean) of x, x, x, 56, and 58 is 51, then $x =$

(A) 43   (B) 47   (C) 49   (D) 51   (E) 53

(B) Use the technique for finding the missing elements of an average. The average of the five numbers is 51, so their sum is $5 \times 51 = 255$. The two known values total 114. So the remaining three numbers total $255 - 114 = 141$. And $141 \div 3 = 47$.

15. For how many integers x is $-2 \leqslant 2x \leqslant 2$?

(A) 1   (B) 2   (C) 3   (D) 4   (E) 5

(C) x could be -1, or 0, or $+1$.

16. If x is an odd integer, all of the following are odd EXCEPT

(A) $x + 2$ (B) $3x + 2$ (C) $2x^2 + x$
(D) $2x^3 + x$ (E) $3x^3 + x$

(E) You can reason to the conclusion using the properties of odd and even numbers. Or you can just substitute a number for x. Say that $x = 1$, an odd number:

(A) $x + 2 = 1 + 2 = 3$ Odd.

(B) $3x + 2 = 3(1) + 2 = 5$ Odd.

(C) $2x^2 + x = 2(1)^2 + 1 = 2 + 1 = 3$ Odd.

(D) $2x^3 + x = 2(1)^3 + 1 = 2 + 1 = 3$ Odd.

(E) $3x^3 + x = 3(1)^3 + 1 = 3 + 1 = 4$ Even.

17. What is the sum of the areas of two squares with sides of 2 and 3 respectively?

(A) 1   (B) 5   (C) 13   (D) 25   (E) 36

(C) Just do the indicated operations. One square has an area of $2 \times 2 = 4$, the other an area of $3 \times 3 = 9$, and the sum of their areas is $4 + 9 = 13$.

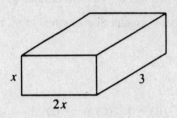

Note: Figure not drawn to scale

18. If the rectangular solid shown above has a volume of 54, then $x =$

(A) 2   (B) 3   (C) 6   (D) 9   (E) 12

(B) You can set up an equation:

$x(2x)(3) = 54$

$2x^2 = 18$

$x^2 = 9$

$x = \sqrt{9} = 3$ (Distances are always positive.)

Or you can "test the test." Try each answer choice as the value of x until you find one that generates a volume of 54.

19. If x is 80 percent of y, then y is what percent of x?

(A) $133\frac{1}{3}\%$ (B) 125%   (C) 120%
(D) 90%   (E) 80%

(B) Since x is 80 percent of y, $x = 0.8y$, and $y = \frac{x}{0.8} = 1.25x$. So y is 125% of x. Or you can just use some numbers. Assume that y is 100. If $y = 100$, the $x = 80\%$ of $y = 80$. Finally, find what percent y is of x: $\frac{100}{80} = \frac{5}{4} = 1.25 = 125\%$.

20. From which of the following statements can it be deduced that $m > n$?

(A) $m + 1 = n$
(B) $2m = n$
(C) $m + n > 0$
(D) $m - n > 0$
(E) $mn > 0$

(D) You can rewrite $m - n > 0$ by adding n to both sides: $m > n$. As for (A), this proves that $m < n$. As for (B), this proves nothing about m and n, since m and n might be either negative or positive. The same is true of (C) which is equivalent to $m > -n$. Finally, as for (E), you have neither relative values for m and n nor their signs.

21. If for any number n, is defined as the least integer that is greater than or equal to n^2, then

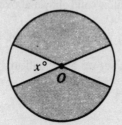 $=$

(A) -2 (B) -1 (C) 0 (D) 1 (E) 2

(E) Here we have a defined function. Just do the indicated operation. $(-1.1)^2 = 1.21$, and the smallest integer greater than that is 2.

22. The circle with center O has a radius of length 2. If the total area of the shaded regions is 3π, then $x =$

(A) 270 (B) 180 (C) 120 (D) 90 (E) 45

(E) First, find the area of the circle: $\pi r^2 = \pi(2)^2 = 4\pi$. Since the shaded area is equal to 3π, it accounts for $\frac{3\pi}{4\pi} = \frac{3}{4}$ of the circle. So the unshaded area accounts for $\frac{1}{4}$ of the circle. This means that angle x plus the angle vertically opposite x are equal to $\frac{1}{4}$ of $360° = 90°$. So $2x = 90$, and $x = 45$. Or, since the figure is drawn to scale, you could have relied on guesstimation.

23. If a bar of metal alloy consists of 100 grams of tin and 150 grams of lead, what percent of the entire bar, by weight, is tin?

(A) 10% (B) 15% (C) $33\frac{1}{3}$% (D) 40%
(E) $66\frac{2}{3}$%

(D) Use the "this-of-that" strategy:

$$\frac{this}{of\ that} = \frac{tin}{entire\ bar} = \frac{100}{(100 + 150)} = \frac{100}{250} = \frac{2}{5} = 40\%$$

24. If $\dfrac{1}{x} + \dfrac{1}{y} = \dfrac{1}{z}$, then $z =$

(A) $\dfrac{1}{xy}$ (B) xy (C) $\dfrac{x+y}{xy}$

(D) $\dfrac{xy}{x+y}$ (E) $\dfrac{2xy}{x+y}$

(D) Rewrite the equation:

$$\frac{1}{x} + \frac{1}{y} = \frac{1}{z}$$

Add the fractions using the "flying x":

$$\frac{y+x}{xy} = \frac{1}{z}$$

Multiply both sides by z:

$$z\left(\frac{y+x}{xy}\right) = 1$$

Multiply both sides by $\dfrac{xy}{y+x}$:

$$z = \frac{xy}{y+x} = \frac{xy}{x+y}$$

Or just assume some values. Assume that $x = 1$ and $y = 1$. On that assumption $z = \frac{1}{2}$. Then substitute 1 for x and 1 for y into the choices. Only (D) generates the value $\frac{1}{2}$.

25. In a certain clothing store, 60 percent of all the articles are imported and 20 percent of all the articles are priced at $100 or more. If 40 percent of the articles priced at $100 or more are imported, what percent of the articles priced *under* $100 are *not* imported?

(A) 28% (B) 12% (C) 8%
(D) 4.8% (E) 2%

(A) Set up a table to show the possibilities:

	Imported	Not Imported	Totals
$100 or more			
Less than $100			
Totals			

Now fill in the numbers that are given:

	Imported	Not Imported	Totals
$100 or more			20%
Less than $100			
Totals	60%		

Since the total must equal 100%:

	Imported	Not Imported	Totals
$100 or more			20%
Less than $100			80%
Totals	60%	40%	100%

Next, 40% of the articles priced at $100 or more are imported, and 40% of 20% = 8%:

	Imported	Not Imported	Totals
$100 or more	8%		20%
Less than $100			80%
Totals	60%	40%	100%

And by adding and subtracting you can complete the table:

	Imported	Not Imported	Totals
$100 or more	8%	12%	20%
Less than $100	52%	28%	80%
Totals	60%	40%	100%

Or you can reach the same conclusion by assuming some numbers.

SECTION 3

CRITICAL READING

1. Burney uses the word *importunities* (line 1) to mean

   (A) cruelties
   (B) refusals
   (C) entreaties
   (D) chances
   (E) openings

   (C) If you have any doubt, Burney uses the word *entreaties* later on in the passage (line 11). It is Mr. Smith's endless pleas that annoy the narrator.

2. By "terms so open and familiar" (lines 16–17), Burney means

   (A) commonly used phrases
   (B) friendly behavior
   (C) brotherly conversation
   (D) truthful and kind words
   (E) intimate and revealing language

   (E) The terms, whatever they are, lead the narrator to express her displeasure "with equal plainness." This would not be true of (A), (B), (C), or (D).

3. The word *demur* (line 27) is used by Burney to mean

   (A) object
   (B) debate
   (C) misgiving
   (D) protest
   (E) reject

   (B) You are probably more used to seeing this word used in its meaning of *protest*, but if you try using the choices in context, only (B) works.

4. How does Burney feel about the character of Mr. Smith?

   (A) He is well-meaning and kind.
   (B) He is a good catch.
   (C) He is shy and diffident.
   (D) He is boorish and absurd.
   (E) He is independent and haughty.

   (D) Mr. Smith does not come off well. Although the author allows us to see him only through the eyes of the narrator and through his own speech, neither of those lead us to believe that he is anything but a clod.

5. The phrase "how should you like to let yourself down all at once into a married man" (lines 40–41) implies that Smith

   (A) finds adultery repugnant
   (B) is insulting toward women
   (C) thinks marriage is a come-down
   (D) both A and B
   (E) both B and C

   (E) You need to look back at this somewhat antiquated phrase in context to decipher its meaning. Mr. Smith is asking the narrator to imagine that she were a popular fellow such as he—someone who appears "smart." How would she like, then, to become the antithesis—a married man? Mr. Smith's assumption, that marriage makes one not smart, is certainly insulting, and his reference to "let yourself down" implies that he thinks it is a degrading state.

6. The word *odious* is used by Austen in line 45 to mean

   (A) attractive
   (B) appealing
   (C) admirable
   (D) burdensome
   (E) loathsome

   (E) Isabella is affecting displeasure at the young men's advances. Therefore, the only suitable descriptors would be those that are negative: (D) or (E). Of those, *burdensome* (D) seems inapplicable; it is really a synonym for *onerous*.

7. By the phrase "unaffected pleasure" (line 55), Austen implies Catherine's

   (A) naïveté
   (B) affectionate nature
   (C) pretentiousness
   (D) self-satisfaction
   (E) recklessness

   (A) Review the phrase in context. Catherine is assuring Isabella that the young men have left, which is not at all what Isabella wants to hear. Since Catherine is doing this with "unaffected pleasure," she clearly does not understand Isabella's true feelings; she is naïve.

8. Catherine is used by Austen in this scene as a

   (A) foil to Isabella's calculations
   (B) mimic of Isabella's speech
   (C) facsimile of Isabella
   (D) watchdog over Isabella
   (E) miniature version of Isabella

   (A) This synthesis/analysis question asks you to determine the author's intent in using the structure she does. Catherine is simple and unaffected;

Isabella bosses her around to a certain degree, and Catherine goes along with her. She is not a mimic (B), facsimile (C), watchdog (D), or miniature version (E) of Isabella; she is Isabella's foil, or antithesis.

9. In contrast to Burney's narrator, Isabella

   (A) treats her admirers scornfully
   (B) feigns lack of interest in her admirers
   (C) does not like men
   (D) both A and B
   (E) both B and C

   (B) Try out all the possibilities before choosing one. Isabella treats her admirers with scorn (A), but Burney's narrator is not much better. There is no evidence that Isabella dislikes men (C); Burney's narrator may or may not. Burney's narrator is certainly not interested in Mr. Smith or in her other potential dance partner. In contrast, Isabella pretends to be uninterested but ends up chasing after the two young men.

10. The passages have in common

    (A) a light tone
    (B) a sense of irony
    (C) moralistic undertones
    (D) both A and B
    (E) both B and C

    (D) Compare the passages to answer this evaluation question. Both are light in tone (A); both have a sense of irony (B). Neither can really be called moralistic (C). Since both (A) and (B) apply, your choice must be (D).

SECTION 4

MATH PROBLEM-SOLVING

1. If p, q, r, s, and t are whole numbers and the expression $2(p(q + r) + s) + t$ is even, which of the numbers *must* be even?

   (A) p (B) q (C) r (D) s (E) t

   (E) The expression $2(p(q + r) + s)$ will be an even number regardless of the values of p, q, r, or s. But whether the whole expression is even depends on t. If t is even, then the whole expression is even; if t is odd, the whole expression is odd.

2. If the area of a square is $9x^2$, what is the length of its side expressed in terms of x?

   (A) $\dfrac{x}{3}$ (B) $3x$ (C) $9x$ (D) $\dfrac{x^2}{3}$ (E) $3x^2$

   (B) Use the formula for finding the area of a square:

Area = side × side
$$s \times s = 9x^2$$
$$s^2 = 9x^2$$
$$s = \sqrt{9x^2} = 3x$$

Or you can assume some values. If $x = 1$, the area of the square is 9, and its side is 3. Substitute 1 for x in the choices. Both (B) and (E) yield the value 3. So pick another number, say 3. If $x = 3$, the area of the square is 81, and its side is 9. Substitute 3 for x in both (B) and (E); only (B) yields the correct value of 9.

3. The sum, the product, and the average (arithmetic mean) of three different integers are equal. If two of the integers are x and $-x$, the third integer is

   (A) $\dfrac{x}{2}$ (B) $2x$ (C) 1 (D) 0

   (E) It cannot be determined from the information given.

   (D) You can arrive at the correct answer in several ways. First, you can reason that if the product of three different integers is 0, one of them is 0. Of x and $-x$, one is positive and the other negative, so they cannot be 0. The missing number must be 0.

   You can also set up equations, but that seems unnecessarily complicated. You would be better off using a third method, just substituting some values for x. You'll find that the missing number must be 0.

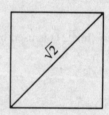

4. The perimeter of the square above is

   (A) 1   (B) $\sqrt{2}$ (C) 4   (D) $4\sqrt{2}$ (E) 8

   (C) The diagonal of a square creates an isosceles right triangle. So the side of the square is equal to $\frac{1}{2} \times \sqrt{2} \times \sqrt{2} = 1$. Since the side has a length of 1, the perimeter of the square is $4(1) = 4$.

5. A triangle has one side of length 4 and another side of length 11. What are the greatest and least possible *integer* values for the length of the remaining side?

   (A) 7 and 4   (B) 11 and 4   (C) 14 and 8
   (D) 15 and 7   (E) 16 and 7

   (C) The difference between 11 and 4 is 7, so 7 marks the limit of the shorter side of a triangle with sides of 11 and 4. But the side must be an integer. So the shortest possible side is 8. Conversely, the sum of 4 and 11 is 15. So 15 marks the limit of the longer side. Since the longer side must have an integral value, its maximum length is 14.

6. If $2x + 3y = 19$, and x and y are positive integers, then x could be equal to which of the following?

(A) 3   (B) 4   (C) 5   (D) 6   (E) 7

(C) You might reason that the only permissible values for x are those which when multiplied by 2 and subtracted from 19 yield a number that is divisible by 3. That's a lot of reasoning. Just "test the test." Try (A). If x is 3, then $2x$ is 6, and $3y = 13$. But then y cannot be an integer, so (A) is wrong. The correct answer is (C). If x is 5, then $3y = 9$, and $y = 3$, an integer.

7. If the cost of N nails is C cents, what is the cost, *in dollars*, of X nails?

(A) $100CX$ (B) $\dfrac{100CX}{N}$ (C) $\dfrac{100NX}{C}$

(D) $\dfrac{NX}{100C}$ (E) $\dfrac{CX}{100N}$

(E) You can create a formula by setting up a direct proportion:

$$\frac{N}{C} = \frac{X}{100z}$$

Where z is the cost of N nails in dollars:

$$100zN = CX$$

$$z = \frac{CX}{100N}$$

Or you can use the technique of assuming some values for the variables.

8. If $a^2b^3c < 0$, then which of the following must be true?

(A) $b^3 < 0$ (B) $b^2c < 0$ (C) $b < 0$
(D) $c < 0$ (E) $bc < 0$

(E) Since the expression is less than zero, either one or three of the factors must be negative. a^2 cannot be negative. So either b^3 is negative, or c is negative, but not both. And this means either b or c is negative but not both. So bc must be negative. You can eliminate (A), (B), (C), and (D) since they might be, but are not necessarily, true.

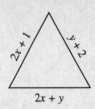

$2x + y$

9. If the figure above is an equilateral triangle, what is its perimeter?

(A) 1   (B) 3   (C) 9   (D) 12
(E) It cannot be determined from the information given.

(C) Since this is an equilateral triangle, the sides are equal. Set up equations:

$$2x + 1 = 2x + y$$

$$y = 1$$

And

$$2x + y = 2y + 1$$

$$2x + (1) = 2(1) + 1$$

$$2x + 1 = 2 + 1$$

$$2x = 2$$

$$x = 1$$

Now pick any side: $2x + y = 2(1) + 1 = 3$. So the perimeter of the triangle is $3(3) = 9$.

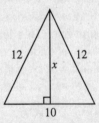

10. In the figure above, what is x?

(A) 5   (B) 7.5   (C) 13   (D) $\sqrt{119}$
(E) Cannot be determined from the information given

(D) Don't be fooled by the answer "13"; this is not a 5–12–13 right triangle. In that case, the side of length 12 would be the second longest leg, not the hypotenuse. You know that in a right triangle $a^2 + b^2 = c^2$, where c is the length of the hypotenuse. Plugging in the numbers you have, you see that $5^2 + b^2 = 12^2$, or $25 + b^2 = 144$. Since $144 - 25 = 119$, b must be the square root of 119.

SECTION 5

SENTENCE COMPLETION

1. The history book, written in 1880, was tremendously
   ----, unfairly blaming the South for the Civil War.

   (A) biased   (B) objective   (C) suppressed
   (D) questionable   (E) complicated

   (A) The sentence gives you a very strong clue with
   the word *unfairly*. You can eliminate (B) since
   something that is unfair could not be objective.
   You can also eliminate (C) and (D) because they
   do not create meaningful sentences. (A), *biased*, is
   the best word to convey the idea that the book
   blamed unfairly.

2. In the Middle Ages, scientists and clergymen thought
   the universe was well-ordered and ----; today scientists are more likely to see the world as ----.

   (A) baffling..dogmatic
   (B) harmonious..chaotic
   (C) transient..predictable
   (D) emancipated..intriguing
   (E) divergent..galling

   (B) This sentence contains both a thought-extender and a thought-reverser. The first blank extends
   the thought that the universe was *well-ordered*.
   You can eliminate (A) since it is not logical that
   something would be *well-ordered* and *baffling*.
   (C), (D), and (E) are not words you would use to
   describe the universe. This leaves you with (B).
   There is a *but* or *yet* understood in this sentence,
   so the next blank will be something opposite to
   harmonious. The second element of (B) works
   because *chaotic* is the opposite of *harmonious*.

3. Hot milk has long been a standard cure for insomnia
   because of its ---- quality.

   (A) malevolent   (B) amorphous   (C) soporific
   (D) plaintive   (E) desultory

   (C) This is a vocabulary question. You must
   know that something that cures *insomnia* is a
   soporific—something that induces sleep.

4. Since the results of the experiment were ---- the
   body of research already completed, the committee
   considered the results to be ----.

   (A) similar to..speculative
   (B) inconsistent with..anomalous
   (C) compounded by..heretical
   (D) dispelled by..convincing
   (E) contradicted by..redundant

   (B) Given that there is a *body of research* already
   existing, the results can only be irrelevant to it,

consistent with it, or inconsistent with it. This
eliminates choice (C). Then you have to substitute
both words of the remaining choices in order to
determine the correct answer. (A) cannot be correct, since results would not be *speculative* if they
were similar to the research already done. (D) is
not possible because the body of research would
not be *dispelled* by *convincing* results. (E) makes
no sense because if the results were *redundant*,
then they would not *contradict* the existing research. This leaves you with (B), which works very
well. Results might be considered *anomalous* if they
were *inconsistent with* the research already done.

5. Psychologists believe that modern life ---- neurosis
   because of the ---- of traditional values which define
   acceptable behavior.

   (A) copes with..inundation
   (B) strives for..condoning
   (C) concentrates on..plethora
   (D) fosters..disappearance
   (E) corroborates..dispelling

   (D) The logical clue here is a thought-extender.
   But the order in which the ideas are presented in
   the sentence makes this difficult to see. The idea
   which follows the *because* specifies the cause of
   the first idea: *The ---- of traditional values* causes
   modern life to ---- *neurosis*. Substitute each of
   the choices into this new sentence. Only (D) produces a sentence that fits the logical structure.

6. The millionaire was such a ---- that any appearance
   he made in public was ----.

   (A) philistine..negligible
   (B) recluse..noteworthy
   (C) gourmand..distorted
   (D) lecher..unexpected
   (E) traitor..protracted

   (B) This sentence does not have a logical structure
   that will help you select the correct answer. The
   first blank merely asks that you supply an adjective. All of the first elements are possible things to
   say about a millionaire. The second part of the
   sentence, however, tells you that something about
   his public appearances is an issue. The only word
   among the first possibilities that has anything to do
   with going out is *recluse*. So start with that choice
   and see if it works. If he is a *recluse*, then his public
   appearances will indeed be *noteworthy* and you
   have your answer. If you check the other possibilities, you will see that once their second words are
   substituted, the sentence does not say anything
   meaningful.

7. Because of the ---- of acupuncture therapy in China, Western physicians are starting to learn the procedure.

(A) veracity　　(B) manipulation　(C) liquidity
(D) effectiveness　(E) inflation

(D) This is basically a vocabulary question. You do, however, have one clue to the meaning of the sentence. The sentence tells you that Western physicians are learning a procedure. Logically, they are doing this because it is desirable, so you should look for the noun that has a positive connotation. This eliminates (B) and (E). If you substitute (A) or (C), you have a meaningless sentence. So the answer must be (D).

8. Being a celebrity has its ----, one of which is the almost complete lack of ----.

(A) delusions..repression
(B) presumptions..income
(C) drawbacks..privacy
(D) frustrations..notoriety
(E) confrontations..intimacy

(C) This sentence really depends on the second blank. You can eliminate (A), (B), and (E). The phrases "Being a celebrity has its *presumptions*" (or *confrontations* or *delusions*) is extremely unlikely. The second blank tells you to look for a lack of something that would create the situation described in the first blank. (B) won't work because a celebrity does not lack *notoriety* (fame is part of the definition of celebrity). So the correct choice is (C).

9. The program concluded with a modern symphony that contained chords so ---- that the piece produced sounds similar to the ---- one hears as the individual orchestra members tune their instruments before a concert.

(A) superfluous..melody
(B) pretentious..roar
(C) melodious..applause
(D) versatile..harmony
(E) discordant..cacophony

(E) The second blank is an extension of the first idea. You can eliminate (A) because the idea of hearing a melody does not explain why a chord is *superfluous*. You can eliminate (B) because the idea of hearing a roar doesn't explain why a chord might be *pretentious*. You can eliminate (C) because the idea of hearing *applause* doesn't explain why a chord might be *melodious*. And you can eliminate (D) because hearing *harmony* doesn't explain why a chord might be *versatile*. (E) preserves the sense and logic of the sentence. Hearing *cacophony* explains that the chord is *discordant*.

10. The king was a haughty aristocrat, but he was not a ----; he ruled his country ---- with genuine affection for his people.

(A) sycophant..benevolently
(B) diplomat..complacently
(C) monarch..stringently
(D) despot..magnanimously
(E) tyrant..superciliously

(D) You have a thought-reverser and a thought-extender in this sentence. The key to the first half of the sentence is "but." The king was *not* something that is like a haughty aristocrat. You can eliminate (A) and (C). Sycophant doesn't provide a logical contrast. And putting "monarch" into the first blank results in a contradiction (because a king is a monarch). The second blank must be filled by a word that can later be extended by the phrase "genuine affection." Of the remaining choices, only (D) has a second element with positive overtones needed to complete that extension.

11. There is a ---- of verbiage in your writing; try not to be so ----.

(A) dearth..pompous
(B) preponderance..verbose
(C) predilection..long-winded
(D) element..prolix
(E) fraction..detrimental

(B) The second choice must extend the first. You would never say *predilection of* or *fraction of*, so (C) and (E) are eliminated. If there were a *dearth* (shortage) of verbiage, the writer would not seem *pompous* (A). A mere *element* (D) would not make the writer *prolix* (wordy). However, a *preponderance* (great amount) would seem *verbose* (wordy).

12. My dog is a rare breed found ---- in the Arctic.

(A) ultimately
(B) comprehensively
(C) exclusively
(D) vitally
(E) extensively

(C) This is a straight vocabulary question. The clues are *rare* and *in the Arctic*. Of the choices, only *exclusively* echoes the quality of rarity. You would never say that a breed was found *vitally* (D), and if it were found *extensively* (E), it would not be rare.

13. Great minds think alike: This old ---- is a favorite of mine.

   (A) draft
   (B) opus
   (C) term
   (D) maxim
   (E) logo

   (D) This is another straight vocabulary question. A *draft* (A) is a plan or first attempt; an *opus* (B) is a composition. A phrase cannot be a *term* (C), which implies a single word; and a *logo* (E) is an emblem. A phrase of this sort is a *maxim*, or saying.

14. Most sitcoms are ----, but this new one is actually ----.

   (A) banal..engaging
   (B) vapid..ordinary
   (C) profound..solemn
   (D) unsightly..atrocious
   (E) passionate..repugnant

   (A) This may be tricky, because it is not immediately clear whether the second phrase extends or contradicts the first. Try the first word of each choice in the first blank, and you can quickly omit *unsightly* (D) and *passionate* (E). It is quite unlikely that sitcoms would be described as *profound*, so that gets rid of (C). A sitcom may be *vapid* (senseless), but that is neither extended nor contradicted by *ordinary* (B). (A) works: Most sitcoms are *banal* (trite), but this one is *engaging* (enjoyable).

15. Paul is ---- and ----; he volunteers for everything.

   (A) saintly..appreciative
   (B) flighty..moody
   (C) unappreciated..misunderstood
   (D) generous..altruistic
   (E) underpaid..insignificant

   (D) The second word extends the first, and the clue is *volunteers*. Paul may be *saintly* (A), but it does not follow that he is *appreciative*. (B), (C), and (E) are illogical, given the rest of the sentence. However, a volunteer may be described as both *generous* (giving) and *altruistic* (charitable).

ANALOGIES

16. BALLAD : SONG::

   (A) spire : church
   (B) ode : poem
   (C) novel : chapter
   (D) envelope : letter
   (E) leopard : jaguar

   (B) This is a "type of" analogy. A BALLAD is a type of SONG and an *ode* is a type of *poem*.

17. TEACHER : CLASSROOM::

   (A) student : library
   (B) minister : church
   (C) horse : carriage
   (D) desert : heat
   (E) curb : highway

   (B) This is a "place where" analogy. A TEACHER works in a CLASSROOM and a *minister* in a *church*.

18. UNIFORM : SOLDIER::

   (A) silks : jockey
   (B) leash : dog
   (C) pasture : cow
   (D) farmer : tractor
   (E) costume : scenery

   (A) This analogy does not fit a category, but the relationship is quite clear. A SOLDIER wears a UNIFORM, and a *jockey* wears *silks*.

19. MURAL : WALL::

   (A) pen : letter
   (B) tree : forest
   (C) painting : canvas
   (D) tobacco : smoke
   (E) museum : curator

   (C) Here there is a clear relationship. A MURAL is painted on a WALL and a *painting* is painted on a *canvas*.

20. BEGIN : PROCRASTINATION::

   (A) terminate : prolongation
   (B) show : demonstration
   (C) frighten : terror
   (D) guarantee : refund
   (E) capture : torture

   (A) This is a variation on the "lack of" relationship. PROCRASTINATION is a lack of BEGINNING, and *prolongation* is a lack of *termination*. Note that in this analogy it is helpful to change the parts of speech.

21. LUBRICANT : FRICTION::

   (A) machine : operator
   (B) spasm : muscle
   (C) dessert : sugar
   (D) balm : pain
   (E) drawer : chest

   (D) The relationship here is quite easy to formulate. Your diagnostic sentence might read "a LUBRICANT eliminates FRICTION," and "a *balm* eliminates *pain*."

22. REGRETTABLE : LAMENT::

   (A) praiseworthy : applaud
   (B) verbose : rejoice
   (C) incongruous : detect
   (D) reliable : defend
   (E) obnoxious : boast

(A) This is a "defining characteristic" analogy. By definition that which is LAMENTED is REGRETTABLE and that which is *applauded* is *praiseworthy*.

23. FASTIDIOUS : CLEANLINESS::

    (A) pliant : fabrication
    (B) meticulous : detail
    (C) timorous : hostility
    (D) bereft : animosity
    (E) enervated : activity

    (B) This is an analogy of degree. To be FASTIDIOUS is to be extremely preoccupied with CLEANLINESS, and to be *meticulous* is to be extremely preoccupied with *detail*.

24. DISAPPROBATION : CONDEMN::

    (A) solvency : deploy
    (B) calumny : laud
    (C) enigma : enlighten
    (D) fallacy : disseminate
    (E) exhortation : urge

    (E) This is a "defining characteristic" analogy. CONDEMNING presupposes DISAPPROBATION, and *urging* presupposes *exhortation*.

25. AMBIVALENCE : COMMITMENT::

    (A) perfidy : profitability
    (B) gullibility : discernment
    (C) travesty : justice
    (D) enthusiasm : predicament
    (E) conundrum : epigram

    (B) This is a "lack of" analogy. AMBIVALENCE is a lack of COMMITMENT and *gullibility* is a lack of *discernment*.

CRITICAL READING

26. The word *diffusion* (line 5) means

    (A) wandering
    (B) redundancy
    (C) concentration
    (D) rambling
    (E) circulation

    (E) Any of the choices may be a synonym for *diffusion*, but only (E) corresponds to the idea of the passing around of knowledge suggested by the context.

27. Locke uses the word *peculiar* (line 15) to mean

    (A) outlandish
    (B) quaint
    (C) characteristic
    (D) unique
    (E) odd

    (D) Again, any of the choices is a possible synonym, but by rereading the sentence in question, you can see that only (D) fits the context: The Negro colleges have a unique chance to enter the academic arena.

28. The *Journal of Negro History* is introduced as an example of

    (A) an analysis of African pioneers
    (B) scholarship on Africa by African-Americans
    (C) work that African-Americans should support
    (D) both A and B
    (E) both B and C

    (E) This kind of synthesis/analysis question asks you to understand the author's reasoning in including a particular example or citation. By returning to the passage and looking for the reference, you can discover Locke's meaning: The journal is doing pioneer scholarship (*not* scholarship on pioneers) and deserves "financial support." Since both (B) and (C) apply, the answer is (E).

29. Locke's "*reconnaisance* trip" apparently included

    (A) trips to Howard University
    (B) tours of archaeological digs
    (C) talks with Dr. Woodson
    (D) a journey to Cairo
    (E) none of the above

    (D) Locke says that "later" he will write about research as he has seen it on his trip (line 25); he then later goes on to discuss work in Cairo. It is more than likely that the trip he mentioned took him to Cairo; that is the only choice that is supported by the text.

30. Why does Locke include the citation from Arthur Weigall?

    (A) to show the racism inherent in white researchers
    (B) to establish a target for his audience
    (C) to support his goal of African–American participation
    (D) both A and B
    (E) both B and C

    (C) Again, this is a synthesis/analysis question, asking you to determine the reasoning behind the inclusion of a citation. Reread the citation, which deals with the study of African traditions by "their own students." It is clear that Locke wants support for his opinion that African–Americans should study Africa.

31. The phrase "substantially concurred" (line 39) means

    (A) agreed for the most part
    (B) significantly differed
    (C) grossly overrated
    (D) largely preferred
    (E) mostly defeated

(A) This interpretation question is fairly easily answered, but if you do not know the words, you can return to the cited line and read the entire sentence. "All save two" substantially concurred with Locke's opinion, and those two saw no advantage to participation, so clearly they disagreed. If two disagreed, all but two agreed.

32. How does Locke feel toward scientifically neutral studies?

   (A) approving
   (B) derogatory
   (C) tolerant
   (D) frustrated
   (E) infuriated

(C) This is an evaluation question. Locke has his own opinion about the usefulness of African–Americans studying Africa, but he is not particularly critical of the two scientists who disagree; he says that "naturally enough" they consider physical anthropology scientifically neutral. He does not indicate approval (A); but he shows that he tolerates their opinion.

33. The Museum for Coptic Antiquities is discussed in order to

   (A) show that African studies are overrun by white scholars
   (B) demonstrate the need for more funding of archaeology
   (C) provide an example of important African cultural studies
   (D) both A and B
   (E) both B and C

(C) This synthesis/analysis question can be botched if you go beyond what is stated or implied in the text. Nowhere does Locke say anything about white scholars (A); he states that the museum has limited funds, but he does not suggest that they need more (B). Only (C) reflects the actual passage itself.

34. By "the great intangible capital" (lines 56–57), Locke means

   (A) loyalty and cooperation cannot be bought
   (B) loyalty and cooperation are abstract but invaluable
   (C) nothing is worthwhile but loyalty and cooperation
   (D) transient loyalty and cooperation are worthless
   (E) the museum is a headquarters for loyal workers

(B) This is an interpretation question. Look back at the line cited. Locke refers to limited funds but intangible capital of loyalty and cooperation; he is contrasting one with the other. Such capital may be intangible (abstract), but it is certainly helpful in the case of the museum.

35. Locke's main goal in this passage is to

   (A) encourage students to expand their horizons
   (B) urge African–Americans to study Africa
   (C) show the difference between African and American art
   (D) demonstrate a way of saving African culture
   (E) convince archaeologists to research African history

(B) An evaluation question of this sort requires you to summarize the passage and determine the author's purpose. (A) is too vague; (E) is too specific (Locke is addressing others besides archaeologists). (C) is irrelevant, and (D) is not supported by the text.

SECTION 6

QUANTITATIVE COMPARISON

Column A	Column B

$$\frac{x}{2} = 18$$

$$\frac{y}{3} = 18$$

1.

x	y

(B) Solve the centered equations:

$$\frac{x}{2} = 18$$

$$x = 36$$

$$\frac{y}{3} = 18$$

$$y = 54$$

So Column B is larger.

2.

10% of 50	50% of 10

(C) Do the indicated operations. 10% of 50 is $0.10 \times 50 = 5$, and 50% of 10 is $0.5 \times 10 = 5$. So the columns are equal.

3.

The sum of the 5 greatest odd integers less than 20	The sum of the 5 least even integers greater than 10

(B) Set up the indicated calculations:

Column A: $19 + 17 + 15 + 13 + 11 =$

Column B: $12 + 14 + 16 + 18 + 20 =$

There is no need to do the addition. Since $20 > 19$, $18 > 17$, and so on, the total in Column B is larger.

Column A	Column B

4.
| The fraction of a day represented by 8 hours | The fraction of an hour represented by 40 minutes |

(B) Again, set up the calculations. Column A is $\frac{8}{24}$, which is $\frac{1}{3}$, and Column B is $\frac{40}{60}$, which is $\frac{2}{3}$. So Column B is larger.

$$x \cdot 1 = x$$

5.
| x | 1 |

(D) The centered equation is equivalent to $x = x$. But x can be any number at all. Substituting numbers for x will quickly prove that the correct answer is (D).

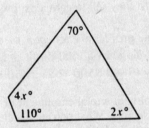

70°

4x°

110°   2x°

Note: Figure not drawn to scale.

6.
| x | 30 |

(C) Since the sum of the measures of the interior angles of a four-sided figure is 360°:

$$2x + 4x + 70 + 110 = 360$$

$$6x + 180 = 360$$

$$6x = 180$$

$$x = 30$$

So the two columns are equal.

7.
| $\sqrt{6} \times \sqrt{10}$ | $\sqrt{3} \times \sqrt{20}$ |

(C) Do the indicated operations. Column A is $\sqrt{6} \times \sqrt{10} = \sqrt{60}$. And Column B is $\sqrt{3} \times \sqrt{20} = \sqrt{60}$. The good enough principle says this is as far as you need to go. The two columns are equal.

Column A	Column B

$$x < 0$$

8.
| x^{15} | x^{16} |

(B) x is negative. And a negative number raised to an odd power is negative while a negative number raised to an even power is positive.

$$x < 50$$

9.
| $50 + x$ | 100 |

(B) You can easily prove that the correct choice is (B) by simplifying across the comparison. Subtract 50 from both sides. Column A becomes x and Column B becomes 50. The centered information establishes that x is less than 50; so Column B is greater.

The average of x, y, and z is y.

10.
| x | z |

(D) The centered statement establishes that $x + y + z = 3y$, so $x + z = 2y$. But that is one equation with three variables. So there is no way to relate x and z. Substituting a couple of numbers will also prove that the correct choice is (D).

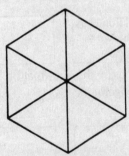

The figure above consists of 6 equilateral triangles, each with a perimeter of 6.

11.
| 36 | The sum of the lengths of all the line segments in the figure |

(A) The answer to the question is not $6 \times 6 = 36$. The length of each side of the small triangles is $6 \div 3 = 2$. So the outer perimeter of the larger figure is $6 \times 2 = 12$. Then each of the three diagonals

Column A	Column B

has a length of 2 + 2 = 4. So the sum of their lengths is 3 × 4 = 12. The total of the lengths of all the lines in the figure (the outer perimeter plus three diagonals) is 12 + 12 = 24. So Column A is larger.

$$50M$$
$$\times \quad 7$$
$$\overline{3,56N}$$
M and N represent digits

12.

M	N

(A) You can solve this by setting up equations:

$7(500 + 0 + M) = 3,000 + 500 + 60 + N$

$3500 + 7M = 3560 + N$

$7M = 60 + N$

Since there is only one digit which, when multiplied by 7, will yield a number over 60, M must be 9 and N must be 3.

You can reach the same conclusion just by reasoning that since the tens' digit of 50M is 0, the 6 in the product had to have come from the multiplication of M and 7. And the only number that M could be is 9.

Smithtown is 20 kilometers from Jamestown.
Jamestown is 50 kilometers from Charlestown.

13.

Distance in kilometers from Smithtown to Charlestown	70

(D) Nothing in the information establishes any spatial arrangement.

14.

$\dfrac{1}{9}$	0.11

(A) $\frac{1}{9}$ is equal to the repeating decimal $0.\overline{11}$. Since 0.111 is larger than 0.110, Column A is larger.

$x < 0$
$y > 0$

15.

$x^2 + y^2$	$(x + y)^2$

(A) First, do the operations indicated for Column B:

618

$(x + y)^2 = (x + y)(x + y) \quad = x^2 + 2xy + y^2$

Next, simplify across the comparison by subtracting both x^2 and y^2 from both sides. Column A becomes 0, and Column B becomes $2xy$. Since x is negative and y is positive (given in the centered information), xy must be negative. So the expression in Column B is less than 0.

STUDENT-PRODUCED RESPONSES

16. If $3x + 2 = 8$, then $6x = ?$

(12) Just solve for x:
$3x + 2 = 8$
$3x = 6$
$x = 2$
So $6(2) = 12$.

17. Members of a civic organization purchase boxes of candy for $1 apiece and sell them for $2 apiece. If no other expenses are incurred, how many boxes of candy must they sell to earn a net profit of $500?

(500) The profit on each box of candy is $2 − $1 = $1. To earn a total profit of $500, it will be necessary to sell $500 ÷ $1 = 500 boxes.

18. In a school with a total enrollment of 360, 90 students are seniors. What percent of all students enrolled in the school are seniors?

(25) This is a simple percent question. Use the "this-of-that" strategy. The "of that" is "of all students enrolled." The other number, the "this," is seniors:

$$\frac{seniors}{total} = \frac{90}{360} = \frac{1}{4} = 25\%$$

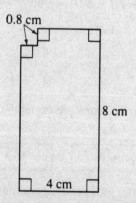

19. The figure above is a scale drawing of the floor of a dining hall. If 1 centimeter on the drawing represents 5 meters, what is the area, in square meters, of the floor?

(784) If the floor were a perfect rectangle, it would have a width of 4 × 5 = 20 meters, a length of 8 × 5 = 40 meters, and total area of 20 × 40 = 800 square meters. But the floor is not a perfect rectangle. Its actual area is smaller. Subtract the area of the missing "corner." It has actual dimensions of 0.8 × 5 = 4. So its actual area is 16. 800 − 16 = 784.

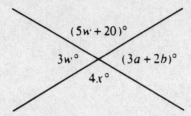

20. If two straight lines intersect as shown, what is the value of *x*?

(30) The angles labeled 3*w* and (5*w* + 20) form a straight line:

$3w + (5w + 20) = 180$

$8w + 20 = 180$

$8w = 160$

$w = 20$

And the angles labeled 3*w* and 4*x* also form a straight line:

$3w + 4x = 180$

$3(20) + 4x = 180$

$60 + 4x = 180$

$4x = 120$

$x = 30$

You can also guesstimate the value of *x*. The angle labeled 4*x* appears to be 120°, so *x* must be about 30°.

21. A school club spent $\frac{2}{5}$ of its budget for one project and $\frac{1}{3}$ of what remained for another project. If the club's entire budget was equal to $300, how much of the budget, in dollars, was left after the two projects?

(120) If the club spent $\frac{2}{5}$ of the budget on the first project, it was left with $\frac{3}{5}$ of $300 = $180. If it spent $\frac{1}{3}$ of $180, it was left with $180 − $60 = $120.

22. If the average of six numbers—10, 12, 15.1, 15.2, 28, and *x*—is 16, what is *x*?

(15.7) It is easy enough to figure that for six numbers to average 16, they must add up to 6 x 16, or 96. The numbers given add up to

$10 + 12 + 15.1 + 15.2 + 28 = 80.3$

$96 − 80.3 = 15.7$, which must be the missing *x*.

23. At the zoo, 25% of the animals are birds, 30% are reptiles or amphibians, and the rest are mammals. If there are 12 geese, representing 20% of the birds, how many mammals are there at the zoo?

(108) This problem has multiple steps, but the arithmetic is simple. The only amount you have to work with is 12 geese, so start there.

12 geese = 20% of birds

$12 = \frac{20}{100} x$

$12 = \frac{1}{5} x$

$x = 12 × 5 = 60$

Now you know that there are 60 birds in all. If 25% of the animals are birds,

60 birds = 25% of animals

$60 = \frac{25}{100} y$

$60 = \frac{1}{4} y$

$y = 60 × 4 = 240$

This is still not the answer — remember, you want a number representing mammals. You must find what part of this 240-animal total is mammals.

% of mammals = 100% − (25% + 30%) = 45%

45% (240) = 108 mammals

24. Jerry grew 5 inches in 1993, and 2 inches more in 1994 before reaching his final height of 5 feet 10 inches. What percentage of his final height did his 1993–1994 growth represent?

(10) First convert Jerry's final height to inches:
    5 × 12 = 60   60 + 10 = 70
Jerry's 7-inch growth is 10% of 70 inches.

25. A circle with radius 2 is superimposed upon a square with sides measuring 5 so that the center of the circle and the center of the square are identical. At how many points will the square and circle intersect?

(0) If you can't picture it in your head, draw it on paper. A circle with radius 2 has a diameter of 4, so when it is imposed on a square with sides of 5, it never intersects that square, assuming the centers are the same.

Practice Test 4

ANSWER SHEET
PRACTICE TEST 4

If a section has fewer questions than answer ovals, leave the extra ovals blank.

SECTION 1

1 Ⓐ Ⓑ Ⓒ Ⓓ Ⓔ	11 Ⓐ Ⓑ Ⓒ Ⓓ Ⓔ	21 Ⓐ Ⓑ Ⓒ Ⓓ Ⓔ	31 Ⓐ Ⓑ Ⓒ Ⓓ Ⓔ
2 Ⓐ Ⓑ Ⓒ Ⓓ Ⓔ	12 Ⓐ Ⓑ Ⓒ Ⓓ Ⓔ	22 Ⓐ Ⓑ Ⓒ Ⓓ Ⓔ	32 Ⓐ Ⓑ Ⓒ Ⓓ Ⓔ
3 Ⓐ Ⓑ Ⓒ Ⓓ Ⓔ	13 Ⓐ Ⓑ Ⓒ Ⓓ Ⓔ	23 Ⓐ Ⓑ Ⓒ Ⓓ Ⓔ	33 Ⓐ Ⓑ Ⓒ Ⓓ Ⓔ
4 Ⓐ Ⓑ Ⓒ Ⓓ Ⓔ	14 Ⓐ Ⓑ Ⓒ Ⓓ Ⓔ	24 Ⓐ Ⓑ Ⓒ Ⓓ Ⓔ	34 Ⓐ Ⓑ Ⓒ Ⓓ Ⓔ
5 Ⓐ Ⓑ Ⓒ Ⓓ Ⓔ	15 Ⓐ Ⓑ Ⓒ Ⓓ Ⓔ	25 Ⓐ Ⓑ Ⓒ Ⓓ Ⓔ	35 Ⓐ Ⓑ Ⓒ Ⓓ Ⓔ
6 Ⓐ Ⓑ Ⓒ Ⓓ Ⓔ	16 Ⓐ Ⓑ Ⓒ Ⓓ Ⓔ	26 Ⓐ Ⓑ Ⓒ Ⓓ Ⓔ	36 Ⓐ Ⓑ Ⓒ Ⓓ Ⓔ
7 Ⓐ Ⓑ Ⓒ Ⓓ Ⓔ	17 Ⓐ Ⓑ Ⓒ Ⓓ Ⓔ	27 Ⓐ Ⓑ Ⓒ Ⓓ Ⓔ	37 Ⓐ Ⓑ Ⓒ Ⓓ Ⓔ
8 Ⓐ Ⓑ Ⓒ Ⓓ Ⓔ	18 Ⓐ Ⓑ Ⓒ Ⓓ Ⓔ	28 Ⓐ Ⓑ Ⓒ Ⓓ Ⓔ	38 Ⓐ Ⓑ Ⓒ Ⓓ Ⓔ
9 Ⓐ Ⓑ Ⓒ Ⓓ Ⓔ	19 Ⓐ Ⓑ Ⓒ Ⓓ Ⓔ	29 Ⓐ Ⓑ Ⓒ Ⓓ Ⓔ	39 Ⓐ Ⓑ Ⓒ Ⓓ Ⓔ
10 Ⓐ Ⓑ Ⓒ Ⓓ Ⓔ	20 Ⓐ Ⓑ Ⓒ Ⓓ Ⓔ	30 Ⓐ Ⓑ Ⓒ Ⓓ Ⓔ	40 Ⓐ Ⓑ Ⓒ Ⓓ Ⓔ

SECTION 2

1 Ⓐ Ⓑ Ⓒ Ⓓ Ⓔ	11 Ⓐ Ⓑ Ⓒ Ⓓ Ⓔ	21 Ⓐ Ⓑ Ⓒ Ⓓ Ⓔ	31 Ⓐ Ⓑ Ⓒ Ⓓ Ⓔ
2 Ⓐ Ⓑ Ⓒ Ⓓ Ⓔ	12 Ⓐ Ⓑ Ⓒ Ⓓ Ⓔ	22 Ⓐ Ⓑ Ⓒ Ⓓ Ⓔ	32 Ⓐ Ⓑ Ⓒ Ⓓ Ⓔ
3 Ⓐ Ⓑ Ⓒ Ⓓ Ⓔ	13 Ⓐ Ⓑ Ⓒ Ⓓ Ⓔ	23 Ⓐ Ⓑ Ⓒ Ⓓ Ⓔ	33 Ⓐ Ⓑ Ⓒ Ⓓ Ⓔ
4 Ⓐ Ⓑ Ⓒ Ⓓ Ⓔ	14 Ⓐ Ⓑ Ⓒ Ⓓ Ⓔ	24 Ⓐ Ⓑ Ⓒ Ⓓ Ⓔ	34 Ⓐ Ⓑ Ⓒ Ⓓ Ⓔ
5 Ⓐ Ⓑ Ⓒ Ⓓ Ⓔ	15 Ⓐ Ⓑ Ⓒ Ⓓ Ⓔ	25 Ⓐ Ⓑ Ⓒ Ⓓ Ⓔ	35 Ⓐ Ⓑ Ⓒ Ⓓ Ⓔ
6 Ⓐ Ⓑ Ⓒ Ⓓ Ⓔ	16 Ⓐ Ⓑ Ⓒ Ⓓ Ⓔ	26 Ⓐ Ⓑ Ⓒ Ⓓ Ⓔ	36 Ⓐ Ⓑ Ⓒ Ⓓ Ⓔ
7 Ⓐ Ⓑ Ⓒ Ⓓ Ⓔ	17 Ⓐ Ⓑ Ⓒ Ⓓ Ⓔ	27 Ⓐ Ⓑ Ⓒ Ⓓ Ⓔ	37 Ⓐ Ⓑ Ⓒ Ⓓ Ⓔ
8 Ⓐ Ⓑ Ⓒ Ⓓ Ⓔ	18 Ⓐ Ⓑ Ⓒ Ⓓ Ⓔ	28 Ⓐ Ⓑ Ⓒ Ⓓ Ⓔ	38 Ⓐ Ⓑ Ⓒ Ⓓ Ⓔ
9 Ⓐ Ⓑ Ⓒ Ⓓ Ⓔ	19 Ⓐ Ⓑ Ⓒ Ⓓ Ⓔ	29 Ⓐ Ⓑ Ⓒ Ⓓ Ⓔ	39 Ⓐ Ⓑ Ⓒ Ⓓ Ⓔ
10 Ⓐ Ⓑ Ⓒ Ⓓ Ⓔ	20 Ⓐ Ⓑ Ⓒ Ⓓ Ⓔ	30 Ⓐ Ⓑ Ⓒ Ⓓ Ⓔ	40 Ⓐ Ⓑ Ⓒ Ⓓ Ⓔ

SECTION 3

1 Ⓐ Ⓑ Ⓒ Ⓓ Ⓔ	6 Ⓐ Ⓑ Ⓒ Ⓓ Ⓔ	11 Ⓐ Ⓑ Ⓒ Ⓓ Ⓔ	16 Ⓐ Ⓑ Ⓒ Ⓓ Ⓔ
2 Ⓐ Ⓑ Ⓒ Ⓓ Ⓔ	7 Ⓐ Ⓑ Ⓒ Ⓓ Ⓔ	12 Ⓐ Ⓑ Ⓒ Ⓓ Ⓔ	17 Ⓐ Ⓑ Ⓒ Ⓓ Ⓔ
3 Ⓐ Ⓑ Ⓒ Ⓓ Ⓔ	8 Ⓐ Ⓑ Ⓒ Ⓓ Ⓔ	13 Ⓐ Ⓑ Ⓒ Ⓓ Ⓔ	18 Ⓐ Ⓑ Ⓒ Ⓓ Ⓔ
4 Ⓐ Ⓑ Ⓒ Ⓓ Ⓔ	9 Ⓐ Ⓑ Ⓒ Ⓓ Ⓔ	14 Ⓐ Ⓑ Ⓒ Ⓓ Ⓔ	19 Ⓐ Ⓑ Ⓒ Ⓓ Ⓔ
5 Ⓐ Ⓑ Ⓒ Ⓓ Ⓔ	10 Ⓐ Ⓑ Ⓒ Ⓓ Ⓔ	15 Ⓐ Ⓑ Ⓒ Ⓓ Ⓔ	20 Ⓐ Ⓑ Ⓒ Ⓓ Ⓔ

SECTION 4

1 Ⓐ Ⓑ Ⓒ Ⓓ Ⓔ	6 Ⓐ Ⓑ Ⓒ Ⓓ Ⓔ	11 Ⓐ Ⓑ Ⓒ Ⓓ Ⓔ	16 Ⓐ Ⓑ Ⓒ Ⓓ Ⓔ
2 Ⓐ Ⓑ Ⓒ Ⓓ Ⓔ	7 Ⓐ Ⓑ Ⓒ Ⓓ Ⓔ	12 Ⓐ Ⓑ Ⓒ Ⓓ Ⓔ	17 Ⓐ Ⓑ Ⓒ Ⓓ Ⓔ
3 Ⓐ Ⓑ Ⓒ Ⓓ Ⓔ	8 Ⓐ Ⓑ Ⓒ Ⓓ Ⓔ	13 Ⓐ Ⓑ Ⓒ Ⓓ Ⓔ	18 Ⓐ Ⓑ Ⓒ Ⓓ Ⓔ
4 Ⓐ Ⓑ Ⓒ Ⓓ Ⓔ	9 Ⓐ Ⓑ Ⓒ Ⓓ Ⓔ	14 Ⓐ Ⓑ Ⓒ Ⓓ Ⓔ	19 Ⓐ Ⓑ Ⓒ Ⓓ Ⓔ
5 Ⓐ Ⓑ Ⓒ Ⓓ Ⓔ	10 Ⓐ Ⓑ Ⓒ Ⓓ Ⓔ	15 Ⓐ Ⓑ Ⓒ Ⓓ Ⓔ	20 Ⓐ Ⓑ Ⓒ Ⓓ Ⓔ

SECTION 5

1 Ⓐ Ⓑ Ⓒ Ⓓ Ⓔ	11 Ⓐ Ⓑ Ⓒ Ⓓ Ⓔ	21 Ⓐ Ⓑ Ⓒ Ⓓ Ⓔ	31 Ⓐ Ⓑ Ⓒ Ⓓ Ⓔ
2 Ⓐ Ⓑ Ⓒ Ⓓ Ⓔ	12 Ⓐ Ⓑ Ⓒ Ⓓ Ⓔ	22 Ⓐ Ⓑ Ⓒ Ⓓ Ⓔ	32 Ⓐ Ⓑ Ⓒ Ⓓ Ⓔ
3 Ⓐ Ⓑ Ⓒ Ⓓ Ⓔ	13 Ⓐ Ⓑ Ⓒ Ⓓ Ⓔ	23 Ⓐ Ⓑ Ⓒ Ⓓ Ⓔ	33 Ⓐ Ⓑ Ⓒ Ⓓ Ⓔ
4 Ⓐ Ⓑ Ⓒ Ⓓ Ⓔ	14 Ⓐ Ⓑ Ⓒ Ⓓ Ⓔ	24 Ⓐ Ⓑ Ⓒ Ⓓ Ⓔ	34 Ⓐ Ⓑ Ⓒ Ⓓ Ⓔ
5 Ⓐ Ⓑ Ⓒ Ⓓ Ⓔ	15 Ⓐ Ⓑ Ⓒ Ⓓ Ⓔ	25 Ⓐ Ⓑ Ⓒ Ⓓ Ⓔ	35 Ⓐ Ⓑ Ⓒ Ⓓ Ⓔ
6 Ⓐ Ⓑ Ⓒ Ⓓ Ⓔ	16 Ⓐ Ⓑ Ⓒ Ⓓ Ⓔ	26 Ⓐ Ⓑ Ⓒ Ⓓ Ⓔ	36 Ⓐ Ⓑ Ⓒ Ⓓ Ⓔ
7 Ⓐ Ⓑ Ⓒ Ⓓ Ⓔ	17 Ⓐ Ⓑ Ⓒ Ⓓ Ⓔ	27 Ⓐ Ⓑ Ⓒ Ⓓ Ⓔ	37 Ⓐ Ⓑ Ⓒ Ⓓ Ⓔ
8 Ⓐ Ⓑ Ⓒ Ⓓ Ⓔ	18 Ⓐ Ⓑ Ⓒ Ⓓ Ⓔ	28 Ⓐ Ⓑ Ⓒ Ⓓ Ⓔ	38 Ⓐ Ⓑ Ⓒ Ⓓ Ⓔ
9 Ⓐ Ⓑ Ⓒ Ⓓ Ⓔ	19 Ⓐ Ⓑ Ⓒ Ⓓ Ⓔ	29 Ⓐ Ⓑ Ⓒ Ⓓ Ⓔ	39 Ⓐ Ⓑ Ⓒ Ⓓ Ⓔ
10 Ⓐ Ⓑ Ⓒ Ⓓ Ⓔ	20 Ⓐ Ⓑ Ⓒ Ⓓ Ⓔ	30 Ⓐ Ⓑ Ⓒ Ⓓ Ⓔ	40 Ⓐ Ⓑ Ⓒ Ⓓ Ⓔ

SECTION 6

1 Ⓐ Ⓑ Ⓒ Ⓓ Ⓔ	6 Ⓐ Ⓑ Ⓒ Ⓓ Ⓔ	11 Ⓐ Ⓑ Ⓒ Ⓓ Ⓔ
2 Ⓐ Ⓑ Ⓒ Ⓓ Ⓔ	7 Ⓐ Ⓑ Ⓒ Ⓓ Ⓔ	12 Ⓐ Ⓑ Ⓒ Ⓓ Ⓔ
3 Ⓐ Ⓑ Ⓒ Ⓓ Ⓔ	8 Ⓐ Ⓑ Ⓒ Ⓓ Ⓔ	13 Ⓐ Ⓑ Ⓒ Ⓓ Ⓔ
4 Ⓐ Ⓑ Ⓒ Ⓓ Ⓔ	9 Ⓐ Ⓑ Ⓒ Ⓓ Ⓔ	14 Ⓐ Ⓑ Ⓒ Ⓓ Ⓔ
5 Ⓐ Ⓑ Ⓒ Ⓓ Ⓔ	10 Ⓐ Ⓑ Ⓒ Ⓓ Ⓔ	15 Ⓐ Ⓑ Ⓒ Ⓓ Ⓔ

Note: ONLY the answers entered on the grid are scored.
Handwritten answers at the top of the column are NOT scored.

16. 17. 18. 19. 20.

21. 22. 23. 24. 25.

624

SECTION 1 Time—30 Minutes For each question in this section, choose the best answer and
35 Questions blacken the corresponding space on the answer sheet.

The passage below is followed by questions based on its content. Answer the questions following the passage on the basis of what is stated or implied in the passage.

Questions 1–12 are based on the following passage.

William Jennings Bryan is perhaps best known for acting as prosecutor in the Scopes Trial of 1925. Twenty-five years earlier, Bryan was a candidate for President. This anti-imperialist passage is from his speech accepting the Democratic nomination on August 8, 1900.

What is our title to the Philippine Islands? Do we hold them by treaty or by conquest? Did we buy them or did we take them? Did we purchase the people? If not, how did
(Line) we secure title to them? Were they thrown in with the
(5) land? Will the Republicans say that inanimate earth has value but that when the earth is molded by the divine hand and stamped with the likeness of the Creator it becomes a fixture and passes with the soil? If governments derive their just powers from the consent of the governed, it is
(10) impossible to secure title to people, either by force or by purchase.

We could extinguish Spain's title by treaty, but if we hold title we must hold it by some method consistent with our ideas of government. When we made allies of the
(15) Filipinos and armed them to fight against Spain, we disputed Spain's title. If we buy Spain's title we are not innocent purchasers.

There can be no doubt that we accepted and utilized the services of the Filipinos, and that when we did so we
(20) had full knowledge that they were fighting for their own independence, and I submit that history furnishes no example of turpitude baser than ours if we now substitute our yoke for the Spanish yoke.

Let us consider briefly the reasons which have been
(25) given in support of an imperialistic policy. Some say that it is our duty to hold the Philippine Islands. But duty is not an argument; it is a conclusion. To ascertain what our duty is, in any emergency, we must apply well-settled and generally accepted principles. It is our duty to avoid stealing,
(30) no matter whether the thing to be stolen is of great or little value. It is our duty to avoid killing a human being, no matter where the human being lives or to what race or class he belongs.

Every one recognizes the obligation imposed upon
(35) individuals to observe both the human and the moral law, but as some deny the application of those laws to nations, it may not be out of place to quote the opinions of others. Jefferson, than whom there is no higher political authority, said: "I know of but one code of morality for men,
(40) whether acting singly or collectively."

Franklin, whose learning, wisdom, and virtue are a part of the priceless legacy bequeathed to us from the revolutionary days, expressed the same idea in even stronger language when he said:

Justice is strictly due between neighbor nations as (45) between neighbor citizens. A highwayman is as much a robber when he plunders in a gang as when single; and the nation that makes an unjust war is only a great gang.

Many may dare to do in crowds what they would not (50) dare to do as individuals, but the moral character of an act is not determined by the number of those who join it. Force can defend a right, but force has never yet created a right. If it was true, as declared in the resolutions of intervention, that the Cubans "are and of right ought to be free (55) and independent" (language taken from the Declaration of Independence), it is equally true that the Filipinos "are and of right ought to be free and independent."

1. The word *title* (line 1) is used throughout to mean

   (A) name
   (B) station
   (C) charter
   (D) interest
   (E) claim

2. By "stamped with the likeness of the Creator" (line 7), Bryan refers to land that is

   (A) inhabited by humans
   (B) mountainous
   (C) beautiful
   (D) utopian
   (E) wracked by natural disasters

3. What, according to Bryan, would be wrong with the United States' purchase of Spain's title?

   (A) It would not jibe with U.S. theories of government.
   (B) It would be hypocritical, because the United States challenged Spain's right to the Philippines.
   (C) Spain would have aided in the Filipinos' move to self-rule.
   (D) both A and B
   (E) both B and C

4. The word *turpitude* (line 22) probably means

   (A) wickedness
   (B) flamboyance
   (C) passion
   (D) lethargy
   (E) tumult

GO ON TO THE NEXT PAGE

625

5. By "substitute our yoke for the Spanish yoke" (line 22–23), Bryan implies that the Filipinos

(A) will be better off under U.S. rule
(B) work like oxen for their citizens
(C) are trading one servant for another
(D) are simply switching masters
(E) cannot rule themselves

6. Bryan uses the images of stealing and killing to show that

(A) war can drive men mad
(B) some things are indisputable moral obligations
(C) our control of the Philippines can only lead to trouble
(D) a civilized nation has much to teach an uncivilized one
(E) none of the above

7. Bryan quotes Jefferson to support his contention that

(A) every man has a price
(B) without morality, conquest means nothing
(C) nations must act according to moral law
(D) people behave differently in groups than alone
(E) none of the above

8. By "a great gang" (line 49), Franklin implies that nations

(A) should always act in concert
(B) sometimes behave like hoodlums
(C) achieve strength through numbers
(D) succeed through teamwork
(E) support their member citizens

9. How does Bryan feel about the use of force?

(A) It may be useful in defending freedom.
(B) It does not excuse a bad policy.
(C) It must be used sparingly.
(D) both A and B
(E) both B and C

10. The "resolutions of intervention" (lines 54–55) must be decrees governing

(A) intercession in other countries' affairs
(B) originality and discoveries
(C) treaties and pacts
(D) post-war reconstruction
(E) conflicts between nations

11. Bryan mentions the Declaration of Independence (lines 56–57) to

(A) show the parallels among nations' fights for freedom
(B) remind his listeners of Jefferson's role in our nation
(C) shock his listeners with a little-known fact
(D) both A and B
(E) both B and C

12. This passage could be entitled

(A) "Our National Destiny"
(B) "The Goals of U.S. Imperialism"
(C) "Without Fear or Favor"
(D) "Standing by Our Allies"
(E) "Our True Duty to the Philippines"

Each sentence below has one or two blanks, each blank indicating that something has been omitted. Beneath the sentence are five lettered words or sets of words. Choose the word or set of words that best fits the meaning of the sentence as a whole.

Example:

Although its publicity has been ----, the film itself is intelligent, well-acted, handsomely produced, and altogether ----.

(A) tasteless..respectable
(B) extensive..moderate
(C) sophisticated..amateur
(D) risqué..crude
(E) perfect..spectacular

● ⒝ ⒞ ⒟ ⒠

13. The victim confronted his attacker in the courtroom calmly, with ---- and without apparent ---- although he had been severely traumatized by the incident.

(A) woe..composure
(B) ineptitude..obstinacy
(C) tempering..philanthropy
(D) equanimity..rancor
(E) scorn..malingering

14. The politician hungered for power; as a result of his ----, he succeeded in winning the election but ---- his closest friends and supporters.

(A) furtiveness..dissuaded
(B) winsomeness..disgruntled
(C) malevolence..mesmerized
(D) acerbity..seduced
(E) cupidity..alienated

15. With the evidence ---- from numerous X-ray studies, scientists are beginning to form a picture of the atomic structure of the cell.

(A) remanded   (B) gleaned   (C) pilfered
(D) atrophied   (E) implored

16. According to recent studies, prices in supermarkets are considerably higher in the inner city, thus ---- the poor who receive assistance to buy the food.

(A) reprimanding   (B) intimidating (C) alleviating
(D) assuaging   (E) exploiting

17. Legislation to stop smoking in public places has
   been ---- by some as a move to save lives, while it is
   ---- by the tobacco industry which calls the action
   "alarmist."

   (A) heralded..condemned
   (B) thwarted..buffered
   (C) initiated..condoned
   (D) prejudiced..supported
   (E) extolled..elicited

Each question below consists of a related pair of
words or phrases, followed by five lettered pairs of
words or phrases. Select the lettered pair that best
expresses the relationship similar to that expressed in
the original pair

Example:

YAWN : BOREDOM::

(A) dream : sleep
(B) anger : madness
(C) smile : amusement
(D) face : expression
(E) impatience : rebellion   Ⓐ Ⓑ ● Ⓓ Ⓔ

---

18. NEST : SPARROW::

   (A) cave : drawing
   (B) flight : wing
   (C) lair : lion
   (D) meadow : lake
   (E) pond : water

19. HANDWRITING : SIGNATURE::

   (A) biography : confession
   (B) eulogy : speech
   (C) painting : self-portrait
   (D) sculptor : model
   (E) sonnet : verse

20. CONTENT : EUPHORIC::

   (A) puzzled : candid
   (B) obvious : complete
   (C) afraid : bold
   (D) sad : morose
   (E) sincere : calm

21. TRIVIAL : IMPORTANCE::

   (A) tiny : magnitude
   (B) repetitious : pattern
   (C) portable : mobility
   (D) miraculous : faith
   (E) urgent : fallibility

22. SQUANDER : ASSETS::

   (A) pronounce : judgment
   (B) exhaust : resources
   (C) fulfill : dream
   (D) accumulate : balance
   (E) obtain : goods

23. MOTE : DUST::

   (A) summit : mountain
   (B) drizzle : flood
   (C) gable : eave
   (D) bead : water
   (E) grain : particle

24. CLANDESTINE : SECRECY::

   (A) personal : servant
   (B) imaginative : narrative
   (C) tumultuous : quiet
   (D) predictable : precision
   (E) confidential : privacy

25. REDOLENT : ODOR::

   (A) recurrent : expenditure
   (B) savory : taste
   (C) passive : aggression
   (D) constricted : vacuum
   (E) harmful : injury

The passage below is followed by questions based on its content. Answer the questions following the passage on the
basis of what is stated or implied in the passage.

Questions 26–35 are based on the following passage.

*The Honorable Emily Eden was born into the British
nobility in 1797, part of the same family from which one-
time Prime Minister Anthony Eden later descended. She
served as an important hostess to her brother, a Governor-
General of India, and in her spare time she wrote anonymous novels. This passage is from her bestseller,* The
Semi-detached House. *It features a housing situation rather
new at the time: two families sharing a double cottage.*

'The only fault of the house is that it is semi-detached.'

   'Oh, Aunt Sarah! you don't mean that you expect me
to live in a semi-detached house?'

   'Why not, my dear, if it suits you in other respects?'

(5)   'Why, because I should hate my semi-detachment, or
whatever the occupants of the other half of the house may
call themselves.'

'They call themselves Hopkinson,' continued Aunt
Sarah coolly.

(10)   'I knew it,' said Blanche triumphantly. 'I felt certain
their name would be either Tomkinson or Hopkinson — I
was not sure which — but I thought the chances were in
favour of Hop rather than Tom.'

   Aunt Sarah did not smile, but drew the mesh out of
her netting and began a fresh row. (15)

   'Go on, Aunt Sarah,' said Blanche demurely.

   'I am going on, thank you, my dear, very nicely; I
expect to finish this net this week.'

   Blanche looked at her aunt to ascertain if she looked
angry, or piqued, or affronted; but Aunt Sarah's count- (20)

Line (10)

Line (15)

Line (20)

Line (5)

GO ON TO THE NEXT PAGE →

nance was totally incapable of any expression but that of imperturbable stolid sense and good-humour. She did not care for Blanche's little vivacities.

Line
(25)

'Do you know the Hopkinsons, Aunt Sarah?'

'No, my dear.'

'Nor their history, nor their number, nor their habits? Recollect, Aunt Sarah, they will be under the same roof with your own pet Blanche.'

'I have several pets, my dear — Tray, and Poll, and
(30) your sister, and —'

'Well, but she will be there, too, for I suppose the Lees will let Aileen come to me, now that I am to be deserted by Arthur,' and Blanche's voice quivered, but she determined to brave it through. 'Did you see any of the
(35) Hopkinsons when you went to look at the house?'

'Yes, they went in at their door just as I went in at yours. The mother, as I suppose, and two daughters, and a little boy.'

'Oh dear me! a little boy, who will always be throw-
(40) ing stones at the palings and making me jump; daughters who will always be playing *Partant pour la Syrie*; and the mother —'

'Well, what will she do to offend your Highness?'

'She will be immensely fat, wear mittens — thick,
(45) heavy mittens — and contrive to know what I have for dinner every day.'

There was a silence, another row of netting and turn of the mesh, and then Aunt Sarah said in her most composed tone:

'I often think, my dear, that it is a great pity you are so imaginative, and a still greater pity that you are so fastidious. You would be happier if you were as dull and as matter-of-fact as I am.'

26. The impression we are given of Blanche is that

(A) she thinks she is clever
(B) she is intolerant
(C) she is sensitive
(D) both A and B
(E) both B and C

27. Why did Blanche feel sure the neighbors would be named Tomkinson or Hopkinson?

(A) She knows both families.
(B) She expected foreigners to move in.
(C) Those are middle-class names.
(D) The neighbors are American.
(E) Blanche's surname is Hopkinson.

28. The word *imperturbable* (line 22) means

(A) impassive
(B) dense
(C) preposterous
(D) unrealistic
(E) sensitive

29. The word *vivacities* (line 23) is used to mean

(A) pep talks
(B) lectures
(C) buoyancies
(D) vitality
(E) jokes

30. When Blanche refers to "their number" (line 26), she wishes to know

(A) the Hopkinsons' rank
(B) Mr. Hopkinson's line of work
(C) the Hopkinsons' net worth
(D) the address of the Hopkinsons
(E) how many Hopkinsons there are

31. *Palings* (line 40) are probably

(A) fences
(B) buckets
(C) beds
(D) tables
(E) stones

32. "As I suppose" (line 37) implies that Aunt Sarah

(A) assumes the woman she saw was the mother
(B) thinks the mother is just as she imagined she'd be
(C) expected to see the mother when she appeared
(D) both A and B
(E) both B and C

33. The word *contrive* (line 45) is used to mean

(A) fashion
(B) originate
(C) improvise
(D) scheme
(E) invent

34. How does the author feel toward Blanche?

(A) charmed
(B) shocked
(C) vexed
(D) patient
(E) somber

35. The character of Aunt Sarah is used as a

(A) counterpart to that of Blanche
(B) contrast to that of Blanche
(C) foil to that of the Hopkinsons
(D) target of old-fashioned witticisms
(E) symbol of change

IF YOU FINISH BEFORE TIME IS CALLED, YOU MAY CHECK YOUR WORK ON THIS SECTION ONLY. DO NOT WORK ON ANY OTHER SECTION IN THE TEST.

STOP

<table>
</table>

SECTION **2**	Time—30 Minutes 25 Questions	In this section, solve each problem, using any available space on the page for scratchwork. Then decide which is the best of the choices given and fill in the corresponding oval on the answer sheet.

Reference:

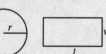   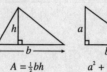

Circle: $C = 2\pi r$, $A = \pi r^2$ Rectangle: $A = lw$ Rectangular Solid: $V = lwh$ Cylinder: $V = \pi r^2 h$ Triangle: $A = \frac{1}{2}bh$, $a^2 + b^2 = c^2$

- The measure in degrees of a straight angle is 180.
- The number of degrees of arc in a circle is 360.
- The sum of the measures of the angles of a triangle is 180.

Notes: The figures accompanying the problems are drawn as accurately as possible unless otherwise stated in specific problems. Again, unless otherwise stated, all figures lie in the same plane. All numbers used in these problems are real numbers. Calculators are permitted for this test.

---

1. If $x + 2 = 7$ and $x + y = 11$, then $y =$
   (A) 2   (B) 4   (C) 6   (D) 7   (E) 9

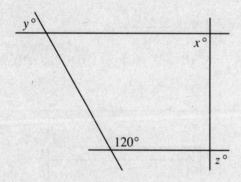

2. In the figure above, if $y + z = 150$, then $x =$
   (A) 30   (B) 45   (C) 75   (D) 90   (E) 120

The product of x and 5 is equal to one-half the sum of $3x$ and 3.

3. Which of the following equations correctly expresses the relationship described above?

   (A) $5x = \dfrac{9x}{2}$ (B) $5x = 2(3x + 3)$

   (C) $5x = \dfrac{(3x + 3)}{2}$ (D) $\dfrac{x}{5} = 2(3x + 3)$

   (E) $\dfrac{x}{5} = \dfrac{(3x + 3)}{2}$

---

4. If $x > -5$, then $(x + 7)$ could be
   (A) -1 (B) 0   (C) 1   (D) 2   (E) 3

---

5. During a sale, 3 of a certain item can be purchased for the usual cost of 2 of the items. If John buys 36 of the items at the sale price, how many of the items could he have bought at the regular price?

   (A) 18   (B) 24   (C) 30   (D) 48   (E) 72

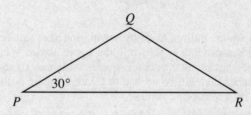

Note: Figure not drawn to scale

6. In PQR above, if $PQ = QR$, then $x =$
   (A) 30   (B) 60   (C) 90   (D) 120   (E) 150

GO ON TO THE NEXT PAGE

7. If $px + 2 = 8$ and $qx + 3 = 10$, what is the value of $\dfrac{p}{q}$?

   (A) $\dfrac{3}{5}$ (B) $\dfrac{8}{15}$ (C) $\dfrac{10}{13}$

   (D) $\dfrac{6}{7}$ (E) $\dfrac{16}{13}$

8. If $2^x = 16$ and $x = \dfrac{y}{2}$, then $y =$

   (A) 2   (B) 3   (C) 4   (D) 6   (E) 8

9. The figure above shows a correctly done addition problem. What is the value of ■?

   (A) 2   (B) 4   (C) 6   (D) 8   (E) 9

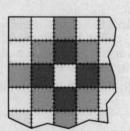

10. A square quilt is made by sewing together square pieces of cloth as shown in the figure above. What is the least number of cloth squares with area 16 square inches that will be needed to create a square quilt with a side of 32 inches?

   (A) 16   (B) 32   (C) 64   (D) 128   (E) 256

11. If a triangle has a height of $\dfrac{1}{x}$ and an area of 2, what is the length of the base of the triangle?

   (A) $4x$ (B) x (C) $\dfrac{1}{2x}$ (D) $\dfrac{1}{4x}$ (E) x^2

12. If the sum of three numbers if $4x$ and the sum of four other numbers is $3x$, then the average (arithmetic mean) of all seven numbers is

   (A) $7x$ (B) x (C) $\dfrac{x}{7}$ (D) 7   (E) 1

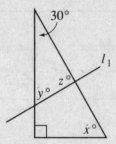

13. In the figure above, if $x = y$, then $z =$

   (A) 30   (B) 45   (C) 60   (D) 75   (E) 90

14. If $6 \leqq x \leqq 30$, $3 \leqq y \leqq 12$, and $2 \leqq z \leqq 10$, then what is the least possible value of $\dfrac{x+y}{z}$?

   (A) $\dfrac{9}{10}$ (B) $\dfrac{9}{5}$ (C) $\dfrac{21}{5}$ (D) $\dfrac{9}{2}$ (E) 21

15. If $x \neq 0$, then $\dfrac{(-3x)^3}{-3x^3} =$

   (A) -9 (B) -3 (C) -1 (D) 3   (E) 9

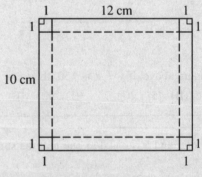

16. The figure above shows a rectangular piece of cardboard with sides of 10 centimeters and 12 centimeters. From each of the four corners, a square 1 centimeter by 1 centimeter is cut out. If an open rectangular box is then formed by folding along the dotted lines, what is the volume of the box in cubic centimeters?

   (A) 80   (B) 96   (C) 99   (D) 120   (E) 168

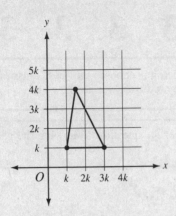

17. If the area of the triangle in the figure above is 12, then $k =$

(A) 1 (B) 2 (C) 3 (D) 4 (E) 6

18. A machine produces 18 widgets every 5 seconds. How many widgets does it produce in an hour?

(A) 720 (B) 1,000 (C) 1,296
(D) 10,000 (E) 12,960

19. If x and y are two different positive integers and $x^3y^2 = 200$, then $xy =$

(A) 5 (B) 6 (C) 10 (D) 25 (E) 40

20. After trimming, a sapling has $\frac{9}{10}$ of its original height. If it must grow $\frac{9}{10}$ foot to regain its original height, what was its original height?

(A) 8 (B) 9 (C) 10 (D) 16 (E) 18

21. A tank contains g gallons of water. Water flows into the tank by one pipe at the rate of m gallons per minute, and water flows out by another pipe at the rate of n gallons per minute. If $n > m$, how many minutes will it take to empty the tank?

(A) $\dfrac{(g-m)}{n}$ (B) $\dfrac{g}{(m-n)}$ (C) $\dfrac{(n-g)}{m}$

(D) $\dfrac{(n-m)}{g}$ (E) $\dfrac{g}{(n-m)}$

B

22. If $\dfrac{13t}{7}$ is an integer, then t could be any of the following EXCEPT

(A) −91 (B) −7 (C) 3 (D) 70 (E) 91

23. If $\dfrac{(x+y)}{x} = 4$ and $\dfrac{(y+z)}{z} = 5$, what is the value of $\dfrac{x}{z}$?

(A) $\dfrac{1}{4}$ (B) $\dfrac{1}{3}$ (C) $\dfrac{3}{4}$ (D) $\dfrac{4}{3}$ (E) $\dfrac{3}{1}$

24. On Monday, Juan withdraws $\frac{1}{2}$ of the money in his savings account. On Tuesday, he withdraws another $60, leaving $\frac{1}{5}$ of the original amount in the account. How much money was originally in Juan's savings account?

(A) $600 (B) $300 (C) $200
(D) $150 (E) $120

25. A painter is planning to paint a row of three houses, using the colors red, gray, and white. If each house is to be painted a single color, and if the painter must use each of the three colors, how many different ways are there of painting the three houses?

(A) 1 (B) 2 (C) 3 (D) 6 (E) 9

IF YOU FINISH BEFORE TIME IS CALLED, YOU MAY CHECK YOUR WORK ON THIS SECTION ONLY. DO NOT WORK ON ANY OTHER SECTION IN THE TEST. **STOP**

631

SECTION **3**   Time—15 Minutes   For each question in this section, choose the best answer and
10 Questions   blacken the corresponding space on the answer sheet.

The passages below are followed by questions based on their content. Answer the questions following the passages on the basis of what is <u>stated</u> or <u>implied</u> in the passages.

Questions 1-10 are based on the following passages.

William Congreve (1670–1729) was a British playwright best known for The Way of the World *(1700). He is considered a master of the English comedy of manners. Henri-Louis Bergson (1859–1941) was a French philosopher and winner of the Nobel Prize for Literature in 1928. In these passages, both men expound on the nature of humor.*

Passage 1 — Congreve, "Concerning Humor in Comedy" (1696)

To define humor perhaps were as difficult as to define wit; for, like that, it is of infinite variety. To enumerate the several humors of men were a work as endless as to sum
Line
(5) up their several opinions. . . . And since I have mentioned wit and humor together, let me make the first distinction between them, and to observe to you that *wit is often mistaken for humor.*

I have observed that when a few things have been wittily and pleasantly spoken by any character in a comedy, it
(10) has been very usual for those who make their remarks on a play while it is acting, to say, *Such a thing is very humorously spoken; There is a great deal of humor in that part.* Thus the character of the person speaking, may be, surprisingly and pleasantly mistaken for a character of humor,
(15) which indeed is a character of wit. But there is a great difference between a comedy wherein there are many things *humorously*, as they call it, which is *pleasantly*, spoken, and one where there are several characters of humor, distinguished by the particular and different humors appropri-
(20) ated to the several persons represented, and which naturally arise from the different constitutions, complexions, and dispositions of men. . . .

As wit, so its opposite, *folly, is sometimes mistaken for humor.*

(25) When a poet brings a character on the stage committing a thousand absurdities, and talking impertinencies, roaring aloud, and laughing immoderately on every or rather upon no occasion, this is a character of humor. . . . As I don't think humor exclusive of wit, neither do I think it incon-
(30) sistent with folly; but I think the follies should be only such as men's humors may incline 'em to, and not follies entirely abstracted from both humor and nature. . . .

I should be unwilling to venture even on a bare description of humor, much more to make a definition of it, but
(35) now my hand is in, I'll tell you what serves one instead of either. I take it to be *A singular and unavoidable manner of doing or saying anything, peculiar and natural to one man only, by which his speech and actions are distinguished from those of other men.*

Passage 2 — Bergson, "The Comic Element" (1900)
Line
(40) The comic, we said, appeals to the intelligence pure and simple; laughter is incompatible with emotion. Depict some fault, however trifling, in such a way as to arouse sympathy, fear, or pity; the mischief is done, it is impossible for us to laugh. On the other hand, take a downright
(45) vice, — even one that is, generally speaking, of an odious nature, — you may make it ludicrous if, by some suitable contrivance, you arrange so that it leaves our emotions unaffected. Not that the vice *must* then be ludicrous, but it *may*, from that time forth, become so. *It must not arouse*
(50) *our feelings*; that is the sole condition really necessary. . . .

To sum up, whether a character is good or bad is of little moment; granted he is unsociable, he is capable of becoming comic. We now see that the seriousness of the case is of no importance either: whether serious or trifling,
(55) it is still capable of making us laugh, provided that care be taken not to arouse our emotions. Unsociability in the performer and insensibility in the spectator — such, in a word, are the two essential conditions. . . .

The third condition is automatism. We have pointed it
(60) out from the outset of this work, continually drawing attention to the following point: what is essentially laughable is what is done automatically. In a vice, even in a virtue, the comic is that element by which the person unwittingly betrays himself — the involuntary gesture or
(65) the unconscious remark. Absentmindedness is always comical. Indeed, the deeper the absentmindedness the higher the comedy. Systematic absentmindedness, like that of Don Quixote, is the most comical thing imaginable: it is the comic itself, drawn as nearly as possible from its very
(70) source. Take any other comic character: however unconscious he may be of what he says or does, he cannot be comical unless there be some aspect of his person of which he is unaware, one side of his nature which he overlooks; on that account alone does he make us laugh.

1. The main point of Congreve's second paragraph is that

   (A) wit is more important to comedy than humor is
   (B) audiences do not know the difference between wit and folly
   (C) there is a difference between humorous language and a humorous character
   (D) playwrights give humorous lines to tragic characters
   (E) characters who speak pleasantly are often humorous

2. The word *appropriated* (lines 19–20) is used by Congreve to mean

   (A) commandeered
   (B) seized
   (C) corrected
   (D) assigned
   (E) fitted

3. The word *abstracted* in Congreve's piece (line 32) means

   (A) disturbed
   (B) confounded
   (C) summarized
   (D) removed
   (E) condensed

4. Congreve believes that humor must be

   (A) self-sufficient
   (B) natural
   (C) pointed
   (D) rare
   (E) unexpected

5. Congreve uses the word *peculiar* (line 37) to mean

   (A) characteristic
   (B) quaint
   (C) outlandish
   (D) odd
   (E) unusual

6. When Bergson remarks, "the mischief is done" (line 43), he means

   (A) the playwright has ruined his play
   (B) an element of tragedy has been injected
   (C) the possibility of humor has been removed
   (D) both A and B
   (E) both B and C

7. The word *moment*, used by Bergson in line 52, means

   (A) flash
   (B) period
   (C) minute
   (D) importance
   (E) time

8. What does Bergson think about emotional response to drama?

   (A) It is a prerequisite to understanding.
   (B) It is especially inappropriate nowadays.
   (C) It has no place in a comedy.
   (D) both A and B
   (E) both B and C

9. Both passages are essentially

   (A) fictional
   (B) definitional
   (C) comical
   (D) argumentative
   (E) lyrical

10. Bergson and Congreve agree that one important element of humor is

    (A) folly
    (B) unsociability
    (C) wit
    (D) involuntary behavior
    (E) absentmindedness

IF YOU FINISH BEFORE TIME IS CALLED, YOU MAY CHECK YOUR WORK ON **S T O P** THIS SECTION ONLY. DO NOT WORK ON ANY OTHER SECTION IN THE TEST.

SECTION **4**	Time—15 Minutes 10 Questions	In this section, solve each problem, using any available space on the page for scratchwork. Then decide which is the best of the choices given and fill in the corresponding oval on the answer sheet.

Reference:

Circle: Rectangle: Rectangular Solid: Cylinder: Triangle:

$C = 2\pi r$
$A = \pi r^2$

$A = lw$

$V = lwh$

$V = \pi r^2 h$

$A = \frac{1}{2}bh$

$a^2 + b^2 = c^2$

- The measure in degrees of a straight angle is 180.
- The number of degrees of arc in a circle is 360.
- The sum of the measures of the angles of a triangle is 180.

Notes: The figures accompanying the problems are drawn as accurately as possible unless otherwise stated in specific problems. Again, unless otherwise stated, all figures lie in the same plane. All numbers used in these problems are real numbers. Calculators are permitted for this test.

Dimensions of 5 different boxes

Box A:	$2 \times 3 \times 4$
Box B:	$2 \times 3 \times 3$
Box C:	$3 \times 4 \times 5$
Box D:	$5 \times 4 \times 2$
Box E:	$4 \times 4 \times 2$

1. If the sides of each box described above are perpendicular to each other, which box has the greatest volume?

(A) A   (B) B   (C) C   (D) D   (E) E

2. The product of an even, positive number and an odd, negative number is

(A) negative and even
(B) negative and odd
(C) negative and either even or odd
(D) positive and odd
(E) positive and even

3. If w, x, y, and z are positive numbers, each of the following expressions equals $w(x + y + z)$ EXCEPT

(A) $wx + wy + wz$
(B) $wx + w(y + z)$
(C) $w(x + y) + wz$
(D) $w(x + z) + wy$
(E) $w(xy) + w(yz)$

4. Originally, a group of 11 students were supposed to share equally a cash prize. If 1 more student is added to the group and the 12 students share the prize equally, then each new share is worth what fraction of each original share?

(A) $\dfrac{1}{12}$ (B) $\dfrac{1}{11}$ (C) $\dfrac{1}{10}$ (D) $\dfrac{10}{11}$ (E) $\dfrac{11}{12}$

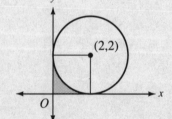

5. In the figure above, the center of the circle has coordinates (2,2). What is the area of the shaded portion of the figure?

(A) $2 - \pi$ (B) $4 - \pi$ (C) $8 - 2\pi$
(D) $8 - \pi$ (E) $16 - 4\pi$

634

Having X and Y	10
Having X but not Y	30
Having Y but not X	20
Having neither X nor Y	40

6. The table above gives the distribution of two genetic characteristics, X and Y, in a population of 100 subjects. What is the ratio of the number of people having characteristic X to the number of people having the characteristic Y?

(A) 1:3　(B) 1:2　(C) 2:3　(D) 4:3　(E) 3:2

7. If $x - y = 42$, then $2x - 2y =$

(A) 21　(B) 42　(C) 84　(D) $2(x + y)$
(E) Cannot be determined from the information given.

8. You can buy $4\frac{1}{2}$ pounds of scallops for $40.50. How much would you pay for 3 pounds?

(A) $25.50　(B) $27　(C) $30　(D) $35　(E) $45

9. A bowling team has 5 members, 40% of whom averaged over 230 this fall. Of those over-230 scorers, 50% had scores averaging 250 or better. How many people had scores averaging below 250?

(A) 1　(B) 2　(C) 3　(D) 4　(E) 5

10. If $x = -21$, what is the value of $x + (x - x)$?

(A) −42　(B) −21　(C) 0　(D) 21　(E) 42

IF YOU FINISH BEFORE TIME IS CALLED, YOU MAY CHECK YOUR WORK ON THIS SECTION ONLY. DO NOT WORK ON ANY OTHER SECTION IN THE TEST. **STOP**

635

SECTION **5**   Time—30 Minutes   For each question in this section, choose the best answer and
35 Questions   blacken the corresponding space on the answer sheet.

Each sentence below has one or two blanks, each
blank indicating that something has been omitted.
Beneath the sentence are five lettered words or sets of
words. Choose the word or set of words that <u>best</u> fits
the meaning of the sentence as a whole.

Example:

Although its publicity has been ----, the film itself
is intelligent, well-acted, handsomely produced, and
altogether ----.

(A) tasteless..respectable
(B) extensive..moderate
(C) sophisticated..amateur
(D) risqué..crude
(E) perfect..spectacular

---

1. His seemingly casual and ---- tone ---- a serious concern for the welfare of his clients.

(A) flippant..belied
(B) worried..displayed
(C) effective..disputed
(D) callous..betrayed
(E) contentious..minimized

2. The actress owed her reputation to her ---- public
and not to the ---- reviews which bordered on being
cruel.

(A) diffident..approbatory
(B) congenial..simpering
(C) trusting..didactic
(D) adoring..scathing
(E) innocent..deferential

3. Treason is punishable by death because ---- constitutes a threat to the very ---- of the state.

(A) perfidy..survival
(B) grief..existence
(C) veracity..foundation
(D) pacifism..dismantling
(E) patriotism..well-being

4. Although scientists have sought to measure time,
only writers and poets have truly ---- its quality and
our ---- experience of it.

(A) neglected..uniform
(B) understood..benign
(C) captured..ephemeral
(D) belied..credulous
(E) devised..fractious

5. Although a gala performance, the conducting was
---- , and the orchestra less than enthusiastic, but the
audience seemed ---- the defects and was enthralled.

(A) auspicious..sensitive to
(B) perfunctory..oblivious to
(C) decimated..mindful of
(D) voracious..excited by
(E) animated..impaired by

6. Since there are so few conservative thinkers on the
committee, their influence on its recommendations is
---- .

(A) monumental   (B) negligible
(C) discriminatory   (D) impractical
(E) cathartic

7. Laboratory tests which often maim animals and
depend solely on observation to determine results are
not only ---- but highly ---- since no two people see
the same thing.

(A) safe..consistent
(B) patented..conclusive
(C) controversial..valuable
(D) gratifying..explosive
(E) cruel..unreliable

8. Execution by lethal injection, although horrifying, is
certainly more civilized than the ---- penalty of death
by torture or dismemberment.

(A) pervasive   (B) viler   (C) humane
(D) prolific   (E) complacent

9. Although vitamins are helpful for maintaining good
health, alcohol, caffeine, and other drugs severely ----
their effectiveness, leaving the body's defenses ----

(A) augment..weakened
(B) reduce..indelible
(C) inhibit..impaired
(D) confuse..allied
(E) duplicate..activated

10. To understand a work of art it is necessary to place it
in ---- context to capture its ---- significance as well
as its present meaning.

(A) a specious..referential
(B) a random..cumulative
(C) an inventive..partial
(D) a historical..original
(E) a sophisticated..international

11. He is an ---- student and a ---- to teach.

 (A) intrepid..hazard
 (B) exceptional..joy
 (C) exuberant..power
 (D) insipid..threat
 (E) ironic..jubilation

12. My work in the field of ---- takes me to ---- around the world.

 (A) spelunking..homes
 (B) geology..castles
 (C) psychiatry..sanity
 (D) ichthyology..gardens
 (E) archaeology..ruins

13. Do you like foreign films, or do you prefer your art ---- ?

 (A) scenic
 (B) alien
 (C) customary
 (D) domestic
 (E) eleemosynary

14. Tears of the ---- are common in ---- .

 (A) sorrow..rulers
 (B) cartilage..competitors
 (C) spine..athletes
 (D) helmet..sports
 (E) lesion..activity

15. A small ---- meandered lyrically through the pasture.

 (A) wellhead
 (B) kine
 (C) gulch
 (D) brine
 (E) rivulet

Each question below consists of a related pair of words or phrases, followed by five lettered pairs of words or phrases. Select the lettered pair that best expresses a relationship similar to that expressed in the original pair.

Example:

YAWN : BOREDOM::

 (A) dream : sleep
 (B) anger : madness
 (C) smile : amusement
 (D) face : expression
 (E) impatience : rebellion   Ⓐ Ⓑ ● Ⓓ Ⓔ

16. SCISSORS : CUTTING::

 (A) knife : cooking
 (B) scalpel : medicine
 (C) arrow : quiver
 (D) needle : sewing
 (E) hatchet : hunting

17. RECIPE : FOOD::

 (A) blueprint : building
 (B) formula : scientist
 (C) ingredient : concoction
 (D) liquid : consumption
 (E) score : performer

18. DEBATER : ARGUMENT::

 (A) minister : congregation
 (B) poet : artist
 (C) chauffeur : passenger
 (D) boxer : ring
 (E) musician : instrument

19. GRAIN : SILO::

 (A) vitamin : nutrition
 (B) farm : tractor
 (C) van : warehouse
 (D) water : reservoir
 (E) money : investor

20. IMPROMPTU : PLANNING::

 (A) gratuitous : ticket
 (B) dramatic : rehearsal
 (C) cursory : care
 (D) ravenous : appetite
 (E) enlightened : knowledge

21. LACONIC : WORDS::

 (A) affable : friends
 (B) hesitant : action
 (C) monotonous : address
 (D) tolerant : laughter
 (E) ambitious : calamity

22. RECIDIVISM : CRIMINAL::

 (A) justice : plaintiff
 (B) bankruptcy : lawyer
 (C) condemnation : authority
 (D) finesse : magician
 (E) relapse : patient

23. INAUGURATE : BEGINNING::

 (A) encapsulate : thought
 (B) advise : dissension
 (C) prevaricate : prank
 (D) forbid : sanction
 (E) consecrate : dedication

24. ELEGIAC : MOURNING

 (A) contemptuous : disdain
 (B) rambunctious : enervation
 (C) profligate : lassitude
 (D) amorphous : spontaneity
 (E) deferential : veracity

25. DISCERNING : PERCEPTION::

 (A) moribund : defilement
 (B) oblivious : forgetfulness
 (C) interminable : brevity
 (D) ambiguous : clarity
 (E) loathsome : decrepitude

637

Questions 26–35 are based on the following passage.

Claude McKay was born in Jamaica in 1890 and later lived in Harlem and London. He is most famous as a poet and short story writer. This is an autobiographical sketch about his boyhood home.

My village was beautiful, sunny, sparsely populated. It was set upon a hill. Except when it was foggy or raining, it was always bathed by the sun. The hills came like chains
Line from the other villages—James Hill, Taremont, Croft's
(5) Hill, Frankfield, and Ballad's River. They came to form a centre in my village of Sunny Ville.

The village was set, something like a triangle, between two streams. The parochial or dirt road, along which it grew on both sides, jutted off abruptly from the
(10) main macadamized road. We were about twenty-one families living between those two streams—one so large we called it a river, the other just a tributary which further down emptied itself into a larger river. Our lives were linked with streams. In fact, the Indian word *Xaymaca*
(15) means "land of springs."

The road was red, very red. I remember during the rainy season how that red clay would cake up on the legs and feet of the old folks going to work their patches of land, and the kids going to school. On Sunday, during that
(20) kind of weather, the peasant men went to Church with their shoes slung over their shoulders, and the peasant women carrying theirs either on their arms and on their heads. When they got to the brook near the Church, they would wash their feet, put on their shoes, and step gingerly
(25) on the grass leading to the Church doors. What used to tickle us children was the quietness of the Church and the squeaking of the shoes of our elders, as they walked down the aisle to the front benches.

Sometimes the rainy season came in with a fierce hur-
(30) ricane which would sweep everything before it, uprooting the strongest trees and destroying the best crops of bananas, sugar cane, corn, and yams. Sometimes it knocked down the peasants' huts. Everything was flattened like reeds by a wind. Fortunately the hurricanes did not
(35) come regularly—sometimes for five or six years we did not have one, and again suddenly we might have two within a period of two years.

Many of the peasants believed that hurricanes, like floods, diseases, and other evils, were caused by Obi or
(40) Obeah, a West African god. Obeahmen who could appease the god, or who could pit their strength against his by exorcism, were accordingly popular. With all the best crops destroyed and the fruit trees uprooted, the villages were faced with starvation. Somehow I recall that we
(45) always used to pull through. Those peasants who had money saved up (and most of them did) used to buy barrels and bags of flour from the town. We would mix it with corn meal and make all kinds of food—johnny cakes, dumplings and mush.

(50) Most of the time there was hardly any way of telling the seasons. To us in Jamaica, as elsewhere in the tropics, there were only two seasons—the rainy season and the dry season. We had no idea of spring, summer, autumn and winter like the peoples of northern lands. Springtime, how-
(55) ever, we did know by the new and lush burgeoning of grasses and the blossoming of trees, although we had blooms all the year round. The mango tree was especially significant of spring, because it was one of the few trees that used to shed its leaves. Then, in springtime, the new
(60) leaves sprouted—very tender, a kind of sulphur brown, as if they had been singed by fire. Soon afterwards the white blossoms came out and we knew that we would be eating juicy mangoes by August. . . .

26. The word *parochial* (line 8) means

    (A) church
    (B) religious
    (C) unlimited
    (D) boundless
    (E) local

27. Why does McKay define an Indian word in paragraph 2?

    (A) to show how the Indians lived long ago
    (B) to explain how his country got its name
    (C) to amuse his audience with jargon
    (D) to impress readers with his erudition
    (E) to reveal that his land once belonged to Indians

28. The word *cake* (line 17) is used to mean

    (A) batter
    (B) sweet
    (C) encrust
    (D) dance
    (E) fill

29. Paragraph 4 is mostly about

    (A) rain
    (B) crops
    (C) rituals
    (D) hurricanes
    (E) seasonal change

30. The Obeahmen were "accordingly popular" (line 42) because they could

    (A) rebuild flattened buildings
    (B) cast out demons
    (C) calm the gods
    (D) both A and B
    (E) both B and C

31. McKay lists the foods made from corn meal (line 48) to show

    (A) how dull the Jamaican peasant's diet was
    (B) how little one could buy with money in those days
    (C) how cleverly the peasants used meager foodstuffs
    (D) both A and B
    (E) both B and C

32. The word *burgeoning* (line 55) means

    (A) planting
    (B) waving
    (C) flowering
    (D) withering
    (E) sprouting

33. How does McKay feel about the place and time about which he is writing?

    (A) uncomfortable
    (B) self-consciously critical
    (C) unemotional and matter-of-fact
    (D) fondly nostalgic
    (E) flippantly casual

34. How can you tell that this piece reflects bygone times?

    (A) The author uses phrases such as "I remember" and "I recall."
    (B) There are no peasants left in Jamaica; times have changed.
    (C) The village of Sunny Ville was long ago destroyed by a hurricane.
    (D) both A and B
    (E) both B and C

35. The main focus of the passage is

    (A) descriptive
    (B) didactic
    (C) preachy
    (D) persuasive
    (E) instructive

IF YOU FINISH BEFORE TIME IS CALLED, YOU MAY CHECK YOUR WORK ON THIS SECTION ONLY. DO NOT WORK ON ANY OTHER SECTION IN THE TEST. **S T O P**

SECTION **6**	Time—30 Minutes 25 Questions	This section contains two types of problems with separate directions for each. You may use any available space for scratchwork.

Reference:

Circle:

$C = 2\pi r$
$A = \pi r^2$

Rectangle:

$A = lw$

Rectangular Solid: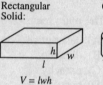

$V = lwh$

Cylinder:

$V = \pi r^2 h$

Triangle:

$A = \frac{1}{2}bh$

$a^2 + b^2 = c^2$

- The measure in degrees of a straight angle is 180.
- The number of degrees of arc in a circle is 360.
- The sum of the measures of the angles of a triangle is 180.

Notes: The figures accompanying the problems are drawn as accurately as possible unless otherwise stated in specific problems. Again, unless otherwise stated, all figures lie in the same plane. All numbers used in these problems are real numbers. Calculators are permitted for this test.

Directions for Quantitative Comparison Questions

Questions 1–15 each consist of two quantities, one in Column A and one in Column B. You are to compare the two quantities and on the answer sheet fill in oval

A if the quantity in Column A is greater;
B if the quantity in Column B is greater;
C if the two quantities are equal;
D if the relationship cannot be determined from the information given.

AN E RESPONSE WILL NOT BE SCORED.

EXAMPLES	Column A	Column B	Answers
E1.	2×6	$2 + 6$	● Ⓑ Ⓒ Ⓓ Ⓔ
E2.	$180 - x$	y	Ⓐ Ⓑ ● Ⓓ Ⓔ
E3.	$p - q$	$q - p$	Ⓐ Ⓑ Ⓒ ● Ⓔ

(E2 figure: lines with angles $x°$ and $y°$)

Notes:

1. In certain questions, information concerning one or both of the quantities to be compared is centered above the two columns.
2. In a given question, a symbol that appears in both columns represents the same thing in Column A as it does in Column B.
3. Letters such as x, n, and k stand for real numbers.

GO ON TO THE NEXT PAGE

Column A	Column B		Column A	Column B

Column A   **Column B**   **Column A**   **Column B**

$$x > 0$$
$$3x = 4y$$

1. | x | | y |

GO ON TO THE NEXT PAGE

$$4x + 3y = 11$$
$$3x + 3y = 9$$

7. | x | | 1 |

$$4.5 < x < 5.5$$
x is an integer

2. | x | | 5 |

$$\boxed{x} = x^2 - x$$

8. | $\boxed{2}$ | | 4 |

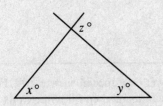

Note: Figure not drawn to scale

3. | $x + y$ | | z |

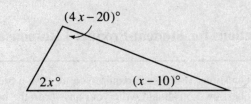

9. | x | | 30 |

4. | $5^7 + (-2)^4$ | | $5^7 + (-2)^5$ |

$$x = y$$

10. | $x(y + 1)$ | | $y(x - 1)$ |

$$x \neq 0$$

5. | $\sqrt{x^2}$ | | $\sqrt{x^2 + 1}$ |

11. | $\dfrac{1}{6}(x + y)$ | | $\dfrac{x}{6} + \dfrac{y}{6}$ |

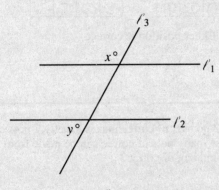

$l1 \parallel l2$

12. | $\dfrac{\frac{3}{4}}{\frac{4}{3}}$ | | 1 |

6. | x | | $180 - y$ |

641

Column A	Column B

The seating capacity of the Red Room is less than the seating capacity of the Blue Room.

The seating capacity of the Blue Room is greater than the seating capacity of the Green Room.

13.

The seating capacity of the Red Room	The seating capacity of the Green Room

14.

17.5% of 123	12.3% of 175

Column A	Column B

$$\frac{x}{9} = \frac{y}{17}$$

x and y are positive integers

15.

$9x$	$17y$

Directions for Student-Produced Response Questions

<u>Questions 16–25</u> each require you to solve a problem and mark your answer on a special answer grid. For each question, you should write your answer in the boxes at the top of each column and then fill in the ovals beneath each answer you write. Here are some examples.

Answer: 3/4 (= .75; show answer either way)

Answer: 325

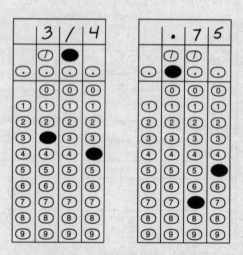

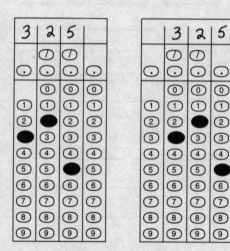

Note: A mixed number such as 3½ must be gridded as 7/2 or as 3.5. If gridded as "31/2," it will be read as "thirty-one halves."

Note: Either position is correct.

16. If $x = 2$, then $x^2 - 2x = ?$

17. If 2 pounds of coffee makes exactly 7 pots of coffee, how many pots of coffee can be made from a 10-pound bag of coffee?

18. If roses cost $1.00 apiece and carnations cost $0.50 apiece, how many more carnations than roses can be purchased for $10.00?

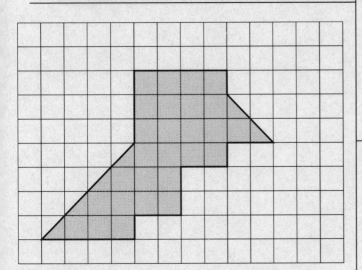

19. In the figure above, each of the small squares has side of length 1. What is the area of the shaded region?

20. If $(x + y)^2 = (x - y)^2 + 4$, then $xy = ?$

21. If $\frac{2}{3}$ of a number is 5 more than $\frac{1}{4}$ of the number, what is the number?

22. If a square has the same area as a rectangle with sides of 9 and 4, what is the length of the side of the square?

23. $D(w)$ is defined as the number of times in a sequence of letters, w, that any letter is followed by itself. For example, if w is *aabbc*, $D(w) = 2$. If w is "*aaabbbcc*," what is the value of $D(w)$?

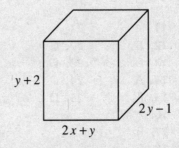

24. What is the volume of the cube shown above?

25. Of the dogs at the kennel, $\frac{1}{10}$ are over 2 years old. Of those, $\frac{3}{5}$ are between 3 and 5 years old, and $\frac{2}{5}$ are over 5 years old. In lowest terms, what fraction of the entire kennel population is over 5 years old?

IF YOU FINISH BEFORE TIME IS CALLED, YOU MAY CHECK YOUR WORK ON THIS SECTION ONLY. DO NOT WORK ON ANY OTHER SECTION IN THE TEST. **S T O P**

643

Answer Key

SECTION 1

1. E	11. A	21. A	31. A
2. A	12. E	22. B	32. A
3. D	13. D	23. D	33. D
4. A	14. E	24. E	34. C
5. D	15. B	25. B	35. B
6. B	16. E	26. D	
7. C	17. A	27. C	
8. B	18. C	28. A	
9. D	19. C	29. E	
10. A	20. D	30. E	

SECTION 2

1. C	11. A	21. E
2. D	12. B	22. C
3. C	13. E	23. D
4. E	14. A	24. C
5. B	15. E	25. D
6. D	16. A	
7. D	17. B	
8. E	18. E	
9. A	19. C	
10. C	20. B	

SECTION 3

1. C
2. D
3. D
4. B
5. A
6. E
7. D
8. C
9. B
10. D

SECTION 4

1. C
2. A
3. E
4. E
5. B
6. D
7. C
8. B
9. D
10. B

SECTION 5

1. A	11. B	21. B	31. C
2. D	12. E	22. E	32. E
3. A	13. D	23. E	33. D
4. C	14. B	24. A	34. A
5. B	15. E	25. B	35. A
6. B	16. D	26. E	
7. E	17. A	27. B	
8. B	18. E	28. C	
9. C	19. D	29. D	
10. D	20. C	30. E	

SECTION 6

1. A	6. C	11. C	16. 0	21. 12
2. C	7. A	12. B	17. 35	22. 6
3. C	8. B	13. D	18. 10	23. 5
4. A	9. C	14. C	19. 30	24. 125
5. B	10. D	15. B	20. 1	25. 1/25

Explanatory Answers

CRITICAL READING

1. The word *title* (line 1) is used throughout to mean

   (A) name
   (B) station
   (C) charter
   (D) interest
   (E) claim

   (E) *Title* is a word with multiple meanings, some of which are included in the answer choices. Only one meaning, however, fits the context, which has to do with the United States' right to the Philippines.

2. By "stamped with the likeness of the Creator" (line 7), Bryan refers to land that is

   (A) inhabited by humans
   (B) mountainous
   (C) beautiful
   (D) utopian
   (E) wracked by natural disasters

   (A) This is an interpretation question, and you must return to the citation in order to decipher the phrase. Earth "stamped with the likeness of the Creator" is contrasted with "inanimate earth" (line 5); therefore, it must refer to earth containing life. The lifeform that supposedly is in the likeness of the Creator is humankind.

3. What, according to Bryan, would be wrong with the United States' purchase of Spain's title?

   (A) It would not jibe with U.S. theories of government.
   (B) It would be hypocritical, because the United States challenged Spain's right to the Philippines.
   (C) Spain would have aided in the Filipinos' move to self-rule.
   (D) both A and B
   (E) both B and C

   (D) Check each choice, and, if necessary, reread the section of the passage where this is discussed. Bryan says two things in that paragraph: (1) that if the United States takes title, it must be held by a method "consistent with our ideas of government" (A), and (2) that the United States allied itself with the Filipinos to dispute Spain's right to the Philippines (B). Since (A) and (B) are true, the answer is (D).

4. The word *turpitude* (line 22) probably means

   (A) wickedness
   (B) flamboyance
   (C) passion
   (D) lethargy
   (E) tumult

   (A) The main clue in the sentence is the word *baser* (lower). Of all the choices, only (A) could refer to a *base* attribute. (B) is a synonym for *turgidity*, (C) is a synonym for *torridness*, (D) is a synonym for *torpor*, and (E) is a synonym for *turbulence*.

5. By "substitute our yoke for the Spanish yoke" (lines 22–23), Bryan implies that the Filipinos

   (A) will be better off under U.S. rule
   (B) work like oxen for their citizens
   (C) are trading one servant for another
   (D) are simply switching masters
   (E) cannot rule themselves

   (D) This is a straightforward metaphor. Yokes do apply to oxen, and the master is he who owns the yoke and harnesses the oxen. If the Filipinos are substituting one yoke for another, they are simply trading masters.

6. Bryan uses the images of stealing and killing to show that

   (A) war can drive men mad
   (B) some things are indisputable moral obligations
   (C) our control of the Philippines can only lead to trouble
   (D) a civilized nation has much to teach an uncivilized one
   (E) none of the above

   (B) To answer this synthesis/analysis question, return to the point in the passage where stealing and killing are discussed. Bryan begins by talking about duty and goes on to say that certain duties are imposed by "generally accepted principles." Included are the duty not to steal and the duty not to kill.

7. Bryan quotes Jefferson to support his contention that

   (A) every man has a price
   (B) without morality, conquest means nothing
   (C) nations must act according to moral law
   (D) people behave differently in groups than alone
   (E) none of the above

(C) This, too, is a synthesis/analysis question. You must understand the context in which the citation appears. In this case, Bryan is remarking that "some deny the application of [moral] laws to nations," but Jefferson would disagree.

8. By "a great gang" (line 49), Franklin implies that nations

   (A) should always act in concert
   (B) sometimes behave like hoodlums
   (C) achieve strength through numbers
   (D) succeed through teamwork
   (E) support their member citizens

   (B) As in question 7, understanding the context in which the citation appears will help you here. Franklin compares nations making unjust war to highwaymen plundering in a gang.

9. How does Bryan feel about the use of force?

   (A) It may be useful in defending freedom.
   (B) It does not excuse a bad policy.
   (C) It must be used sparingly.
   (D) both A and B
   (E) both B and C

   (D) This is an evaluation question that requires you to summarize and restate a sentence: "Force can defend a right, but force has never yet created a right." In other words, force may be useful in defending what is right, but it cannot put right what is wrong.

10. The "resolutions of intervention" (lines 54–55) must be decrees governing

    (A) intercession in other countries' affairs
    (B) originality and discoveries
    (C) treaties and pacts
    (D) post-war reconstruction
    (E) conflicts between nations

    (A) This is really more of a vocabulary question than an interpretation question, but if you do not know the word *intervention* in its connotation of *intercession*, you should still be able to determine the answer by looking at the context.

11. Bryan mentions the Declaration of Independence (lines 56–57) to

    (A) show the parallels among nations' fights for freedom
    (B) remind his listeners of Jefferson's role in our nation
    (C) shock his listeners with a little-known fact
    (D) both A and B
    (E) both B and C

    (A) Bryan did not need this parenthetical remark, but his inclusion of it emphasizes the parallels among the Philippines, Cuba, and the young United States.

12. This passage could be entitled

    (A) "Our National Destiny"
    (B) "The Goals of U.S. Imperialism"
    (C) "Without Fear or Favor"
    (D) "Standing by Our Allies"
    (E) "Our True Duty to the Philippines"

    (E) Look at the passage as a whole to answer this kind of evaluation question. (A) and (B) are too broad. (C) and (D) seem irrelevant. Only (E) gets to the focus of the passage: to open listeners' eyes to the United States' responsibility toward its ally, the Philippines.

SENTENCE COMPLETION

13. The victim confronted his attacker in the courtroom calmly, with ---- and without apparent ---- although he had been severely traumatized by the incident.

    (A) woe..composure
    (B) ineptitude..obstinacy
    (C) tempering..philanthropy
    (D) equanimity..rancor
    (E) scorn..malingering

    (D) This sentence has a thought-extender and a thought-reverser as its logical structure. The first blank is an extension of the word *calmly*. Eliminate (A), (B), and (C) on the grounds of usage. This leaves you with (D) and (E). *Scorn* does not extend the idea of calm, but *equanimity* does. Test the second element of (D). It should reverse the idea of *equanimity*, and it does.

14. The politician hungered for power; as a result of his ----, he succeeded in winning the election but ---- his closest friends and supporters.

    (A) furtiveness..dissuaded
    (B) winsomeness..disgruntled
    (C) malevolence..mesmerized
    (D) acerbity..seduced
    (E) cupidity..alienated

    (E) This question is basically a matter of vocabulary. The first blank requires a word that describes someone who is hungry for power. If you know that the word is *cupidity*, you have the question answered. Otherwise you will have to eliminate choices containing words you know cannot be correct and make your guess.

15. With the evidence ---- from numerous X-ray studies, scientists are beginning to form a picture of the atomic structure of the cell.

    (A) remanded   (B) gleaned   (C) pilfered
    (D) atrophied   (E) implored

    (B) This question is also a matter of vocabulary. You have two hints—the words *numerous* and *evidence.* There is only one word (if you know the definitions) that makes any sense in the blank. You can *glean* evidence from numerous studies.

16. According to recent studies, prices in supermarkets are considerably higher in the inner city, thus ---- the poor who receive assistance to buy the food.

    (A) reprimanding   (B) intimidating   (C) alleviating
    (D) assuaging   (E) exploiting

    (E) You can immediately eliminate choice (A) on the grounds of usage. Next, the blank must describe the consequences for the poor of high prices in the inner city. As for the remaining choices, the strongest connection is between high prices and exploitation.

17. Legislation to stop smoking in public places has been ---- by some as a move to save lives, while it is ---- by the tobacco industry which calls the action "alarmist."

    (A) heralded..condemned
    (B) thwarted..buffered
    (C) initiated..condoned
    (D) prejudiced..supported
    (E) extolled..elicited

    (A) This sentence contains a thought-reverser. Since the legislation is described as a move to save lives, you should be looking for a word with a positive connotation. (B) can be eliminated since no one would want to thwart something that saved lives. (A), (C), (E), and (D) remain possibilities. The second part of the sentence reverses the first part with the word *while*. The adjective *alarmist* tells you that you are looking for a word with negative overtones. (C), (D), and (E) can now be eliminated. This leaves you with (A).

ANALOGIES

18. NEST : SPARROW::

    (A) cave : drawing
    (B) flight : wing
    (C) lair : lion
    (D) meadow : lake
    (E) pond : water

    (C) This is a typical "place where" analogy. A SPARROW lives in a NEST, and a *lion* lives in a *lair*.

19. HANDWRITING : SIGNATURE::

    (A) biography : confession
    (B) eulogy : speech
    (C) painting : self-portrait
    (D) sculptor : model
    (E) sonnet : verse

(C) Although this analogy does not fit into any specific category, the relationship is quite clear. You might want to think of it as a highly specific "type of" analogy. HANDWRITING is general, and a SIGNATURE is a personal type of handwriting. A *painting* is general, but a *self-portrait*, like a SIGNATURE, is individual.

20. CONTENT : EUPHORIC::

    (A) puzzled : candid
    (B) obvious : complete
    (C) afraid : bold
    (D) sad : morose
    (E) sincere : calm

    (D) This is an analogy of degree. EUPHORIA is a more intense form of CONTENTMENT, and *moroseness* is a more intense degree of *sadness*.

21. TRIVIAL : IMPORTANCE::

    (A) tiny : magnitude
    (B) repetitious : pattern
    (C) portable : mobility
    (D) miraculous : faith
    (E) urgent : fallibility

    (A) This is a "lack of" analogy. Something lacking IMPORTANCE is TRIVIAL, and something lacking *magnitude* is *tiny*.

22. SQUANDER : ASSETS::

    (A) pronounce : judgment
    (B) exhaust : resources
    (C) fulfill : dream
    (D) accumulate : balance
    (E) obtain : goods

    (B) This analogy does not fit into any category, but the relationship is clear. ASSETS are SQUANDERED when they are used up, and *resources* are said to be *exhausted* when they are used up. Notice the echoes between SQUANDER and *exhaust*, and ASSETS and *resources*.

23. MOTE : DUST::

    (A) summit : mountain
    (B) drizzle : flood
    (C) gable : eave
    (D) bead : water
    (E) grain : particle

    (D) This is a type of part to whole analogy. A MOTE is a single unit of DUST. A *bead* is a single unit of *water*. Do not be distracted by *grain : particle*. Do not look for a secondary relationship unless you have first screened the choices. (E) would be more nearly correct if it were *grain : sand*.

24. CLANDESTINE : SECRECY::

    (A) personal : servant
    (B) imaginative : narrative
    (C) tumultuous : quiet
    (D) predictable : precision
    (E) confidential : privacy

    (E) This is a "defining characteristic" analogy. Something CLANDESTINE must be SECRET, and something *confidential* must be *private*.

25. REDOLENT : ODOR::

    (A) recurrent : expenditure
    (B) savory : taste
    (C) passive : aggression
    (D) constricted : vacuum
    (E) harmful : injury

    (B) This is a type of "defining characteristic" analogy. Part of the definition of REDOLENT is ODOR (redolent is a pleasing odor), and part of the definition of *savory* is *taste* (savory is a pleasing taste).

CRITICAL READING

26. The impression we are given of Blanche is that

    (A) she thinks she is clever
    (B) she is intolerant
    (C) she is sensitive
    (D) both A and B
    (E) both B and C

    (D) Blanche certainly thinks she is clever; words such as *triumphantly* indicate this. Aunt Sarah is not amused, however, because Blanche's cleverness is at the expense of her neighbors-to-be, about whom she says the most intolerant things. Since (A) and (B) are true, (D) must be the answer.

27. Why did Blanche feel sure the neighbors would be named Tomkinson or Hopkinson?

    (A) She knows both families.
    (B) She expected foreigners to move in.
    (C) Those are middle-class names.
    (D) The neighbors are American.
    (E) Blanche's surname is Hopkinson.

    (C) This is an interpretation question that requires some ability to interpret Blanche's motives. Most of her objections to the neighbors are class-related; she assumes that the family will not be upper class, and their name confirms this.

28. The word *imperturbable* (line 22) means

    (A) impassive
    (B) dense
    (C) preposterous
    (D) unrealistic
    (E) sensitive

(A) The clue here is the word *stolid*, which echoes *imperturbable*. A second clue is the phrase "incapable of any expression." The image is one of a calm, impassive woman.

29. The word *vivacities* (line 23) is used to mean

    (A) pep talks
    (B) lectures
    (C) buoyancies
    (D) vitality
    (E) jokes

    (E) (C) is almost right, but it is not a word that is used in plural form. (D) is close, but it is not Blanche's vitality that annoys Aunt Sarah; it is her silly jokes.

30. When Blanche refers to "their number" (line 26), she wishes to know

    (A) the Hopkinsons' rank
    (B) Mr. Hopkinson's line of work
    (C) the Hopkinsons' net worth
    (D) the address of the Hopkinsons
    (E) how many Hopkinsons there are

    (E) Go with your instincts, and you will probably choose correctly here. Blanche wants to know all about the Hopkinsons, from their history, to their habits, to their number. (A), (B), and (C) would probably be covered under history or habits, and Blanche already knows (D); she plans to be living there, too.

31. *Palings* (line 40) are probably

    (A) fences
    (B) buckets
    (C) beds
    (D) tables
    (E) stones

    (A) Toward what might a little boy throw a stone? Not toward (B), (C), (D), or (E), surely. Only (A) is correct; *palings* are fences made of *pales*, or pickets.

32. "As I suppose" (line 37) implies that Aunt Sarah

    (A) assumes the woman she saw was the mother
    (B) thinks the mother is just as she imagined she'd be
    (C) expected to see the mother when she appeared
    (D) both A and B
    (E) both B and C

    (A) Return to the context, and this question is easy to answer. Aunt Sarah is listing the people she saw. She never states or implies that she had any expectations, as (B) and (C) would indicate.

33. The word *contrive* (line 45) is used to mean

(A) fashion
(B) originate
(C) improvise
(D) scheme
(E) invent

(D) *Contrive* has many meanings, but only one of the meanings listed works in context. Blanche worries that Mrs. Hopkinson will be nosy and scheme to know what she has for dinner.

34. How does the author feel toward Blanche?

(A) charmed
(B) shocked
(C) vexed
(D) patient
(E) somber

(C) Blanche comes off as a silly creature, and that is entirely the author's doing. The author feels somewhat the way Aunt Sarah feels: annoyed, or vexed.

35. The character of Aunt Sarah is used as a

(A) counterpart to that of Blanche
(B) contrast to that of Blanche
(C) foil to that of the Hopkinsons
(D) target of old-fashioned witticisms
(E) symbol of change

(B) Blanche is flighty and talkative; Aunt Sarah, by her own admission, is dull and matter-of-fact. The last paragraph highlights the contrast between them.

SECTION 2

MATH PROBLEM-SOLVING

1. If $x + 2 = 7$ and $x + y = 11$, then $y =$

(A) 2   (B) 4   (C) 6   (D) 7   (E) 9

(C) Use the technique for solving simultaneous equations:

$x + 2 = 7$

$x = 5$

Therefore:

$5 + y = 11$

$y = 6$

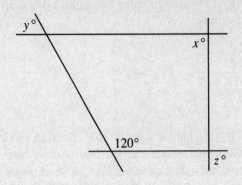

2. In the figure above, if $y + z = 150$, then $x =$

(A) 30   (B) 45   (C) 75   (D) 90   (E) 120

(D) $x + y + z + 120 = 360$

$x + y + z = 240$

$x + 150 = 240$

$x = 90$

The product of x and 5 is equal to one-half the sum of $3x$ and 3.

---

3. Which of the following equations correctly expresses the relationship described above?

(A) $5x = \dfrac{9x}{2}$ (B) $5x = 2(3x + 3)$

(C) $5x = \dfrac{(3x + 3)}{2}$ (D) $\dfrac{x}{5} = 2(3x + 3)$

(E) $\dfrac{x}{5} = \dfrac{(3x + 3)}{2}$

(C) The product of x and 5 is $5x$. And the sum of $3x$ and 3 is $3x + 3$. Since the first expression is equal to $\frac{1}{2}$ of the second expression, the entire statement can be written in "algebrese" as $5x = \frac{1}{2}(3x + 3)$.

4. If $x > -5$, then $(x + 7)$ could be

(A) -1 (B) 0   (C) 1   (D) 2   (E) 3

(E) If x is more than -5, then $x + 7$ must be more than 2. The only answer choice greater than 2 is (E), 3.

5. During a sale, three of a certain item can be purchased for the usual cost of 2 of the items. If John buys 36 of the items at the sale price, how many of the items could he have bought at the regular price?

(A) 18   (B) 24   (C) 30   (D) 48   (E) 72

(B) One way to solve this question is with a proportion:

$$\frac{3}{2} = \frac{36}{x}$$

$$3x = 72$$

$$x = 24$$

Or you can assume some concrete values. For example, assume that the item usually costs $3. So two such items usually cost $6. And on sale, John can buy three for $6, which is $2 apiece. If he buys 36 items at $2 apiece, he pays $72. For $72, at the regular price, he could have purchased $72 ÷ 3 = 24 items.

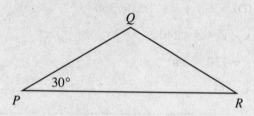

Note: Figure not drawn to scale

6. In *PQR* above, if *PQ = QR*, then *x* =
   (A) 30   (B) 60   (C) 90   (D) 120   (E) 150

(D) Since *PQ = PR*, angle *PRQ* = 30°, and

$$30 + 30 + x = 180$$

$$60 + x = 180$$

$$x = 120$$

7. If $px + 2 = 8$ and $qx + 3 = 10$, what is the value of $\frac{p}{q}$?

   (A) $\frac{3}{5}$ (B) $\frac{8}{15}$ (C) $\frac{10}{13}$

   (D) $\frac{6}{7}$ (E) $\frac{16}{13}$

(D) Here you have simultaneous equations. Look for a way to make a direct substitution of one quantity for another or for a way to compare two quantities directly. In this case, $px = 6$ and $qx = 7$. So $\frac{px}{qx} = \frac{6}{7}$, and $\frac{p}{q} = \frac{6}{7}$.

   You can also solve the problem by assuming a value for *x*, say 1. On that assumption $p = 6$, $q = 7$, and $\frac{p}{q} = \frac{6}{7}$. Which is choice (D).

8. If $2^x = 16$ and $x = \frac{y}{2}$, then $y =$
   (A) 2   (B) 3   (C) 4   (D) 6   (E) 8

(E) You can arrive at the correct answer by reasoning that since $2^x = 16$, $x = 4$. Therefore, $4 = \frac{y}{2}$ and $y = 8$. Or you can work backwards by substituting answers. If $y = 8$, then $x = 4$, and it is true that $2^4 = 16$.

9. The figure above shows a correctly done addition problem. What is the value of ■?
   (A) 2   (B) 4   (C) 6   (D) 8   (E) 9

(A) You can arrive at the correct answer by reasoning that there is only one digit that, when added to 2, will yield 6. That digit is 4. And 4 + 8 = 12, so ■ = 2.

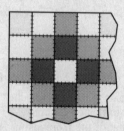

10. A square quilt is made by sewing together square pieces of cloth as shown in the figure above. What is the least number of cloth squares with an area of 16 square inches that will be needed to create a square quilt with a side of 32 inches?
    (A) 16   (B) 32   (C) 64   (D) 128   (E) 256

(C) This is really just a composite figure problem. Each individual square has an area of 16 and therefore a side of 4. A square quilt with a side of 32 inches will have 32 ÷ 4 = 8 squares to a side. So the entire quilt will consist of 8 × 8 = 64 squares.

11. If a triangle has a height of $\frac{1}{x}$ and an area of 2, what is the length of the base of the triangle?

    (A) $4x$ (B) x (C) $\frac{1}{2}x$ (D) $\frac{1}{4}x$ (E) x^2

(A) Use the formula for finding the area of a triangle.

Area = $\frac{1}{2}$ × altitude (or height) × base

$2 = \frac{1}{2}\left(\frac{1}{x}\right)$ (base)

$4 = \left(\frac{1}{x}\right)$ (base)

$4x$ = base

So the base of the triangle is equal to $4x$.

12. If the sum of three numbers is $4x$ and the sum of four other numbers is $3x$, then the average (arithmetic mean) of all seven numbers is

(A) $7x$ (B) x (C) $\frac{x}{7}$ (D) 7   (E) 1

(B) Use the formula for finding an average:

$\frac{4x + 3x}{7}$ = Average

$\frac{7x}{7}$ = Average

x = Average

Of course, you can also substitute numbers. Assume that $x = 10$. The average of 7 numbers would be $[4(10) + 3(10)] \div 7 = \frac{70}{7} = 10$. When you substitute 10 for x into the choices, only (B) yields the value 10.

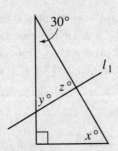

13. In the figure above, if $x = y$, then $z =$
(A) 30   (B) 45   (C) 60   (D) 75   (E) 90

(E) $x + 30 + 90 = 180$

$x = 60$

Since $x = y$, $y = 60$:

$60 + 30 + z = 180$

$z = 90$

14. If $6 \leqq x \leqq 30$, $3 \leqq y \leqq 12$, and $2 \leqq z \leqq 10$, then what is the least possible value of $\frac{x + y}{z}$?

(A) $\frac{9}{10}$ (B) $\frac{9}{5}$ (C) $\frac{21}{5}$ (D) $\frac{9}{2}$ (E) 21

(A) The least possible value for the expression $\frac{x + y}{z}$ will occur when x and y are the least and z is greatest:

$\frac{(6 + 3)}{10} = \frac{9}{10}$

15. If $x \neq 0$, then $\frac{(-3x)^3}{-3x^3} =$

(A) -9 (B) -3 (C) -1 (D) 3   (E) 9

(E) Just use the rules for manipulating exponents to do the indicated operations:

$\frac{(-3x)^3}{-3x^3} = \frac{-27x^3}{-3x^3} = 9$

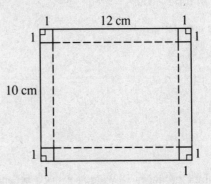

16. The figure above shows a rectangular piece of cardboard with sides of 10 centimeters and 12 centimeters. From each of the four corners, a square 1 centimeter by 1 centimeter is cut out. If an open rectangular box is then formed by folding along the dotted lines, what is the volume of the box in cubic centimeters?

(A) 80   (B) 96   (C) 99   (D) 120   (E) 168

(A) The dimensions of the box will be 1, 8, and 10. The volume, therefore, is $1 \times 8 \times 10 = 80$.

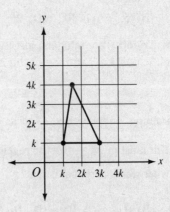

17. If the area of the triangle in the figure above is 12, then $k =$

(A) 1   (B) 2   (C) 3   (D) 4   (E) 6

(B) The base of the triangle is $3k - k = 2k$, and the altitude of the triangle is $4k - k = 3k$:

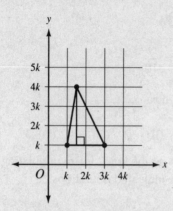

$$\frac{1}{2} \times \text{altitude} \times \text{base} = \text{area}$$

So the area is:

$$\frac{1}{2}(2k)(3k) = 12$$

$$3k^2 = 12$$

$$k^2 = 4$$

$$k = 2$$

18. A machine produces 18 widgets every 5 seconds. How many widgets does it produce in an hour?

(A) 720   (B) 1,000   (C) 1,296
(D) 10,000   (E) 12,960

(E) The calculation is not that difficult to do:

$$18 \times \left(\frac{60}{5}\right) \times 60 = 12,960$$

19. If x and y are two different positive integers and $x^3 y^2 = 200$, then $xy =$

(A) 5   (B) 6   (C) 10   (D) 25   (E) 40

(C) Since x and y are integers, just try substituting numbers: y must be 5 and x must be 2.

20. After trimming, a sapling has $\frac{9}{10}$ of its original height. If it must grow $\frac{9}{10}$ foot to regain its original height, what was its original height?

(A) 8   (B) 9   (C) 10   (D) 16   (E) 18

(B) You can set up an equation. Let h be the original height of the sapling:

$$\frac{9h}{10} + \frac{9}{10} = h$$

And solve for h:

$$\frac{h}{10} = \frac{9}{10}$$

$$h = 9$$

You can also test the choices.

21. A tank contains g gallons of water. Water flows into the tank by one pipe at the rate of m gallons per minute, and water flows out by another pipe at the rate of n gallons per minute. If $n > m$, how many minutes will it take to empty the tank?

(A) $\dfrac{(g - m)}{n}$ (B) $\dfrac{g}{(m - n)}$ (C) $\dfrac{(n - g)}{m}$

(D) $\dfrac{(n - m)}{g}$ (E) $\dfrac{g}{(n - m)}$

(E) Since $n > m$, the net drain from the tank per minute will be $n - m$. So the time required to empty the tank is $\frac{g}{(n-m)}$. You can arrive at the same conclusion by substituting numbers.

22. If $\dfrac{13t}{7}$ is an integer, then t could be any of the following EXCEPT

(A) -91 (B) -7 (C) 3   (D) 70   (E) 91

(C) The easiest way to attack this problem is to test the test. Each of the numbers given in the choices will produce an integer except for the value given in (C): $\frac{13(3)}{7} = \frac{39}{7}$, which is not an integer.

23. If $\dfrac{(x + y)}{x} = 4$ and $\dfrac{(y + z)}{z} = 5$, what is the value of $\dfrac{x}{z}$?

(A) $\dfrac{1}{4}$ (B) $\dfrac{1}{3}$ (C) $\dfrac{3}{4}$ (D) $\dfrac{4}{3}$ (E) $\dfrac{3}{1}$

(D) Rewrite the equations:

$$\frac{(x + y)}{x} = 4$$

$$4x = x + y$$

$$3x = y$$

$$\frac{(y + z)}{z} = 5$$

$$y + z = 5z$$

$$4z = y$$

Since $3x$ and $4z$ are both equal to y,

$$3x = 4z$$

$$\frac{x}{z} = \frac{4}{3}$$

24. On Monday, Juan withdraws $\frac{1}{2}$ of the money in his savings account. On Tuesday, he withdraws another $60, leaving $\frac{1}{5}$ of the original amount in the account. How much money was originally in Juan's savings account?

    (A) $600   (B) $300   (C) $200
    (D) $150   (E) $120

    (C) Set up an equation, using x for the original amount:

    $$\frac{1}{2}(x) - \$60 = \frac{1}{5}(x)$$

    $$\frac{1}{2}x - \frac{1}{5}x = \$60$$

    $$\frac{3}{10}x = 60$$

    $$x = 200$$

    You can also test choices.

25. A painter is planning to paint a row of three houses, using the colors red, gray, and white. If each house is to be painted a single color, and if the painter must use each of the three colors, how many different ways are there of painting the three houses?

    (A) 1   (B) 2   (C) 3   (D) 6   (E) 9

    (D) Just count the different possibilities: RGW, RWG, GRW, GWR, WRG, WGR.

SECTION 3

CRITICAL READING

1. The main point of Congreve's second paragraph is that

   (A) wit is more important to comedy than humor is
   (B) audiences do not know the difference between wit and folly
   (C) there is a difference between humorous language and a humorous character
   (D) playwrights give humorous lines to tragic characters
   (E) characters who speak pleasantly are often humorous

   (C) This evaluation question asks you to summarize a paragraph and determine its main idea. If you do not immediately spot the answer, use the process

of elimination. Nowhere does Congreve state (A); he does not mention *folly* (B) until later in the essay. He does not speak of tragedy at all (D), and (E) is exactly the opposite of the point he is trying to make.

2. The word *appropriated* (lines 19–20) is used by Congreve to mean

   (A) commandeered
   (B) seized
   (C) corrected
   (D) assigned
   (E) fitted

   (D) Substituting the choices for the word in question proves that only one of the many meanings of *appropriated* works in context: "different humors [are assigned] to the several persons represented."

3. The word *abstracted* in Congreve's piece (line 32) means

   (A) disturbed
   (B) confounded
   (C) summarized
   (D) removed
   (E) condensed

   (D) (A) and (B) are synonyms for *distracted*. The other words are synonyms for *abstracted*, but only (D) works in context.

4. Congreve believes that humor must be

   (A) self-sufficient
   (B) natural
   (C) pointed
   (D) rare
   (E) unexpected

   (B) This is Congreve's main idea: that humor is not humor when it is "abstracted from nature."

5. Congreve uses the word *peculiar* (line 37) to mean

   (A) characteristic
   (B) quaint
   (C) outlandish
   (D) odd
   (E) unusual

   (A) Each of the choices is a synonym for *peculiar*, but only (A) fits in the context of a trait "natural to one man only."

6. When Bergson remarks, "the mischief is done" (line 43), he means

   (A) the playwright has ruined his play
   (B) an element of tragedy has been injected
   (C) the possibility of humor has been removed
   (D) both A and B
   (E) both B and C

(E) The characteristics Bergson lists—sympathy, fear, and pity—are elements of tragedy, not comedy. Bergson's point is that when appeals are made to the emotions, humor is removed, and comedy becomes tragedy.

7. The word *moment*, used by Bergson in line 52, means

   (A) flash
   (B) period
   (C) minute
   (D) importance
   (E) time

   (D) "Of little moment" means "of little importance." None of the time-related meanings of *moment* makes sense here.

8. What does Bergson think about emotional response to drama?

   (A) It is a prerequisite to understanding.
   (B) It is especially inappropriate nowadays.
   (C) It has no place in a comedy.
   (D) both A and B
   (E) both B and C

   (C) This evaluation question tests your understanding of Bergson's main idea. If emotions are aroused, comedy is lost. This is not bad, necessarily, but emotional response cannot co-exist with humor.

9. Both passages are essentially

   (A) fictional
   (B) definitional
   (C) comical
   (D) argumentative
   (E) lyrical

   (B) Both passages give the authors' definitions of humor. They are fairly straightforward, and although one might argue with them, they are not, of themselves, argumentative (D).

10. Bergson and Congreve agree that one important element of humor is

    (A) folly
    (B) unsociability
    (C) wit
    (D) involuntary behavior
    (E) absentmindedness

    (D) This kind of evaluation question asks you to compare the passages and find an element in common. Review the choices. Congreve mentions *folly* (A) and *wit* (C), but Bergson does not. Bergson mentions *unsociability* (B) and *absentmindedness* (E), but Congreve does not. Both, however, discuss the naturalness of humor, its *unavoidability* (according to Congreve) and its *automatism* (according to Bergson).

654

SECTION 4

MATH PROBLEM-SOLVING

Dimensions of 5 different boxes	
Box A:	$2 \times 3 \times 4$
Box B:	$2 \times 3 \times 3$
Box C:	$3 \times 4 \times 5$
Box D:	$5 \times 4 \times 2$
Box E:	$4 \times 4 \times 2$

1. If the sides of each box described above are perpendicular to each other, which box has the greatest volume?

   (A) A   (B) B   (C) C   (D) D   (E) E

   (C) You can solve the problem just by multiplying the numbers shown to find the volume of each box. But a better attack strategy is to use a benchmark. For example, Box A, which is 2 x 3 x 4, must be larger than Box B, which is 2 x 3 x 3.

2. The product of an even, positive number and an odd, negative number is

   (A) negative and even
   (B) negative and odd
   (C) negative and either even or odd
   (D) positive and odd
   (E) positive and even

   (A) An even number times an odd number yields an even number, and a positive number times a negative number yields a negative number. So the multiplication described in the question stem results in a number that is both negative and even. Or you can just try numbers to test the choices.

3. If w, x, y, and z are positive numbers, each of the following expressions equals $w(x + y + z)$ EXCEPT

   (A) $wx + wy + wz$
   (B) $wx + w(y + z)$
   (C) $w(x + y) + wz$
   (D) $w(x + z) + wy$
   (E) $w(xy) + w(yz)$

   (E) If you can't do the algebra, assume some values. Let w, x, y, and z all be 1. On that assumption $w(x + y + z) = 1(1 + 1 + 1) = 1(3) = 3$. Then substitute 1 for w, x, y, and z into the answer choices. Every choice yields the value 3 except for (E).

4. Originally, a group of 11 students were supposed to share equally a cash prize. If 1 more student is added to the group and the 12 students share the prize equally, then each new share is worth what fraction of each original share?

   (A) $\frac{1}{12}$ (B) $\frac{1}{11}$ (C) $\frac{1}{10}$ (D) $\frac{10}{11}$ (E) $\frac{11}{12}$

(E) You can reason to a conclusion as follows. If the prize is x, originally each student would receive $\frac{x}{11}$. When another student is added, each student will receive only $\frac{x}{12}$. So each student will finally receive $\frac{\frac{x}{12}}{\frac{x}{11}} = \frac{11}{12}$ of what he would originally receive.

You can also solve the problem by assuming some values. For example, assume the prize is worth \$132 (a convenient assumption since 11 x 12 = 132). Originally a student would have received \$12. After the addition of another student to the group, the prize is worth only \$11. So the second prize is worth only $\frac{11}{12}$ of the first.

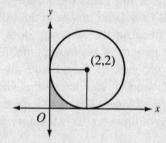

5. In the figure above, the center of the circle has coordinates (2,2). What is the area of the shaded portion of the figure?

(A) $2 - \pi$ (B) $4 - \pi$ (C) $8 - 2\pi$
(D) $8 - \pi$ (E) $16 - 4\pi$

(B) This is a shaded area problem. The shaded area is the square minus $\frac{1}{4}$ of the circle. The square has a side of 2 and an area of $2 \times 2 = 4$. The circle has a radius of 2 and an area of $\pi r^2 = \pi(2)^2 = 4\pi$. $\frac{1}{4}$ of the circle is simply π, so the shaded area is $4 - \pi$.

Having X and Y	10
Having X but not Y	30
Having Y but not X	20
Having neither X nor Y	40

6. The table above gives the distribution of two genetic characteristics, X and Y, in a population of 100 subjects. What is the ratio of the number of people having characteristic X to the number of people having the characteristic Y?

(A) 1:3   (B) 1:2   (C) 2:3   (D) 4:3   (E) 3:2

(D) The number of people having x is $10 + 30 = 40$ and the number of people having y is $10 + 20 = 30$. So the ratio is 4:3.

7. If $x - y = 42$, then $2x - 2y =$
(A) 21   (B) 42   (C) 84   (D) $2(x + y)$
(E) Cannot be determined from the information given.

(C) Solve this, if you do not immediately see the answer, by plugging values of your choice into the equations.

If $43 - 1 = 42$, then $2(43) - 2(1) = 86 - 2 = 84$.

Test with two other values:

If $50 - 8 = 42$, then $2(50) - 2(8) = 100 - 16 = 84$.

8. You can buy $4\frac{1}{2}$ pounds of scallops for \$40.50. How much would you pay for 3 pounds?

(A) \$25.50   (B) \$27   (C) \$30   (D) \$35   (E) \$45

(B) If you do this in your head, you might choose (C) accidentally. The first step is to find the price per pound.

$\$40.50 \div 4\frac{1}{2} = \$40.50 \div 4.5 = 9 \ (not \ 10)$.

Scallops are \$9 per pound, so 3 pounds cost \$27.

9. A bowling team has 5 members, 40% of whom averaged over 230 this fall. Of those over-230 scorers, 50% had scores averaging 250 or better. How many people had scores averaging below 250?

(A) 1   (B) 2   (C) 3   (D) 4   (E) 5

(D) Begin by finding 40% of 5:

$$\frac{40}{100}(5) = \frac{200}{100} = 2$$

Now find 50% of that: 1

If 1 person had a score averaging 250 or better, and there are 5 people in all, 4 had a score averaging below 250.

10. If $x = -21$, what is the value of $x + (x - x)$?
(A) -42 (B) -21 (C) 0   (D) 21   (E) 42

(B) Plug in -21 in place of x.

$-21 + (-21 - -21) = -21 + (-21 + 21)$

$= -21 + 0$

$= -21$

SECTION 5

SENTENCE COMPLETIONS

1. His seemingly casual and ---- tone ---- a serious concern for the welfare of his clients.

   (A) flippant..belied
   (B) worried..displayed
   (C) effective..disputed
   (D) callous..betrayed
   (E) contentious..minimized

   (A) This sentence contains a thought-extender and a thought-reverser. The first blank must extend the idea of *casual*, and only (A) can possibly do that. Checking the second element of (A), *belie* means to disguise, a word which does reverse the *seemingly casual* part of the sentence. He seemed casual but he wasn't.

2. The actress owed her reputation to her ---- public and not to the ---- reviews which bordered on being cruel.

   (A) diffident..approbatory
   (B) congenial..simpering
   (C) trusting..didactic
   (D) adoring..scathing
   (E) innocent..deferential

   (D) This sentence contains a thought-reverser and a thought-extender. Start with the second blank. You need to describe reviews which border on cruel, and only (D) does that. (A) would convey exactly the opposite and therefore wrong meaning. (C) has nothing at all to do with cruelty; and (B) and (E) do not create meaningful phrases. Based on the second blank alone the answer is (D). Now let's check the first element of (D). It should reverse the idea of *scathing* reviews, and it does; she has *adoring* fans, and thus a reputation.

3. Treason is punishable by death because ---- constitutes a threat to the very ---- of the state.

   (A) perfidy..survival
   (B) grief..existence
   (C) veracity..foundation
   (D) pacifism..dismantling
   (E) patriotism..well-being

   (A) This question is largely a test of vocabulary. The first blank asks for a synonym for *treason*. This can only be *perfidy*. Even if you do not know the meaning of the correct choice, you can eliminate (B) and (E) because neither *grief* nor *patriotism* means *treason*. Now, you are left with (A) and (C), so look at the second elements of both choices. Both seem to create meaningful phrases. Ulti-

mately, then, the question turns on the meaning of *perfidy*. But even if you don't know the meanings of *perfidy* and *veracity* you still have a 50–50 chance of answering correctly—so guess!

4. Although scientists have sought to measure time, only writers and poets have truly ---- its quality and our ---- experience of it.

   (A) neglected..uniform
   (B) understood..benign
   (C) captured..ephemeral
   (D) belied..credulous
   (E) devised..fractious

   (C) This sentence has a thought-reverser introduced by the word *although*. The sentence says that writers and poets have done something that scientists have been unable to do. (A) is not a good choice because the sentence does not mean to say that they have *neglected* time. (D) and (E) fail on the grounds of usage. You are left with (B) and (C); and if you know the vocabulary, the answer is obvious. One can't have a *benign* experience of time, so (C) is the answer.

5. Although a gala performance, the conducting was ----, and the orchestra less than enthusiastic, but the audience seemed ---- the defects and was enthralled.

   (A) auspicious...sensitive to
   (B) perfunctory..oblivious to
   (C) decimated..mindful of
   (D) voracious..excited by
   (E) animated..impaired by

   (B) This sentence contains two thought-reversers. *Although* tells you that the conducting was something not expected at a gala or special occasion. You can immediately eliminate (C) and (D) because when substituted into the blanks they don't create meaningful phrases. Then, the fact that the orchestra was not enthusiastic is an extender of the word in the blank, so it is not likely that the conducting was *auspicious* or *animated*. You are left with (B).

6. Since there are so few conservative thinkers on the committee, their influence on its recommendations is ---- .

   (A) monumental   (B) negligible   (C) discriminatory
   (D) impractical   (E) cathartic

   (B) This sentence gives you a logical clue with the word *since*. You know that because of something, something else will be true. The next important word is *few*. Since there are only a few conservatives, their influence must be ----. So you might anticipate a choice such as *slight* or *insignificant*. Eliminate (D) and (E) on the ground of usage. (A) makes no sense because it is not logical that only a few would have a *monumental* influence. (C), *discriminatory*, doesn't have anything to do with the fact that there are only a few conservatives. You are left with (B). It does make perfect sense to say that the influence of a few would be *negligible*.

7. Laboratory tests which often maim animals and depend solely on observation to determine results are not only ---- but highly ---- since no two people see the same thing.

   (A) safe..consistent
   (B) patented..conclusive
   (C) controversial..valuable
   (D) gratifying..explosive
   (E) cruel..unreliable

   (E) This sentence begins with a thought-extender. The first blank requires an adjective that extends the idea of a test which maims animals. (D) is not a possible choice because one would not be gratified by the maiming of animals. Although (A) and (B) makes some sense, the fact that maiming is mentioned gives you a clue that the adjective will have a negative connotation. This leaves you with (C) and (E). Now you have to look at the second blank. This also requires an adjective that summarizes what comes after the blank. Since no two people see the same thing, the test is something. Only the second element of (E), *unreliable*, works.

8. Execution by lethal injection, although horrifying, is certainly more civilized than the—penalty of death by torture or dismemberment.

   (A) pervasive   (B) viler   (C) humane
   (D) prolific   (E) complacent

   (B) This is a fairly easy sentence. There is one thought-reverser introduced by *although*. Although something is *horrifying*, something else is worse. The answer choices are easy vocabulary words. What word is stronger than *horrifying*? (A) and (D) make no sense. (C) and (E) are not adjectives one would use to describe torture or dismemberment. (B), *viler*, is the only possibility.

9. Although vitamins are helpful for maintaining good health, alcohol, caffeine, and other drugs severely ---- their effectiveness, leaving the body's defenses ----.

   (A) augment..weakened
   (B) reduce..indelible
   (C) inhibit..impaired
   (D) confuse..allied
   (E) duplicate..activated

   (C) This sentence contains a thought-reverser and a thought-extender as its logical keys. The *although* tells you that what comes after the comma will be an idea which is the opposite of good health. You can eliminate (D) and (E) on the grounds of usage. You can eliminate (A) because *augment* means to increase, extending rather than reversing the thought. This leaves you with (B) and (C). The second part of the sentence is an extension of the first blank. You can immediately eliminate (B) because a body's defenses cannot be *indelible*. This leaves you with (C). The body's defenses are *impaired* if the effectiveness of vitamins is *inhibited*.

10. To understand a work of art it is necessary to place it in ---- context to capture its ---- significance as well as its present meaning.

    (A) a specious..referential
    (B) a random..cumulative
    (C) an inventive..partial
    (D) a historical..original
    (E) a sophisticated..international

    (D) There is not much you can do with this sentence except to substitute the words into the blanks. Eliminate (B), (C), and (E) on the grounds that they make meaningless phrases. (A) is not really logical because you can't capture the significance of something by putting it into a false context. This leaves you with (D), which clearly works.

11. He is an ---- student and a ---- to teach.

    (A) intrepid..hazard
    (B) exceptional..joy
    (C) exuberant..power
    (D) insipid..threat
    (E) ironic..jubilation

    (B) The second phrase extends the first. Whatever kind of student he is results in his being a ---- to teach. An *intrepid* student (A) might be tricky to teach, but you would never call him a *hazard*. No one would ever be called a *power*, a *threat* or a *jubilation* to teach (C), (D), and (E). However, a student who is *exceptional* (outstanding) could be a *joy* to teach.

12. My work in the field of ---- takes me to ---- around the world.

    (A) spelunking..homes
    (B) geology..castles
    (C) psychiatry..sanity
    (D) ichthyology..gardens
    (E) archaeology..ruins

(E) This is a vocabulary question. If you know that *spelunking* is the art of caving, you know that (A) makes no sense. *Geology* is the study of the earth, so (B) makes no sense, either. You can't be taken to *sanity* around the world, so (C) is out. *Ichthyology* is the study of fish, so (D) is out. *Archaeology* is the study of ancient cultures, so it makes sense that you would visit ruins to pursue it.

13. Do you like foreign films, or do you prefer your art ----?

    (A) scenic
    (B) alien
    (C) customary
    (D) domestic
    (E) eleemosynary

    (D) *Or* signals you that you need to find a word that reverses the notion expressed in the first phrase; in other words, you need an antonym for *foreign*. The only such word is *domestic; customary* (C) does not have the correct shade of meaning. *Eleemosynary* (E) means "philanthropic."

14. Tears of the ---- are common in ----.

    (A) sorrow..rulers
    (B) cartilage..competitors
    (C) spine..athletes
    (D) helmet..sports
    (E) lesion..activity

    (B) This question plays on the word *tears*, which can be pronounced two ways with very different meanings. Because you would not say "the sorrow" in English, (A) is incorrect. Of the remaining choices, only *cartilage* is something one might *tear*.

15. A small ---- meandered lyrically through the pasture.

    (A) wellhead
    (B) kine
    (C) gulch
    (D) brine
    (E) rivulet

    (E) The clues are *small, meandered,* and *lyrically.* A *gulch* (C) might meander, but it would not do so lyrically (musically). Only a small stream such as a *rivulet* could do that.

ANALOGIES

16. SCISSORS : CUTTING::

    (A) knife : cooking
    (B) scalpel : medicine
    (C) arrow : quiver
    (D) needle : sewing
    (E) hatchet : hunting

(D) The relationship in this simple analogy is clear. SCISSORS are tools used for CUTTING, and *needles* are tools used for *sewing.*

17. RECIPE : FOOD::

    (A) blueprint : building
    (B) formula : scientist
    (C) ingredient : concoction
    (D) liquid : consumption
    (E) score : performer

    (A) You might formulate a diagnostic sentence for this analogy such as "RECIPES are instructions for preparing FOOD," and *"blueprints* are instructions for constructing *buildings."* (E) is an attractive distractor, but it doesn't fit the diagnostic sentence as precisely as (A) does, and you can prove it wrong by improving on it. *Score : music* would fit the diagnostic sentence much more precisely.

18. DEBATER : ARGUMENT::

    (A) minister : congregation
    (B) poet : artist
    (C) chauffeur : passenger
    (D) boxer : ring
    (E) musician : instrument

    (E) This is like a "tool" analogy. The tool of a DEBATER is an ARGUMENT, and the tool of a *musician* is an *instrument.*

19. GRAIN : SILO::

    (A) vitamin : nutrition
    (B) farm : tractor
    (C) van : warehouse
    (D) water : reservoir
    (E) money : investor

    (D) This a fairly easy analogy. A SILO is a place to store GRAIN, and a *reservoir* is a place to store *water.* Don't be distracted by the secondary relationship between SILO and *warehouse.* Your diagnostic sentence will eliminate (C).

20. IMPROMPTU : PLANNING::

    (A) gratuitous : ticket
    (B) dramatic : rehearsal
    (C) cursory : care
    (D) ravenous : appetite
    (E) enlightened : knowledge

    (C) This is a "lack of" analogy. Something that is IMPROMPTU is characterized by a lack of PLANNING, and something that is *cursory* is characterized by a lack of *care.*

21. LACONIC : WORDS::

(A) affable : friends
(B) hesitant : action
(C) monotonous : address
(D) tolerant : laughter
(E) ambitious : calamity

(B) This is also a "lack of" analogy. A defining characteristic of LACONIC is a lack of WORDS and a defining characteristic of *hesitant* is a lack of *action*. In more idiomatic English, one who is LACONIC speaks little, and one who is *hesitant* does not take *action*.

22. RECIDIVISM : CRIMINAL::

(A) justice : plaintiff
(B) bankruptcy : lawyer
(C) condemnation : authority
(D) finesse : magician
(E) relapse : patient

(E) Since RECIDIVISM means return to CRIMINAL behavior, the best analogy is (E). A *relapse* is a *patient's* return to illness.

23. INAUGURATE : BEGINNING::

(A) encapsulate : thought
(B) advise : dissension
(C) prevaricate : prank
(D) forbid : sanction
(E) consecrate : dedication

(E) This is an analogy based on a defining characteristic. By definition, an INAUGURATION is a BEGINNING, and a *consecration* is a *dedication*.

24. ELEGIAC : MOURNING

(A) contemptuous : disdain
(B) rambunctious : enervation
(C) profligate : lassitude
(D) amorphous : spontaneity
(E) deferential : veracity

(A) This is also a defining characteristic analogy. By definition, that which is ELEGIAC is MOURNFUL, and that which is *contemptuous* is *disdainful*.

25. DISCERNING : PERCEPTION::

(A) moribund : defilement
(B) oblivious : forgetfulness
(C) interminable : brevity
(D) ambiguous : clarity
(E) loathsome : decrepitude

(B) This is a defining characteristic relationship. A defining characteristic of DISCERNING is PERCEPTION, and a defining characteristic of *oblivious* is *forgetfulness*.

CRITICAL READING

26. The word *parochial* (line 8) means

(A) church
(B) religious
(C) unlimited
(D) boundless
(E) local

(E) The parochial road is contrasted with the main road in this paragraph. Unlike the main road, it is unpaved. Only (E) works in this context.

27. Why does McKay define an Indian word in paragraph 2?

(A) to show how the Indians lived long ago
(B) to explain how his country got its name
(C) to amuse his audience with jargon
(D) to impress readers with his erudition
(E) to reveal that his land once belonged to Indians

(B) *Xaymaca* is, of course, the Indian word from which Jamaica derives its name. McKay's purpose is to explain this, not to reveal an Indian past (E), although that revelation is implicit in his statement.

28. The word *cake* (line 17) is used to mean

(A) batter
(B) sweet
(C) encrust
(D) dance
(E) fill

(C) It is clay that is "caking"; in other words, clay is encrusting the legs of the peasants.

29. Paragraph 4 is mostly about

(A) rain
(B) crops
(C) rituals
(D) hurricanes
(E) seasonal change

(D) This kind of evaluation question simply asks you to summarize a paragraph. McKay mentions rain (A) and crops (B), but his focus is on hurricanes.

30. The Obeahmen were "accordingly popular" (line 42) because they could

(A) rebuild flattened buildings
(B) cast out demons
(C) calm the gods
(D) both A and B
(E) both B and C

(E) This interpretation question requires you to return to the passage and interpret the lines that surround the citation. Obeahmen use "exorcism" or "appease the god"; they cast out demons (B) and calm the gods (C). Since both (B) and (C) are correct, the answer is (E).

31. McKay lists the foods made from corn meal (line 48) to show

    (A) how dull the Jamaican peasant's diet was
    (B) how little one could buy with money in those days
    (C) how cleverly the peasants used meager food-stuffs
    (D) both A and B
    (E) both B and C

    (C) The clue to McKay's meaning is the phrase "all kinds of food." He is listing the kinds to show variety, not dullness (A). The fact that the peasants use their money to buy "barrels and bags of flour" belies (B) as well.

32. The word *burgeoning* (line 55) means

    (A) planting
    (B) waving
    (C) flowering
    (D) withering
    (E) sprouting

    (E) The answer could be (C), but grass is more likely to sprout than to flower. This is an example of a question that requires careful rereading of the text.

33. How does McKay feel about the place and time about which he is writing?

    (A) uncomfortable
    (B) self-consciously critical
    (C) unemotional and matter-of-fact
    (D) fondly nostalgic
    (E) flippantly casual

    (D) This evaluation question focuses on tone. Go with your first impression here; this is a nostalgic piece. McKay's memories are charming, not depressing or sordid, and his tone is upbeat rather than flat (C) or indifferent (E).

34. How can you tell that this piece reflects bygone times?

    (A) The author uses phrases such as "I remember" and "I recall."
    (B) There are no peasants left in Jamaica; times have changed.
    (C) The village of Sunny Ville was long ago destroyed by a hurricane.
    (D) both A and B
    (E) both B and C

(A) There is no support for (B) or (C), so (A) is the only possible choice. The author does indeed use phrases such as "I remember" and "I recall"; see lines 16 and 44.

35. The main focus of the passage is

    (A) descriptive
    (B) didactic
    (C) preachy
    (D) persuasive
    (E) instructive

    (A) McKay's purpose is to evoke a time and place — to describe. He spends no time teaching (B) or (E) and no time preaching (C) or (D).

SECTION 6

QUANTITATIVE COMPARISON

Column A	Column B

$$3x = 4y$$
$$x > 0$$

1. | x | y |

(A) The centered equation can be rewritten as $x = \frac{4y}{3}$. Given that x (and so too y) is positive, x is larger than y. You can reach the same conclusion by substituting some values for x and y.

$$4.5 < x < 5.5$$
$$x \text{ is an integer}$$

2. | x | 5 |

(C) There is only one integer between 4.5 and 5.5, and that is 5.

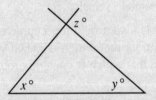

Note: Figure not drawn to scale

3. | $x + y$ | z |

(C) Let the unlabeled angle of the triangle be w:

$$x + y + w = 180$$
$$z + w = 180$$
$$x + y + w = z + w$$
$$x + y = z$$

	Column A	Column B
4.	$5^7 + (-2)^4$	$5^7 + (-2)^5$

(A) Simplify across the comparison by subtracting 5^7 from both sides. Column A becomes $(-2)^4$ and Column B becomes $(-2)^5$. Since $(-2)^4$ is positive and $(-2)^5$ is negative, Column A is larger.

$$x \neq 0$$

	Column A	Column B
5.	$\sqrt{x^2}$	$\sqrt{x^2 + 1}$

(B) You can square both sides. Column A becomes x^2, and Column B becomes $x^2 + 1$. Then subtract x^2 from both sides. The final comparison is 0 in Column A with 1 in Column B.

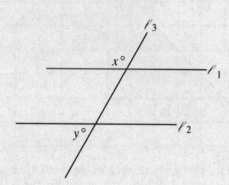

$$l1 \parallel l2$$

	Column A	Column B
6.	x	$180 - y$

(C) Use the "big angle/little angle" theorem:

$$x + y = 180$$

$$x = 180 - y$$

$$4x + 3y = 11$$
$$3x + 3y = 9$$

	Column A	Column B
7.	x	1

(A) Treat the two centered equations as simultaneous equations:

$$4x + 3y = 11$$

$$-(3x + 3y = 9)$$

$$x = 2$$

	Column A	Column B
	$\boxed{x} = x^2 - x$	
8.	$\boxed{2}$	4

(B) This is a defined function problem. So perform the indicated operation:

$$\boxed{2} = (2)^2 - 2 = 4 - 2 = 2$$

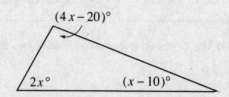

	Column A	Column B
9.	x	30

(C) The measures of three angles total 180°:

$$(2x) + (x - 10) + (4x - 20) = 180$$

$$7x - 30 = 180$$

$$7x = 210$$

$$x = 30$$

$$x = y$$

	Column A	Column B
10.	$x(y + 1)$	$y(x - 1)$

(D) Perform the indicated operations:

$$xy + x \qquad\qquad xy - y$$

Subtract xy from both sides of the comparison:

$$x \qquad\qquad -y$$

And this is like comparing x and $-x$. Without a specific value of x there is no way to determine which is larger.

	Column A	Column B
11.	$\frac{1}{6}(x + y)$	$\frac{x}{6} + \frac{y}{6}$

(C) Just do the operation indicated in Column A. And, of course, you might try substituting some values for x and y.

	Column A	Column B
12.	$\dfrac{\frac{3}{4}}{\frac{4}{3}}$	1

(B) Do the operations indicated in Column A.

661

$$\frac{3}{4} \div \frac{4}{3} = \frac{3}{4} \times \frac{3}{4} = \frac{9}{16}$$

The seating capacity of the Red Room is less than the seating capacity of the Blue Room.

The seating capacity of the Blue Room is greater than the seating capacity of the Green Room.

13.

The seating capacity of the Red Room	The seating capacity of the Green Room

(D) The centered information establishes only:

$R < B$

$G < B$

But that is not enough to determine the relationship between R and G.

14.

17.5% of 123	12.3% of 175

(C) Simplify across the comparison. Clear the "%" by multiplying both sides of the comparison by 100. The result is:

$$175 \times 123 \qquad 123 \times 175$$

At this point you can see the two quantities are equal.

$$\frac{x}{9} = \frac{y}{17}$$

x and y are positive integers

15.

$9x$	$17y$

(B) Solve the centered equation for x or y, say x: $x = \frac{9y}{17}$. Substitute this value for x into Column A. Column A becomes $9\left(\frac{9y}{17}\right)$. Now, since $y > 0$, you can divide both columns by y. Column A becomes $\frac{81}{17}$, and Column B becomes 17. Column B is larger.

STUDENT-PRODUCED RESPONSES

16. If $x = 2$, then $x^2 - 2x = ?$

(0) Just evaluate the expression by substituting 2 for x:

$$x^2 - 2x = (2)^2 - 2(2) = 4 - 4 = 0$$

17. If 2 pounds of coffee makes exactly 7 pots of coffee, how many pots of coffee can be made from a 10-pound bag of coffee?

(35) You can reason that a 10-pound bag will make five times as much coffee as a 2-pound bag. And $7 \times 5 = 35$. Or if need be, you can set up a direct proportion. $\frac{2}{10} = \frac{7}{x}$.

18. If roses cost $1.00 apiece and carnations cost $0.50 apiece, how many more carnations than roses can be purchased for $10.00?

(10) $10.00 buys $10.00 \div $1.00 = 10 roses and $10.00 \div $0.50 = 20 carnations. And $20 - 10 = 10$.

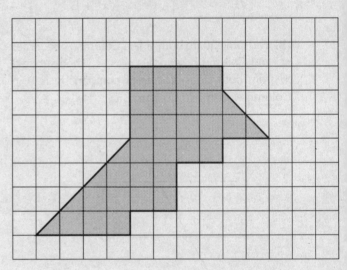

19. In the figure above, each of the small squares has side length 1. What is the area of the shaded region?

(30) The trick is to see that this figure is composed of several smaller figures:

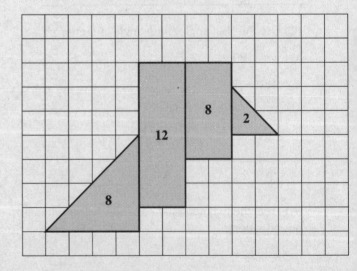

The areas of the rectangles are easy to calculate. As for the triangles, instead of using the formula for

662

finding the area of a triangle, just analyze the triangles as half of squares:

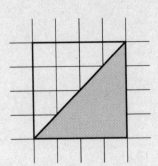 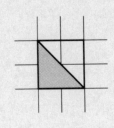

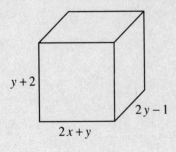

20. If $(x + y)^2 = (x - y)^2 + 4$, then $xy = ?$

(1) Do the indicated operations:

$(x + y)^2 = (x - y)^2 + 4$

$x^2 + 2xy + y^2 = x^2 - 2xy + y^2 + 4$

$2xy = -2xy + 4$

$4xy = 4$

$xy = 1$

21. If $\frac{2}{3}$ of a number is 5 more than $\frac{1}{4}$ of the number, what is the number?

(12) You can set up an equation:

$\frac{2}{3}x = 5 + \frac{1}{4}x$

$\frac{8}{12}x = 5 + \frac{3}{12}x$

$\frac{5}{12}x = 5$

$x = 12$

22. If a square has the same area as a rectangle with sides of 9 and 4, what is the length of the side of the square?

(6) The rectangle has an area of $9 \times 4 = 36$. And a square with an area of 36 has a side of:

$s \times s = 36$

$s^2 = 36$

$s = \sqrt{36} = 6$

23. $D(w)$ is defined as the number of times in a sequence of letters, w, that any letter is followed by itself. For example, if w is *aabbc*, $D(w) = 2$. If w is "*aaabbbcc*," what is the value of $D(w)$?

(5) This is a variation on a defined problem. w has 5 occurrences of double letters: (*aa*)*abbbcc*, *a*(*aa*)*bbbcc*, *aaa*(*bb*)*bcc*, *aaab*(*bb*)*cc*, and *aaabbb*(*cc*).

24. What is the volume of the cube shown above?

(125) The sides of a cube are all equal so set up equations:

$y + 2 = 2x + y$

$2 = 2x$

$x = 1$

And,

$2x + y = 2y - 1$

$2(1) + y = 2y - 1$

$2 + y = 2y - 1$

$y = 3$

Using the values $x = 1$ and $y = 3$, find the length of any side. Since one side of the cube has a length of $y + 2$, the length of the side is $(3) + 2 = 5$. So the volume of the cube is $5 \times 5 \times 5 = 125$.

25. Of the dogs at the kennel, $\frac{1}{10}$ are over 2 years old. Of those, $\frac{3}{5}$ are between 3 and 5 years old, and $\frac{2}{5}$ are over 5 years old. In lowest terms, what fraction of the entire kennel population is over 5 years old?

(1/25) This is an easy problem with extra information thrown in to confuse you. All you need to know is that $\frac{1}{10}$ are over 2 years old, and of those, $\frac{2}{5}$ are over 5 years old. You want to find $\frac{2}{5}$ of $\frac{1}{10}$, so multiplying the fractions gives you the answer:

$\frac{2}{5} \times \frac{1}{10} = \frac{2}{50}$, which reduces to $\frac{1}{25}$

Remember, the question asks for lowest terms. Therefore, $\frac{2}{50}$ is incorrect and will be graded that way.

Practice Test 5

Practice Test 5

ANSWER SHEET
PRACTICE TEST 5

If a section has fewer questions than answer ovals, leave the extra ovals blank.

SECTION 1

1 (A) (B) (C) (D) (E) 11 (A) (B) (C) (D) (E) 21 (A) (B) (C) (D) (E) 31 (A) (B) (C) (D) (E)
2 (A) (B) (C) (D) (E) 12 (A) (B) (C) (D) (E) 22 (A) (B) (C) (D) (E) 32 (A) (B) (C) (D) (E)
3 (A) (B) (C) (D) (E) 13 (A) (B) (C) (D) (E) 23 (A) (B) (C) (D) (E) 33 (A) (B) (C) (D) (E)
4 (A) (B) (C) (D) (E) 14 (A) (B) (C) (D) (E) 24 (A) (B) (C) (D) (E) 34 (A) (B) (C) (D) (E)
5 (A) (B) (C) (D) (E) 15 (A) (B) (C) (D) (E) 25 (A) (B) (C) (D) (E) 35 (A) (B) (C) (D) (E)
6 (A) (B) (C) (D) (E) 16 (A) (B) (C) (D) (E) 26 (A) (B) (C) (D) (E) 36 (A) (B) (C) (D) (E)
7 (A) (B) (C) (D) (E) 17 (A) (B) (C) (D) (E) 27 (A) (B) (C) (D) (E) 37 (A) (B) (C) (D) (E)
8 (A) (B) (C) (D) (E) 18 (A) (B) (C) (D) (E) 28 (A) (B) (C) (D) (E) 38 (A) (B) (C) (D) (E)
9 (A) (B) (C) (D) (E) 19 (A) (B) (C) (D) (E) 29 (A) (B) (C) (D) (E) 39 (A) (B) (C) (D) (E)
10 (A) (B) (C) (D) (E) 20 (A) (B) (C) (D) (E) 30 (A) (B) (C) (D) (E) 40 (A) (B) (C) (D) (E)

SECTION 2

1 (A) (B) (C) (D) (E) 11 (A) (B) (C) (D) (E) 21 (A) (B) (C) (D) (E) 31 (A) (B) (C) (D) (E)
2 (A) (B) (C) (D) (E) 12 (A) (B) (C) (D) (E) 22 (A) (B) (C) (D) (E) 32 (A) (B) (C) (D) (E)
3 (A) (B) (C) (D) (E) 13 (A) (B) (C) (D) (E) 23 (A) (B) (C) (D) (E) 33 (A) (B) (C) (D) (E)
4 (A) (B) (C) (D) (E) 14 (A) (B) (C) (D) (E) 24 (A) (B) (C) (D) (E) 34 (A) (B) (C) (D) (E)
5 (A) (B) (C) (D) (E) 15 (A) (B) (C) (D) (E) 25 (A) (B) (C) (D) (E) 35 (A) (B) (C) (D) (E)
6 (A) (B) (C) (D) (E) 16 (A) (B) (C) (D) (E) 26 (A) (B) (C) (D) (E) 36 (A) (B) (C) (D) (E)
7 (A) (B) (C) (D) (E) 17 (A) (B) (C) (D) (E) 27 (A) (B) (C) (D) (E) 37 (A) (B) (C) (D) (E)
8 (A) (B) (C) (D) (E) 18 (A) (B) (C) (D) (E) 28 (A) (B) (C) (D) (E) 38 (A) (B) (C) (D) (E)
9 (A) (B) (C) (D) (E) 19 (A) (B) (C) (D) (E) 29 (A) (B) (C) (D) (E) 39 (A) (B) (C) (D) (E)
10 (A) (B) (C) (D) (E) 20 (A) (B) (C) (D) (E) 30 (A) (B) (C) (D) (E) 40 (A) (B) (C) (D) (E)

SECTION 3

1 (A) (B) (C) (D) (E) 6 (A) (B) (C) (D) (E) 11 (A) (B) (C) (D) (E) 16 (A) (B) (C) (D) (E)
2 (A) (B) (C) (D) (E) 7 (A) (B) (C) (D) (E) 12 (A) (B) (C) (D) (E) 17 (A) (B) (C) (D) (E)
3 (A) (B) (C) (D) (E) 8 (A) (B) (C) (D) (E) 13 (A) (B) (C) (D) (E) 18 (A) (B) (C) (D) (E)
4 (A) (B) (C) (D) (E) 9 (A) (B) (C) (D) (E) 14 (A) (B) (C) (D) (E) 19 (A) (B) (C) (D) (E)
5 (A) (B) (C) (D) (E) 10 (A) (B) (C) (D) (E) 15 (A) (B) (C) (D) (E) 20 (A) (B) (C) (D) (E)

SECTION 4

1 (A) (B) (C) (D) (E) 6 (A) (B) (C) (D) (E) 11 (A) (B) (C) (D) (E) 16 (A) (B) (C) (D) (E)
2 (A) (B) (C) (D) (E) 7 (A) (B) (C) (D) (E) 12 (A) (B) (C) (D) (E) 17 (A) (B) (C) (D) (E)
3 (A) (B) (C) (D) (E) 8 (A) (B) (C) (D) (E) 13 (A) (B) (C) (D) (E) 18 (A) (B) (C) (D) (E)
4 (A) (B) (C) (D) (E) 9 (A) (B) (C) (D) (E) 14 (A) (B) (C) (D) (E) 19 (A) (B) (C) (D) (E)
5 (A) (B) (C) (D) (E) 10 (A) (B) (C) (D) (E) 15 (A) (B) (C) (D) (E) 20 (A) (B) (C) (D) (E)

SECTION 5

1 (A) (B) (C) (D) (E) 11 (A) (B) (C) (D) (E) 21 (A) (B) (C) (D) (E) 31 (A) (B) (C) (D) (E)
2 (A) (B) (C) (D) (E) 12 (A) (B) (C) (D) (E) 22 (A) (B) (C) (D) (E) 32 (A) (B) (C) (D) (E)
3 (A) (B) (C) (D) (E) 13 (A) (B) (C) (D) (E) 23 (A) (B) (C) (D) (E) 33 (A) (B) (C) (D) (E)
4 (A) (B) (C) (D) (E) 14 (A) (B) (C) (D) (E) 24 (A) (B) (C) (D) (E) 34 (A) (B) (C) (D) (E)
5 (A) (B) (C) (D) (E) 15 (A) (B) (C) (D) (E) 25 (A) (B) (C) (D) (E) 35 (A) (B) (C) (D) (E)
6 (A) (B) (C) (D) (E) 16 (A) (B) (C) (D) (E) 26 (A) (B) (C) (D) (E) 36 (A) (B) (C) (D) (E)
7 (A) (B) (C) (D) (E) 17 (A) (B) (C) (D) (E) 27 (A) (B) (C) (D) (E) 37 (A) (B) (C) (D) (E)
8 (A) (B) (C) (D) (E) 18 (A) (B) (C) (D) (E) 28 (A) (B) (C) (D) (E) 38 (A) (B) (C) (D) (E)
9 (A) (B) (C) (D) (E) 19 (A) (B) (C) (D) (E) 29 (A) (B) (C) (D) (E) 39 (A) (B) (C) (D) (E)
10 (A) (B) (C) (D) (E) 20 (A) (B) (C) (D) (E) 30 (A) (B) (C) (D) (E) 40 (A) (B) (C) (D) (E)

SECTION 6

1 Ⓐ Ⓑ Ⓒ Ⓓ Ⓔ   6 Ⓐ Ⓑ Ⓒ Ⓓ Ⓔ   11 Ⓐ Ⓑ Ⓒ Ⓓ Ⓔ
2 Ⓐ Ⓑ Ⓒ Ⓓ Ⓔ   7 Ⓐ Ⓑ Ⓒ Ⓓ Ⓔ   12 Ⓐ Ⓑ Ⓒ Ⓓ Ⓔ
3 Ⓐ Ⓑ Ⓒ Ⓓ Ⓔ   8 Ⓐ Ⓑ Ⓒ Ⓓ Ⓔ   13 Ⓐ Ⓑ Ⓒ Ⓓ Ⓔ
4 Ⓐ Ⓑ Ⓒ Ⓓ Ⓔ   9 Ⓐ Ⓑ Ⓒ Ⓓ Ⓔ   14 Ⓐ Ⓑ Ⓒ Ⓓ Ⓔ
5 Ⓐ Ⓑ Ⓒ Ⓓ Ⓔ   10 Ⓐ Ⓑ Ⓒ Ⓓ Ⓔ   15 Ⓐ Ⓑ Ⓒ Ⓓ Ⓔ

Note: ONLY the answers entered on the grid are scored.
Handwritten answers at the top of the column are NOT scored.

16. 17. 18. 19. 20.

21. 22. 23. 24. 25.

SECTION **1**	Time—30 Minutes 35 Questions	For each question in this section, choose the best answer and blacken the corresponding space on the answer sheet.

The passage below is followed by questions based on its content. Answer the questions following the passage on the basis of what is <u>stated</u> or <u>implied</u> in the passage.

Questions 1–12 are based on the following passage.

Ciro Alegría was born in the Andes of Peru in 1909. Although most of his works were published in Chile, his most popular works are tales of the lives of Peruvian Indians. This passage is from a short story entitled "The Stone and the Cross."

The trees became smaller as the grade got steeper. The trail heaved, tracing violent curves between scrawny cacti, squat bushes, and angular rocks. The two horses were
(5) panting, and their riders had stopped talking. If a stone rolled off the path, it continued to bounce downhill sometimes dislodging others in its fall, and all were as grains of sand sliding down the grandeur of the Andes.

Suddenly there were not even bushes or cacti. The rocks increased in size, expanding into slabs, grey and red,
(10) pointing toward the summit, standing vertically in dark boulders like immense stair-steps, or wrought into round peaks that pierced the taut sky. Large rocks were scattered like huts in the distance, or stacked wall-like, forming a gigantic circle around the infinite. Where there was some
(15) earth, wild grass known as *ichu* grew tenaciously. The sun's brilliance formed pools in the yellow-grey grass.

The horses' and riders' breath began to freeze into fleeting, whitish puffs. The men felt the cold in their goose-pimpled skin, in spite of their thick woolen clothes
(20) and compact vicuña ponchos. The one in the lead turned his head as he halted his horse, and said:

"Won't you feel *soroche* (altitude sickness), child?"

The boy he addressed answered, "I don't think so. I have climbed as high as the Manancancho with my
(25) father."

Then the one who had asked the question eyed the road that struggled upward, and spurred on. He was an old Indian, with an expressionless face. Beneath the rush hat whose shade somewhat concealed the coarseness of his
(30) face, his eyes sparkled like two black diamonds buried in stone. The boy following him was a white child about ten years old, still new to long trips in the bramble thickets of the craggy Andes, for which reason his father had assigned the Indian to him as a guide. The road to the village where
(35) the school was, crossed a country whose reaches grew ever lonelier and higher.

That the child was white could easily be seen, although the child knew very well through his mother's veins coursed a few drops of Indian blood. However, the
(40) child was considered white because of his color and also because he belonged to the landed class which had dominated the Indian village for more than four centuries.

The boy traveled behind the old man without any consideration for the fact that the latter was doing him a ser-
(45) vice. He was completely accustomed to having the Indians serve him. At that moment, the boy was thinking about his home and some of the events of his short life. It was certainly true that he had climbed with his father as far as Manancancho, the mountain on their hacienda that had
(50) attracted his attention because occasionally it was covered with snow. But the mountains he was climbing now were higher, and perhaps the *soroche*, the sickness of the high passes of the Andes, would attack him when he reached its frozen summit. And where might that famous cross be
(55) anyway?

On rounding the slope of the mountain, the riders ran into some men leading a string of tired mules that could hardly be seen under their immense loads. The packs smelled of coca and were covered by blankets that the
(60) muleteers would use at the inn. The vivid colors of the blankets were jubilant brushstrokes against the uniformly grey rocks and grass fields.

The guide and the child, with some difficulty, got through the slow-moving mules. On top of the two packs
(65) on one of the mules there was a large, beautifully blue, almost lustrous stone.

"The devotional stone," the guide remarked.

1. It is clear from the first paragraph that the riders are going
   (A) uphill
   (B) downhill
   (C) in circles
   (D) to school
   (E) across a ridge

2. By "all were as grains of sand" (lines 6–7), Alegría emphasizes the
   (A) meaninglessness of life
   (B) immensity of the Andes
   (C) beauty of the stones
   (D) contrast between mountain and seashore
   (E) insignificance of man

3. By "immense stair-steps" (line 11), Alegría means that the rocks
   (A) are man-made
   (B) look wooden
   (C) are carved for people to walk on
   (D) have railings
   (E) lead upward

GO ON TO THE NEXT PAGE

669

4. The word *wrought* (line 11) means

   (A) composed
   (B) drafted
   (C) manufactured
   (D) formed
   (E) hammered

5. "The sun's brilliance formed pools" (lines 15–16) means that the sun

   (A) melted the ice
   (B) blended with the clouds
   (C) reflected off the grass
   (D) both A and B
   (E) both B and C

6. The word *rush* (line 28) means

   (A) grass
   (B) sally
   (C) dash
   (D) haste
   (E) advance

7. Paragraph 6 introduces the concept of

   (A) race
   (B) class
   (C) poverty
   (D) both A and B
   (E) both B and C

8. The word *hacienda* (line 49) is used to mean

   (A) house
   (B) castle
   (C) plantation
   (D) villa
   (E) dwelling

9. By "jubilant brushstrokes" (line 61), the author is

   (A) differentiating the muleteers from artists
   (B) comparing the blankets to a painting
   (C) contrasting the blankets with the grey mountains
   (D) both A and B
   (E) both B and C

10. The word *devotional* (line 67) means

    (A) tender
    (B) zealous
    (C) ardent
    (D) venerated
    (E) affectionate

11. The passage is primarily

    (A) persuasive
    (B) instructive
    (C) factual
    (D) descriptive
    (E) informative

12. By the end of the passage, the author has introduced

    (A) the main characters
    (B) the symbols mentioned in the title
    (C) the problem and its solution
    (D) both A and B
    (E) both B and C

Each sentence below has one or two blanks, each blank indicating that something has been omitted. Beneath the sentence are five lettered words or sets of words. Choose the word or set of words that best fits the meaning of the sentence as a whole.

Example:

Although its publicity has been ----, the film itself is intelligent, well acted, handsomely produced, and altogether ----.

(A) tasteless..respectable
(B) extensive..moderate
(C) sophisticated..amateur
(D) risqué..crude
(E) perfect..spectacular

13. Van Gogh's shapes and colors are so ---- that some art historians have attributed his view of the world to illness or to madness.

    (A) inaccessible (B) startling (C) intermediate
    (D) corrupt (E) trivial

14. Although he was usually ----, he ---- the hostess and was never invited back.

    (A) tidy..flattered
    (B) disinterested..suspected
    (C) forgetful..enchanted
    (D) tactful..insulted
    (E) careful..concealed

15. The will was ---- according to the law because there was ---- evidence that the deceased had been mentally incompetent.

    (A) sanctimonious..chronological
    (B) invalid..overwhelming
    (C) punitive..subsequent
    (D) signed..irrefutable
    (E) suspect..inadequate

16. The treatment of the mental illnesses for which there is no cure can only ---- the symptoms, not ---- the disease.

    (A) defend..eradicate
    (B) disrupt..deflate
    (C) ameliorate..eliminate
    (D) confine..restore
    (E) augment..delineate

17. Although Senator Jones had the ---- needed to run for office, it was his ---- that the party considered his greatest asset.

    (A) credentials..charisma
    (B) experience..apathy
    (C) esteem..wrongdoing
    (D) greed..altruism
    (E) serenity..haughtiness

Each question below consists of a related pair of words or phrases, followed by five lettered pairs of words or phrases. Select the lettered pair that best expresses the relationship similar to that expressed in the original pair.

Example:

YAWN : BOREDOM::

(A) dream : sleep
(B) anger : madness
(C) smile : amusement
(D) face : expression
(E) impatience : rebellion

(A) (B) ● (D) (E)

18. DUCK : WADDLE::

   (A) eagle : hunt
   (B) gait : amble
   (C) worm : wriggle
   (D) boat : row
   (E) horse : race

19. COMPOSER : SCORE::

   (A) writer : manuscript
   (B) athlete : exercise
   (C) comedian : laugh
   (D) worker : apprentice
   (E) librarian : books

20. TARANTULA : SPIDER::

   (A) roof : cabin
   (B) cobra : snake
   (C) parrot : jungle
   (D) camel : desert
   (E) poetry : prose

21. AIRPLANE : HANGAR::

   (A) beach : sand
   (B) car : garage
   (C) bird : flight
   (D) mountain : peak
   (E) vault : bank

22. TREE : ORCHARD::

   (A) member : congregation
   (B) priest : church
   (C) animal : mammal
   (D) officer : uniform
   (E) leader : organization

23. RESILIENT : BUOYANCY::

   (A) useful : extravagance
   (B) pliable : flexibility
   (C) enticing : elusiveness
   (D) eccentric : practicality
   (E) harmonious : discord

24. PETTY : SIGNIFICANCE::

   (A) preserved : security
   (B) tempered : variety
   (C) obstinate : fortitude
   (D) abundant : lassitude
   (E) brief : duration

25. FERTILE : PROGENY::

   (A) verdant : vegetation
   (B) inept : ability
   (C) infamous : secrecy
   (D) flagrant : nobility
   (E) affable : insight

The passage below is followed by questions based on its content. Answer the questions following the passage on the basis of what is stated or implied in the passage.

Questions 26–35 are based on the following passage.

With his partner, Richard Steele, Joseph Addison (1672–1719) published one of England's most popular periodicals, the Spectator, *daily from March 1711 until December 1712. For their paper, they invented and developed a new form of essay, the "periodical essay." Such essays were informal but not intimate, informational but not preachy. In this essay, published in the tenth issue of the* Spectator, *Addison discusses the paper's burgeoning popularity.*

It is with much satisfaction that I hear this great city inquiring day by day after these my papers, and receiving my morning lectures with a becoming seriousness and attention. My publisher tells me that there are already three thousand of them distributed every day. So that if I allow twenty readers to every paper, which I look upon as a modest computation, I may reckon about three-score thousand disciples in London and Westminster, who I hope will take care to distinguish themselves from the thoughtless herd of their ignorant and unattentive brethren. Since I (10)

have raised to myself so great an audience, I shall spare no pains to make their instruction agreeable, and their diversion useful. For which reasons I shall endeavor to enliven morality with wit, and to temper wit with morality, that my readers may, if possible, both ways find their account (15) in the speculation of the day. And to the end that their virtue and discretion may not be short, transient, intermitting starts of thought, I have resolved to refresh their memories from day to day, till I have recovered them out of that desperate state of vice and folly into which the age (20) is fallen. The mind that lies fallow but a single day sprouts up in follies that are only to be killed by a constant and assiduous culture. It was said of Socrates that he brought philosophy down from heaven, to inhabit among men; and I shall be ambitious to have it said of me that I have (25) brought philosophy out of closets, libraries, schools and colleges, to dwell in clubs and assemblies, at tea tables and in coffeehouses.

GO ON TO THE NEXT PAGE

671

(30)   I would therefore in a very particular manner recommend these my speculations to all well-regulated families
that set apart an hour in every morning for tea and bread
and butter; and would earnestly advise them for their good
to order this paper to be punctually served up, and to be
looked at as a part of the tea equipage. . . .

(35)   I know several of my friends and well-wishers are in
great pain for me, lest I should not be able to keep up the
spirit of a paper which I oblige myself to furnish every
day: but to make them easy in this particular, I will
promise them faithfully to give it over as soon as I grow
(40) dull. This I know will be a matter of great raillery to the
small wits; who will frequently put me in mind of my
promise, desire me to keep my word, assure me that it is
high time to give over, with many other little pleasantries
of the like nature, which men of a little smart genius can-
(45) not forbear throwing out against their best friends, when
they have such a handle given them of being witty. But let
them remember that I do hereby enter my caveat against
this piece of raillery.

26. By "receiving my morning lectures" (lines 2–3),
Addison means

(A) listening to my radio program
(B) paying attention to my scolding voice
(C) reading my column in the morning paper
(D) both A and B
(E) both B and C

27. The word *disciples* (line 8) is used to mean

(A) patrons
(B) neophytes
(C) converts
(D) apostles
(E) followers

28. "The thoughtless herd" (lines 9–10) refers to

(A) any ill-educated people
(B) people who don't read the *Spectator*
(C) illiterate people
(D) people who live outside London and
Westminster
(E) women

29. By "make their instruction agreeable, and their
diversion useful" (line 12), Addison means that he
will

(A) remove all didactic flavor from the *Spectator*
(B) try to teach a moral lesson in each essay
(C) make lectures humorous and entertainment
meaningful
(D) not include humor unless it is enlightened
(E) try to divert his audience from their everyday
woes

30. The word *temper* (line 14) is used to mean

(A) moderate
(B) dispose
(C) anger
(D) compose
(E) harden

31. Which of these best summarizes Addison's intent in
lines 16–21 ("And to the end . . . to which the age is
fallen")?

(A) No newspaper can restore a reader's virtue.
(B) He will remind his audience of their vices.
(C) Daily publication will save his audience from
folly.
(D) He expects his audience to return to wickedness.
(E) Only he can restore his readership to health.

32. Addison compares himself to Socrates in terms of
their

(A) popularization of philosophy
(B) instructive natures
(C) heavenly beginnings
(D) both A and B
(E) both B and C

33. "To make them easy in this particular" (line 38)
means

(A) to finish this project easily
(B) to ease their minds on this subject
(C) to simplify this matter
(D) to make fastidiousness less complicated
(E) to fashion comfortable items

34. The word *raillery* (line 40) means

(A) balustrade
(B) garments
(C) forcing
(D) teasing
(E) scolding

35. The general tone of this passage is

(A) serious and earnest
(B) cautious and deliberate
(C) flighty and frivolous
(D) shrewd and calculating
(E) congenial and humorous

IF YOU FINISH BEFORE TIME IS CALLED, YOU MAY CHECK YOUR WORK ON **S T O P**
THIS SECTION ONLY. DO NOT WORK ON ANY OTHER SECTION IN THE TEST.

SECTION **2**   Time—15 Minutes   15 Questions

In this section, solve each problem, using any available space on the page for scratchwork. Then decide which is the best of the choices given and fill in the corresponding oval on the answer sheet.

Reference:

Circle:

Rectangle:

Rectangular Solid:

Cylinder:

Triangle:

$C = 2\pi r$
$A = \pi r^2$

$A = lw$

$V = lwh$

$V = \pi r^2 h$

$A = \frac{1}{2}bh$

$a^2 + b^2 = c^2$

- The measure in degrees of a straight angle is 180.
- The number of degrees of arc in a circle is 360.
- The sum of the measures of the angles of a triangle is 180.

Notes: The figures accompanying the problems are drawn as accurately as possible unless otherwise stated in specific problems. Again, unless otherwise stated, all figures lie in the same plane. All numbers used in these problems are real numbers. Calculators are permitted for this test.

1. If $\dfrac{1}{2N} + \dfrac{1}{2N} = \dfrac{1}{4}$, then $N =$

    (A) 4   (B) 2   (C) 1   (D) $\dfrac{1}{2}$ (E) $\dfrac{1}{4}$

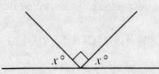

2. In the figure above, $x =$
    (A) 30   (B) 45   (C) 60   (D) 75   (E) 90

3. In a certain game, a person's age is multiplied by 2 and then the product is divided by 3. If the result of performing the operations on John's age is 12, what is John's age?

    (A) 2   (B) 8   (C) 12   (D) 18   (E) 36

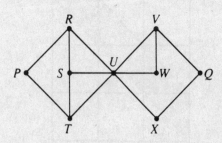

4. The figure above is a map showing the stations and connecting subway lines for a city's subway system. If a person wishes to travel by subway from station P to station Q, without passing through any station more than once, which of the following must be true?

    (A) If he passes through T, he must next pass through S.
    (B) If he passes through S, he must next pass through U.
    (C) If he passes through U, he must next pass through V.
    (D) If he passes through R, he cannot later pass through T.
    (E) If he passes through V, he cannot later pass through W.

GO ON TO THE NEXT PAGE

673

5. A helper must load 38 bricks onto a truck. Given that she can carry at most 4 bricks at a time, what is the fewest number of trips she must make to move all of the bricks from the brickpile onto the truck?

(A) 9 (B) 9.5 (C) 10 (D) 10.5 (E) 12

6. For all numbers, $(a - b)(b - c) - (b - a)(c - b) =$

(A) -2 (B) -1 (C) 0 (D) $ab - ac - bc$
(E) $2ab - 2ac - 2bc$

7. n is a positive integer. If n is a multiple of 6 and a multiple of 9, what is the least possible value of n?

(A) 12 (B) 18 (C) 27 (D) 36 (E) 54

8. For any positive integer k, $\langle\!\langle k \rangle\!\rangle = k^2 - k$. What is the value of $\langle\!\langle 2 \rangle\!\rangle$?

(A) 0 (B) 1 (C) 2 (D) 4 (E) 8

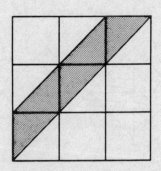

9. The figure above shows a square piece of land that is divided into 9 smaller square lots. The shaded portion is a railroad right-of-way. If the area of the shaded portion of the figure is 5 square miles, what is the area, in square miles, of the entire piece of land?

(A) 9 (B) 10 (C) 13 (D) 18 (E) 36

List X	List Y
1	1
2	2
3	3
4	4

10. For how many different ordered pairs (x, y), where x is a number selected from List X and y is a numbered selected from List Y, is $x - y > 0$?

(A) 24 (B) 18 (C) 15 (D) 12 (E) 6

11. If x and y are negative integers, and $x > y$, which of the following is the greatest?

(A) $-(xy)^2$ (B) x^2y (C) xy
(D) $x + y$ (E) $y - x$

12. A student receives an average of 75 on three exams that are scored on a scale of 0 to 100. If one of her test scores was 75, what is the lowest possible score she could have received on any of the three tests?

(A) 0 (B) 1 (C) 25 (D) 40 (E) 50

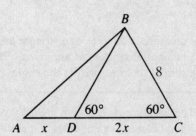

13. In ABC above, what is the length of side AC?

(A) 4 (B) 8 (C) 12 (D) 18
(E) It cannot be determined from the information given.

14. During a certain shift, a quality control inspector inspects 6 out of every 30 items produced. What was the ratio of inspected to uninspected items during that shift?

(A) 1:4 (B) 1:5 (C) 1:6 (D) 5:1 (E) 6:1

15. For which of the following pairs of numbers is it true that their sum is 9 times their product?

(A) $1, \dfrac{1}{9}$ (B) $1, \dfrac{1}{8}$ (C) $1, \dfrac{1}{19}$

(D) $1, 8$ (E) $1, 9$

16. Initially, 24 people apply for jobs with a firm, and $\dfrac{1}{3}$ of those are turned down without being given an interview. If $\dfrac{1}{4}$ of the remaining applicants are hired, how many applicants were given jobs?

(A) 2 (B) 4 (C) 6 (D) 8 (E) 12

GO ON TO THE NEXT PAGE

674

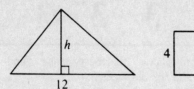

17. In the figures above, if the area of the rectangle is equal to the area of the triangle, then $h =$

(A) 2   (B) 3   (C) 4   (D) 6   (E) 9

18. If 8 francs equal 1 pound, and 2 pounds equal 3 dollars, then 6 dollars is equal to how many francs?

(A) 48   (B) 32   (C) 16   (D) 8   (E) 4

19. The price of a book, after it was reduced by $\frac{1}{3}$, is B dollars. What was the price of the book, in dollars, before the reduction?

(A) $\frac{2B}{3}$ (B) $\frac{3B}{4}$ (C) $\frac{6B}{5}$

(D) $\frac{4B}{3}$ (E) $\frac{3B}{2}$

20. Y years ago, Tom was three times as old as Julie was. If Julie is now 20 years old, how old is Tom in terms of Y?

(A) $60 + 2Y$
(B) $30 + 2Y$
(C) $30 - 2Y$
(D) $60 - 2Y$
(E) $60 - 3Y$

21. If S is the sum of x consecutive integers, then S must be even if x is a multiple of

(A) 6   (B) 5   (C) 4   (D) 3   (E) 2

22. If the radius of circle O is 20 percent less than the radius of circle P, the area of circle O is what percent of the area of circle P?

(A) 60%   (B) 64%   (C) 72%
(D) 80%   (E) 120%

23. If the average (arithmetic mean) of 20, 23, 24, x, and y is 26 and $\frac{x}{y} = \frac{3}{4}$, then $x =$

(A) 25   (B) 27   (C) 36   (D) 41   (E) 63

24. The price of 5 boxes of candy is d dollars. If each box contains 30 pieces of candy, what is the price, in *cents*, of 12 pieces of candy?

(A) $8d$ (B) $12d$ (C) $\frac{25d}{2}$ (D) $50d$ (E) $72d$

25. If a cube has a side of length 2, what is the distance from any vertex to the center of the cube?

(A) $\frac{\sqrt{2}}{2}$ (B) $\sqrt{3}$ (C) $2\sqrt{2}$

(D) $2\sqrt{3}$ (E) $\frac{3}{2}$

IF YOU FINISH BEFORE TIME IS CALLED, YOU MAY CHECK YOUR WORK ON THIS SECTION ONLY. DO NOT WORK ON ANY OTHER SECTION IN THE TEST.   **S T O P**

The passages below are followed by questions based on their content. Answer the questions following the passages on the basis of what is <u>stated</u> or <u>implied</u> in the passages.

Questions 1-10 are based on the following passages.

For months before the United States entered World War II, debate raged regarding U.S. military involvement. Here, two viewpoints are presented. The first speaker, Dorothy Thompson, was a journalist and foreign correspondent. The second, Norman Thomas, was head of the Socialist party and at the time of this speech, a four-time candidate for the Presidency of the United States.

Passage 1 — Dorothy Thompson, Speech in Toronto (May 2, 1941)

Every nation on this globe and every individual on this globe will presently learn what a few have always known: that there are times in history when the business of one is
Line the business of all, when life or death is a matter of choice,
(5) and when no one alive can avoid making that choice. These times occur seldom in history, these times of inevitable decisions. But this is one of those times.

Before this epoch is over, every living human being will have chosen, every living human being will have lined up
(10) with Hitler or against him, every living human being will either have opposed this onslaught or supported it. For if he tries to make no choice that in itself will be a choice. If he takes no side, he is on Hitler's side; if he does not act that is an act — for Hitler. . . .
(15) In this world people get what they passionately desire, and woe unto them if they desire the wrong thing. If we desire isolation, we shall have it — the isolation of a prison camp in a hostile community. We shall be penned up on this Continent, while hostile nations east of us, and
(20) west of us, and north of us, and south of us, do their level best, their vicious scheming, organized, subsidized, ruthless best to destroy us from inside; to set Canadians against the people of the States; to set labor against capital and capital against labor; the masses against the intelli-
(25) gentsia, and the intelligentsia against the masses; the Irish against the English; the Catholics against the Protestants, the Negroes against the whites, the whites against the Negroes, and everybody against the Jews, in order that the war which we sought to avoid elsewhere may occur here
(30) in an internecine fight, the running amok and berserk of an imprisoned colony.

Passage 2 — Norman Thomas, Speech in New York (June 29, 1941)

I insist that if once we let ourselves be plunged into this war, our liberties will be gone. The same oceans which are so mighty a barrier for our own defense will prove an
Line insuperable obstacle to our conquest of distant continents
(35) by any price we can afford to pay. The probable cost of this war in the lives of our sons staggers the imagination. Its cost in money means bankruptcy, something close to a subsistence level of life during the war, and a post-war economic crisis besides which 1932 will be remembered
(40) as a year of prosperity. To make the people maintain so insensate a conflict, propaganda, censorship, and conscription, raised to the highest degree, will become necessary. Every bitterness of division among us will be increased. The last chance for the orderly development of a nobler
(45) democracy on the face of the earth will have gone. It will not come again with the signing of some sort of peace. Instead there will be a bitter and confused reaction; dictatorship, either of the government in office or some stronger, more demagogic rival, will appear the only alter-
(50) native to chaos. The idealists who will have helped put us into another war for democracy or the survivors among them will live to see democracy slain in America by the war they sought. . . .

I am not affirming that we can ignore the dangers of the
(55) world in which we live, or that a Hitler victory far more complete than he has yet won will not add to those dangers. I am denouncing the hysteria which grossly exaggerates those dangers and even more dangerously minimizes the perils of our involvement in war. I am insisting that a
(60) determined America which will keep its sons out of war, can, if it will, make its own democracy work, and by the contagion of its example in a world where alleged democracy has failed, do far more for mankind than by involving itself in a war for which neither Churchill nor Roosevelt
(65) has dared to state specific aims. . . .

I am against our participation in this war not only because I hate war, but because I hate Fascism and all totalitarianism, and love democracy. I speak not only for myself, but for my Party in summoning my fellow coun-
(70) trymen to demand that our country be kept out of war, not as an end in itself, but as a condition to the fulfillment of all our hopes and dreams for a better life for ourselves and our children, yes, and all the children of this great land.

1. The main point of Thompson's introductory paragraph is that

   (A) not everyone knows the importance of decision-making
   (B) the time has come to choose
   (C) choices are made seldom in history
   (D) life and death are inevitable
   (E) this is an important time in history

2. The word *onslaught* (line 11) is used by Thompson to mean

   (A) command
   (B) retreat
   (C) pillage
   (D) resistance
   (E) attack

3. According to Thompson, isolationism will mean

   (A) reduction in forces
   (B) international debt
   (C) imprisonment
   (D) the fall of the economy
   (E) all of the above

4. The word *internecine* (line 30) means

   (A) between friends
   (B) foreign
   (C) global
   (D) territorial
   (E) mutually destructive

5. Thomas uses the word *insuperable* (line 35) to mean

   (A) irresistible
   (B) desperate
   (C) surmountable
   (D) formidable
   (E) unusual

6. Thomas discusses the cost of the war in terms of

   (A) lives
   (B) money
   (C) freedom
   (D) democracy
   (E) all of the above

7. The word *affirming*, used by Thomas in line 55, means

   (A) proving
   (B) validating
   (C) disputing
   (D) denying
   (E) asserting

8. Judging by this passage, Thomas might consider Thompson

   (A) uninformed
   (B) undemocratic
   (C) hysterical
   (D) determined
   (E) noble

9. Unlike Thompson, Thomas believes that isolationism will

   (A) lead to chaos
   (B) result in censorship
   (C) cause riots
   (D) lead to Hitler's victory
   (E) safeguard democracy

10. Thompson and Thomas agree that

    (A) war is avoidable
    (B) war is expensive
    (C) Hitler is dangerous
    (D) democracy is admirable
    (E) idealism is worthless

IF YOU FINISH BEFORE TIME IS CALLED, YOU MAY CHECK YOUR WORK ON THIS SECTION ONLY. DO NOT WORK ON ANY OTHER SECTION IN THE TEST. **S T O P**

SECTION **4**   Time—15 Minutes   In this section, solve each problem, using any available space on the
10 Questions   page for scratchwork. Then decide which is the best of the choices
given and fill in the corresponding oval on the answer sheet.

Reference:

Circle: Rectangle: Rectangular Solid: Cylinder: Triangle:

$C = 2\pi r$ $A = lw$ $V = lwh$ $V = \pi r^2 h$ $A = \frac{1}{2}bh$ $a^2 + b^2 = c^2$
$A = \pi r^2$

- The measure in degrees of a straight angle is 180.
- The number of degrees of arc in a circle is 360.
- The sum of the measures of the angles of a triangle is 180.

Notes: The figures accompanying the problems are drawn as accurately as possible unless otherwise stated in specific problems. Again, unless otherwise stated, all figures lie in the same plane. All numbers used in these problems are real numbers. Calculators are permitted for this test.

---

1. If 1 mill = 0.1 cents, how many mills are there in $3.13?

   (A) 0.313   (B) 3.13   (C) 31.3
   (D) 313   (E) 3,130

2. Which of the following is a pair of numbers that are not equal?

   (A) $\frac{63}{6}$, $\frac{21}{2}$ (B) 0.3%, 0.003   (C) $\frac{44}{77}$, $\frac{4}{7}$

   (D) $\frac{3}{8}$, 0.375   (E) $\sqrt{3^2}$, 9

3. If x and y are different positive integers and $\frac{x}{y}$ is an integer, then which of the following must be true?

   I. $x > y$
   II. $xy > 0$
   III. $y - x < 0$

   (A) I only   (B) II only   (C) III only
   (D) I and II only   (E) I, II, and III

Questions 4–5

   For all positive integers n,
    $= 2n$ if n is even
    $= 3n$ if n is odd

4. If n is a prime number greater than 2, then

    $=$

   (A) $3n$ (B) $2n$ (C) $3n - 3$
   (D) $2n - 2$ (E) n

5. 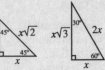 $=$
   (A) ⑥   (B) ⑦   (C) ⑫
   (D) ⑱   (E) ㊱

6. If $\frac{x}{z} = k$ and $\frac{y}{z} = k - 1$, then $x =$

(A) $y - 1$ (B) $y + 1$ (C) $y + z$

(D) $z - y$ (E) $\frac{y}{z}$

9. If x is 25% of y, then y is what percent of x?

(A) 400%   (B) 300%   (C) 250%
(D) 125%   (E) 75%

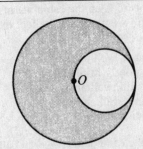

7. In the figure above, O is the center of the circle. What is the ratio of the area of the shaded portion of the figure to the area of the unshaded portion of the figure?

(A) $\frac{4}{1}$ (B) $\frac{\pi}{1}$ (C) $\frac{3}{1}$ (D) $\frac{5}{2}$ (E) $\frac{2}{1}$

10. If x is an integer which is a multiple of both 9 and 5, which of the following must be true?

I. x is equal to 45.
II. x is a multiple of 15.
III. x is odd.

(A) I only   (B) II only   (C) III only
(D) II and III only   (E) I, II, and III

8. If a cube has a surface area $54x^2$, what is its volume?

(A) $3x$ (B) $3x^2$ (C) $3x^3$ (D) $9x^3$ (E) $27x^3$

IF YOU FINISH BEFORE TIME IS CALLED, YOU MAY CHECK YOUR WORK ON THIS SECTION ONLY. DO NOT WORK ON ANY OTHER SECTION IN THE TEST.   **STOP**

SECTION 5
Time—30 Minutes
35 Questions

For each question in this section, choose the best answer and blacken the corresponding space on the answer sheet.

Each sentence below has one or two blanks, each blank indicating that something has been omitted. Beneath the sentence are five lettered words or sets of words. Choose the word or set of words that best fits the meaning of the sentence as a whole.

Example:

Although its publicity has been ----, the film itself is intelligent, well-acted, handsomely produced, and altogether ----.

(A) tasteless..respectable
(B) extensive..moderate
(C) sophisticated..amateur
(D) risqué..crude
(E) perfect..spectacular

● Ⓑ Ⓒ Ⓓ Ⓔ

1. The manuscripts of Thomas Wolfe were so ---- that the publisher was forced to ---- them in order to make them coherent and concise.

(A) obscure..expand
(B) lengthy..edit
(C) unpopular..recall
(D) interesting..organize
(E) depressing..inspire

2. The changes in the organization were so gradual that they seemed almost ----.

(A) hasty   (B) spontaneous   (C) imperceptible
(D) distorted   (E) omitted

3. Although it is difficult to be ---- the plight of one's adversary, it is not necessary to be ---- or cruel.

(A) sympathetic to..callous
(B) excited about..capricious
(C) pessimistic about..dilatory
(D) jealous of..rigorous
(E) ignorant of..esoteric

4. Professor Gray's translation of the work is so ---- that it completely ---- the material and renders it incomprehensible.

(A) thematic..retards
(B) grandiose..obviates
(C) accurate..obscures
(D) ubiquitous..transforms
(E) idiosyncratic..distorts

5. The customers were so incensed at the obvious ---- of the waiter that they could not be ---- and refused to pay their check.

(A) exigence..disconcerted
(B) volubility..condoned
(C) ineptitude..assuaged
(D) lassitude..thwarted
(E) fortitude..mollified

6. All attempts to keep the cabin warm were ---- due to the frigid weather and the fact that the cabin was ----.

(A) delegated..well constructed
(B) futile..poorly insulated
(C) successful..well appointed
(D) punctual..well situated
(E) profitable..extremely spacious

7. Although the candidate is ---- and a popular media figure, her platform is not ---- the general populace and she will probably lose the election.

(A) reclusive..accessible to
(B) distressed..opposed by
(C) personable..supported by
(D) diminutive..injurious to
(E) rabid..relevant to

8. Traditionally, clubs with ---- membership are ---- admit new members without a thorough investigation of their backgrounds.

(A) a raucous..anxious to
(B) an elite..reluctant to
(C) a turgid..fearful to
(D) a sensible..urged to
(E) a disruptive..elated to

9. The ability to compose music depends on a solid background in theory, but the musical talent is essentially ---- and cannot be taught.

(A) destroyed   (B) experienced   (C) innate
(D) forgotten   (E) assured

10. Although the professor had ---- support from the faculty who were either indifferent or downright hostile, he continued to teach using his ---- methods.

(A) adequate..similar
(B) minimal..idiosyncratic
(C) resounding..archaic
(D) adverse..popular
(E) bracing..suspicious

11. Have you ever ---- the ---- of a macaw?

    (A) witnessed..screech
    (B) felt..hoof
    (C) heard..squawk
    (D) remarked..cry
    (E) noticed..vowels

12. He views himself as a ---- who has ---- his health for the cause.

    (A) martyr..sacrificed
    (B) cherub..given
    (C) victim..wounded
    (D) martinet..lost
    (E) athlete..aided

13. That poor woman — she was ---- by the clever con artists.

    (A) curbed
    (B) conjoined
    (C) deceased
    (D) rused
    (E) duped

14. We might divert the ---- by building a ----.

    (A) snow..fort
    (B) castle..moat
    (C) flowage..weir
    (D) carport..retaining wall
    (E) savannah..corral

15. The speech was ----; it reviewed the main themes of the convention.

    (A) holistic
    (B) abstract
    (C) quantitative
    (D) reprisal
    (E) summational

Each question below consists of a related pair of words or phrases, followed by five lettered pairs of words or phrases. Select the lettered pair that best expresses a relationship similar to that expressed in the original pair

Example:

YAWN : BOREDOM::

(A) dream : sleep
(B) anger : madness
(C) smile : amusement
(D) face : expression
(E) impatience : rebellion

16. PIG : STY::

    (A) chicken : egg
    (B) horse : stable
    (C) tree : lawn
    (D) water : mud
    (E) goat : mountain

17. ARCHAEOLOGY : RELICS::

    (A) biology : science
    (B) cartography : geography
    (C) botany : plants
    (D) philosophy : religion
    (E) meteorology : ocean

18. COACH : TEAM::

    (A) director : cast
    (B) athlete : champion
    (C) writer : editor
    (D) manager : secretary
    (E) clergyman : sermon

19. PARAGRAPH : ESSAY::

    (A) gossip : newspaper
    (B) verse : poem
    (C) curse : evil
    (D) pun : wit
    (E) diary : journal

20. CRINGE : FEAR::

    (A) pout : amusement
    (B) blush : embarrassment
    (C) fight : sullenness
    (D) muse : apathy
    (E) tremble : suspicion

21. ROGUE : MISCHIEF::

    (A) charlatan : expertise
    (B) scholar : pedantry
    (C) philanthropist : avarice
    (D) malefactor : evil
    (E) dilettante : creativity

22. BANAL : ORIGINALITY::

    (A) rigorous : enthusiasm
    (B) moribund : vitality
    (C) flagrant : comprehensibility
    (D) dauntless : bravado
    (E) affable : guile

23. REPENT : CONTRITION::

    (A) demur : hesitation
    (B) condone : resentment
    (C) restore : fabrication
    (D) denote : disavowal
    (E) curtail : danger

24. VOLATILE : CHANGEABILITY::

    (A) tangled : obtuseness
    (B) dilapidated : disrepair
    (C) emancipated : reluctance
    (D) constricted : flexibility
    (E) embroiled : sensitivity

25. SOPHISTRY : FALLACIOUS::

    (A) rhetoric : obnoxious
    (B) misnomer : erroneous
    (C) consciousness : incantatory
    (D) volubility : hortatory
    (E) criticism : agrarian

GO ON TO THE NEXT PAGE

The passage below is followed by questions based on its content. Answer the questions following the passage on the basis of what is <u>stated</u> or <u>implied</u> in the passage.

Questions 26–35 are based on the following passage.

Red Jacket was chief of the Seneca Tribe and spokes-
person for the Six Nations when he gave this speech to
Christian missionaries in 1805. In the speech, he makes
an eloquent argument for freedom of religion.

Friend and Brother: It was the will of the Great Spirit that
we should meet together this day. He orders all things and
has given us a fine day for our council. He has taken His
garment from before the sun and caused it to shine with
(5) brightness upon us. Our eyes are opened that we see
clearly; our ears are unstopped that we have been able to
hear distinctly the words you have spoken. For all these
favors we thank the Great Spirit, and Him only.

Brother, this council fire was lit by you. It was at your
(10) request that we came together at this time. We have lis-
tened with attention to what you have said. You requested
us to speak our minds freely. This gives us great joy; for
we now consider that we stand upright before you and can
speak what we think. All have heard your voice and all
(15) speak to you now as one man. Our minds are agreed. . . .

Brother, listen to what we say. There was a time when
our forefathers owned this great island. Their seats
extended from the rising to the setting sun. The Great
Spirit had made it for the use of Indians. He had created
(20) the buffalo, the deer, and other animals for food. He had
made the bear and the beaver. Their skins served us for
clothing. He had scattered them over the country and
taught us how to take them. He had caused the earth to
produce corn for bread. All this He had done for His red
(25) children because He loved them. If we had some disputes
about our hunting-ground they were generally settled without the shedding of much blood.

But an evil day came upon us. Your forefathers
crossed the great water and landed on this island. Their
(30) numbers were small. They found friends and not enemies.
They told us they had fled from their own country for fear
of wicked men and had come here to enjoy their religion.
They asked for a small seat. We took pity upon them,
granted their request, and they sat down among us. We
(35) gave them corn and meat; they gave us poison in return.

Brother, our seats were once large and yours were
small. You have now become a great people, and we have
scarcely a place left to spread our blankets. You have got
our country, but are not satisfied; you want to force your
(40) religion upon us.

Brother, continue to listen. You say that you are sent
to instruct us how to worship the Great Spirit agreeably to
His mind; and, if we do not take hold of the religion which
you white people teach we shall be unhappy hereafter.
(45) You say that you are right and we are lost. How do we
know this to be true? We understand that your religion is
written in a Book. If it was intended for us, as well as you,
why has not the Great Spirit given to us, and not only to
us, but why did He not give to our forefathers the knowl-
(50) edge of that Book, with the means of understanding it
rightly. We only know what you tell us about it. How shall
we know when to believe, being so often deceived by the
white people?

Brother, you say there is but one way to worship and   Line
serve the Great Spirit. If there is but one religion, why do   (55)
you white people differ so much about it? Why do not all
agree, as you can all read the Book?

Brother, we do not understand these things. We are
told that your religion was given to your forefathers and
has been handed down from father to son. We also have a   (60)
religion which was given to our forefathers and has been
handed down to us, their children. We worship in that
way. It teaches us to be thankful for all the favors we
receive, to love each other, and to be united. We never
quarrel about religion. . . .   (65)

Brother, we do not wish to destroy your religion or
take it from you. We only want to enjoy our own.

26. By "this council fire was lit by you" (line 9), Red
Jacket means that

(A) his audience started the conflagration
(B) his listeners convened the meeting
(C) the people he sees lit the fire of hope
(D) his people began the peace process
(E) his listeners are responsible for his passion

27. By "all speak to you now as one man" (lines 14–15),
Red Jacket implies that

(A) the Indians are in agreement
(B) the Indians and whites agree
(C) he has been chosen as spokesperson
(D) both A and B
(E) both B and C

28. Red Jacket uses the word *seat* throughout to mean

(A) place of authority
(B) right of occupation
(C) posture
(D) membership
(E) chair

29. The transition between paragraphs 3 and 4 corresponds to

(A) a change in the weather
(B) the introduction of Christianity to the Indians
(C) the white settlement of America
(D) the departure of the Great Spirit
(E) the eradication of bears and beavers

30. How does Red Jacket feel about the coming of
Europeans?

(A) He is tolerant of their behavior.
(B) He feels that they cast evil upon the Indians.
(C) He does not understand their desire to leave
their native lands.
(D) both A and B
(E) both B and C

682

31. One of Red Jacket's main objections to the Bible is that

(A) It tells only about white people.
(B) Indians do not read books.
(C) It has no pictures.
(D) God did not give it to the Indians.
(E) It tells of things that happened long ago.

32. The word *rightly* (line 51) means

(A) ethically
(B) honestly
(C) directly
(D) virtuously
(E) correctly

33. The main idea of paragraph 7 can be restated as which of these?

(A) White people worship one way, but Indians worship another.
(B) Why doesn't the Bible explain the correct way to worship?
(C) If there were only one right way to worship, why would white people disagree about that one right way?
(D) How can Indians trust people who do not agree?
(E) The Great Spirit may be served in any number of ways.

34. Red Jacket compares Indians to whites in terms of their

(A) respect for nature
(B) desire for freedom of religion
(C) generational bequeathing of religious beliefs
(D) both A and B
(E) both B and C

35. The main focus of the passage is

(A) descriptive
(B) academic
(C) sermonizing
(D) persuasive
(E) demanding

IF YOU FINISH BEFORE TIME IS CALLED, YOU MAY CHECK YOUR WORK ON THIS SECTION ONLY. DO NOT WORK ON ANY OTHER SECTION IN THE TEST.   **STOP**

SECTION **6**	Time—30 Minutes 25 Questions	This section contains two types of problems with separate directions for each. You may use any available space on the page for scratchwork.

Reference:

Circle:

$C = 2\pi r$
$A = \pi r^2$

Rectangle:

$A = lw$

Rectangular Solid:

$V = lwh$

Cylinder:

$V = \pi r^2 h$

Triangle:

$A = \frac{1}{2}bh$

$a^2 + b^2 = c^2$

- The measure in degrees of a straight angle is 180.
- The number of degrees of arc in a circle is 360.
- The sum of the measures of the angles of a triangle is 180.

Notes: The figures accompanying the problems are drawn as accurately as possible unless otherwise stated in specific problems. Again, unless otherwise stated, all figures lie in the same plane. All numbers used in these problems are real numbers. Calculators are permitted for this test.

Directions for Quantitative Comparison Questions

Questions 1–15 each consist of two quantities, one in Column A and one in Column B. You are to compare the two quantities and on the answer sheet fill in oval

A if the quantity in Column A is greater;
B if the quantity in Column B is greater;
C if the two quantities are equal;
D if the relationship cannot be determined from the information given.

AN E RESPONSE WILL NOT BE SCORED.

EXAMPLES		
Column A	Column B	Answers
E1. 2×6	$2 + 6$	● Ⓑ Ⓒ Ⓓ Ⓔ
E2. $180 - x$	y	Ⓐ Ⓑ ● Ⓓ Ⓔ
E3. $p - q$	$q - p$	Ⓐ Ⓑ Ⓒ ● Ⓔ

Notes:

1. In certain questions, information concerning one or both of the quantities to be compared is centered above the two columns.
2. In a given question, a symbol that appears in both columns represents the same thing in Column A as it does in Column B.
3. Letters such as x, n, and k stand for real numbers.

GO ON TO THE NEXT PAGE

$$a + b = 11$$
$$b + 2 = 7$$

1. a | b

2. $\dfrac{2}{3} + \dfrac{3}{5}$ | $\dfrac{5}{8}$

3. $37{,}142$ | $3(10{,}000) + 7(1{,}000) + 1(100) + 4(10) + 2$

4. $\dfrac{665}{999}$ | $\dfrac{2}{3}$

5. The number of days in a year | The number of hours in a month

p, q, and r are consecutive odd integers
$$p < q < r$$

6. $r - p$ | $q - 2$

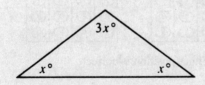

7. x | 45

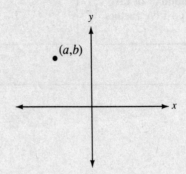

8. a | b

$$x > \dfrac{5}{y} > 0$$

9. x | y

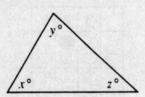

10. The average of x, y, and z | 65

$$x^2 y > 0$$

11. y | 0

The cost per pound of steel is less than the cost per pound of copper. The cost per pound of copper is greater than the cost per pound of zinc.

12. The cost per pound of steel | The cost per pound of zinc

GO ON TO THE NEXT PAGE

$$x = 5 \cdot 13^5$$

13.	The number of distinct positive factors of x	2

For all nonzero numbers x and y

$$x \bigcirc y = \frac{x}{y}$$

$$x \bigtriangledown y = \frac{y}{x}$$

14.	$3 \bigcirc 2$	$2 \bigcirc 3$

15.	$x \bigcirc (y \bigtriangledown x)$	y

Directions for Student-Produced Response Questions

Questions 16–25 each require you to solve a problem and mark your answer on a special answer grid. For each question, you should write your answer in the boxes at the top of each column and then fill in the ovals beneath each answer you write. Here are some examples.

Answer: 3/4 (= .75; show answer either way)

Answer: 325

Note: A mixed number such as 3½ must be gridded as 7/2 or as 3.5. If gridded as "31/2," it will be read as "thirty-one halves."

Note: Either position is correct.

16. If $x + 1 + 2x + 2 + 3x + 3 = 6$, then $x = ?$

17. If a horse gallops at an average speed of 40 feet per second, how many seconds will it take for the horse to gallop 500 feet?

18. If n is a positive integer greater than 6, and if the remainder is the same when 13 and 21 are divided by n, then $n = $?

19. If $\dfrac{64}{x} - 6 = 2$, then $x = $?

20. If x, y, and z are consecutive integers, and $x > y > z$, then $(x - y)(x - z)(y - z) = $?

21. If x is an odd number less than 10, and y is an even number less than 10, what is the greatest number xy can equal?

22. Cyrus worked 8 hours Monday. On each successive day, he worked half as long as on the previous day. How many hours had he worked all week by the end of the day on Friday?

23. Imagine a right triangle ABC with AB congruent to BC. What is the measure, in degrees, of $< BAC$?

24. At Auburn Mills High, 80% of the graduating seniors go on to college. Of those college-bound seniors, 75% will attend school in the state. If there are 150 graduating seniors in all, how many will attend college out of state?

25. Danielle sliced a pizza into sixths. She then sliced each slice in thirds. She served 4 of the small slices to Pete. In lowest terms, what fraction of the whole pizza did Pete have?

IF YOU FINISH BEFORE TIME IS CALLED, YOU MAY CHECK YOUR WORK ON **S T O P** THIS SECTION ONLY. DO NOT WORK ON ANY OTHER SECTION IN THE TEST.

Answer Key

SECTION 1

1. A	11. D	21. B	31. C
2. B	12. D	22. A	32. A
3. E	13. B	23. B	33. B
4. D	14. D	24. E	34. D
5. C	15. B	25. A	35. E
6. A	16. C	26. C	
7. D	17. A	27. E	
8. C	18. C	28. B	
9. E	19. A	29. C	
10. D	20. B	30. A	

SECTION 2

1. A	11. C	21. C
2. B	12. E	22. B
3. D	13. C	23. B
4. E	14. A	24. A
5. C	15. B	25. B
6. C	16. B	
7. B	17. D	
8. C	18. B	
9. D	19. E	
10. E	20. D	

SECTION 3

1. B
2. E
3. C
4. E
5. D
6. E
7. E
8. C
9. E
10. C

SECTION 4

1. E
2. E
3. E
4. D
5. E
6. C
7. C
8. E
9. A
10. B

SECTION 5

1. B	11. C	21. D	31. D
2. C	12. A	22. B	32. E
3. A	13. E	23. A	33. C
4. E	14. C	24. B	34. E
5. C	15. E	25. B	35. D
6. B	16. B	26. B	
7. C	17. C	27. A	
8. B	18. A	28. B	
9. C	19. B	29. C	
10. B	20. B	30. B	

SECTION 6

1. A	6. D	11. A	16. 0	21. 72
2. A	7. B	12. D	17. 12.5	22. 15.5
3. C	8. B	13. C	18. 8	23. 45
4. B	9. D	14. A	19. 8	24. 30
5. B	10. B	15. C	20. 2	25. 2/9

Explanatory Answers

CRITICAL READING

1. It is clear from the first paragraph that the riders are going

   (A) uphill
   (B) downhill
   (C) in circles
   (D) to school
   (E) across a ridge

   (A) The "grade got steeper," which could mean uphill or downhill. The fact that the horses are panting implies a climb upward, and the fact that the trees are shrinking in size corroborates this; trees get smaller and sparser as one approaches the treeline.

2. By "all were as grains of sand" (lines 6–7), Alegría emphasizes the

   (A) meaninglessness of life
   (B) immensity of the Andes
   (C) beauty of the stones
   (D) contrast between mountain and seashore
   (E) insignificance of man

   (B) Place the phrase in context to answer this interpretation question. Some stones are bouncing downhill, dislodging others, and "all were as grains of sand sliding down the grandeur of the Andes." *All* refers to the stones, which become insignificant compared to the mountains around them.

3. By "immense stair-steps" (line 11), Alegría means that the rocks

   (A) are man-made
   (B) look wooden
   (C) are carved for people to walk on
   (D) have railings
   (E) lead upward

   (E) The vertical nature of the boulders is described, so that (E) is the only choice supported by the text.

4. The word *wrought* (line 11) means

   (A) composed
   (B) drafted
   (C) manufactured
   (D) formed
   (E) hammered

   (D) The rocks are not man-made, so they cannot be drafted (B) or manufactured (C) or hammered (E). (A) is possible, but (D) is better.

5. "The sun's brilliance formed pools" (lines 15–16) means that the sun

   (A) melted the ice
   (B) blended with the clouds
   (C) reflected off the grass
   (D) both A and B
   (E) both B and C

   (C) To interpret this phrase requires a certain ability to envision the author's scene. He does not mention snow or ice (A), although he says that the riders' breath is beginning to freeze. The pools are being formed on the grass, not in the sky, so (B) seems impossible. Only (C) makes sense; the "pools" are pools of light, not water.

6. The word *rush* (line 28) means

   (A) grass
   (B) sally
   (C) dash
   (D) haste
   (E) advance

   (A) The only meaning of *rush* that does not have the connotation of *hurry* is the meaning involving a kind of plant used to make baskets and hats, a plant similar to a grass.

7. Paragraph 6 introduces the concept of

   (A) race
   (B) class
   (C) poverty
   (D) both A and B
   (E) both B and C

   (D) This evaluation question asks you to summarize the main points in a paragraph. The child's race and class are discussed; poverty is never mentioned. Since both (A) and (B) are true, the answer is (D).

8. The word *hacienda* (line 49) is used to mean

   (A) house
   (B) castle
   (C) plantation
   (D) villa
   (E) dwelling

   (C) We normally use the word *hacienda* to mean a kind of house, but the context in which it is used here makes that interpretation nonsensical — there cannot be a mountain in a house. There could, however, be one on a plantation, and that is the other meaning of *hacienda* — it can mean a plantation or a plantation house.

9. By "jubilant brushstrokes" (line 61), the author is

   (A) differentiating the muleteers from artists
   (B) comparing the blankets to a painting
   (C) contrasting the blankets with the grey mountains
   (D) both A and B
   (E) both B and C

   (E) This is an example of the use of metaphor in the passage. The author compares the vivid colors of the blankets to the brushstrokes of a painting, and in doing so, he contrasts them with the "uniformly grey rocks."

10. The word *devotional* (line 67) means

   (A) tender
   (B) zealous
   (C) ardent
   (D) venerated
   (E) affectionate

   (D) *Devotional* is a word with many meanings; but a stone can only be devotional in one way — if it is an object of worship.

11. The passage is primarily

   (A) persuasive
   (B) instructive
   (C) factual
   (D) descriptive
   (E) informative

   (D) Figurative language, including vivid descriptors and many similes, marks the passage. The author's purpose is to set a scene, not to persuade, instruct, or give facts.

12. By the end of the passage, the author has introduced

   (A) the main characters
   (B) the symbols mentioned in the title
   (C) the problem and its solution
   (D) both A and B
   (E) both B and C

   (D) The main characters (A) appear to be the boy and the Indian, both of whom we have met

by the end of the passage. The title (B) mentions a stone and a cross, both of which have been alluded to (in lines 67 and 54, respectively). The problem faced by the characters, unless it is crossing the mountains, is unclear, and the solution is certainly not clear. Since (A) and (B) are true, the answer is (D).

SENTENCE COMPLETION

13. Van Gogh's shapes and colors are so ---- that some art historians have attributed his view of the world to illness or to madness.

   (A) inaccessible   (B) startling
   (C) intermediate   (D) corrupt   (E) trivial

   (B) It is best to start this question at the end. Ask yourself what adjective you would need to describe images that are attributed to madness or illness. You might anticipate a word such as "unusual," and (B), *startling,* is a good choice.

14. Although he was usually ----, he ---- the hostess and was never invited back.

   (A) tidy..flattered
   (B) disinterested..suspected
   (C) forgetful..enchanted
   (D) tactful..insulted
   (E) careful..concealed

   (D) Here again it is best to work backwards. What would someone have to do to never be invited back? Something negative, obviously. Eliminate (A). If he *flattered* the hostess, he would surely be invited back! (B) and (E) fail to make a meaningful statement. The *although* tells you this behavior is not usual. Which second element provides a contrast? It is *tactful.*

15. The will was ---- according to the law because there was ---- evidence that the deceased had been mentally incompetent.

   (A) sanctimonious..chronological
   (B) invalid..overwhelming
   (C) punitive..subsequent
   (D) signed..irrefutable
   (E) suspect..inadequate

   (B) There isn't much you can do with this sentence except fill in the blanks. Eliminate (A) immediately because it doesn't make any sense to say that a will is *sanctimonious* by law. Although the other words seem possible on first reading, you can eliminate all but (B). The key word is *because.* One blank depends on the other. When you do the substitutions it becomes apparent that only (B) forms a logical idea.

690

16. The treatment of the mental illnesses for which there is no cure can only ---- the symptoms, not ---- the disease.

(A) defend..eradicate
(B) disrupt..deflate
(C) ameliorate..eliminate
(D) confine..restore
(E) augment..delineate

(C) The key to this sentence is the phrase *for which there is no cure.* Whatever can be done to the symptoms is an extension of this thought, which is then contrasted with what cannot be done to the disease itself. You can eliminate (A) on the grounds of usage. Although (B) looks possible at first, the second element does not make sense in the sentence and does not contrast with disrupt. (D) makes some sense, but again, when you substitute the second element you get a meaningless sentence. And the same is true of (E). (Delineate a disease makes no sense.) (C) works perfectly. Since there is no cure, you can only *ameliorate* the symptoms, not (contrasting idea), *eliminate* the disease.

17. Although Senator Jones had the ---- needed to run for office, it was his ---- that the party considered his greatest asset.

(A) credentials..charisma
(B) experience..apathy
(C) esteem..wrongdoing
(D) greed..altruism
(E) serenity..haughtiness

(A) This sentence begins with a thought-reverser. Although he had something, it was something else (the reverse) which was important. All of the first choices seem plausible with the possible exception of (D), *greed.* You can, however, eliminate several choices on the basis of the second element. No one would say that *apathy, wrongdoing,* or *haughtiness* were assets to a politician. You are left with (A), which fits the logic of the sentence. It was not *credentials* (something very tangible) but *charisma* (something intangible) that was the Senator's greatest asset.

ANALOGIES

18. DUCK : WADDLE::

(A) eagle : hunt
(B) gait : amble
(C) worm : wriggle
(D) boat : row
(E) horse : race

(C) This is a variation of defining characteristic analogies. It is characteristic of a DUCK that it WADDLES (that's the way it moves), and it is characteristic of a *worm* that it *wriggles* because that's the way it moves.

19. COMPOSER : SCORE::

(A) writer : manuscript
(B) athlete : exercise
(C) comedian : laugh
(D) worker : apprentice
(E) librarian : books

(A) This is another twist on the defining characteristic analogy. A COMPOSER creates a SCORE and a *writer* creates a *manuscript.* Or, a SCORE is the product of a COMPOSER, and a *manuscript* is the product of a *writer.*

20. TARANTULA : SPIDER::

(A) roof : cabin
(B) cobra : snake
(C) parrot : jungle
(D) camel : desert
(E) poetry : prose

(B) This is a simple "type of" analogy. A TARANTULA is a type of SPIDER, and a *cobra* is a type of *snake.*

21. AIRPLANE : HANGAR::

(A) beach : sand
(B) car : garage
(C) bird : flight
(D) mountain : peak
(E) vault : bank

(B) This is a "place where" analogy. By definition, a HANGAR is a place for an AIRPLANE, and a *garage* is a place for a *car,* so you could also look at it as a defining characteristic analogy.

22. TREE : ORCHARD::

(A) member : congregation
(B) priest : church
(C) animal : mammal
(D) officer : uniform
(E) leader : organization

(A) This is a straightforward part-to-whole analogy. A TREE is part of an ORCHARD and a *member* is part of a *congregation.* They are both one element in the group.

23. RESILIENT : BUOYANCY::

(A) useful : extravagance
(B) pliable : flexibility
(C) enticing : elusiveness
(D) eccentric : practicality
(E) harmonious : discord

(B) This is a defining characteristic analogy. That which is RESILIENT has BUOYANCY, and that which is *pliable* has *flexibility.*

24. PETTY : SIGNIFICANCE::

   (A) preserved : security
   (B) tempered : variety
   (C) obstinate : fortitude
   (D) abundant : lassitude
   (E) brief : duration

   (E) This is a "lack of" analogy. That which is PETTY lacks SIGNIFICANCE, and that which is *brief* lacks *duration*.

25. FERTILE : PROGENY::

   (A) verdant : vegetation
   (B) inept : ability
   (C) infamous : secrecy
   (D) flagrant : nobility
   (E) affable : insight

   (A) This is a defining characteristic analogy. That which is FERTILE has PROGENY, and that which is *verdant* has *vegetation*.

CRITICAL READING

26. By "receiving my morning lectures" (line 2), Addison means

   (A) listening to my radio program
   (B) paying attention to my scolding voice
   (C) reading my column in the morning paper
   (D) both A and B
   (E) both B and C

   (C) If you understand the beginning of Addison's essay, you know that he is speaking of the growing readership of his paper. His "morning lectures," then, must be his own columns of information or advice in that paper.

27. The word *disciples* (line 8) is used to mean

   (A) patrons
   (B) neophytes
   (C) converts
   (D) apostles
   (E) followers

   (E) *Disciples* is a word with many shades of meaning, but the meaning Addison has in mind is (E). He is referring to those people who read the *Spectator*, his followers.

28. "The thoughtless herd" (line 9) refers to

   (A) any ill-educated people
   (B) people who don't read the *Spectator*
   (C) illiterate people
   (D) people who live outside London and Westminster
   (E) women

   (B) Find the phrase and reread the context that surrounds it to answer this interpretation question. Addison is contrasting his "disciples" with "the

thoughtless herd"; in other words, he is contrasting his readers with those people who do not read his work.

29. By "make their instruction agreeable, and their diversion useful" (line 12), Addison means that he will

   (A) remove all didactic flavor from the *Spectator*
   (B) try to teach a moral lesson in each essay
   (C) make lectures humorous and entertainment meaningful
   (D) not include humor unless it is enlightened
   (E) try to divert his audience from their everyday woes

   (C) This interpretation question calls for a paraphrase of the author's phrase. The phrase in question has two parts, both of which must appear in the paraphrase. Only (C) covers both parts of the original phrase

30. The word *temper* (line 14) is used to mean

   (A) moderate
   (B) dispose
   (C) anger
   (D) compose
   (E) harden

   (A) *Temper* has many meanings, some of which are reflected in the answer choices above. Only *moderate* fits the context of the sentence, however.

31. Which of these best summarizes Addison's intent in lines 16–21 ("And to the end . . . to which the age is fallen")?

   (A) No newspaper can restore a reader's virtue.
   (B) He will remind his audience of their vices.
   (C) Daily publication will save his audience from folly.
   (D) He expects his audience to return to wickedness.
   (E) Only he can restore his readership to health.

   (C) An evaluation question of this type asks you to paraphrase a sentence. Begin by rereading the sentence and restating it in your own words. Then compare your restatement with the choices (A) to (E). "Refresh their memories from day to day" refers to daily publication, which Addison will use to "recover [his readers] out of that desperate state of vice and folly."

32. Addison compares himself to Socrates in terms of their

   (A) popularization of philosophy
   (B) instructive natures
   (C) heavenly beginnings
   (D) both A and B
   (E) both B and C

   (A) First locate the allusion to Socrates (line 23), and then reread the context in which it is found.

Socrates "brought philosophy down from heaven, to inhabit among men," and Addison wishes to bring philosophy out of the academic and into the daily lives of his readers.

33. "To make them easy in this particular" (line 38) means

(A) to finish this project easily
(B) to ease their minds on this subject
(C) to simplify this matter
(D) to make fastidiousness less complicated
(E) to fashion comfortable items

(B) As with any such interpretation question, you should replace the phrase in context with each of the choices in order to determine which choice is best. Addison says that his friends are in pain for him, but he wishes to "make them easy"; that is, to ease their minds.

34. The word *raillery* (line 40) means

(A) balustrade
(B) garments
(C) forcing
(D) teasing
(E) scolding

(D) Addison is envisioning the teasing he will take by asserting that he will retire when he feels too dull to continue writing. He imagines that people will constantly accuse him of being dull and try to force his hand. Of the other choices, (A) is a synonym for *railing*, (B) is a synonym for *raiment*, (C) is a synonym for *railroading*, and (E) is a synonym for *railing (at)*.

35. The general tone of this passage is

(A) serious and earnest
(B) cautious and deliberate
(C) flighty and frivolous
(D) shrewd and calculating
(E) congenial and humorous

(E) Addison is generally lighthearted in his appeal to readers. As he says himself, his aim is to combine wit and instruction.

SECTION 2

MATH PROBLEM SOLVING

1. If $\dfrac{1}{2N} + \dfrac{1}{2N} = \dfrac{1}{4}$, then $N =$

(A) 4   (B) 2   (C) 1   (D) $\dfrac{1}{2}$ (E) $\dfrac{1}{4}$

(A) Here you have a simple equation, so you can just solve for N:

$$\frac{1}{2N} + \frac{1}{2N} = \frac{1}{4}$$

$$\frac{2}{2N} = \frac{1}{4}$$

$$\frac{1}{N} = \frac{1}{4}$$

$$N = 4$$

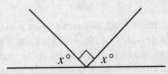

2. In the figure above, $x =$
(A) 30   (B) 45   (C) 60   (D) 75   (E) 90

(B) $x + 90 + x = 180$

$2x = 90$

$x = 45$

3. In a certain game, a person's age is multiplied by 2 and then the product is divided by 3. If the result of performing the operations on John's age is 12, what is John's age?

(A) 2   (B) 8   (C) 12   (D) 18   (E) 36

(D) You can set up an equation:

$$\frac{2J}{3} = 12$$

$$2J = 36$$

$$J = 18$$

Or you could just test answer choices until you found one that worked. 18 times 2 is 36, and 36 divided by 3 is 12.

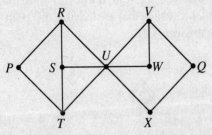

4. The figure above is a map showing the stations and connecting subway lines for a city's subway system. If a person wishes to travel by subway from station P to station Q, without passing through any station more than once, which of the following must be true?

(A) If he passes through T, he must next pass through S.
(B) If he passes through S, he must next pass through U.

(C) If he passes through U, he must next pass through V.

(D) If he passes through R, he cannot later pass through T.

(E) If he passes through V, he cannot later pass through W.

(E) If the passenger is at station V; he got there either via W or directly from U. If it is the first, he cannot go back to W. If it is the second, he cannot go to W because that would force him to return to U.

5. A helper must load 38 bricks onto a truck. Given that she can carry at most 4 bricks at a time, what is the fewest number of trips she must make to move all of the bricks from the brickpile onto the truck?

(A) 9　(B) 9.5　(C) 10　(D) 10.5　(E) 12

(C) $38 \div 4 = 9$ with a remainder of 2. So she will make 9 trips carrying 4 bricks, but she has to make an additional trip with the last 2 bricks.

6. For all numbers, $(a - b)(b - c) - (b - a)(c - b) =$

(A) -2　(B) -1　(C) 0　(D) $ab - ac - bc$
(E) $2ab - 2ac - 2bc$

(C) You can do the multiplication very easily:

$(a - b)(b - c) = ab - ac - b^2 + bc$

$(b - a)(c - b) = bc - b^2 - ac + ab$

Now subtract:

$$ab - ac - b^2 + bc$$
$$- (ab - ac - b^2 + bc)$$
$$\overline{0 - 0 - 0 - 0}$$

7. n is a positive integer. If n is a multiple of 6 and a multiple of 9, what is the least possible value of n?

(A) 12　(B) 18　(C) 27　(D) 36　(E) 54

(B) Just test choices until you find the smallest available value that is divisible by both 6 and 9. The answer is 18.

8. For any positive integer k, ⟨k⟩ $= k^2 - k$. What is the value of ⟨⟨2⟩⟩ ?

(A) 0　(B) 1　(C) 2　(D) 4　(E) 8

(C) Here we have a defined function problem. Do the indicated operation:

⟨2⟩ $= 2^2 - 2 = 2$

And when that operation is repeated for the second time (as required by the problem) the result is still 2.

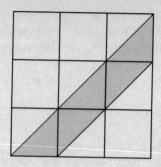

9. The figure above shows a square piece of land that is divided into 9 smaller square lots. The shaded portion is a railroad right-of-way. If the area of the shaded portion of the figure is 5 square miles, what is the area, in square miles, of the entire piece of land?

(A) 9　(B) 10　(C) 13　(D) 18　(E) 36

(D) The easiest way to handle this problem is to recognize that the shaded area takes up half of five of the squares. So the shaded area is $\frac{\frac{5}{2}}{9} = \frac{5}{18}$ of the entire piece of land. Since $\frac{5}{18}$ of the total is equal to 5, the total is equal to 18 square miles.

List X	List Y
1	1
2	2
3	3
4	4

10. For how many different ordered pairs (x, y), where x is a number selected from List X and y is a numbered selected from List Y, is $x - y > 0$?

(A) 24　(B) 18　(C) 15　(D) 12　(E) 6

(E) Just count the pairs that fit the requirement:

$(2,1)$, $(3,1)$, $(3,2)$, $(4,1)$, $(4,2)$, $(4,3)$

11. If x and y are negative integers, and $x > y$, which of the following is the greatest?

(A) $-(xy)^2$　　(B) $x^2 y$　　(C) xy
(D) $x + y$　　(E) $y - x$

(C) This question becomes easy once you recognize that (C) is the only expression that generates a positive result.

12. A student receives an average of 75 on three exams that are scored on a scale of 0 to 100. If one of her test scores was 75, what is the lowest possible score she could have received on any of the three tests?

(A) 0　(B) 1　(C) 25　(D) 40　(E) 50

(E) Use the technique for finding a missing element in an average. Since the three scores average 75, she earned a total score $3 \times 75 = 225$. We know that one score is 75, and $225 - 75 = 150$. The maximum she could receive on any test is 100, and $150 - 100 = 50$. So the lowest score she could have received (and still maintain a 75 average) is 50.

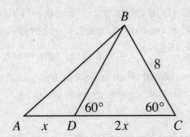

13. In *ABC* above, what is the length of side *AC*?
    (A) 4   (B) 8   (C) 12   (D) 18
    (E) It cannot be determined from the information given.

    (C) The triangle on the right is an equilateral triangle, so $2x = 8$, which means that $x = 4$. So the length of *AC* is $8 + 4 = 12$.

14. During a certain shift, a quality control inspector inspects 6 out of every 30 items produced. What was the ratio of inspected to uninspected items during that shift?
    (A) 1:4   (B) 1:5   (C) 1:6   (D) 5:1   (E) 6:1

    (A) Since 6 items out of 30 are inspected, $30 - 6 = 24$ are not inspected, and the ratio 6:24 is equal to 1:4.

15. For which of the following pairs of numbers is it true that their sum is 9 times their product?

    (A) $1, \frac{1}{9}$ (B) $1, \frac{1}{8}$ (C) $1, \frac{1}{19}$

    (D) 1, 8   (E) 1, 9

    (B) Just test the choices. The sum of 1 and $\frac{1}{8}$ is $\frac{9}{8}$, which is 9 times the product of 1 and $\frac{1}{8}$, which is $\frac{1}{8}$.

16. Initially, 24 people apply for jobs with a firm, and $\frac{1}{3}$ of those are turned down without being given an interview. If $\frac{1}{4}$ of the remaining applicants are hired, how many applicants were given jobs?
    (A) 2   (B) 4   (C) 6   (D) 8   (E) 12

(B) Just work out the calculation. Out of the 24, $\frac{1}{3}$, or 8, are rejected without an interview, leaving only 16. If $\frac{1}{4}$ of those are hired, then $\frac{1}{4}$ of 16 = 4 are hired.

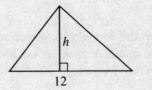 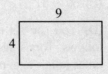

17. In the figures above, if the area of the rectangle is equal to the area of the triangle, then $h =$
    (A) 2   (B) 3   (C) 4   (D) 6   (E) 9

    (D) The rectangle has an area of $4 \times 9 = 36$. Since the triangle also has that area:

    $$\frac{1}{2} \times h \times 12 = 36$$
    $$12h = 72$$
    $$h = 6$$

18. If 8 francs equal 1 pound, and 2 pounds equal 3 dollars, then 6 dollars is equal to how many francs?
    (A) 48   (B) 32   (C) 16   (D) 8   (E) 4

    (B) Use "pounds" as a common term. Since 8 francs is equal to 1 pound, 16 francs is equal to 2 pounds. So 16 francs is equal to 2 pounds is equal to 3 dollars. Since 3 dollars is equal to 16 francs, 6 dollars is equal to 32 francs.

19. The price of a book, after it was reduced by $\frac{1}{3}$, is B dollars. What was the price of the book, in dollars, before the reduction?

    (A) $\frac{2B}{3}$ (B) $\frac{3B}{4}$ (C) $\frac{6B}{5}$

    (D) $\frac{4B}{3}$ (E) $\frac{3B}{2}$

    (E) You can set up an equation here:

    Original Price $- \frac{1}{3}$ Original Price $= B$

    $$O - \frac{1}{3}O = B$$
    $$\frac{2}{3}O = B$$
    $$O = \frac{3B}{2}$$

    Or you can assume some numbers, a technique we have used often.

20. Y years ago, Tom was three times as old as Julie was. If Julie is now 20 years old, how old is Tom in terms of Y?

(A) $60 + 2Y$
(B) $30 + 2Y$
(C) $30 - 2Y$
(D) $60 - 2Y$
(E) $60 - 3Y$

(D) You can set up the formula by reasoning as follows. Tom's age, minus Y years, is equal to 3 times Julie's age, minus Y years:

$$T - Y = 3(20 - Y)$$

$$T - Y = 60 - 3Y$$

$$T = 60 - 2Y$$

You can reach the same conclusion by assuming some values and substituting them into the formulas.

21. If S is the sum of x consecutive integers, then S must be even if x is a multiple of

(A) 6 (B) 5 (C) 4 (D) 3 (E) 2

(C) The sum of 4 consecutive integers must always be even. You have two even numbers, and an odd number added to an odd number which yields another even number.

22. If the radius of circle O is 20 percent less than the radius of circle P, the area of circle O is what percent of the area of circle P?

(A) 60%   (B) 64%   (C) 72%
(D) 80%   (E) 120%

(B) This is not an easy question, so don't be fooled into selecting (D). Let r be the radius of P, the larger circle. It has an area of πr^2. Then the radius of O, the smaller circle, will be $0.8r$, and it will have an area of $\pi(0.8r)^2 = 0.64\pi r$. So the area of the smaller circle is only 64% of that of the larger circle.

23. If the average (arithmetic mean) of 20, 23, 24, x, and y is 26 and $\dfrac{x}{y} = \dfrac{3}{4}$, then $x =$

(A) 25 (B) 27 (C) 36 (D) 41 (E) 63

(B) Solve using the technique for finding the missing elements of an average. Since the average of the 5 numbers is 26, their sum is $26 \times 5 = 130$. The sum of 20, 23, and 24 is 67, and $130 - 67 = 63$. So $x + y = 63$. Now you can use the method for solving simultaneous equations: x is equal to 27 and y is equal to 36.

24. The price of 5 boxes of candy is d dollars. If each box contains 30 pieces of candy, what is the price, in *cents*, of 12 pieces of candy?

(A) $8d$ (B) $12d$ (C) $\dfrac{25d}{2}$ (D) $50d$ (E) $72d$

(A) You can set up the formula in the following way. If the price of 5 boxes of candy is d dollars, the price of 5 boxes of candy is $100d$ cents. Since each box contains 30 pieces of candy, the price is $100d$ cents per $5 \times 30 = 150$ pieces, or $\dfrac{100d}{150}$. The cost of 12 pieces of candy is 12 times that, or $\dfrac{100d(12)}{150} = 8d$. You can reach the same result without the algebra by assuming some value and testing the answer choices.

25. If a cube has a side of length 2, what is the distance from any vertex to the center of the cube?

(A) $\dfrac{\sqrt{2}}{2}$ (B) $\sqrt{3}$ (C) $2\sqrt{2}$

(D) $2\sqrt{3}$ (E) $\dfrac{3}{2}$

(B) This problem really needs a diagram:

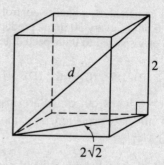

Notice that the diagonal of the face, the edge of the cube, and the diagonal of the cube form a right triangle, the hypotenuse of which is the diagonal of the cube. Since the edge has a length of 2, the diagonal of the face has a length of $2\sqrt{2}$. Now use the Pythagorean Theorem:

$$2^2 + (2\sqrt{2})^2 = d^2$$

$$4 + 8 = d^2$$

$$d^2 = 12$$

$$d = \sqrt{12} = 2\sqrt{3}$$

This is the length of the diagonal. The distance from any vertex to the center of the cube is one half of that or $\sqrt{3}$.

SECTION 3

CRITICAL READING

1. The main point of Thompson's introductory paragraph is that

   (A) not everyone knows the importance of decision-making
   (B) the time has come to choose
   (C) choices are made seldom in history
   (D) life and death are inevitable
   (E) this is an important time in history

   (B) (E) is close, but it is too vague. (A) and (C) are mentioned, but they are not the main point. Thompson introduces her topic with a bang: *Now* is the time to make a decision.

2. The word *onslaught* (line 11) is used by Thompson to mean

   (A) command
   (B) retreat
   (C) pillage
   (D) resistance
   (E) attack

   (E) The onslaught is the continuing attack of Hitler's forces on the people of the world. Substituting each choice in context proves that only (E) fits.

3. According to Thompson, isolationism will mean

   (A) reduction in forces
   (B) international debt
   (C) imprisonment
   (D) the fall of the economy
   (E) all of the above

   (C) This is the only choice that reflects Thompson's fears. Her final paragraph deals with the result of isolationism as she sees it: "a prison camp in a hostile community."

4. The word *internecine* (line 30) means

   (A) between friends
   (B) foreign
   (C) global
   (D) territorial
   (E) mutually destructive

   (E) If you do not know the word, the meaning will not be immediately obvious, but it can be determined from the context in which it is found. Thompson speaks of a number of peoples being set against one another, but the examples she uses are certainly not friends (A). The fight she speaks of is local, not foreign (B) or global (C), but it does not seem to involve territory (D).

Since every group is pitted against every other, however, it could prove mutually destructive (E).

5. Thomas uses the word *insuperable* (line 35) to mean

   (A) irresistible
   (B) desperate
   (C) surmountable
   (D) formidable
   (E) unusual

   (D) As with any vocabulary-in-context question, this one is easily answered if you substitute the choices in place of the word in question. The word being modified is *obstacle*; that might be (A), but is more likely to be (D).

6. Thomas discusses the cost of the war in terms of

   (A) lives
   (B) money
   (C) freedom
   (D) democracy
   (E) all of the above

   (E) This is actually a synthesis/analysis question; it requires that you look at paragraph 1 as a whole. Thomas begins on line 37 by discussing the cost of the war "in the lives of our sons," goes on to discuss the "cost in money" (line 38), continues with the need for censorship and accompanying loss of liberty, and concludes with the slaying of democracy.

7. The word *affirming*, used by Thomas in line 55, means

   (A) proving
   (B) validating
   (C) disputing
   (D) denying
   (E) asserting

   (E) The rather awkward phrasing of this line might lead you to substitute (C) or (D) for the correct answer, but look at the meaning of the sentence as a whole. Thomas is not saying that we can ignore dangers — he is not asserting that.

8. Judging by this passage, Thomas might consider Thompson

   (A) uninformed
   (B) undemocratic
   (C) hysterical
   (D) determined
   (E) noble

   (C) There is no evidence to support any answer but (C) if you stick to the text. In line 58, Thomas denounces the "hysteria which grossly exaggerates" the dangers of the world. Thompson's scenario of the isolated prison camp run amok would surely be considered a hysterical exaggeration by Thomas.

9. Unlike Thompson, Thomas believes that isolationism will
    (A) lead to chaos
    (B) result in censorship
    (C) cause riots
    (D) lead to Hitler's victory
    (E) safeguard democracy

    (E) This question asks you to contrast the opinions of both speakers. Thompson believes (A), (C), and (D); Thomas does not. Thomas believes that *war* will result in (B). He does believe that entering war will threaten democracy, and that staying out will protect it.

10. Thompson and Thomas agree that
    (A) war is avoidable
    (B) war is expensive
    (C) Hitler is dangerous
    (D) democracy is admirable
    (E) idealism is worthless

    (C) Only this one point is touched upon by both speakers. Thompson may well believe (D), but she never says anything about democracy. Thomas mentions (A) and (B), but Thompson does not, and neither implies (E). Any evaluation question of this nature requires you to look at both passages as a whole and not to go beyond what is stated.

SECTION 4

MATH PROBLEM-SOLVING

1. If 1 mill = 0.1 cents, how many mills are there in $3.13?
    (A) 0.313   (B) 3.13   (C) 31.3
    (D) 313   (E) 3,130

    (E) This question just asks you to manipulate the decimal point: $3.13 = 313 cents, and $313 \div 0.01 = 3,130$.

2. Which of the following is a pair of numbers that are not equal?

    (A) $\frac{63}{6}$, $\frac{21}{2}$ (B) 0.3%, 0.003   (C) $\frac{44}{77}$, $\frac{4}{7}$

    (D) $\frac{3}{8}$, 0.375   (E) $\sqrt{3^2}$, 9

    (E) Don't bother with any fancy mathematic theorizing. Just test the test. $\sqrt{3^2} = 3$, which is not equal to 9.

3. If x and y are different positive integers and x/y is an integer, then which of the following must be true?
    I. $x > y$
    II. $xy > 0$
    III. $y - x < 0$
    (A) I only   (B) II only   (C) III only
    (D) I and II only   (E) I, II, and III

    (E) Since $\frac{x}{y}$ is an integer (and x and y are different integers and so can't both be 1), x must be greater than y (otherwise x would not be evenly divisible by y). So I is part of the correct answer. As for II, since x and y are positive integers, their product is greater than 0. Finally, $y - x < 0$ is equivalent to $y < x$, which is really statement I again. So all three statements belong in the correct choice.

Questions 4–5

For all positive integers n,
$\widehat{n}$ = 2n if n is even
$\widehat{n}$ = 3n if n is odd

4. If n is a prime number greater than 4, then
    $\widehat{n-1}$ =
    (A) 3n   (B) 2n   (C) 3n − 3
    (D) 2n − 2   (E) n

    (D) Here we have another defined function problem. If n is a prime number greater than 2, then the next smaller number must be an even number. And $\widehat{n}$ = 2n when n is even, so $\widehat{n-1}$ = 2n − 2.

5. $\widehat{3} \cdot \widehat{4}$ =
    (A) $\widehat{6}$ (B) $\widehat{7}$ (C) $\widehat{12}$
    (D) $\widehat{18}$ (E) $\widehat{36}$

    (E) First, perform the defined function on the values given:

    $\widehat{3}$ = 3 × 3 = 9

    $\widehat{4}$ = 2 × 4 = 8

    So $\widehat{3} \times \widehat{4}$ = 72. Now you can reason that since 72 is an even number, it is the result of performing our defined function on a number $\frac{1}{2}$ of 72, and $\frac{1}{2}$ of 72 = 36. Or you can test answer choices until you find one that generates the value 72.

6. If $\dfrac{x}{z} = k$ and $\dfrac{y}{z} = k - 1$, then $x =$

(A) $y - 1$ (B) $y + 1$ (C) $y + z$

(D) $z - y$ (E) $\dfrac{y}{z}$

(C) Use the method for solving simultaneous equations. Since $\dfrac{y}{z} = k - 1$, $k = \dfrac{y}{z} + 1$. And since $\dfrac{x}{z} = k$:

$$\dfrac{x}{z} = \dfrac{y}{z} + 1$$

$$x = z\left(\dfrac{y}{z} + 1\right)$$

$$x = y + z$$

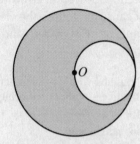

7. In the figure above, O is the center of the circle. What is the ratio of the area of the shaded portion of the figure to the area of the unshaded portion of the figure?

(A) $\dfrac{4}{1}$ (B) $\dfrac{\pi}{1}$ (C) $\dfrac{3}{1}$ (D) $\dfrac{5}{2}$ (E) $\dfrac{2}{1}$

(C) Let r be the radius of the smaller circle. Its area is πr^2. Then the radius of the larger circle is $2r$, and its area is $\pi(2r)^2 = 4\pi r^2$. The shaded part of the diagram is the larger circle minus the smaller one. So the area of the shaded part of the diagram is $4\pi r^2 - \pi r^2 = 3\pi r^2$. And the ratio of the shaded area to the unshaded area is $\dfrac{3}{1}$.

8. If a cube has a surface area $54x^2$, what is its volume?

(A) $3x$ (B) $3x^2$ (C) $3x^3$ (D) $9x^3$ (E) $27x^3$

(E) Since a cube has six faces, the area of each face is:

$6(\text{edge} \times \text{edge}) = 54x^2$

$\text{edge}^2 = 9x^2$

$\text{edge} = \sqrt{9x^2} = 3x$

So the volume of the cube is $(3x)(3x)(3x) = 27x^3$

9. If x is 25% of y, then y is what percent of x?

(A) 400%   (B) 300%   (C) 250%
(D) 125%   (E) 75%

(A) If $x = 0.25y$, then $y = x/0.25 = 4x$. So y is 400 percent of x.

10. If x is an integer which is a multiple of both 9 and 5, which of the following must be true?

 I. x is equal to 45.
 II. x is a multiple of 15.
 III. x is odd.

(A) I only   (B) II only   (C) III only
(D) II and III only   (E) I, II, and III

(B) Since 3 is a factor of 9, and 5 is a factor of 5, any multiple of both 9 and 5 will be a multiple of 15. So II belongs in the correct choice. I, however, is not correct. x could be any multiple of 45, e.g., 90, which also proves that III does not belong in the correct choice.

SECTION 5

SENTENCE COMPLETION

1. The manuscripts of Thomas Wolfe were so ---- that the publisher was forced to ---- them in order to make them coherent and concise.

(A) obscure..expand
(B) lengthy..edit
(C) unpopular..recall
(D) interesting..organize
(E) depressing..inspire

(B) The sentence is characterized by two thought-extenders. First, the second blank must give the reason for what is described by the first blank. On this score you can eliminate (A), (D), and (E). But the second blank also looks forward toward the end of the sentence. It must be something that will result in something that is coherent and concise. Thus, you eliminate (C).

2. The changes in the organization were so gradual that they seemed almost ----.

(A) hasty   (B) spontaneous
(C) imperceptible   (D) distorted   (E) omitted

(C) The only logical feature of the sentence is the thought-extender. The blank must describe changes that are very gradual. And very gradual changes would be almost unnoticeable or imperceptible.

3. Although it is difficult to be ---- the plight of one's adversary, it is not necessary to be ---- or cruel.

(A) sympathetic to..callous
(B) excited about..capricious
(C) pessimistic about..dilatory
(D) jealous of..rigorous
(E) ignorant of..esoteric

699

(A) The overall structure of the sentence is a contrast between two ideas. Additionally, within the first clause there is an extender (the blank must be consistent with the idea of adversary), and in the second clause the blank must parallel cruel. Perhaps the easiest way to find the correct choice is to look for an answer having a second element parallel to cruel. Only (A) is acceptable.

4. Professor Gray's translation of the work is so ---- that it completely ---- the material and renders it incomprehensible.

   (A) thematic..retards
   (B) grandiose..obviates
   (C) accurate..obscures
   (D) ubiquitous..transforms
   (E) idiosyncratic..distorts

   (E) The logical key to this sentence is a thought-extender. The second blank must explain or parallel the first blank. Only (E) provides the needed continuation: since the translation is idiosyncratic (unusual), it distorts the meaning of the original.

5. The customers were so incensed at the obvious ---- of the waiter that they could not be ---- and refused to pay their check.

   (A) exigence..disconcerted
   (B) volubility..condoned
   (C) ineptitude..assuaged
   (D) lassitude..thwarted
   (E) fortitude..mollified

   (C) The sentence is one long thought-extender. The first blank must explain why the customers were incensed. The second blank must further describe their feelings. And the second blank must also describe something that explains why the customers failed to pay the check. On the first score, you can eliminate (A), (B), and (E), for these are not numbered among the sins of bad waiters. (D) is close in meaning to a word that might be used to complete that blank. Lassitude means a weary feeling. Logically, it would not be the waiter's feelings but his actions that would offend the customers. So (C) is a better answer.

6. All attempts to keep the cabin warm were ---- due to the frigid weather and the fact that the cabin was ----.

   (A) delegated..well constructed
   (B) futile..poorly insulated
   (C) successful..well appointed
   (D) punctual..well situated
   (E) profitable..extremely spacious

   (B) The only hint you have in this sentence is *due to the frigid weather*. This tells you that the cabin was probably not warm and leads you to (B). If you don't see (B) immediately, substitute each pair. You'll find that (B) provides the best completion.

7. Although the candidate is ---- and a popular media figure, her platform is not ---- the general populace and she will probably lose the election.

   (A) reclusive..accessible to
   (B) distressed..opposed by
   (C) personable..supported by
   (D) diminutive..injurious to
   (E) rabid..relevant to

   (C) This sentence starts with a thought-extender. What comes after the blank extends the blank, so the blank must somehow parallel the idea of popular. (A), (B), (D), and (E) all fail on this count. This leaves you with (C) (*personable*) which is compatible with the idea of the candidate's popularity. The sentence also has a thought-reverser in the word *although*. She may be popular, but she may lose the election. So you need words that indicate what might cause her to lose the election. The second element of (C) works, and confirms the answer choice.

8. Traditionally, clubs with ---- membership are ---- admit new members without a thorough investigation of their backgrounds.

   (A) a raucous..anxious to
   (B) an elite..reluctant to
   (C) a turgid..fearful to
   (D) a sensible..urged to
   (E) a disruptive..elated to

   (B) Let's start with the second half of this sentence. The *without a thorough investigation* gives you an idea of reluctance, and in fact, that is one of the answer choices. When you substitute the first element of (B) you will see that the sentence works perfectly.

9. The ability to compose music depends on a solid background in theory, but the musical talent is essentially ---- and cannot be taught.

   (A) destroyed   (B) experienced   (C) innate
   (D) forgotten   (E) assured

   (C) This is essentially a vocabulary question. The blank needs an adjective that means "something that isn't taught." This can only be (C), *innate*, which means "inborn."

10. Although the professor had ---- support from the faculty who were either indifferent or downright hostile, he continued to teach using his ---- methods.

    (A) adequate..similar
    (B) minimal..idiosyncratic
    (C) resounding..archaic
    (D) adverse..popular
    (E) bracing..suspicious

    (B) The sentence begins with a thought-extender. You need a word in the first blank that parallels the idea of hostility or indifference. You would not choose (C) or (E); neither *resounding* support nor *bracing* support sounds like indifference or hostility. (D), *adverse* support, is a contradiction in terms. (B) and (A) are left and when you substitute the second element, it is clear that (B) is the correct answer.

11. Have you ever ---- the ---- of a macaw?

(A) witnessed..screech
(B) felt..hoof
(C) heard..squawk
(D) remarked..cry
(E) noticed..vowels

(C) A macaw is a bird; it does not have *hoofs* (B). It might *screech* (A), but you would hear that, not *witness* it. *Remarked* (D) is an unlikely word in this context, and *vowels* (E) makes no sense.

12. He views himself as a ---- who has ---- his health for the cause.

(A) martyr..sacrificed
(B) cherub..given
(C) victim..wounded
(D) martinet..lost
(E) athlete..aided

(A) The second word extends the meaning of the first. *Victim* (C) almost works, but one's health cannot be *wounded*. One's health might be *lost* (D), but that does not make one a *martinet* (disciplinarian). Only (A) has two elements that work in the context of the sentence.

13. That poor woman — she was ---- by the clever con artists.

(A) curbed
(B) conjoined
(C) deceased
(D) rused
(E) duped

(E) She was certainly not *conjoined* (connected) (B). *Deceased* (C) is an adjective, not a verb, and *rused* (D) is not a word. She might have been *curbed*, or restrained (A), but, more likely she was *duped* (deceived).

14. We might divert the ---- by building a ----.

(A) snow..fort
(B) castle..moat
(C) flowage..weir
(D) carport..retaining wall
(E) savannah..corral

(C) The key here is *divert*, meaning "deflect" or "turn." A fort would not divert snow (A), a moat would not divert a castle (B), a wall would not

divert a carport (D), and a corral would not divert a savannah (E). Only a *weir*, or dam, might divert *flowage*, or outflow.

15. The speech was ----; it reviewed the main themes of the convention.

(A) holistic
(B) abstract
(C) quantitative
(D) reprisal
(E) summational

(E) The clues here are *reviewed* and *main themes*. *Holistic* (A) implies integration of parts and wholes; it does not fit the context. *Abstract* (B), as a noun, means "summary," but used adjectivally, as it is here, it means "complex." (C) makes no sense, and (D) is a play on *reprise*, meaning "repeat"; however, *reprisal* is a noun meaning "counterattack." *Summational* (E), meaning "reviewing," fits the context.

ANALOGIES

16. PIG : STY::

(A) chicken : egg
(B) horse : stable
(C) tree : lawn
(D) water : mud
(E) goat : mountain

(B) This analogy is based on the "place where found" connection. A PIG lives in a STY, and a *horse* lives in a *stable*.

17. ARCHAEOLOGY : RELICS::

(A) biology : science
(B) cartography : geography
(C) botany : plants
(D) philosophy : religion
(E) meteorology : ocean

(C) This is an analogy based on the "is the study of" connection. It doesn't appear so frequently that we need to include it as a common form, and it is easily recognized when it does appear. ARCHAEOLOGY is the study of RELICS, and *botany* is the study of *plants*.

18. COACH : TEAM::

(A) director : cast
(B) athlete : champion
(C) writer : editor
(D) manager : secretary
(E) clergyman : sermon

(A) This analogy doesn't fit neatly into a category, but it can be explained in the following way. The COACH is the head of the TEAM, and the *director* is the head of the *cast*. And you should hear a nice confirming echo. A *cast* is like a TEAM (a team of actors), and the *director* is their COACH.

19. PARAGRAPH : ESSAY::

    (A) gossip : newspaper
    (B) verse : poem
    (C) curse : evil
    (D) pun : wit
    (E) diary : journal

    (B) This analogy is based on the "part of" connection. A PARAGRAPH is a part of an ESSAY, and a *verse* is a part of a *poem*.

20. CRINGE : FEAR::

    (A) pout : amusement
    (B) blush : embarrassment
    (C) fight : sullenness
    (D) muse : apathy
    (E) tremble : suspicion

    (B) This analogy is based on the "is a sign of" connection. CRINGING is a sign of FEAR, and *blushing* is a sign of *embarrassment*.

21. ROGUE : MISCHIEF::

    (A) charlatan : expertise
    (B) scholar : pedantry
    (C) philanthropist : avarice
    (D) malefactor : evil
    (E) dilettante : creativity

    (D) This analogy is based on the "defining characteristic" connection. MISCHIEF is a defining characteristic of a ROGUE, and *evil* is a defining characteristic of a *malefactor*. And you can hear a very nice confirming relationship between ROGUE and *malefactor* and between MISCHIEF and *evil*.

22. BANAL : ORIGINALITY::

    (A) rigorous : enthusiasm
    (B) moribund : vitality
    (C) flagrant : comprehensibility
    (D) dauntless : bravado
    (E) affable : guile

    (B) This analogy is based on the "lack of" connection. Something that is BANAL is lacking in ORIGINALITY, and something that is *moribund* is lacking in *vitality*.

23. REPENT : CONTRITION::

    (A) demur : hesitation
    (B) condone : resentment
    (C) restore : fabrication
    (D) denote : disavowal
    (E) curtail : danger

    (A) This analogy is based on the "defining characteristic" connection. By definition, to REPENT is to show CONTRITION; and by definition, to *demur* is to show *hesitation*.

24. VOLATILE : CHANGEABILITY::

    (A) tangled : obtuseness
    (B) dilapidated : disrepair
    (C) emancipated : reluctance
    (D) constricted : flexibility
    (E) embroiled : sensitivity

    (B) This analogy is also based on the "defining characteristic" connection. CHANGEABILITY is a defining characteristic of that which is VOLATILE, and *disrepair* is a defining characteristic of that which is *dilapidated*.

25. SOPHISTRY : FALLACIOUS::

    (A) rhetoric : obnoxious
    (B) misnomer : erroneous
    (C) consciousness : incantatory
    (D) volubility : hortatory
    (E) criticism : agrarian

    (B) Here we have one more item based on the "defining characteristic" connection. By definition, SOPHISTRY is argumentation that is FALLACIOUS, and by definition, a *misnomer* is terminology that is *erroneous*.

CRITICAL READING

26. By "this council fire was lit by you" (line 9), Red Jacket means that

    (A) his audience started the conflagration
    (B) his listeners convened the meeting
    (C) the people he sees lit the fire of hope
    (D) his people began the peace process
    (E) his listeners are responsible for his passion

    (B) The phrase sounds metaphorical, but it is actually literal. There probably was a council fire blazing at this meeting, but it was not Red Jacket and his people who started it. The missionaries called the meeting.

27. By "all speak to you now as one man" (line 15), Red Jacket implies that

    (A) the Indians are in agreement
    (B) the Indians and whites agree
    (C) he has been chosen as spokesperson
    (D) both A and B
    (E) both B and C

    (A) Red Jacket may be the spokesperson (C), but that is not what this phrase means. It certainly does not mean that the Indians and whites agree (B). When Red Jacket says *we*, he refers to the Indians in the audience, who have listened to the white missionaries. It is those Indians who "have heard your voice and all speak to you now as one man."

28. Red Jacket uses the word *seat* throughout to mean

(A) place of authority
(B) right of occupation
(C) posture
(D) membership
(E) chair

(B) This is an unusual connotation for a common word. The only way to answer the question is to return to the passage and find references to the vocabulary word (see lines 17, 33, and 36). Then test the choices in place of the word. Of the choices, (C), (D), and (E) are certainly incorrect. (A) is close, but (B) is better.

29. The transition between paragraphs 3 and 4 corresponds to

(A) a change in the weather
(B) the introduction of Christianity to the Indians
(C) the white settlement of America
(D) the departure of the Great Spirit
(E) the eradication of bears and beavers

(C) Return to paragraphs 3 and 4 and summarize them in order to respond to this synthesis/analysis question. Paragraph 3 speaks of the time when the Indians ruled the land. Paragraph 4 speaks of the arrival of the whites. The transition, then, is the white settlement of America.

30. How does Red Jacket feel about the coming of Europeans?

(A) He is tolerant of their behavior.
(B) He feels that they cast evil upon the Indians.
(C) He does not understand their desire to leave their native lands.
(D) both A and B
(E) both B and C

(B) This evaluation question calls for a quite literal reading of Red Jacket's words. He speaks of the white settlers' arrival as "an evil day" (line 28). Whereas the Indians gave the settlers food, the settlers gave them poison.

31. One of Red Jacket's main objections to the Bible is that

(A) It tells only about white people.
(B) Indians do not read books.
(C) It has no pictures.
(D) God did not give it to the Indians.
(E) It tells of things that happened long ago.

(D) Only (D) is touched on in Red Jacket's discussion. He asks why, if the Bible were meant for Indians as well as whites, the Great Spirit did not give the Book to Indians as well as to whites? Does the Great Spirit really mean that whites must interpret religion for Indians?

32. The word *rightly* (line 51) means

(A) ethically
(B) honestly
(C) directly
(D) virtuously
(E) correctly

(E) Red Jacket is speaking of the desire to understand the Bible rightly, which is to say correctly, in the manner in which it was written.

33. The main idea of paragraph 7 can be restated as which of these?

(A) White people worship one way, but Indians worship another.
(B) Why doesn't the Bible explain the correct way to worship?
(C) If there were only one right way to worship, why would white people disagree about that one right way?
(D) How can Indians trust people who do not agree?
(E) The Great Spirit may be served in any number of ways.

(C) Red Jacket makes the cogent point that even white people differ in their modes of worship, so how, that being so, can these white people say that there is but one way to worship?

34. Red Jacket compares Indians to whites in terms of their

(A) respect for nature
(B) desire for freedom of religion
(C) generational bequeathing of religious beliefs
(D) both A and B
(E) both B and C

(E) Red Jacket mentions the Europeans' leaving of their own country "to enjoy their religion" (line 32). He later speaks of religion "handed down from father to son" (line 60). Both the bequeathing of religion and the wish to enjoy it in peace are things the Europeans and Indians share.

35. The main focus of the passage is

(A) descriptive
(B) academic
(C) sermonizing
(D) persuasive
(E) demanding

(D) This evaluation question asks you to look at Red Jacket's motivation in giving the speech. He is attempting to persuade his audience to let the Indians worship in peace.

SECTION 6

QUANTITATIVE COMPARISON

Column A	Column B

$$a + b = 11$$
$$b + 2 = 7$$

1.
a	b

(A) Here you have simultaneous equations, so solve for a and b:

$$a + b = 11$$
$$- (2 + b = 7)$$
$$a - 2 = 4$$
$$a = 6$$

And $b = 5$.

So Column A is greater.

2.
$\frac{2}{3} + \frac{3}{5}$	$\frac{5}{8}$

(A) Using the "flying x" to perform the operations indicated in Column A:

$$\frac{2}{3} + \frac{3}{5} = \frac{10 + 9}{15} = \frac{19}{15}$$

So Column A is larger.

3.
37,142	3(10,000) + 7(1,000) + 1(100) + 4(10) + 2

(C) The expression in Column B is just another way of writing the number in Column A.

4.
$\frac{665}{999}$	$\frac{2}{3}$

(B) Since $\frac{666}{999}$ is equal to $\frac{2}{3}$, $\frac{665}{999}$ is less than $\frac{2}{3}$.

5.
The number of days in a year	The number of hours in a month

(B) At first you might think the answer to this question is (D) since the months of the year vary in length, and even a year might have 366 days instead of 365. But even if you select February as your month, 28×24 is still greater than 366.

---

p, q, and r are consecutive odd integers
$$p < q < r$$

6.
$r - p$	$q - 2$

(D) There are at least two ways to attack this question. First, you could substitute $p + 4$ for r in Column A and $p + 2$ for q in Column B. Column A then becomes $(p + 4) - p = 4$, and Column B becomes $p + 2 - 2 = p$. Since no information is given about p, you can't make the comparison. You can reach the same conclusion just by picking a couple of different values for p.

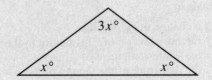

7.
x	45

(B)

$$3x + x + x = 180$$
$$5x = 180$$
$$x = 36$$

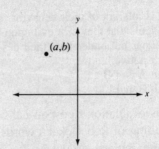

8.
a	b

(B) In the upper-left quadrant, all of the x coordinates are negative and all of the y coordinates are positive. So a is less than b.

$$x > \frac{5}{y} > 0$$

9.
x	y

(D) The easiest way to see that the relationship is indeterminate is just to assume some values. For example, assume that $x = 5$. Then y might also be 5, and the two Columns would be equal.

(Eliminate (A) and (B).) Or y might be 2, and Column A would be greater. (Eliminate (C).) So the correct answer is (D).

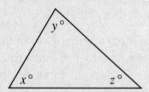

10.

The average of x, y, and z	65

(B) The average of x, y, and z is $\frac{180}{3}$ = 60. So Column B is larger.

$$x^2y > 0$$

11.

y	0

(A) Since $x^2y > 0$, both x^2 and y must have the same signs. (Either both are positive or both are negative.) Since x cannot be equal to 0 (otherwise x^2y would also be equal to 0), y must be positive.

The cost per pound of steel is less than the cost per pound of copper. The cost per pound of copper is greater than the cost per pound of zinc.

12.

The cost per pound of steel	The cost per pound of zinc

(D) The centered information can be summarized as follows:

$S < C$

$Z < C$

Without further information it is impossible to compare the price of steel and the price of zinc.

$$x = 5 \cdot 13^5$$

13.

The number of distinct positive factors of x	2

(C) Whatever x is, it has the factors 5 and 13, and only those factors. (5 and 13 are primes.)

Questions 14–15

For all nonzero numbers x and y

$$x \bigtriangleup y = \frac{x}{y}$$

$$x \bigtriangledown y = \frac{y}{x}$$

14.

$3 \bigtriangleup 2$	$2 \bigtriangleup 3$

(A) This is a defined function problem, so do the indicated operations:

$$3 \bigtriangleup 2 = \frac{3}{2}$$

$$2 \bigtriangleup 3 = \frac{2}{3}$$

So Column A is greater.

15.

$x \bigtriangleup (y \bigtriangledown x)$	y

(C) Perform the indicated operations. First do $y \bigtriangledown x$:

$$y \bigtriangledown x = \frac{x}{y}$$

Now do $x \bigtriangleup \left(\frac{x}{y}\right)$:

$$x \bigtriangleup \left(\frac{x}{y}\right) = \frac{x}{\frac{x}{y}} = y$$

So the two columns are equal.

STUDENT-PRODUCED RESPONSES

16. If $x + 1 + 2x + 2 + 3x + 3 = 6$, then $x = ?$

(0) Just do the indicated operations:

$$x + 1 + 2x + 2 + 3x + 3 = 6$$

$$6x + 6 = 6$$

$$6x = 0$$

$$x = 0$$

17. If a horse gallops at an average speed of 40 feet per second, how many seconds will it take for the horse to gallop 500 feet?

(12.5) The easiest solution is to use a direct proportion:

$$\frac{40 \text{ feet}}{500 \text{ feet}} = \frac{1 \text{ second}}{x \text{ seconds}}$$

$$\frac{40}{500} = \frac{1}{x}$$

$$40x = 500, \text{ so } x = 12.5 \text{ seconds}$$

18. If n is a positive integer greater than 6, and if the remainder is the same when 13 and 21 are divided by n, then $n = ?$

   (8) $6 < n < 13$ because if n were greater than 13, $13 \div n$ would have no remainder. Now start plugging in numbers:

   $13 \div 7 = 1$ with remainder 6; $21 \div 7 = 3$ with no remainder (wrong).

   $13 \div 8 = 1$ with remainder 5; $21 \div 8 = 2$ with remainder 5 (right!).

19. If $\dfrac{64}{x} - 6 = 2$, then $x = ?$

   (8) Here is a simple equation with one variable, so solve for x:

   $$\frac{64}{x} - 6 = 2$$
   $$\frac{64}{x} = 8$$
   $$8x = 64, \text{ so } x = 8$$

20. If x, y, and z are consecutive integers, and $x > y > z$, then $(x - y)(x - z)(y - z) = ?$

   (2) You can solve this by setting up equations. Since x, y, and z are consecutive integers, and since $x > y > z$, $y = x - 1$ and $z = x - 2$.

   $(x - (x - 1)(x - (x - 2))((x - 1) - (x - 2)) =$

   $(x - x + 1)(x - x + 2)(x - 1 - x + 2) =$

   $(1)(2)(1) = 2$

   You can reach the same conclusion with a lot less effort just by assuming some numbers for x, y, and z. Say $x = 3$, $y = 2$, and $z = 1$. The result of plugging those numbers into the expression in the problem is 2.

21. If x is an odd number less than 10, and y is an even number less than 10, what is the greatest number xy can equal?

   (72) Odd numbers less than 10 are 1, 3, 5, 7, and 9. Even numbers less than 10 are 2, 4, 6, and 8. For the greatest xy, take the greatest numbers in each list: 9 and 8. $9 \times 8 = 72$.

22. Cyrus worked 8 hours Monday. On each successive day, he worked half as long as on the previous day. How many hours had he worked all week by the end of the day on Friday?

   (15.5) It is easiest to see this in chart form:

Monday	Tuesday	Wednesday	Thursday	Friday
8	$\dfrac{8}{2} = 4$	$\dfrac{4}{2} = 2$	$\dfrac{2}{2} = 1$	$\dfrac{1}{2} = 0.5$

   $8 + 4 + 2 + 1 + 0.5 = 15.5$

   Notice that the fractional form of this number, 15 1/2, will not fit into the grid. You must express the number in decimal form, or convert it to an improper fraction.

23. Imagine a right triangle ABC with AB congruent to BC. What is the measure, in degrees, of $< BAC$?

   (45) Draw a picture of the triangle.

   Clearly, the right, or 90°, angle is $< ABC$, so congruent angles BAC and ACB must each measure 45°.

24. At Auburn Mills High, 80% of the graduating seniors go on to college. Of those college-bound seniors, 75% will attend school in the state. If there are 150 graduating seniors in all, how many will attend college out of state?

   (30) You know that 80% of the 150 graduating seniors go to college, so that means 80% $\times$ 150, or 120, seniors go to college. Of those, 75% attend school in the state, so 25% attend school out of state. 25% of 120 = 30.

25. Danielle sliced a pizza into sixths. She then sliced each slice in thirds. She served 4 of the small slices to Pete. In lowest terms, what fraction of the whole pizza did Pete have?

   (2/9) This is an easy problem, but you may wish to draw a picture to help you solve it. If you solve it mathematically, you do it this way:

   Each big slice equals $\frac{1}{6}$ of the whole. They are then cut into thirds.

   $$\frac{1}{6} \times \frac{1}{3} = \frac{1}{18}$$

   Therefore, each small slice is $\frac{1}{18}$ of the whole.

   Pete had 4 small slices, or $\frac{4}{18}$ of the whole. In lowest terms, he had $\frac{4}{18} \div \frac{2}{2}$, or $\frac{2}{9}$, of the whole.